Enterprise Java™ Security

Enterprise Java™ Security

Building Secure J2EE™ Applications

Marco Pistoia
Nataraj Nagaratnam
Larry Koved
Anthony Nadalin

♦♦Addison-Wesley

Boston • San Francisco • New York • Toronto • Montreal
London • Munich • Paris • Madrid
Capetown • Sydney • Tokyo • Singapore • Mexico City

Many of the designations used by manufacturers and sellers to distinguish their products are claimed as trademarks. Where those designations appear in this book, and Addison-Wesley was aware of a trademark claim, the designations have been printed with initial capital letters or in all capitals.

The authors and publisher have taken care in the preparation of this book, but make no expressed or implied warranty of any kind and assume no responsibility for errors or omissions. No liability is assumed for incidental or consequential damages in connection with or arising out of the use of the information or programs contained herein.

The publisher offers discounts on this book when ordered in quantity for bulk purchases and special sales. For more information, please contact:

> U.S. Corporate and Government Sales
> (800) 382-3419
> corpsales@pearsontechgroup.com

For sales ouside of the U.S., please contact:

> International Sales
> (317) 581-3793
> international@pearsontechgroup.com

Visit Addison-Wesley on the Web: www.awprofessional.com

Library of Congress Cataloging-in-Publication Data

Enterprise Java security : building secure J2EE applications / Marco Pistoia . . . [et al.].
    p. cm.
    Includes bibliographical references and index.
    ISBN 0-321-11889-8 (pbk ; alk paper)
    1. Java (Computer program language)   2. Computer security. I. Pistoia, Marco.
QA76.73.J3E58 2004
005.8—dc22

                                     2003063781

ISBN: 0-321-11889-8
Text printed on recycled paper
1 2 3 4 5 6 7 8 9 10 — CRS — 0807060504
First printing, February 2004

To my wife, Paolina,
for giving me the strength and courage
to be the man God wants me to be.
— *Marco*

In loving memory of my father,
who continues to inspire my quest for knowledge.
To my wife, Sowmya,
for her understanding and support to pursue my dreams.
To my daughter, Divya,
for giving me a new perspective on life.
To my mother and my family,
for making me who I am.
— *Nataraj*

To Karen, Sam, and Max,
for the love, support, and joy they bring to my life.
To my mother, who taught me,
"Life is short. Eat dessert first."
To my father, who is always there when I need him.
To my brother, who taught me how to count.
— *Larry*

To my wife, Paula, and my daughter, Sarah.
Thanks for keeping my life in check
and reminding me that there is life beyond "geekdom."
You both are the joys of my life.
— *Anthony*

Contents

Foreword

E-BUSINESS, one of the fastest-growing segments of the information technology industry, is changing the face of commerce as we know it. Conducting business on the Web is rapidly becoming a fundamental element of how organizations conduct business with each other, as well as with their customers. Web-based systems do not stand alone. Rather, they are the integration of many existing enterprise systems, processes, and protocols, oftentimes reengineered to leverage the capabilities inherent in the Web-based systems and to afford new capabilities. The value is not in the technology piece parts but in the rapid creation of new business solutions.

All technologies introduce risks into businesses. The challenge is in managing these risks. Some of the risks originate from the complexity of the solutions designed to address a company's business needs; other risks are inherent in the technologies chosen to address these needs. To meet these risks, we have seen the rise of various security technologies, such as antivirus scanners, firewalls, intrusion-detection systems, virtual private networks (VPNs), public-key cryptography, and the Secure Sockets Layer (SSL) protocol.

The Web is no exception. Although it offers new opportunities for creating markets and marketplaces, the risks it introduces have driven the creation of new and innovative solutions. These include authenticating and authorizing users of the system, protecting transactions from malevolent hackers, enforcing access control, guaranteeing privacy, and offering federated identity management.

An enterprise system usually comprises heterogeneous systems. Enabling these systems to communicate and integrate to form useful end-to-end solutions is essential, as much of the growth is not in the creation of entirely new systems but in making legacy systems and services accessible via the Web. This is achieved with greater ease when the enterprise system's key elements, including security, are based on open standards. Using open standards greatly simplifies the complexity and cost of development. Enabling open standards in the industry can happen only when there is an open exchange of ideas and cooperation between vendors.

This book takes an in-depth look at the development of enterprise applications based on the Java 2 Platform, Enterprise Edition (J2EE), which enables integration of existing subsystems into more powerful Web-based enterprise systems. This book focuses on the set of security standards that support and enhance a J2EE environment, including SSL, Kerberos authentication and authorization, secret- and public-key cryptography, Public-Key Cryptography Standards (PKCS), Secure/Multipurpose Internet Mail Extensions, and the Web Services Security specification. Rather than taking a piecewise view of security, this book's perspective is broader. The industry is making a shift from programmatic security to declarative security. The goal is to manage security through policies rather than via security code being written into every application, which is much more expensive to maintain and upgrade as new threats and risks are identified.

This book is the result of IBM's technical leadership and strength in security, middleware, and on-demand computing, as well as a long-standing collaboration between IBM's Software Group and Research Division. This collaboration has brought together people from around the world, creating a partnership dedicated to providing value to the marketplace in a dynamic business and technical environment.

For a long time, there has been a need for a J2EE security book. I am very happy to see that there is now such a book to answer many of the technical questions that developers, managers, and researchers have about such a critical topic. I am sure that this book will contribute greatly to the success of the J2EE platform and e-business.

Steven A. Mills
Senior Vice President and Group Executive
Software Group, IBM Corporation

Preface

THE purpose of this book is to illustrate the applicability of Java 2 Platform, Enterprise Edition (J2EE), and Java 2 Platform, Standard Edition (J2SE), security technologies in building a secure enterprise infrastructure containing Java-based enterprise applications. With a pragmatic approach, the book explains why Java security is a key factor in an e-business environment and how application developers can use this technology in building secure enterprise applications.

The book introduces the J2EE and J2SE security architectures, showing how these architectures relate to each other and how they are augmented by Java Authentication and Authorization Service (JAAS) to provide authentication and authorization. Then, the book delves into the J2EE security technologies: The security aspects of servlets, JavaServer Pages (JSP), and Enterprise JavaBeans (EJB) are treated in detail because these technologies constitute the core of the J2EE architecture. To satisfy the needs of developers who need to build J2EE applications and want to do so securely and reliably, the book covers in great detail the relationship between J2EE and cryptographic technologies; Java Cryptography Architecture, Java Cryptography Extension, Public-Key Cryptography Standards, Secure/Multipurpose Internet Mail Extensions, and Java Secure Socket Extension are also described in detail. The book explains how to work with J2EE in practice and shows how the technologies presented work together and are integrated. The scenarios described are targeted to J2EE developers and deployers needing to build an integrated, secure, component-based system. Finally, Web Services security and other emerging technologies are discussed, along with a description of how the underlying middleware works. The book ends by summarizing the impact of J2EE security in today's e-business environments.

Unlike other treatments of Java security, this book discusses the J2SE and J2EE security architectures, providing practical solutions and use patterns to address the challenges that lie ahead as these architectures evolve to address enterprise e-business needs. The goal is to give practical guidance to groups involved in making Java-based applications or Web sites into industrial-strength commercial propositions. Examples are provided to give the reader a clearer understanding of the underlying technology.

To achieve the goals of portability and reusability, J2EE security has been designed to be mainly declarative. Most of the authentication, authorization, integrity, confidentiality, and access-control decisions on a J2EE platform can be made through configuration files and deployment descriptors, which are external to the applications. This reduces the burden on the programmer and allows Java enterprise programs to be portable, reusable, and flexible. For this reason, Parts I and II focus on the declarative approach of Java security by showing examples of configuration files and deployment descriptors. Additionally, these parts of the book explain how to use the programmatic approach if declarative security alone is insufficient. (Sample programs can be found in Chapters 4 and 5.) The majority of the sample code of this book can be found in Parts III and IV.

This book has its roots in several articles we wrote for the *IBM Systems Journal* and *IBM developerWorks*, describing the origins of Java security and the security for enterprise applications using the J2EE programming model. Although we are geographically dispersed around the United States, we had gathered in Santa Clara, California, at the O'Reilly Conference on Java in March 2000 to present on a number of security topics. It was clear that developers and managers were not familiar with Java security features, J2EE security, and how to manage security in a J2EE environment. Inquiries on Java and J2EE security were being routed to us via e-mail and through our colleagues. We had already written a book on J2SE security, but a book on security for enterprise applications, including those written for server-based applications and Web Services, was needed.

This book draws and expands on material from multiple sources, including the J2SE security book and articles mentioned. Specifically, this book covers J2SE V1.4 and J2EE V1.4. The relevant specifications for J2EE covered in this book include the J2EE V1.4 specification, the Java Servlet V2.4 specification, the EJB V2.1 specification, and the Web Services specifications. The list of the sources used in this book can be found in Appendix D.

About the Authors

THIS book was written by a team of IBM security researchers and architects who have had a major impact in the definition of the Java security architecture and its related technologies. The leader of this project was Marco Pistoia.

Marco Pistoia is a Research Staff Member in the Java and Web Services Security department, a part of the Networking Security, Privacy and Cryptography department at the IBM Thomas J. Watson Research Center in Yorktown Heights, New York. He has written ten books and several papers and journal articles on all areas of Java and e-business security. His latest book, *Java 2 Network Security*, *Second Edition*, was published by Prentice Hall in 1999. He has presented at several conferences worldwide: Sun Microsystems' JavaOne, the Association for Computing Machinery (ACM) conference on Object-Oriented Programming, Systems, Languages, and Applications (OOPSLA), the O'Reilly Conference on Java, IBM Solutions, and Colorado Software Summit. He has been invited to teach graduate courses on Java security and has presented at the New York State Center for Advanced Technology in Telecommunications (CATT), Brooklyn, New York. Marco received his M.S. in Mathematics summa cum laude from the University of Rome, Italy, in 1995 and is working toward a Ph.D. in Mathematics from Polytechnic University, Brooklyn, New York. His technical interests are in mobile-code security, component software, and static analysis of object-oriented languages.

Nataraj Nagaratnam is a Senior Technical Staff Member and the lead security architect for IBM's WebSphere software family in Raleigh, North Carolina. He leads the security architecture for IBM WebSphere and the IBM Grid infrastructure. He is also a core member of the IBM Web Services security architecture team. He has coauthored the Web Services security specifications and Open Grid Services Architecture (OGSA) documents. He actively participates in the Java Community Process on the topics related to J2EE security by either leading or participating in the Java Specification Requests related to J2EE security. Nataraj received his Ph.D. in Computer Engineering from Syracuse University, Syracuse, New York. His thesis deals with the aspects of secure delegation in distributed object environments. He has widely presented on Java and security topics at various conferences and symposiums and has published extensively in numerous journals, conferences, and magazines. Nataraj was the lead author of one of the first books on Java networking, *Java Networking and AWT API SuperBible*, published by Waite Group Press in 1996.

Larry Koved is a Research Staff Member and the manager of the Java and Web Services Security department, a part of the Networking Security, Privacy, and Cryptography department at the IBM Thomas J. Watson Research Center in Yorktown Heights, New York. With Anthony Nadalin, he has served as IBM's Java security architect, including being a liaison to Sun Microsystems for Java security design and development collaboration. He was actively involved in the design of the Java Authentication and Authorization Services (JAAS) and then Enterpise JavaBeans (EJB) V1.1 security architecture. Larry has published more than 25 articles and technical reports on user interface technologies, virtual reality, hypertext and mobile computing, static analysis of Java code, and security. He has presented at several conferences, including ACM OOPSLA, the Institute of Electrical and Electronics Engineers (IEEE) Symposium on Security and Privacy, the O'Reilly Conference on Java, IBM's developerWorks Live!, and Sun Microsystems' JavaOne. His current interests include security of mobile code, component software, and static analysis of OO languages.

Anthony Nadalin is IBM's lead security architect for Java and Web Services in Austin, Texas. As Senior Technical Staff Member, he is responsible for security infrastructure design and development across IBM, Tivoli, and Lotus. He serves as the primary security liaison to Sun Microsystems for Java security design and development collaboration and to Microsoft for Web Services security design and development collaboration. In his 20-year career with IBM, Anthony has held the following positions: lead security architect for VM/SP, security architect for AS/400, and security architect for OS/2. He has authored and coauthored more than 30 technical journal and conference articles, and the book *Java and Internet Security*, which was published by iUniverse.com in 2000. He has been on the technical committee of three major scientific journals and one conference and has extensively reviewed work published by peers in the field. He has given several presentations and invited speeches at numerous technical security conferences.

Thanks to the following people for their invaluable contributions to this project:

- **Rosario Gennaro, Kenneth Goldman, Bob Johnson, Jeff Kravitz, Michael McIntosh, Charles Palmer, Darrell Reimer, Kavitha Srinivas,**

Ray Valdez, Paula Austel, Michael Steiner
IBM Thomas J. Watson Research Center, Yorktown Heights, New York

- **Steve Mills**
  IBM Software Group, Somers, New York

- **Peter Birk, Joyce Leung, Kent Soper, Audrey Timkovich, Krishna Yellepeddy**
  IBM Enterprise Security, Austin, Texas

- **Matt Hogstrom, Bert Laonipon**
  IBM WebSphere Performance and Security, Raleigh, North Carolina

- **Keys Botzum**
  IBM WebSphere Services, Bethesda, Maryland

- **Tom Alcott**
  IBM WebSphere Sales and Technology Support, Costa Mesa, California

- **Tony Cowan**
  IBM Customer Solutions Center, Seattle, Washington

- **Charlie Lai**
  Sun Microsystems, Cupertino, California

- **Chris Kaler**
  Microsoft Web Services Security, Redmond, Washington

- **Paolina Centonze**
  Polytechnic University, Brooklyn, New York

- **Ann Sellers**
  Addison-Wesley Professional, San Francisco, California

- **Julie B. Nahil**
  Addison-Wesley Professional, Boston, Massachusetts

- **Mike Hendrickson**
  Formerly of Addison-Wesley Professional, Boston, Massachusetts

- Thanks also to our able copy editor, **Evelyn Pyle**

ENTERPRISE SECURITY AND JAVA

CHAPTER 1

An Overview of
Java Technology and Security

As e-business matures, companies require enterprise-scalable functionality for their corporate Internet and intranet environments. To support the expansion of their computing boundaries, businesses have embraced Web application servers (WASs). These servers provide simplified development and deployment of Web-based applications. Web applications contain the presentation layer and encapsulate business logic connecting to back-end data stores and legacy applications. However, securing this malleable model presents a challenge. Savvy companies recognize that their security infrastructures need to address the e-business challenge. These companies are aware of the types of attacks that malevolent entities can launch against their servers, and can plan appropriate defenses.

Java technology has established itself as important in the enterprise, both for the ease with which developers can create component software and for the platform independence of the language. Java-based enterprise application servers support Java Servlet, JavaServer Pages (JSP), and Enterprise JavaBeans (EJB) technologies, providing simplified development and flexible deployment of Web-based applications.

To provide security for e-business, the Java 2 Platform, Enterprise Edition (J2EE), builds on the Java 2 Platform, Standard Edition (J2SE), core technologies. J2SE introduced a fine-grained, policy-based security model that is customizable and configurable into numerous security protection domains. This approach is a useful addition to security for component-based software. J2SE security also builds on an additional set of relatively new core technologies: Java Authentication and Authorization Service (JAAS), Java Cryptography Architecture (JCA), Java Cryptography Extension (JCE), Java Secure Socket Extension (JSSE), Public-Key Cryptography Standards (PKCS), and support for the Public Key Infrastructure (PKI).

1.1   Why Java Technology for Enterprise Applications?

Few programming languages and runtimes span heterogeneous multitier distributed computing environments. Prior to the introduction of Java, the client processed Hypertext Markup Language (HTML), Perl, and C/C++, in addition to other programming and scripting languages.

The middle tiers contained the same languages, though often in different combinations, as well as additional languages for performing database queries and messaging. The back-end tier usually contained database query languages, messaging, some amount of scripting, C/C++, and COBOL to access enterprise and legacy resources. Figure 1.1 shows a traditional multitier enterprise environment. Creating an integrated application or suite to address corporate needs across these tiers was a daunting task, especially in a heterogeneous computing environment with multiple languages, development tools, and operating systems.

1.1.1   Java 2 Platform, Standard Edition

As a programming language and runtime environment, J2SE—in the clients, middle tiers, and back-end servers—addresses the challenge of heterogeneous multitiered computing environment by providing a common programming language and runtime environment supported on multiple operating systems. The Java environment acts as a glue to bind these heterogeneous and legacy systems together. Libraries and components exist in J2SE, as well as from other organizations, such as the World Wide Web Consortium (W3C) and Apache, to manipulate the data as

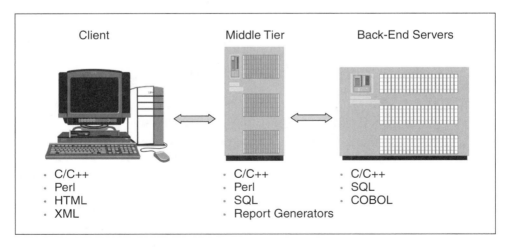

Figure 1.1.   Language Heterogeneity in a Traditional Multitiered Enterprise Environment

it is transformed between the client and back-end servers. These libraries include support for managing and transforming eXtensible Markup Language (XML) documents. However, a single language and its runtime support are insufficient. Additional frameworks are needed to provide structure and design patterns that enable architects, designers, and developers to create and deploy enterprise-scalable applications.

1.1.2   Java 2 Platform, Enterprise Edition

J2EE encompasses a set of enterprise technologies, all integrated through Java Application Programming Interfaces (APIs). These APIs provide the structure needed by enterprise applications. The J2EE technologies include distributed transaction support, asynchronous messaging, and e-mail. In addition, a number of enterprise-critical technologies, including authentication, authorization, message integrity, and confidentiality, are related to security. The J2EE security technologies described in this book afford portable security technologies and APIs that enable interoperable security across the enterprise, even in the presence of heterogenous computing platforms.

1.1.3   Java Components

Before looking at the Java security technologies, it is important to understand the structure of the Java language and runtime environments and how each of the components shown in Figure 1.2 contributes to security.

1.1.3.1   Development Environment and Libraries

The Java 2 Software Development Kit (SDK) contains the tools and library code needed to compile and test Java programs. A significant advantage of the Java 2 libraries is that they include integrated support for networking, file input/output (I/O), multithreading, high-level synchronization primitives, graphical user interface (GUI) support, and key security services.

For the most part, the services found in the Java 2 libraries are those found in typical modern operating systems. The difference is that these libraries have been designed to be portable across operating environments. In addition, these libraries contain integrated security features. For example, to open a network connection to another process, the `Socket` class not only provides the required interfaces but also defines the security authorization requirements for being allowed to open a network connection.

Also, Java code must be written to be type safe. Non-type-safe code will be rejected by the compiler or the runtime. Unlike in C or C++, unsafe type-cast

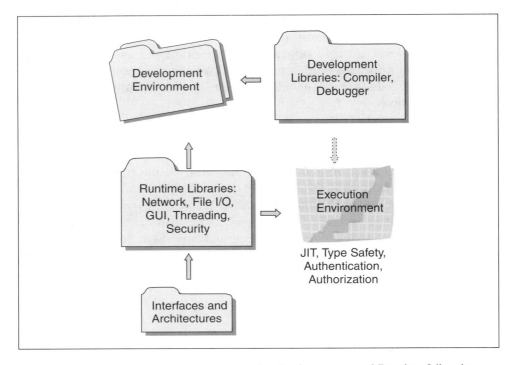

Figure 1.2.   Java Development and Execution Environments and Runtime Libraries,
Interfaces, and Architectures

operations are not allowed. For example, in the Java language, it is not possible to cast a `String` object to be a `StringBuffer` object in order to modify the value in the `String` object. In contrast, other languages, such as C and C++, allow sequences of type-safety-violating cast operations.

1.1.3.2   *Execution Environment and Runtime Libraries*

Execution of a Java program is not a strictly compiled or interpreted program environment. Instead, it is typically a mixed environment that relies on advanced compiler/optimization technologies to enable it to perform well, regardless of the underlying hardware or operating system. The Java Runtime Environment (JRE) processes compiled Java classes at execution time. In particular, the standard Java compiler does not perform many optimizations. Instead, the runtime computes and performs optimizations on the classes during program execution, on the fly. This advanced technology is sometimes referred to as a just-in-time (JIT) compiler.

Like most runtime environments, the JRE includes a set of libraries—for networking, file I/O, threading, GUI support, and security—for application developers to use. The J2EE execution environment may include the compiler, debugger, and other tools, although their presence is not guaranteed and depends on the runtime configuration.

It is the responsibility of the runtime to provide the security mechanisms necessary to enforce security at multiple levels. As code is loaded into the runtime, the runtime ensures type safety of the code. For example, even though the compiler made a first-pass attempt at ensuring type safety, it is possible to mismatch classes at runtime. The code may have been compiled with a library version earlier than the one in the execution environment. This mismatch could cause a type-safety failure if not caught. When loading code, the runtime by default performs a type-safety verification, checking for mismatched types. When type-safety violations are identified, the offending code is not loaded into the runtime. In addition, for those cases in which type safety cannot be verified statically, the runtime performs dynamic type safety. Some of the more familiar runtime safety tests include array-bounds checking and type casting.

As code is loaded into the Java runtime, the location from which the code was obtained is recorded, and when the code is digitally signed, the digital signatures are verified. The combination of the location from which the code was loaded and the set of digital signatures used to sign the code is known as a *code source* and is implemented as a `java.security.CodeSource` object. The `CodeSources` are used to determine whether classes executing in a thread are authorized to access protected resources. In particular, whenever the runtime libraries perform authorization tests, the `CodeSource` for each class is used in determining whether the class is authorized to access a protected resource.

As of J2SE V1.4, the runtime also contains an integrated framework for authenticating and authorizing principals (users, systems, or other accountable entities). This framework is called JAAS. Principal-based authentication and authorization are familiar to most users of computing systems. JAAS usually manifests itself through a login process and restrictions placed on access to computing resources. The support for JAAS both supplements and complements the previously existing support for `CodeSource`-based authorization mechanisms. J2EE V1.3 does not require J2SE V1.4 but must support the JAAS API and framework, as explained in Section 9.4 on page 338.

1.1.3.3   Interfaces and Architectures
Java programs interact with the non-Java world through a set of standard interfaces, or APIs. This interaction includes accessing databases, messaging systems, and processes running in other systems. Many of these interfaces interact with architected subsystems that enable multiple vendors to provide the services in a vendor-neutral manner. Thus, the application can access a set of services without writing to proprietary APIs.

Examples of nonsecurity interfaces and architectures include Java Database Connectivity (JDBC), for access to databases; and Java Message Service (JMS), for access to messaging systems. In the security arena, JCA supplies standard interfaces and architectures for creating and accessing message digests and digital signatures, whereas JCE adds support for encryption. JAAS provides a standard architecture and interfaces for defining and using authentication and authorization services.

1.1.4   Java Security Technologies: Integral, Evolving, and Interoperable

Java security has not been an afterthought, as it is in most programming languages and environments. From its early days as a client-side programming technology, Java security features have included type safety and the ability to create a security *sandbox* that prevents code from unauthorized access to protected computing resources, such as networking and file I/O.

From a security perspective, Java has grown and matured to include an architecture and a set of interfaces to enable a wide range of cryptographic services via JCA and JCE, support for Secure Sockets Layer (SSL) and Transport Layer Security (TLS) via JSSE, Secure/Multipurpose Internet Mail Extensions (S/MIME), and PKI support, including digital certificate path validation via CertPath. One of the main goals for Java has been to support those cryptographic security services, as well as authentication and authorization services through JAAS. In particular, Java supports Kerberos, a network authentication protocol designed to provide strong authentication for client/server applications by using secret-key cryptography; and Generic Security Services (GSS), a protocol for securely exchanging messages between communicating applications. Support for GSS is embedded in the Java GSS API (JGSS-API).

All these services are based on a set of widely recognized and supported standards. Because they are founded on existing standards, Java-based applications can interoperate with existing, or legacy, computing services. The Java development community has expended substantial effort in compliance and interoperability testing. Thus, application and system developers can be assured that Java-based services, including those for security, are interoperable and portable. Figure 1.3 shows the Java security technologies and how they interrelate.

The Java technology had security as a primary design goal from the very beginning. Originally, however, Java technology lacked a number of important security features. The technology has since matured to include some essential cryptographic services, as previously mentioned. Also, one of the security services lacking in the earlier Java versions was a standard architecture and interfaces for performing principal-based authentication and authorization. Although

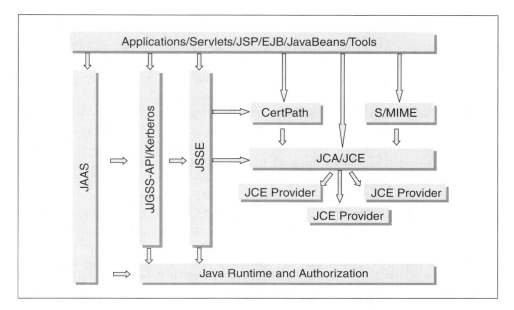

Figure 1.3.   Java Security Technologies

it had a well-developed architecture for authenticating the origins of code executing in the Java runtime, the Java technology lacked standard mechanisms for
authentication typically found in server environments. JAAS has filled this gap-
ing hole by providing the means for authenticating a principal and performing
authorization based on whether the authenticated principal is authorized to access
a specific protected resource.

What is unique about Java support for security is its ability to provide essentially the same collection of security services across a set of heterogeneous
computing platforms. Because of these cross-platform capabilities, the set of
server-side security features is available on all server platforms, making Java
application code and security services highly portable, able to work in heterogeneous computing environments, and able to communicate with non-Java applications and services. For example, a Java program can communicate through an
SSL connection or use Kerberos and interoperate with other services and processes not written in the Java language. This book describes how Java technology
is used to create sophisticated server-side applications that can be protected using
the security technologies found in an enterprise application development and
deployment environment.

1.1.5 Portability in a Heterogeneous World

Most enterprises comprise heterogeneous computing environments. The client-side operating systems include various versions of Microsoft Windows and several flavors of UNIX or Linux, which may be different from the operating systems running on the enterprise servers. Larger enterprises have a server computing environment that also is heterogeneous. This heterogeneity can pose a significant cost to the organization in terms of development, deployment, and interoperability. Heterogeneity can be an impediment to interoperability and integration of computing resources. When this happens, the organization is unable to integrate the services that make it more efficient and competitive.

One of the really tough challenges for enterprises is the creation of applications that can be written and tested on one platform and run on other platforms. Java technology, including J2EE, strives to enable application developers to write and test applications in development environments that are familiar to the developers but that allow deployment and testing in less familiar environments. For example, the development can be performed on a desktop operating system and the code deployed on a mainframe. Few programming languages and development environments can make such a claim.

In addition, few environments can claim to support a broad and common set of security services on the same range of platforms. This level of portability is a tremendous benefit to many organizations that have applications running across a set of heterogeneous computing environments. The cross-platform development and deployment, along with the broad industry support for security, database, and messaging services, are tremendous benefits to organizations that are under pressure to develop and deploy secure applications in heterogeneous environments.

Much of the portability and interoperability of applications are derived from the broad set of services available via the Java runtime libraries. These libraries eliminate or vastly reduce the need for *native,* or non-Java, code. In fact, J2EE discourages the use of native code by bundling a broad range of services most often needed by enterprise application developers.

1.2 Enterprise Java Technology

The three-tier computing model, represented in Figure 1.4, is well established in the computing industry. In fact, this model has been generalized into an *n*-tier model to handle some of the more sophisticated environments that have evolved.

The important question is, How does Java technology fit into a multitier computing model? As previously described, Java technology can run in all the tiers. However, what is more important to recognize is that to develop an application, it is not necessary that the technology run in all the tiers; nor is it required that all the

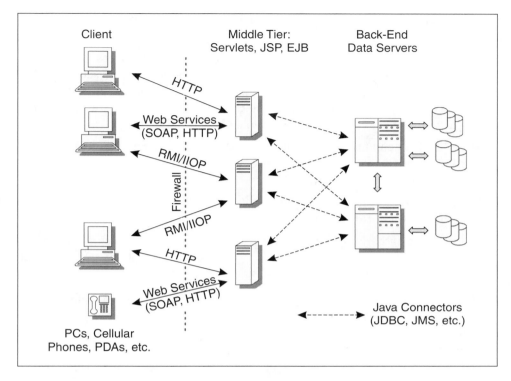

Figure 1.4. Three-Tier Computing Model

computing platforms across the tiers use the same software or hardware architectures. It is quite likely that some of the tiers will not be written using Java-based technologies. Because of the Java set of interoperable technologies, it is possible to write a Java-based application for one or more of the tiers and interface to existing technologies in the same or other tiers.

Enterprise Java applications can connect to other non-J2EE application systems, such as mainframe and enterprise resource planning (ERP) systems. This capability can be achieved through the functionality offered by the Java Connector Architecture (JCA).[1] JCA allows *resource adapters*, or *connectors*, including JDBC and JMS drivers, to provide access to non-J2EE systems. These adapters can be plugged into any J2EE environment.

---

1. Unfortunately, the acronym JCA is also used to indicate another technology: the Java Cryptography Architecture. We will spell this acronym out whenever it is not clear from the context which technology it refers to.

- A servlet in the middle tier uses a JDBC connector to access a database and send the result to an HTML- or XML-enabled client.

- A company's C-based application can send a Web Services XML document through an existing message-queuing-based system, such as IBM WebSphere Message Queuing (MQ).[2] The XML document drives a set of servlets and EJB components, resulting in e-mail being sent to customers to notify them of a set of the company's new services.

- The client and the middle tier use non-Java technologies, whereas the database stored procedures in the back-end server are written in Structured Query Language for Java (SQLJ).

- A Java-based client application can be written to drive non-Java-based Web servers or databases.

- A non-Java-based system can send messages via a wireless communication service to a Java-based application running in a cell phone or a personal digital assistant (PDA).

Connecting heterogeneous applications and systems written in different languages and running on different platforms is one of the most complex tasks that enterprises face. To address the issues in this space, the emerging *Web Services* technology views resources and applications as services. These services can be accessed through a combination of language-agnostic message format over a transport protocol. Such a combination is called a *binding*. A popular binding consists of sending Simple Object Access Protocol (SOAP) messages over HyperText Transfer Protocol (HTTP). SOAP is a proposed standard format for exchanging business messages between applications using standard Internet technologies.

To summarize, it is clear that Java technologies can interoperate with any of the computing tiers in the enterprise. Therefore, the important question is not so much, "How does Java technology fit into a multitier computing model?" but rather, "Which Java technologies are most appropriate for your enterprise and where?"

1.2.1   The Middle Tier: Servlets, JSP, and EJB

When the Web-based computing environment was emerging, developing content that extended beyond static HTML pages was difficult, particularly when more than one vendor's Web server was involved. Extending the server with scripts

---

2. Formerly known as IBM MQSeries.

often required the use of proprietary APIs, making the scripts written for one Web server incompatible with other Web servers. For a variety of reasons, the number of Web servers and proprietary APIs has been greatly reduced. Even so, without portable scripting languages, developing portable extensions to Web servers remained challenging.

The original Common Gateway Interface (CGI) programming model for Web servers was problematic from both scalability and security perspectives. Simple HTTP servers did not support multithreading. CGI scripts were a target of hackers; poorly designed and tested CGI programs failed to test parameters and passed them on to the remainder of the CGI program, resulting in buffer overflows that crashed the CGI script or the HTTP server itself. In some cases, the malicious request caused rogue code to get installed and executed in the server.

The emergence of the Java Servlet programming model simplified server-side Web server programming. Servlets offer server application developers a useful set of APIs for Web application development. In fact, servlets, which are written in the Java language, are often portable across a number of WASs and operating systems. Through servlets, it is possible to write platform-neutral scripts that can call enterprise beans; handle database transactions via JDBC; send messages via JMS and e-mail via JavaMail; generate output, such as HTML or XML, to send to the client; call other servlets; or perform other computing tasks. The *servlet container*—the Web server component responsible for running and managing servlets through their life cycle—also performs optimizations. For example, the servlet container can provide *servlet pooling*, which reduces the overhead of servicing a Web request by pooling instances of servlets so that a servlet is ready to be dispatched as soon as a Web service request arrives. Additionally, the container can provide sharing of HTTP session state across servlet invocations.

The Java Servlet API and runtime simplify writing Web applications and also improve security. As described in Part II of this book, much of the authentication and authorization processes are also now handled by the servlet container through its declarative security architecture, which reduces the burden on the application developer when developing or updating an application. Because the security services are part of the servlet architecture, many of them are easy to enable. For example, the *servlet deployment descriptor*—an XML file containing instructions on how to run servlets—can specify that communication to a particular servlet via HTTP requires confidentiality. The Web server and the servlet container will require that a client communicate with that particular servlet via an HTTP over SSL (HTTPS) session, which uses SSL for encryption. If the deployment descriptor specifies a requirement for client-side authentication based on a digital certificate, the digital certificates exchanged to establish the SSL session will be used to perform client authentication.

Although experienced software developers understand the business logic required to create enterprise applications, the details of how to correctly implement this sort of sophisticated security are often beyond their expertise. Even developers who do have some experience with security technologies do not always implement and deploy these security technologies in a secure manner. It is the responsibility of the Web server and the servlet container to correctly implement and integrate these technologies. By doing so, the security burden on the application developer is greatly reduced.

Servlets have been a boon to Web application developers. However, developing new content could be tedious, particularly when the result to be sent to the client is in HTML, XML, or other formats. The JSP technology was created to address this shortcoming. Rather than writing explicit code to produce the HTML or XML content that will be sent back to the client, a compiler converts an HTML, XML, and Java mixed-content file into a servlet that is then executed.

The servlet and JSP programming models are quite flexible and may be, relatively speaking, long running. However, many enterprise applications often require high throughput, scalability, and multiuser secure distributed transaction processing. The EJB model was created to address this need. Just as servlets run on a servlet container, EJB components run on an *EJB container*, designed to reduce the burden on application developers by providing a set of services common for transaction-based applications. These services include sophisticated distributed transaction management and security. Unlike the servlet and JSP programming model, however, the EJB programming model has additional constraints. For example, EJB components are single threaded, and they may not read from the file system. All I/O operations are intended to be via transactional subsystems using Java connectors, including database I/O operations via JDBC and messaging I/O operations via JMS. Exceptions to this rule are e-mail via JavaMail and printing. Specifically, EJB components are not to manipulate threads and perform file I/O and GUI operations. At first glance, this limitation may seem overly restrictive when compared to servlets and JSP files. However, these restrictions have an advantage in attempts to perform optimizations that result in overall improvements in transaction throughput and scalability. In many regards, this programming model is similar to the IBM Customer Information Control System (CICS) programming model used by large corporations for high-performance transaction processing. In fact, IBM supports the EJB programming model in CICS.

Like servlets and JSP, an EJB component uses a deployment descriptor to define its transaction characteristics, identify other enterprise beans that it will be calling, and specify the security requirements for calling its methods. The security part of the deployment descriptor focuses on authorization issues: specifically, which security roles are allowed to call the methods in an enterprise bean.

1.2.2   Component Software: A Step in the Right Direction

One of the most difficult tasks in the computing industry is the creation of reusable software components. The servlet, JSP, and EJB technologies are all steps in the right direction because they allow creation of clearly defined interfaces, encapsulated state, and transactional and security requirements. The security requirements are defined within the deployment descriptors for each specific component. Well-architected software creates components that can be reused across an enterprise or even used within multiple enterprises. These components communicate via the defined interfaces. The containers in which the components run act as mediators that manage access to the resources they encapsulate, such as database records, and manage the transactional state. The protocols used include HTTP, SOAP, and Java Remote Method Invocation (RMI) over the Internet Inter-Object Request Broker (ORB) Protocol (IIOP) (RMI-IIOP). These protocols allow the container to mediate the communication between the client and the server. The client includes the traditional desktop client, servers located in the same or another enterprise, and handheld devices. Figure 1.5 shows a few ways in which J2EE software components can be combined to create complex applications. Many other combinations, including connection to other services, are possible.

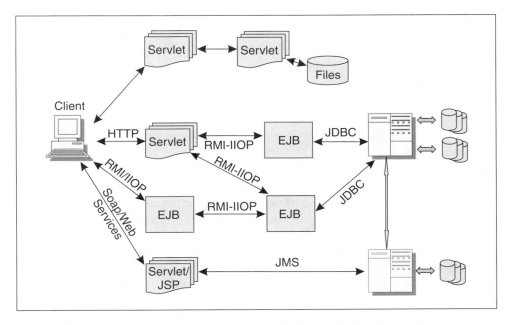

Figure 1.5.   Composing Software Components to Create Applications

Separation of components and their mediation by a container suggests a model in which the security policies can be declarative rather than hard-coded within the applications themselves. In fact, this is the preferred approach because it is difficult, if not impossible, to change corporate security policies once they are written into applications.

The software life cycle takes an application from design and development through to maintenance. After a while, the developers and the maintainers move on to new projects or leave the company. People's lack of familiarity with the application leads to an environment in which there is increasing reluctance to modify functioning software, out of a fear of making changes that result in its failure. When security policies are embedded within the logic of the application, they tend to ossify, becoming rigid and inflexible. It is necessary to break this cycle by extricating the security policy from the application and making it the responsibility of the container and deployer of the application. The use of declarative security is discussed in the context of J2EE (see page 90).

1.2.3   Secure Communication in an Enterprise

One aspect of secure communication in an enterprise is confidentiality: protecting the contents of a communication session from eavesdroppers. The industry-standard protocol for such communication is SSL, which encrypts message content via a combination of public- and private-key encryption. Java technology supports SSL via JSSE, which is a framework and API for using SSL from within Java programs. As with many aspects of the J2EE and J2SE architectures, JSSE is designed so that any vendor's implementation can be installed and used without having to recompile the application, thereby enabling the desirable feature of vendor-neutral applications.

JSSE also supports both server and client authentication and data integrity. The authentication aspect of SSL allows the server and the client to be authenticated by using their private keys to digitally sign documents; the other party can authenticate via the use of public-key cryptography. Also, data integrity is supported so that it is possible to ascertain whether someone tampered with the message contents. JSSE is discussed in Section 13.4.1 on page 460.

In the enterprise realm, communication solely via SSL may be insufficient. Because enterprise applications are often transactional, transactional state needs to be communicated between applications. Some applications require that security information, including principal information for delegation, be transmitted between systems. One of the most common distributed communication models that supports complex enterprise applications is the Object Management Group (OMG) Common Object Request Broker Architecture (CORBA). Within Java, the OMG CORBA model is supported via RMI-IIOP. This protocol can be carried over SSL communication between processes to ensure confidentiality, in addition to the transport of transaction and security information.

SSL provides security between two end points. If messages are sent over message queues and enterprises need end-to-end security, SSL may not satisfy those requirements. In those cases, it is possible to achieve message protection and to carry security information within a message itself and remain independent of the underlying protocol. For example, a SOAP message can be encrypted and digitally signed, while carrying principal information in the message itself.

1.3   Java Technology as Part of Security

Java technology is not an island. It is part of a larger, often heterogenous, computing environment. For example, a stand-alone Java application is not running in isolation. It is running on top of an operating system and functions within an existing enterprise security infrastructure.

Enterprise operating systems offer authentication and authorization services via a directory service, a system used to manage user identities and services within an enterprise. Enterprises invest resources in training their staffs and developing tools to use these directory services. Therefore, it is incumbent on Java technology to integrate with these security services rather than to operate independently, which would make it difficult, if not impossible, to create integrated applications and security. This is why JAAS is designed to interact with existing authentication and authorization services. Examples of this integration can be found in the set of J2SE classes that allow JAAS to use Kerberos for authentication. JAAS also interoperates with existing directory services, including those on such operating systems as UNIX, z/OS,[3] Linux, and Windows.

An enterprise's security infrastructure may include an existing PKI from one or more vendors. This infrastructure includes support for digital certificates used for a variety of cryptographic services, such as authentication. Java components must interface with a PKI and indeed do so via JCA, JCE, and CertPath.

An e-business is more than the Java language and its runtime libraries. A WAS includes an HTTP server, the application containers for servlets and JSP applications and for EJB components, and support for messaging via JMS, database access via JDBC, database-stored procedures via SQLJ, e-mail via JavaMail, and other services. Many of these services are not written in the Java language. These computing elements do not stand alone. Security must be integrated and interoperable. As previously mentioned, J2SE contains an integrated set of

---

3. Previously known as Operating System/390 (OS/390) and Multiple Virtual Storage (MVS).

security services. In fact, it would have been detrimental to create a new set of Java-specific security services or one for each of the elements of aWAS, as they may not seamlessly integrate, generating opportunities for an adversary to slide in between the cracks. Java technology provides many advantages for component and application developers to create portable applications, particularly in a heterogeneous computing environment. That is why its security must be and is integrated into the enterprise.

1.4   An Overview of Enterprise Security Integration

Enterprises typically use a number of security technologies, including authentication and authorization, cryptography and related services, firewalls, SOCKS,[4] and proxy servers. It is essential for Java components and J2EE to interoperate with these technologies, as they provide essential services. When Java technology can plug into existing security technology infrastructures, J2EE can leverage the existing services, thus avoiding duplication of administrative and processing overhead. It also leads to greater consistency between legacy and Java applications. Tying into existing security services will prevent Java technology and J2EE from operating as an island.

1.4.1   Authentication and Authorization Services

Typical authentication and authorization services include some, such as Resource Access Control Facility (RACF) on z/OS and Active Directory on Microsoft Windows, that are native to operating systems. Distributed system support for authentication and authorization technologies exists for Web-based applications and services, including Tivoli's Access Manager product. Kerberos, developed at Massachusetts Institute of Technology (MIT), has been in use for many years in support of distributed systems applications.

Since its inception, the Java 2 platform has provided a means to enforce access control based on where code came from and who signed it. The need for this type of access control derives from the distributed nature of Java technology, whereby mobile code may be downloaded over a public network and then run locally. The original design, however, lacked the means to enforce similar access control based on who runs the code. To provide this type of access control, the Java 2 security architecture required additional support for authentication—determining who is running the code—and extensions to the existing authorization

---

4. SOCKS is a shortened version of *socket secure*. *Socket* is the term used for the data structures that describe a TCP (Transmission Control Protocol) connection.

components to enforce new access controls, based on who was authenticated. The JAAS framework, which is now integrated into the core Java platform, augments the Java 2 security architecture with such support and allows existing authentication and authorization services, such as those listed earlier, to be tied into Java technologies and J2EE, as described in Section 9.4 on page 338.

1.4.2 Cryptographic Services

Cryptography is a key element of enterprise security. The Java platform offers cryptographic support through JCA and JCE.

The basic JCA offers support for message digests and digital signatures. Support for encryption is provided through JCE, a JCA extension that was introduced to respond to the export restrictions on encryption imposed by the United States.

JCA is described as a provider architecture. The primary design principle of the JCA has been to separate the cryptographic concepts from their algorithmic implementations. JCA is designed to allow vendors to provide their own implementations of the cryptographic tools and other administrative functions. Providers may be updated transparently to the application: for example, when faster or more secure versions are available. The result is a flexible framework that will cater to future requirements and allow vendor independence and interoperability.

Even though JCA and JCE offer a flexible and powerful cryptographic support to Java applications, most programmers and application designers would prefer ready-built cryptographic protocols rather than having to create them from the basic elements of encryption and digital signatures. The JSSE framework allows Java programs to communicate with other programs and services using SSL, which is the most widely used cryptographic service provided in the Web.

1.4.3 Firewalls

Firewalls are intended to keep malicious entities from attacking systems within the enterprise. One way to let applications within the firewall access network resources outside the firewall is to use the SOCKS protocol within the intranet and a SOCKS server at the firewall. SOCKS encapsulates a client's network request and sends the data packets to a SOCKS server. SOCKS requests are allowed through the firewall; the SOCKS server unwraps the request and forwards it to the target system. Responses from the target system are encapsulated, sent through the firewall, and sent back to the system that originated the request. Unauthorized network messages are still blocked at the firewall. SOCKS is often enabled by replacing or wrapping the Transmission Control Protocol/Internet Protocol (TCP/IP) APIs on an underlying operating system with a SOCKSified version. This makes SOCKS transparent to applications.

Proxy servers work in a similar way by sending a network request through a third system. A proxy server's function is to receive a request from a Web client, perform that request on behalf of the client—possibly after authorization—and return the results to the browser. Like a SOCKS server, a proxy server prevents requests coming from the external network from accessing the internal network. Unlike a SOCKS server, however, a proxy server does not require TCP to be encapsulated within another protocol.

New network routers and firewalls are eliminating the need for SOCKS and proxy servers by integrating the filtering function directly rather than through a separate server or service. J2EE leverages firewalls to enhance the security of a system, as described in Section 2.4 on page 36, and in Chapter 6.

1.5   Time to Market

The success of an enterprise depends on its agility. The ability of an enterprise to remain competitive means that it must innovate, adapt, and evolve rapidly to meet a continually changing marketplace. This agility includes support for standards and reusable software components.

1.5.1   Support for Essential Technical Standards

An e-business must contend with a broad range of technical standards and evolving technologies to meet the demands of the marketplace, regardless of whether the customer is internal to the organization or a third party. The set of important technical standards is broad, including HTML, XML, SQL, OMG's CORBA, SSL, PKI, Kerberos, Web Services, and SOAP. One of the key benefits of the Java development and deployment environment is that it supports these standards. In fact, unlike other programming languages, the Java language supports a broad range of technologies that bind an enterprise application together:

- Relational databases accessibility via JDBC and SQLJ
- Distributed systems via RMI-IIOP
- Asynchronous messaging via JMS
- XML, SOAP, and Web services
- Cryptography using JCA, JCE, CertPath, and JSSE
- Authentication and authorization via JAAS

1.5.2 Engineering Software in a Heterogeneous World

One of the difficult challenges in software design, development, and deployment is to engineer software to help achieve modularity. Although modularity can be achieved in many ways, one popular approach is to organize components or objects that can be mixed and matched to provide an integrated solution. Although the concept of object-oriented (OO) software has evolved over the past two decades, the current approach is to create and compose course-grained components that can be assembled to create applications. J2EE supports this model.

The classic design pattern for J2EE is to use servlets and JSP for presentation—generation of HTML or XML and interaction with the client—and transactional components via EJB. The development and deployment models treat these components as reusable, with well-defined interfaces that may be developed by multiple vendors and assembled to create applications. J2EE is intended to facilitate the creation and deployment of these software components. An emerging and popular approach to achieve modularity is the service-oriented software methodology that is being realized in the form of Web services.

Enterprises are not homogeneous islands of software technology purchased from a single software vendor. The reality is that the information technology propelling enterprises is purchased from multiple vendors, creating heterogeneous environments that are often difficult to integrate. J2EE and evolving standards, such as Web Services, work to bridge the gaps by offering a set of interoperable and platform-independent technologies. It is possible to produce J2EE applications that can be written on one platform and deployed in another. Servlets, JSP, and EJB applications can be developed and tested on a workstation and deployed on multiple mainframes or departmental servers. Each of these platforms may have radically different hardware and operating system architectures, but the J2EE model isolates the applications from many of these differences.

One of the most challenging aspects of application development and deployment is security. Most application developers are domain experts, not well versed in the nuances of information technology (IT) security. Correctly configuring software to prevent security breaches can be daunting, as witnessed by the number of security flaws discovered in popular desktop operating systems, applications, and Web servers. In fact, some enterprises have chosen to outsource their IT security to external security services providers. J2EE mitigates the difficulty of developing new secure applications by providing a development and deployment model that separates security policy and enforcement from application implementation. The design of J2EE is structured such that the developers are not required to be versed in security design and implementation. Security-configuration decisions can be deferred until the application is deployed, or installed. The J2EE containers—the middleware that runs the servlet, JSP, and EJB software—provide a broad range of standard security services that can be configured during the deployment of the applications. Removing security-related code from application code has a significant benefit. Security policies are no longer embedded within the applications. Therefore, it is far easier to change enterprise security policies and upgrade security services. In fact, it is no longer necessary to modify the application code to effect the changes. Changes to security policies are managed through the J2EE containers by the system administrator.

1.5.3   Time Is of the Essence

No matter what business you are in, bringing your product to market at a reasonable cost in a timely manner is essential. Software development and IT security are critical tasks, particularly in a complex world with many important technical standards. Java technologies, and J2EE in particular, simplify what would otherwise be a formidable task. J2EE brings together the elements essential for creating useful and secure applications that can be developed and deployed in a heterogeneous world. The J2EE framework provides high-value function and structure that reduce the time to market for the development of new applications and integration with existing systems and services. The remainder of this book elaborates on Java and J2EE security, providing a practical approach that includes examples.

CHAPTER 2

Enterprise Network Security and Java Technology

COMPUTER security must be holistic, as attackers concentrate on the weakest links. Therefore, the security of a system that uses Java technology must be reviewed as a whole, following the flow of data and applications and considering the potential for attack at each point. This process applies even more forcefully when many computer systems are connected through a network, as more points are subject to attack.

This chapter describes a number of architectural approaches for enterprises, illustrated with real-life examples. We consider the security implications of these approaches, as well as the effects of using Java technology on the server side.

Firewalls are often touted as a defense against network attacks. This chapter describes how firewalls work and explains what the implications are to Web browser users, server administrators, and Java application designers.

2.1 Networked Architectures

The most common architectural approaches for today's enterprises are the two- and three-tier models.

2.1.1 Two-Tier Architectures

In a *two-tier architecture*, two applications—the *client* and the *server*—exchange information over a network. The client makes requests to the server, and the server sends responses back to the client. Such responses can contain any combination of static and dynamic information. *Static responses* are identical for each client, such as static HTML documents. *Dynamic responses* are generated based on the particular input from the user; the generation of a dynamic response requires a program running on the server. To perform transactions, the server may need to access a database.

In a Web environment, the client application is usually a Web browser, and the server application is a Web server. The Web browser can be enhanced by a number of plug-ins, including a Java Plug-in to run applets. The Web server can be enhanced by a servlet container, an EJB container, and other transactional applications, as discussed in Section 2.3 on page 32.

Perhaps the simplest use of a Java application in a two-tier architecture is the browser add-on Java virtual machine (JVM) to run applets and extend the facilities provided by a Web browser. Applets may be used to enhance the user interface by providing interactivity, such as context-sensitive help or local-search functions. Applets may also be used to handle additional data types, such as compressed astronomical images or packed database records. These examples depend directly on the Java security architecture, which prevents unauthorized access to protected resources.

The next level of complexity is seen in *network-aware* applets, which perform network operations other than simply reading data. Terminal emulators are in this category. These applets provide the functions of a nonprogrammable terminal, or visual display unit (VDU), connected via a local area network (LAN) to a z/OS or Application System/400 (AS/400) host system, where the applications are run. An example is IBM Host On-Demand, which emulates a 3270 or 5250 mainframe display session, communicating with a mainframe over TCP/IP. Figure 2.1 shows an IBM Host On-Demand system.

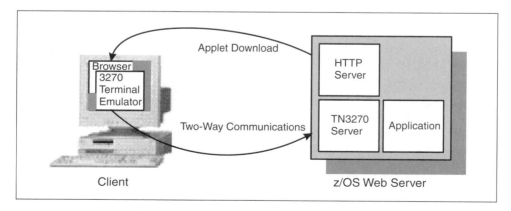

Figure 2.1. IBM Host On-Demand System

When run as applets, such programs are subject to the restrictions imposed by the Java authorization mechanisms. By default, they may open a network connection only back to the system from which they were downloaded. However, terminal emulation programs usually need to communicate with many different host systems, not just one. If the host is a large mainframe, crucial to business, its owners may be reluctant to install the TCP/IP software, preferring to remain with Systems Network Architecture (SNA) LANs. On other host systems, it might not be desirable to install, configure, run, and maintain a Web server simply to download the Java emulator applet, and this approach would still restrict access to that single host.

The Java 2 security architecture solves that problem. It is still true that downloaded applets are restricted to connect back only to the system from which they are downloaded; that is the default configuration. Using the fine-grained Java 2 access control mechanisms, it is possible to modify this default restriction. Java system administrators can specify the range of socket connections that a particular Java program is allowed to use. Java 2 supports a *declarative* policy configuration, which means that the policy definition can be external to the application. Therefore, modifying the default restrictions does not require hard-coding the security policy in the application or altering the Java system's security manager, which is implemented as a `java.lang.SecurityManager` object. This makes it easy to change the policy, extend the application, and port the application to various platforms.

Another possibility is to run the Java emulator as a stand-alone application, thereby relaxing the restrictions on which hosts the emulator may connect to. This is the classic two-tier client/server application architecture. The security issues are very similar to running any other executable program, namely, that it is wise to use only trusted sources of programs. Java technology has several safety and security advantages over other binary programs; its executable files and digitally signed Java programs can provide a cryptographic guarantee about the code author's identity.

2.1.2 Three-Tier Architectures

Another design is to run *middleware software* on the Web server. The client will communicate over TCP/IP with the middleware software, which can then pass through the messages to the ultimate destination. For example, in the case of 3270 terminal emulation, IBM's Communications Server, which runs on several operating systems, can provide the TCP/IP connection to the Java 3270 Terminal Emulator and can connect to hosts over both TCP/IP and SNA. Figure 2.2 shows the architecture for this *three-tier* client/server application.

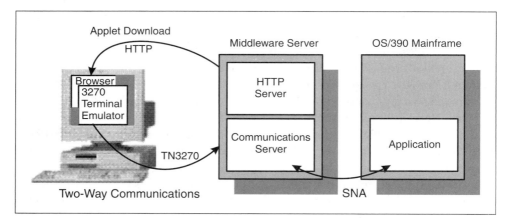

Figure 2.2.   Three-Tier Architecture Example

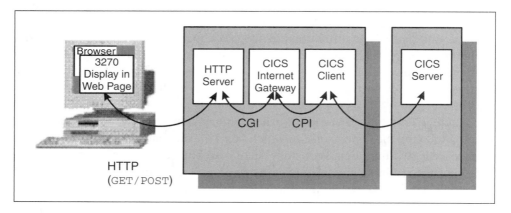

Figure 2.3.   CICS Internet Gateway

Another possibility is to use Web server CGI programs[1] to provide the middle tier. The IBM CICS Internet Gateway takes this approach: to the application server, emulating the functions of a 3270 terminal but downstream, generating HTML code, which is displayed in the Web browser window (see Figure 2.3). This approach avoids using Java technology in the client but does not provide as much flexibility, as the display is restricted to what can be done in HTML.

---

1. Often termed *CGI-BIN* programs after the name of the directory in which they are conventionally stored.

A better design, described in Section 2.3 on page 32, is to use Java servlets and/or JSP applications in place of CGI programs in the middle tier and then take advantage of the J2EE and J2SE security services. The servlet and JSP programming model offer a simple way to present data to the client by generating HTML and/or XML code that is sent to the client, based on the client/server interaction. Servlets and JSP applications can interact with EJB components via Java RMI-IIOP (see Appendix A on page 547). The JDBC protocol allows interaction with databases. This architecture is shown in Figure 2.4.

The gateway server approach can also be used to provide extended facilities to Java applets. The IBM CICS Gateway for Java is a good example of this; it allows a Java applet to access transaction-processing capabilities of CICS servers running on a variety of server platforms. The IBM CICS Gateway for Java provides a class library package to access CICS functions. The class library itself does not perform the bulk of the functions; instead, it transmits the request to the gateway server and returns the server's response to the applet. The gateway server is a small program that receives the requests and calls the CICS client library, which communicates with the CICS system itself.

The CICS transaction-processing engine is commonly run on its own system, separate from the Web server, as shown in Figure 2.5. The CICS client application, residing on the midlle tier, and the CICS server applications, located on the third tier, communicate using the External Presentation Interface (EPI) and the External Call Interface (ECI). Several communication protocols are supported, such as TCP/IP and Network Basic Input-Output System (NetBIOS). The CICS client and the CICS server application can also communicate through Advanced Peer-to-Peer Communication (APPC), an application programming interface (API) for peer-to-peer communication on SNA.

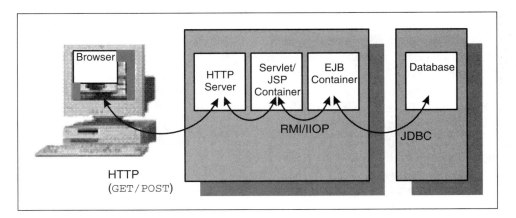

Figure 2.4. Three-Tier Architecture Using Servlets and EJB Technology

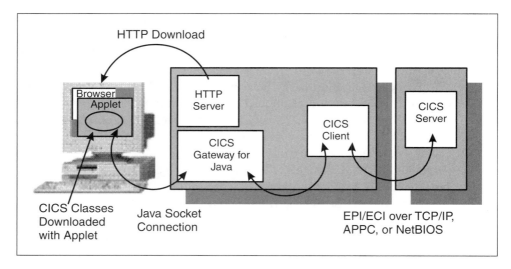

Figure 2.5.   CICS Gateway for Java Example

Enforcing security for the type of system shown in Figure 2.5 is more complex. The security of both the gateway system and the systems with which it connects must be ensured, especially if the server is on the public Internet, where any malicious hacker may attempt to access it. Intranet systems should already have some defenses in place to restrict access to company personnel, but security is still of concern, especially if sensitive data is at risk.

The usual approach is to provide a number of barriers that must be overcome before data access is granted. Often, the first barrier is the company's firewall system. As discussed in more detail in Section 2.4 on page 36, a *firewall* is a system combining hardware and software enforcing an access control policy between two networks. Typically, a firewall checks that requests are coming from, and responses are going to, apparently valid addresses. Some firewalls check the data content of selected protocols, but there are limits to what can be checked. There have been several embarrassingly public demonstrations of Web servers whose content has been replaced by derogatory pages, despite the presence of firewalls. Often, these hackers have succeeded because valid HTTP uniform resource locator (URL) requests to the Web server allowed software to be run that contained unintended security holes in it, such as permitting any data file to be read or written or even executing arbitrary binary code.

Therefore, it is necessary to secure the Web server against as many vulnerabilities as possible and to ensure that if the Web server is compromised, the attacker's access to data is limited. Hardening Web servers against attack has been the subject of several books, such as *Practical Unix & Internet Security* by Simson

Garfinkel, Gene Spafford, and Alan Schwartz[2] so only a brief checklist is given here.

- Disable all network services that do not need to be present; where possible, allow only HTTP and the gateway protocol.
- Check the Web server configuration files to allow access only to the required set of pages.
- Delete any CGI-BIN and other executable programs that are not required; if they are not present, they cannot be run.
- Use Java servlets and/or JSP applications in place of CGI programs.
- Restrict the privileges of the Web server program, if possible. On UNIX, the Web server can be run as a normal user with restricted access rights.

These guidelines also apply to any gateway software. Ensure that it does not provide access to resources that are not required for it to run. In particular, do not depend on the client to validate requests. Assume that a hacker has constructed a modified client that can generate any possible request, including a wide variety of invalid requests. For example, for a 3270 gateway, do not assume that the client will request connection to only a limited set of hosts. Configure the gateway so that the minimal number of hosts have connections available. No other host names must be visible. For database access and transaction processing, make sure that the gateway allows no more than the set of permitted requests and that its authorizations are limited to a minimal set.

2.2 Network Security

The classic three-tier architecture pictures can hide other attack routes. Figures 2.2, 2.3, and 2.5 imply that there are separate connections between the client and the Web server/gateway and between the gateway and the end server. However, the real network may not be configured that way. For simplicity or cost, there might be only a single network interface on the Web server, as shown in Figure 2.6.

In this case, the third-tier server is on the same network and can potentially be accessed directly from the firewall. Perhaps the firewall is configured correctly and will prevent direct access to the end server. However, will this be true tomorrow, after additional services have been added? For very little extra cost, the

---

2. S. Garfinkel, G. Spafford, and A. Schwartz. *Practical Unix & Internet Security,* 3rd Edition. (Sebastopol, CA: O'Reilly & Associates, 2003).

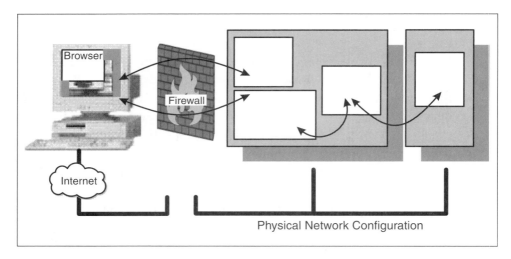

Figure 2.6.   Web Server with One Network Interface

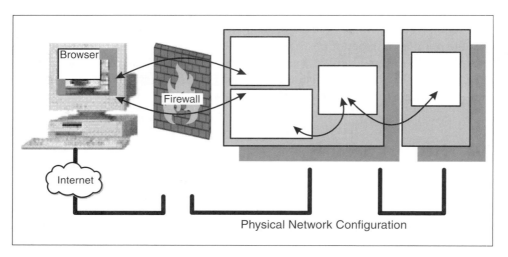

Figure 2.7.   Separating the Third Tier

networks can be physically separated by providing two network interfaces in the Web server, as shown in Figure 2.7.

Or, a second firewall system can be used. This configuration has the benefit that even if the Web server is compromised, the second firewall still restricts access to the rest of the network. It is more expensive to provide such a demilitarized zone (DMZ) (Figure 2.8), but if such a configuration is already required to provide

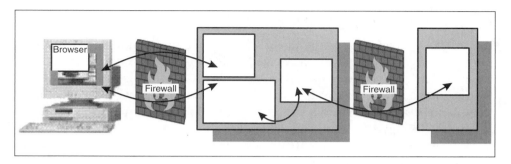

Figure 2.8.   DMZ Network Environment

safe Internet connection, there is no extra cost. The cost of a second firewall is likely to be less than the value of the data it protects, so a value assessment needs to be made.

One additional security barrier to consider using is the type of network. The gateway and the end server could be linked by using SNA protocols or by a small custom-built program communicating over a dedicated serial link. These approaches effectively use the network connection as another firewall; if TCP/IP cannot travel over it, many hacking techniques are simply not possible. However, if the Web server is totally compromised, the hackers have all the communications software at their disposal if they can discover it. Therefore, the third-tier server still needs to be guarded (see Figure 2.9).

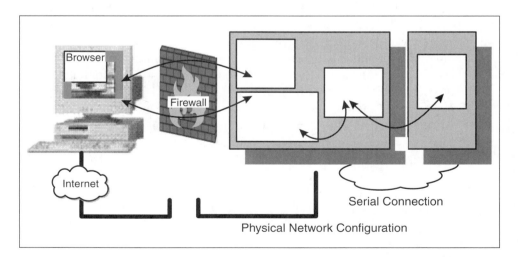

Figure 2.9.   Protection Using Mixed Connection Protocols

2.3   Server-Side Java Technology

Running Java technology on the server side can greatly simplify the work of software developers, especially of distributed architectures. Although the majority of client systems might be personal computers (PCs) running some version of Microsoft Windows, most of the world's crucial business data is kept on mainframe, Linux, and UNIX servers. A server-side distributed application developed in Java technology can be run on almost any of these servers, whether they run z/OS,[3] Virtual Machine (VM), Windows, Operating System/2 (OS/2), AS/400, one of the many flavors of UNIX, or Linux.

In many ways, the Java environment is ideal for server applications. The multithreaded environment is well suited for supporting simultaneous requests to a server. Even the standard classes are simplified, as many server programs are unlikely to need the `java.awt` windowing classes as well as several others, which is where most cross-platform problems often arise. As an example, because it is written in the Java language, the gateway component of the CICS Java gateway can run on any Web server system, reducing porting and testing costs.

Web application servers supplement and even surpass traditional Web servers in their use and functionality in enterprise environments. Unlike a traditional Web server, a WAS provides a robust and flexible foundation for dynamic transactions and objects. Traditional Web servers are constrained to servicing standard HTTP requests, returning the contents of static HTML pages and images or the output from executed CGI scripts. Some Web servers have extended their functionality by including support for Java servlets, JSP applications, and EJB components.

- Servlets allow Java applications to be executed on the server side and return dynamically generated information, in much the same way that a CGI script can dynamically generate information. However, servlets have additional capabilities. A *servlet,* a Java class residing on a Web server, accepts requests and generates responses over various communication protocols. The most common type of servlet is an HTTP servlet, which is implemented by the `javax.servlet.http.HttpServlet` class. An `HttpServlet` accepts HTTP requests and generates HTTP responses. As a server resource, a servlet has access to other server resources, such as other servlets, EJB components, JSP applications, and databases. The purpose of a servlet is to generate a dynamic response.

  However, grafting servlet support onto a Web server does not provide a complete solution to meet e-business requirements. A WAS provides a

---

3. Previously known as Operating System/390 (OS/390) and Multiple Virtual Storage (MVS).

more scalable environment for modeling enterprise solutions, partly through the use of Java technology. A WAS supports Java objects in their simple and compound manifestations. Servlet support plays an important role, but a WAS also supports EJB and JSP technologies.

- EJB technology provides an architecture for distributed, transaction-based objects, called *enterprise beans*, which allow developers to concentrate on the business logic rather than its interaction with the underlying infrastructure.

- Similarly, JSP technology provides developers and administrators with a convenient way to produce HTML or XML via template data, custom elements, scripting languages, and server-side Java objects to generate dynamic information and return it to a client.

The blend of EJB, servlets, and JSP provides the foundation for representing a Model-View-Controller (MVC) architecture[4] to developers. Typically, the modularity and focus of purpose in EJB represents the model; JSP and servlets represent the view through their ability to dynamically generate HTML and XML information; the client system represents the controller.

2.3.1   WAS Components

A Web application server must contain a servlet container and an EJB container.

2.3.1.1   Servlet Container

A *servlet container*, a Java environment within which servlets execute, constitutes an intermediary between the Web server and the servlets in the WAS. The servlet container is responsible for managing the life cycle of servlets by loading, initializing, and executing them (see Section 4.3 on page 107). A servlet container ensures that memory contains a single instance of a servlet and dispatches a thread that executes the servlet for each request.

When a request arrives, a servlet container maps the request to a servlet and then passes the request to the servlet. The servlet processes the request and produces a response. The servlet container translates the response into the network

---

4. The *MVC architecture* is a popular object-oriented (OO) design pattern for the creation of user interfaces. Its goal is to separate the application object—*model*—from the way it is represented to the user—*view*—and from the way in which the user controls it—*controller*. Before MVC, user interface designs tended to lump such objects together. MVC decouples them, thus allowing greater flexibility and possibility for reuse. MVC also provides a powerful way to organize systems that support multiple presentations of the same information.

format and sends the response back to the Web server. For this process to work, a servlet container must provide the network services over which the requests and responses are sent and is responsible for decoding and formatting MIME-type requests and responses. All servlet containers must support HTTP as a protocol for requests and responses but may also support additional request/response protocols, such as HTTP over SSL (HTTPS).

A servlet container is designed to perform well while serving large numbers of requests. A servlet container can hold any number of active servlets. Both a servlet container and the objects in it are multithreaded. A servlet container creates and manages threads as necessary to handle incoming requests. It can handle multiple requests concurrently, and more than one thread may enter an object at a time. Therefore, each object within a servlet container must be thread safe. Additionally, to support JSP applications, a servlet container provides an engine that interprets and processes JSP pages into servlets.

A servlet container can manage numerous distinct applications. As noted in Section 4.4 on page 111 and Section 4.10.3 on page 150, an application may consist of any number of servlets, JSP applications, filters, listeners, utility classes, and static Web pages. A collection of such components working together is a *Web application*. A servlet container uses a *context* to group-related components. The servlet loads the objects within a context as a group; objects within the same context can easily share data. Therefore, each context corresponds to a distinct Web application. A context is represented as an instance of the `javax.servlet.ServletContext` interface. Therefore, a servlet container is responsible for creating one `ServletContext` instance for each invocation of a Web application. Programmers can use the `ServletContext` object to make resources available to all servlets within a Web application.

2.3.1.2   EJB Container

An *EJB container* is a runtime environment that manages one or more enterprise beans. It manages the life cycles of enterprise bean objects, coordinates distributed transactions, and implements object security. Generally, each EJB container is provided by a WAS and contains a set of enterprise beans that run on the WAS.

An EJB container acts as the interface between an enterprise bean and the WAS. In essence, the EJB container is an abstraction that manages one or more EJB classes while making the required services available to EJB classes through standard interfaces as defined in the EJB specification. The EJB container vendor is also free to provide additional services implemented at either the container or the server level. An EJB client never accesses an enterprise bean directly. Any access to the enterprise bean is done through the methods of the container-generated classes, which in turn invoke the enterprise bean's methods. Multiple EJB component instances typically exist inside a single EJB container.

Having an EJB container interposed on all enterprise bean invocations allows the EJB container to manage transactions and resources, load enterprise bean instances, and provide such services as versioning, scalability, mobility, persistence, concurrency, deployment, and security to the EJB components it contains. Because the EJB container handles all these functions, the Enterprise Bean Provider can concentrate on business rules and leave database manipulation and other details to the EJB container. For example, if it needs to abort the current transaction, a single EJB component simply tells its EJB container; the EJB container is responsible for performing all rollbacks and doing whatever is necessary to cancel a transaction in progress.

2.3.2 WAS Security Environment

A WAS is more than a grouping of Java objects. In the multiuser enterprise environment, a WAS also provides integrated authentication and authorization support for user transactions, whether they originate from Web browsers, client applications, or another WAS. This complex environment of both friendly and potentially malicious entities requires answers to a number of questions:

- How can users be authenticated to a WAS?
- After authentication, to which objects and actions are the users authorized?
- How can the details of users' transactions remain hidden from unauthorized entities?

These questions deal with the security issues of authentication, authorization, and encryption.

Objects that play a major role in the WAS environment are client objects and server objects. *Client objects* include Web clients and application clients. *Server objects* include Web servers, WASs, security servers, and user registry servers.

The physical WAS executing the supported Java objects plays an important role, but it is only one member of the entire ensemble of processes that complete the WAS environment. Note the distinction between the WAS and the WAS environment, depicted in Figure 3.1 on page 56. The WAS represents the server that handles requests for EJB objects, servlets, and JSP pages. The *WAS environment* encompasses all the client and server objects that have a direct or indirect interaction with the WAS, including the WAS itself.

Clients to a WAS include Web browsers, Java client applications or applets, and pervasive devices, such as mobile appliances. Client objects can originate from many different sources but can be categorized into those from traditional Web browsers and those from stand-alone applications.

A WAS typically does not directly service client requests. Web servers respond to HTTP requests for HTML pages or to execute CGI scripts. For more complex tasks, such as the manipulation of EJB objects, Web servers pass the service requests to the WAS.

The security server is an essential element in the WAS environment, maintaining a consistent security schema and arbitrating user authentication and authorization access to objects. To authenticate users, as well as to obtain the user's authorization attributes and digital certificate information, the security server obtains the information from an enterprise user registry, such as a Lightweight Directory Access Protocol (LDAP) server, RACF, or IBM Tivoli Access Manager.

Security in the WAS environment is not limited to authentication and authorization. Between the various server and client objects, security also comes into play through the use of encryption technologies.

2.4   Java and Firewalls

This section considers how Java security can be affected when firewall systems are used on the network. Various firewall implementations can affect the proper working of a network connection through a firewall.

A *firewall* is any computer system, network hardware, or system/hardware combination that links two or more networks and enforces an access control policy between them. The intent is that one side of the network, the *secure network*, is protected from malicious entities in the other part of the network, the *nonsecure network*, as shown in Figure 2.10. This concept is analogous to a building's solid firewalls, which prevent a fire from spreading from one part of the building to another.

Sometimes, a single hardware system is called a *firewall*; other times, a complex collection of multiple routers and servers implement the firewall function. The National Computer Security Association (NCSA) has created tests to enforce minimum standards for a firewall, but that has not stopped some vendors from using the term creatively. Here, we are concerned only about the policies enforced by the firewall and what the effect is on the data traffic.

Depending on their configuration, firewalls can affect any type of network traffic. Two such types of traffic are

1. The loading of Java applets from a server to a client

2. Network accesses by Java applets to a server

Firewalls may be present in the client network, the server network, or both.

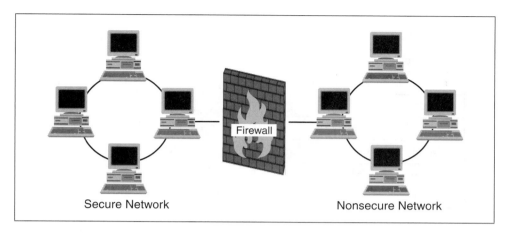

Secure Network

Nonsecure Network

Figure 2.10. Firewall Representation

Current literature on firewalls is filled with buzzwords describing the various software techniques used to create firewalls. Techniques include packet filtering, application gateways, proxy servers, dynamic filters, bastion hosts, DMZs, and dual-homed gateways. For the purpose of this book, we concentrate on the data packets flowing through the firewall. The basic security functions of any firewall are to examine data packets sent through the firewall and to accept, reject, or modify the packets according to the security policy requirements. Most of today's firewalls work only with TCP/IP data.

2.4.1 TCP/IP Packets

All network traffic exchange is performed by sending blocks of data between two connected systems. The blocks of data are encapsulated within a data packet by adding header fields to control what happens to the data block en route and when it reaches its final destination. Network architectures are constructed of layers of function, each built on the services of the layer beneath it. The most thorough layered architecture is the Open Systems Interconnection (OSI) model, whereas other architectures, such as TCP/IP, use broader layer definitions. On the wire, these layers are translated into a series of headers placed before the data being sent, as shown in Figure 2.11.

The first part of the header, the data link/physical header, is determined by the type of network. Ethernet, token-ring, serial lines, Fiber Distributed Data Interface (FDDI) networks: Each type has its own headers, containing synchronization,

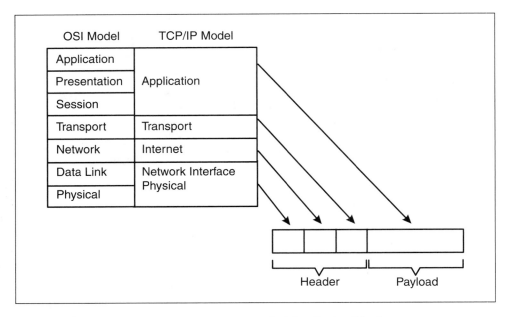

Figure 2.11. Mapping the Layered Network Model to Packet Headers

start-of-packet identifiers, access control, and physical addresses[5] as required by the network type. There may be fields to distinguish IP packets from other types of packets, such as NetBIOS or SNA. We consider only IP packets here.

The next part of the header of IP packets is the standard IP header, which specifies the originator, or *source* address, and the intended recipient, or *destination* address, together with fields to control how the packet is forwarded through the Internet. IP headers adhere to the IP standard.

Next is the transport layer header, which controls what happens to the packet when it reaches its destination. Almost all the user-level protocols commonly referred to as TCP/IP use either a TCP or a User Datagram Protocol (UDP) header

---

5. Network devices require an adapter to physically attach to the LAN. This adapter must provide both physical and logical capabilities for the device. The adapter contains a unique 48-bit address, called media access control (MAC), assigned to it during the manufacturing process. All MAC addresses are assigned by the Institute for Electrical and Electronic Engineers (IEEE) 802 committee. The IEEE provides the vendor building adapters with a range of MAC addresses to use for assigning adapters their unique 48-bit addresses, so that no two adapters should ever have the same address. Ethernet and token-ring networks require the MAC address for both the origin and the destination adapters when communicating over a LAN. Besides the IP address, the MAC address also must be known when sending data to a LAN-attached device.

at the transport layer. Finally, application protocol headers and data are contained in the payload portion of the packet and are passed from the sending process to the receiving process.

Each packet header contains a number of data fields, which may be examined by a firewall and used to decide whether to accept or reject the data packet. The most important data fields are

- *Source IP address*, a 32- or 128-bit address, depending on the IP version
- *Destination IP address*, a 32- or 128-bit address, depending on the IP version
- *Source port number*, a 16-bit value
- *Destination port number*, a 16-bit value

The source and destination IP addresses logically identify the machines at each end of the connection and are used by intermediate machines to route the packet through the network. An IP address identifies a physical or logical network interface on the machine, which allows a single machine to have several IP addresses.

The TCP/IP networking software uses the source and destination port numbers at each end to send the packets to the appropriate program running on the machines. Standard port numbers are defined for the common network services; for example, by default, a File Transfer Protocol (FTP) server expects to receive TCP requests addressed to port 21; an HTTP Web server, to port 80.

However, nonstandard ports may be used. It is quite possible to put a Web server on port 21 and access it with a URL of `http://serverName:21/`. Because of this possibility, some firewall systems examine the inside details of the protocol data, not just headers, to ensure that only valid data can flow through.

As an elementary security precaution, port numbers less than 1024 are *privileged* ports. On some systems, such as UNIX, programs without the appropriate privileges are prevented from listening to these ports. On less secure operating systems, a program can listen on any port. HTTP Web servers, in particular, are often run on nonstandard ports, such as 8000 or 8080, to avoid requiring the privileged standard port 80.

The nonprivileged ports of 1024 and above can be used by any program; when a connection is created, a free port number will be allocated to the program. For example, a Web browser opening a connection to a Web server might be allocated port 1044 to communicate with server port 80. But what happens if a Web browser from another client also gets allocated port 1044? The two connections are distinguished by looking at all four values—source IP address, source port, destination IP address, destination port—as this group of values is guaranteed to be unique by the TCP standards.

2.4.2   Program Communication through a Firewall

Simple packet-filtering firewalls use the source and destination IP addresses and ports to determine whether packets may pass through the firewall. The firewall may permit packets going to a Web server on destination port 80 and the replies on source port 80 but reject packets to other port numbers. This restriction may be allowed in one direction only and may be further restricted by allowing only packets to and from a particular group of Web servers, as shown in Figure 2.12.

Data may need to pass through more than one firewall. Users in a corporate network often have a firewall between them and the Internet in order to protect the entire corporate network. And at the other end of the connection, the remote server often has a firewall to protect it and its networks.

These firewalls may enforce different rules on what types of data are allowed to flow through. This difference can have consequences for Java programs and programs written in any other language. It is not uncommon to find Java-enabled Web pages that work over a home Internet connection simply fail to run on a corporate network.

Two problem areas, discussed in Section 2.4.3 on page 45, are as follows.

1. Can the Java program be downloaded from a remote server?

2. Can the Java program create the network connections it requires?

Proxy servers and SOCKS gateways are two common approaches used to provide Internet access through corporate firewalls. The primary goal is to allow people within the company network the ability to access the World Wide Web (WWW) but to prevent people outside from accessing the company's internal networks.

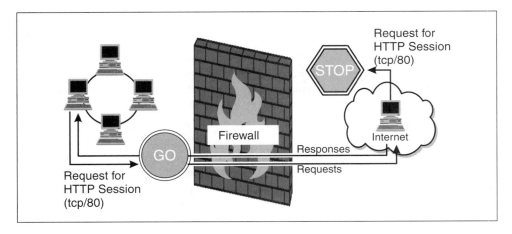

Figure 2.12. Asymmetric Firewall Behavior

2.4.2.1   Proxy Servers

A proxy server receives a request from a Web browser, performs that request on behalf of the browser—possibly after authorization checks—and returns the results to the browser (see Figure 2.13). Instead of sending a specific request to a particular server, a browser sends the request to a proxy system. Then, the proxy system contacts the server. This indirect approach has several advantages.

- All external Web access can be forced to go through the proxy server, creating a single control point. This is achieved by blocking all HTTP data, except from the proxy server itself.

- All pages being transferred can be logged, together with the address of the requesting machine.

- Requests for certain sites can be restricted or banned.

- The IP addresses or names of the internal systems never appear on the Internet; only the address of the proxy server appears. Thus, attackers cannot use the addresses to gain information about internal system names and network structure.

- The proxy can be configured as a caching proxy server and will save local copies of Web pages retrieved. Subsequent requests will return the cached copies, thus providing faster access and reducing the load on the connection to the Internet.

- Web proxy servers usually support several protocols, including HTTP, FTP, Gopher, and HTTPS.

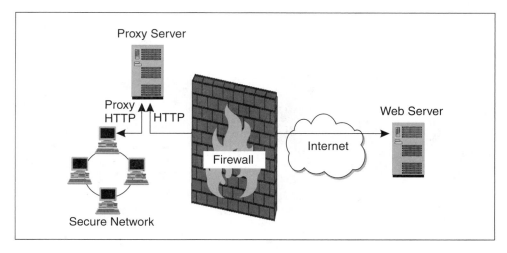

Figure 2.13.   Where a Proxy Server Fits

- Proxy servers can themselves use the SOCKS protocol to provide additional security, without affecting the browser configuration.

The disadvantages are that browser configuration is more complex, the added data transfers can add an extra delay to page access, and proxies sometimes impose additional restrictions, such as a timeout on the length of a connection, preventing very large downloads.

2.4.2.2 SOCKS

The other common approach to providing Internet access through a firewall is to use a SOCKS gateway. The SOCKS protocol allows users within a corporate firewall to access almost any TCP or UDP service outside the firewall but without allowing outsiders to get back inside. This approach works through TCP and SOCKS, together with a SOCKS server program running in the firewall system (see Figure 2.14).

SOCKS is a means of encapsulating any TCP within the SOCKS protocol. On the client system, within the corporate network, the data packets to be sent to an external system will be put inside a SOCKS packet and sent to a SOCKS server. For example, a request for `http://www.fabrikam456.com/page.html` would, if sent directly, be contained in a packet with the characteristics shown in Listing 2.1.

Listing 2.1. Example of TCP Packet for a Direct HTTP Request

```
Destination address: www.fabrikam456.com
Destination port: 80 (HTTP)
Data: "GET /page.html"
```

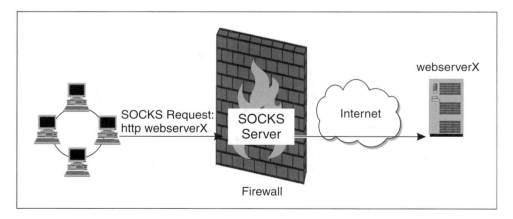

Figure 2.14. A SOCKS Connection

If SOCKS were used, the packet sent would be, effectively, as in Listing 2.2.

Listing 2.2. Example of a SOCKS Packet Encapsulating an HTTP Request

```
Destination address: socks_server.local456.com
Destination port: TCP 1080 (SOCKS)
Data: Destination address = www.fabrikam456.com
Destination port = TCP 80 (HTTP)
Data = "GET /page.html"
```

When it receives this packet, the SOCKS server extracts the required destination address, port, and data and sends this packet; naturally, the source IP address will be that of the SOCKS server itself. The firewall will have been configured to allow these packets from the SOCKS server program, so they will not be blocked. Returning packets will be sent to the SOCKS server, which will encapsulate them similarly and pass on to the original client, which in turn strips off the SOCKS encapsulation, giving the required data to the application.[6] The advantage of all this is that the firewall can be configured very simply to allow any TCP/IP connection on any port, from the SOCKS server to the nonsecure Internet, trusting it to disallow any connections that are initiated from the Internet (see Figure 2.15).

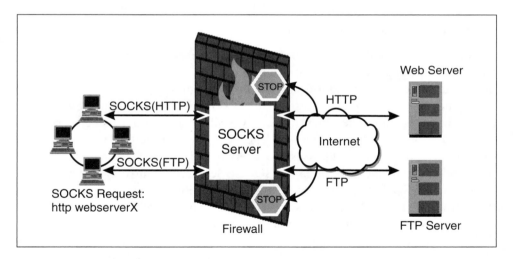

Figure 2.15. SOCKS Flexibility

---

6. This description is simplified; in reality, requests between the client and the SOCKS server are in a socket API format, rather than the pure protocol data as shown.

The disadvantage is that the client software must be modified to use SOCKS. The original approach was to recompile the network client code with a new SOCKS header file, which translated TCP system calls—`connect`, `getsockname`, `bind`, `accept`, `listen`, `select`—into new names: `Rconnect`, `Rgetsockname`, `Rbind`, `Raccept`, `Rlisten`, `Rselect`. When linked with the `libsocks` library, these new names will access the SOCKS version rather than the standard system version, resulting in a new, *SOCKSified* version of the client software.

This approach is still used for clients running on UNIX. On Windows operating systems, the dynamically linked libraries that implement the TCP calls can be replaced by a SOCKSified version, usually termed a *SOCKSified TCP/IP stack*. This SOCKSified stack can then be used with any client code, without the need to modify the client, requiring only the SOCKS configuration to be specified, that is, the address of the SOCKS server and information on whether to use SOCKS protocol or to make a direct connection.

2.4.2.3 *Proxy Servers versus SOCKS Gateways*

The three options of providing secure Internet access through corporate firewalls are to use

1. A proxy server
2. A SOCKS gateway with a SOCKSified client application
3. A SOCKS gateway with a SOCKSified TCP/IP stack

Each of these options has its own advantages and disadvantages for the company network security manager to evaluate for the company's particular environment. But what does the end user need to do to use these options?

Rather than sending all requests to the SOCKS server, which may overload it, as well as supporting other clients, the SOCKSified stack provides better support for deciding whether to use SOCKS. The stack is controlled by a configuration file that specifies which addresses are internal and can be handled directly and which addresses must go through the SOCKS server. Of course, if a SOCKSified stack is used, SOCKS should not be enabled in the client application configuration. However, as a SOCKSified stack is not available for all platforms, the client application's SOCKS configuration may have to be used.

The SOCKSified stack approach will also work with Java programs, as the classes in the `java.net` package will use the underlying TCP stack. Therefore, this approach provides a simple way of running Java programs using a SOCKS server through a firewall. But if a SOCKSified stack is not available, you will need to SOCKSify the library classes yourself if you have source code or look for a vendor that supports SOCKS.

2.4.3   The Effect of Firewalls on Java Programs

The effect of firewalls on Java programs can be considered from three points of view: loading them, stopping them, and the network connections that the programs themselves may create.

2.4.3.1   *Using HTTP for Applet Downloading*

Java applets within a Web page are transferred using HTTP when the browser fetches the class files referred to by the `<APPLET>` tag. So, if a Web page contains a tag like the one in Listing 2.3, the browser would transfer the Web page itself first, then the file `Example.class`, and then any class files referred to in `Example.class`.

Listing 2.3.   Example of `<APPLET>` Tag in an HTML Page

```
<APPLET Code="Example.class" Width=300 Height=300>
    <PARAM NAME=pname VALUE="example1">
</APPLET>
```

Each HTTP transfer would be performed separately, unless HTTP V1.1 is used. Starting with Java Development Kit (JDK) V1.1, the Java language allows a more efficient transfer, whereby all the classes are combined into a compressed Java Archive (JAR) file. In this case, the Web page contains a tag like the one in Listing 2.4.

Listing 2.4.   Example of `<APPLET>` Tag Pointing to a JAR File

```
<APPLET Archive="example.jar" Code="Example.class"
    Width=300 Height=300>
</APPLET>
```

If there are problems finding `example.jar` or if an older browser that still runs a JDK V1.0 JVM is used, the archive option is ignored, and the code option is used instead, as in the previous example.

2.4.3.2   *Using a Firewall to Stop Java Downloads*

What effect do firewalls have on the downloading of Java class files? If the security policy is to allow HTTP traffic to flow through the firewall, Java programs and JAR files will simply be treated like any other component of a Web page and be transferred. But on the other hand, if HTTP is prohibited, it is going to be very difficult to obtain the applet class files, unless there is another way of getting them, such as using FTP. Quite frequently, Web servers using nonstandard TCP ports, such as 81, 8000, and 8080, may be blocked by the firewall, so if you are running a Web server, stick to the standard port 80 if you want as many people as possible to see your Web pages and applets.

Because Java programs are transferred using HTTP, the IP and TCP headers are indistinguishable from any other element of a Web page. Simple packet filtering based on IP addresses and port numbers will therefore not be able to block only Java programs. If more selective filtering is needed, an additional step beyond basic packet filtering will be required: examining the packet payload, or the HTTP data itself. This can be done with a suitable Web proxy server or an HTTP gateway that scans the data transferred.

If a Web proxy server is used, a common arrangement is to force all clients to go through the proxy server—inside the firewall—by preventing all HTTP access through the firewall, unless that access came from the proxy server itself (Figure 2.16). A user who does not have an arrangement like this can bypass the checking by connecting directly.

How can a Java class file inside the HTTP packet be identified? In an ideal world, there would be a standard MIME data type for Java classes. Thus, a Web browser might request:

```
Accept: application/java, application/jar
```

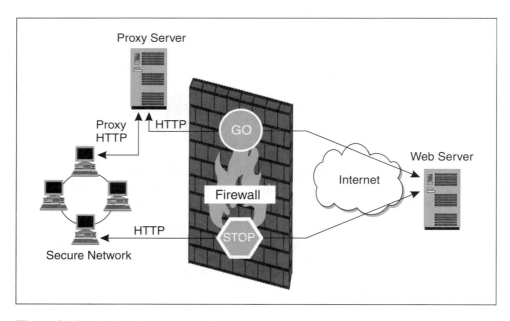

Figure 2.16. Forcing Connections through a Proxy

Firewalls could quite easily check for these requests and the Web server `Content-Type:` replies. In practice, however, servers respond with a variety of MIME types, such as:

```
application/octet-stream⁷
www/unknown
text/plain
multipart/x-zip⁸
application/zip
```

This means that it is necessary to examine the data being transferred to see whether it might be Java bytecode or JAR files. Bytecode files must start with hexadecimal number `0XCAFEBABE` in the first four bytes (see Figure 7.13 on page 236). This string, called the *magic number*, will also be found in bytecode files that are embedded in JAR files, but as a JAR file may be compressed, a scanner must work harder to find the signature. Commercial products are available that can perform this inspection. They usually work as, or with, an HTTP proxy server and check all HTTP requests passing through.

Of course, in these restrictive environments, any other types of executable content that are less secure than Java, such as ActiveX and JavaScript executable files, would need to be filtered out. In addition, other protocols, such as FTP, HTTP or FTP encapsulated in SOCKS, and HTTP encapsulated in SSL—which adds the problem of decoding the type of encrypted data—would have to be considered.

Searching for the class file signature is an effective way to stop Java classes, but it indiscriminately prohibits good code and bad. The cleanest solution to the problem of selectively stopping Java code is the use of signed code. By certifying the originator of the code, one can permit Java bytecode from sites where the signer is trusted, such as your own company sites, and disallow other sites.

Another question may be whether to allow Java or any other type of executable content to travel through the firewall. A site with public Web servers would probably allow Java code to be sent to the Internet. But that site might wish to make restrictions on Java code that can be received.

The most permissive policy is to allow Java to be received and to let users adopt their own defenses or trust in the Java security model. More restrictive policies might allow Java classes only from trusted Web sites or not at all. The question is the degree of risk. As shown in this book, Java programs run on a well-configured JVM are very safe, compared with other types of executable content. Thus, if applets are to be blocked, other downloads also should be prevented. For

---

7. This is valid for class files.
8. This is valid for JAR files.

example, macro viruses contained in word processor files are a major problem, but few companies prevent employees from exchanging such files with customers and suppliers.

2.4.3.3   *Java Network Connections through the Firewall*

In creating its own network connections through a firewall, a Java program faces all the difficulties described earlier, as well as the default SecurityManager restrictions that allow Java programs to contact only the server from which they were downloaded. One of the major problems people have encountered with Java programs and firewalls is trying to get the Java programs to communicate back to the server through a firewall. This problem becomes particularly evident

- On the client side, when applets attempt to open a network connection with a server located outside the firewall
- On the server side, especially in the DMZ architecture shown in Figure 2.8 on page 31

For example, the middle tier may be a fully functional WAS, hosting both servlets and enterprise beans, and the third tier may be the database system (see Figure 2.4 on page 27). Alternatively, the Web server may be located in the DMZ, and the servlet and EJB engines may constitute the third tier, safely positioned in the intranet behind the firewall (see Figure 6.3 on page 199 and Figure 6.4 on page 200). With this architecture, all requests from the Internet get handled within the DMZ, and only authorized requests are allowed to proceed to enter into the intranet. In a more complicated architecture, an additional firewall may be used to separate the EJB engine from the servlet engine (see Figure 6.5 on page 201). The additional firewall further restricts the requests that can reach the business applications.

From behind a firewall, a program can adopt two major approaches to retrieve data from a server outside the firewall: a URL connection or a socket connection. The first approach means using the URL classes from the `java.net` package to request data from a server using HTTP. Using a URL connection is easier to implement and is also likely to be the more reliable, as the Java runtime passes the URL request to the underlying application—browser or WAS—to process. Thus, if a proxy is defined, the Java code will automatically use it. However, URL connections suffer from the fact that the server side of the connection has limited capability; it can be only a simple file retrieval, a Common Gateway Interface (CGI) program, a servlet, or similar.

The second approach—a socket connection from a Java program to a remote server—involves the use of classes from the `java.net` package to create socket connections to a dedicated server application. The program will need to choose a port number to connect to, but many programs will not be allowed to open a socket connection through the firewall. Some types of programs have no real choice as to port number. For example, IBM Host On-Demand, shown in Figure 2. 1 on page 24, is a Java applet that is a 3270 terminal emulator and hence needs to use the tn3270 protocol to TELNET port 23. It is quite likely that this standard port would be allowed through the firewall; otherwise, encapsulation of tn3270 inside the SOCKS protocol may be the only answer.

Other programs need to make a connection to the server but do not need any special port. It may be that they can use a nonprivileged server port of 1024 or greater, but often these, too, are blocked by simple packet-filtering firewalls. A flexible approach is to let the Java program be configurable to allow direct connections, if allowed, or to use the SOCKS protocol to pass through the firewall.

Many HTTP proxy servers implement the *connect method*. This allows a client to send to the proxy an HTTP request that includes a header telling it to connect to a specific port on the target system. The connect method was developed to allow SSL connections to be handled by a proxy server, but it has since been extended to other applications. For example, Lotus Notes servers can use it. The connect method operates in a very similar way to SOCKS, and Java program connections can be implemented with it in much the same way as with SOCKS.

Another approach is to disguise the packets in another protocol, most likely HTTP, as this will have been permitted through the firewall. This approach will allow a two-way transfer of data between the client program and the server but will require a special type of server, which must be able to communicate with the client programs to process their disguised network traffic.

Finally, Java client/server applications in the network can use remote object access mechanisms, such as Java RMI. A practical implementation of this approach is described in the next section.

2.4.3.4   RMI through the Firewall
Java RMI (see Appendix A on page 547) allows developers to distribute Java objects seamlessly across the Internet. This implies that RMI too needs to be able to cross firewalls.

The normal approach that RMI uses, in the absence of firewalls, is that the client applet will attempt to open a direct network connection to the RMI port (default is port 1099) on the server. The client will send its request to the server and receive its reply over this network connection.

The RMI designers have made provisions for two firewall scenarios, both using RMI calls embedded in HTTP requests, under the reasonable assumption that HTTP will be allowed through the firewall. The RMI server itself will accept either type of request and format its reply accordingly. The client sends an HTTP

POST request, with the RMI call data sent as the body of the POST request, and the server returns the result in the body of an HTTP response.

In the first scenario (Figure 2.17), the proxy server is permitted by the firewall to connect directly to the remote server's RMI port (1099). The client code will make an HTTP POST request to http://rmi_server:1099/. This request passes across the Internet to the remote server, where it is found to be an encapsulated RMI call. Therefore, the reply is sent back as an HTML response. In theory, this method could also be used with a SOCKS server, instead of a proxy server, if run by a SOCKSified application or if the TCP/IP stack is SOCKSified.

As well as assuming that the firewall on the client passes the RMI port, this scenario assumes that the remote firewall also accepts incoming requests directly to the RMI port. But in some organizations, the firewall manager may be reluctant to permit traffic to additional ports, such as the RMI port. An alternative configuration is available in case RMI data is blocked by either firewall (see Figure 2.18).

In the second scenario, the proxy server cannot use the RMI port directly, so the remote server, which supplied the applet, has a CGI-BIN program configured to forward HTTP on the normal port (80) to the RMI server's port 1099. This CGI-BIN program needs to be installed on the Web server in the cgi-bin directory. Once installed, the CGI-BIN program invokes the Java interpreter on the server to forward the request to the appropriate RMI server port and copies the standard CGI environment variables to Java properties. The CGI-BIN program passes the request on to the RMI port. The reply will be passed back to the Web

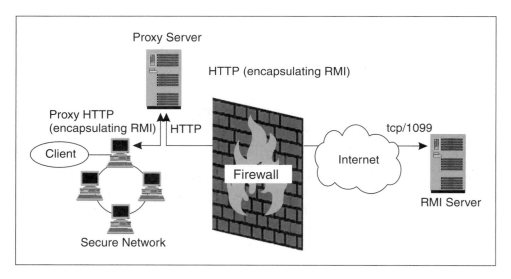

Figure 2.17. Proxy Configuration for RMI: First Scenario

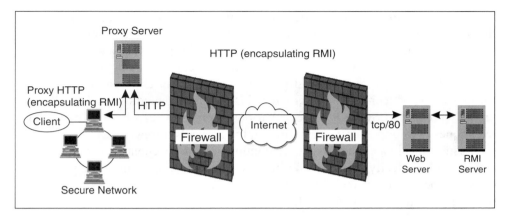

Figure 2.18. Proxy Configuration for RMI: Second Scenario

server, which adds the HTML header line and returns the response to the client. In principle, this scenario would allow the RMI server to reside on a different system from the remote Web server in a three-tier model (see Section 2.1.2 on page 25).

Fortunately, all this work is performed automatically in the `java.rmi` package, so the software developer need not be concerned about the details. It is necessary only to configure the RMI server correctly and to ensure that the client uses the automatic mechanism for encapsulating RMI.

In the current version of RMI, the client stub code checks for the presence—ignoring the value—of system properties `proxyHost` or `http.proxyHost`, in order to decide whether to try using the HTTP encapsulation. If you are using a Web browser and encapsulated RMI does not seem to work, try explicitly setting these properties, as the browser may be using its own proxy HTTP, without setting `proxyHost`.

All this automatic encapsulation is not free, of course. Encapsulated RMI calls are at least an order of magnitude slower than direct requests, and proxy servers may add extra delays to the process as they receive and forward requests.

2.5   Summary

At the beginning of this chapter, we stated that computer security must be holistic because attackers will concentrate on the weakest link. Because Java is an essential part of today's e-business environments, it is clear that Java security must be viewed in relation to the security of the enterprise.

In this chapter, we showed the most common network architectures and high-lighted where Java can play a role. In particular, we investigated the effects of running Java on the server side, especially from a security point of view.

We also showed how firewalls provide added security to an organization's network, at the expense of some restrictions on what client users can do. Firewalls use a variety of techniques to provide this security, including packet filtering, proxy servers, and SOCKS servers. Various approaches can be used with these techniques to allow secure access through the firewalls. Firewalls can impose certain restrictions in a client/server Java communication. A client/server application would work perfectly in a normal setup, but the same application might not execute as expected in a firewall environment. Finally, we described the implications of using RMI through the firewall.

ENTERPRISE JAVA COMPONENTS SECURITY

CHAPTER 3

Enterprise Java Security Fundamentals

THE J2EE platform has achieved remarkable success in meeting enterprise needs, resulting in its widespread adoption. The security infrastructure plays a key role in the e-business strategy of a company. J2EE provides a standard approach to allow enterprise applications to be developed without hard-coded security policies. Instead, declarative policies are bundled with an assembled set of application components. Security policies specified using this security model are enforced in any operational environments and deployed in any of the application servers that host them.

The J2EE security model addresses authentication, authorization, delegation, and data integrity for the components that make up a J2EE environment. This environment includes J2EE applications—Web components, such as servlets and JSP files, EJB components, Java 2 connectors, and JavaMail—and secure interoperability requirements. The J2EE security model also considers the organizational roles that define and enforce these security policies:

- Application Component Provider
- Application Assembler
- Deployer
- System Administrator
- J2EE Product Provider

This chapter provides an overview of J2EE, exploring the J2EE security model. The chapter explains how various J2EE components are tied into enterprise security, describes how the J2EE security model addresses the security of J2EE components, and identifies the responsibility of each of the organizational roles in enforcing security. Declarative security policies and programmatic security APIs are explained, in addition to the security requirements on Java-Mail, Java connectors, client applications, and containers. This chapter also outlines the secure interoperability requirements that exist between various application servers.

Since its inception, one of the top requirements of the J2EE security model has been to support secure application deployments that do not rely on private networks or other application runtime isolation techniques. This allows application portability between containers. Another requirement has been to reduce the application developer's burden by delegating the security responsibilities to the J2EE roles. Finally, the policy-driven security model enables much of security enforcement to be handled without custom code.

3.1   Enterprise Systems

An *enterprise Java environment,* or WAS environment, is nominally viewed as a three-tier architecture (see Section 2.1.2 on page 25). Clients access the information made available through middle-tier systems, which connect to the back-end enterprise systems, as shown in Figure 3.1.

In an enterprise Java environment, the clients can be both Java based and non-Java based. Clients access the servers over a variety of protocols, including HTTP,

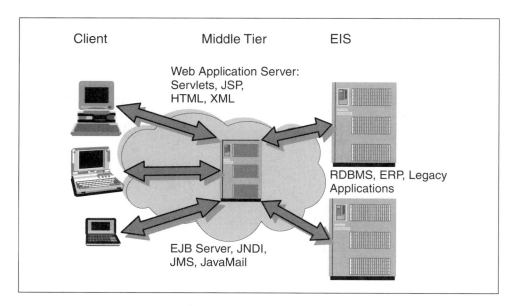

Figure 3.1.   WAS Environment

IIOP, SSL, and other messaging protocols accessible through JMS. These clients connect to and access a J2EE-based server environment providing a hosting system for the enterprise components. These components constitute a presentation layer in the form of servlets, JSP files, HTML files, or XML documents. Alternatively, the components can abstract out the business logic in the form of enterprise beans. Clients may also submit their requests by using e-mail protocols through the JavaMail framework or connect to naming and directory services by using the Java Naming and Directory Interface (JNDI). In an enterprise environment, middle-tier applications are likely to connect to back-end enterprise information systems (EISs). Examples of back-end EISs include relational database management systems (RDBMSs) and ERP applications.

Before delving into the security implications of this architecturally rich environment, it is important to understand the technologies that comprise a J2EE environment.

3.2 J2EE Applications

A *J2EE application*, an enterprise application that conforms to the J2EE specification, is structured as shown in Figure 3.2 and consists of the following:

- Zero or more EJB modules
- Zero or more Web modules
- Zero or more application client modules

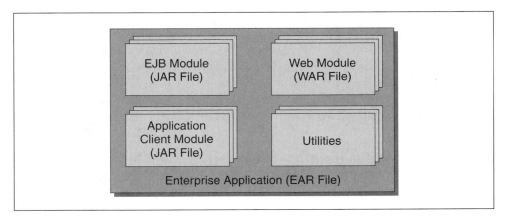

Figure 3.2. Contents of a J2EE Application

- Optionally, JAR files containing dependent classes or components required by the application

- Any combination of the preceding, as long as it contains at least one module

A J2EE application is represented by, and packaged in, an Enterprise Archive (EAR) file. The modules that comprise the EAR file are themselves packaged in archive files specific to their types. For example, a Web module is packaged in a Web Archive (WAR) file, and an EJB module, containing one or more enterprise beans, is packaged in a JAR file. WAR files can exist as independent deployment units from EAR files.

EAR files also contain a *deployment descriptor* file—an XML document describing the contents of the application and containing instructions for the deployment of the application. In particular, the deployment descriptor specifies the security settings to be enforced by the runtime environment. Each WAR file packaging a Web module, JAR file packaging enterprise beans, or JAR file packaging an application client module contains its own deployment descriptor as well.

3.2.1   EJB Modules

An *enterprise bean* is a Java component that can be combined with other resources to create distributed client/server applications. Instantiated enterprise beans reside in *enterprise bean containers*, or *EJB containers*. An EJB container provides an interface between the enterprise beans and the application server on which the enterprise beans reside. An enterprise bean is typically accessed using Java RMI-IIOP. An ORB manages the interaction between clients and enterprise beans, using IIOP. ORBs enable clients to make requests and receive responses from servers in distributed computing environments. Alternatively, enterprise beans are accessible through JMS. It is also possible to invoke an enterprise bean as a Web service via SOAP, as explained in Chapter 14 on page 497.

There are three types of enterprise beans: entity beans, session beans, and message-driven beans. *Entity beans* store persistent data and typically use database connections. Entity beans are of two types: CMP entity beans and BMP entity beans.

- Entity beans with *container-managed persistence* (CMP) let the EJB container transparently and implicitly manage the persistent state. The enterprise bean developer does not need to code any database access functions within the enterprise bean class methods.

- Entity beans with *bean-managed persistence* (BMP) manage persistent data in a manner defined by the application developer in the bean code. This usually includes writing to databases.

Session beans do not require database access, although they can obtain it indirectly, as needed, by accessing entity beans. Session beans can also obtain direct access to databases and other resources through the use of *resource references*, which include the use of JDBC. Session beans can be either stateless or stateful.

- A session bean is said to be *stateless* if it provides a stateless service to the client. A business method on a stateless session bean is similar to a procedural application or static method; there is no instance state. Therefore, all the data needed to execute a stateless session bean's method is provided by the method arguments.

- A session bean is said to be *stateful* if it acts as a server-side extension of the client that uses it. A stateful session bean is created by a client and will work for only that client until the client connection is dropped or the bean is explicitly removed. Unlike a stateless session bean, a stateful session bean has state or instance fields that can be initialized and changed by the client with each method invocation.

Message-driven beans are enterprise beans accessible asynchronously via JMS rather than synchronously through such protocols as RMI-IIOP. The EJB V2.1 specification expands the scope of message-driven beans beyond JMS to support any messaging system.

An *EJB module* is one or more enterprise beans assembled into a single deployable unit. As we have observed, an EJB module is stored in a standard JAR file, commonly referred to as *ejb-jar*. This file contains

- One or more deployable enterprise beans
- A deployment descriptor, stored in an XML file

Specifically, an EJB module's deployment descriptor file declares the contents of the module, specifies the structure and external dependencies of the enterprise beans in the module, explains how the enterprise beans are to be used at runtime, and defines the security policies applicable to the enterprise beans within the module. The format of the security policy is defined by the EJB specification (see Chapter 5 on page 157).

3.2.2   Web Modules

A *Web module* represents a *Web application*—an application that can be accessed over the Web using HTTP. A Web module is used to assemble servlets and JSP files, as well as static content, such as HTML pages, into a single deployable unit.

As we said earlier, Web modules are stored in WAR files, which are enhanced JAR files with a `.war` file extension, and contain

- One or more servlets, JSP files, and other supporting files
- A deployment descriptor, stored in an XML file

The deployment descriptor file, `web.xml`, declares the contents of the Web module. This file contains information about the structure and external dependencies of the components in the Web module and describes the components' runtime use. In addition, the deployment description file is used to declare the security policies applicable to the universal resource identifiers (URIs) that are mapped to the resources within the Web module. These security policies include both the authorization policy and the login configuration information. The format of the security policy is defined by the Java Servlet specification.

Servlets are Java programs running on a WAS and extend the Web server's capabilities. For example, servlets support generation of dynamic Web page content, provide database access, concurrently serve multiple clients, and filter data by MIME type. Servlets use the Java Servlet API. By analogy, servlets are the server-side equivalent of client-side browser applets.

JSP files enable the separation of the HTML coding from the business logic in Web pages, allowing HTML programmers and Java programmers to more easily collaborate in creating and maintaining pages. This process is described in greater detail in Section 4.1.2 on page 104.

3.2.3   Application Client Modules

Application clients are first-tier Java-based client programs. Even though it is a regular Java application, an application client depends on an *application client container* to provide system services. An *application client module* packages application client code in a JAR file. This JAR file includes a deployment descriptor XML file, which specifies the enterprise beans and external resources referenced by the application.

The security configuration of an application client determines how the application will access enterprise beans and Web resources. If the J2EE components that the client application accesses are secured, the client will be authenticated accordingly. In order for an application client to retrieve authentication data from an end user, configuration information must be specified in a deployment descriptor XML file, `application-client.xml`, associated with the client application. Application clients typically run in an environment that has a Java 2 security manager installed and the security policies enforced based on the J2SE security policy framework (see Chapter 8 on page 253).

3.3   Secure Interoperability between ORBs

J2EE applications are required to use RMI-IIOP when accessing EJB components. This allows enterprise beans to be portable between container implementations.

A *J2EE container* provides the runtime support for the J2EE components. A J2EE container vendor enables access to the enterprise beans via IIOP. This facilitates interoperability between containers by using the Common Secure Interoperability (CSI) protocol. Security is enabled and enforced by the ORBs, ensuring authenticity, confidentiality, and integrity. Version 2 of this protocol specification (CSIv2) is the accepted industry standard and is mandated by the J2EE specification.

3.4   Connectors

A *resource adapter* is defined in the J2EE Connector Architecture specification as a system-level software driver that a Java application uses to connect to an EIS. The resource adapter plugs into an application server and provides connectivity between the EIS, the J2EE application server, and the enterprise application.

The Java Connector Architecture (JCA) specification allows resource adapters that support access to non-J2EE systems to be plugged into any J2EE environment. Resource adapter components implementing the JCA API are called *connectors*.

The JCA specification describes standard ways to extend J2EE services with connectors to other non-J2EE application systems, such as mainframe systems and ERP systems. The JCA architecture enables an EIS vendor to provide a standard resource adapter for a J2EE application to connect to the EIS. A resource adapter is used by a Java application to connect to an EIS. For example, Web enablement of business applications, such as IBM's Customer Information Control System (CICS), would imply that the J2EE-based presentation layer would connect to a CICS application using a CICS connector. With this approach, protocol details of connecting to a CICS system are transparent to the Web application and are handled by the CICS connector implementation.

JCA defines a standard set of *system-level contracts* between a J2EE server and a resource adapter. In particular, these standard contracts include a *security contract* and enable secure access to non-J2EE EISs. The security contract helps to reduce security threats to the information system and protects valuable information resources managed by such a system. Given that most of these EIS systems have facilities to accept some form of authentication data representing an identity connecting to the system, the JCA security contract deals with the authentication aspects of the EIS. Essentially, it is about a J2EE application *signing on* to an EIS system. This means that the J2EE application accesses a connection to the EIS system by providing authentication information. As discussed in Section 3.9.4 on page 87 and Section 3.10.3 on page 94, two organizational roles are involved in addressing this issue: the Application Component Provider and the Deployer. Specifically, the Application Component Provider can use either of two choices related to EIS sign-on: the declarative approach or the programmatic approach.

- The *declarative approach* allows the Deployer to set up the resource principal and EIS sign-on information. For example, the Deployer sets the user ID and password—or another set of credentials—necessary to establish a connection to an EIS instance.

- With the *programmatic approach*, the Application Component Provider can choose to perform sign-on to an EIS from the component code by providing explicit security information. For example, the user ID and password—or another set of credentials—necessary to establish a connection to an EIS instance are coded into the application code.

The Application Component Provider uses a deployment descriptor element, such as `res-auth` for EJB components, to indicate the requirement for one of the two approaches. If the `res-auth` element is set to `Container`, the application server sets up and manages EIS sign-on. If the `res-auth` element is set to `Application`, the component code performs a programmatic sign-on to the EIS.

Further details of the security aspects of a JCA-based connection to an EIS from a J2EE application are discussed in Section 3.9.4 on page 87 and Section 3.10.3 on page 94.

3.5   JMS

JMS is a standard Java messaging API that provides a common mechanism for Java-language programs to access messaging systems. Java clients and middle-tier components must be capable of using messaging systems to access the J2EE components that are enabled via a messaging layer.

- Application clients, EJB components, and Web components can send or synchronously receive a JMS message. Application clients can also receive JMS messages asynchronously.

- A new kind of enterprise bean introduced in EJB V2.0, the message-driven bean, enables the asynchronous consumption of messages. A message-driven bean can be accessed by sending a method invocation request over a messaging infrastructure. A JMS provider may optionally implement concurrent processing of messages by message-driven beans.

The J2EE specification requires JMS providers to implement both the reliable point-to-point messaging model and the publish/subscribe model. The *reliable point-to-point messaging model* allows one entity to send messages directly to another entity that understands the format of the messages and the requests. The *publish/subscribe model* is event driven; a message is published, and the message is delivered to all subscribers of the event. One example is a StockQuote application, with multiple traders wanting to get the latest stock quote. In this scenario, the traders' applications subscribe to the stock-quote messaging service. When the stock values are published, the information is made available to all the subscribers. In a Java environment, both the StockQuote server and the traders' applications can use the JMS mechanism with a JMS provider to achieve the required messaging fucntionality.

However, JMS does not specify a security contract or an API for controlling message confidentiality and integrity. Security is considered to be a JMS-provider-specific feature. It is controlled by a System Administrator rather than implemented programmatically or by the J2EE server runtime.

3.6 Simple E-Business Request Flow

It would be helpful to understand a simple e-business request flow in an enterprise Java environment. Figure 3.3 presents a simple request flow that does not involve security.

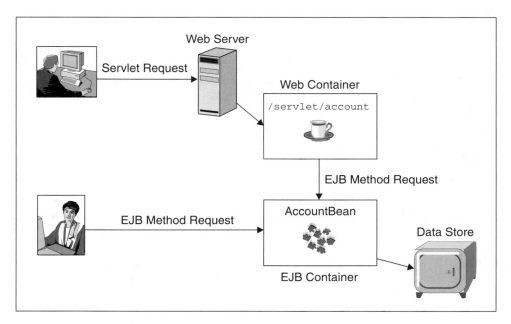

Figure 3.3. Simple E-Business Request Flow

Let us consider two types of clients: *HTTP clients*, such as Web browsers, and *IIOP clients*, regular applications capable of using IIOP to send requests and receive responses over the network. An HTTP client invokes a URL: for instance, `/servlet/account/`. The request from the user's browser gets handled by the Web server, which routes the request to a Web, or servlet, container serving the URL resource. The logic behind the URL is implemented as a Java servlet. This servlet, packaged in a Web module, is hosted in a J2EE Web container, which in turn invokes an enterprise bean, AccountBean, via IIOP. AccountBean is an entity bean, packaged in an EJB module, with its business data stored in a data store. The same enterprise bean is accessed directly from an IIOP client, packaged in an application client module. In this case, the request is not routed by the servlet but is directly accessed as a remote object from the Java client.

The request flow just described does not involve security considerations. The next sections in this chapter provide an overview of the J2EE specification as it pertains the security of an enterprise. The platform roles reflect the organizational responsibilities, from application development, application assembly, and application deployment, to administration.

3.7   J2EE Platform Roles

J2EE defines roles that reflect the responsibilities within an organization. Any person or software involved in the process of making an application available within an enterprise can usually be categorized into organization roles, called *J2EE platform roles*. The J2EE platform roles having security responsibilities are the Application Component Provider, Application Assembler, Deployer, System Administrator, J2EE Product Provider, and Tool Provider. The J2EE security model is defined with respect to these J2EE roles.

Figure 3.4 shows the interactions among the Application Component Provider, Application Assembler, Deployer, and System Administrator. These are the roles involved, from a security perspective, in the stages between development and deployment.

Figure 3.4 depicts the software process cycle from the perspective of J2EE platform roles.[1] In a typical J2EE software process cycle, application component developers build enterprise application components, such as servlets or enterprise

---

1. The J2EE V1.3 platform role called *Tool Provider* is responsible for supplying tools used for the development and packaging of application components. Because it depicts the software life cycle in development and deployment of a J2EE application and the users involved in the process, Figure 3.4 does not include the roles of Tool Provider and J2EE Product Provider.

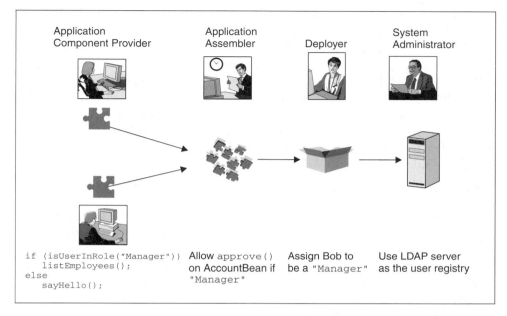

Figure 3.4.   J2EE Platform Roles with Security Responsibilities in the Development and Deployment of a J2EE Application

beans. The greatest opportunity for component reuse and flexibility in reconfiguring security policy is when the components are written to be *security unaware*, meaning that they do not contain embedded security policy code. Conversely, components containing embedded security policy code are said to be *security aware*. Security-aware components are difficult to reuse, and flexibility is limited because it often requires changing the source code to reflect various security policies. For some applications, this may be unavoidable.

An Application Assembler integrates a set of components supplied by one or more Application Component Providers. The Application Assembler has the in-depth knowledge of the application. The Application Assembler specifies security policies as hints to the Deployer. For example, the Application Assembler can provide hints such that the `approve()` method of an enterprise bean should be accessed only by those principals granted the role of a Manager.

A Deployer deploys enterprise applications, assembled by Application Assemblers, into an operational environment. When tailoring the security policies to the operational environment, the Deployer consults the security policy hints provided by the Application Assembler. For example, the Deployer can assign the role of a Manager to a user named Bob.

A System Administrator is responsible for administering the system, including security. This may include configuring the J2EE product to use an LDAP server for managing security information, including user and group membership.

The following subsections provide a more detailed description of the four J2EE roles. The J2EE platform roles that we have listed are considered to be the typical roles, although in practice, the roles are adapted to better match the organization's application development and deployment work flow. The rest of this section summarizes the major responsibilities of the individual J2EE platform roles with respect to security management.

3.7.1   Application Component Provider

The *Application Component Provider* is the J2EE platform role responsible for implementing the business logic as a set of J2EE application components—enterprise beans, servlets, and/or JSP files. These components are packaged in an ejb-jar file containing one or more enterprise beans and/or aWAR file containing one or more servlets and/or JSP files, and/or a JAR file containing an application client module.

The Application Component Provider has numerous responsibilities in code development. These responsibilities range from resource access to programmatic access of the caller's security context. Following are the Application Component Provider's key security responsibilities:

3.7.1.1   *Access of Resources in the Underlying Operating System*
The J2EE architecture does not define the operating system principal—for example, the operating system user—under which EJB methods or servlets execute. Therefore, the Application Component Provider cannot rely on a specific principal for accessing the underlying operating system resources. The Application Component Provider should design the applications so that special privileges are not required to access system resources.

3.7.1.2   *Security Recommendations*
The Application Component Provider should avoid implementing security mechanisms or hard-coded security policies in the component but instead should rely on the security mechanisms provided by the J2EE container. The Application Component Provider should let the Application Assembler and the Deployer define the appropriate security policies for the application. The Application Component Provider can use the deployment descriptors to convey security-related information to the Application Assembler.

3.7.1.3 *Programmatic Access to the Caller's Security Context*

Programmatic-security APIs should be avoided when possible. However, they should be used when the J2EE component methods need access to security-context information because the J2EE declarative security model is insufficient to implement application security requirements.

3.7.1.4 *Conveying the Use of Role References*

A *security role* is a set of J2EE authorizations. The Application Component Provider may build a security-aware application and use *role references*—security role names within the application components. For example, a component may call `isUserInRole("Manager")` on a `javax.servlet.http.HttpServlet-Request` object. When security role names are hard-coded in an application component, the Application Component Provider must identify these role names for the Application Assembler so that it can map component-defined security role references in each of the components in the deployment to a single application-level security role name. For example, two components in an application may use the security role references `Manager` and `Boss` within the component, whereas both of these roles imply the application security role of a Supervisor.

3.7.2   Application Assembler

The *Application Assembler* is the J2EE platform role responsible for combining J2EE components into deployable application units. The Application Assembler also simplifies the Deployer's job by providing a security view of the enterprise beans, servlets, and JSP files in the relevant deployment descriptors. A *security view* consists of a set of J2EE security roles. A security role is a semantic grouping of J2EE authorizations, or permissions—implemented as `java.security.Permission` objects—that a given type of application users must have in order to successfully use the application. The Application Assembler defines one or more security roles in the deployment descriptor and specifies and associates J2EE permissions with these roles. For example, the security role Manager could be granted the J2EE permissions to invoke an enterprise bean to grant loans and view the loan status of all the customers using Web applications. In contrast, the security role HelpDesk could be granted only a subset of these J2EE permissions—for example, only the J2EE permission to view the loan status of the customers—by having been granted access to the relevant URIs.

Following are some of the Application Assembler's security responsibilities.

3.7.2.1   Defining EJB Method Permissions

The home, local home, remote, and local interfaces of an enterprise bean are defined as part of the EJB specification.

- The *home interface* of an enterprise bean is a Java interface used to create, find, or delete an instance of the enterprise bean. The methods defined in the remote interface can be accessed from within the same container or remotely via RMI-IIOP.

- The *local home interface* of an enterprise bean is functionally similar to the home interface, but the methods defined in the local home interface are accessible only from within the same container.

- The *remote interface* of an enterprise bean is a Java interface that defines the operations that can be performed on the enterprise bean to access the business logic associated with the enterprise bean itself. The methods defined in the remote interface can be accessed from within the same container or remotely via RMI-IIOP.

- The *local interface* of an enterprise bean is functionally similar to the remote interface, but the methods defined in the local interface are accessible only from within the same container.

The home, local home, remote, and local interfaces of an enterprise bean define which methods the enterprise bean exposes to a client. An EJB method permission is defined by an XML `method-permission` element in an EJB module's deployment descriptor and is used to assign groups of methods of the home, local home, remote, and local interfaces of an enterprise bean packaged in that EJB module to the security roles. This way, the Application Assembler can define the security view of the enterprise bean.

An EJB method permission specifies the methods of the home, local home, remote, and local interfaces that each of the listed security roles is allowed to invoke. This implies that an EJB method permission may include a list of one or more security roles and a list of one or more methods. In addition, a security role or a method may appear in multiple XML `method-permission` elements. Users of particular security roles are granted access to all the methods listed in all the EJB method permission elements where those security roles appear. EJB method permissions and the deployment descriptor are discussed further in Chapter 5 on page 157.

3.7.2.2   Defining Web Resources Security Constraints

An Application Assembler uses a Web module's deployment descriptor to define security constraints for a Web application packaged in that module. The Web module's deployment descriptor's `auth-constraint` element is used for this purpose. This element consists of one or more security roles and a list of URL patterns that users with any of those security roles are authorized to invoke. Specifically, deployment descriptors are used to assign groups of URL patterns to the security roles, thus defining security views of Web applications. Login configuration information, such as requiring a user to be authenticated using a form-based login mechanism, and transport guarantee constraints, such as requiring access to a URL pattern to be submitted only using an HTTPS connection, can also be specified in the deployment descriptor.

3.7.2.3   *Declaring Security Roles within a J2EE Application*

An Application Assembler defines each security role by using the `security-role` XML element in the relevant deployment descriptor.

- If the deployment descriptor belongs to an ejb-jar file, the `security-role` element is scoped to that ejb-jar file and applies to all the enterprise beans in that EJB module.

- If the deployment descriptor belongs to a WAR file, the security role element is scoped to that WAR file and applies to all the servlets and/or JSP files in that Web module.

- If the deployment descriptor belongs to an EAR file, the `security-role` element applies to all the JAR and WAR files that are packaged within that EAR file. Effectively, the set of security roles declared in the EAR file's deployment descriptor is the union of the security roles defined in the deployment descriptors of the JAR and WAR files packaged within that EAR file. Technically, however, the security roles described in the constituent modules of an EAR file are the ones that are used to enforce authorization, because those roles are associated with authorization policies. The roles declared in the EAR file's deployment descriptor are typically used for administration and management purposes only. For example, they can be used to assign security roles to principals with regard to the whole application packaged in the EAR file.

The deployment descriptor of an application client module does not contain security role elements, because security roles are specific to the server side of a J2EE application, not for the client.

Within each `security-role` element, the Application Assembler will use the `role-name` subelement to define the name of the security role and, optionally, will use the `description` subelement to provide a description of the security role.

3.7.3   Deployer

For each J2EE application, the Deployer takes the modules comprising that application and deploys the module components into a specific operational, or runtime, environment. The modules were produced by an Application Assembler. The operational environment in which the application is deployed includes a specific J2EE container. The Deployer is also responsible for ensuring the security of an assembled application when it is deployed in the target operational environment.

The Deployer has the following responsibilities with respect to security management.

3.7.3.1   *Reading the Security View of the J2EE Application*
The Deployer uses the deployment tools supplied by the J2EE Product Provider to read the security view of the application. The Deployer should treat the security policies specified in a deployment descriptor as hints and modify those policies as appropriate to the operational environment in which the application is being deployed.

3.7.3.2   *Configuring the Security Domain*
A *security domain* within an enterprise represents an instance of an authentication authority and relevant security infrastructure. For example, a security domain may point to a particular Kerberos domain for authentication and an LDAP user repository to deduce user and group membership to be used for authorization. In the case of multiple security domains within the enterprise, the Deployer is responsible for configuring the J2EE product to use the appropriate security domains.

3.7.3.3   *Assigning of Principals to Security Roles*
The Deployer is responsible for assigning principals and/or groups of principals used for managing security in the runtime to the security roles defined in the XML `security-role` elements of the deployment descriptors. The process of assigning the logical security roles defined in the J2EE application's deployment descriptor to the operational environment's security concepts is specific to the configuration capabilities of a particular J2EE product.

3.7.3.4   *Configuring Principal Delegation*
Delegation allows an intermediary to perform a task, initiated by a client, under an identity based on a *delegation policy*. The Deployer is responsible for configuring principal delegation for intercomponent calls by using the appropriate deployment descriptor elements, as follows.

- If the deployment descriptor belongs to an ejb-jar file, the Deployer uses the `security-identity` deployment descriptor element for this purpose.

When the value of the `security-identity` element is `use-caller-identity`, the identity of the caller of the enterprise bean will be used when calling other components from the enterprise bean. When the value specified is `run-as`, the identity of the caller to the enterprise bean will be propagated in terms of the security role name defined in the `run-as` element of the descriptor. For example, if the caller to an enterprise bean is user Bob, Bob's identity will be used if the `security-identity` element is set to `use-caller-identity`. If the `security-identity` element is set to `run-as` and the role name is `Teller`, the downstream calls from the enterprise bean will be performed in terms of the Teller role.

- If the deployment descriptor belongs to a WAR file, the Deployer uses the `run-as` deployment descriptor element for this purpose. If the `run-as` element is not declared in the WAR file, the identity of the servlet's caller will be used for components called from the servlet. If the `run-as` element is declared in the deployment descriptor, the identity passed when the servlet makes calls to other components will be that of the security role name defined in the `run-as` element of the descriptor. For example, if the caller to a servlet is user Bob, Bob's identity will be used if no `run-as` element is declared in the WAR file's deployment descriptor. If the `run-as` element is declared in the deployment descriptor and the role name is `Teller`, the downstream calls from the servlet will be performed in terms of the Teller role.

3.7.4   System Administrator

The System Administrator is responsible for the configuration and administration of the enterprise's computing and networking infrastructure, including the J2EE container. The System Administrator is also responsible for the overall management and operational aspects of the J2EE applications at runtime. The following list describes the security-related responsibilities of the System Administrator. Some of these responsibilities may be carried out by the Deployer or may require the cooperation of both the Deployer and the System Administrator.

3.7.4.1   *Administering the Security Domain*

The System Administrator is responsible for administering the security domain. This includes the principal administration, user account management, group membership assignment, deployment of J2EE products within an enterprise environment, including configuration of DMZs, firewalls, user registries, and so on. These are typically performed using the tools provided by the relevant product vendor; for example, user registry management is performed using an LDAP server product, firewall configuration using the firewall product, and so on.

3.7.4.2   Assigning Application Roles to Users and Groups

The System Administrator is responsible for assigning principals and/or groups of principals used for managing security in the runtime to the security roles defined in the XML `security-role` elements of the deployment descriptors. The process of assigning the logical security roles defined in the J2EE application's deployment descriptor to the operational environment's security concepts is specific to the configuration capabilities of a particular J2EE product. For example, using the tools provided by a J2EE product, the System Administrator can assign a Teller role scoped to a J2EE application FinanceApp to user Bob and group TellerGroup.

3.7.5   J2EE Product Provider

The J2EE Product Provider has the following areas of responsibility.

3.7.5.1   Supplying Deployment Tools

The J2EE Product Provider is responsible for supplying the deployment tools that the Deployer uses to perform all the deployment tasks, including the security-related tasks. For example, the J2EE Product Provider will supply tools to perform security-role-to-principal and/or -user and/or -group assignment.

3.7.5.2   Configuring Security Domains

The J2EE Product Provider is responsible for configuring the J2EE product to use appropriate security domains. For example, the J2EE Product Provider needs to supply facilities to configure the J2EE product to use a particular authentication mechanism—for example, to use a Kerberos domain.

3.7.5.3   Supplying Mechanisms to Enforce Security Policies

The J2EE Product Provider is responsible for supplying the security mechanisms necessary to enforce the security policies set by the Deployer. This includes authentication of principals, authorization to perform EJB/servlet calls, configuration of resource adapters defined in the JCA, and secure communication with remote clients, integrity, and confidentiality.

3.7.5.4   Providing Tools for Principal Delegation

The J2EE Product Provider is responsible for passing principals on EJB/servlet calls. In particular, the J2EE Product Provider is responsible for providing the deployment tools that allow the Deployer to configure principal delegation for calls from one J2EE component to another.

3.7.5.5   Providing Access to the Caller's Security Context

The J2EE Product Provider is responsible for providing access to the caller's security context information when programmatically queried from enterprise beans and servlets using the J2EE-defined security APIs. For example, when a servlet calls `getUserPrincipal()` on a `javax.servlet.http.HttpServletRequest` object, the J2EE Product Provider must return the `java.security.Principal` object representing the caller of the servlet.

3.7.5.6 Supplying Runtime Security Enforcement

One of the most significant responsibilities of the J2EE Product Provider is to supply *runtime security enforcement*, as follows.

- Provide enforcement of the client access control as specified by the current security policy.

- Isolate an enterprise bean instance from other instances and other application components running on the server, thus preventing unauthorized access to privileged information.

- Provide runtime facilities to implement the principal-delegation policies set in the deployment descriptor.

- Allow a J2EE application to be deployed independently multiple times, each time with a different security policy.

3.7.5.7 Providing a Security Audit Trail

Optionally, the J2EE Product Provider may provide a *security audit trail* mechanism whereby secure access to enterprise beans and Web resources is logged. Such audit logs can be used to determine the information about the activity on the J2EE components. For example, these logs can be used to discover unauthorized attempts to access enterprise beans and Web resources.

3.8 J2EE Security Roles

The J2EE authorization model is based on the concept of security roles. Security roles are different from J2EE platform roles. As noted in Section 3.7.2 on page 67, a security role is a semantic grouping of permissions that a given type of application users must be granted to be authorized to use the application. In contrast, a J2EE platform role represents the organizational responsibility in making a J2EE application available to an enterprise, as described in Section 3.7 on page 64. Both declarative and programmatic security are based on the security roles.

Security roles are defined by the Application Component Provider and the Application Assembler. The Deployer then maps each security role to one or more security identities, such as users and groups, in the runtime environment. Listing 3.1 is an example of an XML description of two security roles declared within the deployment descriptor of an application's EAR file.

Listing 3.1.   Description of Security Roles Teller and Supervisor

```
<assembly-descriptor>
    <security-role>
        <description>
            This role is intended for employees who provide
            services to customers (tellers).
        </description>
        <role-name>Teller</role-name>
    </security-role>
    <security-role>
        <description>
            This role is intended for supervisors.
        </description>
        <role-name>Supervisor</role-name>
    </security-role>
</assembly-descriptor>
```

Declarative authorization can be used to control access to an enterprise bean method. This contract is specified in the deployment descriptor. Enterprise bean methods can be associated with `method-permission` elements in EJB modules' deployment descriptors. As described in Section 3.7.2 on page 67, a `method-permission` element specifies one or more EJB methods that are authorized for access by one or more security roles. In Section 3.7.3 on page 70, we observed that the mapping of principals to security roles is performed by the Deployer. If the calling principal is in one of the security roles authorized access to a method, the caller is allowed to execute the method. Conversely, if the calling principal is not a member of any of the roles, the caller is not authorized to execute the method. Listing 3.2 is an example of an XML `method-permission` element in an EJB module's deployment descriptor.

Listing 3.2.   Example of an XML `method-permission` Element in an EJB Module's Depolyment Descriptor

```
<method-permission>
    <role-name>Teller</role-name>
    <method>
        <ejb-name>AccountBean</ejb-name>
        <method-name>getBalance</method-name>
    </method>
    <method>
        <ejb-name>AccountBean</ejb-name>
        <method-name>getDetails</method-name>
    </method>
</method-permission>
```

Access to Web resources can be similarly protected. An action on a Web resource URI can be associated with an XML `security-constraint` element in a

Web module's deployment descriptor. The `security-constraint` element contains one or more URI patterns that can be authorized for access by one or more security roles. If the calling principal is a member of one or more of the security roles authorized to access an HTTP method on a URI, the principal is authorized to access the URI. Conversely, if the calling principal is not a member of any of the roles, the caller is not allowed to access the URI. Listing 3.3 shows a Web module's deployment descriptor fragment that defines access authorization requirements for a Web application.

Listing 3.3.   Example of an XML `security-constraint` Element in a Web Module's
Deployment Descriptor

```
<security-constraint>
    <web-resource-collection>
        <web-resource-name>
            Account servlet protected area
        </web-resource-name>
        <url-pattern>/finance/account/</url-pattern>
        <http-method>GET</http-method>
    </web-resource-collection>
    <auth-constraint>
        <description>Teller can access the URIs</description>
        <role-name>Teller</role-name>
    </auth-constraint>
</security-constraint>
```

In a J2EE environment, the security roles form the basis for the security provided by the containers that host the components. A container can provide two types of security: declarative and programmatic.

In the *declarative security model*, an application expresses its security policies through security constraints in a form external to the application. In J2EE, security constraints are specified in the deployment descriptors. This allows the application to be *security-mechanism agnostic*, or *security unaware*. Application code is not required to enable security or enforce the application security policy.

With declarative security, the application's logical security requirements are defined in the deployment descriptors and then mapped by the Deployer and the System Administrator to a deployment environment. The Deployer uses container-deployment tools to process the deployment descriptors. At runtime, the container uses the security policy configured by the Deployer and the System Administrator to enforce authorization.

Declarative security allows greater opportunities for application portability because all the security issues related to the underlying container and operating system are defined in configuration files external to the application. In addition, an application that makes use of declarative security is easier to develop because security and policy configuration issues are managed outside the application.

Application developers need not to be security experts, and an application based on declarative security can be more easily extended. Therefore, declarative security should always be used instead of programmatic security unless declarative security alone is insufficient to describe the security requirements of an application.

In the *programmatic security model*, the application programmer is responsible for explicitly writing the code that defines and enables security. The application security policy is an integral part of the application. An application conforming to this model is said to be *security aware*.

Programmatic security makes application development more difficult and severely limits the portability and extensibility of an application, because security issues related to the specific application, container, and operating system on which the application is running must be hard-coded. For these reasons, programmatic security should be used only when declarative security alone is insufficient to express the security model of an application. For example, the declarative security capabilities of J2EE V1.3 do not allow expressing a policy whereby a user cannot withdraw more than $1,000 from an automatic teller machine (ATM). Similarly, instance-level authorization to impose that only Bob can access Bob's account cannot be defined declaratively. In these cases, the application needs to enforce these rules programmatically.

3.9   Declarative Security Policies

Security policies associated with URIs and enterprise beans include the following:

- Login configurations associated with URIs: for example, use of form-based login

- Authorization policies associated with URIs and enterprise beans based on J2EE security roles

- Principal-delegation policies that apply to Web applications and enterprise beans

- Connection policies associated with JCA connectors that dictate how applications access EIS in a secure manner

Such authorization and delegation policies can be specified declaratively within the relevant deployment descriptors.

3.9.1   Login-Configuration Policy

Authentication is the process of proving the identity of an entity. Authentication generally is performed in two steps: (1) acquiring the authentication data of a principal and (2) verifying the authentication data against a user (principal) registry.

J2EE security authenticates a principal on the basis of the authentication policy associated with the resource the principal has requested. When a user requests a protected resource from a Web application server, the server authenticates the user. J2EE servers use authentication mechanisms based on validating credentials, such as digital certificates (see Section 10.3.4 on page 372), and user ID and password pairs. Credentials are verified against a user registry that supports the requested authentication scheme. For example, authentication based on user ID and password can be performed against an LDAP user registry, where authentication is performed using an LDAP bind request.

A Web server is responsible for servicing HTTP requests. In a typical J2EE environment, a Web server is a component of a J2EE WAS. In this case, the WAS hosts servlets, JSP files, and enterprise beans. The login—authentication—configuration is managed by the WAS, which drives the authentication challenges and performs the authentication. Similarly, if the Web server is independent of the WAS and the Web server is the front end for the WAS, the Web server acts as a proxy for J2EE requests. Again, the authentication is typically performed by the WAS.

The authentication policy for performing authentication among a user, a Web server, and a WAS can be specified in terms of the J2EE login configuration elements of a Web application's deployment descriptor. The authentication policy can specify the requirement for a secure channel and the authentication method. The requirement to use a secure channel when accessing a URI is specified through the `user-data-constraint` descriptor.

The authentication method is specified through the `auth-method` element in the `login-config` descriptor. There are three types of authentication methods:

1. **HTTP authentication method.** The credentials that the client must submit to authenticate are user ID and password, sent to the server as part of an HTTP header and typically retrieved through a browser's dialog window. The two modes of HTTP authentication are *basic* and *digest*. In both cases, the user ID is sent as cleartext.[2] In basic authentication, the password is transmitted in cleartext as well; in digest authentication, only a hash value of the password is transmitted to the server (see Section 10.2.2.4 on page 356).

---

2. More precisely, the cleartext is encoded in *base64 format*, a commonly used Internet standard. Binary data can be encoded in base64 format by rearranging the bits of the data stream in such a way that only the six least significant bits are used in every byte. Encoding a string in base64 format does not add security; the algorithm to encode and decode is fairly simple, and tools to perform encoding and decoding are publicly available on the Internet. Therefore, a string encoded in base64 format is still considered to be in cleartext.

2. **Form-based authentication method.** The credentials that the client must submit to authenticate are user ID and password, which are retrieved through an HTML form.

3. **Certificate-based authentication method.** The credential that the client must submit is the client's digital certificate, transmitted over an HTTPS connection.

3.9.1.1   *Authentication Method in Login Configuration*

The `auth-method` element in the `login-config` element specifies how a server challenges and retrieves authentication data from a user. As noted previously, there are three possible authentication methods: HTTP (user ID and password), form based (user ID and password), and certificate based (X.509 certificate).

With the *HTTP authentication method*, the credentials provided by the user consist of a user ID and password pair, transmitted as part of an HTTP header. When HTTP authentication is specified, a user at a Web client machine is challenged for a user ID and password pair. The challenge usually occurs in the following way:

1. A WAS issues an HTTP unauthorized client error code (401) and a `WWW_Authenticate` HTTP header.

2. The Web browser pops up a dialog window.

3. The user enters a user ID and password pair in this dialog window.

4. The information is sent to the Web server.

5. The WAS extracts the information and authenticates the user, using the authentication mechanism with which it has been configured.

With HTTP authentication, a realm name also needs to be specified. *Realms* are used to determine the scope of security data and to provide a mechanism for protecting Web application resources. For example, a user defined as `bob` in one realm is treated as different from `bob` in a second realm, even if these two IDs represent the same human user, Bob Smith.

Once specified, the realm name is used in the HTTP 401 challenge to help the Web server inform the end user of the name of the application domain. For example, if the realm is SampleAppRealm, the dialog window prompting the user for a user ID and password pair during authentication will include that the user ID and password are to be supplied for the SampleAppRealm realm.

HTTP authentication can be either basic or digest. In *basic authentication*, the credentials requested of the user are user ID and password, and both are transmitted as cleartext. In order for the authentication method to be basic, the `auth-method` element in the `login-config` descriptor must be set to `BASIC`. Listing 3.4

is a deployment descriptor fragment showing an example of login configuration requiring basic authentication.

Listing 3.4.   Login Configuration for Basic Authentication

```
<login-config>
    <auth-method>BASIC</auth-method>
    <realm-name>SampleAppRealm</realm-name>
</login-config>
```

This scheme is not considered to be a secure method of user authentication, unless used in conjunction with some external secure systems, such as SSL.

In *digest authentication*, the user ID and a hash value of the password are transmitted to the server as part of an HTTP header. Therefore, the password does not appear in cleartext, which is the biggest weakness of basic authentication.

When digest authentication is specified, the Web server responds to the client's request by requiring digest authentication. A one-way hash of the password (see Section 10.2.2.4 on page 356), as specifed by the Request for Comments (RFC) 2617,[3] is computed by the client, based on a random number, called *nonce*, uniquely generated by the server each time a 401 response is made. The hash value of the password is sent to the server, which computes the digest of the password for the user ID and compares the resulting hash value with the one submitted by the client. The requesting user is considered to be authenticated if the hash values are identical.

This mode of authentication assumes that the server has access to the user's password in cleartext—a necessary requirement in order for the server to compute the hash of the password. However, this is rarely the case in most enterprise environments, as the password in cleartext is not retrievable from a user repository containing the user ID and password information. Rather, the server typically delegates responsibility to the user repository to validate a user's password. Therefore, digest authentication is not widely adopted in enterprise environments and hence is not required to be supported by a J2EE container.

J2EE servers that do support digest authentication can be configured to issue a digest authentication challenge by setting the value of the `auth-method` element in the `login-config` descriptor to `DIGEST`. Listing 3.5 is a deployment descriptor fragment illustrating how a J2EE server can be configured to require digest authentication.

---

3. See `http://www.ietf.org/rfc/rfc2617.txt`.

Listing 3.5. Login Configuration for Digest Authentication

```
<login-config>
    <auth-method>DIGEST</auth-method>
    <realm-name>SampleAppRealm</realm-name>
</login-config>
```

The second authentication method is form based. With this method, the `auth-method` element in the `login-config` element must be set to `FORM`. The form-based authentication method assumes that the server is configured to send the client an HTML form to retrieve the user ID and password from the Web user, as opposed to sending a 401 HTTP unauthorized client error code as in the basic challenge type.

The configuration information for a form-based authentication method is specified through the `form-login-config` element in the `login-config` element. This element contains two subelements: `form-login-page` and `form-error-page`.

- The Web address to which a user requesting the resource is redirected is specified by the `form-login-page` subelement in the Web module's deployment descriptor. When the form-based authentication mode is specified, the user will be redirected to the specified `form-login-page` URL. An HTML form on this page will request a user ID and password.

- If the authentication fails, the user is redirected to the page specified by the `form-error-page` subelement.

Listing 3.6 is a sample HTML page for the login form.

Listing 3.6. Login Page Contents

```
<HTML>
    <HEAD>
        <TITLE>Sample Login page.</TITLE>
    </HEAD>
    <BODY>
        <TR><TD>
        <HR><B>Please log in!</B><BR><BR>
        </TD></TR>
        <CENTER>
        Please enter the following information:<BR>
        <FORM METHOD=POST ACTION="j_security_check">
            Account <INPUT TYPE=text NAME="j_username"
                SIZE=20><BR>
            Password <INPUT TYPE=password
                NAME="j_password" SIZE=20><BR>
```

```
                    <INPUT TYPE=submit NAME=action
                          VALUE="Submit Login">
            </FORM><HR>
            </CENTER>
        </BODY>
    </HTML>
```

Listing 3.7 is a deployment descriptor fragment showing an example of login configuration that requires form-based authentication.

Listing 3.7.   Login Configuration for Form-Based Authentication

```
<login-config>
    <auth-method>FORM</auth-method>
    <form-login-config>
        <form-login-page>/login.html</form-login-page>
        <form-error-page>
            /login-failed.html
        </form-error-page>
    </form-login-config>
</login-config>
```

The third type of authentication method is *certificate based* (X.509 certificate). In order for the authentication method to be certificate based, the `auth-method` element in the `login-config` descriptor must be set to `CLIENT-CERT`. The certificate-based authentication method implies that the Web server is configured to perform mutual authentication over SSL. The client is required to present a certificate to establish the connection. When the `CLIENT-CERT` mode is specified, the client will be required to submit the request over an HTTPS connection. If the request is not already over HTTPS, the J2EE product will redirect the client over an HTTPS connection. Successful establishment of an SSL connection implies that the client has presented its own certificate and not anyone else's. The details of how the server ensures that the client certificate really belongs to the client are explained in Section 10.3.4 on page 372 and Section 13.1.2 on page 452. The certificate used by the client is then mapped to an identity in the user registry the J2EE product is configured to use.

Listing 3.8 is a deployment descriptor fragment showing an example of login configuration that requires certificate-based authentication.

Listing 3.8.   Login Configuration for Certificate-Based Authentication

```
<login-config>
    <auth-method>CLIENT-CERT</auth-method>
</login-config>
```

Note that the user registry is not specified in this XML deployment descriptor fragment because it is not part of the J2EE specification.

3.9.1.2   *Secure-Channel Constraint*

Establishing an HTTPS session between the client and the Web server is often a necessary requirement to provide data confidentiality and integrity for the information flowing between the HTTP client and the server. In a J2EE environment, the security policy can require the use of a secure channel, specified through the `user-data-contraint` deployment descriptor element. When the requirement for a secure channel is specified, the request to the URI resource should be initiated over an HTTPS connection. If access is not already via a HTTPS session, the request is redirected over an HTTPS connection.

Specifying `INTEGRAL` or `CONFIDENTIAL` as the value for the `transport-guarantee` element in the `user-data-constraint` descriptor will be treated as a requirement for the HTTP request to be over SSL. This requirement can be specified as part of the `user-data-constraint` element in a Web application's login configuration. In theory, `INTEGRAL` should enforce communitcation integrity, whereas `CONFIDENTIAL` should enforce communication confidentiality, and it could be possible to select different cipher suites to satisfy these requirements. However, a J2EE server typically does not differentiate `INTEGRAL` from `CONFIDENTIAL` but instead treats both of these values to indicate the need to require an SSL connection with a particular cipher suite, not based on whether `INTEGRAL` or `CONFIDENTIAL` was specified.

Listing 3.9 is a deployment descriptor fragment showing an example of login configuration that contains the `user-data-constraint` element. More details are provided in Section 4.6.6 on page 132.

Listing 3.9.   Specifying the Requirement for a Secure Channel

```
<user-data-constraint>
   <transport-guarantee>CONFIDENTIAL</transport-guarantee>
</user-data-constraint>
```

3.9.2   Authorization Policy

The *role-permission interpretation* of the J2EE security model treats a security role to be a set of permissions. The security role uses the `role-name` label defined in the `method-permission` element of an EJB module's deployment descriptor and in the `security-constraint` element of a Web module's deployment descriptor as the name of the set of permissions. The set of permissions defines a number of *resources*—the enterprise beans and the Web resources to which the `method-permission` and `security-constraint` elements refer, respectively—and a set of *actions*—the methods listed by the `method-permission` and the `security-constraint` descriptors. For example, in Listing 3.2 on page 74, the security role Teller is associated with the permissions to invoke the `getBalance()` and `getDetails()` methods on the AccountBean enterprise bean. Similarly, in Listing 3.3 on page 75, the security role Teller is associated with the permission to perform a GET invocation over HTTP to the `/finance/account/` URI. If multiple `method-permission` and `security-constraint` descriptors refer to the same security role, they are all taken to contribute to the same role permission. In other words, the sets of permissions associated with that security role are merged to form a single set.

This model has the advantage of dramatically reducing the number of objects in a *security object space*—a set of pairs (*subject*, *<target, operation>*), where the *subject* is an entity requesting to perform a security-sensitive *operation* on a given *target*. The Deployer and the System Administrator can define authorization policies, associated with EJB or URI targets and the operations of enterprise bean methods and HTTP methods, respectively, for the security roles in their applications. Then, they associate subjects to security roles; by extension, those subjects are granted the permissions to perform the operations permitted by the security roles.

Based on the J2EE security model, a protected action can be performed by a subject who has been granted at least one of the security roles associated with the action. The security roles associated with a protected action are the *required security roles*—the permissions necessary to perform the action itself. The roles associated with a subject are the *granted security roles*—the permissions that have been given to that subject. This means that the subject will be allowed to perform an action if the subject's granted security roles contain at least one of the required security roles to perform that action. For example, if the action consisting of accessing the EJB method `getDetails()` on the AccountBean enterprise bean can be performed only by the security roles Teller and Supervisor and if subject Bob has been granted the security role of Teller, Bob will be allowed to perform that action, even if Bob has not been granted the security role of Supervisor.

The table that represents the association of security roles to sets of permissions is called the *method-permission table*. A method-permission table (see Table 3.1) can be used to deduce the set of required security roles. The rows in the table represent security roles; the columns represent protected actions.

It can be inferred from Table 3.1 that in order to access the `getBalance()` method on AccountBean, the required security roles are Teller and Supervisor. In order to access any URI that matches the pattern `/public/*`, a PublicRole is required.

Table 3.1.   Example of Method-Permission Table

	`/finance/` `accountGET`	`/finance/` `accountPUT`	`/public/*`	`AccountBean.` `getBalance()`	`AccountBean.` `getDetails()`
Teller	Yes	No	No	Yes	Yes
Supervisor	Yes	Yes	No	Yes	Yes
PublicRole	No	No	Yes	No	No

The table that represents the association of roles to subjects is called the *authorization table*, or *protection matrix*. In such a table, the security role is defined as the *security object*, and users and groups are defined as *security subjects*. An authorization table (see Table 3.2) can be used to deduce the set of granted security roles. The rows in the table refer to the users and user groups that are security subjects in the protection matrix; the columns represent the J2EE security roles that are security objects in the protection matrix.

The method-permission table and the protection matrix reflect the configuration specified in the deployment descriptors. For example, the first row in Table 3.1 reflects the deployment descriptor obtained from the deployment descriptor fragments of Listing 3.2 on page 74 and Listing 3.3 on page 75. It can be inferred from Table 3.2 that user Bob and group TellerGroup are granted the security role of Teller, everyone is granted the PublicRole, and only users in the ManagerGroup are granted the security role of Supervisor.

Combining Table 3.1 and Table 3.2, it follows that Bob can access the `getBalance()` and `getDetails()` methods on the AccountBean enterprise bean and can issue an HTTP `GET` request on the `/finance/account/` URI. Bob cannot, however, issue an HTTP `PUT` request on the `/finance/account/` URI. Note that Bob will be able to access any URI that matches `/public/*`, as everyone has been granted the role PublicRole, which is the role necessary to get access to `/public/*`.

In the J2EE security model, the Application Assembler defines the initial mapping of actions on the protected resources to the set of the required security

Table 3.2.   Example of Authorization Table

	Teller	**Supervisor**	**PublicRole**
TellerGroup	Yes	No	No
ManagerGroup	No	Yes	No
Everyone	No	No	Yes
Bob	Yes	No	No

roles (see Section 3.7.2 on page 67). This can be done using the application assembly tool. Subsequently, the Deployer will refine the policies specified by the Application Assembler when installing the application into a J2EE environment (see Section 3.7.3 on page 70). The Deployer also can use the application assembly tool to redefine the security policies, when necessary, and then install the application into the J2EE container. The method-permission table is formed as a result of the required security roles getting specified through the process of application assembly and refinement during deployment.

Authorization policies can be broadly categorized into *application policies*, which are specified in deployment descriptors and map J2EE resources to roles, and *authorization bindings*, which reflect role to user or group mapping. As discussed in Section 3.7.2 on page 67, a set of security roles is associated with actions on J2EE protected resources. These associations are defined in the J2EE deployment descriptors when an application is assembled and deployed. The security roles specified in this way are the required security roles—the sets of permissions that users must be granted in order to be able to perform actions on protected resources. Pragmatically, before a user is allowed to perform an action on a protected resource, either that same user or one of the groups that user is a member of should be granted at least one of the required security roles associated with that protected resource. The authorization table that relates the application-scoped required security roles to users and user groups is managed within the J2EE Product Provider using the J2EE Product Provider configuration tools.

3.9.3   Delegation Policy

Earlier in this chapter, we defined *delegation* as the process of forwarding a principal's credentials with the cascaded downstream requests. Enforcement of delegation policies affects the identity under which the intermediary will perform the downstream invocations on other components. By default, the intermediary will impersonate the requesting client when making the downstream calls. The downstream resources do not know about the real identity, prior to impersonation, of the intermediary. Alternatively, the intermediary may perform the downstream invocations using a different identity. In either case, the access decisions on the downstream objects are based on the identity at the outbound call from the intermediary. To summarize, in a J2EE environment, the identity under which the intermediary will perform a task can be either

- The client's identity—the identity under which the client is making the request to the intermediary

- A specified identity—an identity in terms of a role indicated via deployment descriptor configuration

The application deployment environment determines whether the client or a specified identity is appropriate.

The Application Assembler can use the `security-identity` element to define a delegation identity for an enterprise bean's method in the deployment descriptor. Consider an example in which a user, Bob, invokes methods on a SavingsAccountBean enterprise bean. SavingsAccountBean exposes three methods—`getBalance()`, `setBalance()`, and `transferToOtherBank()`—and its delegation policy is defined as in Table 3.3. Figure 3.5 shows a possible scenario based on the delegation policy specified in Table 3.3.

The method `setBalance()` will execute under the client's identity because the delegation mode is set to `use-caller-identity`. The method `getBalance()` will execute under the client's identity as well because no delegation mode is specified, and the default is `use-caller-identity`. Therefore, if Bob invokes the method `getBalance()` on AccountBean, the method will execute under Bob's identity, `bob`. Suppose that the `getBalance()` method invokes a `lookup()` method on

Table 3.3.   SavingsAccountBean Enterprise Bean's Delegation Policy

Method	Delegation Mode	Specified Role
`getBalance()`		
`setBalance()`	`use-caller-identity`	
`transferToOtherBank()`	`run-as`	Supervisor

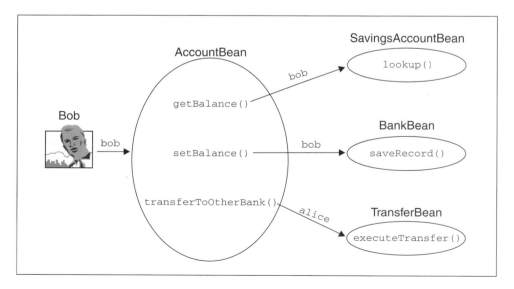

Figure 3.5.   Delegation Policy Scenario

SavingsAccountBean. This invocation will still be executed under Bob's identity and will succeed only if Bob has been granted the permission to invoke `lookup()` on SavingsAccountBean.

Any downstream call from `transferToOtherBank()` will perform method calls on a TransferBean enterprise bean. These invocations will need to execute under a principal that has been granted the Supervisor role. The Deployer or the System Adminstrator needs to map the Supervisor role to a principal that has been granted the Supervisor role. This can be done by specifying a valid user ID and password pair corresponding to a user who has been granted that role. For example, if user Alice has been granted the Supervisor role and if the user ID and password pair for Alice is associated with the Supervisor role, the calls to `transferToOtherBank()` will occur under Alice's identity.

3.9.4   Connection Policy

Information in any EIS must be protected from unauthorized access. An EIS system is likely to have its own authorization model. At a minimum, most of these systems have facilities to accept some form of authentication data representing an identity connecting to the EIS. The JCA is designed to extend the end-to-end security model for J2EE-based applications to include integration with EISs. A WAS and an EIS collaborate to ensure the proper authentication of a resource principal when establishing a connection to a target EIS. As discussed in Section 3.4 on page 61, the JCA allows for two ways to sign on to an EIS: container-managed sign-on and component-managed sign-on.

With container-managed sign-on, the connection to an EIS is obtained through declarative security. In order for a connection to be container managed, the deployment descriptor will indicate that the `res-auth` element associated with a resource definition is declared as `Container`. If the connection is obtained by passing the identity information programmatically, the value for `res-auth` should be set to `Application`. Details of component-managed sign-on are discussed in Section 3.10.3 on page 94.

A deployment descriptor fragment that declares that the authentication facilitated by the resource adapter should be set to be `Container` is shown in Listing 3.10.

Listing 3.10. An XML `res-auth` Element in a Deployment Descriptor

```
<resource-ref>
    <description>Connection to myConnection</description>
    <res-ref-name>eis/myConnection</res-ref-name>
    <res-type>javax.resource.cci.ConnectionFactory</res-type>
    <res-auth>Container</res-auth>
</resource-ref>
```

The container is responsible for obtaining appropriate user authentication information needed to access the EIS. The connection to the EIS is facilitated by the specified resource adapter. The JCA allows specifying the authentication mechanism. The `authentication-mechanism-type` element in the deployment descriptor is used to specify whether a resource adapter supports a specific authentication mechanism. This XML element is a subelement of the `authentication-mechanism` element. The JCA specification supports the following authentication mechanisms:

- **Basic authentication.** The authentication mechanism is based on user ID and password. In this case, the `authentication-mechanism-type` XML element in the deployment descriptor is set to `BasicPassword`.

- **Kerberos V5.** The authentication mechanism is based on Kerberos V5. In this case, the `authentication-mechanism-type` element in the deployment descriptor is set to `Kerbv5`.

Other authentication mechanisms are outside the scope of the JCA specification.

In a secure environment, it is likely that a J2EE application component, such as an enterprise bean, and the EIS system that is accessed through the component are secured under different security domains, where a *security domain* is a scope within which certain common security mechanisms and policies are established. In such cases, the identity under which the J2EE component is accessed should be mapped to an identity under which the EIS is to be accessed. Figure 3.6 depicts a possible scenario.

In this scenario, an enterprise bean in a J2EE container is accessed by a user, Bob Smith. The enterprise bean is protected in a way that it allows only users from a specified LDAP directory to access it. Therefore, the identity under which Bob Smith will access the enterprise bean must be registered in that LDAP directory. Bob Smith uses the identity of `bsmith` when he accesses the enterprise bean.

In a simplistic case, where the `run-as` policy of the enterprise bean is set to be the caller identity, the connections to the EIS will be obtained on behalf of Bob Smith. If the connections are obtained through user ID and password, when the enterprise bean obtains a connection to a back-end system, such as a CICS system, the J2EE container will retrieve a user ID and password to act on behalf of user `bsmith`. The application invokes the `getConnection()` method on the `javax.resource.cci.ConnectionFactory` instance (see Listing 3.10 on page 87) with no security-related parameters, as shown in Listing 3.11, a fragment of Java code.

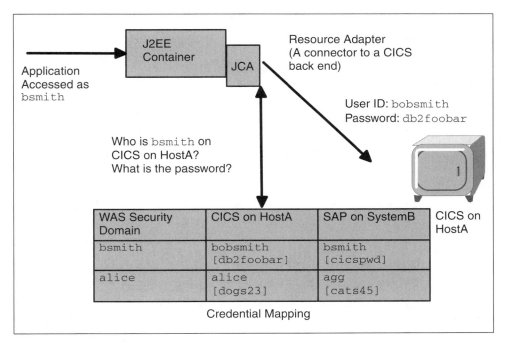

Figure 3.6.   Credential Mapping when Accessing an EIS from a J2EE Container

Listing 3.11.   Getting a Connection to an EIS with Container-Managed Sign-On

```
// Construct the InitialContext
Context initctx = new InitialContext();

// Perform a JNDI lookup to obtain a ConnectionFactory
javax.resource.cci.ConnectionFactory cxf =
    (javax.resource.cci.ConnectionFactory) initctx.lookup
    ("java:comp/env/eis/MyEIS");

// Invoke the ConnectionFactory to obtain a connection.
// The security information is not passed to the
// getConnection() method
javax.resource.cci.Connection cx = cxf.getConnection();
```

The application relies on the container to manage the sign-on to the EIS instance. This is possible in simple deployment scenarios in which the identity under which the EIS system is accessed is specified by the Deployer. This effectively means that all identities accessing the application are mapped to a single identity to access the EIS system: a *many-to-one identity mapping*.

In more sophisticated deployment scenarios, a many-to-one identity mapping may not be sufficient for security policy reasons. For example, it may be necessary for the EIS system to log all the identities that accessed it. For this logging facility to be useful, the identities accessing a J2EE application must not all be mapped to the same identity on the EIS system. A *one-to-one* or *many-to-many identity mapping* is recommended in this case. In particular, the container may use a credential mapping facility whereby `bsmith` is mapped to user ID `bobsmith` and password `db2foobar`, as shown in Figure 3.6.

If connections require Kerberos credentials or other generic credentials to be passed, the mapping facility is responsible for mapping one form of the credential to another that can be used by the target security domain. The manner in which these mappings happen and the level of sophistication in mapping available in J2EE application servers are server specific and not dictated by the J2EE specification.

In enterprise environments consisting of multiple departments, organizations, and even acquired companies, it is typical for systems to be interconnected and the applications shared. In such environments in which J2EE applications are deployed, it is a good architectural approach to design the application integration in a way that applications use JCA to obtain connections to other applications and to follow the declarative approach to define connection sign-on, as explained in this section. The use of JCA will make applications unaware of cross-security domains when accessing non-J2EE systems, and the use of declarative security will enhance application flexibility and portability. JCA with declarative security will also help manage the mapping of credentials and identities outside the application as enforced and facilitated by the enterprise-level mapping infrastructure.

3.10 Programmatic Security

Declarative security should always be used instead of programmatic security whenever possible. However, when declarative security is insufficient, it may be necessary to retrieve security-sensitive information programmatically from the container. This section explains how to retrieve the user's identity and privilege information programatically.

Applications that make use of programmatic security typically invoke the following EJB and servlet/JSP security APIs:

* **EJB method `isCallerInRole()` in interface `javax.ejb.EJBContext`.** This method is used to test whether the current caller, the client, has been assigned to a specified security role.

- **EJB method** `getCallerPrincipal()` **in interface** `javax.ejb.EJB-Context`. This method is used to obtain a `Principal` object representing the current caller, the client.

- **Servlet/JSP method** `isUserInRole()` **in interface** `javax.servlet.http.HttpServletRequest`. This method, similar to the EJB method `isCallerInRole()`, returns a `boolean` indicating whether the authenticated user, the client, is a member of the specified security role.

- **Servlet/JSP method** `getUserPrincipal()` **in interface** `javax.servlet.http.HttpServletRequest`. This method, similar to the EJB method `getCallerPrincipal()`, returns a `Principal` object representing the current authenticated user, the client.

3.10.1 Retrieving Identity Information

The Java Servlet and EJB specifications provide mechanisms to programmatically obtain identity information about the user invoking a method on a servlet or an enterprise bean.

3.10.1.1 From a Servlet or JSP File

The `HttpServletRequest` object passed to a servlet method can be used to obtain information about the user invoking the method. Invoking the `getRemoteUser()` method on the `HttpServletRequest` object returns the name of the user if the user has been authenticated, `null` otherwise.

The `getRemoteUser()` method can be invoked as shown in Listing 3.12.

Listing 3.12. Retrieving the User Name from a Servlet

```
public void doGet(HttpServletRequest req,
    HttpServletResponse res)
{
    // other code...

    // obtain the user name
    String userName = req.getRemoteUser();

    // other code...
}
```

The `getUserPrincipal()` method in the `HttpServletRequest` object returns the `Principal` object corresponding to the user if the user has been authenticated, `null` otherwise. The name of the user can then be obtained by calling the `getName()` method on the `Principal` object, if this not `null`, as shown in Listing 3.13.

Listing 3.13. Retrieving the `Principal` Object and the User Name from a Servlet

```
public void doGet(HttpServletRequest req,
    HttpServletResponse res)
{
    // other code...

    // obtain the user Principal
    Principal userPrincipal = req.getUserPrincipal();

    // obtain the user name
    String userName;

    if (userPrincipal != null)
        userName = userPrincipal.getName();

    // other code...
}
```

3.10.1.2 From an Enterprise Bean

The `getCallerPrincipal()` method can be called on a `javax.ejb.EJBContext` object to obtain the `Principal` object corresponding to the user making the enterprise bean method invocation. The `Principal` object can then be used to obtain information about the user. A code example is shown in Listing 3.14.

Listing 3.14. Retrieving the User Name from an Enterprise Bean

```
public String getUserName(EJBContext context)
{
        // obtain and return the user name
        return context.getCallerPrincipal().getName();
}
```

3.10.2   Proactive Authorization

The Java Servlet and EJB specifications provide mechanisms to programmatically obtain information about the user's privileges by invoking a method on a servlet or an enterprise bean.

3.10.2.1 From a Servlet or JSP File

The `HttpServletRequest` object passed to a servlet method can be interrogated to obtain information about whether the user invoking the method has been granted a particular security role. Based on the result, the servlet may make decisions on how to proceed. For example, if the caller is granted the Boss role, the servlet redirects to a page that has managerial capabilities; otherwise, it might redirect to a different page. Note that when the servlet checks for the Boss role, this role is scoped to the servlet. The Application Assembler performs the mapping of this role reference to an enterprise application role by using the `role-link` tag in the deployment descriptor, as shown in Listing 3.15.

Listing 3.15. An XML `role-link` Element in a Deployment Descriptor

```
<security-role-ref>
    <role-name>Boss</role-name>
    <role-link>Manager</role-link>
</security-role-ref>
```

A code example is shown in Listing 3.16.

Listing 3.16. Retrieving the User's Role Information from a Servlet

```
public void doGet(HttpServletRequest req,
    HttpServletResponse res)
{
    // other code...

    if (req.isUserInRole("Boss"))
    {
        // code to redirect to Manager's page...
    }
    else
    {
        // code to redirect to generic page...
    }

    // other code...
}
```

3.10.2.2 *From an Enterprise Bean*

The `isCallerInRole()` method on an `EJBContext` object can be used to obtain information about the roles granted to a particular user. This is similar to what we saw in Section 3.10.1.1 on page 91. A code fragment example is shown in Listing 3.17.

Listing 3.17. Retrieving the User's Role Information from an Enterprise Bean

```
public Object getOrganizationInfo(EJBContext context)
{
    // other code...

    // obtain the user name
    if (context.isCallerInRole ("Boss")
    {
```

(continues)

Listing 3.17. Retrieving the User's Role Information from an Enterprise Bean

```
        // code to access the Boss entity bean and get the
        // budget info...
    }
    else
    {
        // code to access the employee bean and get the
        // organization chart...
    }

    // other code...
}
```

3.10.3 Application-Managed Sign-On to an EIS

Section 3.9.4 on page 87 described container-managed sign-on, whereby a connection to an EIS is obtained through declarative security. An alternative approach is to use programmatic security by allowing the sign-on to an EIS to be managed directly by the application. In order for a connection to be application managed, the value of the `res-auth` XML element associated with a resource definition in the deployment descriptor must be set to `Application`, as shown in Listing 3.18.

Listing 3.18. Setting the `res-auth` Deployment Descriptor Tag to `Application`

```
<resource-ref>
    <description>Connection to myConnection</description>
    <res-ref-name>eis/myConnection</res-ref-name>
    <res-type>javax.resource.cci.ConnectionFactory</res-type>
    <res-auth>Application</res-auth>
</resource-ref>
```

In the case of application-managed sign-on, the application is responsible for retrieving appropriate user information, such as the user ID and password, necessary to connect to the EIS. The connection is facilitated by a resource adapter. The application invokes the `getConnection()` method on the `ConnectionFactory` instance with the security information: user ID and password. Specifying security information is dependent on the resource adapter type and the way in which the adapter accepts the user ID and password. For example, in order to connect to an EIS system called MyEIS, the application may be required to pass user ID and password through a `com.myeis.ConnectionSpecImpl` object. Listing 3.19 is a Java code fragment showing such a scenario, which is similar to the one discussed in Section 3.9.4 on page 87, except that the security information is coded into the application and is passed to the `getConnection()` method.

Listing 3.19. Getting a Connection to an EIS with Container-Managed Sign-On

```
// Method in an application component
Context initctx = new InitialContext();

// Perform a JNDI lookup to obtain a ConnectionFactory
javax.resource.cci.ConnectionFactory cxf =
    (javax.resource.cci.ConnectionFactory) initctx.lookup
    ("java:comp/env/eis/MyEIS");

// Insert here the code to get a new ConnectionSpec
com.myeis.ConnectionSpecImpl props = // ...

// Set user ID and password
props.setUserName("bobsmith");
props.setPassword("db2foobar");

// Invoke the ConnectionFactory to obtain a connection.
// The security information is passed explicitly to the
// getConnection() method.
javax.resource.cci.Connection cx = cxf.getConnection(props);
```

3.11 Secure Communication within a WAS Environment

A fundamental aspect of any distributed computing system is remote communication. In an enterprise environment, components, such as Web servers, plug-ins, and WASs; external servers, such as LDAP directory servers; and clients communicate with one another over multiple protocols.

- HTTP clients invoke URL requests to Web servers over HTTP.

- WASs communicate with one another over IIOP.

- Some WASs may communicate with external systems by using other protocols. For instance, a WAS can communicate with an LDAP directory server over LDAP.

Because these components can host and distribute security-sensitive information, it is necessary to provide secure communication channels. The quality-of-service (QoS) should include encryption, integrity, and, possibly, authentication. The SSL protocol is generally used to meet these QoS requirements. Typically, two modes of SSL connections are used in J2EE:

1. **Server-side SSL.**   The client connects to the server and attempts to verify the authenticity of the server's identity. The server does not verify the client's identity. If the client can authenticate the server successfully, the client/server communication is performed over an encrypted channel.

2. **Mutual-authentication SSL.** The client connects to the server. Both client and server attempt to authenticate to each other. If the mutual-authentication process is successful, client and server communicate over an encrypted channel.

The SSL configuration on the server side dictates whether a client connecting to the server should connect over server-side SSL or mutual-authentication SSL. In both cases, the strength of encryption depends on the configured cipher suite. In a Java environment, JSSE-compliant SSL providers are used to establish secure communication using SSL between the end points (see Chapter 13 on page 449).

The following list shows possible combinations of securely communicating parties:

- **Web client to Web server.** Any Web browser can issue a request to a Web server over a secure connection. This communication can be over either server-side SSL or mutual-authentication SSL. The Web server should be configured to accept connections from Web browsers over a secure-socket port—typically, port 443. If a WAS requires a client to present a client certificate in order to be authenticated to access a servlet, the underlying Web server should be configured to require mutual-authentication SSL connections from Web browsers. This configuration is specific to the underlying Web server that is used, whereas the client certificate information is configured on the Web browser and is specific to the browser settings.

- **Web server to WAS.** In general, a Web server needs a plug-in to communicate with a back-end WAS, unless the Web server and the WAS are integrated to form a single component. In a typical scenario, a Web server plug-in may communicate with an application server over HTTP. This can be configured to be over SSL, in which case the resulting protocol is HTTPS. In order for this to happen, the WAS transport must be configured to accept only secure connections. In the case of mutual-authentication SSL, the WAS transport can also be configured to trust only a set of selected clients to connect to the WAS. By properly configuring the digital-key storage facility—for example, a key file—both the plug-in and the WAS can be configured to accept a list of trusted Certificate Authorities (CAs), so that a trusted communication link can be established with only the clients whose certificates have been authenticated by one of the trusted CAs (see Section 10.3.4 on page 372).

- **WAS to WAS.** WASs communicate to other WASs by using IIOP. In a secure environment, all these communications are over SSL. The digital-key databases can be configured to reflect the trust policy by using the tools provided with J2EE. In general, it is also possible to configure the strength of encryption enforced in such a secure connection.

- **Application client to WAS.** Similar to a Web browser's making a request to a Web resource, Java clients can use the EJB programming model to invoke methods on an enterprise bean by connecting to the WAS that hosts the enterprise bean. In a secure environment, the communication from the client to the protected resources should be protected by the SSL protocol. At that point, an application client can securely communicate with a WAS over SSL. This is achieved by configuring the WAS with a list of trusted application clients. Alternatively, the WAS can be configured to accept a list of trusted CAs, so that a trusted communication link can be established with only the application clients whose digital certificates have been authenticated by one of the trusted CAs.

- **WAS to LDAP directory server.** A WAS may need to connect to external systems. For example, a WAS may be configured to use an LDAP directory server as a user registry. In this case, the WAS will make calls against the LDAP directory. The protocol of communication between these two entities is LDAP. User ID and password pairs are verified by performing LDAP bind operations against the LDAP directory. In a scenario like this, these values will flow over the wire unencrypted unless the communication is protected by the SSL protocol. For this reason, an LDAP directory server should be configured to require that all connections be over SSL. The set of digital certificates trusted by the directory server can be imported into the WAS's digital-key storage facility so that the WAS can successfully establish an SSL connection with the LDAP directory server.

3.12 Secure E-Business Request Flow

We are now ready to revisit the simple e-business request flow presented in Section 3.6 on page 63 with the security semantics added to the flow. The secure e-business request flow takes the security model and security technologies available in the J2EE environment into account and depicts the use of those components.

Figure 3.7 enhances the diagram depicted in Figure 3.3 on page 63 and shows how the J2EE security technologies presented in this chapter can play a role in a secure e-business request flow.

Let us consider the request flow discussed in Section 3.6 on page 63 and understand how security technologies play a role when that request is secured. A user, say, Bob, invokes URL `http://samples.com/servlet/account`, which is handled by the Web container that hosts the account servlet. Based on the security

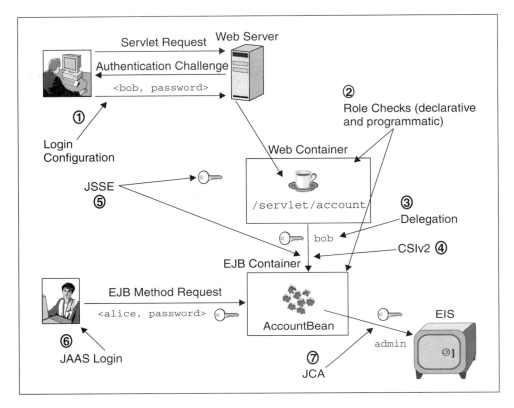

Figure 3.7.   Secure E-Business Request Flow

constraints defined, the URI /servlet/account is a protected resource. The login configuration associated with the Web application is set to BASIC. Therefore, when the request arrives, the Web container issues an HTTP 401 response back to the browser. Bob resubmits his request by providing his user ID (bob) and his password (see step 1 in Figure 3.7). The Web container validates the user ID and password by authenticating the pair against the underlying user registry.

After the credentials are validated, the Web container performs an authorization check. The URI is protected in a way to grant access only to the Teller role. The container checks whether user Bob is granted the role (see step 2 in Figure 3.7). As Bob has been granted the Teller role, he is allowed to access the URI.

The servlet invokes the AccountBean enterprise bean, and the request is dispatched to the enterprise bean. The delegation policy on the servlet is not set to run-as, which means that the downstream requests will be performed by using the caller's identity. In this case, the caller is Bob, and therefore the identity under which the enterprise bean is called consists of Bob's credentials, as depicted in step 3 in Figure 3.7.

The Web container dispatches the request to the EJB container when the account servlet makes a call to the AccountBean enterprise bean. The request is sent over IIOP. Given that this request is sent over a secure environment, the CSIv2 protocol is in effect (see Section 3.3 on page 61). The servers hosting the Web container and the EJB container establish a secure association using the CSIv2 technology as depicted in step 4 in Figure 3.7. Based on a successful establishment of the connection and the validity of Bob's credentials, the received identity at the EJB container is Bob's.

The connections between the Web server and the Web container, and the Web container and the EJB container are over SSL. This ensures confidentiality and integrity of the messages sent over the wire. It is essential for all communications in an enterprise to be over a secure connection. JSSE is used to establish the SSL connection as depicted in step 5 in Figure 3.7.

The AccountBean enterprise bean can also be invoked from a Java client. In this case, a user, say, Alice, sends the request directly over IIOP. The request is made from a J2EE client. In this case, the J2EE security technology used for authentication and authorization is JAAS, which is discussed in detail in Chapter 9 on page 289. The client is configured with a `javax.security.auth.callback.CallbackHandler` and performs a JAAS login against the server hosting the EJB container (step 6 in Figure 3.7). Alice needs to provide a valid user ID and password pair. Then, she can perform a method invocation on the AccountBean enterprise bean. J2EE supports a Java client to submit a user ID and password pair over an IIOP message. Using the CSIv2 protocol, the user ID and password pair is in a Generic Security Services Username Password (GSSUP) token within the CSIv2 `ESTABLISH_CONTEXT` message.[4] In order for this communication to be protected, transport-level SSL is recommended.

The AccountBean enterprise bean is protected by J2EE declarative security. A method permission definition declares the enterprise bean's methods to be accessible only by those who are granted the Teller role. Both users, Bob and Alice, are granted the Teller role. Therefore, the requests that come through the servlet and the one directly submitted are allowed to be invoked. The AccountBean enterprise bean is succesfully accessed after the authorization check.

The AccountBean enterprise bean needs to access the data source in order to retrieve the account information. The bean uses a JCA connection manager to obtain a connection to an EIS. When the connection is obtained, based on the connector security configuration, an identity is associated with the connection. The

---

4. Note that there is no standard declarative way to specify this type of authentication. The details are specific to the J2EE container.

`admin` identity is used to obtain the connection and access the back-end EIS. This access is enforced by the JCA capability and ensures that the EIS is accessed securely, based on the security configuration, as depicted in step 7 in Figure 3.7.

As illustrated in the simple request flow enhanced with security characteristics, the J2EE security model provides the capability and infrastructure to perform secure transactions in an e-business environment.

CHAPTER 4

Servlet and JSP Security

An enterprise solution has come to be considered incomplete if the applications it enables cannot be accessed over the Web. Along with the advantages of Web enablement of enterprise applications comes the inherent vulnerability of security breaches into an enterprise system. Security must be considered from the design through deployment and administration. This chapter describes the security policies and features defined for use by J2EE Web modules, which assemble Java servlets and JSP files, as well as static content, such as HTML pages, into a single deployable unit (see Section 3.2.2 on page 59).

The sections in this chapter use concrete examples to illustrate how the security policy can be declaratively specified in a Web module's deployment descriptor. The chapter first describes a Web module's deployment descriptor and then explains how it can be used to enforce authentication, authorization, and delegation policies. This chapter also discusses how applications can programmatically enforce security to address any additional enterprise security requirements that are not addressed by the J2EE specification at this time. The chapter concludes by describing future directions of Web application security.

4.1   Introduction

In the Web-based world, many of the servers run an HTTP Web server. The traditional way to add customized functions to a Web server has been to write CGI programs—stand-alone programs called by an HTTP server when it receives requests for specific pages. Rather than returning static HTML text, the HTTP server starts a CGI program and passes on the user's request, together with many details about the server environment. The CGI program handles the request and returns HTML text to the HTTP server, which transfers it to the user. Figure 4.1 shows this process.

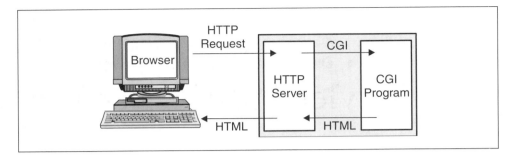

Figure 4.1.   How a CGI Program Works

Starting the execution of any program—not just a CGI program—can be a lengthy process. Memory needs to be allocated, the program code needs to be read from disk into memory, references to dynamic libraries need to be linked, standard I/O streams need to be created and connected, and the program needs to process the request.

In a very simple HTTP Web server, multithreading may not be implemented, which means that pending HTTP requests cannot be served until the CGI program returns, possibly after many seconds. However, most modern HTTP servers support multithreading, so this is less of an issue. Yet limits remain on the number of process threads that can be created. When there are large numbers of outstanding requests to an HTTP server, individual threads still need to wait for the previously started CGI programs to complete.

CGI programs are also the target of malicious hacking. Many successful attacks on Web servers have been through poorly written CGI programs, which too often fail to test the parameters passed to them, causing, for example, input-buffer overflows when passed data that is longer than the allocated buffers.

Several alternatives to CGI have been implemented, such as Netscape Connection Application Programming Interface (NSAPI) from Netscape and Internet Connection Application Programming Interface (ICAPI) from IBM. These interfaces permit native software routines to be directly called by the Web server, significantly reducing the startup overhead. However, the add-on routines still need to be compiled for each platform. The various programming interfaces are not fully compatible, restricting the choice of Web server to a particular vendor, although ICAPI, for example, has been designed to include the NSAPI calls. Program testing is even more important, to prevent poorly written software from corrupting the Web server itself.

4.1.1 Java Servlets

Java servlets can be used to overcome these CGI programming issues. A *servlet* is a platform-independent server-side software component written in the Java language. Servlets run inside a servlet, or Web, container. They extend the capabilities of the underlying Web server because they provide services over the Web, using a request/response paradigm, similar to the CGI programs'.

Servlets were introduced to interactively view and modify data and to generate dynamic Web content. From a high-level perspective, the process flow sequence is as follows.

1. A client sends a request to a Web server.
2. The Web server forwards the request to a servlet container.
3. The servlet container sends the request information to the servlet.
4. The servlet builds a response and passes it to the servlet container. Depending on the client's request, the content of the response is dynamically constructed.
5. The servlet container sends the response back to the Web server.
6. The Web server forwards the response to the client.

This flow is shown in Figure 4.2.

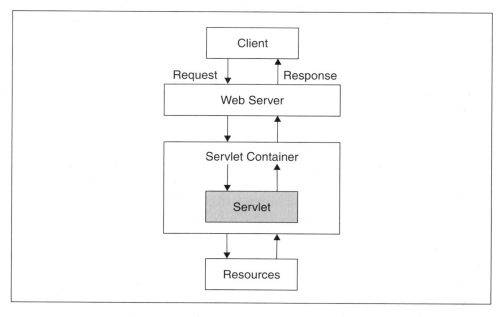

Figure 4.2. Process Flow from a High-Level Perspective

4.1.2   JSP Technology

JSP technology, an extension of the Java servlet technology, offers support for dynamic page content through XML-like tags and scriptlets written in the Java language to encapsulate the logic that generates the content for the page. The code of a simple JSP application, Welcome, is shown in Listing 4.1.

Listing 4.1.   `Welcome.jsp`

```
<!DOCTYPE HTML
    PUBLIC "-//W3C//DTD HTML 4.01 Transitional//EN">
<HTML>
    <HEAD>
        <META http-equiv="Content-Type" content="text/html">
        <META name="GENERATOR" content="IBM WebSphere Studio">
        <TITLE>Welcome.jsp</TITLE>
    </HEAD>
    <BODY>
        Welcome,
        <%=request.getParameter("firstName")%>
        <%=request.getParameter("lastName")%>!
    </BODY>
</HTML>
```

The request to the Welcome application must come from a form that posted two parameters: `firstName` and `lastName`. Alternatively, the values of the `first-Name` and `lastName` variables can be passed to the JSP application as part of the URL. This can be done by appending the following to the URL invoking the JSP application:

`?firstName=John&lastName=Smith`

In this case, the output of the Welcome application is an HTML page displaying the message:

`Welcome, John Smith!`

Listing 4.1 shows that the Java expressions in a JSP application are enclosed by pairs of delimiters: `<%=` and `%>`. The HTML and XML portion of a JSP application is called *fixed-template data*, or *fixed-template text*. Fixed-template text often helps a programmer decide whether to use a servlet or a JSP application. JSP applications are more appropriate when most of the content sent to the client is fixed-template data and only a small portion of the content is generated dynamically with Java code. Conversely, servlets are more appropriate when only a small portion of the content sent to the client is fixed-template data. In fact, some servlets do not produce any content. Rather, they perform a task on behalf of their clients and then invoke other servlets or JSP applications to provide a response. In most cases, servlets and JSP applications are interchangeable.

JSP technology allows producing dynamic Web pages with server-side scripting. For flexibility, JSP files can include any combination of in-line Java, `<SERVLET>` tags, National Center for Supercomputing Applications (NCSA) tags, and JavaBeans. The result is a separation of the presentation logic from the business logic. The objective is to separate the HTML-generation code, which defines the Web page appearance, from the Java code, which implements the business logic, including access to databases.

When a servlet container receives the first request for a JSP application, the runtime translates that JSP application into a Java servlet that handles the current request and future requests to the JSP application. Any errors compiling the new servlet result in translation-time errors. Some servlet containers translate JSP applications to servlets at installation time. This eliminates the translation overhead for the first client that requests each JSP application. In any case, any security considerations about servlets also apply to JSP applications.

4.2 Advantages of Servlets

Java servlet technology offers many advantages.

- A servlet can interact with other resources—file systems, databases, applets, applications written in the Java language or in other languages—to construct the response that is sent back to the client. When needed, the servlet can save information about the request/response interaction.

- With the servlet approach, the servlet container can grant full access to local facilities, such as databases, and trust that the servlet itself will control the amount and precise nature of access that is effectively afforded to external users. For example, the Java Servlet API provides methods to monitor and verify the origin of all requests. Moreover, the servlet code is not passed to the client, only the results that it produces. If the code is not passed to the client, malicious users cannot save it or disassemble it. This protects proprietary algorithms within the servlet.

- Servlets can be client programs of other services. For example, servlets are often used in distributed application systems and are typically used to invoke EJB components.

- Servlets can be *chained*. This means that one servlet can call another servlet, thus becoming its client. Several servlets can be called in sequence.

- Servlets can be dynamically called from within HTML pages, using the special HTML `<SERVLET>` tag. This function is also known as *servlet-tag technique*. With this technique, a servlet container converts a section of an HTML file into an alternative dynamic portion each time the document is sent to the client's browser. This dynamic portion invokes an appropriate servlet and passes to it the parameters it needs. The HTML document must carry the extension `.shtml` rather than the usual `.html`. In addition, the point at which the inclusion should be made is marked with the special `<SERVLET>` and `</SERVLET>` tag pair, as shown in Listing 4.2.

Listing 4.2.   Servlet-Tag Technique

```
<HTML>
    <HEAD>
        <TITLE>Simple SHTML Page</TITLE>
    </HEAD>
    <BODY>
        <H1>Simple SHTML Page</H1>
        <SERVLET Code=Welcome.class>
            <param firstName=John lastName=Smith>
        </SERVLET>
    </BODY>
</HTML>
```

- A servlet service routine is only a thread, not an entire operating system process. That is why a servlet can handle connections with multiple clients, accepting requests and downloading responses back to the multiple clients. This is a more efficient mechanism than using CGI.

- Servlets are portable. They run on a variety of servers and operating systems without needing to be rewritten and recompiled.

- Java servlets must respect the security rules of the Java platform where they run.

- Like all Java programs, servlets can use all the capabilities of the object-oriented Java language. That is, they can be rapidly developed, and their lack of pointers promotes robust applications (unlike C). Also, memory access violations are not possible, so faulty servlets will not crash servers.

From a high-level perspective, servlets can perform the same functions as CGI programs. However, there are some important differences.

- CGI applications may be difficult to develop, as technical knowledge is needed to work with parameter passing, and this is not a commonly available skill. They are not portable; a CGI application written for a specific platform will be able to run only in that environment. Each CGI application is part of a specific process that is activated by a client's request and is destroyed after the client has been served. This causes high start-up, memory, and central processing unit (CPU) costs and implies that multiple clients cannot be served by the same process.

- On the other hand, servlets offer all the advantages of Java programs; they are portable and robust applications and are easy to develop. Servlets also allow you to generate dynamic portions of HTML pages embedded in static HTML pages using the `<SERVLET>` tag. However, the main advantage of servlets over CGI programs is that a servlet is activated by the first client that sends it a request. The servlet then continues running in the background, waiting for further requests. Each request dispatches a thread, not an entire process. Multiple clients may be served simultaneously inside the same process, and typically, the servlet process is destroyed only when the servlet container is shut down. In fact, servlets generally follow what is known as a *singleton pattern*; at the appropriate time, the servlet container creates a single instance of a servlet. Once the single instance is created, multiple threads, each handling a single client request and generating a response, use the same common instance of the servlet. Although this may at first seem counterintuitive, it has performance advantages when there are thousands of requests to the servlet every second. Having a single instance of the servlet eliminates the need to create and garbage collect the servlet instances.

From a security perspective, it must be noted that

- CGI programs are typically written in C, C++, or Perl. This means that they are subjected to the security limitations of the operating system only. If further security restrictions need to be applied, these must be coded into the program by the CGI programmer.
- In contrast, servlets are written in the Java language and run in a servlet container—an enhanced Java runtime. Hence, they are subjected to the security restrictions imposed by the `java.lang.SecurityManager` of the servlet container in which they run.

4.3 Servlet Life Cycle

Servlets use packages found in the Java Servlet API. When you write code for a Java servlet, you must use at least one of the following two packages: `javax.servlet` for any type of servlet and/or `javax.servlet.http` for servlets specific to HTTP.

Servlets are usually created by extending from the `javax.servlet.http.HttpServlet` abstract class, which in turn extends the `javax.servlet.GenericServlet` abstract class, or from the `GenericServlet` class itself, which implements the `javax.servlet.Servlet` interface. Both the `GenericServlet` and the `HttpServlet` classes contain three methods that they inherit from the `Servlet` interface: `init()`, `service()`, and `destroy()`. These methods, used by the servlet to communicate with the servlet container, are called *life-cycle methods.* You work with these three methods in a slightly different way, depending on whether you are extending the `GenericServlet` class or the `HttpServlet` class. The `init()` and the `destroy()` methods have the same properties for the `GenericServlet` and the `HttpServlet` classes; the `service()` method must be handled differently when it is based on the `GenericServlet` class or on the `HttpServlet` class.

The `init()` method is run only once after the servlet container loads the servlet class and the servlet is instantiated, regardless of how many clients access the servlet. This method is guaranteed to finish before any `service()` requests are processed. The servlet can be activated when the servlet container starts or when the first client accesses the servlet.

A custom `init()` method is typically used to perform setup of servlet-wide resources only once rather than once per request, as in the `service()` method. For example, a customized `init()` can load Graphics Interchange Format (GIF) images once, whereas the servlet `service()` method returns the images multiple times in response to multiple client requests to the servlet. Further examples include initializing sessions with other network services or establishing access to persistent data, such as databases and files.

The `destroy()` method is run only once when the servlet container stops the servlet and unloads it. Usually, servlets are unloaded when the servlet container is shut down. The default `destroy()` method can be accepted as is, without the need to override it, because it is not abstract. Servlet writers may, if they wish, override the `destroy()` call, providing their own custom `destroy()` method. A custom `destroy()` method is often used to manage servletwide resources. For example, the `destroy()` method can be used to release shared servletwide resources allocated in the `init()` method.

The `service()` method is the heart of a servlet. The simplest servlets define only the `service()` method. Unlike the `init()` and `destroy()` methods, `service()` is called for each client request.

The `service()` method must be handled differently when it is based on the `GenericServlet` class or on the `HttpServlet` class.

- If the servlet is based on the `GenericServlet` class, the `service()` method is abstract, so it must be overriden. The `service()` method obtains information about the client request, prepares the response, and returns this response to the client. As multiple clients might access the `service()` method at the same time, multiple threads will be executing the code in the single instance of the servlet. Therefore, the `service()` method must include any required synchronization code.

- If the servlet is based on the `HttpServlet` class—the majority of the cases—the `service()` method is not abstract. Therefore, it can be used as is. More commonly, the servlet overrides one or more of the methods `doGet()`, `doPut()`, `doPost()`, and `doDelete()`. The default implementation of `service()` calls one of these methods, based on the client request. For example, if the client request is an HTTP GET method, the servlet's `service()` method will invoke the `doGet()` method; if the request is an HTTP POST method, the `service()` method will invoke the `doPost()` method, and so on.

It is through the `service()` method that the servlet and the servlet container exchange data. When it invokes the servlet's `service()` method, the servlet container also passes in two objects as parameters. These objects are known as the *request* and *response* objects, and their implementation depends on the servlet's superclass.

- If the servlet is based on the `GenericServlet` class, the two objects are instances of the `javax.servlet.ServletRequest` and `javax.servlet.ServletResponse` interfaces, respectively.

- If the servlet is based on the `HttpServlet` class, the two objects are instances of the `javax.servlet.http.HttpServletRequest` and `javax.servlet.http.HttpServletResponse` interfaces, respectively.

The request and response objects encapsulate the data sent by the client, providing access to parameters and allowing the servlets to report status information, including any errors that occurred. The servlet container creates an instance for the request and response objects and passes them to the servlet. Both of these objects are used by the servlet container to exchange data with the servlet.

- The servlet invokes methods on the request object in order to discover information about the client and server environments, as well as the parameter names and values. For example, the servlet can call methods on the request object to obtain all the data entered on a form on the client's Web browser and set by the HTTP GET and POST methods.

- The servlet invokes methods from the response object to send the response information back to the servlet container, which then sends it to the client.

The servlet life cycle involves a series of interactions among the client, the servlet container, and the servlet, as shown in Figure 4.3. The steps are as follows.

1. The servlet is loaded. This operation is typically performed when the first client accesses the servlet. In most servlet containers, options are provided to force the loading of the servlet when the servlet container starts up.

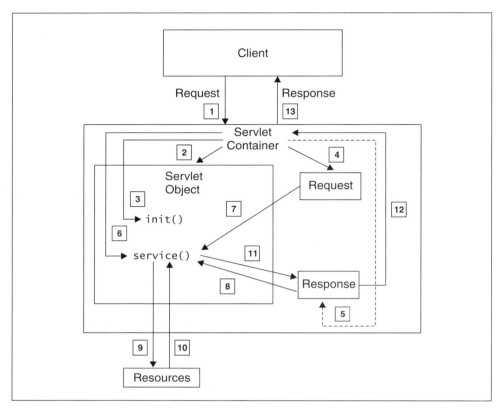

Figure 4.3.   Servlet Life Cycle

2. The servlet container creates an instance of the servlet.

3. The servlet container calls the servlet's `init()` method. This method is called only once during the lifetime of the servlet.

4. A client request arrives at the servlet container, and the servlet container creates a request object: `ServletRequest` or `HttpServletRequest`.

5. The servlet container creates a response object: `ServletResponse` or `HttpServletResponse`.

6. The servlet container invokes the servlet's `service()` method.

7. The `service()` method takes the request object as one of its two parameters.

8. The `service()` method takes the response object as the other parameter.

9. The `service()` method gets information about the request object and processes the request accessing other resources, such as databases and files.

10. The `service()` method retrieves the necessary information from the resources accessed.

11. The `service()` method uses methods of the response object.

12. The `service()` method passes the response back to the servlet container.

13. The servlet container passes the response back to the client.

For additional client requests, the servlet container creates new request and response objects, invokes the `service()` method of the servlet, and passes the request and response objects as parameters. This loop is repeated for every client request but without the need to call the `init()` method every time. When the servlet container no longer needs the servlet—typically when the servlet container is shut down—the servlet container invokes the servlet `destroy()` method.

As discussed earlier, a servlet based on the `HttpServlet` class generally overrides one or more of the HTTP methods `doGet()`, `doPut()`, `doPost()`, and `doDelete()`, and the default implementation of the `service()` method calls one of these methods, based on the client request. In this case, the servlet life cycle just described should take into account the additional call that the `service()` method makes to the HTTP method.

4.4   The Deployment Descriptor of a Web Module

A *Web application* is a collection of servlets, JSP applications, and static content, such as HTML pages, that can be accessed over the Internet. A Web application is packaged in a single deployable unit called a *Web module* (see Section 3.2.2 on page 59). Each Web module is stored in a WAR file—an enhanced JAR file having a `.war` extension.

A Web module always contains a special XML file, called *deployment descriptor*, which declares the contents of the Web module, contains information about the structure and external dependencies of the Web module's components, and declares the security policies applicable to the URIs that are mapped to the resources within the Web module. These security policies include both the authorization policy and the login configuration information. The deployment descriptor of a Web module is specified in a file named web.xml. This file is packaged along with the Web application in the Web module's WAR file. As discussed in Section 3.7 on page 64, a deployment descriptor contains hints about the deployment of a Web application. These hints are specified by an Application Assembler, who packages the various Web components forming the Web application. The

Application Assembler is expected to be familiar with the Web application. In particular, the Application Assembler has to know which parts of the Web application are to be exposed to other services and the outside world. It is the responsibility of the Deployer to take the Application Assembler's hints in the deployment descriptor and make them relevant to the operational environment into which the application is deployed.

In terms of security, a Web application's deployment descriptor defines

- The mechanisms by which users should be authenticated to access the Web resources (see Section 3.9.1 on page 76)

- The privileges users are expected to have in order to access these resources (see Section 3.9.2 on page 82)

- The delegation policies that specify the principals whose credentials are propagated with the cascaded downstream requests (see Section 3.9.3 on page 85)

It is important to understand that the deployment descriptor is merely a hint for deployment. It is expected that the effective policy for a Web application will be different from what is originally specified in the deployment descriptor. For example, a Web application's deployment descriptor may say that the URI `/travelAgent/*` may be accessed only by those users with TravelAgent role. In the enterprise in which the Web application is deployed, however, the enterprise security policy may require that the same URI also be accessible by those users with Supervisor role. Even though the deployment descriptor may be modified at a later time, it is important to convey the intended security policy in the deployment descriptor. This allows the Deployers and the System Administrators to know less about the application logic itself.

The following sections explain how security policies can be described and specified in a Web application's deployment descriptor. These sections explain the semantics of the deployment descriptors and how they can be altered to achieve various security policies.

4.5   Authentication

Authentication is the process to prove the identity of an entity or principal. In a J2EE environment, a principal may be

- An end user—for example, Bob—invoking a J2EE component

- A WAS—for example, a server hosting a finance application—delegating a request downstream to another WAS

- A WAS that has to access a resource adapter—for example, a JDBC connector—using a resource-specific connection pattern (see Section 3.4 on page 61)

- Any combination of the preceding

The requests to access Web resources are submitted as HTTP requests. Therefore, the means of authentication are tied to HTTP capabilities, with certain enhancements introduced at the J2EE Web application layer.

4.5.1 Login-Configuration Policy

In order to authenticate the caller, authentication data needs to be retrieved so that it can be used to perform the authentication. The authentication data—for example, user ID and password—can be retrieved in many ways. In the case of HTTP, it is possible to use the HTTP authentication mechanism, whereby user ID and password are expected in a specific HTTP header. Because the HTTP authentication mechanism does not involve a user-friendly HTML form, J2EE allows for an enhanced mode by which the user ID and password can be sent to the WAS. As part of the login-configuration details of a J2EE Web application, an Application Assembler and/or a Deployer can specify the approach by which a user's authentication data should be obtained. This is done in the deployment descriptor, `web.xml`, bundled in the Web application's WAR file. The authentication method is specified through the `auth-method` element in the `login-config` descriptor. The `auth-method` element indicates which authentication mechanism should be used to obtain the authentication data.

As we saw in Section 3.9.1.1 on page 78, there are three types of authentication methods:

1. **HTTP.** The credentials submitted by the client are user ID and password, transmitted as part of an HTTP header. The HTTP authentication method can be either basic or digest. With basic authentication, the user ID and password are sent as cleartext (see footnote 2 on page 77). For this to happen, the `auth-method` element in the `login-config` descriptor must be set to `BASIC`. With digest authentication, the user ID is sent in cleartext, but for security reasons, only a hash value of the password is transmitted to the server. For this to happen, the `auth-method` element in the `login-config` descriptor must be set to `DIGEST`.

   With HTTP standard authentication, it is also necessary to specify a realm name. This is done by setting a value for the `auth-method` element in the `login-config` descriptor. Recall that realms are used to determine the scope of security data and provide a mechanism for protecting Web application resources. The realm name indicates the HTTP security realm for which the user ID and password should be supplied and typically has a significance about the security registry against which an authenticating user must be verified. For example, a value of HRDept would mean that the user ID and password must be valid in a registry that is associated with the enterprise's human resources (HR) department. Section 4.5.1.1 describes how the realm name is used in HTTP authentication.

2. **Form based.**   With form-based authentication, the credentials required of a user are user ID and password. A user submits these credential from within an HTML form. Form-based authentication requires that the auth-method element in the login-config descriptor be set to FORM. The form-login-config element in the login-config descriptor indicates the URL of the Web page containing the login HTML form and the URL of an error page to which the user will be redirected if the authentication fails.

3. **Certificate based.**   If a user is to be authenticated using client-side X.509 certificates (see Appendix B on page 553), the auth-method element in the login-config descriptor must be set to CLIENT-CERT.

The following subsections describe each of these authentication methods in detail.

4.5.1.1   HTTP Authentication Method

The specification for HTTP authentication is described in Request for Comments (RFC) 2617.[1] The two modes of HTTP authentication—basic and digest—are implemented by HTTP. Therefore, when an HTTP client, such as a Web browser or a Java program, authenticates itself to an HTTP server, the communication between the client and the server is based on the HTTP specification.

When the HTTP authentication mode is basic, the user ID and password of the end user are submitted in cleartext as part of an HTTP header. When a client submits a request without the authentication data, a server that has been configured to perform basic authentication responds by indicating that this type of authentication is required. The client must resubmit the request with a user ID and password pair. A typical HTTP communication flow with basic authentication request is summarized in Figure 4.4.

Suppose that the www.fabrikam456.com Web site hosts travel reservations on-line. When a user visits the site to make reservations, the client submits a request to http://www.fabrikam456.com/travel/reserve. The Web site has secured access to reservations by means of HTTP basic authentication. Therefore, the Web server receiving the request will send an error response indicating that basic

---

1. See http://www.ietf.org/rfc/rfc2617.txt.

Figure 4.4. Communication Flow with HTTP Basic Authentication

authentication is required. The client will be asked to submit authentication data relative to a user registry, which is specified in terms of an HTTP security realm.

It is possible for an end user to have accounts in multiple security realms. Therefore, in order to help the end user provide a valid user ID and password for the target realm, the Web server will also indicate a realm name when it issues an authentication response. In HTTP terminology, the Web server sends back an HTTP 401 error code. Along with the error code, the server sends back a WWW-Authenticate HTTP header, asking the client to authenticate with basic authentication by submitting a valid user ID and password pair specific to a named realm. In the scenario depicted in Figure 4.4, the server issues an HTTP 401 response with an HTTP WWW-Authenticate header, indicating that the server expects basic authentication specific to the fabrikam456 HTTP realm.

A WAS can be configured to protect a Web resource with HTTP basic authentication by setting the auth-method element in the login-config descriptor to BASIC. The name of the realm to which the user must authenticate must be specified by setting the realm-name element. A sample login configuration for basic authentication requiring a user to authenticate to the fabrikam456 realm is shown in Listing 4.3.

Listing 4.3. Sample Login Configuration for HTTP Basic Authentication

```
<login-config>
    <auth-method>BASIC</auth-method>
    <realm-name>fabrikam456</realm-name>
</login-config>
```

On receiving an HTTP 401 error response from a Web server, a Web browser prompts the user for a user ID and password in a dialog box, which also shows the realm name. In the context of the scenario of Figure 4.4, the user is prompted for user ID and password for the fabrikam456 realm.

When the client responds with a user ID and password, the original request— for example, `http://www.fabrikam456.com/travel/reserve`—must also be re-submitted. The authentication information is sent over as an HTTP header named `Authorization`. The client sends a base64-encoded version (see footnote 2 on page 77) of the user ID and password, with a colon separating these two values. For example, if user Bob Smith has user ID `bob` and password `bobpass`, the base64 encoding of the string `bob:bobpass` will be computed and sent as an authorization header.

As discussed in Section 4.10.2 on page 147, HTTP is a stateless protocol. Therefore, the WAS processes this request as if it were a new request. The WAS will find out that the URL is protected and that it requires HTTP basic authentication. The WAS will then look for the `Authorization` HTTP header in the submitted request to find the userID and password information. The server extracts the user ID and password from the header by decoding the base64-encoded value and validates the values within the specified realm. In the example of Figure 4.4, the server validates the user ID and password pair in the frbrikam456 realm. If the values are correct , the client will be considered to have been successfully authenticated. If not, the WAS responds with an error message.

Because the user ID and password are encoded in base64 format, which from a security point of view is equivalent to cleartext, it is highly recommended that this transaction take place over an SSL connection (see Chapter 13 on page 449). Specifically, whenever user ID and password will be sent in response to an HTTP 401 challenge, the request is recommended to be an HTTP over SSL (HTTPS) request.[2] For example, in the scenario depicted in Figure 4.4, the URL invoked by the client would be `https://www.fabrikam456.com/travel/reserve`. In J2EE, one can require basic authentication to be sent over a secure channel, as explained in Section 4.6.6 on page 132.

With digest authentication, the user ID and a hash value of the password (see Section 10.2.2.4 on page 356) are transmitted to the HTTP server as part of an HTTP header. This way, the password does not appear in cleartext, which is the biggest weakness of basic authentication.

---

2. With HTTP basic authentication, the credentials required of the client for authentication are user ID and password. Therefore, SSL is not used to authenticate the client but only to protect the communication between the client and the server. For this reason, it is not necessary for the server to require mutual-authentication SSL. Typically, in these scenarios, user ID and password information is transmitted over an SSL session with server-side authentication only.

The details of how digest authentication works are explained in Chapter 3 on page 55. The authentication flow in digest authentication is similar to that in basic authentication mode. With digest authentication, however, the `WWW-Authenticate` HTTP header indicates that the HTTP server expects digest authentication.

As we observed in Chapter 3 on page 55, in order for an HTTP server to compute the hash value of a user's password, the server must have access to the passwords of all the users. This is rarely the case in most enterprise environments, as passwords in cleartext are not retrievable from a user repository containing user ID and password information. Therefore, digest authentication has not been widely adopted in enterprise environments and hence is not required to be supported by a J2EE container.

A WAS that supports digest authentication can be configured to protect a Web resource with HTTP digest authentication by setting the `auth-method` element in the `login-config` descriptor to `DIGEST`. The name of the realm to which the user must authenticate must also be specified by setting the `realm-name` element. A sample login configuration for digest authentication requiring a user to authenticate to the fabrikam456 realm is shown in Listing 4.4.

Listing 4.4. Sample Login Configuration for HTTP Digest Authentication

```
<login-config>
    <auth-method>DIGEST</auth-method>
    <realm-name>fabrikam456</realm-name>
</login-config>
```

4.5.1.2 *Form-Based Authentication Method*

A user-friendly presentation layer is a key part of an enterprise's e-business Web design. Usually, the home page of an enterprise contains information about the company and the services it offers, as well as links to detailed information about the business. When online transactions are involved, a user is typically redirected to a Web page asking for user ID and password, thus enabling the user to log on to one or more applications. Typically, a Web page or section of a Web page is provided with an HTML form for a user to enter user ID and password and a button to submit the authentication data to the HTTP server. Providing the user ID and password will take the user to a page that is customized to that user and from where all the user account information can be securely accessed. For example, in our travel service scenario described on page 114, a user could log in and update credit information or view his or her travel itinerary, frequent flyer account details, and monthly billing statement.

Because basic authentication has virtually no customization capabilities and is also specific to a browser's characteristics, enterprise environments choose to use a login method whereby the user ID and password information are captured in an

HTML form. This *form-based login* is not an option in the HTTP specification and is therefore specific to the application layer. Because this is a common enterprise scenario, this mode of authentication is standardized under the Java Servlet specification by allowing the value of the `auth-method` element in the `login-config` descriptor to be set to `FORM`.

The form-based login approach allows the WAS to use an HTML form to retrieve the user ID and password, as opposed to sending a 401 error code response as in the basic challenge type. When the value of `auth-method` is set to `FORM`, the user is redirected to the URL specified within the `form-login-page` element of the deployment descriptor. The form login page must contain the form elements `j_username` and `j_password`. The `ACTION` attribute associated with the form must be set to `j_securitycheck`. An example of such a login page is shown in Listing 4.5.

Listing 4.5.   Sample Login Web Page for Form-Based Login

```
<HTML>
    <HEAD>
        <TITLE>Fabrikam456 Login page</TITLE>
    </HEAD>

    <BODY BGCOLOR="#FFFFFF" TEXT="#000000">
        <TR><TD><HR NOSHADE SIZE="1">
        <FONT SIZE="-1" FACE="Helvetica,Arial" COLOR="#996600">
        <B>Please log in!</B></FONT><BR><BR></TD></TR>
        <CENTER>
        <FONT SIZE=1 COLOR="Blue">
        Enter your travel account name and password in order
        to access our services
        </FONT><BR>
        <FORM METHOD=POST ACTION="j_security_check">
        <FONT SIZE=1>Account
        <INPUT TYPE=TEXT NAME="j_username" SIZE=20></FONT><BR>
        <FONT SIZE=1>Password
        <INPUT TYPE=PASSWORD NAME="j_password" SIZE=20>
        </FONT><BR>
        <INPUT TYPE=SUBMIT NAME=ACTION VALUE="Submit Login">
        </FORM><HR>
        </CENTER>
    </BODY>
</HTML>
```

When the `ACTION` attribute associated with the form is set to `j_security-check` as in Listing 4.5, the WAS extracts the user ID and password from the form and validates them. The WAS recognizes the user ID and password because these are the values that the user entered in the `j_username` and `j_password` text boxes, respectively. If the authentication fails, the user is redirected to the Web page specified by the deployment descriptor's `form-error-page` element. An example of deployment descriptor login configuration using FORM as the authentication method is shown in Listing 4.6.

Listing 4.6. Sample Login Configuration for Form-Based Authentication

```
<login-config>
<auth-method>FORM</auth-method>
    <form-login-config>
        <form-login-page>/login.jsp</form-login-page>
        <form-error-page>/login-failed.html</form-error-page>
    </form-login-config>
</login-config>
```

Typically, the URLs specified in the form-login-page and the form-error-page are relative to the context path of the Web application to which the deployment descriptor refers. The *context path* of a Web application is the path prefix associated with the javax.servlet.ServletContext that the servlet or the JSP application is a part of. For example, let us consider again the URL http://www.fabrikam456.com:80/travel/reserve, which we used in the scenario described on page 000. A *path prefix* in a URL is a substring of the URL that excludes the protocol part, host name, and port number (http://www.fabrikam456.com:80); it can either be a single forward slash (/) or start with a forward slash and end with the last character before a subsequent forward slash. For example, in the preceding URL, the possible path prefixes are / and /travel. Of these two path prefixes, the context path for the travel Web application is /travel. Therefore, the values /login.jsp and /login-failed.html are relative to /travel.

A typical HTTP communication flow with a form-based authentication request is summarized in Figure 4.5. A user who tries to access the secured resource, http://www.fabrikam456.com/travel/reserve, is redirected to the login Web page at http://www.fabrikam456.com/travel/login.jsp and presented with a login form. In the case of authentication failure, the user is redirected to the error page at http://www.fabrikam456.com/travel/login-failed.html. To protect the user ID and password during transmission, the entire HTTP transaction should be carried over the SSL protocol.[3] This implies that all the URLs in Figure 4.5 should start with https rather than http.

---

3. As we observed on page 116, when the credentials required of the user are user ID and password, it is not necessary for a server to require mutual-authentication SSL. The user ID and password transmission can be protected by using an SSL session with server-side authentication only.

Figure 4.5.   Form-Based Login Request Flow Scenario

4.5.1.3   *Certificate-Based Authentication Method*

In public-key cryptography-based systems, the private key of a client stays with the client and is never sent over the network. The public key is available to the server, wrapped in a digital certificate (see Chapter 10 on page 372).

The SSL protocol is a public-key cryptography-based mechanism widely used in a Web environment. In particular, SSL is commonly adopted to achieve integrity and confidentiality of HTTP message transactions. As we discussed on page 96, when a Web server is configured to require mutal authentication with the end client over SSL, the client authenticates the server, using the server's digital certificate, and the server authenticates the client, using the client's digital certificate. These digital certificates are exhanged during the SSL *handshake*—the phase in which the client and the server establish the SSL connection (see Section 13.1.2, on page 452).

Because a client's certificate is associated with a given principal on the client side of a mutual-authentication SSL connection, the client's certificate is considered a form of client authentication in a Web environment (see Figure 4.6). In such cases, successful negotiation of an SSL connection implies that the client certificate is signed by a CA trusted by the server and that the client who presented the certificate possesses the correct private key—the one corresponding to the public key wrapped in the client certificate. It is also possible, and highly

Figure 4.6. Establishing a Principal's Identity Based on Mutual-Authentication SSL

recommended, that a digital certificate be validated against a certificate revocation list (CRL) to ensure that it is still valid. The client-certificate contents can be used to derive the identity of the requester. This enables using client digital certificates to infer the identity of the clients and prove authenticity when performing authorization checks. The concepts of digital certificate, CA, and CRL are described in Section 10.3.4 on page 372.

In a J2EE environment, the authentication method for a Web application can be set to be certificate based by properly configuring the deployment descriptor in the Web application's Web module. In particular, the `auth-method` element in the `login-config` descriptor must be set to CLIENT-CERT, as shown in Listing 4.7.

Listing 4.7. Sample Login Configuration for Certificate-Based Authentication

```
<login-config>
   <auth-method>CLIENT-CERT</auth-method>
</login-config>
```

After the SSL handshake, the client's digital certificate can be made accessible to the WAS designated to handle the client's request. The WAS can then use the contents of the client's digital certificate to derive the identity of the requester. In particular, the WAS uses the client's digital certificate to represent a unique user, a group of users, or an organization. For example, the subject's name obtained from the client's digital certificate may be mapped to the short name of a user in an LDAP directory. Each certificate contains a field called the subject's Distinguished Name (DN). A subject's DN is a string representing the name of the entity whose public key the certificate identifies. The DN uniquely identifies the name of that subject across the Internet. According to the X.509 standard, a subject's DN contains the following attributes:

- Common Name (CN)
- Organizational Unit (OU)
- Organization (O)
- Location (L)
- State (ST)
- Country (C)

Let us consider the example of a subject whose DN is

```
CN=Bob Smith, OU=Travel Division, O=Fabrikam456, L=Raleigh,
ST=North Carolina, C=United States
```

Because a subject's DN is unique, a direct match against the DN is the preferred way to obtain the corresponding user ID in the registry. If this option is not available, imperfect mappings can be used. For example, in the subject's DN, the CN attribute, `Bob Smith`, can be mapped to a user entry in an LDAP directory where the user's short name is `bob`. In this example, the policy to map the certificate is as simple as using the CN in the subject's DN to map directly to a user ID in the registry. Other attributes in the client certificate may be used to establish the user's identity. How a certificate-based authentication can be used to deduce the identity of the requester and details of mapping rules are outside the scope of the J2EE specification and depend on the J2EE product implementation.

Note that a J2EE WAS gets to handle a request after the SSL handshake is established at the transport layer, as shown in Figure 4.6. In many enterprise topologies, an SSL connection is established with a reverse proxy server that sits in a DMZ (see Section 6.2.2 on page 193). A reverse proxy server can accomplish several tasks, including content caching, load balancing, user authentication, and access-control enforcement. The machines that host the WASs are often different from the machine hosting the reverse proxy server. Therefore, it is common that the WAS designated to handle the client's request does not directly participate in the SSL handshake. Because the client's identity is derived from the client's digital certificate and is the basis for identifying the principal accessing the Web resource, the trust relationship between the WASs and the reverse proxy server acting as the server-side SSL end point must be properly designed. This may be achieved by establishing a mutual-authentication SSL connection between each WAS and the reverse proxy server.

4.5.2 Single Sign-On

As we discuss in Section 4.10.2 on page 147, the stateless nature of HTTP implies that every request a client submits is treated by a server as a new request. Therefore, if user authentication is required, a user will be asked to authenticate on every request. For example, if the authentication method is based on user ID and password, as in HTTP and form-based authentication, the user will be prompted to type and submit a user ID and password pair on every request. This scenario is annoying for the user and is considered user unfriendly. WASs offer a mechanism providing single sign-on (SSO), which means that users are prompted for their credentials only once. SSO can be achieved at various levels: browser, J2EE Web application, J2EE Web container, and others.

- **HTTP realm.**   When HTTP basic authentication is used to retrieve user ID and password, a realm is specified as part of the challenge. When a user gets prompted for user ID and password for the first time in a browser session with an HTTP server, the browser typically caches the user ID and password information. When the user requests another secured resource from the same HTTP server and the HTTP server challenges the user for user ID and password under the same realm, the browser does not prompt the user again. Instead, it retrieves the information from its local cache and sends it back to the HTTP server. This is the least sophisticated level of SSO that is provided when using HTTP basic authentication as implemented by Web browsers.

- **HTTP state management mechanisms.**   If a user is authenticated with user ID and password using form-based login, the browser-supported SSO is not feasible. The J2EE specification formalizes the notion of SSO over multiple HTTP requests and requires J2EE products to provide some form of SSO so that users will be prompted only once for all authentication requests that target the same WAS. In order to satisfy this requirement with form-based authentication, WASs maintain the user authentication information across multiple requests using HTTP state-management mechanisms, such as HTTP cookies (see Section 4.10.2.1 on page 148), HTTP sessions (see Section 4.10.2.2 on page 149), or SSL sessions.

- **SSL session.**   In the case of certificate-based authentication, an SSL connection is maintained across multiple HTTPS requests. Therefore, the client's certificate information is available on every request without the user's being prompted multiple times. SSO in these scenarios comes for free because all the HTTP requests are carried over a single SSL session.

  It must be noted, however, that this option is not always available. As observed in Section 4.10.2.2 on page 149, some Web servers are configured to renegotiate the SSL session with the client from time to time. This results in a change of the session ID and hence the loss of session information.

An e-business scenario may involve multiple organizations participating in the same transaction. For example, a user contacting a real estate agency on the Internet may be temporarily redirected to an associated home mortgage organization. After having been preapproved for a mortgage, the user is then readmitted to the real estate agency's Web site. The real estate agency's WAS can now personalize the response sent back to the client by showing the user only those houses that the user can afford, based on the mortgage amount calculated by the home mortgage organization. A scenario like this involves multiple HTTP servers, each belonging to a different Domain Name Service (DNS) system. In such scenarios, if various organizations require client authentication, none of the previous solutions would achieve SSO, for the following reasons.

- Browser-supported SSO for HTTP basic authentication is not applicable, because the organizations requiring client authentication belong to different DNS systems and therefore fall within different HTTP security realms.
- Cookie-based SSO in form-based authentication would not work, because HTTP cookies are valid for hosts that fall within a specified DNS system. A securely configured Web browser would refuse to allow an organization's HTTP server to retrieve the cookie set by another organization's HTTP server if the two servers belong to different DNS systems.
- Finally, it should be noted that an SSL session between a client and a server cannot be transferred from one server to another. The second server should engage in a new SSL handshake with the client. Therefore, the SSO intrinsically supported by certificate-based authentication cannot be used when an enterprise spans multiple organizations, each having its own HTTP server belonging to a different DNS system.

In such cases, sophisticated enterprise SSO solutions are typically deployed. These solutions are outside the scope of the J2EE specification and depend on the implementation of the J2EE product and other external security products that can work with the J2EE product.

4.6 Authorization

Once a client is authenticated, a J2EE container needs to perform authorization checks. Authorization policies configured in an enterprise describe which users or groups are allowed to access protected J2EE resources. The Application Assembler specifies, in the deployment descriptor of the Web module packaging a Web application, which security roles are required in order to access a URI managed by a J2EE container (see Section 3.7.2 on page 67). Because an Application Assembler is probably not familiar with the deployment environment of the enterprise in which the application is deployed, the Application Assembler specifies authorization policies in terms of J2EE security roles, with a security role being a named collection of J2EE authorizations, implemented as `java.security.Permission` objects. When a security role is mapped to a user or a group in an enterprise, that user or group is authorized to access the resources protected by those permissions associated with the security role. For example, if the Fabrikam456 travel organization has established that access to online reservations should be allowed only to customers, the deployment descriptor can specify that only the principals corresponding to the Customer security role are authorized to access the travel reservation URLs.

The default behavior of a WAS is to authorize access to all the J2EE resources unless they are explicitly protected. Therefore, System Administrators (see Section 3.7.4 on page 71) can deploy Web resources without declaring them explicitly in a Web module's deployment descriptor.

Web resources are accessed by the URL to which they are mapped. For example, a ReservationServlet can be invoked through the URL `http://www.fabrikam456.com/travel/reserve`. An Application Assembler, therefore, declares authorization policies in the Web module's deployment descriptor in terms of URLs. In the deployment descriptor, security constraints are defined to restrict access to URLs. Such constraints are associated with a set of URLs relative to the Web application's context path using the `security-constraint` XML element. For example, if the context path of the Fabrikam456 travel application is `/travel`, the relative URL to access the ReservationServlet will be specified in terms of the relative URL `/reserve`.

The relative URLs to which the restriction applies can be defined via URL patterns. In the Web module's deployment descriptor, such a collection of URLs, known as a *Web resource collection*, is specified through a `web-resource-collection` XML element. Associated with a Web resource collection is its authorization constraint policy, specified by an `auth-constraint` element. An authorization constraint policy is specified in terms of J2EE security roles. An example of this is shown in Listing 3.3 on page 75. Security administrators are responsible for managing authorization policies for the users and groups authorized to access the protected URIs. The following subsections describe how protected Web resources can be accessed by authorized users and groups.

4.6.1 Invocation Chain

When building a Web application, it is often useful to forward processing of a request to another servlet or to include the output of another servlet in the response. The `javax.servlet.RequestDispatcher` interface provides a mechanism to accomplish this through its methods `forward()` and `include()`. The `RequestDispatcher` interface defines an object that receives requests from the client and sends them to any resource, such as a servlet, HTML file, or JSP file, on the server. The servlet container creates the `RequestDispatcher` object, which is used as a wrapper around a server resource located at a particular path or given by a particular name.

- The `forward()` method forwards a request from a servlet to another resource on the server. This method allows one servlet to do preliminary processing of a request and another resource to generate the response.

- The `include()` method includes the content of a resource in the response.

The operations of invoking the `forward()` and `include()` methods on the `RequestDispatcher` object are known as *servlet forwards* and *servlet includes*, respectively. Servlet forwards and includes allow for servlet internal invocations. Basically, a servlet can dispatch a request to another servlet or resource on the server without involving the HTTP server. Performing a servlet forward or a servlet include generates an *invocation chain*—a chain of multiple servlet, JSP application, and/or HTML file invocations.

From a security point of view, it should be noted that the protection rules for a Web resource accessed through a J2EE container are based on the invocation chain leading to the protected Web resource. In particular, in a J2EE container, only the first servlet or JSP application in an invocation chain is subject to authorization tests. Authorization tests are not performed by the Web container if the request is a result of an entry servlet or a JSP application performing a servlet forward or include; they are performed only on the first, or *entry*, servlet or JSP application in the invocation chain.

For example, let us consider a scenario in which the servlet AgentInfoServlet, accessible through the `/travel/agentInfo` relative URL, is to be protected; only users with TravelAgents role are allowed access to it. Likewise, the Agent-AddressServlet, associated with the relative URL `/travel/agentAddress`, is to be protected; in this case, however, the protection is specified such that no one should have direct access to it. Whenever a user with TravelAgent requests the `/travel/agentInfo` relative URL, the serlvet AgentInfoServlet is invoked. Let us assume that AgentInfoServlet contains a servlet include directive for the Agent-AddressServlet by invoking the relative URL `/travel/agentAddress`. In this scenario, access to the AgentAddressServlet is allowed because it is the result of a

servlet include rather than a direct call to the AgentAddressServlet, which would
not be allowed. In contrast, if a user tries to directly access the /travel/agent-
Address URL directly from a browser, the request is denied, as Agent-
AddressServlet would be the first servlet handled by the Web container for that
particular request. This scenario is depicted in Figure 4.7.

4.6.2   Protecting a Specific URL

Authorization is declared at the granularity of a specific URL by indicating the
exact URL path in the web-resource-collection element of the deployment
descriptor. Cases exist in which all resources within a directory are to be generally
accessible with only a few exceptions; conversely, almost all the resources in another directory should be inaccessible except for a few.

Consider the travel service Web application; the relative URL /travel/
reserve is mapped to the ReservationServlet. The context path for the Web application is /travel. The request URL for the servlet would be http://www.
fabrikam456.com/travel/reserve. If the ReservationServlet is to be protected
such that only a user with Customer or TravelAgent role can access the HTTP
methods GET, POST, and PUT—typically implemented within an HttpServlet as
the methods doGet(), doPost(), and doPut(), respectively—the authorization
policy must be declared in terms of the URLs that will be used to access the servlet. This policy is shown in Listing 4.8.

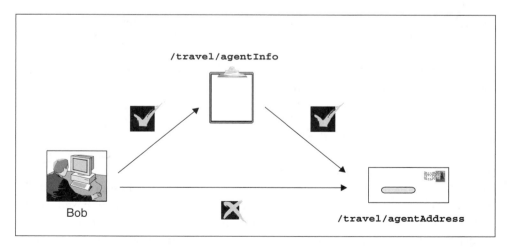

Figure 4.7.   Access Dependent on an Invocation Chain

Listing 4.8.   Security Constraint Definition for a Specific URL

```
<security-constraint>
    <web-resource-collection>
        <web-resource-name>
            ReservationServlet
        </web-resource-name>
        <url-pattern>/travel/reserve</url-pattern>
        <http-method>GET</http-method>
        <http-method>POST</http-method>
        <http-method>PUT</http-method>
    </web-resource-collection>
    <auth-constraint>
        <role-name>Customer</role-name>
        <role-name>TravelAgent</role-name>
    </auth-constraint>
</security-constraint>
```

A URL can be protected by explicitly stating it under the `url-pattern` element of the `web-resource-collection` descriptor. Note that the URL is a relative URL—relative to the Web application's context path. All the HTTP methods that are to be protected are also declared within the `web-resource-collection` element.

4.6.3   Protecting a URL Pattern

When a set of URLs needs to be protected, it is adminstratively easier to express and manage the authorization policies in terms of URL patterns instead of listing every URL separately. These patterns are used by a Web container when handling URL requests based on servlet-processing rules as defined by the Java Servlet specification.

URL patterns can be specified in a couple of ways in a Web module's deployment descriptor. The following subsections describe URL path-prefix and extension patterns that can be used in addition to using specific URLs.

4.6.3.1   URL Path-Prefix Protection

In Section 4.5.1.2 on page 117, we noted that a specific URL can have multiple path prefixes. Let us consider the URL `http://www.fabrikam456.com/travel/travelAgent/reserve`. Given that `/travel` is the context path of the Fabrikam456 Web application, we can specify the protection rules based on the URL `/travelAgent/reserve`, which is relative to `/travel`. This URL has two path prefixes: `/` and `/travelAgent`. Path prefixes are an administrative convenience. For example, let us assume that the structure of the Fabrikam456 Web site is designed so that all the resources under the URL path `http://www.fabrikam456.com/travel/travelAgent/` must be protected and are to be accessible only to users having the TravelAgent security role. Instead of specifying all the resources by name, it is easier to specify the policy by combining a path prefix with a wildcard expression. In the scenario described, the URL path pattern `/travelAgent/*` can be declared protected such that only users granted the TravelAgent security role can access the resources underneath it. This policy is specified using the `security-constraint` element in the Web application's deployment descriptor, as shown in Listing 4.9.

Listing 4.9. Deployment Descriptor Fragment Showing Path-Prefix Protection

```
<security-constraint>
   <web-resource-collection>
      <web-resource-name>
         Travel agents information
      </web-resource-name>
      <url-pattern>/travelAgent/*</url-pattern>
   </web-resource-collection>
   <auth-constraint>
      <role-name>TravelAgent</role-name>
   </auth-constraint>
</security-constraint>
```

4.6.3.2 URL Extension Protection

A URL *extension* is defined as the substring starting with the last dot character. For example, in the JSP URL `http://www.fabrikam456.com/travel/welcome.jsp`, the extension is the string `.jsp`. An extension does not, however, include fragments or references. Therefore, in the URL `http://www.fabrikam456.com/travel/index.html#WELCOME`, the extension includes only the part `.html`. If several resources with many different extensions are served from a specific path prefix and if only some of them are to be protected, protection based on extension patterns provides an efficient mechanism for this purpose.

Protecting all the URL patterns with extension `.jsp` under the `status` directory can be specified by using the security constraint shown in Listing 4.10.

Listing 4.10. Deployment Descriptor Fragment Showing Extension Protection

```
<security-constraint>
   <web-resource-collection>
      <web-resource-name>
         Protect only the JSP files
      </web-resource-name>
      <url-pattern>/status/*.jsp</url-pattern>
   </web-resource-collection>
   <auth-constraint>
      <role-name>TravelAgent</role-name>
   </auth-constraint>
</security-constraint>
```

Besides the standard extensions, such as `.jsp` and `.html`, it is possible to define custom extensions.

4.6.4   Protecting from Everyone

A Web application may be designed to contain multiple directories and entry points. There may be assumptions about how a resource is to be accessed. For example, it could be established that a resource or group of resources should be accessible only internally from a servlet and never directly from a client. In such cases, security constraints should be specified in terms of specific URLs or URL patterns, as discussed in Section 4.6.1 on page 126, Section 4.6.2 on page 127, and Section 4.6.3 on page 128. However, instead of specifying a list of authorized roles, an empty `auth-constraint` descriptor implies that no external access is allowed, as is shown in Listing 4.11.

Listing 4.11. Deployment Descriptor Fragment Forbidding External Access

```
<security-constraint>
    <web-resource-collection>
        <web-resource-name>Not accessible</web-resource-name>
        <url-pattern>/private/*</url-pattern>
    </web-resource-collection>
    <auth-constraint></auth-constraint>
</security-constraint>
```

4.6.5   Understanding the Precedence Rules

Understanding the precedence of authorization policy constraints is essential, as it has implications on which security constraints are applicable. When a URL request is presented to a Web container, the Web container selects a Web application that has the longest context path matching the start of the requested URL. For example, consider two Web applications, Default and Travel, with respective context paths `/` and `/travel`. When a request is submitted for the URL `/travel/travelAgent/reserve`, the request is mapped to the Travel Web application because the longest matching context path, `/travel`, is mapped to the Travel Web application. Because the matched prefix is the Web application's context path, the rest of the URL, other than that matched context path, needs to be mapped to a Web component—for example, a servlet—that can handle the incoming request. In our example, `/travelAgent/reserve` is mapped to the TravelAgent-ReservationServlet. Because a URL may be matched by multiple URL patterns, precedence rules are defined for the Web container.

Precedence rules for matching security constraints are the same as the ones used by a Web container to map URLs to servlets. The Web container will attempt to map a given URL to a security constraint, based on those rules. If no matching rules are found, the URL is assumed to be unprotected. The precedence rules for mapping URLs to servlets are based on case-sensitive matching in the following order:

1. **Exact match.** If the requested URL path is an exact match to a defined URL mapping for the servlet, the matched servlet is determined to be the target servlet.

2. **Path mapping through the longest path prefix.** The Web container walks down the directory path one directory at a time by using the forward slash character, /, as path separator. The first successful match is deemed to be the longest matching prefix to handle the request.

3. **Extension match.** If the last part of the URL is an extension, such as .jsp, the Web container tries to match a servlet that is defined to handle the extension.

When none of these rules matches a requested URL, the Web container passes the request to a servlet that is configured to handle requests by default.

For example, let us assume that a Web application's deployment descriptor defines security constraints for the URL /travelAgent/reserve, the path-prefix URL pattern /travelAgent/*, and the URL extension pattern status/*.jsp.

- An incoming request for the URL http://www.fabrikam456.com/ travel/travelAgent/reserve matches both the specific URL /travel-Agent/reserve and the URL pattern /travelAgent/*. The precedence rules dictate that owing to an exact match, the security constraints applied by the Web container are the ones associated with the relative URL /travelAgent/reserve.

- An incoming request for the URL http://www.fabrikam456.com/ travel/travelAgent/info matches the URL pattern /travelAgent/*. In this case, therefore, the precedence rules dictate that the security constraints applied by the Web container are the ones associated with the URL path-prefix pattern /travelAgent/*.

- An incoming request for the URL http://www.fabrikam456.com/ travel/status/info.jsp matches the URL extension pattern status/*. jsp. In this case, the precedence rules dictate that the security constraints applied by the Web container are the ones associated with the URL extension pattern /status/*.jsp.

This scenario is illustrated in Table 4.1.

Table 4.1. Example Showing Application of Precedence Rules

Requested URL	Matched Security Constraints
http://www.fabrikam456.com/travel/travelAgent/reserve	/travelAgent/reserve
http://www.fabrikam456.com/travel/travelAgent/info	/travelAgent/*
http://www.fabrikam456.com/travel/status/info.jsp	/status/*.jsp

4.6.6 Data Constraints—Only over SSL!

Transactions between an HTTP client and an HTTP server frequently contain security- or privacy-sensitive data. Such data should be kept confidential to prevent its unauthorized disclosure and modification, especially when it is transmitted over the Internet. One approach is to secure the communication channel itself. Another approach is to protect the data by using programmatic cryptography. The latter approach requires special client-side capabilities that may not be available in a pure Web browser environment. The most common solution to the former approach—to secure the communication channel—is obtained by using SSL, a widely adopted protocol that maintains confidentiality and integrity in network communications between clients and servers.

HTTP requests and responses are sent over an SSL connection when the protocol specified is HTTPS. This approach secures the communication between the client and the first server that handles the HTTP requests. This guarantees that client authentication is protected by the SSL protocol. The remainder of the communication connections within an enterprise may also be over SSL for the same reasons of confidentiality and integrity. In order for a Deployer to specify that a particular URL request must be accessed over a secure channel, the Java Servlet specification introduces the concept of a *user data constraint*. By specifying this constraint in the Web application's deployment descriptor, the Deployer conveys the security constraint to a J2EE Web container to serve a URL only over an HTTPS connection. A user data constraint is used to enforce integrity and confidentiality requirements for the transport layer of the communication between the client and the server. When a request is over HTTP and the transport-guarantee element in the user-data-constraint descriptor is set to INTEGRAL or CONFIDENTIAL, the Web container will redirect the request to be resubmitted over HTTPS.

Listing 4.12 shows an example of a security constraint imposing that the URL /travel/reserve be accessed only over an SSL connection:

Listing 4.12. Deployment Descriptor Fragment Enforcing Integrity and Confidentiality

```
<security-constraint>
    <web-resource-collection>
        <web-resource-name>
            ReservationServlet
        </web-resource-name>
        <url-pattern>/travel/reserve</url-pattern>
    </web-resource-collection>
    <user-data-constraint>
        <transport-guarantee>
            CONFIDENTIAL
        </transport-guarantee>
    </user-data-constraint>
</security-constraint>
```

As we observed in Section 3.10.1.2 on page 92, the server does not typically differentiate INTEGRAL from CONFIDENTIAL; both of these values indicate the need to require an SSL connection.

4.7   Principal Delegation

Frequently, multiple software components are aggregated to create a Web application. Often, these components call other components to perform specific tasks of the application. For example, in our travel agent scenario, the Web user interface calls components that look up travel fares, make reservations, and perform financial transactions. Some of these components need to be executed as though they were called by someone other than the user who initiated the transaction on the client side—the person using the Web browser. The J2EE security model addresses this requirement through the use of principal delegation (see Section 3.10.3 on page 94). *Principal delegation* allows an intermediary to perform a task, initiated by a client, using an identity specified in a delegation policy. This is achieved through the declarative security support in J2EE.

In the case of Web applications, a delegation policy specifies whether downstream calls (see Section 3.7.3.4 on page 70) should occur with the authority of a particular J2EE security role. The principal-delegation behavior for downstream calls depends on whether a run-as element in a Web application's deployment descriptor is specified.

- When no run-as element is specified, the default behavior is that the identity calling the servlet is used for downstream method calls. As shown in Figure 4.8, bob is the identity under which both the servlet Travel-CustomerServlet and the enterprise bean CustomerInfoBean are invoked.

- When the Web application's deployment descriptor contains a run-as element, the identity under which the downstream method calls are

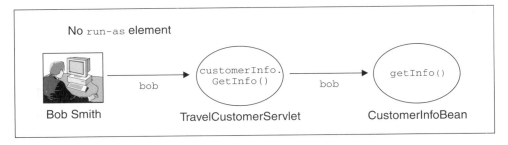

Figure 4.8.   Principal-Delegation Scenario with No `run-as` Element

performed is based on the value of its `role-name` subelement. As shown in Figure 4.9, if the `role-name` element in the `run-as` descriptor is set to the `TravelAgent` security role, all downstream method calls will be performed under an identity—for example, `agent`—that has been granted Travel-Agent role. Which identity is picked to perform the downstream calls depends on the J2EE product implementation. The only requirement is that the identity the J2EE product uses to perform the downstream calls has been granted the specified security role. Listing 4.13 shows a deployment descriptor fragment setting the `run-as` security `role-name` element to `TravelAgent`.

Listing 4.13. Deployment Descriptor Fragment Containing a `run-as` Element

```
<servlet>
   <servlet-name>TravelCustomer</servlet-name>
   <description>
      Travel customer specific information
   </description>
   <servlet-class>TravelCustomerServlet</servlet-class>
   <run-as>
      <role-name>TravelAgent</role-name>
   </run-as>
</servlet>
```

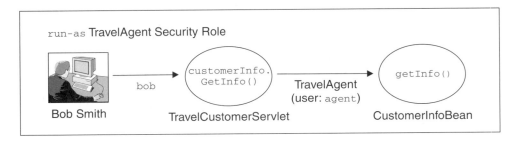

Figure 4.9.   Principal-Delegation Scenario with a `run-as` Element

4.8   Programmatic Security

Declarative security facilities in the Java Servlet specification define the primary mechanisms by which the Web container manages and enforces security. However, in some scenarios, these policies are insufficient to handle the security requirements of an enterprise. In these cases, applications themselves must include security code. APIs are available to address these scenarios. This section describes these APIs and the scenarios in which they are likely to be useful.

4.8.1   Principal Information

Many Web applications want to get information about the user making the request. This information is used for various reasons. For example, it may be important to provide personalized presentation based on the user's profile and achieve fine-grained control of information access and presentation. To faciliate these scenarios, the Java Servlet specification provides access to the user name through the `getUserPrincipal()` method available in the `HttpServletRequest` object. This method returns a `java.security.Principal` object that represents the user who submitted the servlet request. The `getName()` method on the `Principal` object is of particular interest for Web applications, as it returns the name of the calling user. Unfortunately, the format of the user name returned is dependent on the J2EE product implementation, so the `java.lang.String` value that `getName()` returns is not likely to be consistent across J2EE implementations. For example, if the end user logs onto the Fabrikam456 travel agency Web site as `bob`, the `getName()` method may return `bob`, `bob@fabrikam456`, and so on.

In our travel agency scenario, a reservation portal can use the user name to present the information in a personalized fashion. In that environment, the user information can also be used to retrieve the user's profile and display user-specific information. For example, when customer Bob Smith flying out of the Raleigh-Durham (RDU) airport visits the travel agency Web site and logs on, he may be presented with the latest air fares out of the RDU airport, weather information at RDU, and information about his frequent destination(s). This result can be achieved by finding out the name of the user via the `getUserPrincipal()` and `getName()` APIs and then using that information to retrieve the user's profile.

In Web applications that are developed in non-Java environments, principal information is typically obtained through CGI variables that the Web server makes available. In particular, to obtain the name of the requesting user, CGI programmers can access the `REMOTE_USER` variable. In the Java Servlet specification, the information equivalent to the `REMOTE_USER` CGI variable is made available through a `getRemoteUser()` method call on an `HttpServletRequest` object. This method returns a `String`, which is likely, though not guaranteed, to be identical to the `String` obtained by calling `getName()` on the `Principal` object returned by `getUserPrincipal()`.

Listing 4.14 shows a JSP application, Home, invoking `getRemoteUser()` on an `HttpServbletRequest` object to obtain the name of the user making the request.

Listing 4.14. `Home.jsp`

```
<HTML>
    <HEAD>
        <TITLE>Fabrikam456 Online</TITLE>
    </HEAD>
    <BODY>
        <H1>Hi <%=(request.getRemoteUser() != null? ", " +
        request.getRemoteUser() : "")%>, welcome to
        Fabrikam456!</H1>
        <!-- the rest of the JSP code goes here ... --!>
    </BODY>
</HTML>
```

Figure 4.10 shows a scenario involving the Home application. In this scenario, user Bob Smith logs on to the Fabrikam456 Web site and is presented personalized Web contents, such as his recent travels, destinations of interest, weather information at his frequent destinations, and promotions he is entitled to by virtue of his mileage.

4.8.2   Authorization Information

It is common practice for an application's user interface to be based on the user's security authority. For example, for usability reasons, it is considered important to present links to only the information that the requester can access. Presenting contents based on the entitlements of a user is sometimes known as *proactive authorization*—the ability to find out whether a user can access a resource even before presenting a way to access it (see Section 3.10.2 on page 92). Alternatively, in a *reactive authorization* mode, users have to try accessing a resource to determine whether they are authorized for it. Proactive authorization is clearly useful in many enterprise scenarios, including administration, showing only the resources a user can administer; e-business transactions, making only the offers for which the a user is eligible; and enterprise information management, providing only those pieces of budget information the user is entitled to access and manage.

Consider a scenario in which the company Fabrikam456 wants to provide only its platinum-level customers with special offers (see Figure 4.10). This can be accomplished based on whether the customer belongs to a particular user group, which implies that the application needs to have knowledge of the deploy-

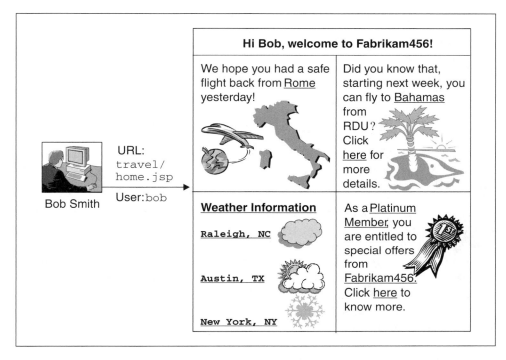

Figure 4.10. Personalized Contents Based on Principal Information

ment environment. Instead of hard-coding the information, J2EE provides the `isUserInRole()` method in the `HttpServletRequest` interface. This method takes a `String` value representing the security role name used within the application code and returns a `boolean` value indicating whether the requesting user has been granted that security role. The TravelCustomerServlet illustrated in Listing 4.15 provides an implementation of the `doGet()` method that uses `isUserInRole()`.

Listing 4.15. `TravelCustomerServlet.java`

```
import java.io.IOException;

import javax.servlet.ServletException;

import javax.servlet.http.HttpServlet;
import javax.servlet.http.HttpServletRequest;
import javax.servlet.http.HttpServletResponse;
```

(continues)

Listing 4.15. `TravelCustomerServlet.java` (*continued*)

```
public class TravelCustomerServlet extends HttpServlet
{
    public void doGet (HttpServletRequest request,
        HttpServletResponse response) throws ServletException,
        IOException
    {
        if (request.isUserInRole("PlatinumCust"))
            response.sendRedirect("PlatinumCustomer.jsp");
        else
            response.sendRedirect("Customer.jsp");
    }
}
```

A security role name programmatically referenced within a Web application is called a *role reference* (see page 67). The Web container must be able to map a Web application's role references to the security role names declared in the Web application's deployment descriptor. This mapping is configured by the Application Assembler in the Web application's deployment descriptor. Listing 4.16 shows a deployment descriptor fragment mapping both the role references `PlatinumCust` in TravelCustmerServlet and `PlatCustomer` in TravelOffers-Servlet to the security role `PlatinumCustomer`.

Listing 4.16. Mapping Role References to Security Roles

```
<servlet>
    <servlet-name>TravelCustomer</servlet-name>
    <description>
        Travel customer specific information
    </description>
    <servlet-class>TravelCustomerServlet</servlet-class>
    <security-role-ref>
        <role-name>PlatinumCust</role-name>
        <role-link>PlatinumCustomer</role-link>
    </security-role-ref>
</servlet>
<servlet>
    <servlet-name>TravelOffers</servlet-name>
    <description>Travel deals</description>
    <servlet-class>TravelOffersServlet</servlet-class>
    <security-role-ref>
        <role-name>PlatCustomer</role-name>
        <role-link>PlatinumCustomer</role-link>
    </security-role-ref>
</servlet>
```

This deployment descriptor example demonstrates how to use `security-role-ref` elements to define the mapping between the security role names embedded in a Web application and the security role names that will be used for defining URL authorizations. A `security-role-ref` element is embedded within a `servlet` element that specifies a servlet containing a call to the `isUserIn-Role()` API. A `security-role-ref` element contains two entries: `role-name` and `role-link`.

1. The `role-name` entry within a `security-role-ref` element refers to the role name `String` value passed as an argument to `isUserInRole()` in the application code. The deployment descriptor fragment relevant to Travel-CustomerServlet in Listing 4.16 sets the `role-name` element to `Platinum-Cust` because the TravelCustomerServlet code shown in Lisitng 4.15 calls `isUserInRole("PlatinumCust")`. In a similar way, the deployment descriptor fragment relevant to the TravelOffersServlet sets the `role-name` element to `PlatCustomer`.

2. Once `role-name` values have been assigned in the `security-role-ref` elements, the role references need to be mapped to the security role names used for authorization of Web resources. The `role-link` elements within the `security-role-ref` elements allow the Application Assembler to map the security role names that are hard-coded in the application as used in the calls to `isUserInRole()` to the security role names that are used by the Deployer and the Web container. In the deployment descriptor fragment of Listing 4.16, both role references `PlatinumCust` and `Plat-Customer` are mapped to the security role name `PlatinumCustomer`.

As an example, let us say that the principal calling the servlet Travel-CustomerServlet in Listing 4.15 is granted the PlatinumCustomer security role. When the servlet calls `isUserInRole("PlatinumCust")`, this method call returns `true` because the deployment descriptor in Listing 4.16 tells the servlet container to map the `PlatinumCust` role reference to the `PlatinumCustomer` security role, and the calling principal is granted that security role. However, if the calling principal is not granted the `PlatinumCustomer` security role, the call to `isUserIn-Role("PlatinumCust")` returns `false`.

It is quite possible that modules developed by various Application Component Providers are bundled into the same J2EE application and its JAR file—the application's EAR file (see Section 3.2 on page 57). This could potentially generate confusion in the mapping between role references and security role names. For example, in the code of Listing 4.15, the developer uses the term `PlatinumCust` to refer to a security role associated with a platinum-level customer. Another servlet written by another developer that may also use the same term `PlatinumCust` to refer to a different security role.

One of the purposes of the `security-role-ref` element and its `role-link` subelement is to disambiguate the security `role-name` values. In fact, the `role-link` subelement is used to specify the security role name in the deployment environment. Therefore, when two applications use role references intended to have different meanings, different `role-link` values can be specified to map these role references to different security roles in the deployed environment.

Sometimes, the Application Component Provider and the Application Assembler are the same person. In these cases, you might see that the `role-name` and the `role-link` elements have identical values, as shown in Listing 4.17.

Listing 4.17. Example of Identical `role-name` and `role-link` Values

```
<servlet>
    <servlet-name>TravelCustomer</servlet-name>
    <description>
        Travel customer specific information
    </description>
    <servlet-class>TravelCustomerServlet</servlet-class>
    <security-role-ref>
        <role-name>PlatinumCust</role-name>
        <role-link>PlatinumCust</role-link>
    </security-role-ref>
</servlet>
```

Mapping identical strings is a redundant step, so it is not necessary to explicitly declare it. Therefore, the deployment descriptor fragment shown in Listing 4.17 is considered to be equivalent to the one in Listing 4.18, where the `security-role-ref` element is not even declared in the `servlet` element of the Web module's deployment descriptor.

Listing 4.18. Removing a Redundant `security-role-ref` Element

```
<servlet>
    <servlet-name>TravelCustomer</servlet-name>
    <description>
        Travel customer specific information
    </description>
    <servlet-class>TravelCustomerServlet</servlet-class>
</servlet>
```

4.8.3 SSL Attribute Information: Certificates and Cipher Suites

As explained in Section 4.5 on page 112, when connecting over the HTTPS protocol, client-side certificates can be used to establish a mutual-authentication SSL session between an HTTP client and an HTTP server. The client presents an X.509 certificate during the SSL handshake. On completing a successful SSL handshake, the client's identity is mapped to a principal that is assigned to zero or more J2EE security roles. The client is then authorized to access resources, as was described in Section 4.6 on page 124. In addition, the `isSecure()` method on a `ServletRequest` object returns `true` when the request was made using a secure channel, such as HTTPS.

Once the connection has succeeded, enterprise applications may want to access the client's X.509 certificate and other attributes of the SSL session. The value of the subject's DN attribute in the certificate, other information retrieved from the certificate (see Section 4.5.1.3 on page 120), or the cipher suite used to establish the SSL connection can be used to determine the security level of the connection established. To obtain the X.509 certificate programmatically, the `getAttribute()` method on the `ServletRequest` object can be queried using the key `javax.servlet.request.X509Certificate`, as shown in the following line of code:

```
java.security.cert.X509Certificate[] certs =
    (java.security.cert.X509Certificate[]) request.getAttribute
    ("javax.servlet.request.X509Certificate");
```

This method call returns an array of objects of type `java.security.cert.X509Certificate`. The order of the certificates in the array reflects the ascending order of trust; the first element in the array is the certificate of the client, the second element is the certificate that was used to issue the first certificate (see Section 10.3.4 on page 372), and so on.

Similarly, the `getAttribute()` method of a `ServletRequest` object can be used to programmatically obtain other attributes of an SSL session.

- The size of the key used to establish the SSL connection is obtained by requesting the attribute `javax.servlet.request.key_size`, as shown in the following line of code:

  ```
  Integer keySize = (Integer) request.getAttribute
      ("javax.servlet.request.key_size");
  ```

- The cipher suite used to establish the SSL connection is obtained by requesting the attribute `javax.servlet.request.cipher_suite`, as shown in the following line of code:

  ```
  String cipherSuite = (String) request.getAttribute
      ("javax.servlet.request.cipher_suite");
  ```

The CertAndCipherSuiteInfo servlet in Listing 4.19 shows how to access client-certificate and SSL-attribute information programmatically.

Listing 4.19. `CertAndCipherSuiteInfo.java`

```
import java.io.PrintWriter;
import java.io.IOException;

import java.security.cert.X509Certificate;
```

(continues)

Listing 4.19. `CertAndCipherSuiteInfo.java` (*continued*)

```java
import javax.servlet.ServletException;

import javax.servlet.http.HttpServlet;
import javax.servlet.http.HttpServletRequest;
import javax.servlet.http.HttpServletResponse;


/**
 * This servlet obtains certificate and SSL cipher suite
 * information from the client request.
 */
public class CertAndCipherSuiteInfo extends HttpServlet
{
    public void doGet(HttpServletRequest req,
        HttpServletResponse res) throws ServletException,
        IOException
    {
        PrintWriter out;
        res.setContentType("text/html");
        out = res.getWriter();
        out.println("<HTML><HEAD><TITLE>SSL Attribute " +
            "Information </TITLE></HEAD>" +
            "<BODY BGCOLOR=\"#FFFFEE\">");
        String cipherSuite = (String) req.getAttribute
            ("javax.servlet.request.cipher_suite");

        if (cipherSuite != null)
        {
            X509Certificate certChain[] =
                (X509Certificate[]) req.getAttribute
                ("javax.servlet.request.X509Certificate");
            out.println("<H2>HTTPS Information:</H2>");
            out.println("<TABLE BORDER=\"2\" " +
                "WIDTH=\"65%\" BGCOLOR=\"#DDDDFF\">");
            out.println("<tr><td>Cipher Suite</td><td>" +
                cipherSuite + "</td></tr>");

            if (certChain != null)
                for (int i = 0; i < certChain.length; i++)
                    out.println("Client Certificate Chain [" +
                        i + "] = " + certChain[i].toString());

            out.println("</TABLE><BR><BR>");
        }

        out.println("</BODY></HTML>");
    }
}
```

4.8.4   Programmatic Login

Some scenarios require a servlet to perform a *programmatic login*—a servlet-managed authentication—instead of using the J2EE declarative login configuration to request the user to log in. With programmatic login, servlets should perform the login from within the Web container and access resources based on the authenticated user's identity. Even though JAAS provides authentication APIs (see Section 9.2 on page 291), J2EE V1.3 does not mandate any standard for using JAAS to achieve programmatic login from within a Web container. Containers, including IBM WebSphere Application Server,[4] provide a vendor-specific approach for achieving this functionality.

4.9   Runtime Restrictions for Web Components

A number of programming restrictions must be followed in order to maintain portability of Web components—servlets and JSP applications—between containers, as well as to preserve security. Some of these restrictions can be enforced by the Web Container Provider; others are solely the responsibility of the Web Application Provider.

- Web components must not write to and depend on static fields but should instead use enterprise beans or databases. Writing to static fields can result in inconsistency in deployed applications, as some containers will run all instances of an application in a single Java virtual machine, whereas others will run the same application in multiple containers.

- Web Container Providers may limit the creation of threads. Therefore, Web component developers must not use `java.lang.Thread` objects, and thus multithreading, within their Web applications.

    One important aspect from a security perspective is the fact that a Web application's security context is typically maintained at the granularity of a thread. Managing the context per thread is implementation dependent; therefore, a Web application's security context will not be automatically tranferred when a new thread is created.

- J2SE Abstract Windowing Toolkit (AWT) functionality must not be used to interact with a keyboard or a display. Web components are intended to be server-side components that front end transactional components, and containers are designed to facilitate high-throughput transaction processing. As such, interaction with a keyboard or a display will interfere with these objectives. Therefore, containers do not support keyboard/display interactions.

- Web components are allowed to perform file read and write I/O operations via the `java.io` package, including reading and writing via `java.io.FileDescriptor` objects. That said, owing to inherent security risks in

---

4. See `http://www.ibm.com/websphere`.

letting untrusted components write or even delete files from the file system, Web Container Providers may enforce certain restrictions. (For example, Web components may only read and write files under a directory that maps to the context root of the Web application to which they belong.) Deleting and executing files is forbidden, even though from a practical point of view, granting the permission to write to a file is implicitly equivalent to granting the permission to delete it.

- The network socket operations listen, accept, and multicast are not allowed. Although Web components are server objects, all inbound communication must be routed through the Web container. If a Web component were to become a server via listen and accept operations, it would interfere with the objective of being a server for Web client requests. Additionally, the security policy is likely to be violated, as all communication with a Web component, including authentication and authorization requests, is supposed to be routed through the Web container and its method- and role-based authorization mechanisms.

  A Web component is allowed to be a network client, making requests to other network applications. It may connect to enterprise beans via RMI-IIOP; other resource adapters, such as a database, or other legacy server environments that communicate over socket connections.

- The following operations are not allowed: obtaining a `java.lang.Class-Loader`, including the current `ClassLoader`; setting the context `Class-Loader` and the `SecurityManager`; creating a new `SecurityManager`; stopping the JVM; changing the input, output, or error streams in `java.lang.System`; setting network socket factories and URL stream handlers; starting, stopping, suspending, and resuming `Threads`; or changing `Thread` names or priorities. These functions are reserved for use by the container. Modification of any of these would undermine both security and the container's stability.

  However, Web components are allowed to load native libraries. This flexbility is allowed for Web components to provide a Web front end to native applications.

- Security policy information in the container should not be interrogated or modified. This includes the `java.security.Policy` implementation. The container implements security and may use J2SE security mechanisms but may include mechanisms that are not part of J2SE. There is no guarantee that Web components using the J2SE APIs will get the correct or consistent information about the container's security policies. Interrogating the security policy can also create security exposures, particularly if the results of the interrogation were to be disseminated outside the container: for example, if they were sent to a Web client. This information would enable a malicious entity to better plan an attack against the container and/or enterprise.

- Web components should not be allowed to set system properties by calling `System.setProperty()`. Reading the value of a system property should instead be permitted.

The Web container can enforce some of the preceding programming model restrictions through the use of a J2SE security policy configuration. Such a policy configuration should unconditionally deny `java.security.AllPermission`, `java.awt.AWTPermission`, `java.net.NetPermission`, `java.lang.reflect.ReflectPermission`, `java.security.SecurityPermission`, and `java.io.SerializablePermission` and grant `java.util.PropertyPermission "read"`, `"*"`, `java.lang.RuntimePermission "queuePrintJob"` and `"loadLibrary.*"`, `java.net.SocketPermission "connect"`, `"*"`, and `java.io.FilePermission "<<ALL FILES>>"`, `"read, write"`. These authorizations allow Web components to be portable. However, some containers may enforce further restrictions or may be lenient and allow for more permissions.

4.10 Usage Patterns

The declarative and programmatic security features supported by the Java Servlet specification are used in various ways within enterprise environments. Based on the need, common usage patterns can be used. This section discusses a few usage patterns that have emerged out of common use cases within Web application environments. The patterns identified include connecting to other HTTP servers via HTTPS connections, maintaining the state securely, and performing secure pre- and post-servlet processing.

4.10.1 Using HTTPS to Connect to External HTTP Servers

URL connections from servlets to external HTTP servers can be established programamtically using the `java.net.URL` class. The URL to connect to is passed as a `String` argument to the `URL` constructor. Most URLs start with the string `http://`. When URL connections need to be made over SSL, the protocol is HTTPS, and the URL starts with the string `https://`. By default, a URL starting with `https://` would result in an error—a `java.net.MalformedURLException` would be thrown—unless an HTTPS protocol handler has been installed on the Java system.

For servlets to make HTTPS connections, the Web container hosting the servlet should have the JSSE API (see Section 13.4.1 on page 460) installed and available in the Java runtime class path (see Section 7.2.2 on page 207) with the necessary authorizations granted. Additionally, a JSSE provider must be installed and configured for use by the J2EE programs that need to establish SSL connections (see Section Listing 11.1. on page 384 and Section 11.1.3.3 on page 387).

After JSSE is available to be used by the Web container, the system property `java.protocol.handler.pkgs` may be set to an SSL protocol handler class. This can be done either statically or programmatically. A static configuration usually involves editing a property file on the WAS. A programmatic configuration requires making a `System.setProperty()` method call. The following line of code shows how to set the IBM SSL protocol handler programmatically:

```
System.setProperty("java.protocol.handler.pkgs",
    "com.ibm.net.ssl.internal.www.protocol");
```

As we saw in Section 4.9 on page 143, Web components cannot expect to be allowed to set system properties; they can expect to be allowed only to read them. Also, note that multiple Web components may coexist within the same JVM. Therefore, setting a protocol handler will affect other Web components and may conflict with the provider that the container will want to use. Therefore, setting a JVM-wide provider is not a good option.

By specifying the appropriate `java.net.URLStreamHandler` as the third parameter, Web components can provide the protocol handler programmatically when they construct the `URL` object. For example, the `MalformedURLException` will no longer be thrown, and the appropriate HTTPS protocol handler will be used for the connection when constructing an HTTPS `URL` object, as in the following line of code:

```
URL url = new URL(null, "https://www.fabrikam456.com",
    new com.ibm.net.ssl.internal.www.protocol.https.Handler());
```

When the `URL` object being constructed is intended to connect to the standard SSL port, 443, it is not necessary to specify the port number as part of the URL. However, if the servlet needs to connect to a nonstandard port—for example, 9443—it is necessary to append the port number to the target URL, as shown in the following line of code:

```
URL url = new URL(null, "https://www.fabrikam456.com:9443",
    new com.ibm.net.ssl.internal.www.protocol.https.Handler());
```

If a URL refers to a resource hosted on a server that has an invalid or untrusted certificate, an attempt to retrieve the `java.io.InputStream` or the `java.io.OutputStream` from the associated `java.net.URLConnection` object will throw a `javax.net.ssl.SSLException` with the message `untrusted server cert`

chain. The InputStream and OutputStream can be obtained by calling get-
InputStream() and getOutputStream() on the URLConnection object, respectively. However, if the server has a valid, trusted certificate, no exception will be
thrown. The resultant URL object can be used to open the connection and get the
InputStream or OutputStream, as shown next:

```
URL url = new URL(null, "https://www.fabrikam456.com",
    new com.ibm.net.ssl.internal.www.protocol.https.Handler());
URLConnection con = url.openConnection();
InputStream is = con.getInputStream();
OutputStream os = con.getOutputStream();
```

When a servlet connects to an external HTTP server, it considers the servlet as
a client. If the external HTTP server requires its clients to present their certificates
to perform client authentication, as discussed in Section 4.5.1.3 on page 120, the
Web container hosting the servlet needs to be configured to connect using the appropriate client certificate.

Similar considerations apply when a servlet tries to connect to a server whose
server certificate was issued by a nonstandard CA. In this case, if the server is considered trusted, the key store used by the Web container to establish SSL connections between the servlet and the external HTTP servers needs to be updated to
include the certificate of the external server the servlet is trying to connect to.

4.10.2 Maintaining the State Securely

As we observed in Section 4.5.2 on page 123, HTTP is a *stateless* protocol. The
way HTTP operates is that an HTTP client initiates an HTTP transaction by sending a request to an HTTP server: for example, it asks for a Web page. The server
responds; after that, the HTTP transaction is automatically closed. That request
has no relation to the next request, if any, the client sends.

The advantage of this approach is that it allows an HTTP server to serve multiple clients simultaneously, without incurring the overhead generated by keeping
several sessions opened with all the clients that initiated a request. The negative
implication is that information about the client, including authentication and per-
sonalization information, needs to be resubmitted with every request.

- In the context of a password-protected session, a user would have to enter
  a valid user ID and password pair on every request.

- In the context of an online store, the HTTP server cannot know whether
  the client has selected items to purchase.

- In the context of an online newspaper that allows users to specify which
  types of articles they are most interested in, the HTTP server cannot
  establish whether the client has previously specified preferences.

Resubmitting this information with every request is considered user unfriendly and may also have negative security implications. A solution to this problem would be for the Web server to store the information gathered from all the clients on some permanent storage. However, this solution is considered too expensive if implemented on the server side, especially if the HTTP server is contacted by a large number of users.

The J2EE architecture supports two solutions to maintain session state: HTTP cookies, and HTTP and SSL sessions. The next two subsections examine how these two solutions work and their security implications in a J2EE environment.

4.10.2.1   HTTP Cookies

An *HTTP cookie*[5] is a piece of information passed between an HTTP client and server during an HTTP transaction. The cookie is stored on the client machine under the form of a text file and can be shared across multiple requests. For example, the server may store a customer number in a cookie and send it to the client. On subsequent requests, the client will include the current value of that cookie as part of the requests. On receiving a request, the HTTP server extracts the value from the cookie and uses it to identify the session and process the request based on that information.

As part of a well-defined HTTP header, a cookie flows over the network in cleartext. Therefore, eavesdroppers can get at its value easily. When carrying sensitive information, a cookie should be set to be valid for a limited time period and be restricted to flow only over SSL connections. Cookies can be further restricted by taking advantage of their `Domain` and `Path` attributes.

- The `Domain` attribute of a cookie specifies the domain for which the cookie is valid.

- The `Path` attribute of a cookie specifies the subset of URLs to which the cookie applies.

Servlets can generate secure cookies, store information in them, and retrieve their contents on subsequent client requests by using the `javax.servlet.http.Cookie` class offered by the Java Servlet API:

1. A `Cookie` object is created by passing cookie name and value `String`s to the `Cookie` constructor, as shown in the following line of code:

   ```
   Cookie cookie = new Cookie("Account Number", "1234-5678");
   ```

2. A `Cookie` object can be made *secure*, which means that its `Secure` attribute is set. This is an indication for the client that the cookie should be

---

5. See RFC 2109 at `http://www.ietf.org/rfc/rfc2109.txt`.

sent back to the server using only a secure protocol, such as HTTPS or SSL. The line of code to make a `Cookie` object secure is shown next:

```
cookie.setSecure();
```

3. For increased security, a cookie can be made nonpersistent. This is an indication for the client—typically, a Web browser—that the cookie should not be permanently stored, and should instead be deleted when the client program exits. To make a cookie nonpersistent, a servlet can pass a negative `int` value to the `setMaxAge()` method on the `Cookie` object, as in the following line of code:

```
cookie.setMaxAge(-1);
```

4. A servlet can send a cookie to a client by passing a `Cookie` object to the `addCookie()` method of an `HttpServletResponse`, as shown next:

```
response.addCookie(cookie);
```

This method call adds fields to HTTP response headers to send cookies to the Web browser, one at a time. A Web browser is expected to support 20 cookies for each Web server, 300 cookies total, and may limit cookie size to 4 K each.

5. A Web browser returns cookies to the servlet by adding fields to the HTTP request headers. A servlet can retrieve cookies from a client request in the form of a `Cookie` array by using the `getCookies()` method on an `HttpServletRequest` object.

```
Cookie[] cookies = request.getCookies();
```

4.10.2.2 HTTP and SSL Sessions

HTTP cookies have inherent limited storage capabilities. Another disadvantage is that managing cookies must be handled within the application code. In order to abstract the notion of a session and related state, J2EE supports the notion of an HTTP session, represented as a `javax.servlet.http.HttpSession` object.

Servlets can create an `HttpSession` object associated with an HTTP request. Any information that needs to be associated with the request can be stored in the `HttpSession` object. For example, in our travel agency scenario, a customer's current selection of itinerary can be stored in an `HttpSession` object. Subsequent requests are processed without retrieving all the customer information from the back-end system. Instead, such information is retrieved from the associated `HttpSession` object. In scenarios like this, an `HttpSession` is associated with an identifier, `jsessionid`, that is part of the request. The identifier's value is exchanged either via a cookie or through URL rewriting.

In addition to these mechanisms, WASs support sessions by using an SSL session ID as the identifier for an HTTP session. Even though using SSL session IDs tightly links a request to its underlying transport security, this option is not always possible. One reason is that, as we observed in Section 4.5.1.3 on page 120, multiple HTTP servers might form the end point of an SSL handshake, and they may not always have access to the SSL session ID information. Another reason is that SSL sessions may be renegotiated periodically between HTTP clients and servers, resulting in a change of the session ID and hence the loss of HTTP session information.

If HTTP session identification is to be maintained through cookies, the Deployer must ensure that they are tranported only over SSL, to prevent eavesdropping and tampering. This helps prevent replay attacks[6] when obtaining the session ID can lead to access to the session itself, including the session information and application state.

Because HTTPSession objects may carry reference to sensitive information, it is also wise to choose a short timeout for the underlying HTTP sessions. If these session identifiers can be obtained by an untrusted third party, setting a small timeout will reduce the time window within which attacks may be possible. The timeout can be specified in a Web application's deployment descriptor and is specified in whole minutes. Listing 4.20 shows an example of setting a 30-minute window for an HTTP session.

Listing 4.20. Setting an HTTP Session Timeout

```
<web-app>
   <session-config>
      <session-timeout>30</session-timeout>
   </session-config>
</web-app>
```

4.10.3   Pre- and Post-Servlet Processing

A common pattern within Web applications is to perform some actions before and/or after processing a servlet. One example is monitoring the number of failed login attempts and taking an action, such as locking the account, after a maximum number of login attempts is reached. However, J2EE does not require facilities for user and account management.

One approach to handling pre- and post-servlet processing is through the use of servlet filters. *Filters* are software components that perform filtering tasks on either the request to a resource—a servlet or static content—or on the response

---

6. A *replay attack* consists of intercepting and recording messages in order to send them out later to a recipient unaware that the message is no longer legitimate. A replay attack is a type of denial-of-service attack (see page 237 and Section 7.4.4.1 on page 245).

from a resource or both. They allow dynamic—on-the-fly—manipulation of HTTP header and payload information as it flows in and out of Web containers. The Java Servlet API provides the `javax.servlet.Filter` interface to represent filters. Filters are associated with a servlet or a URI and are invoked on the inbound and outbound call paths.

Multiple filters can be associated with a request by chaining the filters. The servlet being filtered becomes the final component in the chain. Each filter in the chain is given an opportunity to handle requests. In J2EE, filter chains are represented as `javax.servlet.FilterChain` objects.

The use of servlet filters is a programming pattern for using a standard API for plugging security services into applications. Examples include *login filters* to monitor number of login attempts, *auditing filters* to securely log request details, and *encryption filters* to encrypt or decrypt the messages that are exchanged with a servlet. Note that even though servlet filters use a standard API, they are considered to be application code. Therefore, they need to be packaged with the Web applications with which they are associated. Alternatively, a given set of filters for an environment may get explicitly associated with all Web applications.

Let us consider a simple scenario in which a certain set of users must be prevented from logging in. A servlet filter can be designed to check whether a user attempting to log in is on this revocation list. The skeleton code in Listing 4.21 can be customized to address the requirements as appropriate—for example, to obtain the revocation list from a database, LDAP directory, and so on.

Listing 4.21. `CheckUserStatus.java`

```
import java.util.ArrayList;

import java.io.IOException;

import javax.servlet.Filter;
import javax.servlet.FilterConfig;
import javax.servlet.FilterChain;
import javax.servlet.ServletException;
import javax.servlet.ServletRequest;
import javax.servlet.ServletResponse;

import javax.servlet.http.HttpServletRequest;
import javax.servlet.http.HttpServletResponse;


/**
 * A servlet filter that checks if a user trying to login
 * is in a revocation list.
 */
public class CheckUserStatus implements Filter
{
```

(continues)

Listing 4.21. CheckUserStatus.java (*continued*)

```
    protected FilterConfig filterConfig;

    private java.util.List revocationList;

    /**
     * This method is called when the Filter is
     * instantiated. This Filter is instantiated the first
     * time j_security_check is invoked for the application,
     * that is when a protected servlet in the application
     * is accessed.
     *
     * @param filterConfig a FilterConfig object used by a
     *          servlet container to pass information to the
     *          filter during initialization.
     * @throws ServletException if an exception has occurred
     *          that interferes with the Filter's normal
     *          operations.
     */
    public void init(FilterConfig filterConfig)
        throws ServletException
    {
        this.filterConfig = filterConfig;

        // Obtain the user revocation list.
        revocationList = new java.util.ArrayList();
        obtainRevocationList(revocationList);
    }

    /**
     * This method is called when the Filter is taken out of
     * service. This method is only called once all threads
     * within the Filter's doFilter() method have exited or
     * after a timeout period has passed. After the Web
     * container calls this method, it will not call the
     * doFilter() method again on this instance of the
     * Filter.  This method gives the Filter an opportunity
     * to clean up any resources that are being held. In
     * particular, it cleans up the FilterConfig and the
     * revocation list held by this instance of the Filter.
     */
    public void destroy()
    {
        filterConfig = null;
        revocationList = null;
    }

    /**
     * This method is called before the servlet that this
     * Filter is mapped to is invoked. Since this Filter is
     * mapped to j_security_check, this method is called
     * before the j_security_check action is posted.
     * The doFilter() method of the Filter is called by the
     * container each time a request/response pair is passed
     * through the chain due to a client request for a
     * resource at the end of the chain. The FilterChain
```

Listing 4.21. `CheckUserStatus.java`   (*continued*)

```
     * passed in to this method allows the Filter to pass on
     * the request and response to the next entity in the
     * chain.
     *
       * @param request a ServletRequest object representing
     *         a request to the servlet associated with this
     *         Filter.
     * @param response a ServletResponse object representing
     *         a response sent to the servlet associated with
     *         this Filter.
     * @param chain a FilterChain object representing the
     *         invocation chain of a filtered request for a
     *         resource. This FilterChain is used to invoke
     *         the next filter in the chain, or if the
     *         calling filter is the last filter in the
     *         chain, to invoke the rosource at the end of
     *         the chain.
     * @throws IOException if an I/O error has occurred.
     * @throws ServletException if an error has occurred
     *         that interferes with the normal operation of
     *         this Filter.
     */
    public void doFilter(ServletRequest request,
        ServletResponse response, FilterChain chain)
        throws IOException, ServletException
    {
        HttpServletRequest req =
            (HttpServletRequest) request;
        HttpServletResponse res =
            (HttpServletResponse) response;
        // Check if the user can be allowed to access the
        // associated servlet before the authentication
        // takes place.

        // Get the user ID.
        String userName = req.getParameter("j_username");

        // Send error message if the user is among the set
        // of users who are revoked of their access
        // privileges.
        if (revocationList.contains(userName))
        {
            res.sendError
                (HttpServletResponse.SC_UNAUTHORIZED);
            return;
        }

        // Call next filter in the chain. Let
        // j_security_check authenticate user.
        chain.doFilter(request, response);
    }
```

(*continues*)

Listing 4.21. `CheckUserStatus.java` (*continued*)

```
    /**
     * Updates the list of users who are revoked of their
     * access privileges.
     *
     * @param userList an ArrayList containing the users
     *          who have been revoked of their access
     *          privileges.
     */
    private void obtainRevocationlist(ArrayList userList)
    {
        // In this sample, three users are hardcoded as
        // revoked. They are hardcoded to illustrate the
        // concepts. Replace this method implementation
        // using other means to obtain the revocation list
        // (for example, read it from file, obtain it from
        // a database, get it from an LDAP directory, etc.).
        userList.add("bob");
        userList.add("user123");
        userList.add("emp1234");
    }
}
```

4.11 Partitioning Web Applications

Web applications are logical groups of Web resources. Therefore, certain security
constraints, such as login configuration and data constraints, are scoped to a specific Web application. In some scenarios, a single authentication mechanism does
not address the security requirements of all the applications being hosted. For example, some of the applications can suffice with a form-based login. Others have
more stringent security requirements and necessitate the use of certificate-based
authentication. Because it acts as an SSO mechanism, the Web container design
point is limited with respect to authentication in that login information to a Web
application is required to be shared with other Web applications within the same
Web container. To work around this limitation, applications with different authentication requirements need to be hosted in different Web container instances—for
example, the same Web container but running in a separate process—or through
virtual hosting.[7] Therefore, in addition to securing resources based on declarative

---

7. *Virtual hosting* is the provision of the Web server and other services so that a company or
   individual does not have to buy and maintain a Web server host with a line to the Internet
   but can use the Web server of a *virtual hosting provider*, also called a *Web* or *Internet*
   space provider. This is achieved by allowing a Web server to serve contents for more than
   one domain name or IP address. This way, a single machine or Web server can handle
   multiple Web sites.

security and programmatic control, security characteristics can be tuned by appropriately partitioning applications.

Consider two Web applications, WebAppA and WebAppB, and suppose that WebAppA is secured using form-based login, whereas WebAppB is secured using certificate-based login. If both Web applications are deployed in the same Web container, the user accessing these resources will be allowed to access all of them after the inital access, regardless of the authentication mechanism used on that initial access. For instance, if the first request is to WebAppA, the user provides user ID and password through form-based login. Although WebAppB requires the user to exhibit a client digital certificate to log in, this certificate will not be required if the user has already logged on to WebAppA. Therefore, if the intention is to provide a higher level of security for WebAppB by requiring client digital certificates in order to access WebAppB, that cannot be achieved by hosting WebAppA and WebAppB in a single Web container. If two different levels of security are to be provided for WebAppA and WebAppB, the two Web applications must be deployed in two different Web containers.

Owing to other SSO features provided by the J2EE vendor, it may still be the case that login to access one Web application may influence access rights to other applications in other containers. In such cases, the security requirements of the Web resources need to be evaluated and enforced through appropriate partitioning and deployment and by using other vendor-specific security facilities offered by J2EE products.

CHAPTER 5

EJB Security

No enterprise solution is complete without the ability to model business processes and perform transactions. These transactions may use existing, or legacy, systems or newly developed applications and databases. J2EE provides the EJB model for simplified development and deployment of high-performance transactional programs called *enterprise beans*. In particular, WASs specialize in providing containers for deploying and executing enterprise beans. For business applications to progress from small-scale endeavors to the demands of enterprise-wide solutions, the development of EJB objects is usually adopted to model the business processes. As with all enterprise transaction processing, security is a key consideration.

This chapter outlines the basics of the EJB model and the relevant security considerations, including EJB support for authentication, authorization, and delegation. In particular, this chapter explains how each of the J2EE/EJB roles is involved in security, from the Enterprise Bean Provider to the Container Provider and the System Administrator. This discussion includes descriptions of the declarative security policies defined in the EJB deployment descriptor. This chapter also discusses how the EJB container enforces the declarative security policies, as well as how EJB components can programmatically enforce security to address any enterprise security requirements not addressed by the EJB specification. The chapter concludes by describing future directions for EJB security.

5.1 Introduction

EJB technology is a server-side component model for the development and deployment of secure distributed-transaction business programs. The model enables Enterprise Bean Providers to write transactional business logic as a set of components that are deployable in *any* EJB-compliant container. Among the many services it offers, an EJB container provides for the management of concurrency, transactions, persistence, distributed objects, naming, and security.

The EJB component model supports the development of software *black boxes* that can be aggregated to create larger components or systems. These components are written by the *in-house* software development groups of a large organization or may be purchased from a third-party vendor specializing in a particular set of business processes, such as human resources, payroll, general ledger, or other forms of financial processing.

Like EJB components, servlets and JSP applications can engage in transaction processing. However, there are significant differentiators between EJB components versus servlets and JSP components. The EJB architecture defines a simplified programming model oriented toward transaction processing, which makes it easier for developers to focus on business logic. This includes extensive support for distributed-transaction monitor support.

Based on information provided at deployment time, the transaction monitor of the EJB container ensures that the database properties of atomicity, consistency, isolation, and durability (ACID) are preserved:

- *Atomicity*—all-or-nothing
- *Consistency*—internally consistent
- *Isolation*—serializability
- *Durability*—ability to survive transaction processor failure

EJB technology is also designed to be a distributed-component model. The deployed components of an application may reside in a single EJB container or can be distributed across any number of EJB containers and transaction monitors. The interaction between distributed, or remote, EJB components can be carried over a variety of transports. RMI-IIOP is the industry-standard method for interoperability. Aside from assisting the distributed-transaction monitor in managing the transactions, the container is responsible for enforcing the security policy, regardless of whether the components reside in a single EJB container or across multiple EJB containers.

Enterprise beans are intended to be portable, reusable, black-box software components that can be aggregated to create larger components. The contract between components is defined by the home, local home, local, and remote interfaces (see Section 3.7.2.1 on page 68), as well as the EJB deployment descriptor (see Section 3.2.1 on page 58), for each EJB component.

In a distributed computing environment, client code communicates with a server over a communication network, typically using TCP/IP. The protocol required by the EJB specification is RMI-IIOP, which defines the format of a remote

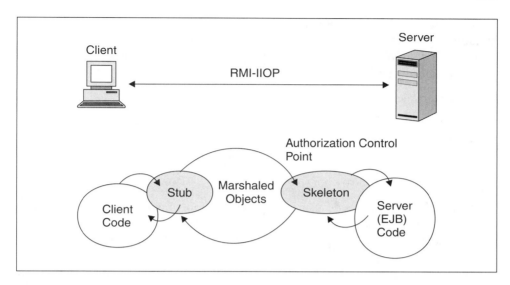

Figure 5.1.   Remote Method Invocation

method request to a (possibly) remote server object, as shown in Figure 5.1. This
format includes the *wire protocol*, or sequence of bits sent in each message across
the network, and the sequence of messages that comprise the remote request and
response from the server. *Marshaling*—packaging—of the RMI request is via a
piece of code called a *stub*, which packages the request and calls the RMI-IIOP
ORB to send the request to the EJB container hosting the EJB code. The server
process's ORB *demarshals*—unpackages—the request via a piece of code called a
skeleton, which then calls the requested server code with the appropriate arguments. Aside from the name of the target object being called and the parameters
for the call, RMI-IIOP transmits transaction and security attributes in a manner
that is transparent to the client and EJB developers. The RMI-IIOP security protocol for EJB containers is based on the Object Management Group's CSIv2 specification, which includes authentication and authorization of the client, or requester.

5.2   EJB Roles and Security

EJB technology defines a set of processes, starting from the application development and following through the administration of the deployed code. The EJB
specification describes a set of contracts to enable the development and deployment of software components and also outlines processes that span from software
development to deployment. *EJB roles* take on specific responsibilities at the

various stages in the development/deployment/administration process. These roles include responsibility for defining and managing transactional characteristics of each of the components, as well as security. The defined EJB roles with security considerations discussed in this chapter are

- Enterprise Bean Provider
- Application Assembler
- Deployer
- System Administrator
- EJB Container Provider

Each of these EJB roles is described with respect to its responsibilities in the definition and management of security.

EJB security is intended to be managed by the EJB container and driven by declarative security policy rather than security policy being hard-coded within the application code. Much of this declarative policy information is encoded within the EJB deployment descriptor. Removing security from the application code greatly reduces the burden on application developers, allowing them to concentrate on modeling business processes. Specifically, most application developers may not be familiar with the intricacies of security and the coding practices that will ensure secure deployed applications. Additionally, application developers are usually unaware of the details of the security environment into which their code is to be deployed. Application code containing security policy decisions for authentication, authorization, secrecy, and integrity usually does not quickly adapt to changes in enterprise security requirements. Externalizing security policy from the EJB code provides greater opportunity for deployment flexibility, code reuse, and portability between container implementations.

EJB delegates security issues to those EJB roles having greater familiarity with the security features of the EJB container and deployment environment. In practice, the effective security policy is defined by the Deployer and the System Administrator, and the EJB container is responsible for enforcement of the policy.

Every enterprise bean goes through the process shown in Figure 5.2.

1. Enterprise Bean Providers are responsible for writing the enterprise beans that embody the business logic.

2. Application Assemblers combine, or assemble, a number of EJB components to create an entire application and also provide hints about the security aspects of the enterprise beans being assembled.

3. Deployers take one or more assembled applications, prepare them, and install them in EJB containers, including setting up resource definitions, such as JNDI and LDAP entries, databases, security attributes, and so on.

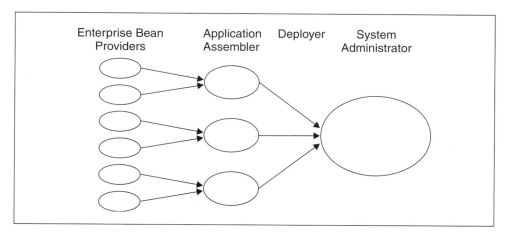

Figure 5.2.   Process of EJB Development to Deployment

4. System Administrators manage the containers and other J2EE resources, including defining new users, or principals, and their mapping to security roles.

5.2.1   Enterprise Bean Provider

The Enterprise Bean Provider is the application developer who is an expert in writing code that embodies enterprise rules. As we saw in Section 3.2.1 on page 58, enterprise beans fall into three broad categories:

1. Nonpersistent beans, or *session beans*
2. Persistent beans, or *entity beans*
3. Message-oriented beans, or *message-driven beans*

For entity beans, persistence managed by code in the enterprise bean is called bean-managed persistence (BMP). Persistence managed by the EJB container is called container managed persistence (CMP).

5.2.1.1   Communicating with an Enterprise Bean

All communication between a remote client and an enterprise bean is mediated by RMI-IIOP, as shown in Figure 5.1 on page 159. If the client and the enterprise bean are colocated in the same container, the request is mediated by the container itself. This architecture allows for

* A clean separation between components
* Proper transaction management, ensuring that the database ACID properties are preserved

- Security policy enforcement by performing necessary authentication and authorization, as well as establishing the security context for the EJB method invocation

Figure 5.3 shows the two types of interfaces that each enterprise bean defines as part of the contract between the container and clients.

1. The first type consists of the home and local home interfaces, which define the enterprise bean life-cycle methods that are used to create, locate, and delete EJB instances. These interfaces include the create, remove, and find methods. All enterprise beans' home interfaces must extend the `javax.ejb.EJBHome` interface. All enterprise beans' local home interfaces must extend the `javax.ejb.EJBLocalHome` interface.

2. The second type of interface specifies the business methods implemented by the enterprise bean and available to the client code. These methods are defined in the remote and local interfaces. All enterprise beans' remote interfaces must extend the `javax.ejb.EJBObject` interface. All enterprise beans' local interfaces must extend the `javax.ejb.EJBLocalObject` interface.

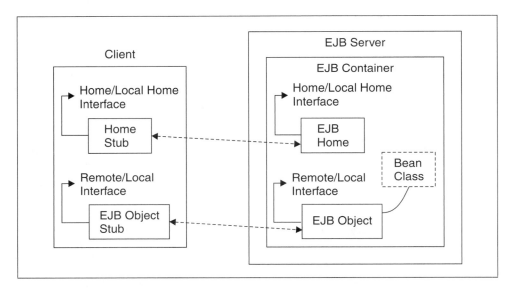

Figure 5.3.   EJB Interfaces

If the client and the enterprise bean reside in different containers, the enterprise bean must implement the methods exposed in the home and remote interfaces. When the client and the enterprise bean reside in the same container, it is still acceptable, but not necessary, for the enterprise bean to implement the home and remote interfaces. Prior to EJB V2.0, there were no local home or local interfaces.

According to the RMI-IIOP specification, all RMI-IIOP method invocations must follow call-by-value (CBV) semantics. When a method is called *by value*, the method sees a copy of any primitives passed to it. Therefore, any changes the method makes to those values have no effect on the caller's variables. This requirement also applies to object references passed as parameters. The callee cannot change the caller's referenced fields and objects. For clients and enterprise beans colocated in the same container and when the parameter and return values contain large data structures, CBV marshaling/demarshaling is a significant performance overhead. To overcome this performance bottleneck, EJB V2.0–compliant containers now allow enterprise beans to define local home and local interfaces that the container will use to perform call-by-reference (CBR) rather than CBV to bypass marshaling/demarshaling of parameters and return values. When a method is called *by reference*, the callee sees the caller's original fields and objects passed as parameters, not copies. References to the callee's objects are treated the same way. Thus, any changes the callee makes to the caller's fields and objects affect the caller's original fields and objects. Regardless of whether an enterprise bean is called via a remote, home, local, or local home interface, the container still performs all required security operations, including authorization, as described in Section 5.4 on page 184.

5.2.1.2   *Scenario*
Listings 5.1, 5.2, and 5.3 show the code fragments for a simple entity bean.

- Listing 5.1 shows the home interface and the methods to create, locate, and destroy beans of this type.

- Listing 5.2 shows the remote interface and the methods for performing operations on the bean instances.

- Listing 5.3 shows the code for implementing the enterprise bean, including the implementations for some of the home methods.

CMP is assumed, to simplify the example. Listing 5.1 shows a simplified example of a home interface.

Listing 5.1. `TravelerCreditCardHome.java`

```
import javax.ejb.EJBHome;
import javax.ejb.CreateException;
import javax.ejb.FinderException;
import javax.ejb.RemoveException;

import java.rmi.RemoteException;


public interface TravelerCreditCardHome extends EJBHome
{
    public TravelerCreditCard create
        (TravelerId travelerId, String cardNumber)
        throws CreateException, RemoteException;

    public TravelerCreditCard findByPrimaryKey
        (TravelerId travelerId)
        throws FinderException, RemoteException;

    public void remove(TravelerId travelerId)
        throws RemoveException, RemoteException;
}
```

This interface exhibits three methods.

1. The first method will create and return a new `TravelerCreditCard` entry in the database by using a `TravelerId` as the primary key for the database query/update. This key uniquely encodes a description of a person booking a specific trip and will be sufficient to identify the credit card that will be used for the trip.

2. The second method takes a `TravelerId` as the primary key and performs a database query to return `TravelerCreditCard`.

3. The third method will locate and delete the record in the database.

In all cases, if an error occurs during the method invocation on the `EJBHome` object, specific `Exceptions` are thrown and must be caught by the client. Also note that the primary key class, `TravelerId`, must be serializable.

Listing 5.2 gives a simplified example of a remote interface.

Listing 5.2. `TravelerCreditCardInterface.java`

```
import javax.ejb.EJBObject;
import javax.ejb.EJBException;

import java.rmi.RemoteException;


```

```
public interface TravelerCreditCardInterface
    extends EJBObject
{
    public void debit(double amount) throws EJBException;

    public void credit(double amount) throws EJBException;

    public double balance() throw EJBException;
}
```

This interface exhibits three methods.

1. The first method charges the specified amount to the traveler's credit card and is called when the traveler needs to pay for travel arrangements.
2. The second method credits the traveler's credit card: for example, when a reservation is canceled.
3. The third method returns the balance—credits and debits—associated with the credit card.

In all cases, if an error occurs during the method invocation on the enterprise bean's business methods, an EJBException is thrown and must be caught by the client.

Listing 5.3 shows a simplified example of an entity bean.

Listing 5.3. TravelerCreditCard.java

```
import javax.ejb.EntityBean;

public class TravelerCreditCard extends javax.ejb.EntityBean
{
    public double balance; // value managed by the container

    public void debit(double amount) throws EJBException;
    {
        // Implementation code goes here...
    }

    public void credit(double amount) throws EJBException;
    {
        // Implementation code goes here...
    }

    public double balance() throws EJBException;
    {
        // Implementation code goes here...
    }

    // Other code goes here...
}
```

This entity bean exhibits the three implemented business methods as described by the remote interface (see Listing 5.2).

As described on page 76, security in J2EE is largely declarative, defined by the Deployer and the System Administrator, and enforced by the container rather than being encoded in the application. Leaving security out of the application enhances the application's portability. Conversely, portablity of an enterprise bean between container implementations or to newer versions of the container from the same vendor is diminished when the enterprise bean contains code that embodies security policy.

The EJB model has no API to influence the security context and the identity under which an enterprise bean method is executed.[1] Aside from adding optional comments into the EJB deployment descriptor, the Enterprise Bean Provider has no other obligations with respect to security.

To call an enterprise bean, a JNDI call locates the target enterprise bean and its stub, as shown in Listing 5.4. The presence of the stub allows RMI calls. It is the responsibility of the Deployer and the System Administrator to determine whether the principal executing the code is authorized to get the stub to invoke the EJB methods. The EJB container is responsible for authenticating the principal making the RMI request and authorizing the principal to invoke the requested method.

Listing 5.4.   Code Fragment Performing the JNDI Lookup

```
import javax.ejb.EJBException;

import javax.naming.InitialContext;
import javax.naming.NamingException;

import javax.rmi.PortableRemoteObject;

import java.rmi.RemoteException;


// Other code goes here...

InitialContext initialContext = null;

try
{
    initialContext = new InitialContext();
}
catch (NamingException ne)
{
```

---

1. JAAS is available inside J2EE. However, using the JAAS API should not affect the security context for the purpose of method invocation, as explained in this chapter.

```
        throw new EJBException
            ("Could not create an InitialContext", ne);
    }

    // Other code goes here...

    try
    {
        Object iclu = initialContext.lookup
            ("java:comp/env/ejb/TravelerCreditCard",
            TravelerCreditCardHome.class);
        TravelerCreditCardHome tcc = (TravelerCreditCardHome)
            javax.rmi.PortableRemoteObject.narrow(iclu);
    }
    catch (NamingException ne)
    {
        throw new EJBException
            ("Attempting to get TravelerCreditCardHome ", ne);
    }
    catch (RemoteException re)
    {
        throw new EJBException
            ("Attempting to get TravelerCreditCardHome ", re);
    }
```

The code fragment in Listing 5.4 shows the use of JNDI and RMI to locate and obtain the stub code for `TravelerCreditCardHome`. Note that each `Exception` is handled for unexpected errors. This makes the code more robust in the presence of network and other failures.

5.2.1.3   Security APIs for Enterprise Beans

Because the Enterprise Bean Provider has no security obligations, gaps do exist in the EJB security model. One of these gaps is the occasional need for instance-level or application-specific authorization. As is described later in this chapter, method-level authorization is provided. However, circumstances arise in which the application needs to apply additional security constraints or needs to obtain information about the security context under which the enterprise bean is executing.

Two APIs for security are found in the `javax.ejb.EJBContext` interface: EJB methods `isCallerInRole()` and `getCallerPrincipal()`.

We introduced the first security-related method, `isCallerInRole()`, in Chapter 3. This method returns a `boolean` indicating whether the caller is defined to be a member of an EJB security role. EJB security roles are discussed in Section 5.2.2.1 on page 177. Of the two security-related methods in the `EJB-Context`, `isCallerInRole()` is the most likely to work across container implementations and yield consistent results. Listing 5.5 shows how to determine whether the caller is a member of the Supervisor security role. The `debit()`

method may be called by a booking agent or a Supervisor. However, the enterprise bean wants to limit the agent's ability to place charges against the credit card. A call to `isCallerInRole()` will enable the method to determine whether a charge limit should apply.

Listing 5.5.   Code Fragment Showing Use of `isCallerInRole()`

```
import javax.ejb.EntityBean;
import javax.ejb.EntityContext;


public class TravelerCreditCard extends EntityBean
{
    EntityContext ejbContext;
    static double agentLimit = 10000.0;

    public void debit(double amount)
        throws AgentChargeLimitExceededException
    {
        // The customer credit card can only be charged up
        // to a limit by the booking agent. Higher charges
        // must be done by the Supervisor.
        if (amount > agentLimit &&
            ! ejbContext.isCallerInRole ("Supervisor"))
            throw new AgentChargeLimitExceededException();

        // Other code goes here...
    }

    // Other code goes here...
}
```

Application-specific authorization uses the `isCallerInRole()` method in the `EJBContext`. This examples shows how application-specific information can be combined with security information—the Supervisor security role—to constrain authorization to execute a method. The Supervisor role name must be specified in the EJB deployment descriptor.

The `isCallerInRole()` method takes a single `String` argument—the name of an EJB security role. Nominally, this is a problem. Each enterprise bean may use a different security role name to describe the same EJB security role. Or, two different enterprise beans may use the same security role name to describe two different security roles. The EJB container needs to know how to map the application-specified security role names to the runtime security roles. A `String` value used in an enterprise bean code to describe a role in the `isCallerInRole()` call is called a `role-name`. Part of the EJB deployment descriptor provides a mapping from `role-name` values to identifiers used by the EJB container. This mapping allows the Deployer and the EJB container to map nonidentical role names as may be found in different enterprise beans to a single security role name at deployment and runtime. The same mechanisms can be used to disambiguate the same `role-name` in different enterprise beans that use the same `String` value but are intended to have different runtime security roles. This mapping is described in Section 5.2.2.3 on page 179.

A fragment of an EJB deployment descriptor is shown in Listing 5.6, which illustrates an example of a `security-role-ref` entry defining a security `role-name` and a description of the purpose of the security role. This description is particularly important when the Enterprise Bean Provider is not also the Application Assembler, because it lets the Application Assembler know the purpose of the security role. This enables the Application Assembler to correctly define the security role mappings between the enterprise beans that are being brought together to form an application.

Listing 5.6.   EJB Deployment Descriptor Fragment for Security `role-name` Definitions

```
<enterprise-beans>
    ...
    <entity>
        <ejb-name>TravelerCreditCard</ejb-name>
        <ejb-class>
            com.travel.booking.TravelerCreditCard
        </ejb-class>
        ...
        <security-role-ref>
            <description>
                This security role should be assigned to
                employees who work in supervisory capacity.
                In particular, this role allows them to
                authorize large charges on customer
                credit cards.
            </description>
            <role-name>Supervisor</role-name>
        </security-role-ref>
        ...
    </entity>
    ...
</enterprise-beans>
```

In Listing 5.6, the enterprise bean is an entity bean called TravelerCreditCard whose class is specified. The `security-role-ref` element defines a security role's name and a description of the role's purpose as it is understood by the Enterprise Bean Provider. The `role-name` is a `String` value used as a parameter to `isCallerInRole()`. The description of the role's purpose is important communication between the Enterprise Bean Provider and the Application Assembler and, ultimately, the Deployer. Depending on how `isCallerInRole()` is used in the enterprise bean, poor communication of the intended use of the security role can have unintended consequences, including incorrect authorizations.

The second security-related method, `getCallerPrincipal()`, was also introduced in Chapter 3. This method returns a `java.security.Principal` object representing the caller as authenticated and defined by the EJB container's security subsystem. Listing 5.7 shows an example of obtaining the caller `Principal`. This method is not guaranteed to provide consistent results across container implementations from different EJB Container Providers, or vendors. In addition, the result of calling `getCallerPrincipal()` can be deployment specific, even from the same EJB Container Provider, as it depends on the user registry against which the users of the container are authenticated.

The EJB specification states that the `Principal` is the client's. However, the Deployer, System Administrator, and EJB container are all involved in defining credential mappings that affect the result of calling `getCallerPrincipal()`. For example, a client that authenticates using an X.509 certificate in its Web browser can be mapped to a Kerberos principal. The enterprise bean's call to `getCaller-Principal()` will return the Kerberos `Principal`, not the X.509 `Principal`. In a large enterprise or for interenterprise method calls, the identity mappings may be more complex. For this reason, we discourage Enterprise Bean Providers from using `getCallerPrincipal()` for making authorization decisions. Finally, even if a `run-as` identity is specified in the EJB deployment descriptor, `getCaller-Principal()` returns the client's `Principal`, not the `Principal` for the `run-as` identity.

Listing 5.7.   Code Fragment Showing Use of `getCallerPrincipal()`

```
import javax.ejb.EntityBean;
import javax.ejb.EntityContext;

import javax.rmi.PortableRemoteObject;

import javax.naming.Context;
import javax.naming.InitialContext;

import java.security.Principal;


public class TravelerCreditCard extends EntityBean
{
    EntityContext ejbContext;

    public void debit(double amount)
        throws AgentChargeLimitExceededException
    {
        Context initialContext = new InitialContext();

        // Get home interface of the employee database.
        Object lookupResult = initialContext.lookup
            ("java:/comp/env/ejb/EmployeeRecord");
```

```
        EmployeeRecordHome employeeRecordHome =
            (EmployeeRecordHome)
            PortableRemoteObject.narrow
            (lookupResult, EmployeeRecordHome.class);

        // Get the caller Principal and name.
        Principal callerPrincipal =
            ejbContext.getCallerPrincipal();
        String callerName = callerPrincipal.getName();

        // Not likely to be portable or work consistently
        // across all deployments.
        EmployeeRecord employeeRecord =
            employeeRecordHome.
            findByPrimaryKey(callerName);
        String businessRole =
            employeeRecord.getJobTitle();

        // The customer credit card can only be charged up
        // to a limit by the booking agent. Higher charges
        // must be done by the supervisor.
        if (amount > agentLimit &&
            ! businessRole.equals("Supervisor"))
            throw new AgentChargeLimitExceededException();

        // Other code goes here...
    }

    // Other code goes here...
}
```

The code fragment in Listing 5.7 shows how to get the caller's `Principal`. The use of `getCallerPrincipal()` is not likely to be portable and useful for authorization purposes in a container- and deployment-independent manner.

Finally, if you should choose to use `getCallerPrincipal()` or `isCallerIn-Role()`, the client security-context information is not available within all EJB methods. In particular, calling `getCallerPrincipal()` or `isCallerInRole()` is not supported if the following method calls are performed from within:

- The constructors of `javax.ejb.EnterpriseBeans`: stateful and stateless `javax.ejb.SessionBeans`, `javax.ejb.EntityBeans`, and `javax.ejb.MessageDrivenBeans`

- The `setSessionContext()` and `ejbRemove()` methods in stateless `SessionBeans`

- The `setSessionContext()` method in stateful `SessionBeans`

- The `setEntityContext()`, `unsetEntityContext()`, `ejbActivate()`, and `ejbPassivate()` methods in `EntityBeans`

Attempts to use `isCallerInRole()` or `getCallerPrincipal()` from EJB methods that do not support these calls should result in the throwing of a `java.lang.IllegalStateException`.

5.2.1.4   *EJB Runtime Restrictions*

J2SE is a rich programming environment, including extensive support for networking, file I/O, and multithreading. However, in the context of high-performance transaction processing, many of the J2SE features conflict with the transaction-processing objectives. Therefore, a number of programming restrictions must be followed[2] in order to maintain portability of enterprise beans between containers and to preserve security. Some of these restrictions can be enforced by the EJB Container Provider; others are solely the responsibility of the Enterprise Bean Provider.

- Home, local, local home, and remote methods must not to write to static fields. This restriction includes modifying values referenced by static fields. The code fragment in Listing 5.8 shows disallowed modifications, both direct and indirect, of static fields.

Listing 5.8.   Enterprise Beans Are Not Allowed to Write to Static Fields

```
import javax.ejb.EntityBean;

import java.util.Hashtable;

public class TravelerCreditCard extends EntityBean
{
    static EmployeeKey emplKey = null;
    static Hashtable lookup = new Hashtable();

    // Other code goes here...

    public void debit(double amount)
        throws AgentChargeLimitExceededException
    {
        // The following line is an example of a value
        // modification of a static field that is not
        // allowed.
        emplKey = getCallerEmployeeKey();
```

---

2. These runtime restrictions are described in the EJB V2.0 specification, Chapter 24.

```
        // The following line is an example of a
        // modification of the state of a static field
        // that is not allowed.
        lookup.put(emplKey.toString(), emplKey);

        // Other code goes here...
    }

    // Other code goes here...
}
```

Writing to static fields can result in inconsistency in deployed enterprise beans. In some cases, all instances of an enterprise bean will run in a single container. In other cases, the enterprise bean instances will run in multiple containers. When an enterprise bean is deployed in multiple containers running on different JVMs, writing to static fields can result in memory leaks. This can happen when an enterprise bean loaded in one container in which a static field is updated is *passivated*—serialized to persistent storage—and subsequently *activated*, or deserialized, in a different container.

If the enterprise bean was written assuming that it would execute in a single JVM and release objects in the static field during its execution and if it is then executed in multiple containers, which are in different JVMs, the values stored in the static field may not be correctly released. An attacker, knowing that an enterprise bean writes values to a static field, can make repeated requests to the enterprise bean in an attempt to a generate lot of garbage in the static field. By doing so, the JVMs can reach their heap capacities and terminate, resulting in a denial of service.

Reading from static fields is acceptable and is often good software engineering style. For example, static fields can be used to hold references to constant information required by the application.

- Thread-synchronization primitives must not be used to synchronize the execution of multiple enterprise bean instances. An enterprise bean can be executed concurrently in multiple JVMs. Thread synchronization is not guaranteed to be supported outside the confines of a single JVM; therefore, thread synchronization in an enterprise bean will not have the desired effect. Also, an excessive use of thread synchronization is likely to degrade application performance and could result in deadlocks because the container also performs locking—for example, to guarantee transaction-processing ACID properties. An attacker, knowing that an application uses synchronization, can rapidly make repeated requests to the method that contains the synchronization. The synchronization forces serialization of the application and can result in a denial-of-service attack.

- J2SE AWT functionality must not be used to interact with a keyboard or a display. Enterprise beans are intended to be transactional, and the containers are designed to facilitate high-throughput transaction processing. Creation of AWT resources will consume memory and CPU cycles in the JVM running the enterprise beans, thus degrading performance. As such, interaction with a keyboard or a display will interfere with an enterprise bean's performance and throughput objectives. Therefore, containers do not support keyboard or display interactions. Additionally, enterprise beans run in servers. As such, they are not intended to have a keyboard or a display for end-user interaction.

- Attempts to perform file I/O operations via the `java.io` package are not allowed, including reading/writing via `FileDescriptors`. File system APIs are not well suited for a transaction environment. All I/O operations must be performed through the resource-manager APIs, such as JDBC, JNDI, JMS, and JavaMail. In particular, there is no assumption of an enterprise bean's having an operating system identity, so it is not clear under which principal any operating system resource would be requested. Because this can be a security violation, file I/O operations are prohibited to enterprise beans.

- The network socket operations listen, accept, and multicast are not allowed. Although enterprise beans are server objects, all inbound communication must be routed through the RMI-IIOP ORB. If an enterprise bean were to become a server via listen/accept operations, it would interfere with the objective of being a server for EJB client requests. Additionally, the security policy is likely to be violated, as all communication with an enterprise bean, including authentication and authorization requests, is supposed to be routed through the RMI-IIOP ORB and its method/role-based authorization mechanisms.

  An enterprise bean is allowed to be a network client. Requests must be made to other enterprise beans via RMI-IIOP, but access to other resource managers supported by EJB containers, including JDBC and JMS, may be over any protocol.

- Access to an enterprise bean's fields and methods not specified by the enterprise bean's home, local home, local, or remote interfaces are not allowed. This includes access via functions provided in the J2SE `java.lang.reflect` package. The home, local home, local, or remote EJB interfaces define the supported contract between a client and an enterprise bean. Access to an enterprise bean other than through its defined interfaces can violate security but is also bad software engineering practice, as the implementation of the enterprise bean could change, resulting in unexpected or incorrect values in the referenced fields or methods.

- The following operations are not allowed: obtaining a `java.lang.ClassLoader`, including the current `ClassLoader`; setting the context `ClassLoader` and the `java.lang.SecurityManager`; creating a new `SecurityManager`; stopping the JVM; changing the input, output, or error streams in `java.lang.System`; setting network socket factories and URL stream handlers; starting, stopping, suspending, and resuming `java.lang.Threads`, or changing `Thread` names or priorities. These functions are reserved for use by the container. Modification of any of these functions would undermine both security and the container's integrity.

- Security policy information in the container should not be interrogated or modified. This restriction includes the `java.security.Policy` implementation (see Section 8.3 on page 261). The container implements security and may use J2SE security mechanisms but may also include mechanisms that are not part of J2SE. There is no guarantee that enterprise beans using the J2SE APIs will get the correct or consistent information about the container's security policies. Interrogating the security policy can also create security exposures, particularly if the results of the interrogation were to be disseminated outside the container: for example, if they were sent to a Web client. This information would enable a malicious entity to better plan an attack against the container and/or enterprise.

- Loading native libraries is not allowed. Native libraries are not portable across all platforms. Also, native code may deliberately or inadvertently circumvent the container's security policies.

- The subclass and object-substitution features of the Java Serialization protocol are not to be used (see the Java Object Serialization Specification[3] for details). These features allow modification of values passed during RMI calls, such as calls to other enterprise beans, and can subvert security.

- The `this` object reference for an enterprise bean must not be passed as an argument or returned as a method result. This restriction can interfere with the container's management of the enterprise bean, perhaps causing unintended modification of the wrong instance of an enterprise bean. Instead, calls to `javax.ejb.SessionContext.getEJBObject()` or `javax.ejb.EntityContext.getEJBOjbect()` calls should be used to get the appropriate object to pass or return.

- Enterprise beans should not be allowed to set system properties by calling `System.setProperty()`. Instead, reading the value of a system property should be permitted.

---

3. The Java Object Serialization Specification is available at `http://java.sun.com`.

The EJB container can enforce some of the preceding programming model restrictions through the use of a J2SE security policy configuration. Such a policy configuration should unconditionally deny `java.security.AllPermission`, `java.awt.AWTPermission`, `java.io.FilePermission`, `java.net.NetPermission`, `java.lang.reflect.ReflectPermission`, `java.security.SecurityPermission`, and `java.io.SerializablePermission` and grant all code `java.util.PropertyPermission` `"read"`, `"*"`, `java.lang.RuntimePermission` `"queuePrintJob"`, and `java.net.SocketPermission "connect"`, `"*"`. These authorizations allow enterprise beans to be portable. However, some containers may allow the Deployer to grant some of the denied permissions.

5.2.2   Application Assembler

Like the Enterprise Bean Provider, the Application Assembler is an expert in modeling business models. Whereas the Enterprise Bean Provider is focused on implementing the business objects and rules, the Application Assembler is combining these business objects and rules into complete applications. The Application Assembler must have a broader perspective, being knowledgable in transaction processing and security issues as they relate to the applications being assembled. This requires having at least some knowledge of the intended target environments into which the application will ultimately be installed.

The Application Assembler's responsibility is to assemble software components into an entire application that models an aspect of an enterprise. Once the Application Assembler has completed the assembly process, a deployment descriptor contains the information needed by a Deployer to install the application in one or more containers. Part of the process is creating a security view of the application. Creation of this view makes it easier to deploy the application, as fewer details of the application need to be known by the Deployer. For security, the Application Assembler

- **Defines a set of security roles for the application.**   The security roles (see Section 3.7.2 on page 67 and Section 3.8 on page 73) are distinct from EJB/J2EE platform roles (see Section 3.7 on page 64). Because the Application Assembler may not know the details of the deployment environment, the security roles define a logical view of the security environment, particularly, the authorization requirements for an application. Each security role represents a type of user of the application. Thus, security roles are logical roles and are defined independently from users or groups. A mapping of users and groups—principals—to security roles is made at deployment time. The security roles defined in a deployment descriptor for an application are limited in scope to the enterprise bean in a single EJB JAR file.

- **Define method permissions, or authorizations, for the EJB methods.**
  These authorizations (see Section 3.7.2.1 on page 68) are for the home, local home, local, and remote methods. Authorizations are defined with respect to the security roles.

The Application Assembler takes one or more enterprise beans from Enterprise Bean Providers and constructs a logical view of authorization requirements for the application. This logical view is provided as guidance to the Deployer and, subsequently, the System Administrator.

5.2.2.1   *EJB Security Roles*

The deployment descriptor contains a set of security roles whose scope is an EJB JAR file. The definition of a security role is provided in a `security-role` deployment descriptor element as part of the `assembly-descriptor` element and includes a `description` subelement and a `role-name` subelement. An example of an `assembly-descriptor` element with two `security-role` subelements is shown in Listing 5.9.

Listing 5.9.   Example of an XML `assembly-descriptor` Element in a Deployment Descriptor

```
<assembly-descriptor>
    ...
    <security-role>
        <description>
            This role is for the travel agency office manager or
            supervisor who has a master-key authority to perform
            any of the transactions allowed by any of the travel
            agents. In addition, this role is allowed to perform
            a number of financial transactions otherwise not
            allowed the travel agents.
        </description>
        <role-name>Manager</role-name>
    </security-role>
    <security-role>
        <description>
            This role is for each of the travel agents who book
            reservations and perform most of the financial
            transactions associated with the reservations.
        </description>
        <role-name>Agent</role-name>
    </security-role>
    ...
<assembly-descriptor>
```

This deployment descriptor fragment shows the definition of two security roles named Manager and Agent. The security roles scope to the applications in the EJB JAR file to which the deployment descriptor belongs. These security role names will be used in defining method authorizations.

5.2.2.2   EJB Method Authorizations

Now that the security roles are defined, it is possible to specify the authorization requirements for each of the methods of the enterprise beans in the JAR file. In particular, the `EJBHome`, `EJBObject`, `EJBLocalHome`, and `EJBLocalObject` methods of the session and entity beans need to have their authorization requirements defined in the deployment descriptor. To invoke one of those EJB methods, the calling principal must be a member of one of the security roles defined in the deployment descriptor that is authorized for the requested method.

In the deployment descriptor, each `method-permission` element contains one or more security roles and EJB methods. This element defines the list of methods that can be accessed by a user granted one or more of the associated security roles. Security roles and methods may appear in more than one `method-permission` element in the deployment descriptor. The deployment descriptor fragments of Listing 5.10, 5.11, and 5.12 demonstrate how to specify EJB methods in the deployment descriptor. Basically, there are three ways to specify EJB methods.

1. The EJB name is specified, along with the wildcard character, *, as the method name. This indicates that all methods are included.

Listing 5.10. How to Include All the Methods of an Enterprise Bean

```
<method>
    <ejb-name>TravelerCreditCard</ejb-name>
    <method-name>*</method-name>
</method>
```

2. The EJB name is specified, along with a method name. This indicates that only the specified methods should be included. If the method name is overloaded and multiple methods have the same name, all the methods are included.

Listing 5.11. How to Include all the Methods with a Given Name in an Enterprise Bean

```
<method>
    <ejb-name>TravelerCreditCard</ejb-name>
    <method-name>debit</method-name>
</method>
```

3. The method name and its parameter(s) are specified. If more than one method had the same name, this element disambiguates the methods. The `method-param` element must be repeated for each of the method's parameters.

Listing 5.12. How to Include a Specific Method of an Enterprise Bean

```
<method>
    <ejb-name>TravelerCreditCard</ejb-name>
    <method-name>debit</method-name>
    <method-params>
        <method-param>double</method-param>
    </method-params>
</method>
```

The deployment descriptor fragment of Listing 5.13 shows that a principal in the role of an Agent is authorized to debit a customer's credit card. Also, a Manager is authorized to perform any operation on methods in the TravelerCredit-Card bean.

Listing 5.13. Deployment Descriptor Fragment Showing how to Assign Security Roles to Methods

```
<method-permission>
    <role-name>Agent</role-name>
    <method>
        <ejb-name>TravelerCreditCard</ejb-name>
        <method-name>debit</method-name>
    </method>
</method-permission>
<method-permission>
    <role-name>Manager</role-name>
    <method>
        <ejb-name>TravelerCreditCard</ejb-name>
        <method-name>*</method-name>
    </method>
</method-permission>
```

If the `role-name` were to be replaced by an `unchecked` element, the method(s) are authorized for every security role. Similarly, if `role-name` were replaced by an `exclude-list` element, no one would be authorized to call the method, even if there were other declarations containing roles for the same method.

5.2.2.3 Linking EJB Security Roles to Role References

The last step is to link the ejb-jar-scoped security roles, as defined by the Application Assembler, to the role references defined by the Enterprise Bean Provider.

This requires mapping the `security-role` elements to the `security-role-ref` elements. This is done with the `role-link` element, as is shown in Listing 5.14.

Listing 5.14. Tying a Security Role to a Security Role Reference

```
<enterprise-beans>
    ...
    <entity>
        <ejb-name>TravelerCreditCard</ejb-name>
        <ejb-class>
            com.travel.booking.TravelerCreditCard
        </ejb-class>
        ...
        <security-role-ref>
            <description>
                This security role should be assigned to
                employees who work in supervisory capacity. In
                particular, this role allows them to authorize
                large charges on customer credit cards.
            </description>
            <role-name>Supervisor</role-name>
            <role-link>Manager</role-link>
        </security-role-ref>
        ...
    </entity>
    ...
</enterprise-beans>
```

This deployment descriptor fragment is the same as in Listing 5.6 on page 169, with the addition of the `role-link` element that ties the TravelerCreditCard security role Supervisor to the ejb-jar file's Manager security role. When called by a principal having the Manager role, the method `isCallerInRole("Supervisor")` returns `true`. It is the responsibility of the container to map the Manager security role to the role name Supervisor as appropriate during the execution of TravelerCreditCard.

5.2.2.4 EJB Principal Delegation

Sometimes, the Application Assembler knows that after a caller has been authenticated and authorized to execute a method, the method should be run using a specific principal, regardless of who the caller was. This is done by using the `run-as` element. The `run-as` identity applies to all methods in an enterprise bean and is used when making subsequent calls from the enterprise bean. The identity of the caller remains unaffected and is still used for authorization to access the enterprise bean's methods. The `run-as` identity is a logical security role name, as the Application Assembler does not know the deployment environment. The `run-as` identity refers to one of the security roles defined by the Application Assembler in the deployment descriptor. The Deployer, using the deployment tools, may be required to assign a principal to this security role at deployment time. Listing 5.15 shows a deployment descriptor fragment illustrating how to use the `run-as` element.

Listing 5.15. Specifying the Identity for Method Execution Using the `run-as` Element

```
<enterprise-beans>
    ...
    <entity>
        <ejb-name>TravelerCreditCard</ejb-name>
        ...
        <security-identity>
            <run-as>
                <role-name>Credit-Card-Agent</role-name>
            </run-as>
        </security-identity>
        ...
    </entity>
    ...
</enterprise-beans>
```

The role name specified in the `role-name` element indicates the security role that will be mapped at deployment time to the principal that will be used for execution of the methods in the enterprise bean.

5.2.3   Deployer

To run an enterprise bean, its ejb-jar file must be deployed into an operational environment. That environment includes the EJB container and the security platform in which the enterprise bean will be operating. To deploy the enterprise bean, the Deployer will be using tools supplied by the EJB Container Provider. These tools process the ejb-jar file's deployment descriptor, as prepared by the Application Assembler, and map the users and groups within the operational environment to the security roles described in the deployment descriptor. The steps in the deployment process are as follows.

1. The Deployer processes the enterprise bean's ejb-jar file, including the deployment descriptor and the security roles and method authorizations as defined by the Application Assembler. The deployment descriptor definitions of security roles and method authorizations are mere recommendations. Ultimately, it is the responsibility of the Deployer to decide whether the Application Assembler's recommendations are reasonable for the deployment environment. The Deployer must make whatever changes are needed to the security role definitions and/or the method authorizations that are appropriate for the deployment environment. The Deployer also specifies which principals are to be granted the security roles.

2. The Deployer is responsible for configuring the EJB container to install and execute the enterprise bean.

3. The Deployer configures the network environment to contain the RMI stubs the client needs in order to communicate with the enterprise bean via the EJB container.

4. Finally, the Deployer provides the necessary directory services, such as JNDI, to enable locating the deployed enterprise bean.

The EJB Container Provider supplies tools for security management at deployment time, as well as for the System Administrator for ongoing security administration of the enterprise beans and container runtime environment. The tools may include support for mapping of principals, such as users and groups, between security realms when more than one security realm is involved in the deployment of the applications. The output of the deployment is container specific.

5.2.4   System Administrator

The Deployer takes one or more assembled ejb-jar files from the Application Assemblers and deploys, or installs, them in one or more EJB containers. This process includes mapping identities from the client to EJB security roles and may include configuration management across multiple security domains. The System Administrator is responsible for overall management of security in the operational environment. In particular, the System Administrator is responsible for configuration of security domains and ongoing user- and group-identity management: defining users and groups, mapping them to the EJB security roles, and providing principal mapping across security domains within the enterprise or between enterprises, as appropriate. When an audit-trail capability is provided by the EJB container, the System Administrator is responsible for management of the facility.

5.2.5   EJB Container Provider

Once an enterprise bean is deployed, it is the responsibility of the container to enforce the security policy defined by the Application Assembler and/or the Deployer. The J2EE specification does not prescribe how containers provide security. However, the container is responsible for principal authentication, access authorization for EJB method calls, resource manager access, and secure communication, including privacy and integrity, with remote clients.

One of the primary responsibilities of the EJB container is the establishment of a security context so that it can be correctly propagated in a chain of EJB calls. In particular, this is necessary to enable the `getCallerPrincipal()` method in the `EJBContext` interface to get the correct result when there is a chain of calls between enterprise beans or calls to resource managers. If principal delegation is used to specify an identity under which an enterprise bean's method should execute, the container must support this identity and be able to propagate it for subsequent calls to enterprise beans and resource managers.

Part of the EJB container's establishment of the security context includes support for the `EJBContext isCallerInRole()` and `getCallerPrincipal()` methods. For `isCallerInRole()`, the container must correctly map the role names, as defined by the Enterprise Bean Provider, to the role names defined by the Application Assembler and the Deployer. All the mappings are transparent to the Enterprise Bean Provider and the Application Assembler, thus making their jobs simpler and enabling greater portablity of applications between containers and deployment environments.

5.3 Authentication

The EJB specification does not directly address the issue of authentication and the authentication process. Most of the specification deals with authenticated principals and the actions they can take, such as invoking EJB methods. In most respects, the model follows a simplified version of the Common Object Request Broker Architecture (CORBA) security model. Authentication is the responsibility of the EJB container and could be implemented using JAAS, as described in Chapter 9 on page 289. It is the EJB Container Provider's responsiblity to use, as appropriate, existing authentication mechanisms provided by the underlying platforms or security providers.

In the CORBA authentication model, an ORB, such as RMI-IIOP, receives a method invocation request and examines the security attributes of the request prior to method dispatch. If the principals are authenticated, the process moves on to the authorization phase.

Aside from the authorization process, the result of authentication appears in several places. In particular, EJB technology includes the concept of a security role. A security role is a set of J2EE permissions to make it easier for the Deployer and the System Administrator to administer authorization. When a client attempts to access an EJB method, the calling principal is logically assigned to zero or more security roles defined by the application, as configured by the Deployer.

For the Enterprise Bean Provider, authenticated-user information appears in two methods in the `EJBContext` interface, as described in Section 5.2.1.3 on page 167.

1. The first method conveying user information is `isCallerInRole()`. After the requesting principal is authenticated, the principal is assigned one or more security roles. If authorization is successful, the target enterprise

bean method is invoked. During the execution of the EJB method, the enterprise bean code can determine whether the caller is a member of a specific security role. The EJB container evaluates whether the user is granted the role, based on the mapping between the `String` argument to the `isCallerInRole()` method and the roles declared in the enterprise bean's deployment descriptor.

2. The second method, `getCallerPrincipal()`, returns a `Principal` object representing the authenticated principal currently executing the enterprise bean. The result of `getCallerPrincipal()` is implementation specific and is discussed in Section 5.5.

From an authentication perspective, the EJB Container Provider is responsible for providing tools and runtime support for

- The EJBContext methods `getCallerPrincipal()` and `isCallerIn-Role()`
- Security role name mappings as defined in the EJB deployment descriptor
- Tools for the Deployer and the System Administrator to perform security administration, including security role mapping and assignment of roles to principals or user groups
- Principal authentication and delegation support in the ORB

5.4   Authorization

Much of EJB security is concerned with authorization. In general, access to a deployed enterprise bean is via an ORB, such as RMI-IIOP. EJB authorization is based on a simplified CORBA security model, through which it is possible to establish whether an authenticated principal is authorized to invoke a method accessible via the ORB. The only architected means for a calling client to call a method on an enterprise bean is by calling it through RMI-IIOP.

As described in Section 5.2.2.1 on page 177 and Section 5.2.2.2 on page 178, the deployment descriptor defines security roles that are authorized to execute each of the EJB methods. If a method anywhere in the deployment descriptor is part of an `exclude-list` element, the method is not accessible from outside the bean itself, so requests from clients to call the method are rejected. Conversely, if a method name appears under the `unchecked` element, any client is authorized to call the method. When a method has more than one security role associated with it, any authenticated client that is a member of one or more of the security roles required for the method is authorized to call the method. The client need not be a member of all the security roles but must be a member of at least one security role.

EJB clients are constrained in how they are allowed to manage their security contexts, as these affect authorization.

- Transactional clients are not allowed to change their principal within a transaction.

- Session bean clients are not allowed to change their principal for the duration of communication with the session object.

- Finally, if a request for a specific transaction arrives from multiple clients, all the clients must have the same security context.

5.5 Delegation

Delegation is the process of forwarding a principal's credentials along with associated tasks that the principal originated or is having performed on its behalf. The EJB specification does not define how delegation is to be handled, as it is tied to a specific container implementation. Other than the `run-as` deployment descriptor element, delegation is left as a container tools issue. If Deployers and/or System Administrators enable delegation, they must configure their delegation policies in order for the EJB container to comply with the security policies of the enterprise.

When a Deployer configures an enterprise bean for a container, the container tools provide any necessary interfaces to configure delegation. One notable problem with delegation is that the `getCallerPrincipal()` method in the `EJB-Context` interface is ill defined. In general, the Enterprise Bean Provider will not know the delegation configuration in the deployment environment. Also, the EJB specification does not indicate who the *caller principal* really is; it could be the client initiating the original call to the EJB container, or it could be the immediate caller to an enterprise bean instance. If delegation is enabled, the result of `get-CallerPrincipal()` may not be the principal that the Enterprise Bean Provider expected when the enterprise bean was being written.

Along with authentication, it is the responsibility of the EJB container implementation to enforce the policies defined and supported within the environment. The EJB container can use the JAAS technology to implement delegation policies. As described in Section 9.3.1 on page 314, the method `doAs()` in class `javax.security.auth.Subject` can be used to execute code under the identity of the specified `Principal`. As this is not yet a part of the EJB specification, an Enterprise Bean Provider cannot yet expect the same behavior when the enterprise beans are deployed in different EJB containers, as these may exhibit different authentication mechanisms and delegation support.

5.6   Security Considerations

Although not specifically a security consideration, the EJB programming model constrains an enterprise bean to a limited set of resources. Specifically, in a J2SE environment, an enterprise bean is prohibited from using many Java resources as a result of EJB's isolation architecture. This architecture scales well in a multi-process and multithreaded WAS environment. Each enterprise bean needs to be designed to run by itself and not interfere with other enterprise beans. For example, enterprise beans must not include native method calls, as native code could adversely affect other enterprise beans, as well as be nonportable. This also means that enterprise beans must not write to static fields or attempt to share state with other enterprise beans except via remote method calls or via resource managers, such as JDBC and JMS. Note that because the EJB container is middleware and acts as a broker, it can make native calls and use restricted Java resources.

Given the isolation architecture of EJB components, each enterprise bean needs to interact with other enterprise beans via remote method calls. As the interaction will be location independent and may cross machine boundaries, it is important to define and enforce a secure association mechanism between EJB components. The channel of communication should provide data confidentiality and integrity. Using SSL communication between the EJB containers may address these requirements. It is also important for the security context associated with the client enterprise bean to be passed on to the target enterprise bean so that the identity of the client gets propagated through the invocation. A mechanism that achieves secure association between the client and the target EJB components needs to address the quality-of-service requirements.

CHAPTER 6

Enterprise Java Security Deployment Scenarios

THE J2EE security model forms a fundamental building block for secure enterprise systems. Such a specification needs to be backed by the solid and secure implementation of a J2EE product and applications hosted within a topology that provides enterprise-level security. The topology considers the common practice whereby business-critical data and applications are shielded from direct Internet access. J2EE applications that make up an enterprise solution should be partitioned and deployed into an environment that considers the security requirements of the enterprise. In addition to J2EE Web application servers, most enterprise environments consist of legacy or other applications accessed through the Java applications. Each of these environments must take the security of non-J2EE products into consideration while ensuring that no part of the environment is exposed owing to lack of security enforcement.

This chapter identifies deployment patterns within enterprise environments. It discusses how firewalls are used to create secure zones, based on the assumption that the farther a zone is from the direct Internet access, the more difficult it should be to access security-sensitive information stored in that zone. If contents are served at the edge of the network, a security policy can be enforced by placing secure reverse proxy servers that ensure a level of authentication and authorization before the content gets served. In the presence of enterprise environments in which various systems are integrated, resource adapters are an important part of the enterprise system. Even if some of the systems that are connected through resources do not have built-in security mechanisms, external network solutions can be used to provide a secure environment. These solutions include using firewalls to isolate zones, using Internet Protocol Security (IPSec), and building virtual private networks (VPNs).

6.1   Planning a Secure-Component System

Identifying the components that need to be secured is an important first step in designing a secure environment. Next, mechanisms that can be used to secure those components need to be identified. In practice, it is then necessary to understand which mechanisms are to be put together to secure the components, thus giving rise to a secure deployment scenario.

In a typical three-tier distributed-computing environment, such as the one represented in Figure 6.1, the presentation logic front ends the business logic. The business-logic layer hosts business applications, interacts with the data tier, and computes the results that will be delivered to the presentation-logic layer. Typically, security sensitivity increases from the first layer toward the last. Such partitioning into zones helps define the security requirements for the environment and the design of the topology to host the components.

In a J2EE environment, the three-tier computing model can be extended to reflect a four-tier model, in which servlets and JSP files form the presentation layer, enterprise beans provide the business-logic abstraction, and the data is stored in the data source layer connected through resource adapters. This four-tier model is depicted in Figure 6.2.

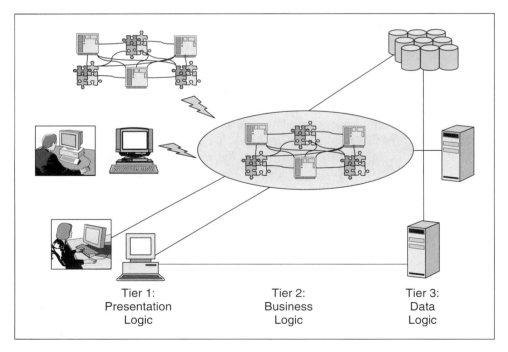

Tier 1:	Tier 2:	Tier 3:
Presentation	Business	Data
Logic	Logic	Logic

Figure 6.1.   Typical Three-Tier Distributed-Computing Environment

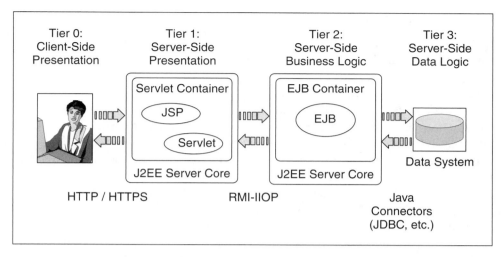

Figure 6.2. J2EE Four-Tier Computing Model

The protocols of communications indicated in Figure 6.2 are as follows.

1. Typically, the client- and server-side presentation layers communicate with each other using HTTP. When confidential information is involved, HTTP can be encrypted using the SSL protocol. HTTP over SSL is known as HTTPS.

2. The server-side presentation and business-logic layer communicate using Java RMI-IIOP.

3. The server-side business-logic and data-logic layers communicate through a Java connector, such as JDBC.

6.1.1   Client Access

Access to an enterprise application is achieved through a variety of client applications. In the context of J2EE, the most common access is through HTTP or IIOP clients. Increasingly, other types of clients are including messaging clients and Web Services clients. The security model of an end-to-end flow must include the capabilities of the end client. In the context of HTTP, client access is over HTTPS routed through a firewall. In the case of IIOP thick clients,[1] security is enforced through the Common Secure Interoperability Version 2 protocol.

---

1. Clients become *thicker* as they use increasing bandwidth and processor power. They become *thinner* as their transmission media decreases bandwidth and portability of devices decreases processing power. Typically, with thin-client computing, the bulk of the processing is not done at the mobile-client level, leaving this task to faster, more powerful controllers.

6.1.2   Presentation Layer

In discussing the presentation layer, we have to distinguish the presentation of static content from the presentation of dynamic content.

6.1.2.1   *Static Content*

When businesses initially connected to the Internet, the Internet was used primarily to share information that was considered public in nature. Such information was usually uploaded at predetermined intervals to the Web server and hence was considered to be static information. Because the information was public, restricting viewing access was not necessary. However, it was important to prevent unauthorized modification of that information. For example, if anyone were allowed to make modifications to a company's mission statement, it could be distorted to affect the company's business. Therefore, although information may be intended to be public and anyone can read it, steps should be taken to ensure that modification and deletion are restricted.

6.1.2.2   *Dynamic Content*

Dynamic Web content is used to tailor an individual's interactions with a Web site and provide users with more interactive information. Dynamic content may be rendered in various forms, including static HTML files or dynamic JSP files rendered using Java servlets in a J2EE environment. Those servlets may invoke business-logic applications hosted in a back-end tier to access business data, so that the data can be presented to the end user.

Depending on the design of such applications, it is possible that servlets go directly to the data source without introducing another layer of abstraction through enterprise beans. For example, servlets may use JDBC to access data in the back end directly, without necessarily encapsulating the business logic in an enterpise bean.

Even though servlets can perform such data access directly through JDBC calls, it is a recommended practice within J2EE environments to abstract out data access by using either enterprise beans or resource adapters, thereby providing a level of separation between the presentation layer and the business-logic layer. Because the presentation layer typically front ends access to the business logic, the presentation layer becomes a first important layer of defense in the access to business-critical data. Protecting servlets and JSP files thus becomes very important. Whether they are protected by a secure reverse proxy server that sits in front of the WAS and/or by the WAS itself depends on the environment topology and the corporate security policy and architecture.

6.1.3 Business Logic

EJB technology provides infrastructure for building business applications. These applications are accessible over the Internet or the intranet and can also be accessed through a variety of clients and client applications. Business-layer components provide the isolation of the presentation layer from the complexity of business logic: back-end resource adapters, connections, and legacy applications. This isolation aids in the design of deployment topologies by clearly delineating the requirements for authentication and authorization.

Connection from the business-logic layer to the back-end legacy applications is hidden from clients accessing the business logic. The connections between the business logic and the back-end applications are typically managed through Java connectors (see Section 3.4 on page 61). Security semantics of connecting to legacy applications are handled through the Java Connector Architecture (JCA), which provides the necessary adapters to those non-J2EE systems.

6.1.4 Resource Adapters and Legacy Applications

Many enterprise environments consist of applications that form the basis of their information technology infrastructure. These applications, known as *legacy applications*, are customized for enterprises and have been in use for a long time. In fact, these applications form the backbone of enterprise information systems and can manage such enterprise systems as banking-account, resource-planning and management, corporate-employee, human-resources, manufacturing-workflow, and inventory-control information systems. Legacy applications have helped streamline automated processes and work-flow systems.

J2EE defines a standard for accessing these data stores and legacy applications through the JCA. Though hidden from end-client applications, the business logic needs to be aware of the resource adapters used. In the case of bean-managed persistence, the enterprise bean is responsible for obtaining the information from the data store and applying the business logic. This is not necessary in the case of container-managed persistence, in which the EJB container transparently and implicitly manages the persistent state of the enterprise bean, and the enterprise bean developer does not need to code any database-access functions within the enterprise bean class methods (see Section 3.2.1 on page 58). The back-end databases and enterprise applications and systems can be protected by using their own proprietary security models.

Depending on the sensitivity of the data or legacy-application topology, access to the data store and applications is protected in a variety of ways.

- At one end of the spectrum is a privileged identity that is allowed access to all the sensitive parts of the EIS. Therefore, once enterprise beans are securely accessed, they are assumed to be allowed access to the data store or other non-J2EE applications under that privileged identity.

- At the other end of the spectrum is the requirement to propagate the identity of the caller, starting at the client, all the way to the back end where the data store or legacy application, which makes its own authorization decisions based on the caller's identity, resides.

By layering the business and presentation logic, it is possible to architect the system topology in a way that J2EE and non-J2EE system security can be carefully and deliberately considered.

6.2   Deployment Topologies

Partitioning a J2EE environment into four tiers as depicted in Figure 6.2 on page 189 helps define the security requirements for the environment and the design of the topology to host the components.

6.2.1   Entry Level

A simple topology in an enterprise environment consists of a DMZ where the Web server is deployed (see Figure 2.8 on page 31). Figure 6.3 shows how to build a DMZ in a J2EE environment. All requests from the Internet get handled within the DMZ, and only authorized requests are allowed to enter into the intranet. Based on the incoming request, the Web server routes the request to a WAS deployed behind the firewall. WASs behind the firewall host both the presentation layer and the business-logic layer. After successfully handling the request, the WAS sends a response back to the end user through the DMZ. This architecture is known as *entry-level topology.*

In the entry-level topology, the security of the environment is enforced by a combination of appropriate DMZ partitioning, firewalls, and configuration of security policies at the Web server and the WASs. In particular, in an entry-level topology, in which typically only one Web server handles all the incoming requests, the firewall policies can be configured in addition to the Web server and WAS security policies to restrict access to resources on the Web server. The firewall policies can be set up such that the firewall locks down a port, which can be used to connect to the systems within the intranet.

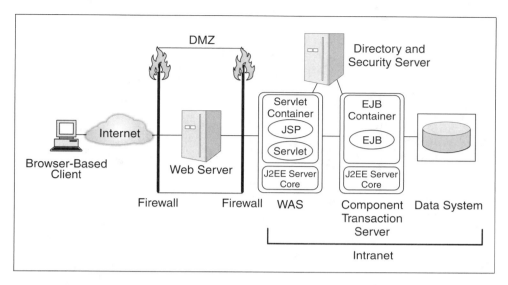

Figure 6.3.   Entry-Level Topology

6.2.2   Clustered Environment

In a *clustered environment* with multiple Web servers and with WASs deployed to handle requests to an enterprise, security requirements tend to be different. It may no longer be simple to lock down a port and host for a Web server or rely only on the firewall functionality to restrict access to WASs and transaction servers, as in the entry-level topology. Given that requests need to be load balanced across a set of servers within a cluster, care should be taken to make sure that when a Web server receives a secure request from a particular client, the secure session that the server establishes with the client can then be reused for subsequent requests.

A clustered environment contains multiple Web servers, WASs, and, possibly, multiple replicated directory and security servers. When a request arrives, it is typically handled by a load-balancing edge server.

In addition to load balancing the incoming requests, the edge server can filter the requests, based on the security requirements for the resources being accessed, acting as a secure *reverse proxy server*. Secure reverse proxy servers provide coarse-grained access control to the resource, in addition to the fine-grained control enforced by the downstream Web servers or WASs. Given the load-balancing characteristics of such an environment, WASs typically share some session state so that requests from a given user within a given period of time can be handled by any of the deployed WASs. Figure 6.4 shows a clustered environment topology in which the edge server also acts as a secure reverse proxy server.

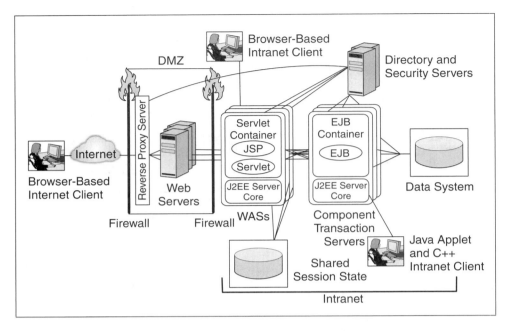

Figure 6.4.   Clustered Environment with Secure Reverse Proxy Server

In the case of intranet applications, clients can issue requests directly to the WASs. Some of these clients, known as *fat clients*, are typically nonbrowser applications, such as Java applications and applets, and C++ programs, as shown in Figure 6.4. An intranet application is sometimes accessible over a protocol specific to the application. For example, an enterprise bean can be accessed from IIOP clients within the intranet, whereas the same enterprise bean is accessed via IIOP from a front-ending servlet invoked by HTTP clients. Even in these cases, in which J2EE applications are accessed from within an intranet, the business-logic components need to be protected; the servers enforce access control by authenticating users over the application-specific protocol, such as IIOP, and enforcing the authorization policies associated with those applications.

6.2.3   Adding Another Level of Defense

A widely adopted deployment topology is to use a portal server as a presentation-layer front end to business applications. Depending on the sensitivity of the data in the back end and the corporate security policies, additional security constraints may be desired. In such cases, portal servers and WASs can be separated by a firewall that restricts the requests that can reach the business applications. As de-

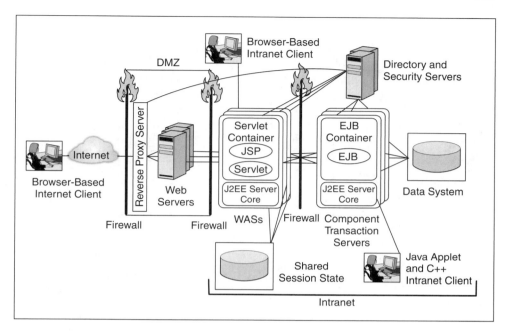

Figure 6.5. Clustered-Environment Topology with Additional Level of Defense

picted in Figure 6.5, such a firewall is placed between the portal servers and the WASs that host the business logic in the form of enterprise beans.

In order for a consistent security policy to be enforced, it is likely that the portal server and the WASs share the same set of security and directory servers. Given the desire not to have the security and directory servers in the DMZ, it is possible for the security and directory servers used in the DMZ to be a subset of the enterprise directory. In Figure 6.5, such servers are placed in a third partitioned zone, which hosts the business-logic and data systems.

6.2.4 Defending with a Secure Caching Reverse Proxy Server

It is possible to introduce a reverse proxy server at the edge of the network to provide high-performance caching capabilities. This *caching reverse proxy server* can enforce security policies that are consistent with the WASs' security policies. In this case, the caching reverse proxy server includes a security plug-in (see Figure 6.6) or is coupled with a separate security server. This coupling helps handle requests securely within a DMZ such that if a request ends up being cached in the caching reverse proxy server, a response can be sent right from the cache without compromising the security of the environment.

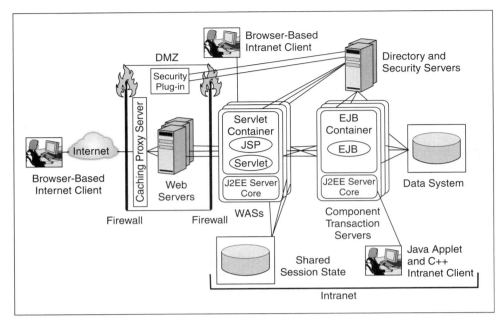

Figure 6.6.   Clustered Environment with a Caching Reverse Proxy Server and a Security
Plug-in

Access to a system or a legacy application usually requires that the user identity be passed to downstream requests. Often, this identity needs to be the same as
the user accessing the presentation- or business-logic layers. In some cases, the
identity needs to be mapped to a different value. For example, some business application environments require that database access control be based on the end
user accessing the presentation logic. In such cases, the credentials associated
with the user can be securely passed to the back-end server. An example of such a
credential is a Kerberos ticket.

In many scenarios, millions of users have access to a portal server. If
enterprise-application access is required, the number of users known to the legacy
application may be far smaller. In such scenarios, back-end applications need to
establish a trust relationship with the WASs so that the end users' identities are
filtered as the end users' requests traverse from the Internet to the back-end systems. At any such boundary—where the users known to a target server are different from or limited compared to those for a front-end WAS—some form of
identity mapping needs to take place so that an end user's credential, or identity,
can be mapped to a different one known and trusted by the target application.

Where J2EE servers host the business logic to access legacy applications or databases, translation of an identity accessing the business logic to another identity meaningful to legacy applications or data systems is handled by a JCA connection manager (see Section 3.12 on page 97). The JCA connection manager constitutes an additional layer, known in this topology as the *connector layer* (see Figure 6.7).

The mapping of an identity in a business-logic layer when accessing a data system depends on the target environment and the policies associated at the connector layer. The relation that dictates the mapping of identities at the business-logic layer to identities known to back-end systems can be a many-to-one relationship. For example, all the requests from an enterprise bean to a database may be performed under a single identity, say db2client, that is known to the database. Alternatively, in a many-to-some relationship, the identity used to access a back-end system will be based on some group membership. For example, all employess of a human resources department will be mapped to the hr_emp identity, which will be used to access the database, and users who have managerial privileges will be mapped to the manager_user identity. In some cases, an end-user identity needs to be conveyed to the back-end system, and in such cases, there will be a

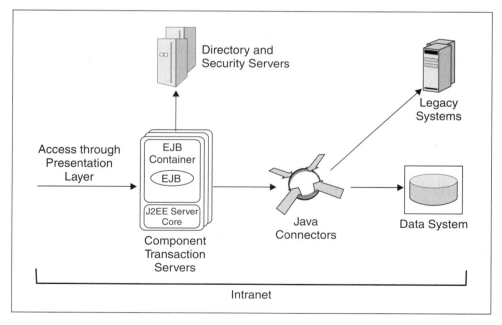

Figure 6.7. Clustered Environment with a Connector Layer

one-to-one mapping. For example, user Bob accessing a Web application will be mapped to his identity, `bob1`, on the database system when the application performs database access.

6.3   Secure Communication Channel

By providing layers of defense, authentication and authorization play critical roles in securing any environment. It is equally important to ensure integrity and confidentiality of information as it is propagated through data networks. Part of hardening the security of an enterprise environment is to ensure that all communication between the servers is over a secure communication channel. It is typical to use SSL when communication is over TCP.

6.3.1   HTTP Connections

When they connect to WASs behind the firewalls, Web servers typically use HTTP to route the requests. To ensure confidentiality and integrity, SSL is used. The resulting protocol is HTTPS. If such connections are long-lived and the SSL sessions are not frequently torn down, the SSL handshake overhead is minimal. Of course, encryption and decryption of every request has its own performance effect, but it should be considered in the context of the time the application takes to execute in the WAS and the payload size itself. For example, for an application that takes a long time to run, the time spent in encryption and decryption may be negligible. This should be combined with the fact that the time it takes to perform encryption and decryption is proportional to the size of the content.

6.3.2   IIOP Connections

If the enterprise beans are distributed across a set of WASs, it is also important to secure the communication between the WASs. These request invocations are performed as RMI-IIOP requests, so the communication can be secured by establishing an SSL session between the servers. Because enterprise beans are hosted within ORBs, the security context must be established between the ORBs. This can be enforced through the use of CSIv2, whereby ORB connections are handled per security requirements of the ORBs. The CSIv2 capabilities of a J2EE WAS can be configured to ensure that all the requests are over SSL. Additional tuning can be achieved by specifying the cipher suites that are acceptable or minimally required for these IIOP communications.

6.3.3   JMS Connections

Java Message Service is increasingly being adopted to enable message-driven enterprise applications. The JMS framework allows messaging providers, such as IBM WebSphere Message Queuing (MQ),[2] to be plugged in and used by J2EE applications. The JMS specification does not define any security functionality. The security of a messaging layer is dependent on the security capabilities of the JMS implementation. Therefore, when requests are sent over a JMS connection, care should be taken to secure the messages. For example, publishers should encrypt their messages, which should be decrypted only by trusted subscribers.

Messages sent over a JMS channel can be secured in at least two ways.

1. Security requirements can be addressed at the application layer, where the messages can be encrypted or digitally signed. In the case of standard message formats, steps should be taken to take advantage of the existing security capabilities. For example, SOAP messages can be secured using the Web Services Security specification (WS-Security), according to which the elements of a SOAP message can be encrypted and/or digitally signed. Note that WS-Security is not part of the J2EE specification. More details on WS-Security are given in Section 14.5.2 on page 506 and Section 14.6 on page 507.

2. Security requirements can be addressed by taking advantage of the built-in security capabilities of the message provider. For example, the encryption of the messages can be achieved by configuring the message endpoints, based on provider-specific mechanisms.

6.3.4   Connections to Non-J2EE Systems

As discussed in Section 6.2.4 on page 195, connections that are established between a J2EE environment and a back-end system are typically handled through Java connectors. The JCA deals with authentication requirements of the back-end system and expresses how credentials are passed to it from the J2EE environment. In addition, it is necessary to inspect each of the connectors and see whether the connection can be secured. This may be dependent on the capabilities of the back-end system. If connections are directly established from applications and not through the JCA framework, care should be taken to evaluate the security of such communications. For instance, a connection to a back-end LDAP directory can be configured to be over SSL.

---

2. Formerly known as IBM MQSeries. See http://www.ibm.com/websphere.

6.3.5   Exploring Other Options

Certain protocols of communications may be proprietary to an enterprise. Such communication channels may be difficult to replace with standard protocols, such as HTTP, or to provide encryption for. In these cases, network security mechanisms, such as VPNs and IPSec, must be evaluated. Because VPNs are configured at the network layer, they do not require changes at the application layer. This may help harden the security of a computer network and meet the security requirements of an enterprise.

6.4   Security Considerations

The administration of all the security policies and the security configuration is the basis for the successful use of any security products, enforcement of a security model, and successful use of deployment topologies. For example, if users are required to authenticate with user ID and password to an enterprise system, user registries must require that passwords be changed periodically.

The SSL protocol guarantees that the keys used during the handshake belong to the respective end points. Typically, certificate validity is performed by the SSL implementation. In other words, the SSL implementation is responsible for ensuring that the certificate has not expired, been revoked, and so on (see Section 10.3.4 on page 372). Some implementations of SSL go a step further to check whether that end point is the one that was originally given those keys; for example, those SSL implementations check whether the Domain Name Service name of the host making the connection matches the name in the certificate that is used.

Wherever SSL connections are established, the keystores must be administered securely. It is a good practice to generate certificates for internal use. Typically, these certificates are issued by a Certificate Authority specially established for a particular enterprise. Also, in systems in which certificates are used either to authenticate or to establish an SSL connection, certificates should be validated against certificate revocation lists.

It is important to understand that the security of an enterprise is not just about topology, secure communication, authentication, and access control. Enterprise security is also about administration of security policies and responsibility of the people who perform the administration. Technology provides tools to enforce the security policies. Any planning of security must also consider the trustworthiness of the administrators who manage the enterprise systems.

PART III

THE FOUNDATIONS OF JAVA 2 SECURITY

CHAPTER 7

J2SE Security Fundamentals

JAVA technology is not just for applets any more. Developers now use Java technology to build stand-alone, enterprise-class applications to enable disparate clients, such as workstations, personal computers, Java-based network computers, mobile telephones, and personal digital assistants, to access legacy databases and share applications across the network.

The J2EE security architecture builds on the basic characteristics of J2SE security. It is therefore helpful to understand J2SE security before studying the advanced features J2EE offers. This chapter describes the basic J2SE security model and introduces all the main concepts related to Java security. Chapter 8 discusses the Java 2 permission model, and Chapter 9 focuses on how Java Authentication and Authorization Service (JAAS) augments the basic permission model by providing user authentication and authorization. Readers who are already experienced with the basic J2SE security model can quickly glance through this part of the book or even skip it entirely. However, readers who do not have a solid background on J2SE security will find that this material will help them understand J2EE security.

The J2SE security model has evolved and matured over the years and has become very complex and articulated.

We begin this chapter by discussing access restrictions to classes, interfaces, methods, and fields. We then cover the *three legs* of Java security, which are three fundamental security components of the Java Runtime Environment:

1. **Class loaders.** Class loaders determine how and when Java programs can load code and are ultimately responsible for loading it. From a security perspective, class loaders ensure that system-level components within the runtime environment are not replaced with untrusted code.

2. **Class file verifier.** The class file verifier ensures proper formatting of nonsystem code by verifying that the bytecode does not violate the type-safety restrictions of the JVM, that internal stacks cannot overflow and

underflow, and that the bytecode instructions will have correctly typed arguments.

3. **Security manager.**   The security manager, implemented as an instance of `java.lang.SecurityManager`, enforces runtime access control restrictions on attempts to perform file and network I/O operations, create a new class loader, manipulate `java.lang.Threads` and `java.lang.Thread-Groups`, start processes on the underlying operating system, terminate the JVM, load non-Java libraries—*native code*—into the JVM, perform certain types of windowing system operations, load certain types of classes into the JVM, instantiate a new `SecurityManager`, change the current `SecurityManager`, access system and security properties, and so on. For example, the *Java sandbox*, which severely constrains downloaded, untrusted applets to a limited set of functions that are considered to be relatively safe, is a function of the `SecurityManager`. No more than one `SecurityManager` can be active at any given time in a JVM.

Figure 7.1 shows a simplified view of the JVM, from which we can see where the three security legs fit in the architecture of the JVM.

This chapter is useful for anyone who wants to understand the foundation of Java security. J2EE product providers in particular will find this chapter helpful in

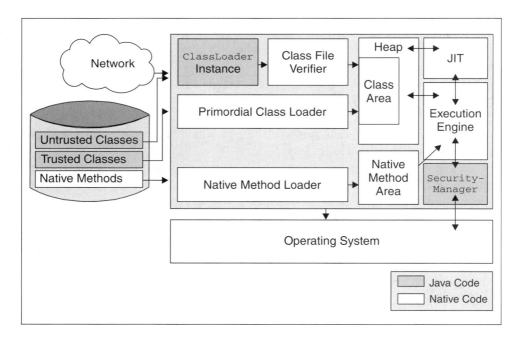

Figure 7.1.   JVM Components

understanding how they can customize class loaders and `SecurityManager` to achieve a more sophisticated control on the security implementation of their J2EE products.

7.1 Access to Classes, Interfaces, Fields, and Methods

The object-oriented Java language provides mechanisms for limiting access to classes, interfaces, fields, and methods. A class or an interface is said to be *public* if it is declared using the `public` keyword, in which case it may be accessed, using its qualified name, by any Java code that can access the package in which the class or interface is declared. A nonpublic class or interface may be accessed only from the package in which it is declared and is said to have *default access*. The effect of the `public` keyword on classes and interfaces is shown in Figure 7.2.

A class member—a field, a method, or a constructor—may be declared using at most one of the `public`, `private`, or `protected` keywords.

- A *private member* may be accessed only from within the class that contains its declaration. In particular, this means that this member may be accessed by any instance of that class type.

- A member that is not declared public, protected, or private is said to have *default access* and may be accessed from, and only from, anywhere in the package in which it is declared.

- A *protected member* of an object may be accessed only by the code responsible for the implementation of that object. To be precise, a protected member may be accessed from anywhere in the package in which it is declared, as well as from within any subclass of the class type that contains

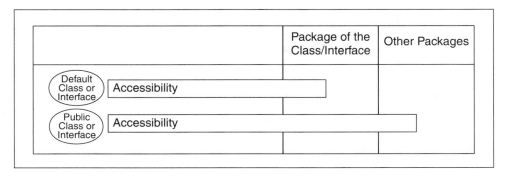

Figure 7.2. Access Restrictions to Classes and Interfaces

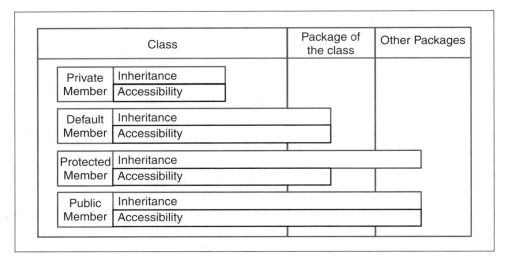

Figure 7.3.   Effect of Access Modifiers on Members

its declaration. This means that a protected member is less protected than a member with default access.

• A *public member* may be accessed by any Java code.

The effect of the access modifiers on class members is shown in Figure 7.3. Note that every field or method of an interface must be public. Every member of a public interface is implicitly public, whether or not the keyword `public` appears in its declaration. If an interface is not public, every one of its fields and methods must be explicitly declared public.

7.2   Class Loaders

A class loader is responsible for loading classes from a specific location. At runtime, multiple class loaders may be in effect at any given time. The set of classes loaded by a particular class loader is known as that class loader's *name space*.

To run a Java program, the JVM needs to locate and load into memory the classes comprising that program. In a traditional execution environment, this service is provided by the loader and linker utilities, which load code from the file system in a platform-specific way. In the JRE, things are complicated by the fact that code may be loaded from multiple locations, some of which may be remote, unsecure, or untrusted. Therefore, loading classes into the JVM at runtime has several security implications.

7.2.1   Security Responsibilities of the Class-Loading Mechanism

Class loaders are the gatekeepers of the JVM, controlling which bytecodes may be loaded and which should be rejected. As such, class loaders have a number of security responsibilities:

- **Name-space separation.**   Separating name spaces prevents intentional and unintentional name-clash problems.

- **Package-boundary protection.**   Class loaders can refuse to load untrusted classes into the core Java packages, which contain the trusted system classes and other restricted packages.

- **Access-right assignment.**   Class loaders have the ability to associate a set of authorizations with each loaded class. In Java parlance, an *authorization*, or *permission,* is the right to access a protected resource. In the Java 2 platform, authorizations are represented as objects of type `java.security.Permission`. The JVM administrator can use a security policy database to specify what `Permissions` loaded code is granted. This association is the basis for runtime authorization checking for access to resources.

- **Search-order enforcement.**   The class-loading mechanism enforces a search order that prevents trusted classes from being replaced by classes from less trusted sources.

The class-loading mechanism has another useful side effect. By controlling how the JVM loads code, all platform-specific file I/O involved in the loading of the classes is channeled through one part of the JVM, thus making porting the JVM to other platforms a much simpler task.

7.2.2   Levels of Trustworthiness of Loaded Classes

Java code can be loaded from various sources. Some of the more common sources, listed from most trusted to least trusted, are

1. The core classes that ship with the JVM: for example, those in packages `java.lang`, `java.io`, `java.net`, `java.util`, and so on. These are also known as the *system classes*. By default, system classes are the only ones to be considered fully trusted. As such, they are not subjected to any security restrictions; nor is their integrity verified by the class file verifier.

2. Any installed JVM extensions, such as cryptographic service providers (CSPs), XML parsers, and so on.

3. Classes stored in the local file system, usually found using the CLASSPATH system environment variable.

4. Classes retrieved from external sources, such as remote Web servers.

Given that code running on a JVM can come from trusted and untrusted sources, the class-loading mechanism must guarantee

- **Protection of trusted classes.** Clearly, a trusted system class should not be overwritten with an identically named class downloaded from a remote, untrusted location, as this would undermine the security of the entire system. For instance, the *default* SecurityManager class—the one in package java.lang—is responsible for a large part of the JVM runtime security and is a trusted local class. Consider what would happen to the JVM's security if the default SecurityManager could be replaced by a class loaded from an untrusted, remote site. The class-loading mechanism must therefore ensure that where a name clash occurs, trusted local classes are loaded in preference to remote or untrusted classes.

- **Protection against name collisions.** Especially where classes are loaded from remote locations, a deliberate or unintentional collision of names could occur, although the Sun Microsystems Java naming conventions[1] exist to prevent unintentional name collisions. If two versions of a class exist and are used by different programs loaded from different URLs, the JVM, through the auspices of the class-loading mechanism, must ensure that the two classes can coexist without any possibility of confusion occurring.

- **Protection of trusted packages.** The class-loading mechanism must protect the boundaries of the trusted class packages and sealed packages.[2] The core Java class libraries that ship with the JVM reside in a series of packages. Because the Java programming language grants special access privileges to classes that reside in the same package, a class that is part of the java.lang package, for instance, has access to other classes' methods and fields that are not accessible to classes outside of the java.lang package. If it were possible for a programmer to add extraneous classes to the

---

1. See http://java.sun.com.
2. When a Java package is *sealed*, all the classes defined in that package originate from the same JAR file. When a JAR file is *sealed*, all the packages defined in that JAR file are sealed. Whether or not a JAR file or a package inside it are sealed can be specified in the manifest file of the JAR file itself. Sealing a package is important because it guarantees that classes external to the JAR file where the sealed package is defined cannot declare themselves as part of that package.

java.lang package, those classes would gain privileged access to the core java.lang classes. This would be an exposure of the JVM and consequently must not be allowed. The class-loading mechanism, therefore, ensures that classes cannot be dynamically added to the various core-language and sealed packages. This result is accomplished by forcing class loaders to check with the SecurityManager every time a request comes to load a class in one of the system or sealed packages.

• **Name-space isolation.**   The class-loading mechanism is responsible for isolating unrelated mobile programs, by placing them in different name spaces. Each class loader is responsible for loading classes from a specific set of URLs. This allows different classes having the same fully qualified name but loaded from different locations to coexist without any possibility of confusion.

   As discussed in Section 7.2.3.2 on page 216, Java class loaders are organized in a tree structure, as shown in Figure 7.4. If two name spaces correspond to class loaders that belong to different branches of the class-loading tree, those name spaces are *isolated* from each other. Classes loaded into isolated name spaces cannot interfere with each other. For example, if classes *A* and *B* are loaded into two isolated name spaces, as shown in Figure 7.4, *A* cannot directly instantiate *B*, invoke static methods on *B* or instance methods on objects of type *B*, refer to static fields on *B* or instance fields on objects of type *B*, or subclass *B*. More important, *A* and *B* are totally unaware of each other's presence. For this reason, they could even have the same fully qualified name without any possibility of confusion.

As discussed in Section 7.2.3.2 on page 216, a correct implementation of the class-loading mechanism must enforce isolation for unrelated name spaces.

Figure 7.4 shows that the JVM may have many class loaders operating at any time, each of which is responsible for locating and loading classes from different sources. However, in general, these sources can be divided into two categories, trusted and untrusted.

7.2.2.1   *Loading Classes from Trusted Sources*

The *primordial class loader*, which is a built-in part of the JVM, is also known as the *internal*, or *null*, or *default class loader*. The primordial class loader is responsible for loading the trusted classes of the Java runtime.

Classes loaded by the primordial class loader are regarded as special insofar as they are not subjected to verification prior to execution. They are assumed to be well-formed, safe Java classes. In addition, they are not subjected to any security

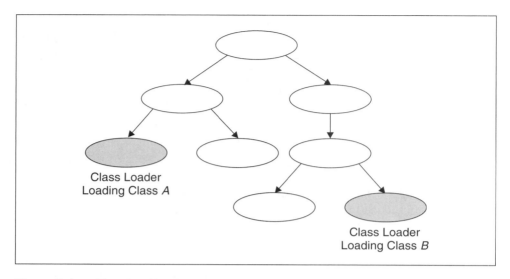

Figure 7.4.   Class-Loading Tree Structure

policy restrictions. In early Java versions, these classes were the JVM core classes, along with any classes that could be found using the CLASSPATH system environment variable. Obviously, if would-be attackers could somehow introduce a malicious class into the CLASSPATH of a JVM, they could cause serious damage. In the Java 2 platform, this exposure is minimized by removing the core-class path information from the CLASSPATH environment variable and subjecting all but the core classes to verification[3] and the security policy.

The core Java 2 classes are located by using a JVM internal property[4] whose value is called the *boot class path*. This internal property is formed internally from install information.[5]

---

3. In the J2SE reference implementation, it is also possible to subject the core classes to verification by using the -verify option of the java command or the -J-verify option of the appletviewer command.

4. In the J2SE reference implementation, this internal property is called sun.boot.class. path.

5. In the J2SE reference implementation, the boot class path can be specified at runtime by the java command option -Xbootclasspath, which becomes -J-Xbootclasspath for the appletviewer command. At compile time, the javac command-line option -bootclasspath is available to cross-compile programs against a specified set of boot classes.

Some J2SE and J2EE implementations allow a system administrator to extend the set of the system classes by placing custom classes in a particular directory.[6] Therefore, if a request arrives to load one of the classes from this directory, the primordial class loader will have responsibility for loading it. From a security point of view, two things should be noted. First, if a request arrives to load a class, this directory, as part of the boot class path, is inspected before the extension class path, application class path, and any remote location. Therefore, classes in this directory can potentially replace extension and application classes, as well as classes located in the network. Second, classes in this particular directory are considered fully trusted, just like the system classes. They will not be subjected to security policy restrictions, nor will the class file verifier check them for safety and integrity. It is therefore recommended to use operating system protections to make sure that only trusted users are allowed to create this directory and add files to it.

7.2.2.2 Loading Classes from Untrusted Sources

Classes from untrusted sources include application classes, extension classes, and classes from remote network locations.

Application Classes.   The Java 2 platform bounds the scope of implicitly trusted classes to only the Java core classes. User classes are not considered fully trusted and are not loaded by the primordial class loader. At JVM start-up, the *application class path* information is copied from the CLASSPATH environment variable into a JVM internal property.[7] This property is used to start an instance of java.net. URLClassLoader, an implementation of java.lang.ClassLoader.[8] This instance,

---

6. For example, in the J2SE reference implementation, this directory is called classes. The Java system administrator needs to explicitly create the classes directory under the JRE installation directory, which, for example, in a Java 2 SDK V1.4.1 installation on a Windows platform is by default C:\Program Files\Java\j2re1.4.1. Once created, however, the classes directory is automatically considered part of the boot class path. By default, the classes directory is the last location where the primordial class loader looks for classes. Note, however, that from Java 2 SDK V1.3 onward, the classes directory exists for use by the SDK only and should not be used for application classes. Application classes should be placed in a directory outside the SDK directory hierarchy. That way, installing a new SDK does not force you to reinstall application classes. For compatibility with older versions, applications that use the classes directory as a class library will run in the current version, but there is no guarantee that they will run in future versions.

7. In the J2SE reference implementation, the name of this internal property is java.class. path.

8. A note on terminology: From now on, we say ClassLoader when it is clear that the loader is an implementation of java.lang.ClassLoader. The term *class loader* is used only to refer to a generic loader, which may include the primordial class loader.

called the *application class loader*, is given a list of URLs generated from CLASS-PATH, which it will use to locate and load user classes. The application class loader is also responsible for associating the appropriate Permissions with the loaded class, based on the security configuration defined by the JVM administrator.[9]

Extension Classes. From a trust viewpoint, classes of the *extension framework* fall logically in between the fully trusted core classes, for which no policy Permission entries are required and no integrity and safety verification is performed, and the completely untrusted application classes, for which explicit policy Permission entries are required and integrity and safety verification is performed. This framework allows for the installation of JAR files in a specific extensions directory referenced by a JVM internal property.[10] The value of this property is called the *extension class path*.[11] A URLClassLoader instance, called the *extension class loader*, is created at JVM start-up and is responsible for loading installed extensions.

Extension classes are subjected to security policy restrictions as well as safety and integrity verification, just like application classes. However, by default, extension classes are typically granted java.security.AllPermission, corresponding to the right to access all the system resources. Therefore, system administrators should allow only trusted users to add files to the extension class path. System administrators can also decide to restrict the access rights granted to the extensions.

Classes from Remote Network Locations. In a Web environment, classes can be loaded from remote network locations. An additional ClassLoader instance is created to load remote classes from a specific set of URLs.[12] Classes from different URLs may result in multiple ClassLoaders being created to maintain separate name spaces. Therefore, there may be multiple instances of the same ClassLoader class at any given time.

On most networks, including the Internet, there are many Web servers from which classes could be loaded. Nothing prevents two webmasters from having

---

9. In most implementations, the application class path can also be set on the command line using the option -classpath (or -cp). This will override the CLASSPATH environment setting.

10. In the J2SE reference implementation, the name of this internal property is java.ext.dirs.

11. In the J2SE reference implementation, the extension class path by default contains only the subdirectory lib/ext of the Java home directory. However, this value can be changed at JVM start-up by using the java command-line option -Djava.ext.dirs and at compile time by using the javac command-line option -extdirs.

12. For example, the Java Applet Viewer application or a Web browser automatically create a URLClassLoader instance, called *applet class loader,* to load applet classes from one or more URLs.

different classes with the same name on their Web sites. Within a name space, duplicate fully qualified class names are prohibited; in other words, a given instance of a `ClassLoader` cannot load multiple classes with the same fully qualified name. If we did not have a specific `ClassLoader` instance for any URL from which classes are loaded, we would very quickly run into problems when loading classes with the same fully qualified name from multiple sites.

Moreover, it is essential for the security of the JVM to separate classes from different sites so that the classes cannot inadvertently or deliberately cross-reference each other. Imagine what could happen if a mobile program downloaded from a bank's Web site to manage financial transactions became accessible to another mobile program downloaded from a hacker's Web site. Classes from different sites are separated by preventing cross-visibility between name spaces corresponding to different URLs, as shown in Figure 7.5. Because classes from separate Web sites are loaded into separate name spaces for which there is no cross-visibility, a class loaded from a particular URL—the bank's Web site—cannot be accessed by a class loaded from a different URL—the hacker's Web site.

Classes loaded from remote network locations are considered fully untrusted. Therefore, they are subjected to the class file verifier's checks for integrity and

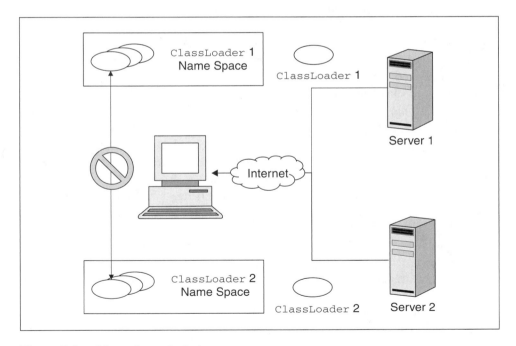

Figure 7.5. Name Space Isolation

safety purposes. In addition, by default those classes will run confined in the sand-box, unless the security policy of the Java system in which they are loaded grants them explicit `Permissions`.

The class-loading mechanism is also used in a J2EE environment to achieve isolation. Some J2EE implementations give system administrators the ability to isolate J2EE applications from each other by loading each J2EE application in a different name space. In other implementations, it is possible to isolate each module; this means that each Web or Enterprise JavaBeans module is loaded into its own name space. Additionally, name-space separation allows loading the same J2EE application multiple times, each time in a different name space.

7.2.3   The Class-Loading Process

It should now be clear that many types of class loaders can be within a Java environment at any time. In addition, multiple instances of a particular type of `ClassLoader` may be operating at once. In this section, we look at how all the class loaders cooperate to load classes in a secure manner. First, we consider the problem from a design viewpoint. Then, we show how that design is implemented in the Java 2 platform and how it should be implemented by any Java product needing to develop a customized class-loading mechanism.

7.2.3.1   *Enforcing the Correct Search Order: The Design*
In this section, we look at some of the design aspects of the Java 2 class-loading architecture. In other words, we describe what is supposed to happen from the viewpoint of the Java architects.

Let us assume that, at a certain time during the execution of a program, class *A*, which was loaded by class loader *x*, makes a reference to class *B*, as shown in point 1 in Figure 7.6. When class *B* is referenced, the JVM execution environment receives the request (point 2 in Figure 7.6) and invokes class loader *x*, associated with the requesting program *A,* to locate and load the referenced class (point 3 in Figure 7.6). Class loader *x* is associated with *A* because *x* was the class loader in-stance that loaded *A*'s class. Identifying the `ClassLoader` instance that loaded *A* is as simple as invoking the method `getClassLoader()` on *A*, as depicted in Figure 7.6. If *A* was loaded by the primordial class loader, invoking `getClassLoader()` returns `null`.

Once *x* has received the request to load *B*, *x* becomes responsible for loading *B* (point 4 in Figure 7.6). First, *x* checks whether it had already loaded *B*. Loaded classes are cached, and there is no reason to load them again. If *x* had already loaded *B*, *x* interacts with the `SecurityManager` to see whether class *A* has the `Permission` to access *B*. If *A* does not have the `Permission`, a `java.lang.SecurityException` is thrown. If, however, *A* has the right `Permission`, *x* returns a reference to the existing `Class` object.

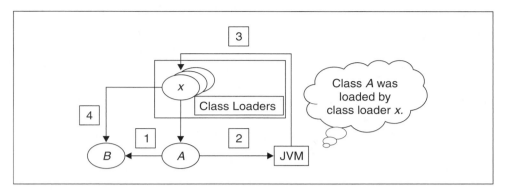

Figure 7.6.   Class-Loading Process Scenario

If *B* has not already been loaded, *x* invokes the SecurityManager to see whether *A* has the Permission to create the requested class, *B*. If it does not, a SecurityException is thrown. Otherwise, *x* first tries to find the requested class in the core Java API in the boot class path. This step prevents the JVM's core classes from being replaced by classes from another, less trusted location. If class *B* is found, it is loaded by the primordial class loader into the class area (see Figure 7.1 on page 204), and a reference to the Class object is returned to *A*.

If *B* is not found in the boot class path, *x* will try to find it in any JVM extensions located in the extension class path. If class *B* is found, it is loaded by the extension class loader into the class area, and a reference to the Class object is returned to *A*. Extensions are less trusted than the core Java classes but more trusted than the local application classes and the classes loaded from remote network locations. The mechanism we have described so far prevents extension classes from replacing the more trusted system classes and from being replaced by classes from less trusted locations.

If we have come to this point without finding *B*, *x* will look through the application class path before going to the network to locate the class. If it is found in the application class path, the class is loaded by the application class loader, and a reference to the Class object is returned to *A*. Otherwise, the ClassLoader responsible for finding classes in the network will look for *B* in the network locations from which it is responsible for loading classes. If this ClassLoader also fails to find the requested class, other user-defined ClassLoaders (see Section 7.2.4 on page 219) may be consulted to see whether they can find it in the other locations from which they are responsible for loading classes: for example, the ROM memory, a database, and so on. If none of the class loaders that received the request can find *B*, *x* will throw a java.lang.ClassNotFoundException.

If *B* is found, the class file verifier is responsible for making sure that the class file is well formed (see Section 7.3.1 on page 226). If the bytecode passes verification, the class is loaded into the class area, a `Class` object is created, and a set of `Permissions` is associated with the class for subsequent resource authorization checking. *B* is then linked by resolving any references to other classes within it. This may result in additional calls to *B*'s class loader to locate and load other classes. Next, static initialization of class *B* is performed; that is, static variables are defined and static initializers are run. Finally, the class is available to be executed, and a reference to it is returned to *A*.

The steps described in the preceding paragraph are performed regardless of the actual `ClassLoader` that loaded *B*. The only exceptional case is if *B* is one of the system classes in the boot class path, which ultimately implies that *B*'s class loader is the primordial loader. As system classes are considered fully trusted and safe to run, the primordial loader will not pass *B* to the class file verifier (see Figure 7.1 on page 204). In addition, given that system classes are implicitly granted full access to all the system resources, the primordial loader will not associate a set of `Permissions` with *B*. Except for these two security-related steps, the rest of the process is the same.

7.2.3.2   *The Class-Loading Delegation Hierarchy: The Implementation*

Every `ClassLoader`'s class, being just another Java class itself, is loaded by a class loader. The primordial class loader, which in general is not a Java class, is not loaded by any class loader and is generated at JVM start-up, and its primary function is to load the Java core classes. This forms a runtime parent/child hierarchical tree relationship between class loaders, with the primordial class loader at the root. This relationship is the basis for the *delegation model*, which is the recommended implementation model for all `ClassLoader`s. Every `ClassLoader` instance, on receiving the request to load a Java class, should immediately delegate the request to its *parent class loader*.

By default, when a program instantiates a `ClassLoader` object, the program's class loader becomes the `ClassLoader` object's parent. For example, in the J2SE reference implementation, the extension class loader is created at JVM start-up by one of the JVM's internal system programs, whose class loader is the primordial class loader. Therefore, the extension class loader's parent is the primordial class loader.

It is also possible to specify the parent `ClassLoader` explicitly via a parameter to the `ClassLoader`'s constructor. In this case, the specified `ClassLoader` is forced to be the parent. For example, at JVM start-up, in the J2SE reference implementation, the same system program that creates the extension class loader also creates the application class loader. Therefore, the primordial class loader should be the application class loader's parent. However, when the application class loader is constructed, the extension class loader is passed as a parameter to the constructor and becomes the application class loader's parent.

If a program creates a user-defined ClassLoader *x*, *x*'s parent is by default going to be the application class loader. The parent/child hierarchical tree relationship between class loaders in this scenario is shown in Figure 7.7.

The runtime parent/child relationship between class loaders always has the primordial class loader at the root and forms the basis for the recommended implementation of the class-loading design. Figure 7.8 illustrates the security advantages coming from the delegation model.

Figure 7.8 shows how the class-loading delegation model guarantees the following.

- A more trusted class cannot be replaced with a less trusted class having the same fully qualified name. In particular, system classes cannot be maliciously replaced with less trusted classes.

- A class *A* and its instances can directly reference a class *B* and its instances if both *A* and *B* are loaded by the same class loader, *x*. For example, any two objects of the same application can reference each other because their classes are part of the same name space. According to the delegation model, the request for *B* will percolate up to the primordial class loader and then down back to *x*, which will load *B*, unless this had already been loaded and cached, in which case it would be simply returned to *A*.

- A class *C* and its instances can directly reference a class *D* and its instances if *C* was loaded by a class loader *y* and *D* was loaded by any of *y*'s

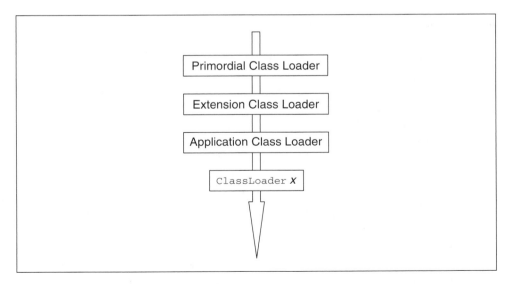

Figure 7.7.   Delegation Hierarchy Scenario

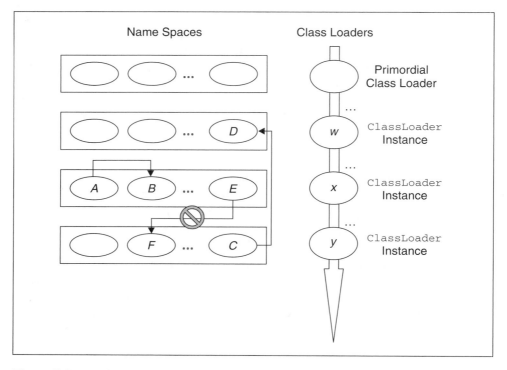

Figure 7.8.　　Referencing Classes in the Delegation Hierarchy

ancestor class loaders, *w*. For example, an application object can call `java.lang.System.out.println()` because the `System` class belongs to the name space of the primordial class loader, which is an ancestor of the application class loader.

According to the delegation model, the request for *D* will percolate up to the primordial class loader, unless *w* had previously loaded *D*, in which case *w* will be able to satisfy the request for *D* on receiving it, without having to delegate it. If, however, the request for *D* reaches the primordial loader, as *D* is not in the boot class path, the primordial loader will propagate the request for *D* back down through all the descendant `ClassLoader` instances recursively, until descendant `ClassLoader` *x* is found that can find the requested class in its own class path, load it, and return it.

- A class *E* and its instances cannot reference a class *F* and its instances if *E* was loaded by a class loader *x* and *F* was loaded by a class loader *y*, where *y* is one of *x*'s proper descendants. According to the delegation model, the request for *F* will percolate from *x* up to the primordial class loader and then back down back to *x* through all the descendant `ClassLoader` instances in the delegation chain recursively. None of these class loaders can find *F* because *F* is known only to *y*, and *y* is not a class loader in the delegation chain.

The class-loading delegation model additionally guarantees that programs whose classes are located in name spaces belonging to different branches of the class-loading delegation tree cannot reference each other, as shown in point 1 in Figure 7.9. This prevents cross-visibility and allows isolation between name spaces belonging to different branches of the delegation tree. Classes loaded in such name spaces are totally unaware of each other, as depicted in the scenario of Figure 7.5 on page 213. However, as shown in Figure 7.8, a class *C* and its instances can directly reference a class *D* and its instances if *C* was loaded by a class loader *y* and *D* was loaded by any of *y*'s ancestor class loaders, *w*. This scenario is also represented in point 2 in Figure 7.9. This implies that though isolated, two classes belonging to different branches of the delegation tree can still theoretically exchange information by setting and getting static state information on a program whose classes have been loaded by a common class loader ancestor. Therefore, developers of core and extension classes, whose class loaders are ancestors for all the other class loaders, should avoid writing classes whose state information can be mutated and subsequently retrieved by application code.

7.2.4   Building a Customized `ClassLoader`

Application writers, including JVM implementers and J2EE container providers, may subclass `ClassLoader` to handle the loading of classes from different sources—the Internet, an intranet, local storage, or perhaps even from read-only memory (ROM) in an embedded system—or to implement additional functions that built-in `ClassLoader`s do not provide. These functions may include security

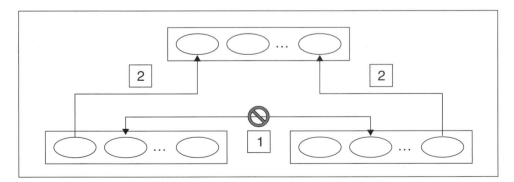

Figure 7.9.   Name Space Isolation through the Class-Loading Delegation Model

and auditing. Custom `ClassLoader`s are not a part of the JVM but rather are part of an application running on top of the JVM.

The ability to create additional `ClassLoader`s is a very powerful feature of Java technology and places a heavy responsibility on the `ClassLoader` implementer. This feature becomes particularly apparent when you realize that user-written `ClassLoader`s have the choice of following the delegation model or not. They get first choice on whether to load a class. They can even take priority over the primordial class loader. This enables a user-written `ClassLoader` to replace any of the system classes, including the `SecurityManager`. A customized `ClassLoader` could even refuse to pass a loaded class to the class file verifier for integrity and safety verification. In addition, because the `ClassLoader` is responsible for associating `Permissions` with each loaded class, a customized `ClassLoader` could decide to assign full access to all the system resources to any loaded class. This shows the high degree of responsibility that `ClassLoader` designers and developers have and justifies the reason why, in order to install a new `ClassLoader` at runtime, programs need to be granted a specific `Permission`.

Starting with the Java 2 platform, the JRE includes a `ClassLoader` implementation, `java.security.SecureClassLoader`, which implements the basic security-related requirements of class loading: checking with the `SecurityManager`, calling the class file verifier, linking the class, and associating it with the `Permissions` that the Java system administrator granted to the class. Its constructor is protected; `SecureClassLoader` is meant to be the basis for the development of other class loaders.

`URLClassLoader` is a general-purpose loader included in the core Java 2 API. `URLClassLoader`, a subclass of `SecureClassLoader`, has the ability to find and load class files from a list of URLs. `URLClassLoader` should meet most of the requirements an application may have for loading class files. If not, developers can easily develop their own `ClassLoader`s by subclassing `SecureClassLoader` or `URLClassLoader`, instead of the `ClassLoader` abstract class. This way, they can benefit from the function and security built into `SecureClassLoader`.

The Java 2 API also includes the `java.rmi.server.RMIClassLoader` class to support dynamic class loading with Java RMI. The methods in this class are static, so they can be called directly to load individual unsigned class files from a single URL. Once a class file has been loaded, the `RMIClassLoader` provides the functionality to define a class from the loaded file. The `RMIClassLoader`'s name is misleading, as this `ClassLoader` is much more general purpose than its name implies and can be used to simply load class files. The `RMIClassLoader` can support several protocols, including HTTP and IIOP.

With the Java 2 existing class-loading architecture, there is much less reason to implement a customized `ClassLoader`. Instances of class `URLClassLoader` can load classes from a list of URLs. The instances can process class files, JAR files, and signed JAR files; can handle associating `Permissions` with loaded classes; and are programmed to interact with the `SecurityManager` during class loading to verify that a class has the right to trigger a reference to another class and that core packages are protected. Finally, `URLClassLoader` instances obey the class-loading delegation model, so they preserve the various levels of class trustworthiness by preventing less trusted classes from replacing more trusted classes with the same fully qualified name.

If, after all this, you still have reason to build your own `ClassLoader`, such as one that performs class-access auditing or works across a network protocol unsupported by the existing `ClassLoaders`, you can still benefit from subclassing one of the provided classes. For instance, if you are not using HTTP but everything else is the same, you can implement your own `ClassLoader` based on `SecureClassLoader`, and model it after `URLClassLoader`.

The example we show in this section is a Java 2 `ClassLoader`, `Audit2ClassLoader`, that extends `URLClassLoader` to provide class-access auditing, a feature that existing `ClassLoaders` do not regularly implement. It is interesting to note how much less work is required on the developer's part to write a Java 2 `ClassLoader`. By simply subclassing `URLClassLoader`, developers can focus on implementing a particular behavior that their new `ClassLoader` should provide, with the major security features automatically inherited from the superclass.

`Audit2ClassLoader` overrides the `loadClass()` method in `URLClassLoader`, simply recording class load requests in a file, whose name is hard-coded as `auditclasses.log`, and then asks its parent `ClassLoader` to load the class (Listing 7.1). By using all of `URLClassLoader`'s function, the code for `Audit2ClassLoader` is very short, but it offers an elegant example of OO design and implementation.

Listing 7.1.   `Audit2ClassLoader.java`

```
import java.io.DataOutputStream;
import java.io.FileOutputStream;
import java.io.IOException;

import java.net.URL;
import java.net.URLClassLoader;


/**
 * This class extends URLClassLoader by providing an
 * additional class-auditing function.
 */
public class Audit2ClassLoader extends URLClassLoader
{
    private DataOutputStream auditlog;
```

(continues)

Listing 7.1. `Audit2ClassLoader.java` (*continued*)

```
/**
 * Public constructor. Calls URLClassLoader's constructor
 * and opens a file for recording class load messages.
 *
 * @param urls an array or URL objects from which this
 *        ClassLoader is responsible for loading classes.
 */
public Audit2ClassLoader(URL[] urls)
{
    super(urls);

    try
    {
        auditlog = new DataOutputStream(
            new FileOutputStream("auditclasses.log"));
        auditlog.writeBytes("Audit Started:\n");
    }
    catch (IOException e)
    {
        System.err.println("Audit file not opened " +
            "properly\n" + e.toString());
    }
}

/**
 * The method that actually loads a class file. This
 * method is invoked to load a new class. The steps that it
 * must carry out are to write a message to a log file and
 * to call the parent findClass() method to load, verify,
 * and resolve the class and associate Permissions with it.
 *
 * @param name the fully qualified name of the class to load
 * @throws ClassNotFoundException if the class was
 *        not found
 */
public Class loadClass(String name)

    throws ClassNotFoundException
{
    try
    {
        auditlog.writeBytes("loading class " + name + "\n");
    }
    catch (IOException ioe)
    {
        System.err.println("Could not write to audit file\n"
            + ioe.toString());
    }

    try
    {
        return super.loadClass(name);
    }
    catch (Exception e)
    {
        throw new ClassNotFoundException(name);
    }
}
}
```

Audit2ClassLoader requires a list of URLs to be passed to its constructor. This is really a requirement of URLClassLoader, thus limiting the scope of where Audit2ClassLoader will look for user class files. Classes in the boot, extension, and application class paths will be found and loaded through delegation by the appropriate class loader, as follows.

1. Audit2ClassLoader will handle the files not found by delegation and will look only in the URL list passed on to its constructor.

2. The application class loader created at JVM start-up will handle the classes not found by the extension class loader and primordial class loader and that it can find in the application class path.

3. The extension class loader created at JVM start-up will handle the classes not found by the primordial class loader and that it can find in the extension class path.

4. The primordial class loader will handle all the core classes, which are located in the boot class path.

7.3   The Class File Verifier

Once it has been located and loaded by a ClassLoader other than the primordial class loader, a class still has another hurdle to cross before being available for execution within the JVM. At this point, we can be reasonably sure that the class file in question cannot supplant any of the core classes, cannot inveigle its way into the trusted packages, and cannot interfere with other safe classes already loaded. We cannot, however, be sure that the class itself is safe. The class might contain illegal bytecode, forge pointers to protected memory, overflow or underflow the program stack, or in some other way attempt to corrupt the integrity of the JVM and runtime. A number of factors could cause a class to be unsafe.

Malicious compilers could cause a class to be unsafe. A well-behaved Java compiler produces well-behaved Java classes. There would not be any harm in running these classes within the JVM, as the Java language itself and the compiler define a high degree of safety. Unfortunately, there is no guarantee that everyone is using a well-behaved Java compiler. Hackers may be using corrupted compilers to produce bytecode designed to crash the JVM or, worse, subvert the security thereof. In fact, the source language may not have been Java in the first place; programs written in Common Business Oriented Language (COBOL) or Net Restructured Extended Executor (NetREXX) can be compiled to Java bytecode.

Class editors, decompilers, and disassemblers too may cause a class to be unsafe. The Java language is like any other high-level programming language, as it is created as source code in an English-like form. Before it can be executed, the source code has to be translated into a more efficient, machine-readable format. In general, to perform this conversion, the code is either *compiled*—converted once and stored as machine code—or *interpreted*—converted and executed at runtime. The Java language combines these two approaches, as shown in Figure 7.10.

Before it can be used, the source code has to be compiled with a Java compiler, such as `javac`. This is a conventional compilation. However, the output that a Java compiler produces is not machine-specific code but instead is *bytecode*, a system-independent format. In order to execute, the bytecode has to be processed by an interpreter, such as `java`, which is part of the JVM. The bytecode is machine code written for the JVM instruction set. The JVM processes bytecode while the program is running and converts it to real machine code that it executes on the fly.

The fact that Java programs are compiled to bytecode instead of to machine code makes them portable across platforms. However, bytecode is a much higher-level language. As such, it lends itself to easy attacks. For example, Java bytecode can be easily edited by using a hexadecimal class editor. Listings 7.2 and 7.3 show the source code and the corresponding bytecode, respectively, of a simple Hello-World program. As you can see, the Java bytecode contains several pieces of information in cleartext, and whoever has an average understanding of the structure of a class file could easily compromise the behavior of the class by editing the bytecode.

Listing 7.2. `HelloWorld.java`

```
class HelloWorld
{
    public static void main(String args[])
    {
        System.out.println("Hello World");
    }
}
```

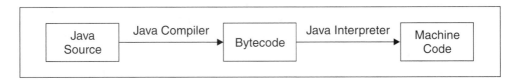

Figure 7.10. Compilation and Interpretation of Java Programs

Listing 7.3. HelloWorld Java Bytecode

```
   0: CA FE BA BE 00 00 00 2E  00 1D 0A 00 06 00 0F 09   Êþº¾..........
  10: 00 10 00 11 08 00 12 0A  00 13 00 14 07 00 15 07   ................
  20: 00 16 01 00 06 3C 69 6E  69 74 3E 01 00 03 28 29   .....<init>...()
  30: 56 01 00 04 43 6F 64 65  01 00 0F 4C 69 6E 65 4E   V...Code...LineN
  40: 75 6D 62 65 72 54 61 62  6C 65 01 00 04 6D 61 69   umberTable...mai
  50: 6E 01 00 16 28 5B 4C 6A  61 76 61 2F 6C 61 6E 67   n...([Ljava/lang
  60: 2F 53 74 72 69 6E 67 3B  29 56 01 00 0A 53 6F 75   /String;)V...Sou
  70: 72 63 65 46 69 6C 65 01  00 0F 48 65 6C 6C 6F 57   rceFile...HelloW
  80: 6F 72 6C 64 2E 6A 61 76  61 0C 00 07 00 08 07 00   orld.java.......
  90: 17 0C 00 18 00 19 01 00  0B 48 65 6C 6C 6F 20 57   .........Hello W
  A0: 6F 72 6C 64 07 00 1A 0C  00 1B 00 1C 01 00 0A 48   orld...........H
  B0: 65 6C 6C 6F 57 6F 72 6C  64 01 00 10 6A 61 76 61   elloWorld...java
  C0: 2F 6C 61 6E 67 2F 4F 62  6A 65 63 74 01 00 10 6A   /lang/Object...j
  D0: 61 76 61 2F 6C 61 6E 67  2F 53 79 73 74 65 6D 01   ava/lang/System.
  E0: 00 03 6F 75 74 01 00 15  4C 6A 61 76 61 2F 69 6F   ..out...Ljava/io
  F0: 2F 50 72 69 6E 74 53 74  72 65 61 6D 3B 01 00 13   /PrintStream;...
 100: 6A 61 76 61 2F 69 6F 2F  50 72 69 6E 74 53 74 72   java/io/PrintStr
 110: 65 61 6D 01 00 07 70 72  69 6E 74 6C 6E 01 00 15   eam...println...
 120: 28 4C 6A 61 76 61 2F 6C  61 6E 67 2F 53 74 72 69   (Ljava/lang/Stri
 130: 6E 67 3B 29 56 00 20 00  05 00 06 00 00 00 00 00   ng;)V. .........
 140: 02 00 00 00 07 00 08 00  01 00 09 00 00 00 1D 00   ................
 150: 01 00 01 00 00 00 05 2A  B7 00 01 B1 00 00 00 01   .......*.·.±....
 160: 00 0A 00 00 00 06 00 01  00 00 00 01 00 09 00 0B   ................
 170: 00 0C 00 01 00 09 00 00  00 25 00 02 00 01 00 00   .........%......
 180: 00 09 B2 00 02 12 03 B6  00 04 B1 00 00 00 01 00   ..²....¶..±.....
 190: 0A 00 00 00 0A 00 02 00  00 00 05 00 08 00 06 00   ................
 1A0: 01 00 0D 00 00 00 02 00  0E                        .........
```

In addition to class editors, several decompilers and disassemblers can operate on Java bytecode. A *decompiler* can usually recreate the source code, except for the original comments; the decompiled code can then be modified and complied back into malicious Java bytecode. Although a regular compiler would refuse to compile back into bytecode a maliciously modified Java source code, a hacker can use a corrupted compiler to generate harmful bytecode. A *disassembler* generates pseudo-assembly code, which can be maliciously modified and reassembled back into corrupted Java bytecode. In this case, there is not even the issue of modifying the compiler to force it to produce bytecode from an illegal source code.

Besides the security attacks just described, class editors, decompilers, and disassemblers can be used to perpetrate privacy and intellectual property attacks.

- Valuable algorithms can easily be stolen.
- Security functions can be revealed and bypassed.
- Confidential information, such as hard-coded passwords and keys, can be easily extracted.

A break in release-to-release binary compatibility too can cause a class to be unsafe. When a new version of an API is released, programs that relied on that API may fail if some of the API members changed.

- A member that was previously accessible has become unaccessible or been removed.

- A member has changed from static to instance.
- The new version of a method has a different return type, or different number or types of parameters.

These conditions imply that the binary-code compatibility between the classes has been broken between releases. These problems exist with all forms of binary-distributable libraries. On most systems, this results in at best a system message and the application's refusing to run. At worst, the entire operating system could crash. The JVM has to perform at least as well as other systems in these circumstances and preferably better.

For all these reasons, an extra stage of checking is required before executing Java code, and this is where the class file verifier comes in. After loading an untrusted class via a `ClassLoader` instance, the class file is handed over to the class file verifier, which attempts to ensure that the class is fit to be run, as shown in Figure 7.1 on page 204. The class file verifier is itself a part of the JVM and as such cannot be removed or overridden without replacing the JVM.

7.3.1   The Duties of the Class File Verifier

After seeing what can make a Java class unsafe and before discussing what the class file verifier does, we want to look at the possible ways in which a class file might be unsafe. By understanding a threat, we can better understand how the Java architecture guards against it. Following are some of the things that a class file could do to compromise the integrity of the JVM:

- **Forge illegal pointers.**   A Java class should not obtain a reference to an object of one type and then treat it as an object of a different type. This type of attack is known as a *class-confusion attack*, as it relies on confusing the JVM about the type, or class, of an object.

- **Contain illegal bytecode instructions.**   The JVM's execution engine is responsible for running the bytecode of a program in the same way as a conventional processor runs machine code. When it encounters an illegal instruction in a program, a conventional processor can only stop execution. Typically, the operating system identifies that an illegal instruction has been executed and displays an error message.

  Similarly, if it finds a bytecode instruction that it cannot execute, the execution engine is forced to stop executing. In a poorly written execution engine, it is possible that the entire JVM, the container in which it is embedded, or even the underlying operating system might be halted. This is obviously unacceptable.

- **Contain illegal parameters for bytecode instructions.** Passing too many or too few parameters to a bytecode instruction or passing parameters of the wrong type can lead to type confusion or errors in executing the instruction.

- **Overflow or underflow the program stack.** If a class file could *underflow* the stack—by attempting to pop more values from it than it had placed on it—or *overflow* it—by placing values on it that it did not remove—it could at best cause the JVM to execute an instruction with illegal parameters or at worst crash the JVM by exhausting its memory.

- **Perform illegal casting operations.** Attempting to convert from one data type to another—for example, from an integer to a floating point or from an `Exception` to an `Object`—is known as *casting*. Some types of casting can result in a loss of precision, such as converting a floating-point number to an integer, or are simply illegal, such as converting an `Exception` to a `java.io.DataInputStream`.

  The legality of other types of casts is less clear; for example, all `Exceptions` are `Objects`—because the `Exception` class is derived from the `Object` class—but not all `Objects` are `Exceptions`. Trying to cast from an `Object` to an `Exception` is legal only if the `Object` was originally an `Exception` or an `Exception` derivative. Allowing illegal casts to be performed will result in type confusion and thus must be prevented.

- **Attempt to access classes, fields, or methods illegally.** A class file may attempt to access a nonexistent class. Even if the class does exist, a class file may attempt to make reference to class's methods or fields that either do not exist or to which it has no access rights (see Section 7.1 on page 205). This may be part of a deliberate hacking attempt or a result of a break in release-to-release binary compatibility.

By tagging each object with its type, the JVM could check for illegal casts. By checking the size of the stack before and after each method call, stack overflows and underflows can be caught. The JVM could also test the stack before each bytecode is executed and thus avoid illegal parameters. In fact, all these tests could be made at runtime, but the performance impact would be significant. Any work that the class file verifier can do in advance of runtime to reduce the performance burden will be done. With some idea of the magnitude of the task before the class file verifier, we now look at how it meets this challenge.

7.3.2   The Four Passes of the Class File Verifier

Before we go into any detail on how the class file verifier works, it is important to note that the Java specification requires the JVM to behave in a particular way when it encounters certain problems with class files, which is usually to throw an error and refuse to use the class. The precise implementation varies from one vendor to the next and is not specified. Thus, some vendors may make all checks prior to making a class file available; other vendors may defer some or all checks until runtime. The following process description is how Sun Microsystems' JVM works; this process has been adopted by most JVM writers, not least because it saves the effort of reinventing a complex process.

The class file verifier makes four passes over the newly loaded class file, each pass examining it in closer detail. Should any of the passes find fault with the code, the class file is rejected. Not all these tests are performed prior to executing the code. The first three passes are performed prior to execution; only if the code passes the tests here will it be made available for use. The fourth pass, really a series of ad hoc tests, is performed at execution time, once the code has already started to run.

7.3.2.1 *File-Integrity Check*

The first and simplest pass checks the structure of the class file. This pass ensures that the file has the appropriate signature—the first four bytes must correspond to the hexadecimal *magic number* 0xCAFEBABE, as shown in the example of Listing 7.3 on page 225—and that each structure within the file is of the appropriate length. This pass checks that the class file itself is neither too long nor too short and that the constant pool contains only valid entries. Of course, class files may have varying lengths, but each of the structures, such as the constant pool, has its length included as part of the file specification. If a file is too long or too short, the class file verifier throws an error and refuses to make the class available for use.

7.3.2.2 *Class-Integrity Check*

The second pass performs all other checking that is possible without examining the bytecode instructions themselves. Specifically, it ensures that

- The class has a superclass, unless this class is Object.
- The superclass is not a final class.
- This class does not attempt to override a final method in its superclass.
- Constant-pool entries are well formed.
- All method and field references have legal names and signatures.

Note that in this pass, no check is made as to whether fields, methods, or classes actually exist, merely that their names and signatures are legal according to the language specification.

7.3.2.3   *Bytecode-Integrity Check*

In this pass, the most complex pass of the class file verifier, the *bytecode verifier* runs. The individual bytecodes are examined to determine how the code will behave at runtime. This examination includes data-flow analysis, stack checking, and static type checking for method arguments and bytecode operands.

The bytecode verifier is responsible for checking that the bytecodes have the correct number and type of operands, that data types are not accessed illegally, that the stack is not overflowed or underflowed, and that methods are called with the appropriate parameter types. Section 7.3.3 on page 231 gives the precise details of how the bytecode verifier operates. For now, it is important to state two points.

1. The bytecode verifier analyzes the code in a class file statically. The bytecode verifier attempts to reconstruct what the behavior of the code would be at runtime but does not run the code.

2. Some very important work has been done, which mathematically demonstrates that it is impossible for static analysis of code to identify all the problems that may occur at runtime. This proof is provided on page 233.

To summarize: Any class file is in one of three categories.

1. Runtime behavior is demonstrably safe.

2. Runtime behavior is demonstrably unsafe.

3. Runtime behavior is neither demonstrably safe nor demonstrably unsafe.

Clearly, the bytecode verifier should accept those class files in category 1 and reject those in category 2. The problem arises with category 3 class files, which may or may not contain code that will cause a problem at runtime, but it is impossible from static analysis of the code to determine which. The more complex the bytecode verifier becomes, the more it can reduce the number of cases that fall in category 3, but no matter how complex the verifier, it can never completely eliminate category 3. For this reason, there will always be bytecode programs that pass verification but that may contain illegal code. This means that simply having the bytecode verifier is not enough to prevent runtime errors in the JVM and that it must perform some runtime checking of the executable code. Lest you begin panicking at this stage, you should comfort yourself with the thought that the level of verification performed by the JVM prior to executing bytecode is significantly higher than that performed by traditional runtime environments for native code: that is, none at all.

7.3.2.4   *Runtime Integrity Check*

As we have hinted, the JVM must make a trade-off between security and efficiency. For that reason, the bytecode verifier does not exhaustively check for the existence of fields, methods, and classes when it performs bytecode-integrity checks. If it did, the JVM would need to load all classes required by a program prior to running it, resulting in a very heavy overhead, which may not be strictly required.

We will examine the following case, which has three classes: `ClassA`, `ClassB`, and `ClassC`. `ClassC` is a subclass of `ClassA`. `ClassB` has two public methods:

1. `methodReturningClassA()`, which returns an instance of `ClassA`

2. `methodReturningClassC()`, which returns an instance of `ClassC`

The architecture of this simple scenario is shown in Figure 7.11.

Against this background, consider the following code snippet:

```
ClassB b = new ClassB();
ClassA a = b.methodReturningClassA();
```

When it did bytecode-integrity checks, the class file verifier ascertained that `methodReturningClassA()` is listed in the constant pool as a method of `ClassB` and that it is reachable from this code because it is public. The class file verifier also checked that the return type of `methodReturningClassA()` is `ClassA`. Having made this check and assuming that the classes and methods involved do exist, the assignment statement in the second line of code is perfectly legal. The bytecode verifier does not in fact need to load and check `ClassA` at this point.

Now consider this similar code:

```
ClassB b = new ClassB();
ClassA a = b.methodReturningClassC();
```

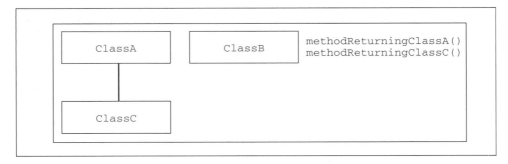

Figure 7.11.   Runtime Integrity Check Scenario

In this case, the return type of the method call does not return an object of ClassA, but the assignment is still legal, as the method returns a subclass of ClassA. This is not, however, obvious from the code alone: The verifier would need to load the class file for the return type ClassC and check that this is indeed a subclass of ClassA. Loading this class involves a possible network access and running the class file verifier for the class, and it may well be that these lines of code are never executed in the normal course of the program's execution, in which case loading and checking the subclass would be a waste of time. For this reason, class files are loaded only when they are required, that is, when a method call is executed or a field in an object of that class is modified. This is determined at runtime, which is when the fourth pass of the verifier is executed.

7.3.3   The Bytecode Verifier in Detail

The first stage of the bytecode verifier process is identifying bytecode instructions and their arguments. This operation is completed in two passes. The first pass locates the start of each instruction and stores it in a table. Having found the start of each instruction, the verifier makes a second pass, parsing the instructions. For each instruction, this involves building a structure storing the instruction itself and its arguments. These arguments are checked for validity at this point.

- All arguments to flow-control instructions must cause branches to the start of a valid instruction.

- All references to local variables must be legal. That is, an instruction may not attempt to read or write to a local variable beyond those that a method declares.

- All references to the constant pool must be to an entry of the appropriate type.

- All opcodes must have the correct number of arguments.

- Each exception handler must have start and end points at the beginning of valid instructions, with the start point before the end point. In addition, the offset of the exception handler must be the start of a valid instruction.

Having established that the bytecodes are syntactically correct, the bytecode verifier now has the task of analyzing the runtime behavior of the code, within the limitations examined on page 233. To perform this analysis, the bytecode verifier has to keep track of two pieces of information for each instruction:

1. The status of the stack prior to executing that instruction in the form of the number and type of items on the stack.

2. The contents of local variables prior to executing that instruction. Only the type of each local variable is tracked. The value is ignored.

Where types are concerned in the preceding two points, the analyzer does not need to distinguish between the various normal integer types, as they all have the same internal representation.

The first stage is the initialization of the data-flow analyzer.

1. Each instruction is marked as unvisited. That is, the data-flow analyzer has not yet examined that instruction.

2. For the first instruction, the stack is marked as empty, and the local variables corresponding to the method's arguments are initialized with the appropriate types.

3. All other local variables declared as used by the method are marked as containing illegal values.

4. The *changed bit* of the first instruction is set, indicating that the analyzer should examine this instruction.

Finally, the data-flow analyzer runs, looping through the following steps.

1. Find a virtual machine instruction whose changed bit is set.

2. If no instruction remains whose changed bit is set, the method has successfully been verified; otherwise, turn off the changed bit of the instruction found and proceed to step 3.

3. Emulate the effect of this instruction on the stack and local variables.

   - If the instruction uses values from the stack, ensure that sufficient elements are on the stack and that the elements on the top of the stack are of the appropriate type.

   - If the instruction pushes values onto the stack, ensure that the stack has sufficient room for the new elements, and update the stack status to reflect the pushed values.

   - If the instruction reads a local variable, ensure that the specified variable contains a value of the appropriate type.

   - If the instruction writes a value to a local variable, change the type of that variable to reflect that change

4. Determine the set of all possible instructions that could be executed next:

   - The next instruction in sequence, if the current instruction is not an unconditional `goto`, a `return`, or a `throw`

   - The target instruction of a conditional or an unconditional branch

   - The first instruction of all exception handlers for this instruction

5. For each of the possible following instructions, merge the stack and local variables as they exist after executing the current instruction with the state prior to executing the following instruction. In the exception-handler case, change the stack so that it contains a single object of the exception type indicated by the exception-handler information. Merging proceeds as follows.

   • If the stacks are of different sizes, this is an error. Stop the execution.

   • If the stacks contain exactly the same types, they are already merged.

   • If the stacks are identical other than having differently typed object references at corresponding places on the stacks, the merged stack will have this object reference replaced by an instance of the first common superclass or common superinterface of the two types. Such a reference type always exists because the type `Object` is a supertype of all class and interface types.

   • If this is the first time the successor instruction has been visited, set up the stack and local variable values by using those calculated in step 2, and set the changed bit for the successor instruction. If the instruction has been seen before, merge the stack and local variable values calculated in steps 2 and 3 into the values already there; set the changed bit if there is any modification.

   • Go to step 1.

If the data-flow analyzer runs on the method without reporting any failures, the method has been successfully verified by the class file verifier during the bytecode integrity checks (see Section 7.3.2.3 on page 229).

The bytecode verifier is a key component of Java security but can be improved by reducing its area of uncertainty. Can you eliminate uncertainty completely? Can you build a complete bytecode verifier that determines whether a program is safe before it runs? The answer is no. It is mathematically impossible.

To demonstrate this, we focus on one aspect of bytecode verification: stack-underflow checking, which involves determining whether a bytecode program will underflow the stack, by removing more items from it than were ever placed on it. Then, we use the argument known as *reductio ad absurdum*. We assume that there is a complete stack-underflow checker and show that this assumption leads to a contradiction. This means that the assumption must have been false—a complete stack-underflow checker is impossible. Because a complete bytecode verifier must contain a complete stack-underflow checker, a complete bytecode verifier is impossible too.

Suppose, then, that there is such a thing as a complete stack-underflow checker. We write a method in standard Java bytecode, which takes as its argument the name of a class file and returns

- The value `true` if the specified class file does not underflow the stack
- The value `false` if it does

We call this method `doesNotUnderflow()`. Figure 7.12 offers a graphical representation of the method's functionality.

We now consider the bytecode program Snarl, whose `main()` method's Java source code contains the lines in Listing 7.4.

Listing 7.4.   Portion of `main()` Method in Java Program Snarl

```
if (doesNotUnderflow(classFileName))
    while (true)
        pop()
else
{
}
```

The `pop()` method, which removes the top element from the stack, may not be pure Java code but can certainly be written in bytecode. The bytecode program Snarl is compiled into the class file `Snarl.class`.

What happens if we give Snarl itself as a parameter? The first thing it does is to invoke the method `doesNotUnderflow()` on `Snarl.class`.

- If `doesNotUnderflow(Snarl)` is `true`, Snarl immediately underflows the stack.
- If `doesNotUnderflow(Snarl)` is `false`, Snarl exits safely, without underflowing the stack.

This contradiction means that there could never have been a method `doesNotUnderflow()` that worked for all class files. The quest for a way of determin-

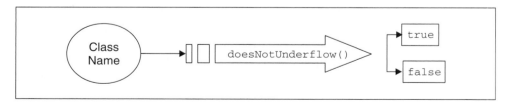

Figure 7.12.   Functionality of Method `doesNotUnderflow()`

ing statically that a class would behave itself at runtime was doomed. Complete checking for stack underflow must be done at runtime if it is to be done at all.

This result can be generalized and applied to any aspect of bytecode verification for which you try to determine statically something that happens at runtime. So all bytecode verifiers are incomplete. This does not, of course, mean that they are not useful—they contribute significantly to Java security—or that they cannot be improved. It does mean, however, that some checking has to be left until runtime.

7.3.4   An Example of Class File Verification

As an example to show the effects of class file verification and to see when classes are subjected to verification, let us consider Listing 7.5, Java method `add()`, which adds two integers initialized to the values 3 and 4 and returns the answer, 7.

Listing 7.5. `add()` Method Code

```
static int add()
{
    int a, b;
    a = 3;
    b = 4;
    return (a + b);
}
```

The `add()` method can be embedded in any Java program, such as an application, a servlet, or an enterprise bean, without any security restrictions. The same program could invoke `add()` through a line of code such as the following:

```
System.out.println("3 + 4 = " + add());
```

This is the output that would be produced:

```
3 + 4 = 7
```

We want to use the `add()` method to determine when and how verification of classes occurs. To do this, we would like to modify the initialization of variable `b` in method `add()`, using a hexadecimal editor to reinitialize variable a, so that variable `b` is never initialized. A regular compiler would refuse to compile a program in which the values of two variables are manipulated, if one of them has not been properly initialized. Therefore, after compiling the program embedding the `add()` method, we need to manually alter the bytecode. To understand what should be changed, let us consider Listing 7.6, the disassembled code of method `add()` produced by the `javap` command line utility.

Listing 7.6.   Disassembled Code of Method `add()` in Class `TestVerify`

```
Method int add()
   0 iconst_3
   1 istore_0
   2 iconst_4
   3 istore_1
   4 iload_0
   5 iload_1
   6 iadd
   7 ireturn
```

Instruction 3 in Listing 7.6 shows an `istore_1` instruction. This is the initialization of variable `b` and has the bytecode `3C`.

Figure 7.13 shows the bytecode of the `add()` method after we changed bytecode `3C` via a hexadecimal editor to `3B`, the bytecode for `istore_0`, which is the same as instruction 1 in Listing 7.6 and reinitializes variable `a`, thereby eliminating the initialization of variable `b`.

The change shown in Figure 7.13 prevents variable `b` from being initialized. Because method `add()` operates on the value of variable `b`, the fact that `b` has not been initialized implies an illegal memory access, which the class file verifier is responsible for detecting. In a Java 2 system, the only classes that are exempted from verification are those loaded by the primordial class loader, which is responsible for loading classes from the boot class path. Therefore, when the corrupted

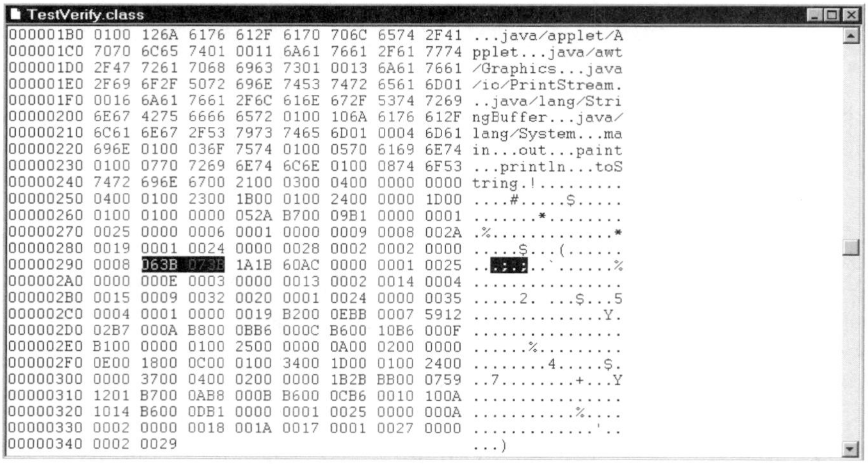

Figure 7.13.   `TestVerify` Class with `istore_1` Instruction Changed to `istore_0`

version of the bytecode is loaded from the application or extension class path or from a remote network location, it always fails verification and does not run. In fact, an attempt to run it produces a `VerifyError` with the message:

```
Accessing value from uninitialized register
```

In early Java versions, the JVM considered application code fully trusted and exempted it from class file verification. As a local application, a user class can be found only by searching the `CLASSPATH` system environment variable. As the current directory is always front appended to `CLASSPATH`, pre-Java 2 version program classes always ran as trusted and were exempted from class file verification. Running the modified version of the `add()` method on a JDK V1.1.6 platform produced a result similar to the following:

```
3 + 4 = 26246588
```

A result like this could still be produced on a Java 2 platform. In the J2SE reference implementation, prevent a class file from being verified by the class file verifier, the `java` command can be run with the `-noverify` option. Alternatively, the JVM can be forced to load the class files of an application from the boot class path via the primordial class loader, which does not pass loaded classes to the class file verifier. Section 7.2.2.1 on page 209 explains how to modify the boot class path.

Note that the results produced by the corrupted version of the `add()` method when it is not verified may be different each time. The reason is that the memory for integer `b` is never initialized, and the `add()` operation simply adds 3 to whatever value happens to be left from some previous use of that memory location.

7.4   The Security Manager

A Java environment can be subjected to four levels of attack:

1. *System modification*, in which a program gets read/write access and makes some changes to the system
2. *Privacy invasion*, in which a program gets read access and steals restricted information from the system
3. *Denial of service*, in which a program uses up system resources without being invited
4. *Impersonation*, in which a program masquerades as the real user of the system

The default Java 2 `SecurityManager`, in package `java.lang`, enforces restrictions based on security policy statements that are designed to prevent the first two

types of attack and, to some extent, the last. In this section, we look at what the
`SecurityManager` does and how it does it. Finally, we briefly consider the tricks
that a program can use to perform the nuisance attacks—denial of service and
impersonation.

7.4.1   What the `SecurityManager` Does

In the Java 2 platform, `SecurityManager` is a concrete class, whose implementation supports the policy-driven security model discussed in Chapter 8 on page
253. Previously, `SecurityManager` was an abstract class that application developers, such as JVM and WAS manufacturers, were forced to extend to implement a
set of access controls. Although the class was abstract, it did implement a set of
check methods: for example, `checkRead()`, `checkWrite()`, and `checkConnect()`.
The intent was for the application developer to override these methods with
something that answered the question, "Is the applet allowed to do this?" either by
quietly returning to the caller an implicit yes or by throwing a `Security-`
`Exception`, an emphatic no. As shipped, each method did have a default behavior
in case the application did not override the method; it simply said no by throwing
a `SecurityException`.

   With the Java 2 platform, `java.lang.SecurityManager` is a fully functional,
resource-level, access-control facility. Application developers need call only one
method, `checkPermission()`, which takes a `Permission` object as a parameter
and forwards the `Permission` checking to the `checkPermission()` method in
class `java.security.AccessController`. `AccessController` is the class that
enforces the security policy configuration imposed by the Java system administrator, which we introduced in Section 7.2.1 on page 207 (see Figure 7.14).

   Even though the Java 2 `SecurityManager` offers a `checkPermission()`
method taking a `Permission` object as a parameter, the other check methods are
still available for backward compatibility. However, they now answer the question

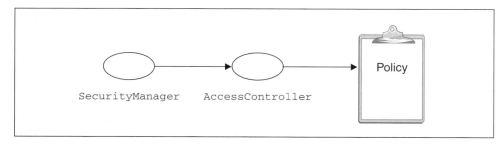

Figure 7.14.   `SecurityManager`, `AccessController`, and the Current Security Policy

using the Java 2 permission model by turning the request into a `Permission` and calling `SecurityManager.checkPermission()`. All the check methods can still be overridden, if necessary.

Figure 7.15 summarizes which system resources are protected by the default `SecurityManager`, the methods that are invoked to check whether the rights to access the resources have been granted, and the `Permission` types that are passed to `checkPermission()` by each check method. This is also the `Permission` type to pass to `checkPermission()` when you call it directly.

The default `SecurityManager` automatically grants a class file the `java.io.FilePermission` necessary to read to all files contained in the class's directory and all its subdirectories recursively, as illustrated in Figure 7.16. No explicit file read `Permission` is necessary in this case. However, this rule does not apply to class files contained in JAR files.

Another `Permission` that is automatically granted by the default `Security-Manager` is the `java.net.SocketPermission` that allows a remote code to connect to, accept, and resolve the local host and the host the code is loaded from, including host name of the local system, if loaded locally, as shown in Figure 7.17. No explicit `SocketPermission` is required in this case.

Areas of Control	Method Names	`Permission` Types Passed to `checkPermission()`
Network	`checkAccept()`	`SocketPermission`
	`checkConnect()`	`SocketPermission`
	`checkListen()`	`SocketPermission`
	`checkMulticast()`	`SocketPermission`
	`checkSetFactory()`	`RuntimePermission`
Thread	`checkAccess()`	`RuntimePermission`
File System	`checkDelete()`	`FilePermission`
	`checkRead()`	`RuntimePermission, FilePermission`
	`checkWrite()`	`RuntimePermission, FilePermission`
Operating System	`checkExec()`	`FilePermission`
	`checkPrintJobAccess()`	`RuntimePermission`
	`checkSystemClipboardAccess()`	`AWTPermission`
	`checkLink()`	`RuntimePermission`
	`checkTopLevelWindow()`	`AWTPermission`
JVM	`checkExit()`	`RuntimePermission`
	`checkPropertyAccess()`	`PropertyPermission`
	`checkPropertiesAccess()`	`PropertyPermission`
	`checkAwtEventQueueAccess()`	`AWTPermission`
	`checkCreateClassLoader()`	`RuntimePermission`
Packages and Classes	`checkPackageAccess()`	`RuntimePermission`
	`checkPackageDefinition()`	`RuntimePermission`
	`checkMemberAccess()`	`RuntimePermission`
Security	`checkSecurityAccess()`	`SecurityPermission`

Figure 7.15. Default `SecurityManager` Controls

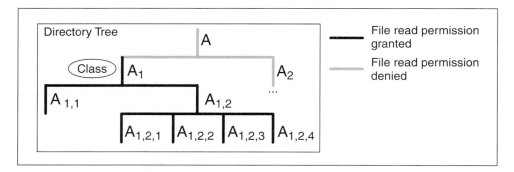

Figure 7.16. Automatic File Read `Permission` Granted to a Class File

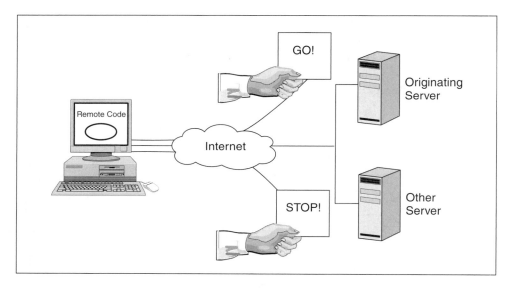

Figure 7.17. `SocketPermission` Automatically Granted to Remote Code

7.4.2   Operation of the `SecurityManager`

Although any Java program, such as a servlet, an enterprise bean, or an application, can instantiate a new `SecurityManager`, the JVM will allow only one `SecurityManager` to be active at a time. To make a `SecurityManager` active programmatically, you have to call the static method `System.setSecurity-Manager()` and pass it an instance of the desired `SecurityManager`.

In the Java 2 platform, the `SecurityManager` can be activated for local applications as well, even though this is not the default option, and an explicit command-line flag must be specified.[13] In other words, local applications can now, on demand, be subjected to the access-control restrictions of the `SecurityManager`, which enforces the security policy configuration imposed by the system administrator. This was not true prior to the Java 2 platform. The reason for this security enforcement is that today's application distribution may be performed through FTP or by shipping a CD-ROM in the mail. An application that has been obtained in one of these ways will be run locally, even though its origin is external to the local file system. It is therefore very important to be able to restrict, if necessary, the system resources that an application can have access to.

Once a `SecurityManager` is active, it cannot be replaced unless the program that attempts the replacement has the authority to create an instance of `Security-Manager` and set a `SecurityManager` instance as the active `SecurityManager`. These two rights translate into two `java.lang.RuntimePermission`s that the Java system administrator has to grant to the code attempting the `SecurityManager` replacement. The target parameters for these two `RuntimePermission`s are, respectively, `"createSecurityManager"` and `"setSecurityManager"`.

The reason a `Permission` is required to set a `SecurityManager` instance as active should be obvious; a `SecurityManager` instance could choose to authorize any operation that running programs attempt to perform. However, it is not so obvious why a `Permission` is required even to simply instantiate a `Security-Manager`, regardless of the fact that the new `SecurityManager` instance might never be set as the current `SecurityManager` of the Java system. The reason for this restriction is that any `SecurityManager` instance, whether active or inactive, can be used to inspect the current execution stack and obtain security-sensitive information about the current execution environment.

Once installed, a `SecurityManager` is active only on request; it does not check anything unless one of its check methods is called by other system functions. Figure 7.18 illustrates the flow for a specific restricted operation: establishing a network connection. The calling code creates a new `java.net.Socket` class, using one of the constructor methods it provides. This method invokes the `check-Connect()` method of the local `SecurityManager` subclass instance, passing a `java.net.SocketPermission` object as a parameter.

---

13. In the J2SE reference implementation, you can set the system property `java.security.manager` as an option on the `java` command. The `-Djava.security.manager` command line option will activate the default `SecurityManager`, which, as we said, is the one in package `java.lang`. The option `-Djava.security.manager=CustomSecurityManager` will load and make class `CustomSecurityManager` the active `SecurityManager`. Note that `CustomSecurityManager` must be a `Security-Manager` subclass and must be reachable through one of the active class search paths (see Section 7.2.2 on page 207).

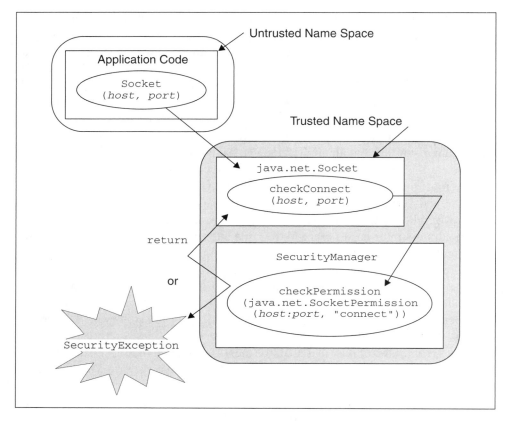

Figure 7.18. `SecurityManager` Operation

The `SecurityManager` has a very simple question to answer when one of its check methods is invoked: "Is this program allowed to perform the security-sensitive operation?" In Figure 7.18, this question becomes, "Can the application code connect to the specified host on the specified port?" In order to answer this question, the `SecurityManager` relies on the underlying `AccessController` class to check whether the running code has been granted the `Permission` entry necessary to perform the socket connection. If the connection is allowed, a `Socket` instance is created and made available to the application code. Otherwise, `AccessController` throws a `SecurityException`.

7.4.3   Types of Attack

Although we do not describe any attacks in detail, it is worth summarizing some of the security holes that have been discovered in previous Java releases. All the bugs reported in this section were found in vendor implementations of the JVM. If application developers and JVM implementors use the fully functional Java 2 `SecurityManager` as a base for their work, the number and variations of security implementations, and therefore possibilities for error, will be greatly reduced.

Flaws and the security exposures they might create are inevitable. However, the Java platform receives a great deal of attention by a wide audience. An encouraging consequence is that most of the flaws found to date were identified by field researchers attempting to find and close all holes. Fixes were provided rapidly by Sun Microsystems and application vendors. All this experience has influenced the evolution of the Java 2 security architecture.

7.4.3.1   *Infiltrating Local Classes*
Prior to the Java 2 platform, David Hopwood, once a student at Oxford and then a Netscape employee, discovered a vendor JVM implementation bug that allowed an applet to load a class from any directory on the browser system. This bug was quickly fixed.

Downloading code packages from the Internet has become a part of everyday life for many people. Any of those packages could have been modified to plant a Trojan horse class file along with their legitimate payload. Of course, this is not just a Java problem but more like a new form of computer virus. One solution lies in signed content, so that you know that the package you download comes from a trusted source and is not likely to have been tampered with.

Fully trusted classes are those that the JVM assumes and depends on being correct and well behaved. Java 2 fully trusted classes are limited to those on the boot class path; all other classes are subject to verification and security policy restrictions. Protecting the Java 2 trusted classes is a matter of limiting access to the directories and files on the boot class path. As part of the boot class path, those files are automatically considered fully trusted. The class-loading mechanism gives them the highest loading priority, as they are loaded by the primordial class loader and are exempted from class file verification and security policy restrictions. The underlying operating system should be configured to restrict writing access to the directories pointed to by the boot class path.

The extension framework, which we described on page 212, also offers a back door to hackers. Because extension classes are by default granted full access to the system resources, it is highly recommended that system administrators allow only trusted users to add extensions to the runtime environment. An alternative is for system administrators to change the policy configuration and reduce the set of authorizations granted to the extensions.

7.4.3.2   *Type Confusion*
The Java platform goes to great lengths to ensure that objects of a particular type are dealt with consistently. We see this both in the compiler and later in the third

pass of the class file verifier. It is crucial that the class of an object and the level of access it allows, as specified by the `private`, `protected`, or `public` keywords, are preserved.

If, somehow, an attacker can create an object reference that is not of the type it claims to be, there is a possibility of breaking down the protection. Several examples have shown ways to achieve type confusion by taking advantage of various JVM implementation flaws, such as:

- A bug that allowed a `ClassLoader` to be created but avoided calling the `ClassLoader` constructor, which normally invokes `SecurityManager.checkCreateClassLoader()`, as shown in Figure 7.15 on page 239

- Flaws in JVM access checking that allowed a method or an object defined as private in one class to be accessed by another class as public

- A JVM bug that failed to distinguish between two classes with the same name but loaded by different class loaders

7.4.3.3   *Network Loopholes*
The first security-related JVM flaw to get worldwide attention was a failure to check the source IP address of a remote program rigorously enough. This was exploited by abusing the DNS, a network service responsible for resolving names to addresses and vice versa, to fool the `SecurityManager` into allowing the remote program to connect to a host that would normally have been invisible to the server from which the program was loaded. In this way, the attacker could access a system that would normally be safe behind a firewall.

7.4.3.4   *JavaScript Back Doors*
A series of JavaScript exploits allowed a script to persist after the Web page it was invoked from had been exited. This flaw was used to track the user's Web accesses. The problem was fixed but then reappeared when Netscape introduced LiveConnect, which allows a JavaScript to create Java objects and invoke Java methods. Both Java and JavaScript have strict limitations on what they are allowed to do, but the limitations are different. By combining them, it was possible to get a union of the two protection schemes.

7.4.4   Malicious Code

Setting the rules for a program's environment is always a question of striking a balance. The program needs some system and/or network resources; otherwise, it will not be useful at all. On the other hand, it must not be allowed to have free reign over the system, especially if this program has been downloaded from a remote site. The need to find a compromise between allowing a program to access some system resources and restricting its access to other resources at the same time poses the conditions for some security exposures.

So far, we have talked about system modification and privacy invasion. What about denial of service and impersonation? These last two categories of exposure are allowed by the Java security framework because they cannot harm a system in a permanent way. However, they can still be annoying or damaging.

In theory, there is also another type of malice that is not Java specific. This is based on *deception*, that is, the attempt to trick users into entering information that they would not normally give away. This sort of thing is not specific to Java. In fact, there are much easier ways to do the same thing by using scripting languages or simple HTML forms, so we will not consider them further here.

7.4.4.1 Cycle Stealing

Denial-of-service attacks have long been a scourge of the Internet. Denial of service implies that the user can no longer use the system, because a server or even a whole site has been taken down. Cycle stealing is much more subtle: a *cycle-stealing program* is any program that consumes resources, whether computer or human, without the user's permission. The most extreme form of these are denial-of-service programs, but the most insidious ones may not be detected by their victim at all.

There are obvious denial-of-service attacks. For example, a program could try to create an infinite number of windows or could sit in a tight loop, using up CPU cycles. These attacks are very annoying and can have a real impact: for example, if the user has to reboot the machine to recover.

The key to this kind of program lies in persistent background threads. Every implementation of the JVM supports threads, implemented as `Thread` objects, and the Java language makes it very easy to use them. Normally, when a Java program stops, it will also stop any `Thread`s it created. However, there is nothing to assist the program in this task or to enforce that this is done. Indeed, if a Java program fails, intentionally or unintentionally, to explicitly stop the `Thread`s it created, they will continue to run until they end on their own or the application—the J2EE container, for instance—ends.

The attack described here is fairly benign. The attacker has obtained free use of machine cycles on your system. What sort of thing might he or she want to do with them?

One example might be to do *brute-force cipher cracking*. A feature of any good symmetric-key encryption algorithm is a uniform key space. That is, if you want to crack the code, there is no mathematical shortcut to finding the key; you simply have to try all possible keys until you find one that works. Several recent encryption challenges have been solved by using spare cycles on a large number of computers working as a loosely coupled complex, each being delegated a range of keys to try, under the direction of a central coordinator.

A number of other attacks along the same lines have been demonstrated, such as programs that kill the `Threads` of other programs executing concurrently. This type of attack can be prevented by controlling which programs are allowed to run on the Java platform.

7.4.4.2   *Impersonation*

Internet e-mail is based on the Simple Mail Transfer Protocol (SMTP). Mail messages are passed from one SMTP gateway to another, using sessions on TCP/IP port 25. Abusing these connections to send bogus e-mail is an established nuisance of the Internet. A hacker can create mail messages that appear to come from someone else, which can be used to embarrass or annoy the receiver of the mail and the apparent sender.

Mail that has been forged in this way is not impossible to tell from the real thing, however. The SMTP gateways keep track of the original IP address, so you can trace the message back, if not to a person at least to a machine, unless the originator was also using a spoofed IP address.

A Java remote program allows this kind of errant behavior to go one stage further. In fact, a remote program is typically allowed to connect to port 25 and appear to be a mail client. However, the only system it can connect to is the one that it was originally loaded from, because of the sandbox restrictions (see Figure 7.17 on page 240). Therefore, if an attacker is able to load a program on a remote machine, the program would be allowed to connect back to the server and send e-mail to the target of the attack. When the recipient checks the IP address, it belongs to a complete stranger, who has no idea that anything has happened.

7.4.5   `SecurityManager` Extensions

The default Java 2 `SecurityManager` is a fully functional class that acts as an interface between programs running on top of the JVM and the underlying Java 2 security access-control system. The structure is very flexible, and most applications will find that the default Java 2 `SecurityManager` will give them all the function they need. However, sometimes an application vendor, such as a J2EE product provider, will want to extend or limit the default `SecurityManager`'s capabilities. Several examples follow.

- You may want to prevent access to a system resource even if someone explicitly grants that `Permission` in the system policy database. This means that the `SecurityManager` overrides the security policy at runtime.

- You may want to log all the requests for access to certain resources.

- You may want to prompt users with a special password before a particular system resource can be accessed.

Because a `SecurityManager` is responsible for enforcing access-control restrictions, a `SecurityManager` extension should not be subjected to any security restrictions. In fact, a custom `SecurityManager` should be granted `All-Permission`.

7.4.5.1 Ignoring Policy

Sometimes, a JVM vendor or a J2SE/J2EE provider may wish to deny a certain `Permission` even when the Java system administrator has explicitly granted that `Permission`. The code fragment in Listing 7.7 shows how to override the `checkPermission()` method in the default `SecurityManager` to deny the `Permission` to print unconditionally.

Listing 7.7.   Overriding `SecurityManager.checkPermission()`

```
public void checkPermission(Permission perm)
{
    if (perm instanceof RuntimePermission &&
    perm.getName() == "queuePrintJob")
    {
        System.out.println("Permission to print is denied");
        throw new SecurityException();
    }
    super.checkPermission(perm);
}
```

The `checkPermission()` method shown in Listing 7.7 behaves exactly as its homonym in the `SecurityManager` superclass, except when it is invoked to check whether a `RuntimePermission` `"queuePrintJob"` has been granted to the running code. In this case, the custom `SecurityManager` will deny the `Permission` unconditionally by throwing a `SecurityException`.

7.4.5.2 Logging

In this section, we take an easy task and continue with our theme by implementing a simple audit log of `Permission` requests. Our example creates a log file during construction of the `SecurityManager` and overrides the `checkPermission()` method. Whenever a `checkPermission()` is received, this implementation of `checkPermission()` will log in file `PermissionRequests.log` that a check is being made to check whether a particular `Permission` is being checked by writing a `String` representation of the `Permission` to the file. Then, it will call the parent `SecurityManager`'s `checkPermission()` method, which will enforce the access-control restrictions as imposed by the security policy currently in effect. A log function such as the one implemented by this `SecurityManager` extension could be useful in a J2EE environment for auditing purposes. The code of this `SecurityManager` extension is shown in Listing 7.8.

Listing 7.8.   `LogSecurityManager.java`

```
import java.io.DataOutputStream;
import java.io.FileOutputStream;
import java.io.IOException;

import java.security.Permission;


/**
 * LogSecurityManager extends the default SecurityManager in
 * package java.lang by overriding the checkPermission()
 * method. The implementation of checkPermission() offered
 * by LogSecurityManager logs all the checkPermission()
 * invocations by registering the name of the Permission
 * being checked.
 */
public class LogSecurityManager extends SecurityManager
{
    private DataOutputStream auditlog;

    /**
     * Public constructor. It calls the constructor in the
     * SecurityManager superclass and then initializes the log
     * function.
     */
    public LogSecurityManager()
    {
        super(); // initilize using parent constructor

        try
        {
            auditlog = new DataOutputStream(new
                FileOutputStream("PermissionRequests.log"));
                auditlog.writeBytes("Log Started:\n");
        }
        catch (IOException e)
        {
            System.err.println
                ("PermissionRequests.log file not opened " +
                "properly\n" + e.toString());
        }

        System.out.println("LogSecurityManager constructed");
    }

    /**
     * This method behaves exactly as checkPermission() in
     * the SecurityManager superclass, the only difference
     * being that all the Permission requests are being
     * logged.
     *
     * @param perm a java.security.Permission object
     *             representing the access right being checked
     *             by this LogSecurityManager.
     */
    public void checkPermission(Permission perm)
    {
```

```
        try
        {
            auditlog.writeBytes("Checking: " + perm.toString() +
                "\n");
        }
        catch (IOException e)
        {
            System.err.println
                ("Could not write to log file\n" + e.
toString());
        }

        // Invoke checkPermission() in the superclass.
        super.checkPermission(perm);
    }
}
```

7.4.5.3   *Enforcing Password-Based Protection*

This section shows how to program a SecurityManager implementing password-based authentication. This SecurityManager subclass asks the user for a password whenever a simple file read or write is attempted. This SecurityManager overrides the default implementation provided by the Java 2 API in package java. lang. We also show how to combine this password-based control with the policy-based access control of the default SecurityManager. Listing 7.9 gives the code.

Listing 7.9.   RWSecurityManager.java

```
import java.io.BufferedReader;
import java.io.IOException;
import java.io.FileDescriptor;
import java.io.InputStreamReader;


/**
 * This class implements a SecurityManager that prompts the
 * user to authenticate with a password every time there is
 * a file read and write attempt.
 */
public class RWSecurityManager extends SecurityManager
{
    private String rpasswd; // private read password
    private String wpasswd; // private write password

    /**
     * Public constructor, used to set the read and write
     * passwords.
     *
     * @param rpwd a String representing the read password.
     * @param wpwd a String representing the write password.
     */
    public RWSecurityManager(String rpwd, String wpwd)
    {
        super();
```

(continues)

Listing 7.9.   `RWSecurityManager.java`   (*continued*)

```
        // The class using this SecurityManager will set
        // both the read and write passwords
        this.rpasswd = rpwd;
        this.wpasswd = wpwd;
    }

    /**
     * This method overrides checkRead() in the superclass
     * by asking the user for a password every time there is
     * an attempt to perform a file read operation.
     * Optionally, this method can call checkRead() in the
     * superclass. In this case, entering the correct
     * password will not be enough, and the code attempting
     * to perform the file read operation will have to have
     * been granted a java.io.FilePermission.
     *
     * @param fileName a String representing the name of
     *        the file from which the code is attempting to
     *        read.
     */
    public void checkRead(String filename)
    {
        String pwdgiven;

        // Ask if the user has the required password
        System.out.println
            ("Enter the password for reading files.");

        try
        {
            pwdgiven = new BufferedReader
                (new InputStreamReader(System.in)).
                    readLine();

            if (pwdgiven.equals(rpasswd))
                System.out.println
                    ("Permission to read files granted.");
            else
                throw new SecurityException
                    ("Permission to read files denied");
        }
        catch (IOException e)
        {
            throw new SecurityException
                ("Permission to read files denied");
        }

        // Uncomment the line below if you want to call
        // SecurityManager.checkRead() at this time

        // super.checkRead(filename);
    }

    /**
     * This method overrides checkWrite() in the superclass
     * by asking the user for a password every time there is
```

```
 * an attempt to perform a file write operation.
 * Optionally, this method can call checkWrite() in the
 * superclass. In this case, entering the correct
 * password will not be enough, and the code attempting
 * to perform the file write operation will have to have
 * been granted a java.io.FilePermission.
 *
 * @param fileName a String representing the name of
 *        the file to which the code is attempting to
 *        write.
 */
public void checkWrite(String filename)
{
    String pwdgiven;

    // Ask if the user has the required password
    System.out.println
        ("Enter the password for writing to files.");

    try
    {
        pwdgiven = new BufferedReader(new
            InputStreamReader(System.in)).readLine();
        if (pwdgiven.equals(wpasswd))
            System.out.println
                ("Permission to write files granted");
        else
            throw new SecurityException
                ("Permission to write files denied");
    }
    catch (IOException e)
    {
        throw new SecurityException
            ("Permission to write files denied");
    }

    // Uncomment the line below if you want to call
    // SecurityManager.checkWrite() at this time

    // super.checkWrite(filename);
    }
}
```

If an instance of RWSecurityManager is set as the active SecurityManager of a Java system, code attempting to read and write files will cause a Security-Exception to be thrown unless the user running the program enters the correct authenticating password. However, it is not necessary to grant the code the File-Permission to read and write files. The reason is that the methods checkRead() and checkWrite() of the superclass SecurityManager are completely over-written. If invoked, those methods would call checkPermission() in Access-Controller. The RWSecurityManager class bases its policy decision on a password. If the application developer wants to keep the behavior of Security-Manager, which requires specific read and write FilePermissions enabled in the active policy, RWSecurityManager has to call super.checkRead() and super.

`checkWrite()`. The code in Listing 7.9 shows the calls to these two methods commented out. Uncommenting those lines will enable the default `SecurityManager` functions. At that point, the Java system administrator will need to modify the active security policy of the Java system in order to have the application work correctly.

7.5 Interdependence of the Three Java Security Legs

Although the three legs of Java security—class-loading system, class file verifier, and security manager—each have unique functions, they are interdependent.

- The class-loading system relies on the security manager to prevent untrusted code from loading its own class loader, which could flag untrusted code as trusted.

- Conversely, the security manager relies on the class-loading system to keep untrusted classes and local classes in separate name spaces and to prevent the local trusted classes from being overwritten.

- Both the security manager and the class-loading system rely on the class file verifier to make sure that class confusion is avoided and that class protection directives are honored.

The bottom line is this: If an attacker can breach one of the three defenses, the security of the whole system is usually compromised.

7.6 Summary

In this chapter, we took a deep look at the foundations of Java 2 security. First, we examined how it is possible to restrict access to classes, interfaces, methods, and fields. Then, we studied in detail the three legs of Java security: class loaders, the class file verifier, and security manager.

In Chapter 8, we see how Java security allows enforcing runtime access control restrictions declaratively. This involves understanding the concepts of `Permission`, `Policy`, `CodeSource`, and `ProtectionDomain`. We also see how `SecurityManager` and `AccessController` collaborate to enforce access-control restrictions based on the security `Policy` in effect and how it is possible to relax some access-control restrictions by using privileged code.

CHAPTER 8

The Java 2 Permission Model

THE Java programming language has been one of the fastest-growing technologies in use on the Internet. The Java advantage is the promise that an application written once in the Java language can be run from any machine that has a Java virtual machine. From the early stages of Java development, it was realized that this feature poses the greatest challenge to Java security because code distribution is risky. For this reason, the Java 2 platform offers a built-in access-control architecture. In this chapter, we examine how access-control restrictions are enforced in the Java 2 platform. In particular, we study

- The foundations of the Java 2 security model, which include the permission API and the concepts of security `Policy`, `CodeSource`, and `ProtectionDomain`
- The Java 2 access-control architecture
- The concept of privileged code

8.1 Overview of the Java 2 Access-Control Model

An obvious handicap with the security architecture of some common mobile-code platforms is the lack of fine-grained access control. Code is in general either completely trusted or completely untrusted, with all trusted code enjoying unrestricted access to all the system resources and all untrusted code not allowed to execute. The Java 2 platform implements a *fine-grained access-control model*, or the ability to grant specific permissions to a particular piece of code about accessing specific resources of the client—say, read and write permission on file x but only read permissions on file y and no permission on file z—depending on the signers of the code and/or the URL location from which the code was loaded. The existence of a fine-grained access control allows a Java system administrator to specify access permissions on a case-by-case basis.

The Java 2 security architecture allows easy fine-tuning of the access-control restrictions. With the Java 2 security model, all code, whether remotely downloaded or local, signed or unsigned, has access to system resources based on what the system administrator defines in a security policy database. The default implementation of this database is a flat file, called the *policy file*. This mechanism allows the client to explicitly specify the access rights to be granted to various signatories of code and originating URL locations.

Prior to the Java 2 platform, the JVM resource access was enforced by the sandbox security model, which was a function of the security controller, implemented as a `java.lang.SecurityManager` object (see Section 7.4 on page 237). Extensions were usually limited to features implemented in the specific platforms such as Web browsers and Java-enabled Web servers. The Java 2 implementation gives you full control over what each program and application is permitted to do, unlike earlier versions. The Java 2 security architecture allows Java system administrators to define the exact operations any program—application, servlet, enterprise bean, and so on—signed by one or more particular entities and coming from a specific URL location can do. Further, in multiuser systems, the system administrator can define a default system policy database, and each system user can have a separate policy database, which is combined with the system default. Additionally, in an intranet, the network administrator can define a corporatewide policy database and install it on a policy server for all the Java systems in the network to download and use. At runtime, the corporatewide policy database is combined with the system policy database and the user-defined policy database to specify the current security policy in effect.

Java 2 access restrictions can be customized without having to write a new `SecurityManager` or modify the underlying platform. The Java 2 access-control model is depicted in Figure 8.1 and shows how a predetermined security policy of the Java system dictates the Java security domains within which a specific piece of code can reside.

8.1.1   Lexical Scoping of Privilege Modifications

A security feature implemented in the Java 2 platform is the *lexical scoping of privilege modification*. Using this technique, a piece of code, typically library code, can be defined as *privileged*. To understand what privileged code is and why it is necessary, consider the scenario depicted in Figure 8.2.

A method in a J2EE-container trusted library class has been programmed to perform a security-sensitive operation, such as opening a socket connection, on behalf of its callers and also to log to a file all the times it has been accessed. It certainly makes sense to require that this method's callers have the necessary `java.net.SocketPermission` but not the `java.io.FilePermission` to write to

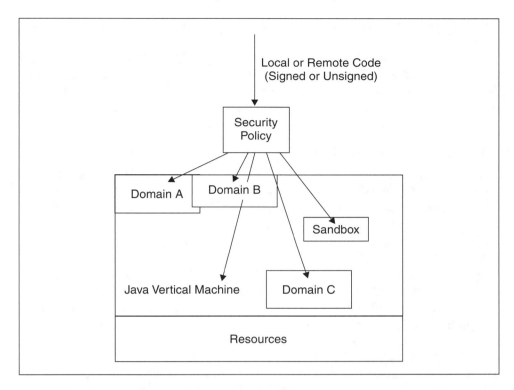

Figure 8.1. Java 2 Fine-Grained Access Control Mechanism

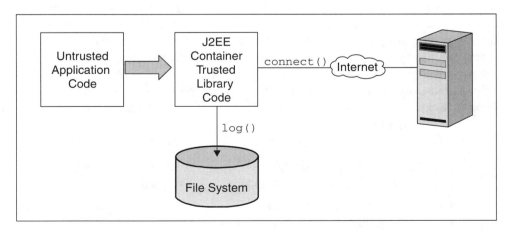

Figure 8.2. Motivation for Privileged Code

the local file system, because technically, they had not requested to perform the log operation.

As we see in more detail in Section 8.7 on page 274, this problem can be overcome by wrapping the portion of code responsible for writing to the log file into a *privileged block*. The API to define privileged code is `java.security.Access-Controller.doPrivileged()`.

8.1.2   Java 2 Security Tools

The Java 2 reference implementation provides four security tools for ensuring confidentiality, integrity, authenticity of data, and adequate control on access to various system and nonsystem resources. These tools are `jar`, `keytool`, `jarsigner`, and the Policy Tool utilities.

8.1.2.1   The `jar` Utility

The `jar` command line tool is used to aggregate and compress collections of Java programs and related resources into a single JAR file. The JAR format acquires specific security significance because only JAR files can be signed. Additionally, JAR files can be sealed (see footnote 2 on page 208).

8.1.2.2   The `keytool` Utility

The `keytool` command line utility creates key pairs; imports and exports X.509 V1, V2, and V3 certificates; generates self-signed X.509 certificates; and manages keystores (see Appendix B on page 553). A *keystore* is a protected database that holds private keys, public keys, and certificates. In the default implementation, a keystore is protected using a password, and each private key stored in the keystore is protected with a possibly different password. The private keys are used to digitally sign programs, whereas public keys are used to verify signed data, and certificates are used to verify whether a public key indeed belongs to the person to whom it is supposed to belong. The `-export` flag of the `keytool` command line utility can be used to export certificates from a keystore. The `-import` flag can be used to import certificates as trusted certificates into a keystore.

The `keytool` utility can also be used to obtain a certificate issued by a Certificate Authority (see Section 10.3.4 on page 372) by following these steps:

1. Use the `-genkey` option of the `keytool` utility to generate a public/private key pair, with the public key wrapped in a self-signed certificate.

2. Use the `-certreq` option of the `keytool` utility to generate a PKCS#10 Certificate Signing Request (see Section 12.1.6 on page 437) that contains the self-signed certificate.

3. Send the certificate request to the CA. The CA will authenticate the certificate requestor, usually off line, and will return a certificate or certificate chain, used to replace the existing certificate chain, which initially consists of the self-signed certificate only.

4. Use the `-import` option of the `keytool` utility to import the response from the CA.

8.1.2.3   The `jarsigner` Utility

The `jarsigner` command line tool signs JAR files and verifies the signatures of signed JAR files. It accesses the keystore when it needs to find

- A private key when signing a JAR file
- A public key when verifying a signature
- A certificate when verifying a public key

8.1.2.4   The Policy Tool

The Policy Tool utility, which is launched through the `policytool` command, creates and modifies the policy configuration files that define the Java system security policy. In the Java 2 reference implementation, policy files are flat files that can be modified with a regular text editor. The Policy Tool offers a graphical user interface to prevent unintentional syntax errors while modifying a policy file.

8.1.3   JAAS

Access control in the basic Java security model allows granting `Permission`s to code, based on the code signers and the URL location from which the code is coming. Even though this powerful concept significantly protects Java systems against malicious programs downloaded from the network, this model would be insufficient in an enterprise environment, where the concept of the user running the code is a fundamental component in access-control decisions.

To compensate for this limitation, the basic Java security model was originally complemented with a standard extension framework: Java Authentication and Authorization Service. By using JAAS, it is possible to refine the security policy of a Java system by taking into account the user who runs the code, besides the signer of the code and the location from which the code is coming. Starting with Java 2 SDK V1.4, JAAS has been promoted to become an integral part of the core Java platform. JAAS and its relation to J2EE are discussed in Chapter 9 on page 289.

8.2   Java Permissions

In the Java language, an *authorization*, or *permission*, is the right to access a protected resource. The `java.security` package provides the abstract class `Permission` to represent the right to access a resource. The `Permission` class is subclassed to represent specific access rights. Several subclasses of this class are available in the Java core API.

You can define your own specific `Permission` classes by subclassing this class or by using available concrete subclasses, such as `java.security.Basic-Permission`. Custom `Permission`s designed for network distribution can be signed. At runtime, the JVM will check the signature to authenticate the originator of the code.

Although each `Permission` class subclasses, directly or indirectly, the `Permission` class in package `java.security`, specific access rights are represented by `Permission` classes that are generally part of the package in which they are most likely to be used. For example, the `Permission` class `FilePermission` is part of the `java.io` package, and the `SocketPermission` class belongs to the package `java.net`. Figure 8.3 shows the inheritance tree of the most commonly used `Permission` classes that are part of J2SE.

8.2.1   Permission Target and Actions

`Permission`s may have a target and an optional list of actions. A *target* represents a protected system resource, and an *action* represents the type of access on the re-

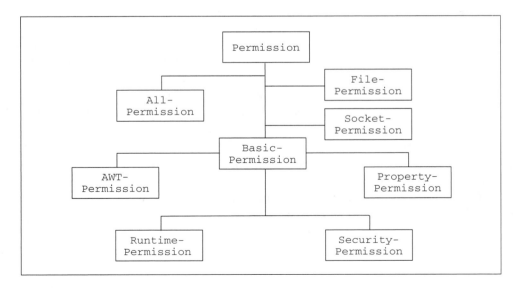

Figure 8.3.   `Permission` API Inheritance Tree

source. For example, in `java.io.FilePermission "C:\AUTOEXEC.BAT"`, `"read, write, execute"`, the target object is the local file `C:\AUTOEXEC.BAT`, and the actions are read, write, and execute. Some `Permission`s have only a target. For example, the `java.lang.RuntimePermission` with target `"exitVM"` protects the JVM against those codes that attempt to exit the JVM, but no action list is associated with this type of resource. Finally, some `Permission`s may not have a target. This is the case, for example, for `java.security.AllPermission`, which grants code full access to all the system resources.

8.2.2   The `PermissionCollection` and `Permissions` Classes

Associated with the `Permission` class are also the abstract class `java.security.PermissionCollection` and the final class `java.security.Permissions`. The former represents a collection of homogeneous `Permissions`, such as a set of `FilePermissions`. The latter is a `PermissionCollection` subclass and is used to group heterogeneous `Permission` objects, organized into `PermissionCollections`. The relation between the classes `Permission`, `PermissionCollection`, and `Permissions` is shown in Figure 8.4.

Permission classes are responsible for defining the type of `Permission-Collection` in which they should be grouped. The type of `Permission-Collection` is defined by overriding the `newPermissionCollection()` method inherited from the `Permission` superclass.

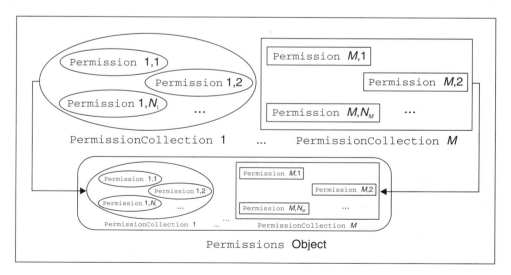

Figure 8.4.   Relation between the `Permission`, `PermissionCollection`, and `Permissions` Classes

8.2.3   The `implies()` Method in the `Permission` Class

When implementing a subclass of the `Permission` class, it is crucial to implement the abstract method `implies()`, which returns a `boolean`. Here, *a implies b* means that granting an application `Permission` *a* automatically grants it `Permission` *b* too. For example, giving some code `AllPermission` implies giving all the rest of the `Permissions`. Similarly, the `Permission` `java.io.FilePermission` `"/tmp/*"`, `"read"` implies the `Permission` `java.io.FilePermission "/tmp/readme.txt", "read"`.

The `BasicPermission` class offers a simple implementation of the `implies()` method, which is sufficient in most cases for those custom `Permissions` that have only a target. If the custom `Permission` requires the concept of an action too, it is advisable to directly subclass the `Permission` class.

8.2.4   The `implies()` Method in `PermissionCollection` and `Permissions`

The `PermissionCollection` class also has an `implies()` method that takes a `Permission` object as a parameter and returns a `boolean`. Because `Permissions` subclasses `PermissionCollection`, an `implies()` method that takes a `Permission` object as a parameter and returns a `boolean` is also available in the `Permissions` class.

When `implies()` is invoked on a `Permissions` object with a `Permission` parameter, the `Permissions` object invokes the `implies()` method on the `PermissionCollection` of the specified `Permission` parameter, passing it the `Permission` object as a parameter. The `PermissionCollection` object, in turn, invokes the `implies()` method with the same `Permission` parameter on the `Permission` objects that it contains. The `implies()` method of the `Permissions` object returns `true` if and only if the `implies()` method of the `PermissionCollection` object returns `true`, which happens if and only if the combination of the `Permission` objects in the `PermissionCollection` implies the specified `Permission`.

8.2.5   `Permissions` Implicitly Equivalent to `AllPermission`

From what we said about `AllPermission`, it is clear that much caution is needed when granting this `Permission`. In this section, we study other `Permissions` that are implicitly equivalent to `AllPermission`. Extreme care should be used when granting `AllPermission` and any of the following `Permissions`.

- **Permission to define the system's `SecurityManager`.** If a code has been granted `java.lang.RuntimePermission "createSecurityManager"` and `java.lang.RuntimePermission` `"setSecurityManager"`, that code is allowed to create and set a new `SecurityManager`, respectively. However, that code is implicitly granted `AllPermission` too because the `Security-Manager` it installs has the authority to enforce its own security policy and may choose to allow access to protected system resources with no restrictions.

- **Permission to create a `ClassLoader`.**   If a code has been granted `java.lang.RuntimePermission` `"createClassLoader"` to create a new `java.lang.ClassLoader` instance, that code has been potentially granted `All-Permission`. In fact, a new `ClassLoader` could choose not to respect the delegation hierarchy, which means that untrusted classes would be allowed to replace trusted classes, including the `SecurityManager`, thus subverting the security of the JVM. Additionally, because the `ClassLoader` assigns `Permission`s to loaded classes, based on the current policy, a malicious `ClassLoader` could choose to assign `AllPermission` to particular classes, regardless of the Java system administrator's security policy settings.

- **Permission to execute native code.**   Java code that has been granted `java.lang.RuntimePermission` `"loadLibrary.library_name"` is allowed to execute native code. This `Permission`, however, is implicitly equivalent to `AllPermission`. In fact, because it runs directly on the underlying operating system, native code bypasses all the Java security restrictions and could potentially steal private information or modify the underlying system.

- **Permission to set the system's security policy.**   Java code that has been granted `java.security.SecurityPermission` `"setProperty.policy.url.1"` to set the security property pointing to the current systemwide policy database is equivalent to `AllPermission` because the systemwide security policy may grant a hacker all the necessary authorizations to successfully mount an attack on the system.

8.3   Java Security Policy

The basic Java 2 security model establishes that a Java system administrator can grant `Permission`s to a given program, based on the location from which the program is coming and the entities that signed the code. This is done in a declarative way, externally to applications. Although Java programmatic security is possible by using the API available in the package `java.security` and in its subpackages, the JRE has been designed to offer declarative security. Configuring the policy can be done externally to programs, which makes the programming task much easier. The advantage is that security-unaware programs are platform independent. In addition, an application's security policy can be easily changed without having to rewrite the application code every time. Therefore, declarative security should always be the preferred choice when configuring the security policy of a Java application, and programmatic security should be used only when declarative security alone is insufficient.

The Java 2 reference implementation uses flat files, called *policy files*, for policy configuration. Even if the default policy implementation is file based, application developers can implement their own `java.security.Policy` subclass, providing an implementation of its abstract methods. For example, a `Policy` implementation more sophisticated than a flat file could be an encrypted file.

A policy file contains a number of `grant` entries, whose syntax is specified in Listing 8.1.

Listing 8.1.   Policy File `grant` Entry Syntax

```
grant [signedBy signers][, codeBase URL] {
permission Perm_class [target][, action][, signedBy signers];
[permission ...]
};
```

The policy file fragment in Listing 8.2 grants the `FilePermission` to read the file `C:\AUTOEXEC.BAT` from the local file system and the `RuntimePermission` to set a new `SecurityManager` to all the programs coming from the IBM Web site and signed by both the entities whose aliases are `bob` and `alice`. Note that the `Permission` class name must be fully qualified.

Listing 8.2.   Example of Policy File `grant` Entry

```
grant signedBy "bob, alice" codeBase "http://www.ibm.com" {
permission java.io.FilePermission "C:\AUTOEXEC.BAT", "read";
permission java.lang.RuntimePermission "setSecurityManager";
};
```

For this policy fragment to have an effect, it is necessary that the keystore used by the JVM at runtime contain the digital certificates belonging to the entities whose aliases are `bob` and `alice`. At runtime, the digital signatures on programs downloaded from the IBM Web site are checked by using the public keys embedded in those certificates.

Note that the syntax of the `grant` entries must be followed exactly; the omission of even a single comma will result in rejection of the policy by the JVM. An inadvertent mistake editing the policy file may cause unexpected changes in the Java security policy, which, in turn, may compromise the security of the whole system. Additionally, in future Java versions, the default policy file may be encrypted or may be stored in a format other than a flat file, which will make manual editing of the policy impractical. For these reasons, the Policy Tool is the recommended utility to create and modify policy files. This tool prevents errors that are likely to happen when manually editing the text of policy files; in the future, this tool will be essential in updating nontext policy data.

8.3.1   Combining Multiple Signers

According to Listing 8.2, *both* bob *and* alice must have signed the code if a restricted action is initiated—a logical AND. If the purpose had been to have the code signed by bob *or* alice, the grant entry should have been duplicated, once for bob and once for alice—a logical OR. This concept is shown in Figure 8.5.

The possibility for multiple signers to sign the code is very powerful. For example, one could grant Permissions to a particular piece of code only if this is signed by the developer who wrote the code and the company for which the developer works. Or, in a joint project between two companies, it may make sense for both companies to sign the code they produced.

8.3.2   Multiple Policy Files, One Active Policy

Multiple policy files can be combined at runtime to form a single Policy object, which represents the current security policy in effect. There is no risk of conflict, as Permissions in Java are only positive; by default, a program is denied any Permission, and through security policy configuration, users and system and network administrators can grant programs positive Permissions to access particular system resources. Once the runtime Policy object has been instantiated, a change in the policy configuration can be enforced by calling its refresh() method.

In addition, in a multiuser system, the user-defined policy file can be combined with a systemwide policy file and, in an intranet, even with a corporatewide policy file, which can be downloaded from a policy server using one of the network protocols implemented in the JVM. It is therefore very important to guarantee policy file portability. To accomplish this result, policy file values that could prevent portability can be replaced with special variables. For example, in a multiuser system, the user home directory changes user by user. In order for a grant entry in the systemwide policy file to specify the Permission to read a particular

Figure 8.5.   Combining Signers in the Policy File

file from the user's home directory, policy files can use the variable ${user. home}. Similarly, when a policy file is downloaded from a policy server at runtime, portability problems may arise if some JVMs are running on Microsoft Windows operating systems, in which the file separator is a back slash, whereas others are running on UNIX systems, in which the file separator is a forward slash. To solve this problem, the Java language introduced the variable ${/}, or ${file. separator}, which at runtime is replaced with the file separator specific to the operating system. The presence of such variables in the policy file guarantees policy file portability and promotes the use of declarative security in place of programmatic security for Java applications.

8.4   The Concept of `CodeSource`

Listings 8.1 and 8.2 show that `Permissions` in the basic Java security model are granted based on the entities that signed the code and the URL location, called *codebase*, from which the code is coming. When a Java class is loaded onto the JVM, these two pieces of information, which are fundamental for access-control decisions, are encapsulated into a `java.security.CodeSource` object. Basically, `Permissions` in Java 2 are granted to `CodeSources`. If two classes have been signed by the same signers and are loaded from the same codebase, they will also have the same `CodeSource` and therefore will be granted the same `Permissions`.

   In a `CodeSource` object, the signers are represented as an array of `java. security.cert.Certificate` objects, whereas the codebase is a `java.net.URL` object, as shown in Figure 8.6. The certificates stored in a `CodeSource` are for the public keys corresponding to the private keys that signed the code.

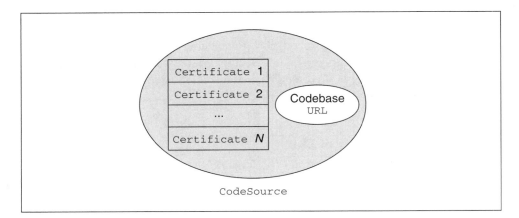

Figure 8.6.   Graphical Representation of a `CodeSource`

8.5 **ProtectionDomains**

When a class is loaded into the JVM by the appropriate Java 2 ClassLoader, the CodeSource of that class is mapped to the Permissions granted to it by the current policy. The Permissions are first organized into PermissionCollections, so that homogeneous Permissions are grouped together, and then the various PermissionCollections are organized into a Permissions object, which becomes a heterogeneous set of PermissionCollections, as depicted in Figure 8.4 on page 259.

These two pieces of information—the CodeSource and the Permissions object—are stored by the ClassLoader in a java.security.ProtectionDomain object, graphically represented in Figure 8.7. It is, therefore, the responsibility of the ClassLoader to interrogate the Policy object currently in effect and to build the ProtectionDomain for each class loaded into the system, based on the class's CodeSource. A set of Permissions is bound to the ProtectionDomain when it is constructed. Starting with Java 2 SDK V1.4, to support dynamic security policies, a ProtectionDomain can also be constructed such that it is dynamically mapped to a set of Permissions by the current Policy whenever a Permission is checked.[1]

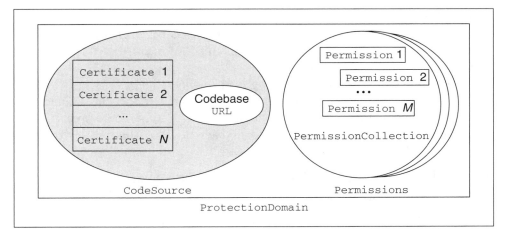

Figure 8.7.   Graphical Representation of a ProtectionDomain

---

1. Prior to Java 2 SDK V1.4, ProtectionDomains were cached and could not be refreshed. A change in the Java system's policy did not reflect in a change in the Protection-Domains. This was a limitation for systems in which the Policy was subject to changes because in order to refresh the ProtectionDomains, it was necessary to restart the JVM.

8.5.1   The `implies()` Method in the `ProtectionDomain` Class

Each `ProtectionDomain` defines an `implies()` method that takes a `Permission` object argument and returns a `boolean`. This `boolean` value indicates whether the `CodeSource` encapsulated in the `ProtectionDomain` has been granted the `Permission` passed as a parameter. If the return value is `true`, classes with that `CodeSource` are allowed to perform the action guarded by that `Permission`.

When `implies()` is invoked on a `ProtectionDomain`, the `ProtectionDomain` turns the request to the `implies()` method on the `Permissions` object that it encapsulates, as explained in Section 8.2.4 on page 260. The `implies()` method of the `ProtectionDomain` returns `true` if and only if the `implies()` method of one of the `Permissions` objects that it encapsulates returns `true`.

8.5.2   System Domain and Application Domains

Java 2 system classes are treated in a special way. Because they are considered fully trusted, they have a prebuilt `ProtectionDomain`, called the *system domain*, that grants them `AllPermission`. The system domain is also known as the *null* `ProtectionDomain` because, from an implementation point of view, the primordial class loader, which is responsible for loading the system classes, does not even build a `ProtectionDomain` for them, and calling `getProtectionDomain()` on one of those `Class` objects returns `null`. This is done for performance purposes. For the same reason, `AccessController` does not even check that a class in the system domain is granted the `Permission` to perform a restricted action; `AllPermission` is implicitly granted.

Nonsystem classes are said to belong to an *application domain*. At JVM start-up, one and only one system domain always contains the system classes, and zero or more application domains contain the nonsystem classes. To be precise, there are as many application domains as the nonsystem `CodeSource`s.

8.5.3   Relation between Classes, `ProtectionDomains`, and `Permissions`

Based on how `ProtectionDomain`s are defined, we can conclude the following.

*   All the classes with the same `CodeSource` belong to the same `ProtectionDomain`.

*   Each class belongs to one and only one `ProtectionDomain`. The `ProtectionDomain` depends on the class's `CodeSource` and the `Permissions` granted to the `CodeSource`.

*   Classes that have the same `Permissions` but are from different `CodeSource`s belong to different `ProtectionDomain`s.

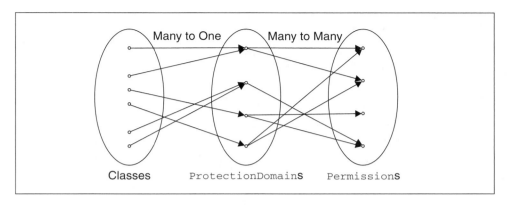

Figure 8.8.   Class/`ProtectionDomain` and `ProtectionDomain`/`Permission`
Mappings

The Java application environment maintains a many-to-one mapping from classes to their `ProtectionDomain`s and a many-to-many mapping from those `ProtectionDomain`s to their `Permission`s, as shown in Figure 8.8.

8.6   The Basic Java 2 Access-Control Model

In the Java platform, all protected resources, such as the file system, networking facility, printing system, AWT, and keyboard, are accessible only via the system domain, as shown in Figure 8.9. At various points during a Java program's execution, access to protected resources may be requested. This includes network I/O attempts, local file I/O, and attempts to create a new `ClassLoader` or to access a program-defined resource.

To verify whether the running program is allowed to perform the operation, the library routine makes a call to the method `SecurityManager.check-Permission()`. This method takes a `Permission` object argument and determines whether that `Permission` is granted to the running program. As we pointed out in Section 7.4.1 on page 238, for backward compatibility with older Java versions, other check methods in the `SecurityManager`, such as `checkRead()` or `check-Connect()`, are still available, and it is possible that the library routine calls them instead of calling `checkPermission()`. These methods, however, turn the request into a `Permission` and end up invoking `checkPermission()` anyway.

How does `SecurityManager.checkPermission()` determine whether the running program has the `Permission` to execute the protected action? `Security-Manager.checkPermission()` is in reality only an interface between the library routines and the underlying Java access-control mechanism. In fact, it relies on

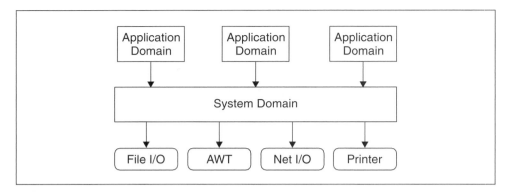

Figure 8.9. `ProtectionDomain` Composition of a Java Application Environment

`AccessController.checkPermission()` to verify whether the `Permission` has been granted to the running program. `SecurityManager.checkPermission()` invokes `AccessController.checkPermission()`, passing it the same `Permission` parameter it was passed. Therefore, it remains to be understood how `AccessController.checkPermission()` performs this verification.

In the Java language, a *thread of execution* may occur completely within a single `ProtectionDomain`—the system domain—or may involve one or more application domains and also the system domain. Logically, each thread in the JVM contains a number of *stack frames*. Simply stated, each frame contains the method instance variables for one of the methods called in the current thread. Therefore, there must be a stack frame for each method invocation. Because `Permissions` are granted to `CodeSources` and implicitly to classes but not to methods, for the purpose of `Permission` verification, each stack frame is mapped to the class in which the method is declared.

The `AccessController.checkPermission()` method walks back through the current thread's stack frames, getting the `ProtectionDomain` for each class on the thread's stack. All these `ProtectionDomains` are collected into a `java.security.AccessControlContext` object. As each `ProtectionDomain` in the thread's stack is located, the `implies()` method on that `ProtectionDomain` is invoked with the `Permission` object to check as a parameter (see Section 8.5.1 on page 266). For each stack frame, if the checked `Permission` is implied by the `ProtectionDomain`, testing of the `Permission` continues with the `ProtectionDomain` associated with the next frame on the stack.

This testing repeats until the end of the stack is reached. That is, all the classes in the thread have the `Permission` to perform the operation. Thus, the access-control check succeeds, typically meaning that the requested operation is able to proceed. However, if even only one `ProtectionDomain` in the thread's stack does not imply the checked `Permission`—which means that the checked `Permission` is not granted to all classes on the stack—a `SecurityException` is thrown, and access to the resource is denied.

Therefore, for a restricted operation to succeed, the `Permission` to perform the operation must be implied by all the `ProtectionDomains` traversed by the thread of execution. We can conclude that the `Permission` set of an execution thread is the intersection of the sets of the `Permissions` implied by all the `ProtectionDomains` traversed by the executing thread. Figure 8.10 shows the `Permissions` granted to the thread of execution as the intersection of the `Permissions` implied by the *N* `ProtectionDomains` traversed by the thread.

The reason for this access-control model is simple. Java security has been designed to prevent a less powerful `ProtectionDomain` from gaining additional `Permissions` as a result of calling or being called by a more powerful `ProtectionDomain`. Let us consider the scenario shown in Figure 8.11.

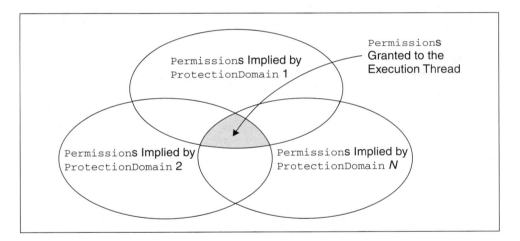

Figure 8.10.   `Permissions` Granted to a Thread Traversing *N* `ProtectionDomains`

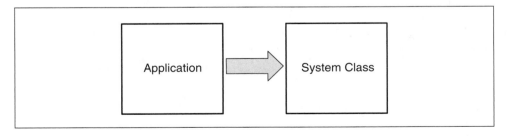

Figure 8.11.   `ProtectionDomain` Interaction from Less Powerful to More Powerful

An application that prints a message interacts with the `java.lang.System` class in the system domain. The application domain is untrusted, whereas the system domain is fully trusted. Both the application domain and the system domain are traversed by the thread of execution. If `AccessController.check-Permission()` verified only the `Permissions` of the `System` class, any operation would be allowed, as the `System` class is fully trusted. As a consequence, the application could force the `System` class to perform restricted operations on its behalf, bypassing the security restrictions imposed by the system's security policy.

The way it has been designed, the Java 2 access-control mechanism grants this thread of execution the intersection of the set of the `Permissions` implied by the application domain and the set of the `Permissions` implied by the system domain. Because the set of the `Permissions` implied by the application domain is a subset of the set of the `Permissions` implied by the system domain, that granted `Permission` set coincides with the set of the `Permissions` implied by the application domain. Therefore, the application domain does not gain any additional privilege from calling a more trusted class.

It is also possible that it is the system domain that calls classes in the application domain. For example, a servlet container's system domain may call a servlet's `init()` method to initialize the servlet, as shown in Figure 8.12. From what we have explained before, the effective access rights of the servlet are the same as the current rights enabled in its application domain.

In more complex scenarios, many `ProtectionDomains` may be involved in a particular thread of execution. By granting the thread only the intersection of the sets of the `Permissions` implied by each of the `ProtectionDomains` involved, the Java security model guarantees that less trusted classes will not gain additional privileges.

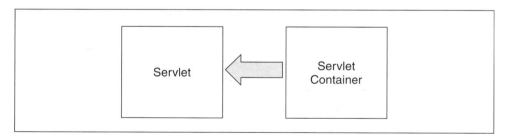

Figure 8.12. `ProtectionDomain` Interaction from More Powerful to Less Powerful

8.6.1   Scenario: Simple Check of the Current Thread

Let us consider Listing 8.3, a Java application called GetProperty.

Listing 8.3.   GetProperty.java

```
import java.security.*;

class GetProperty
{
    public static void main(String[] args)
    {
        String s;

        try
        {
            if (args.length > 0)
            {
                s = System.getProperty(args[0], "name " + args[0]
                    + " not specified");
                System.out.println(args[0] +
                    " property value is: " + s);
            }
            else
                System.out.println("Property name required");
        }
        catch(Exception e)
        {
            System.err.println("Caught exception " +
                e.toString());
        }
    }
}
```

GetProperty expects the name of a system property passed on the command line and, as a result, displays the value of that property. For example, if

```
java GetProperty java.version
```

is entered on the command line of a system running Java 2 SDK V1.4.0, the result would be

```
java.version property value is: 1.4.0
```

To enforce access-control restrictions in this scenario, a SecurityManager needs to be activated. Remember that in the Java 2 reference implementation, Java applications, being local programs, do not run by default under any Security-Manager. In fact, no access-control mechanism is applied unless the application itself programmatically sets a SecurityManager instance as the active Security-Manager or the JVM is launched with the -Djava.security.manager option (see

Section 7.4.2 on page 240). Therefore, we assume that the default `Security-Manager`, the one in package `java.lang`, is activated from the command line. In addition, to really understand how the access-control mechanism works behind the scenes, it is advisable to activate the Java debugger. Therefore, the recommended full command line is

```
java -Djava.security.manager -Djava.security.debug=all GetProperty
java.version
```

The output of the debugger clarifies the steps necessary to verify whether the current thread has access to the system property `java.version`.

1. `System.getProperty()` calls `SecurityManager.checkPropertyAccess()` with argument `"java.version"`.

2. `SecurityManager.checkPropertyAccess()` invokes `AccessController.checkPermission` with the parameter `java.util.PropertyPermission "java.version", "read"`.

3. `AccessController.checkPermission()` performs the following operations:

   a. Walks back through the stack frames of the current thread

   b. Obtains the `ProtectionDomains` of all the classes on the thread's stack

   c. Verifies that all the `ProtectionDomains` obtained in point b imply `java.util.PropertyPermission "java.version", "read"`.

To examine in detail the steps performed by `AccessController` when it walks back through the stack frames of the current thread, let us consider Figure 8. 13, which shows a graphical representation of the thread's stack during the execution of the GetProperty application. When it examines the thread's stack, `AccessController.checkPermission()` starts with the last method call in the calling sequence and proceeds backward up to the top of the stack. For each frame on the stack, the method verifies that the `ProtectionDomain` of the class containing the method implies the `PropertyPermission` to read the system property `java.version`. The details of the process follow.

1. Class `AccessController` is in the system domain—the `PropertyPermission` is implicitly granted. Proceed to the next frame on the thread's stack.

2. Class `SecurityManager` is in the system domain—the `PropertyPermission` is implicitly granted. Proceed to the next frame on the thread's stack.

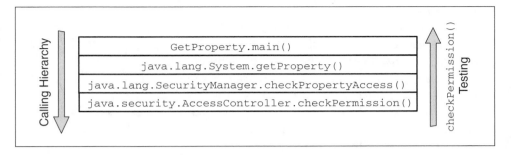

Figure 8.13.   Thread of Execution for the GetProperty Application

3. Class `System` is in the system domain—the `PropertyPermission` is implicitly granted. Proceed to the next frame on the thread's stack.
4. Class `GetProperty` is in an application domain—Is the `Property-Permission` granted?
   - If yes, because this is the top of the stack, the `PropertyPermission` is granted to the entire thread of execution.
   - If no, throw a `SecurityException`.

In practice, as this scenario involves only two `ProtectionDomains`, one of which is the system domain, step 4 is the only crucial point where the access-control decision is made. In fact, this is the point where GetProperty's application domain is interrogated to see whether it implies the required `Property-Permission`.

8.6.2   `SecurityManager` and `AccessController`

In Chapter 7, we defined the class-loading system, class file verifier, and `SecurityManager` as the foundations of Java 2 security. However, we have just seen that another Java 2 class, `AccessController`, complements `Security-Manager` by playing a crucial role in enforcing access-control decisions. This section clarifies how `SecurityManager` and `AccessController` share responsibility for enforcing access control based on the security policy configuration.

Before the `AccessController` class was introduced in the Java 2 platform, the `SecurityManager` class had to rely on its own internal logic to determine the security policy needed to be in effect, and any change in the security policy meant changing the `SecurityManager`. Therefore, prior to the Java 2 platform, implementing customized security policies was possible with the `Security-Manager` alone, but it took a great deal of effort. Now, the `SecurityManager` can defer access-control decisions to the `AccessController`. Determining Java 2 security policies is much more flexible, as the policy to be enforced by the `SecurityManager` can be specified in a file. The `AccessController` provides a simple procedure for giving specific `Permissions` to specific code. For backward-compatibility reasons, the Java 2 API still calls the methods of the `SecurityManager` to enforce system security, but most of these methods call the `AccessController`. The large body of Java programs built on pre-Java 2 versions dictates that the `SecurityManager` not be changed but instead be supplemented by the `AccessController`, which provides a simple method for implementing fine-grained access control.

Even though newly written library code could enforce access-control decisions by directly calling `AccessController.checkPermission()`, this is not considered to be a good programming choice. `SecurityManager.check-Permission()` should always be the primary interface between programs and `AccessController.checkPermission()`, for several reasons.

- The `AccessController` implementation may change in future Java releases. By sticking to the `SecurityManager`'s methods, programmers know that their code will not break.

- The `SecurityManager` can be made active from the command line; the `AccessController` cannot. As a consequence, an application can be run without an active `SecurityManager`, but security would still be partially enforced if `AccessController.checkPermission()` were invoked directly. This could lead to inconsistent security enforcements.

- Once it has been set as the system's current `SecurityManager`, a `SecurityManager` instance becomes the unique `SecurityManager` for the entire JVM system. This instance can, however, be replaced with a different `SecurityManager` instance by programs that are authorized to do so. A change in the active `SecurityManager` may imply a change in the measure the security policy is enforced; a new `SecurityManager` could be, in spite of the security policy, stricter than the previous one, by denying specific `Permissions`, or more relaxed, by allowing other `Permissions`. If some library code calls `AccessController.checkPermission()` directly, without using `SecurityManager.checkPermission()` as an interface, a change in the `SecurityManager` will inconsistently reflect in a corresponding change in the policy enforcement.

8.7   Privileged Java 2 Code

The Java 2 access-control model is very strict. By granting a thread of execution only to the intersection of the sets of `Permissions` implied by the `Protection-`

Domains the thread traverses, this architecture guarantees that less trusted ProtectionDomains do not get extra Permissions that had not been granted to them. Therefore, it is not possible for an application domain to steal Permissions from the system domain by making calls into it (see Figure 8.11 on page 269) or by being called by it (see Figure 8.12 on page 270).

However, there would be an intrinsic limitation in the model that we have just described if library code did not have the possibility of exempting its callers from requiring certain Permissions. Consider again the scenario depicted in Section 8.1.1 on page 254. There may be cases in which a trusted class, typically in a library, implements a security-sensitive operation but does not care about whether its callers have the Permissions to perform that operation.

This problem could be solved by granting application code the additional Permissions needed by the library. This solution, however, is not recommended, because it would violate the *principle of least privilege*,[2] which dictates that an entity be given no more privilege than necessary to perform an operation. Violating this principle would be unwise because (1) malicious application code could misuse the additional Permission and (2) the portability and flexibility of the library code would be limited if its callers were forced to be granted a Permission that they did not directly require.

To address the issue of trusted library code needing to temporarily extend some of its Permissions to its callers, the Java 2 language introduces the concept of privileged code. When a portion of code is wrapped into a call to Access-Controller.doPrivileged(), an annotation is made on the thread's stack frame, indicating that when the AccessController.checkPermission() method searches for ProtectionDomains to see whether they imply the Permission being checked, the search stops at this stack frame (see Figure 8.14). As Figure 8.14 shows, the code that calls doPrivileged() and the code called from the privileged block downward have to have the Permission in order for the security-sensitive operation to succeed. However, the callers are exempted from being granted that particular Permission.

For example, the library code in Figure 8.2 on page 255 will need a Socket-Permission and a FilePermission. However, if the log operation code is wrapped into a call to doPrivileged(), the calling application code will still need the SocketPermission but will be exempted from being granted the File-Permission to write to the log file.

---

2. J. H. Saltzer and M. D. Schroeder. *"The Protection of Information in Computer Systems,"* *Proceedings of the Institute of Electrical and Electronics Engineers* 63, 9 (September 1975), 1278–1308.

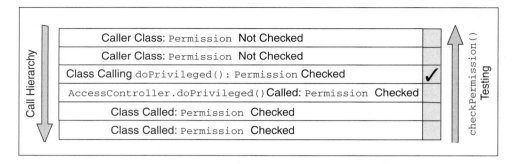

Figure 8.14. Effects of Calling `doPrivileged()` on the Thread's Stack

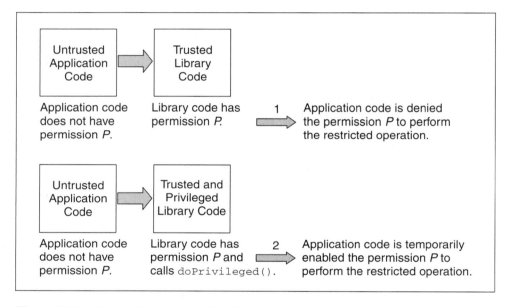

Figure 8.15. Nonprivileged versus Privileged Code Scenario

To summarize, the general rule is that when a `Permission` checking is performed, all the `ProtectionDomains` traversed by the thread of execution must have been granted the `Permission` being checked (see point 1 in Figure 8.15). However, if the code that effectively performs the restricted operation wraps the security-sensitive code into a call to `doPrivileged()`, the callers of that code are exempted from the `Permission` requirement (see point 2 in Figure 8.15).

8.7.1 Security Recommendations on Making Code Privileged

Inappropriate use of the privileged-code construct can create serious security holes.

- To avoid inadvertently violating the principle of least privilege, the privileged-code section should be as small as possible and contain only the code that really needs to extend its `Permissions` to its callers.

- Privileged code should be used only when the restricted operation leading to a call to `AccessController.checkPermission()` is not considered a security threat for the system. (See the discussions about the scenario depicted in Figure 8.2 on page 255.)

- The call to `doPrivileged()` should be made in the code that has direct need to extend its `Permissions`. Utility classes that themselves call `doPrivileged()` should be avoided, as they could create security holes.

8.7.2 How to Write Privileged Code

Privileged code needs to wrapped into a call to `AccessController.doPrivileged()`. This method can take as an argument

- A `java.security.PrivilegedAction` object if the privileged code is not supposed to throw any exceptions

- A `java.security.PrivilegedExceptionAction` object if the privileged code could throw a *checked exception*, that is, an exception listed in the `throws` clause of a method

Besides these two versions of `doPrivileged()`, two additional versions of this method take an `AccessControlContext` object as an additional parameter. An `AccessControlContext` encapsulates an array of `ProtectionDomain`s. Passing an `AccessControlContext` to `doPrivileged()` besides the `PrivilegedAction` or `PrivilegedExceptionAction` object further restricts the privileges granted to a thread of execution. In fact, when an `AccessControlContext` is specified, the restricted action is performed with the intersection of the set of the `Permissions` implied by the caller's `ProtectionDomain` and the set of the `Permissions` implied by the `ProtectionDomain`s encapsulated in the `AccessControlContext`.

`PrivilegedAction` and `PrivilegedExceptionAction` are two interfaces. They have only one method, `run()`, which when implemented will contain the security-sensitive code. This method returns a `java.lang.Object`. `AccessController.doPrivileged()` invokes the `run()` method on the `PrivilegedAction` or `PrivilegedExceptionAction` that was passed to it as a parameter and returns the `run()` method's return value, which could be `null` if there is nothing to return. If the return value is not `null`, an explicit casting may be necessary.

Listing 8.4 is an example of `PrivilegedAction` use when the `run()` method's return value is `null`.

Listing 8.4.   Use of `PrivilegedAction` within a Privileged Block with no
                    Return Value

```
someMethod()
{
    // unprivileged code here...

    AccessController.doPrivileged(new PrivilegedAction()
    {
        public Object run()
        {
            // privileged code goes here, for example:
            System.loadLibrary("awt");
            return null; // nothing to return
        }
    });

    // unprivileged code here...
}
```

If a return value is required, the code should be written as in Listing 8.5.

Listing 8.5.   Use of `PrivilegedAction` within a Privileged Block with a Return Value

```
someMethod()
{
    // unprivileged code here...

    String user = (String) AccessController.doPrivileged(
        new PrivilegedAction()
    {
        public Object run()
        {
            // privileged code goes here, for example:
            return System.getProperty("user.name");
        }
    });

    // unprivileged code here...
}
```

When using the `PrivilegedExceptionAction` interface, a `java.security.PrivilegedActionException` must be caught in a `try{} catch(){}` block, as in Listing 8.6.

Listing 8.6.   Use of `PrivilegedExceptionAction` and
`PrivilegedActionException`

```
someMethod() throws FileNotFoundException
{
    // unprivileged code here...

    try
    {
        FileInputStream fis = (FileInputStream)
            AccessController.doPrivileged(
            new PrivilegedExceptionAction()
        {
            public Object run() throws FileNotFoundException
            {
                // privileged code goes here, for example:
                return new FileInputStream("someFile");
            }
        });
    }
    catch(PrivilegedActionException e)
    {
        throw (FileNotFoundException) e.getException();
    }

    // unprivileged code here...
}
```

Note that the `getException()` method for `PrivilegedActionException`
returns an `Exception` object. Therefore, you must catch this `Exception` to the
type of the specific `Exception` to be thrown, as only a checked exception will be
wrapped in a `PrivilegedActionException`. In fact, `PrivilegedAction-`
`Exception` is a wrapper for an `Exception` thrown by a `PrivilegedException-`
`Action`. In Listing 8.6, the `Exception` that needs to be thrown is a
`FileNotFoundException`.

8.7.3   Privileged-Code Scenario

Let us consider the scenario shown in Figure 8.16. Here, we have two applications, CountFileCaller1 and CountFileCaller2, attempting to get indirect read
access to a local file through the use of library code. The purpose of these applications is to count the number of characters in that file. CountFileCaller1 invokes the
CountFile1 API to access the file, whereas CountFileCaller2 uses the CountFile2
API. Both `CountFile1` and `CountFile2` are granted the `FilePermission` necessary to read the file. However, `CountFile1` does that through a call to `doPrivi-`
`leged()`; `CountFile2` does not. Therefore, CountFileCaller1 is exempted from
being granted the `FilePermission` to read the file; CountFileCaller2 is not.

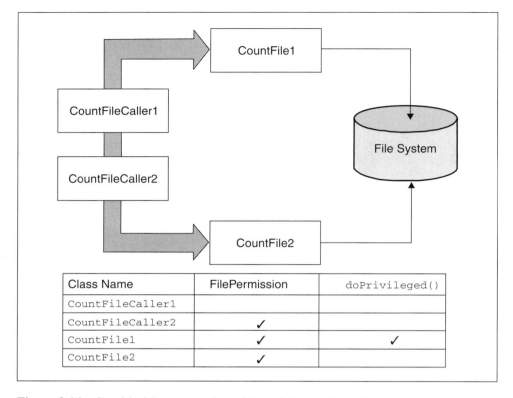

Class Name	FilePermission	`doPrivileged()`
`CountFileCaller1`		
`CountFileCaller2`	✓	
`CountFile1`	✓	✓
`CountFile2`	✓	

Figure 8.16. Graphical Representation of the Privileged-Code Scenario

Listing 8.7 shows the CountFile1 API code. Note that CountFile1 uses the privileged-code mechanism to exempt its callers from the `FilePermission` requirement.

Listing 8.7. `CountFile1.java`

```
import java.io.FileInputStream;
import java.io.FileNotFoundException;

import java.security.PrivilegedExceptionAction;
import java.security.PrivilegedActionException;
import java.security.AccessController;

class MyPrivilegedExceptionAction
    implements PrivilegedExceptionAction
{
    public Object run() throws FileNotFoundException
    {
        FileInputStream fis = new
            FileInputStream("C:\\AUTOEXEC.BAT");
```

```
        try
        {
            int count = 0;

            while (fis.read() != -1)
                count++;

            System.out.println("Counted " + count + " chars.");
        }
        catch (Exception e)
        {
            System.out.println("Exception " + e);
        }
        return null;
    }
}

public class CountFile1
{
    public CountFile1() throws FileNotFoundException
    {
        try
        {
            AccessController.doPrivileged(new
                MyPrivilegedExceptionAction());
        }
        catch (PrivilegedActionException e)
        {
            throw (FileNotFoundException) e.getException();
        }
    }
}
```

CountFile1 is invoked by CountFileCaller1, whose code is given in Listing 8.8.

Listing 8.8.   `CountFileCaller1.java`

```
public class CountFileCaller1
{
    public static void main(String[] args)
    {
        try
        {
            System.out.println("Instantiating CountFile...");
            CountFile1 cf = new CountFile1();
        }
        catch(Exception e)
        {
            System.out.println("Exception " + e.toString());
            e.printStackTrace();
        }
    }
}
```

The CountFileCaller2 API gets access to the local file system directly, without using privileged code. The source code is shown in Listing 8.9.

Listing 8.9. `CountFile2.java`

```
import java.io.FileInputStream;

public class CountFile2
{
    int count = 0;
    public void countChars() throws Exception
    {
        FileInputStream fis = new
            FileInputStream("C:\\AUTOEXEC.BAT");

        try
        {
            while (fis.read() != -1)
                count++;

            System.out.println("Counted " + count + " chars.");
        }
        catch (Exception e)
        {
            System.out.println("No characters counted");
            System.out.println("Exception " + e);
        }
    }
}
```

CountFile2 is invoked by the CountFileCaller2 application, whose code is shown in Listing 8.10.

Listing 8.10. `CountFileCaller2.java`

```
public class CountFileCaller2
{
    public static void main(String[] args)
    {
        try
        {
            System.out.println("Instantiating CountFile2...");
            CountFile2 cf = new CountFile2();
            cf.countChars();
        }
        catch(Exception e)
        {
            System.out.println("" + e.toString());
            e.printStackTrace();
        }
    }
}
```

To apply the Java 2 access-control mechanism, the CountFileCaller1 application must be invoked with an active `SecurityManager`. Section 8.6.1 on page 271 shows how to invoke an application with the default `SecurityManager` and, in addition, how to activate the Java debugger, which gives details on how `Access-Controller` works behind the scenes. Here are the details of the access-control flow as they are revealed by the Java debugger.

1. `CountFileCaller1.main()` calls the constructor of CountFile1.

2. The constructor of CountFile1 calls `AccessController.doPrivileged()` with a parameter of type `MyPrivilegedExceptionAction` (see Listing 8.7 on page 280).

3. `AccessController.doPrivileged()` invokes the `run()` method on the instance of `MyPrivilegedExceptionAction` that it was passed as a parameter.

4. The `run()` method of the instance of `MyPrivilegedExceptionAction` calls the `java.io.FileInputStream` constructor.

5. The constructor of `FileInputStream` invokes `SecurityManager.checkRead()`, passing it the name of the file that has to be accessed, `"C:\\AUTOEXEC.BAT"`.

6. `SecurityManager.checkRead()` turns the file name into a `java.io.FilePermission "C:\\AUTOEXEC.BAT", "read"` object, and passes this `FilePermission` object to `SecurityManager.checkPermission()`.

7. `SecurityManager.checkPermission()` invokes `AccessController.checkPermission()`, passing it the same `FilePermission` object.

8. `AccessController.checkPermission()` performs the following operations:

   a. Walks back through the stack frames of the current thread up to the first call to `AccessContoller.doPrivileged()`

   b. Obtains the `ProtectionDomain`s of all the classes on the thread's stack up to the caller of `doPrivileged()`

   c. Verifies that all the `ProtectionDomain`s obtained in point b imply `java.io.FilePermission "C:\\AUTOEXEC.BAT", "read"`

To examine in detail the steps performed by `AccessController` when it walks back through the stack frames of the current thread, let us consider Figure 8.17, which shows the thread's stack during the execution of the CountFileCaller1 application.

When it examines the thread's stack, `AccessController.checkPermission()` starts with the last method call in the calling sequence and proceeds backward up to the top of the stack. For each frame on the stack, `AccessController.`

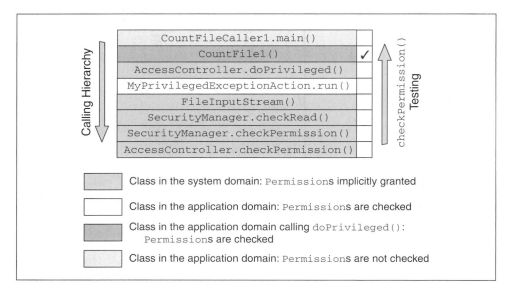

Figure 8.17. Thread's Stack for the CountFileCaller1 Application

`checkPermission()` verifies that the `ProtectionDomain` of the class containing the method implies the `FilePermission` to read the local file `C:\AUTOEXEC.BAT`. However, not all the `ProtectionDomain`s are checked. As soon as a call to `doPrivileged()` is encountered, `AccessController.checkPermission()` stops the `ProtectionDomain` examination with the caller to `doPrivileged()`. The details of the process are as follows.

1. Class `AccessController` is in the system domain; the `FilePermission` is implicitly granted. Proceed to the next frame on the thread's stack.

2. Class `SecurityManager` is in the system domain; the `FilePermission` is implicitly granted. Proceed to the next frame on the thread's stack.

3. Class `SecurityManager` is in the system domain; the `FilePermission` is implicitly granted. Proceed to the next frame on the thread's stack.

4. Class `FileInputStream` is in the system domain; the `FilePermission` is implicitly granted. Proceed to the next frame on the thread's stack.

5. Class `MyPrivilegedExceptionAction` is in the application domain—Is the `FilePermission` granted?

   - If yes, proceed to the next frame on the thread's stack.
   - If no, throw a `SecurityException`.

6. Class `AccessController` is in the system domain—the `FilePermission` is implicitly granted. Proceed to the next frame on the thread's stack.

7. Class `CountFile1` is in the application domain—Is the `FilePermission` granted?

   - If yes, because `CountFile1` is the first `doPrivileged()` caller encountered, the `FilePermission` is granted to the entire thread of execution, and no further verification is required.

   - If no, throw a `SecurityException`.

The `ProtectionDomain` for `CountFileCaller1` is not checked. The restricted action is authorized even if `CountFileCaller1` does not have the `FilePermission` to read the file `C:\AUTOEXEC.BAT`.

8.8 `ProtectionDomain` Inheritance

A potential problem that could arise with the basic access-control model as described in Section 8.6 on page 267 is that when a Java program creates a new `java.lang.Thread` object, the child thread could become more privileged than its parent thread. As each new thread creates a new runtime stack, it would be a serious problem if the `ProtectionDomain`s on the stack of the parent thread were not present on the new thread's stack. Important `ProtectionDomain` information would no longer be available when an `AccessController.checkPermission()` operation is performed, giving new threads more `Permission`s than the threads that created them. Malicious programs could therefore bypass the security restrictions by simply creating new threads. In fact, the `Permission` set granted to a thread is obtained by intersecting the sets of the `Permission`s implied by the `ProtectionDomain`s traversed by the thread itself. Therefore, if a newly created thread's stack did not contain the parent thread's `ProtectionDomain`s, the child thread could be granted more `Permission`s than its parent because the set of the `Permission`s granted to it would be obtained by intersecting fewer `ProtectionDomain`s.

To correct this potential loss of security information, the `ProtectionDomain` objects of the parent thread are attached to any child thread that is created. This process, called `ProtectionDomain` *inheritance*, is shown in Figure 8.18. With `ProtectionDomain` inheritance, unless a `doPrivileged()` operation is performed in the child thread, the parent thread's `ProtectionDomain` objects are also checked during an `AccessController.checkPermission()` operation.

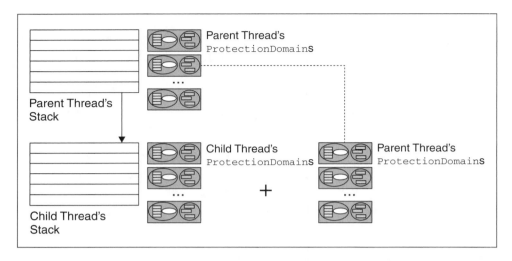

Figure 8.18. `ProtectionDomain` Inheritance

8.9   Performance Issues in the Java 2 Access-Control Model

The Java 2 access-control model is certainly very powerful. It offers a strong security mechanism embedded into the runtime. It is clear, however, that all the access-control checks performed during the execution of a program may add a significant overhead to the performance of the program itself. This should not be a surprise. Security has a price, but it is better to have reduced performance than to be attacked by malicious programs. To reduce the performance hit, the access-control mechanism adopts three optimization measures.

8.9.1   Removal of Duplicate `ProtectionDomains`

When it obtains the `ProtectionDomains` traversed by the thread of execution, `AccessController.checkPermission()` considers each single `Protection-Domain` only once. If a `ProtectionDomain` appears more than one time, its `implies()` method will be invoked only once. This offers a good improvement because the `ProtectionDomain.implies()` method is very expensive in terms of performance (see Section 8.5.1 on page 266).

In Figure 8.17 on page 284, the same application domain is traversed twice by the thread of execution, with classes `MyPrivilegedExceptionAction` and `CountFile1`. However, when `AccessController.checkPermission()` walks back through the stack frames, obtaining the `ProtectionDomains` for all the classes on the thread's stack, the first application domain class encountered is `MyPrivilegedExceptionAction` (see step 5 on page 284). At this point, `Access-Controller.checkPermission()` invokes the `implies()` method on the application domain. When `CountFile1` is encountered (see step 7 on page 285), the application domain is not interrogated again.

8.9.2 Filtering Out of the System Domain

A significant improvement in the performance of the access-control mechanism comes from the fact that the system domain is never interrogated to see whether it implies a particular `Permission`. The system domain, being fully trusted, auto-matically implies `AllPermission` (see Section 8.2 on page 258). Therefore, there would be no point in calling its `implies()` method.

From an implementation standpoint, it should be noted also that the system domain is `null`. Therefore, it would be even impossible to call `implies()` on it. When it encounters the system domain on the thread's stack, `AccessController.checkPermission()` moves directly to the next frame on the stack. In Figure 8.17 on page 284, steps 1, 2, 3, 4, and 6 are filtered out because they involve the system domain.

8.9.3 Verification Stopped at the First Privileged Stack Frame

When it encounters a call to `AccessController.doPrivileged()`, `Access-Controller.checkPermission()` stops the verification process with the `doPriv-ileged()` caller. The `ProtectionDomains` for the class calling `doPrivileged()` is checked for the `Permission`, but the callers of that class are not (see Figure 8.14 on page 276). This may result in several `Permission` checkings being filtered out.

In Figure 8.17 on page 284, the `ProtectionDomain` for `CountFile1` is checked, but because `CountFile1` calls `doPrivileged()`, the `ProtectionDomain` of its caller, `CountFileCaller1`, is not interrogated at all.

8.10 Summary

The Java 2 access-control model is centered on the concept of `CodeSource`. Per-missions are granted based on the URL location from which the code is coming and the entities that certify the origin of the code through their digital signatures. In a multitier architecture, however, this is often insufficient. Access-control decisions in a J2EE environment need to take into account the user who runs the code too. In Chapter 9 we see how JAAS extends and complements the access-control model presented in this chapter so that user information can have a role in access-control decisions.

CHAPTER **9**

Authentication and Authorization with JAAS

Enterprise authentication and authorization requirements can be fairly complex. To make matters worse, all applications or solutions in a given deployment environment may not originate from the same vendor. In addition, these applications may run on different operating systems. The Java language is the language of choice for portability between platforms, and it needs to integrate its authentication and authorization services with those of the containing environment. This chapter explains how the Java Authentication and Authorization Service accomplishes this integration and how it can be used.[1]

In J2EE security, the focus is on the declarative approach to maximize code portability, flexibility, and reusability. As enterprises evolve, their security requirements change. When applications contain code embodying security policies, it is much more difficult for an enterprise to change those security policies as new circumstances and threats arise.

There are limits to what security policies can be expressed using the declarative aspects of the J2EE security model. As such, this chapter introduces some additional mechanisms that applications can use to refine security policies. We start by explaining JAAS and then discuss the limitations on the use of JAAS from within J2EE applications, particularly from within servlet and EJB containers.

9.1 Overview of JAAS and JAAS Terminology

Authentication and authorization are key elements in any secure information-handling system. Initially, much of the Java authentication and authorization focus

---

1. This chapter is based on the Java 2 SDK V1.4 JAAS.

was on downloadable code running in Web browsers. At that time, that focus was valid, as the client systems needed to be protected from mobile code obtained from arbitrary sites on the Internet. Once mobile code had been downloaded into a client system, it was necessary to authenticate and authorize the code to perform privileged operations, including networking and file I/O. Later, the Java language matured and supported RMI. One of the features of Java's RMI is the ability to dynamically download code, including the client-side stubs needed to call the remote code. This feature reinforced the need for authentication of mobile code. In evolving from a client-centric Web technology to a server-side scripting and integration technology, the Java platform required additional authentication and authorization mechanisms to be effective in the server arena.

Traditional computing systems perform authentication on a principal or other accountable entity, typically through a challenge/response mechanism. The most salient of these mechanisms is a user ID and password combination, often used for server or Web resources, such as HTTP basic authentication. However, the challenge may need to be more sophisticated. Variants include the encryption of information, the possession of a specific physical token—for example, a physical key for a locking mechanism, or a fingerprint—or the knowledge of specific information, such as the user's mother's maiden name or the value from a one-time keypad. The response must be valid, based on the type of the challenge.

Similarly, most enterprise computing systems base authorization on a subject and an object. Typically, the *subject* is an authenticated principal, and the *object* is a resource authorized for use by the principal. In UNIX and many other operating systems, a subject is a user ID or group ID, and the objects include file system entries, such as files and/or devices. In particular, the authenticated principal is most often associated with an operating system process, although on some systems, the granularity may be to the thread of execution (see Section 8.6 on page 267). When an attempt is made to access a protected resource, the operating system authorization mechanism verifies whether the currently executing subject is authorized for the object.

Prior to creation of JAAS, the Java authorization mechanisms did not contain the structure necessary to support traditional authentication and authorization. Authentication in J2SE was based on using public-key cryptography for digital signatures applied to the set of methods and classes executing in the Java runtime. Authorization was not based on the principal's making a request for computing or data resources. In practice, authorization was based on the code's attempting to use the computing or data resources. JAAS was designed specifically to address these shortcomings in a manner consistent with the existing J2SE security infrastructure.[2]

---

2. C. Lai, L. Gong, L. Koved, A. Nadalin, and R. Schemers. "User Authentication and Authorization in the Java™ Platform," *Proceedings of the 15th Annual Computer Security Applications Conference*. Phoenix, AZ. December 1999.

As previously described in this book, particularly in Chapter 3 on page 55, the authentication and authorization system is an integral part of the overall framework for enterprise Java security. Much of the security policy information is encoded in *deployment descriptors*—XML documents that describe the application and its transaction/security attributes—and managed by the J2EE containers. However, for completeness, we include this chapter on JAAS to enable you to better understand the mechanisms J2EE containers might use for authentication and authorization. You might also find this chapter useful when developing client code, servlets, or JSP files, for which you need to write authentication or authorization code or need to develop an application-specific fine-grained authorization scheme.

As its name implies, JAAS is divided into two major components: *authentication* and *authorization*. The authentication part of JAAS is designed around Pluggable Authentication Modules (PAMs), usable on both clients and servers. The authorization components are designed as an extension of the authorization mechanisms previously found in J2SE. In J2SE V1.4, the JAAS classes, shipped in the `javax.security.auth` package and its subpackages, are an integral part of the SDK and the JRE. Previously, in J2SE V1.3, JAAS was offered as a standard extension to the SDK and JRE. For the purposes of this chapter, we assume the J2SE V1.4 version of JAAS.

To authorize access to resources, applications first need to authenticate the source of the request. The JAAS framework uses the term *subject* to represent the source of a request. A subject may be any entity, such as a person or a service. A subject is represented by the `javax.security.auth.Subject` class.

Once authenticated, a `Subject` is associated with identities, or *principals*, which in JAAS are represented as `java.security.Principal` objects. A `Subject` may contain multiple `Principals`. For example, a person may have a `Principal` name and a `Principal` Social Security Number (SSN), each of which distinguishes that `Subject` from other `Subjects`.

In addition to associated `Principals`, a `Subject` may possess security-related attributes, or credentials. A *credential* is a user's identifying data. A credential may contain information used to authenticate the subject to other services. Such credentials include passwords, Kerberos tickets, and public-key certificates for signing data. Credentials might also contain data that simply enables the subject to perform specific activities. For example, cryptographic keys can enable the subject to sign or encrypt data. Any class, therefore, can represent a credential; for this reason, credential classes do not have to be part of the JAAS API.

9.2 Authentication

Authentication is the process by which the identity of a subject is verified. Authentication must be performed in a secure fashion; otherwise, a malicious entity may impersonate legitimate entities to gain access to a system.

Unlike the Object Management Group's CORBA and Microsoft's Component Object Model (COM) and Distributed Component Object Model (DCOM), JAAS authentication and authorization are not performed every time a Java method is called. The principal-based Java authentication and authorization processes are integrated with the previously existing J2SE authentication and authorization mechanisms. Authentication and authorization routines must be called explicitly.

An important feature of JAAS is that it can be configured to support a wide variety of authentication mechanisms. For example, the authentication mechanism could require

- An account name or user name, and a password
- The ability to prove identity information that only the subject could produce, such as data signed using a private key or a value from a hardware security device
- A biometric measurement, such as a fingerprint or an iris scan comparison

9.2.1   Pluggable Authentication via `LoginModules`

An *authenticator* is a security component responsible for authenticating the identity of a `Subject`. In JAAS, authenticators are Java classes implementing the `LoginModule` interface in package `javax.security.auth.spi`. `LoginModules` are supplied by authentication technology providers. As one of the goals of JAAS is to have a pluggable authentication mechanism, the `LoginModule` framework methods are generic enough to allow all authentication mechanisms to work and simple enough so that complexity need not be a hindrance to authentication mechanism providers.

Each `LoginModule` must implement the four authentication methods in the `javax.security.auth.spi.LoginModule` API: `login()`, `commit()`, `abort()`, and `logout()`. As shown in Listing 9.1, these methods have no parameters, and a Java return type of `boolean`—`true` if the method succeeded or `false` if the `LoginModule` should be ignored. If the method failed, a `javax.Security.auth.login.LoginException` will be thrown.

Listing 9.1.   The `LoginModule` Interface

```
public interface LoginModule
{
    void initialize(Subject subject,
        CallbackHandler callbackHandler, Map sharedState,
        Map options);

    boolean login() throws LoginException;
```

```
    boolean commit() throws LoginException;

    boolean abort() throws LoginException;

    boolean logout() throws LoginException;
}
```

This approach certainly succeeds in not requiring authentication providers to add constraints to their current interfaces but still leaves the issue of how to provide additional configuration information when required. Additional information is supplied to the LoginModule via the initialize() method, which takes four arguments.

1. The subject argument is the instance that will be updated by the Login-Modules with Principals and credentials during login and logout.

2. The callbackHandler argument provides implementation- and environment-specific information needed to satisfy a particular LoginModule. When it needs to communicate with the user—for example, to ask for a user name and password—a LoginModule does not do so directly. The reason is that there are various ways of communicating with a user, and it is desirable for LoginModules to remain independent of the various types of user interaction. Rather, the LoginModule invokes a javax.security.auth.callback.CallbackHandler to perform the user interaction and obtain the requested information, such as the user name and password. An application typically provides its own CallbackHandler implementation.

   If it needs environment information to authenticate the user, a Login-Module passes the CallbackHandler handle() method an array of appropriate javax.security.auth.callback.Callbacks, such as a NameCallback for the user name and a PasswordCallback for the password. The CallbackHandler performs the requested user interaction and sets appropriate values in the Callbacks. Then, the LoginModule can examine the array of instantiated Callbacks to extract the necessary information. For example, if a user name and password are needed, the LoginModule can examine the Callback array to see whether it contains a javax.security.auth.callback.NameCallback and a javax.security.auth.callback.PasswordCallback. If so, it will use these Callback objects to obtain the authentication information.

3. The sharedState Map argument allows multiple LoginModules to share state information.

4. The options Map argument passes in configuration information from the JAAS LoginModule configuration file (see Section 9.2.2 on page 296). It is a set of key/value pairs for each of the optional arguments specified in the LoginModule configuration file for the LoginModule.

The kind of proof necessary for authentication depends on the security requirements of a particular resource and the enterprise security policies. To provide such flexibility, the JAAS authentication framework is designed around the concept of *configurable authenticators*. This architecture allows system administrators to configure, or *plug in*, the authenticators appropriate for the security requirements of the deployed application. This configuration is typically specified on the command line when the application is started or can be specified with a call to `System.setProperty()`. The configuration location can also be specified in the form of a URL in the security properties file in the `lib/security` directory.

The JAAS architecture also enables applications to remain independent of underlying authentication mechanisms. Therefore, as new authenticators become available or as current authentication services are updated, system administrators can easily replace or add authenticators without having to modify or recompile existing applications. This allows greater portability of applications, as the authentication implementations are not hard-wired into the applications. Porting an application to a new platform does not require rewriting the application. Instead, the JAAS `LoginModule` configuration file is modified to specify the authenticators for the platform, and the `LoginContext` class in package `javax.security.auth.login` handles the rest of the details of calling the configured authenticators. No application coding changes are required. The `LoginContext` class represents a Java implementation of the plug-in framework. The `LoginContext` consults the `LoginModule` configuration file to determine the authenticators, or `LoginModules`, to be used by an application. As we see in Section 9.2.2 on page 296, the first argument to the `LoginContext` constructor is the name of the *stanza*, which describes the set of `LoginModules` to be used, and the second argument is a `CallbackHandler` instance.

JAAS also supports the notion of *stacked authenticators*. This means that an application may be configured to use more than one `LoginModule`. For example, one could configure both a Kerberos `LoginModule` and a smart-card `LoginModule` for an application. The JAAS authentication framework ensures that either all the configured `LoginModules` succeed or none succeed via a two-phase process. It is the responsibility of the `LoginContext` performing the authentication to ensure this all-or-nothing behavior.

1. In the first, or *login,* phase of authentication, the `LoginContext`'s `login()` method invokes the specified `LoginModules`' `login()` methods and instructs each to attempt only the authentication. For example, each `Login-Module` will prompt the user for a user ID and password pair and verify it. The authentication status is saved in each `LoginModule` as private state information. Once finished, each `LoginModule`'s `login()` method either returns `true` when the authentication succeeded or `false` when this `Log-`

`inModule` should be ignored, or throws a `LoginException` to specify an authentication failure. In the failure case, the `LoginModule` must not retry the authentication or introduce delays. The responsibility of such tasks belongs to the application. If the application attempts to retry the authentication, the `LoginModule`'s `login()` method will be called again.

2. In the second, or *commit*, phase, each configured `LoginModule` is instructed to formally commit or abort the authentication process. To accomplish this, the `LoginContext` calls either the `commit()` method or the `abort()` method for each of the configured `LoginModules`. The `commit()` method for each `LoginModule` gets invoked when the overall authentication succeeded. The `abort()` method for each `LoginModule` is invoked when the overall authentication failed. If the `LoginContext` determined that authentication succeeded, the `commit()` method of each `LoginModule` that successfully authenticated a `Principal` associates the appropriate authenticated `Principal` and credential objects with the `Subject`. Conversely, if either login phase fails, the `LoginContext` calls the configured `LoginModule`'s `abort()` method to abort the entire authentication process. Each `LoginModule` is instructed to clean up any state—for example, erase a password—that had been associated with the attempted authentication.

In general, a `LoginModule` in a `LoginModule` configuration file stanza has one of the following four attributes:

1. `required`. The `LoginModule` is required to succeed. If it succeeds or fails, authentication still continues to proceed down the `LoginModule` list.

2. `requisite`. The `LoginModule` is required to succeed. If it succeeds, authentication continues down the `LoginModule` list. If it fails, control immediately returns to the application; authentication does not proceed down the `LoginModule` list.

3. `sufficient`. The `LoginModule` is not required to succeed. If it does succeed, control immediately returns to the application; authentication does not proceed down the `LoginModule` list. If it fails, authentication continues down the `LoginModule` list.

4. `optional`. The `LoginModule` is not required to succeed. If it succeeds or fails, authentication still continues to proceed down the `LoginModule` list.

The overall authentication succeeds only if all required and requisite `LoginModules` succeed. If a sufficient `LoginModule` is configured and succeeds, only the required and requisite `LoginModules` prior to that sufficient `LoginModule` need to have succeeded for the overall authentication to succeed. If no required or requisite `LoginModules` are configured for an application, at least one sufficient or optional `LoginModule` must succeed. A stanza with a single or stand-alone `Login-Module` exhibits identical behavior, regardless of the attribute associated with it.

In addition, it is possible to specify a space-separated list of `LoginModule`-specific *option* keys and values that are passed directly to the underlying `Login-Modules`. Option keys and values are defined by the `LoginModule` itself. The options control the behavior of the `LoginModule` instance. For example, a `LoginModule` may define options to support debugging and testing capabilities. There is no limit to the number of options a `LoginModule` may define.

9.2.2   JAAS `LoginModule` Examples

We examine the richness of the login process through a series of three `LoginModules` (Section 9.2.2.1 on page 301, Section 9.2.2.2 on page 305, and Section 9.2.2.3 on page 308). But first, we provide a sample Main program that shows the context in which `LoginModules` are used (Listing 9.2).

Listing 9.2.   `Main.java`

```
package jaasexample;


import java.security.Principal;

import java.util.Iterator;
import java.util.Set;

import javax.security.auth.Subject;

import javax.security.auth.login.LoginContext;
import javax.security.auth.login.LoginException;


/**
 * Sample application used to demonstrate how to use JAAS
 * LoginModules.
 */
public class Main
{
    /**
     * The main method of this application.
     *
     * @param args an array of Strings to be passed on the
     *        command line. The first argument tells the
     *        LoginContext which LoginModule stanza to use
     *        when selecting LoginModules.
     */
    public static void main(String[] args)
    {
        (new Main()).run(args);
    }
```

```
/**
 * This method performs the actual LoginModule
 * demonstration.
 *
 * @param args an array of Strings to be passed on the
 *        command line. The first argument tells the
 *        LoginContext which LoginModule stanza to use
 *        when selecting LoginModules.
 */
public void run(String[] args)
{
    boolean succeeded; // did the login succeed?
    LoginContext loginContext = null;

    try
    {
        // the first argument tells the LoginContext which
        // LoginModule stanza to use when selecting
        // LoginModules. The second argument is the
        // CallBackHandler to be used by all of the
        // LoginModules.
        loginContext = new LoginContext
            (args[0], new DemoCallbackHandler());

        loginContext.login(); // attempt login(s)

        succeeded = true; // login(s) succeeded
    }
    catch (LoginException le)
    {
        succeeded = false; // login(s) failed.
    }

    System.out.println("Login succeeded? " + succeeded);

    if (! succeeded)
        return;

    // The LoginContext created a Subject.  The
    // LoginModules populated it with Principals and
    // credentials.
    Subject subject = loginContext.getSubject();
    showPrincipals(subject.getPrincipals());
    showCredentials("Public credentials:",
        subject.getPublicCredentials());
    showCredentials("Private credentials:",
        subject.getPrivateCredentials());

    // The next line performs some action that requires a
    // Subject.
    doSomethingInteresting(subject);

    // Attempt to perform a logout on all of the
    // LoginModules
    try
    {
        loginContext.logout();
    }
    catch (LoginException le)
```

(*continues*)

Listing 9.2.   `Main.java` (*continued*)

```
        {
            le.printStackTrace();
        }
    }

    /**
     * Subclasses can override and do something interesting
     * here that requires a Subject.
     * The default implementation does nothing.
     *
     * @param subject is the authenticated Subject.
     */
    protected void doSomethingInteresting(Subject subject)
    {
        // do something with the Subject
    }

    /**
     * Show all of the Principals, and the classes that
     * implement the Principals, contained in the Set passed
     *
     * as an argument.
     *
     * @param principals is a Set of Principals to display.
     */
    public static void showPrincipals(Set principals)
    {
        System.out.println("Principals");
        Iterator principalsIter = principals.iterator();

        if (! principalsIter.hasNext())
            System.out.println("   none.");

        while (principalsIter.hasNext())
        {
            Principal principal =
                (Principal) principalsIter.next();
            System.out.println("Principal: " +
                principal.getName());
            System.out.println("    Class: " +
                principal.getClass().getName());
        }
    }

    /**
     * Show all of the credentials, and the classes that
     * implement the credentials, contained in the Set
     * passed as an argument.
     *
     * @param title a String to display before printing the
     *        credentials.
     * @param credentials is a Set of credentials to
     *        display.
     */
```

```
    public static void showCredentials(String title,
        Set credentials)
    {
        System.out.println(title);
        Iterator credIter = credentials.iterator();

        if (! credIter.hasNext())
            System.out.println("    none.");

        while (credIter.hasNext())
        {
            Object credential = credIter.next();
            System.out.println("    Value: " + credential);
            System.out.println("    Class: " +
                credential.getClass().getName());
        }
    }
}
```

To enable flexibility in selecting an appropriate set of LoginModules, a java.lang.String is passed to the LoginContext constructor. In this example, the String is obtained as the command-line argument to the Main application and is applied as an index into the LoginModule configuration file to select the stanza describing the appropriate LoginModule(s) to be used for authentication. By using a configuration file and an indexing mechanism, it is possible to change the stanza, or the set of selected LoginModules, without requiring modification of the application. This flexibility is demonstrated in the three scenarios in this section. The beauty of this approach is that the LoginModules can be platform specific, but the application code requesting the authentication can remain platform neutral and can be upgraded without requiring changes to the application.

The missing pieces of the Main application are the details of the Callback-Handler instantiated in Main. DemoCallbackHandler, shown in Listing 9.3, is an implementation of a CallbackHandler, providing the function sufficient to demonstrate the LoginModule examples in this chapter.

Listing 9.3. DemoCallbackHandler.java

```
package jaasexample;

import java.io.InputStreamReader;
import java.io.BufferedReader;
import java.io.IOException;

import javax.security.auth.callback.Callback;
import javax.security.auth.callback.CallbackHandler;
import javax.security.auth.callback.NameCallback;
import javax.security.auth.callback.PasswordCallback;
```

(continues)

Listing 9.3.   `DemoCallbackHandler.java`   (*continued*)

```java
import javax.security.auth.callback.
    UnsupportedCallbackException;


/**
 * A minimal CallbackHandler class that will process
 * NameCallback and PasswordCallback objects.
 */
class DemoCallbackHandler implements CallbackHandler
{
    /**
     * Process the Callback objects passed to the
     * CallbackHandler, which then calls this method when
     * CallbackHandler.handle() is called.
     *
     * @param callbacks is the array of Callback objects to
     *        be processed.
     */
    public void handle(Callback[] callbacks)
        throws IOException, UnsupportedCallbackException
    {
        for (int i = 0; i < callbacks.length; i++)
        {
            if (callbacks[i] instanceof NameCallback)
            {
                // Prompt the user for a user ID
                NameCallback nameCallback =
                    (NameCallback) callbacks[i];

                System.err.print(nameCallback.getPrompt());
                System.err.flush();
                nameCallback.setName((new BufferedReader
                    (new InputStreamReader(System.in))).
                    readLine());
            }
            else
                if (callbacks[i] instanceof PasswordCallback)
                {
                    // Prompt the user for sensitive
                    // information
                    PasswordCallback pwCallback =
                        (PasswordCallback) callbacks[i];
                    System.err.print(pwCallback.getPrompt());
                    System.err.flush();
                    pwCallback.setPassword((new BufferedReader
                        (new InputStreamReader(System.in))).
                        readLine().toCharArray());
                }
                else
                    throw new UnsupportedCallbackException
                        (callbacks[i],
                        "Unrecognized Callback");
        }
    }
}
```

9.2.2.1 First Scenario

The first step in the authentication process is to create a `LoginContext`, passing in the name of a `LoginModule` configuration file stanza and a `CallbackHandler`. The `LoginContext` reads the `LoginModule` configuration file and locates the configuration stanza corresponding to the first argument to the `LoginContext`'s constructor. The `LoginContext`, then, instantiates all the `LoginModules` specified in the configuration file stanza. Listing 9.4 shows a simple `LoginModule` configuration file stanza, called Demo1. Note the location of the semicolons. Semicolons terminate `LoginModule` entries and stanzas.

Listing 9.4. Demo1 `LoginModule` Configuration File Stanza

```
Demo1
{
    jaasexample.Demo1LoginModule required
    debug=true
    succeeded=true;
};
```

When `Main.main()` calls `loginContext.login()`, the `LoginContext` finds the Demo1 stanza and instantiates `Demo1LoginModule`, specifying that this is required to succeed for the `LoginContext`'s `login()` method to succeed. Two options, `debug` and `succeed`, with their values, are defined for the `Demo1LoginModule`. The meaning of these options and their value is `LoginModule` specific. The option names and their values are passed to the `LoginModule` via the options argument of the `initialize()` method. Listing 9.5 gives the code for `Demo1LoginModule`.

Listing 9.5. `Demo1LoginModule.java`

```
package jaasexample;

import java.util.Map;

import javax.security.auth.Subject;

import javax.security.auth.callback.CallbackHandler;

import javax.security.auth.login.LoginException;

import javax.security.auth.spi.LoginModule;

```

(continues)

Listing 9.5. `Demo1LoginModule.java` *(continued)*

```
/**
 * A basic LoginModule that records the arguments passed to
 * the initialize() method, prints debug trace messages, and
 * determines whether the methods should succeed.
 * Other than initialize(), other methods return default
 * values.
 */
public class Demo1LoginModule implements LoginModule
{
    // To fill in Principals & credentials
    Subject subject;
    // To acquire challenge/response info
    CallbackHandler callbackHandler;
    // State shared with other LoginModules
    Map sharedState;
    // Key/value options from config file stanza for this
    // LoginModule instance
    Map options;
    // config file debug option value
    boolean debug = false;
    // config file succeeded option value
    boolean succeeded = false;

    /**
     * Initialize this LoginModule; in particular, record the
     * <code>debug</code> and <code>succeeded</code> options
     * for this LoginModule instance as specified in the
     * LoginModule configuration file. If not specified in
     * the configuration file, <code>debug</code> will be
     * false, and <code>succeeded</code> will be true.
     *
     * @param subject is the Subject to be constructed by the
     *          LoginModules associated with the LoginContext
     *          that instantiated this LoginModule.
     * @param callbackHandler is a CallbackHandler that
     *          processes the Callback objects for challenge/
     *          response.
     * @param sharedState is a Map of state shared between
     *          LoginModules associated with the LoginContext
     *          that instantiated this LoginModule.
     * @param options is a Map that defines the options
     *          in the LoginContext configuration file for this
     *          LoginModule.
     */
    public void initialize(Subject subject, CallbackHandler
        callbackHandler, Map sharedState, Map options)
    {
        // Save the arguments for later use
        this.subject = subject;
        this.callbackHandler = callbackHandler;
        this.sharedState = sharedState;
        this.options = options;

        // Get the debug option specified in the
        // configuration file.
```

```
        String debugValue = (String) options.get("debug");
        debug = "true".equalsIgnoreCase(debugValue);

        // See if the succeeded option was specified in the
        // configuration file.
        String succeededValue =
            (String) options.get("succeeded");
        succeeded =
            ! "false".equalsIgnoreCase(succeededValue);

        if (debug)
            System.out.println("Demo1LoginModule.initialize");
    }

    /**
     * Default login routine that returns the
     * <code>succeeded</code> value. If <code>debug</code> is
     * <code>true</code>, a progress message is printed.
     *
     * @return the <code>succeeded</code> value.
     */
    public boolean login() throws LoginException
    {
        if (debug)
            System.out.println("Demo1LoginModule.login: " +
                succeeded);

        return succeeded;
    }

    /**
     * Default logout routine always returns
     * <code>true</code>. If <code>debug</code> is
     * <code>true</code>, a progress message is printed.
     *
     * @return the boolean <code>true</code>.
     */
    public boolean commit() throws LoginException
    {
        if (debug)
            System.out.println("Demo1LoginModule.commit");

        return true;
    }

    /**
     * Default abort routine that returns the
     * <code>succeeded</code> value. If <code>debug</code> is
     * <code>true</code>, a progress message is printed.
     *
     * @return the boolean <code>true</code>.
     */
    public boolean abort() throws LoginException
    {
        if (debug)
            System.out.println("Demo1LoginModule.abort: " +
                succeeded);
```

(continues)

Listing 9.5.   `Demo1LoginModule.java`   (*continued*)

```
        return true; // return true if the abort has succeeded
    }


    /**
     * Default logout routine always returns
     * <code>true</code>. If <code>debug</code> is
     * <code>true</code>, a progress message is printed.
     *
     * @return the boolean <code>true</code>.
     */
    public boolean logout() throws LoginException
    {
        if (debug)
            System.out.println("Demo1LoginModule.logout");

        return true;
    }
}
```

The `initialize()` method saves state information, such as the `debug` and `succeed` options. As is shown in Listing 9.6, when `debug` and `succeed` are both set to `true`, the `Demo1LoginModule.login()` method succeeds, and the progress through the `Demo1LoginModule`'s methods is written to `System.out`, including the eventual call to the `logout()` when `Main.main()` calls `loginContext.logout()`.

Listing 9.6.   Running `Main` with `Demo1LoginModule`

```
java -Djava.security.auth.login.config==jaasexample/
jaasexample.config jaasexample.Main Demo1

Demo1LoginModule.initialize
Demo1LoginModule.login: true
Demo1LoginModule.commit
Login succeeded? true
Principals
   none.
Public credentials:
   none.
Private credentials:
   none.
Demo1LoginModule.logout
```

Although not shown here, if the `succeed` option is changed to `false`, the `login()` fails, and an `Exception` is thrown.

Note that this scenario's `LoginModule` configuration file, `jaasexample/jaasexample.config`, is specified on the command line as the value of the `java.security.auth.login.config` system property. Alternatively, the value can be

set via a call to `java.lang.System.setProperty()` or in the configuration specified in the security properties file, `java.security`, in the `lib/security` directory.

9.2.2.2   Second Scenario

The second scenario builds on the first scenario. The `LoginModule` of this example, `Demo2LoginModule`, extends from `Demo1LoginModule`. The Demo2 `Login-
Module` stanza is shown in Listing 9.7.

Listing 9.7.   Demo2 `LoginModule` Configuration File Stanza

```
Demo2
{
    jaasexample.Demo2LoginModule required
    debug=false;
};
```

The source code for `Demo2LoginModule` is shown in Listing 9.8.

Listing 9.8.   `Demo2LoginModule.java`

```
package jaasexample;

import javax.security.auth.callback.Callback;
import javax.security.auth.callback.NameCallback;
import javax.security.auth.callback.PasswordCallback;
import javax.security.auth.callback.
    UnsupportedCallbackException;

import javax.security.auth.login.LoginException;
import javax.security.auth.login.FailedLoginException;


/**
 * Demonstrate a login() method that uses Callback objects to
 * perform a trivial challenge/response (user ID/password)
 * and validate them using hard-coded values.
 * All other methods are inherited from Demo1LoginModule.
 */
public class Demo2LoginModule extends Demo1LoginModule
{
    String userName = null;// the authenticated user name

    // hard-coded user ID and password for validation
    private String referenceName = "demo";
    private char[] referencePw = {'d', 'e', 'm', 'o'};

    /**
     * Using Callback objects and the CallbackHandler, prompt
     * the user for a user ID and password and see if they
     * match the hard-coded values found in this class.
     *
```

(continues)

Listing 9.8.   `Demo2LoginModule.java`   (*continued*)

```java
 * @return the boolean <code>true</code> if the
 *         authentication succeeds.
 * @throws LoginException if authentication fails.
 */
public boolean login() throws LoginException
{
    super.login(); // Optionally print progress message

    // the default is that authentication failed
    succeeded = false;

    if (callbackHandler == null)
        throw new LoginException("No CallbackHandler " +
            "to get info from the user");

    // Prompt for user ID and password via
    // the CallbackHandler passed to initialize()
    Callback[] callbacks = new Callback[2];
    NameCallback nameCallback =
        new NameCallback("Name: ");
    callbacks[0] = nameCallback;
    PasswordCallback passwordCallback =
        new PasswordCallback("Password: ", false);
    callbacks[1] = passwordCallback;
    String name = null;
    char[] password = null;

    try
    {
        // Prompt for user ID and password
        callbackHandler.handle(callbacks);
    }
    catch (java.io.IOException ioe)
    {
        // Login failed
        throw new LoginException(ioe.toString());
    }
    catch (UnsupportedCallbackException uce)
    {
        // Login failed
        throw new LoginException
            (uce.getCallback().toString());
    }

    // Retrieve the user ID and password from the
    // respective Callback objects.
    name = nameCallback.getName();
    char[] tmpPwd = passwordCallback.getPassword();

    // treat a null as an empty (length 0) password
    if (tmpPwd == null)
        tmpPwd = new char[0];
```

```
        password = new char[tmpPwd.length];
        System.arraycopy
            (tmpPwd, 0, password, 0, tmpPwd.length);
        passwordCallback.clearPassword();

        // check the user ID
        boolean nameOk = name.equals(referenceName);

        if (! nameOk)
        {
            password = clearPassword( password );
            throw new FailedLoginException("Incorrect name");
        }

        // Trivial password check
        if (password.length != referencePw.length)
        {
            password = clearPassword(password);
            throw new FailedLoginException
                ("Incorrect password");
        }
        // Done with the password, so clear it.
        password = clearPassword(password);

        succeeded = true;
        userName = name;
        return succeeded;
    }

    /**
     * Wipe out the password character array and return a
     * null character array.
     *
     * @param password is the char[] to be cleared.
     * @return a null character array.
     */
    private char[] clearPassword(char[] password)
    {
        for (int i = 0; i < password.length; i++)
            password[i] = ' ';

        return null;
    }
}
```

The primary difference with Demo1LoginModule is that the login() method now performs the authentication, and the CallbackHandler is used to prompt the user for a user ID and password and see whether they match the values hard-coded in the class. In login(), a NameCallback and a PasswordCallback are instantiated. These objects are processed via the CallbackHandler's handle() method. Then, the login() method performs a simple authorization test by comparing the user ID and password from the NameCallback and PasswordCallback objects with hard-coded values in the class. It is easy to extend this class to call a user ID registry to perform the authentication. In the remainder of `login()`, if the user ID or password do not match, a `javax.security.auth.login.FailedLogin-Exception` is thrown. In all cases, the password is cleared from memory by calling `clearPassword()` to put blank characters into the password array.

The output from running `Main` with `Demo2LoginModule` is shown in Listing 9.9.

Listing 9.9.   Running `Main` with `Demo2LoginModule`

```
java -Djava.security.auth.login.config==jaasexample/
jaasexample.config jaasexample.Main Demo2

Name: demo
Password: demo
Login succeeded? true
Principals
    none.
Public credentials:
    none.
Private credentials:
    none.
```

9.2.2.3   Third Scenario

The next step after authenticating a principal is to create the associated `Principal` and credential objects and add them to the `Subject` passed to the `LoginModule`. `Demo3LoginModule` demonstrates this by extending `Demo2LoginModule`, as shown in Listing 9.10.

Listing 9.10.   `Demo3LoginModule.java`

```
package jaasexample;


import java.util.Set;

import java.security.Principal;

import javax.security.auth.login.LoginException;


/**
 * If a login() succeeds, the commit() method populates the
 * Subject by adding Principals and credential objects to the
 * authenticated Subject; the logout() method will remove
 * them from the Subject. The abort() method will reset
 * <code>userName</code>.
 * This class extends Demo2LoginModule, which performs the
 * authentication via the login() method.
 */
public class Demo3LoginModule extends Demo2LoginModule
{
```

```
// Create two hard-coded Principals to use when
// populating the subject
private Principal principal1 =
    new DemoPrincipal("Manager");
private Principal principal2 =
    new DemoPrincipal("Agent");

// Create two hard-coded credentials to use when
// populating the subject
private String publicCredential = "Louise";
private String privateCredential =
    "Private DB access password";

/**
 * When the first phase of the LoginContext.login()
 * process succeeds, each of the LoginModules need to
 * associate Principal and credential objects with the
 * Subject.
 * This commit() method adds Principals
 * <code>principal1</code> and <code>principal2</code>,
 * public credential <code>publicCredential</code> to the
 * public credentials, and <code>privateCredential</code>
 * to the privateCredentials for the Subject.
 *
 * @return the current boolean value of the
 *          <code>succeeded</code> variable.
 */
public boolean commit() throws LoginException
{
    if (debug)
        System.out.println("Demo3LoginModule.commit: " +
            succeeded);
    // Add 2 Principals and 2 credentials to the Subject
    Set principalSet = subject.getPrincipals();
    principalSet.add(principal1);
    principalSet.add(principal2);
    subject.getPublicCredentials().add(publicCredential);
    subject.getPrivateCredentials().
        add(privateCredential);

    return succeeded;
}

/**
 * During logout processing, remove the state (Principals
 * and credentials) added by the commit() method to the
 * Subject, and remove <code>userName</code>.
 *
 * @return the boolean <code>true</code>.
 */
public boolean logout() throws LoginException
{
    if (debug)
        System.out.println("Demo3LoginModule.logout");

    // Remove the Principals and credentials added by
    // commit() and clear userName
```

(*continues*)

Listing 9.10. `Demo3LoginModule.java`   (*continued*)

```
        Set principalSet = subject.getPrincipals();
        principalSet.remove(principal1);
        principalSet.remove(principal2);
        subject.getPublicCredentials().
            remove(publicCredential);
        subject.getPrivateCredentials().
            remove(privateCredential);
        userName = null;

        return true;
    }

    /**
     * Reset the state set up by the login() method since the
     * login process failed. In this implementation,
     * <code>userName</code> is reset, and the value of the
     * <code>succeeded</code> variable is returned.
     *
     * @return the current boolean value of the
     *         <code>succeeded</code> variable.
     */
    public boolean abort() throws LoginException
    {
        if (debug)
            System.out.println("Demo3LoginModule.abort");

        userName = null;
        return succeeded;
    }
}
```

The notable differences with the `Demo2LoginModule` code are that `commit()` adds `Principal` and credential objects to the `Subject` being logged in. The `abort()` method removes the reference to the user name. The `logout()` method removes from the `Subject` the `Principal`s and credentials that were added to the `Subject` by `commit()`.

As we said in Section 9.1 on page 289, a credential can be an object of any type, whereas the principals must implement the `Principal` and `Serializable` interfaces. The `Principal`s must implement the `Serializable` interface because `Subject` is `Serializable`. In `Demo3LoginModule`, the public credential is the `String` object `"Louise"`, and the private credential is the `String` object `"Private DB access password"`. `Demo3LoginModule` associates two `Principal`s with the `Subject`: `principal1`, with name `"Manager"`; and `principal2`, with name `"Agent"`. Both of these `Principal`s are instance of the `DemoPrincipal` class, whose code is shown in Listing 9.11.

Listing 9.11. `DemoPrincipal.java`

```java
package jaasexample;

import java.io.Serializable;

import java.security.Principal;


/**
 * The Principal class used by Demo3LoginModule.
 * This class must implement Principal and Serializable.
 */
public class DemoPrincipal implements Principal, Serializable
{
    private String name; // need this for method getName()

    /**
     * Create the Principal instance, remembering the name of
     * the principal.
     *
     * @param principalName is a String representing the
     *        principal's name.
     */
    public DemoPrincipal(String principalName)
    {
        // Remember this for the getName() method
        name = principalName;
    }

    /**
     * Return the principal's name.  Required by the
     * Principal interface.
     *
     * @return the String representing the name of the
     *         principal.
     */
    public String getName()
    {
        return name;
    }

    /**
     * Return the principal's name in a formatted String.
     *
     * @return the principal's name in a formatted String.
     */
    public String toString()
    {
        return "DemoPrincipal: " + name;
    }

    /**
     * Return the hash code for this object.
     *
```

(continues)

Listing 9.11. `DemoPrincipal.java`   (*continued*)

```
   * @return the int value representing the hash code for
   *         this object.
   */
  public int hashCode()
  {
     return name.hashCode();
  }

  /**
   * Return the boolean <code>true</code> when the parameter
   * is the same object as this object; otherwise return
   * the boolean <code>false</code>.
   *
   * @return the boolean <code>true</code> when the
   *         parameter is the same object as this object.
   *         Otherwise return the boolean
   *         <code>false</code>.
   */
  public boolean equals(Object o)
  {
     return this == o;
  }
}
```

Surprisingly, the credentials (both public and private) do not need to be `Serializable`, even though they are part of the `Subject`. For security reasons, the credentials are not serialized with a `Subject`. If they were, an attacker could serialize a `Subject` and then extract the public and private credentials. If the credentials were to include a password or cryptographic key, security would be compromised. Specifically, in the J2SE V1.4 implementation of `Subject`, the fields that hold references to the credentials are marked as `transient` so that they will not be serialized.

Note that the methods `hashCode()` and `equals()` are overridden because the `Principal` objects are stored in a `Set` within the `Subject`.

The Demo3 `LoginModule` configuration file stanza is shown in Listing 9.12.

Listing 9.12. Demo3 `LoginModule` Configuration File Stanza

```
Demo3
{
    jaasexample.Demo3LoginModule required
    debug=true;
};
```

In `Main.run()`, the `LoginContext` is used to retrieve information about the `Subject`, along with its `Principals` and credentials. The output from running `Main` with `Demo3LoginModule` is shown in Listing 9.13.

Listing 9.13. Running `Main` with `Demo3LoginModule`

```
java -Djava.security.auth.login.config==jaasexample/
jaasexample.config jaasexample.Main Demo3

Demo1LoginModule.initialize
Demo1LoginModule.login: true
Name: demo
Password: demo
Demo3LoginModule.commit: true
Login succeeded? true
Principals
Principal: Manager
    Class: jaasexample.DemoPrincipal
Principal: Agent
    Class: jaasexample.DemoPrincipal
Public credentials:
    Value: Louise
    Class: java.lang.String
Private credentials:
    Value: Private DB access password
    Class: java.lang.String
Demo3LoginModule.logout
```

The `Subject`'s `Principal` objects can be used for authorization purposes. This will be demonstrated in Section 9.3.

9.3 Authorization Overview

The challenge in developing of JAAS was to add principal-based authorization to J2SE in a way that would augment, and not disturb, the existing Java authorization mechanisms. This requirement was accomplished by

- Associating a `Subject` and its set of `Principals` with a thread of execution

- Logically extending the `java.security.ProtectionDomain`s of executing code to include the `java.security.Permissions` associated with the `Subject`'s `Principals` (see Section 8.5 on page 265 and Section 8.2 on page 258)

Here, we provide a brief review of the J2SE `ProtectionDomain`-based authorization algorithm, including authorization calls to `java.security.Access-Controller.doPrivileged()` (see Section 8.7 on page 274). We then explain how to add a `Subject` to a thread of execution to extend authorization to an authenticated `Principal` requesting access to a restricted resource. Finally, we show how the basic J2SE authorization algorithm (see Section 8.6 on page 267) is modified to support authorizing `Subject`s.

9.3.1   A Brief Review of J2SE `ProtectionDomain`-Based Authorization

Basic J2SE authorization involves the authorization of classes and their methods to perform privileged operations. Authorization consists of determining whether each of the classes whose methods are executing in a thread is authorized to perform the privileged operation. If one or more of the classes is not authorized, the authorization request fails, resulting in a `java.lang.SecurityException` being thrown. This basic algorithm is slightly modified when a method chooses to enter a privileged mode by calling the `AccessController.doPrivileged()` method. When `doPrivileged()` is called, all methods and their associated classes on the thread runtime stack prior to the method's calling `doPrivileged()` are excluded from the authorization test. Figure 9.1 shows the basic concepts.

To enable authorization, each class needs to be granted a set of authorizations, represented as `Permission` objects. Each class is loaded into the Java runtime via a `java.security.SecureClassLoader`, such as a `java.net.URLClassLoader`. The `ClassLoader` associates a `ProtectionDomain` with each class. The `ProtectionDomain` references the class's `java.security.Code-Source`, representing the URL location from which the class has been loaded and the entities that digitally signed the class's code. The set of `Permissions` to associate with a `ProtectionDomain` are defined by the `Policy` object and are dynami-

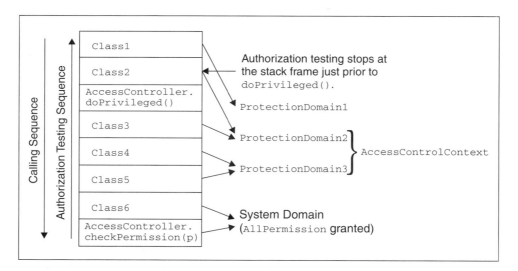

Figure 9.1.   Thread Stack Frames, `ProtectionDomains`, and `AccessControlContext`

cally calculated during each `Permission` check. This dynamic behavior allows for `Policy` refresh without restarting the Java runtime.

When access to a restricted resource is requested, an authorization test is performed by making a call to `AccessController.checkPermission()`. In essence, the following steps are performed.

1. A `Permission` object instance is passed to `checkPermission()`. This `Permission` object represents the right to access the restricted resource. For example:

   ```
   AccessController.checkPermission(new
     java.util.PropertyPermission("user.home", "read"));
   ```

2. A `java.security.AccessControlContext` is constructed by collecting the `ProtectionDomain`s for all the classes whose methods are on the thread stack. This is achieved by walking back through each of the thread stack frames, starting at the `checkPermission()` method. If a `doPrivileged()` call is encountered in the thread stack, the thread stack walkback stops at the method/class just prior to the `doPrivileged()` call. The result of the walkback is a set of unique `ProtectionDomain`s. System classes—those loaded by the primordial class loader via the boot class path—are considered to be fully trusted and essentially are granted `java.security.AllPermission`. In the Sun Microsystems reference implementation of the Java runtime, a `ProtectionDomain` is not included in the `AccessControlContext` for the system classes.

   Figure 9.1 shows a calling sequence that includes a call to `doPrivileged()` and `checkPermission()`. When `checkPermission()` is called, the `AccessControlContext` used for the authorization testing contains only `ProtectionDomain2` and `ProtectionDomain3`. `ProtectionDomain1` is excluded, as the method in `Class1` is called prior to the method that called `doPrivileged()`. The system domain is also excluded, because it is considered to be fully trusted.

3. Authorization is performed by taking the `Permission` object passed to the `checkPermission()` call and calling `ProtectionDomain.implies()` with the same `Permission` object from step 1 for each `ProtectionDomain` in the `AccessControlContext`. The result is that each `ProtectionDomain` in the `AccessControlContext` is queried as to whether it contains a `Permission` that *implies*—is equivalent to or stronger than—the `Permission` checked by the call to `AccessController.checkPermission()`. If all the `ProtectionDomain`s in the `AccessControlContext` imply the `Permission` passed to the `AccessController.checkPermission()` method, the authorization succeeds. If at least one `ProtectionDomain` does not imply

the required `Permission`, authorization fails, and a `SecurityException` is thrown.

In Figure 9.1, if both `ProtectionDomain2` and `ProtectionDomain3` imply the `Permission` passed as an argument to `checkPermission()`, the authorization succeeds. If either `ProtectionDomain.implies()` method fails because it lacks a `Permission` that implies the `Permission` passed as an argument to `checkPermission()`, the authorization fails.

9.3.2   Adding a Subject to a Thread

A key JAAS feature is principal-based authorization, which allows an authenticated `Principal`, referenced by a `Subject` instance, to access restricted resources regardless of the authorization granted to the executing code. As shown in Section 9.2 on page 291, it is possible to use `LoginContext`s and `LoginModule`s to create `Subject`s and attach `Principal` objects to them. The next step is to associate a `Subject` with a thread of execution. This is accomplished via the `doAs()` and `doAsPrivileged()` static methods in class `javax.security.auth.Subject`.

Syntactically, associating the `Subject` with a thread is similar to calling `AccessController.doPrivileged()`. The `Subject.doAs()` method is called with two parameters:

1. A `Subject` instance containing authenticated `Principal`s

2. A `PrivilegedAction` or `PrivilegedExceptionAction` instance

`PrivilegedAction` and `PrivilegedExceptionAction` are the two `java.security` package interfaces that are also used for passing privileged code to an `AccessController.doPrivileged()` call. They have a `run()` method that, when implemented, will contain code to be executed with the `Subject`'s `Permission`s. The `PrivilegedExceptionAction` interface should be used when the code embedded into the `run()` method can throw a *checked* `Exception`, or an `Exception` listed in the `throws` clause of a method. If there are no checked `Exception`s, `PrivilegedAction` should be used. When invoked, `Subject.doAs()` calls the `run()` method in the `PrivilegedAction` or the `PrivilegedExceptionAction` object, executes the code with the set of `Permission`s granted to the thread of execution unioned with the set of `Permission`s granted to the `Subject`'s `Principal`s, and returns the `run()` method's return value.

As we explained in Section 8.6 on page 267, the set of `Permission`s granted to a thread of execution is obtained by intersecting the sets of `Permission`s implied by the `ProtectionDomain`s in the thread's `AccessControlContext`. When `Subject.doAs()` is called, it adds the `Permission`s granted to the `Subject`'s `Principal`s to the `ProtectionDomain`s at the stack frames after the call to `Subject.doAs()`.

The Subject API offers another method to enable a `Subject`'s `Principals`' `Permissions`, `Subject.doAsPrivileged()`. Like `doAs()`, `doAsPrivileged()` takes a `Subject` and a `PrivilegedAction` or a `PrivilegedExceptionAction` parameter, as well as an `AccessControlContext` parameter. `Subject.doAs-Privileged()` behaves exactly like `Subject.doAs()` but uses the `Access-ControlContext` provided as the third parameter instead of retrieving the current thread's `AccessControlContext`. If the provided `AccessControlContext` is `null`, this method instantiates a new `AccessControlContext` with an empty collection of `ProtectionDomains`.

Note that adding a `Subject`'s `Permissions` to a thread of execution is considered a security-sensitive operation. Therefore, if a `SecurityManager` is installed, the `Subject` API will consult it to verify whether the code attempting to perform such an operation is authorized to do so. Specifically, calling `Subject.doAs()` or `Subject.doAsPrivileged()` requires a `javax.security.auth.Auth-Permission`. The `Permission` target is the `String` `"doAs"` for `Subject.doAs()`; the `String` `"doAsPrivileged"` for `Subject.doAsPrivileged()`.

9.3.2.1 Fourth Scenario
The following application, Main2 (Listing 9.14), shows how to use `Subject.doAs()` to run a thread of execution under a particular authenticated `Subject`.

Listing 9.14. `Main2.java`

```
package jaasexample;

import javax.security.auth.Subject;

/**
 * Main2 extends the function of Main by overriding the
 * doSomethingInteresting() method so that it calls
 * Subject.doAs() with an instance of Demo4PrivilegedAction.
 */
public class Main2 extends Main
{
    public static void main( String[] args)
    {
        (new Main2()).run(args);
    }

    /**
     * Associate a Subject with the current thread, calling
     * a Demo4PrivilegedAction that will retrieve the Subject
     * currently executing, and then display the Principals
     * that were active when Demo4PrivilegedAction.run()
     * was executing.
     *
```

(continues)

Listing 9.14. `Main2.java`   (*continued*)

```
    * @param subject is the Subject to associate with the
    *          current thread.
    */
   protected void doSomethingInteresting(Subject subject)
   {
       System.out.println();
       System.out.println("Calling " +
           "Demo4PrivilegedAction.run()");
       System.out.println();

       // Associate the subject argument passed to this
       // method with the current thread, then call
       // Demo4PrivilegedAction.run().
       // Demo4PrivilegedAction will return the thread's
       // current Subject, which will be the subject passed
       // as an argument to this method.
       Subject threadSubject = (Subject) Subject.doAs
           (subject, new Demo4PrivilegedAction());

       showPrincipals(threadSubject.getPrincipals());
       System.out.println();
   }
}
```

`Main2` subclasses `Main` (see Listing 9.2 on page 296) and reuses `Demo3LoginModule` (see Listing 9.10 on page 310). In particular, `Main2` calls `Main`'s `run()` method to perform the authentication. As we saw in Section 9.2.2.3 on page 308, `Demo3LoginModule` creates the `Subject` with two associated `Principal`s—`Manager` and `Agent`—the `String "Louise"` as the public credential, and the `String "Private DB access password"` as the private credential. `Main2` overrides the `doSomethingInteresting()` method, which is called by `Main`'s `run()` method after the `Subject` has been created. `Main2.doSomething-Interesting()` associates the `Subject` with the current thread of execution and runs a `PrivilegedAction`, called `Demo4PrivilegedAction`, from within a `doAs()` block. Finally, `Main.showPrincipals()` displays the `Principal`s for the current `Subject`.

Listing 9.15 shows the `Demo4PrivilegedAction` code, which gets the `Subject` from the current thread by passing the current `AccessControlContext` to the static method `Subject.getSubject()`, which returns the thread's current `Subject`. This operation will be executed with the `Subject`'s `Permission`s. Calling `Subject.getSubject()` requires a `javax.security.auth.AuthPermission "getSubject"`, which must be granted to the application's `CodeSource` or the `Subject`.

Listing 9.15. `Demo4PrivilegedAction.java`

```java
package jaasexample;

import java.security.AccessController;
import java.security.PrivilegedAction;

import javax.security.auth.Subject;


/**
 * A simple class to demonstrate how to get
 * the Subject from the current thread.
 */
public class Demo4PrivilegedAction
    implements PrivilegedAction
{
    /**
     * This method is indirectly called by a Subject.doAs()
     * method, where the current instance of this class is
     * passed as an argument to the Subject.doAs() method.
     * The current thread's Subject is returned by this
     * method.
     *
     * @return the current thread's Subject.
     */
    public Object run()
    {
        // The AccessControlContext contains the current
        // Subject
        return Subject.getSubject
            (AccessController.getContext());
    }
}
```

The command line arguments to run this scenario are as follows.

- `-Djava.security.manager` indicates that the default `SecurityManager`, in package `java.lang`, should be installed by the Java virtual machine launcher.

- `-Djava.security.policy` specifies the location of the Java 2 security policy file, which in this scenario is `jaasexample/jaasexample.policy`.

- `-Djava.security.auth.login.config` indicates the location of the `LoginModule` configuration file, which in this scenario is `jaasexample/jaasexample.config`.

- `jaasexample.Main2` is the program to run.

- `Demo3` is the argument to the `Main2` program. `Demo3` is the name of the stanza in the `LoginModule` configuration file to use for creating `Login-Modules` (see Listing 9.12 on page 312).

Listing 9.16 shows, as expected, that `Manager` and `Agent` are the two `Principal`s associated with the current thread and that the `String`s `"Louise"` and `"Private DB access password"` are the public and private credentials, respectively. The example displays the `Principal`s as they are constructed. Subsequently, `Demo4PrivilegedAction.run()` demonstrates that the thread's current `Subject` has the same `Principal`s.

Listing 9.16. Running `Main2` with `Demo3LoginModule`

```
java -Djava.security.manager -Djava.security.
policy==jaasexample/jaasexample.policy -Djava.security.auth.
login.config==jaasexample/jaasexample.config jaasexample.Main2
Demo3

Demo1LoginModule.initialize
Demo1LoginModule.login: true
Name: demo
Password: demo
Demo3LoginModule.commit: true
Login succeeded? true
Principals
Principal: Manager
    Class: jaasexample.DemoPrincipal
Principal: Agent
    Class: jaasexample.DemoPrincipal
Public credentials:
    Value: Louise
    Class: java.lang.String
Private credentials:
    Value: Private DB access password
    Class: java.lang.String

Inside Demo4PrivilegedAction.run()

Principals
Principal: Manager
    Class: jaasexample.DemoPrincipal
Principal: Agent
    Class: jaasexample.DemoPrincipal

Demo3LoginModule.logout
```

As we said, getting the `Subject` associated with the current thread of execution is considered a security-sensitive operation that requires a special `Permission` to be executed. In the Java 2 language, `Permission`s must be granted to the application's `CodeSource`. Alternatively, JAAS allows granting `Permission`s to the `Principal` that represents the `Subject` associated with the thread of execution. The Java system administrator grants `Permission`s to `CodeSource`s and/or `Principal`s by configuring a security policy database. In Section 8.3 on page 261, we saw that the default implementation of the policy database is file based, and we studied how `Permissions` can be granted based on the `CodeSource`. As a result of the integration of JAAS with the Java 2 SDK V1.4, the Java security `Policy` now considers the `Permissions` granted to `Principals` representing `Subjects` associated with threads of execution.

9.3.3   Security Authorization Policy File

In the Java 2 SDK V1.4, the security policy includes authorization `grant` entries that describe `CodeSources` and/or `Principals` authorized to perform privileged operations. The default implementation of the `Policy` is a flat text file. The sample policy file in Listing 9.17 shows four `grant` statements, each granting a `CodeSource` and/or a `Principal` access to restricted resources.

Listing 9.17. Sample Authorization Policy File

```
grant codeBase "file:./" {
    permission javax.security.auth.AuthPermission
        "createLoginContext.Demo3";
    permission javax.security.auth.AuthPermission
        "modifyPrincipals";
    permission javax.security.auth.AuthPermission
        "modifyPublicCredentials";
    permission javax.security.auth.AuthPermission
        "modifyPrivateCredentials";
    permission javax.security.auth.PrivateCredentialPermission
        "java.lang.String jaasexample.DemoPrincipal
            \"Manager\"", "read";
    permission javax.security.auth.AuthPermission "doAs";
    permission javax.security.auth.AuthPermission
        "getSubject";
    permission javax.security.auth.AuthPermission
        "doAsPrivileged";
};

grant codeBase "file:./", Principal jaasexample.DemoPrincipal
    "Manager" {
    permission jaasexample.DemoPermission "Test";
    permission jaasexample.DemoPermission
        "deploy1:EJB:TravellerCreditCard.*";
    permission jaasexample.DemoPermission
        "deploy1:EJB:WebAccess.lookup(String)";
};

grant Principal jaasexample.DemoPrincipal "Agent" {
};

grant {
    permission jaasexample.DemoPermission
        "deploy1:EJB:WebAccess.bookmark(int)";
};
```

In Listing 9.17, `grant` stanzas for `Permission jaasexample.Demo-Permission` exist for authorization for two `DemoPrincipal`s: `Manager` and `Agent`. This policy file requires J2SE V1.4. Earlier versions of J2SE require multiple policy files. See the corresponding J2SE documentation for setting up the policy files.

The source code for `DemoPermission` is shown in Listing 9.18.

Listing 9.18. `DemoPermission.java`

```
package jaasexample;


import java.security.BasicPermission;


/**
 * A class to demonstrate a J2EE-like Permission.
 */
public class DemoPermission extends BasicPermission
{
    /**
     * Required constructor for use when the security policy
     * is read.
     *
     * @param target a String representing the target
     * resource.
     */
    public DemoPermission(String target)
    {
        super(target);
    }

    /**
     * Each deployment has resource types (for example,
     * <code>WEB</code> or <code>EJB</code>), and the name of
     * the resource. The actual target object for the
     * Permission is a String obtained by colon-concatenating
     * the three parts, deployment, resourceType and
     * resource.
     *
     * @param deployment is a String representing the name of
     *        the deployment (for example,
     *        <code>deploy1</code>).
     * @param resourceType is either the String
     *        <code>WEB</code> or the String
     *        <code>EJB</code>.
     * @param resource is a String representing the name of
     *        the resource, such as a URL or an EJB method.
     */
    public DemoPermission(String deployment,
        String resourceType, String resource)
    {
        super(deployment + ":" + resourceType + ":" +
            resource);
    }
}
```

DemoPermission is a simple custom Permission that subclasses Basic-Permission in package java.security. As we noted in Section 8.2 on page 258, BasicPermission is a nonabstract class that offers a concrete implementation of the implies() method. BasicPermission is the ideal superclass for custom *named* Permissions, which are those Permissions that, just like DemoPermission, have a target but not an action list.

The DemoPermission target is a String composed of three parts that we will loosely define around the J2EE authorization model. In this example, the protected resource is access to EJB methods.

1. The first part is the name of the container instance running the application: for example, deploy1.

2. The second part, EJB, indicates that the resource is an EJB method.

3. The third part is the target method signature, as in WebAccess.lookup(String). Instead of the method name, it is possible to use a wildcard character, as in TravellerCreditCard.*, to indicate that the Principal is authorized for all EJB methods in the target class.

Details of EJB authorization are covered in Section 5.2 on page 159 and Section 5.4 on page 184.

For running the examples in this chapter, the code needs to be authorized to perform privileged operations, including operations on the Subject and Principals, and invoking Subject.doAs(). A detailed explanation of the policy file of Listing 9.17 follows.

1. The first stanza in the security policy file grants all code whose codebase URL is file:./ authorization to perform a set of operations requiring AuthPermission and PrivateCredentialPermission in package javax.security.auth. These Permissions are required to enable the sample code in this chapter to run. Most of the authorizations are for JAAS methods that perform logins and operations on the Subject. The stanza implies that all Principals are granted these Permissions.

2. The second stanza grants three DemoPermissions to all code run by Demo-Principal Manager and whose codebase URL is file:./. The three DemoPermissions are distinguished by their respective targets: "deploy1:EJB:WebAccess.lookup(String)", "Test", and "deploy1:EJB:TravellerCreditCard.*".

3. The third stanza, for DemoPrincipal Agent, does not grant any authorizations. This stanza demonstrates that it is possible to have a grant stanza with no Permissions. This stanza could have been omitted because by default, Java Permissions are denied unless explicitly granted by the security policy.

4. The final stanza grants all code and `Principals` a `DemoPermission` whose target is `"deploy1:EJB:WebAccess.bookmark(int)"`.

9.3.4   Examples of the Subject-Based Authorization Algorithm

Java 2 authorization is performed by the `AccessController`. As described in Section 9.3.1 on page 314, `AccessController.getContext()` creates an `AccessControlContext` containing the `ProtectionDomains` of the classes whose methods are on the thread stack at the time `AccessController.get-Context()` is called. Subsequently, `AccessController.checkPermission()` tests these `ProtectionDomains` to see whether each of them contains a `Permission` that implies the `Permission` to access the requested resource. If so, the authorization test succeeds. If any `ProtectionDomain` in the `AccessControlContext` does not have a `Permission` that implies the `Permission` to access the requested resource, the authorization test fails, and a `SecurityException` is thrown.

With JAAS, the basic Java 2 authorization concepts are extended to `Subjects`. Each `Subject` has a (possibly empty) set of `Principals` associated with it. When `Subject.doAs()` is called, the `Permissions` associated with each `Principal` in the specified `Subject` are added to—unioned with—each subsequent stack frame's `Permissions`. Specifically, the `Subject`'s `Permissions` are added to the `Permissions` of the `ProtectionDomains` associated with each of the stack frames after the call to `Subject.doAs()`.

Figure 9.2 shows the calling sequence for Main2, including the `Permissions` associated with the methods and their classes. The `Permission` set in Figure 9.2 indicated as {default `Permissions`} contains the `Permissions` associated with all `CodeSources`, where the `grant` stanza in the security policy file did not specify a codebase or `Principal` (see point 4 on page 324). The `Permission` set {All-Permission} is for system classes, which are authorized to perform all privileged operations within the Java runtime. As for the rest, each class on the thread stack gets the `Permissions` granted to its `CodeSource`, which in this case is reduced to the simple codebase, and those granted to the `Principals`.

Figure 9.2 also shows the effect of the call to `Subject.doAs()`. At each stack frame after the call to `Subject.doAs()`, the `Subject`'s `Permissions` for Demo-Principals Manager and Agent are added to the `Permissions` associated with the method's class.

From an implementation point of view, `Subject.doAs()` gets the `Access-ControlContext` associated with the current thread of execution and combines it with the `Permissions` granted to the `Subject`. This is done by adding the `Subject`'s `Permissions` to the `ProtectionDomains` associated with each of the

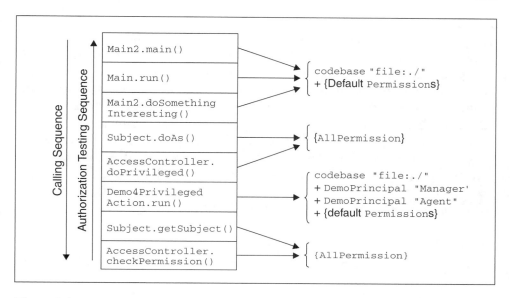

Figure 9.2. Main2 Thread Stack and `Permissions` by Stack Frame

stack frames *after* the call to `Subject.doAs()`. The `ProtectionDomains` prior to the `Subject.doAs()` call remain unaltered in the new `AccessControlContext` that is created. Then, `Subject.doAs()` calls `AccessController.doPrivileged()`, passing it the `PrivilegedAction` or `PrivilegedExceptionAction` along with the modified `AccessControlContext`. The `PrivilegedAction`'s or `PrivilegedExceptionAction`'s `run()` method is executed.

Note that even though `Subject.doAs()` calls `AccessController.doPrivileged()`, this does not mean that the `ProtectionDomains` of the stack frames prior to the call to `Subject.doAs()` are not tested by `AccessController.checkPermission()`. In fact, those `ProtectionDomains` appear unaltered in the modified `AccessControlContext` that `Subject.doAs()` passes to `AccessController.doPrivileged()`.

In conclusion, when an `AccessController.checkPermission()` operation is performed, the basic authorization algorithm works the same as before, but the test of the `ProtectionDomain` for each of the stack frames now includes the `Permissions` added owing to `Subject.doAs()`, as we will see in Section 9.3.4.1. In addition, the `Subject` is now associated with the thread and can be obtained by getting the thread's `AccessControlContext` and passing it to `Subject.getSubject()`, as is shown in Listing 9.15 on page 319 and Listing 9.16 on page 320.

9.3.4.1   Fifth Scenario

The program Main3 shown in this section is similar to the Main2 program shown in Listing 9.14 on page 317 but also includes authorization tests in the doSome-thingInteresting() method, as well as in the PrivilegedAction. The purpose of Main3 is to show the effect of performing authorization tests at various points, including from within Main3 itself and the PrivilegedAction. The Privileged-Action implementation used by Main3 is called Demo5PrivilegedAction. In particular, Demo5PrivilegedAction is called via Subject.doAs() and Subject.doAsPrivileged(); in both cases, the Subject contains the Manager and Agent DemoPrincipals. Main3 also shows the effect of calling Demo5Privileged-Action via Subject.doAsPrivileged() with a Subject containing no Principals. The code of the Main3 application is shown in Listing 9.19.

Listing 9.19. Main3.java

```
package jaasexample;


import java.util.Iterator;
import java.util.Map;

import java.security.PrivilegedAction;

import javax.security.auth.Subject;


/**
 * Main3 extends Main by implementing the
 * doSomethingInteresting() method
 * to perform authorization tests.
 */
public class Main3 extends Main
{
    /**
     * The main method of this application.
     *
     * @param args an array of Strings to be passed on the
     *        command line. The first argument tells the
     *        LoginContext which LoginContext stanza to use
     *        when selecting LoginModules. The second
     *        argument is the CallBackHandler to be used by
     *        all of the LoginModules.
     */
    public static void main(String[] args)
    {
        (new Main3()).run(args);
    }

    /**
     * Demonstrate authorization with and without the Subject
```

```
 *  being associated with the current thread, and by using
 *  Subject.doAs() and Subject.doAsPrivileged().
 *    * @param subject is the Subject to be associated with
 *         the current thread.
 */
protected void doSomethingInteresting(Subject subject)
{
    SecurityManager sm = System.getSecurityManager();

    // This scenario requires a SecurityManager
    // installed.
    if (sm == null)
        throw new RuntimeException
            ("Please, rerun with a SecurityManager");

    // Test whether the current thread is authorized for
    // DemoPermission("TestDeploy", "EJB", "Test"). The
    // test should fail.
    boolean succeeded;
    Permission perm = new DemoPermission
        ("TestDeploy", "EJB", "Test");

    try
    {
        sm.checkPermission(perm);
        succeeded = true;
    }
    catch (SecurityException se)
    {
        succeeded = false;
    }

    System.out.println();
    System.out.println
        ("DemoPermission(\"TestDeploy\", \"EJB\", " +
        "\"Test\") " + "succeeded? " + succeeded);
    System.out.println();

    // The Demo5PrivilegedAction will be used 3 times
    // below
    PrivilegedAction paDemo5PA =
        new Demo5PrivilegedAction();

    // A Map that holds the result of the
    // Demo5PrivilegedAction.run() call.
    Map resultMap;

    // Use doAs() with the Subject.
    // Demo5PrivilegedAction.run() will be called.
    // Authorization requests will fail because the
    // classes in the thread prior to doAs() are not
    // authorized. The exception is for access to
    // WebAccess.bookmark(int), where all of the code in
    // the thread is authorized for access.
```

(continues)

Listing 9.19. `Main3.java`   (*continued*)

```
        System.out.println("doAs() with the Subject:");
        resultMap = (Map) Subject.doAs(subject, paDemo5PA);
        showResult(resultMap);

        // Add the Subject and its Principals to the thread
        // so that any Permissions granted to the Principals
        // will be added to all ProtectionDomains on the
        // stack when an authorization test is performed.
        // Demo5PrivilegedAction.run() will be called.
        // doAsPrivileged() with a null third argument will
        // exclude all ProtectionDomains prior to
        // Demo5PrivilegedAction.run() from the
        // AccessControlContext when the authorization test
        // is performed. In effect, this method and those
        // prior to it in the thread will not be considered
        // in the authorization test.
        System.out.println
            ("doAsPrivileged() with the Subject:");
        resultMap = (Map) Subject.doAsPrivileged
            (subject, paDemo5PA, null);
        showResult(resultMap);

        // Perform the authorization request using a Subject
        // without any Principals. The authorization requests
        // will fail except where all of the code in the
        // thread is authorized: WebAccess.bookmark(int).
        System.out.println
            ("doAsPrivileged() using an empty Subject:");
        Subject emptySubject = new Subject();
        resultMap = (Map) Subject.doAsPrivileged
            (emptySubject, paDemo5PA, null);
        showResult(resultMap);
    }

    /**
     * Show the contents of the Map returned by the
     * Demo5PrivilegedAction.run().
     *
     * @param map is a Map representing results of
     *        authorization tests. For each entry in the Map,
     *        the key is a String representing the target for
     *        an authorization test, and the value is the
     *        boolean <code>true</code> if the authorization
     *        test succeeded and the boolean
     *        <code>false</code> if the authorization test
     *        failed.
     */
    private void showResult(Map resultMap)
    {
        Iterator resultIter =
            resultMap.entrySet().iterator();

        while (resultIter.hasNext())
        {
```

```
                Map.Entry entry = (Map.Entry) resultIter.next();
                System.out.println("Method permission: " +
                    entry.getKey());
                System.out.println("    Succeeded? " +
                    entry.getValue());
            }

        System.out.println();
        }
    }
```

The code of `Demo5PrivilegedAction` is shown in Listing 9.20.

Listing 9.20. `Demo5PrivilegedAction.java`

```
package jaasexample;


import java.util.TreeMap;

import java.security.PrivilegedAction;
import java.security.Permission;


/**
 * This class demonstrates authorization system calls (calls
 * to the SecurityManager). Instances of this class are
 * used by Subject.doAs(), which associates a Subject with
 * the current thread.
 */
public class Demo5PrivilegedAction
    implements PrivilegedAction
{
    /**
     * The set of target EJB methods for which authorization
     * is being tested.
     */
    String[] methodPerms =
    {
        "TravellerCreditCard.balance(),"
        "TravellerCreditCard.credit(int),"
        "TravellerCreditCard.debit(int),"
        "WebAccess.bookmark(int),"
        "WebAccess.lookup(String)"
    };

    /**
     * Perform an authorization test for each target EJB
     * method in the methodPerms array.
     *
     * @return a Map representing results of authorization
     *         tests. For each entry in the Map, the key is
     *         a String representing the target for an
```

(continues)

Listing 9.20. `Demo5PrivilegedAction.java`   (*continued*)

```
 *            authorization test, and the value is the
 *            String <code>true</code> if the authorization
 *            test succeeded and the String
 *            <code>false</code> if the authorization test
 *            failed.
 */
public Object run()
{
    // Get the SecurityManager to call its
    // checkPermission() method.
    SecurityManager sm = System.getSecurityManager();

    // This scenario requires a SecurityManager
    // installed.
    if (sm == null)
        throw new RuntimeException
            ("Please, rerun with a SecurityManager");

    // To record the result of the authorization tests.
    TreeMap resultMap = new TreeMap();

    // Perform an authorization test on each resource
    // listed in methodPerms.
    for (int i=0; i < methodPerms.length; i++)
    {
        // Create a DemoPermission with the specified
        // target method
        Permission perm = new DemoPermission
            ("deploy1", "EJB", methodPerms[i]);

        try
        {
            // See if the current Subject/thread classes
            // are authorized
            sm.checkPermission(perm);

            // We reached here if authorization succeeded
            resultMap.put(methodPerms[i], "true");
        }
        catch (SecurityException se)
        {
            // We reached here if authorization failed
            resultMap.put(methodPerms[i], "false");
        }
    }

    // Return the set of authorizations/failures.
    return resultMap;
    }
}
```

Listing 9.21 shows the output produced by Main3 when it is run with
`Demo3LoginModule` (see Listing 9.21 on page 331). For an explanation of the
command line arguments to run this scenario, see the list on page 319.

Listing 9.21. Running `Main3` with `Demo3LoginModule`

```
java -Djava.security.manager -Djava.security.
policy==jaasexample/jaasexample.policy -Djava.security.auth.
login.config==jaasexample/jaasexample.config jaasexample.Main3
Demo3

DemoLoginModule.initialize
DemoLoginModule.login: true
Name: demo
Password: demo
Demo3LoginModule.commit: true
Login succeeded? true
Principals
Principal: Manager
   Class: jaasexample.DemoPrincipal
Principal: Agent
   Class: jaasexample.DemoPrincipal
Public credentials:
   Value: Louise
   Class: java.lang.String
Private credentials:
   Value: Private DB access password
   Class: java.lang.String

DemoPermission "Test" succeeded? false

doAs() with the Subject:

Inside Demo5PrivilegedAction.run()

Method permission: deploy1:EJB:TravellerCreditCard.debit(int)
   Succeeded? false
Method permission: deploy1:EJB:TravellerCreditCard.credit(int)
   Succeeded? false
Method permission: deploy1:EJB:TravellerCreditCard.balance()
   Succeeded? false
Method permission: deploy1:EJB:WebAccess.lookup(String)
   Succeeded? false
Method permission: deploy1:EJB:WebAccess.bookmark(int)
   Succeeded? true


doAsPrivileged() with the Subject:

Inside Demo5PrivilegedAction.run()

Method permission: deploy1:EJB:TravellerCreditCard.debit(int)
   Succeeded? true
Method permission: deploy1:EJB:TravellerCreditCard.credit(int)
   Succeeded? true
Method permission: deploy1:EJB:TravellerCreditCard.balance()
   Succeeded? true
Method permission: deploy1:EJB:WebAccess.lookup(String)
   Succeeded? true
```

(continues)

Listing 9.21. Running `Main3` with `Demo3LoginModule` (*continued*)

```
Method permission: deploy1:EJB:WebAccess.bookmark(int)
   Succeeded? true

doAsPrivileged() using an empty Subject:

Inside Demo5PrivilegedAction.run()

Method permission: deploy1:EJB:TravellerCreditCard.debit(int)
   Succeeded? false
Method permission: deploy1:EJB:TravellerCreditCard.credit(int)
   Succeeded? false
Method permission: deploy1:EJB:TravellerCreditCard.balance()
   Succeeded? false
Method permission: deploy1:EJB:WebAccess.lookup(String)
   Succeeded? false
Method permission: deploy1:EJB:WebAccess.bookmark(int)
   Succeeded? true


Demo3LoginModule.logout
```

In Main3, an authorization test is performed by calling `SecurityManager.checkPermission()` with a `DemoPermission` whose target resource is called `"Test"`. As shown in Figure 9.3, not all the thread `AccessControlContext` `ProtectionDomain`s, at the point the authorization test is performed, imply `jaasexample.DemoPermission "Test"`. Therefore, the authorization test fails.

Next is a series of authorization tests within `Demo5PrivilegedAction`. The authenticated `Subject` contains the `Manager` and `Agent DemoPrincipal`s and is associated with the thread via the `Subject.doAs()` call performed in Main3. Figure 9.4 shows the `Permissions` associated with each of the stack frames during the call to `Demo5PrivilegedAction`.

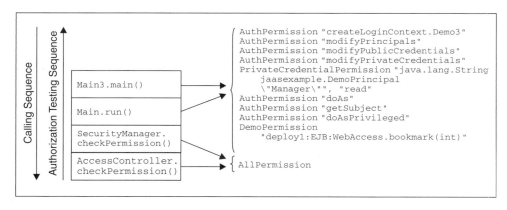

Figure 9.3.   Authorization Test from within Main3

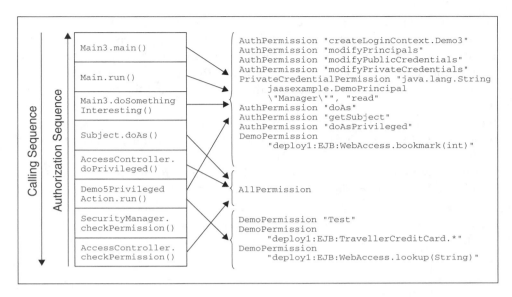

Figure 9.4. Authorization Test after the Call to `Subject.doAs()`

Note that the call to `AccessController.doPrivileged()` is made to associate the `Subject`'s `Permissions` with all the stack frames after the `Subject.doAs()` call. As we have observed, the call to `doPrivileged()` does not exclude any of the `ProtectionDomains` from the stack frames prior to the call to `Subject.doAs()`. Therefore, the authorization test includes checking all the stack frames prior to the call to `Subject.doAs()`. The `ProtectionDomains` of the classes prior to `Subject.doAs()` call do not imply `jaasexample.DemoPermission` with any of the following targets:

- `"deploy1:EJB:TravellerCreditCard.debit(int)"`
- `"deploy1:EJB:TravellerCreditCard.credit(int)"`
- `"deploy1:EJB:TravellerCreditCard.balance()"`
- `"deploy1:EJB:WebAccess.lookup(String)"`

Therefore, all these authorization tests fail. The last authorization test in `Demo5PrivilegedAction`, `jassexample.DemoPermission` with target resource `"deploy1:EJB:WebAccess.bookmark(int)"`, passes because the authorization policy file contains a stanza that grants authorization to all classes and `Principals` (see point 4 on page 324).

Including all the stack frames prior to the `Subject.doAs()` method in an authorization test is not always satisfactory. In J2EE security, the resource authorization process involves defining a `Subject`, associating it with a thread, and determining whether it is authorized to use a resource. In this case, we want to make an authorization decision regardless of the authorizations possessed by the code in the thread. We need a means by which the `Subject` is associated with a thread but ignores the callers to the method that associated the `Subject` with the thread. The effect is to perform the more traditional principal-based authorization typically found in servers. For example, with J2EE resource-access authorizations, such as to access to EJB methods, we are interested in the authorizations for a `Subject`, not the code's access rights.

To accommodate traditional principal-based authorization, `Subject.doAsPrivileged()` is called with the `Subject`, a `PrivilegedAction` or a `PrivilegedExceptionAction`, and an `AccessControlContext`. Main3 passes `Subject.doAsPrivileged()` a null `AccessControlContext`. As shown in Figure 9.5, this call has the same effect as `Subject.doAs()` but also marks the thread stack as

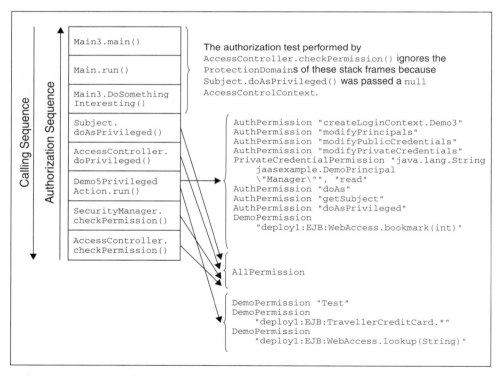

Figure 9.5.   Authorization Test after the Call to `Subject.doAsPrivileged()` with a null `AccessControlContext`

though an `AccessController.doPrivileged()` was called to truncate the authorization test at the stack frame just prior to the `AccessController.do-Privileged()` call. In effect, the authorization test is truncated at the `Subject.doAsPrivileged()` stack frame. When the authorization tests are performed in `Demo5PrivilegedAction`, they all succeed, as all the thread stack frames checked during a call to `AccessController.checkPermission()` contain authorizations for the requested resources. The reason behind this behavior is that the `Access-ControlContext` passed to `doAsPrivileged()` was `null`. If the value were a reference to an actual `AccessControlContext`, it would behave as though there were a call to `AccessController.doPrivileged()` with the `AccessControlContext` passed as the second parameter, as described in Section 8.7.2 on page 277.

The final set of authorization tests in Main3 demonstrates a call to `Subject.doAsPrivileged()` with the same `PrivilegedAction` but with a `Subject` lacking `Principals` authorized for the resources requested in the `PrivilegedAction`. In particular, the `Subject` in this example does not contain any `Principals`, although the effect would be the same even if it did contain `Principals` that lacked authorization for access to the requested resources. As shown in Figure 9.6,

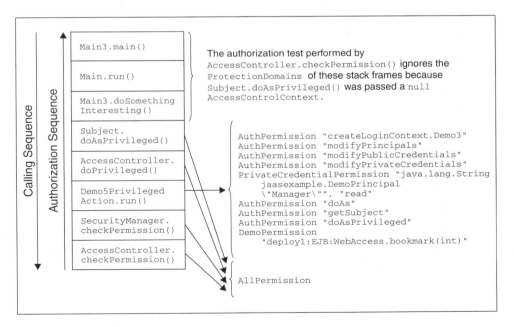

Figure 9.6. Authorization Test after the Call to `Subject.doAsPrivileged()` with a `null AccessControlContext` and a `Subject` Lacking Authorized `Principals`

the authorization test fails because not all the methods on the stack whose `ProtectionDomain`s are being tested have the required `Permissions`. In particular, for those methods, neither the `CodeSource` nor the `Subject`'s `Principals` have the required authorizations.

9.3.5   Additional Observations about JAAS

It is possible to call `Subject.doAs()` multiple times within a thread, but only one `Subject` may be active at a time. As shown in Figure 9.7, when `Subject.doAs()` is called with `Subject` s1 and `PrivilegedAction` or `PrivilegedException-Action` pa1, followed by a call to `Subject.doAs()` with `Subject` s2 and `PrivilegedAction` or `PrivilegedExceptionAction` pa2, pa2 will be executed with s2's `Permissions`, not s1's `Permissions`. The effect of the second call to `Subject.doAs()` is to obscure s1's `Permissions` until the second `Subject.doAs()` completes and returns to its caller, `method1`. Similar considerations apply to `Subject.doAsPrivileged()`.

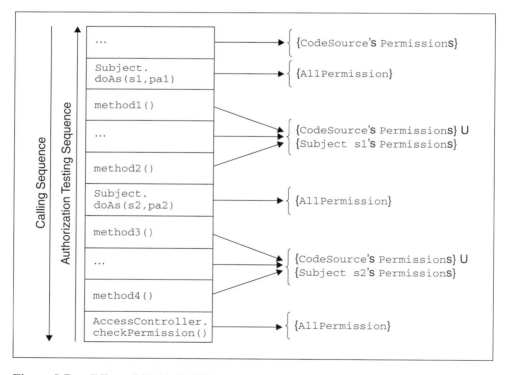

Figure 9.7.   Effect of Multiple Calls to `Subject.doAs()`

JAAS is integrated with the J2SE security and authorization mechanisms, including `AccessController.doPrivileged()`. In the absence of `Subjects` associated with a thread, a call to `doPrivileged()` will mark the thread stack to limit the number of stack frames searched for `ProtectionDomains` and `Permissions` when constructing an `AccessControlContext`. The same is true for JAAS and `Subjects`. If a `doPrivileged()` call is made after a call to `Subject.doAs()`, the `Subject` is not visible when an authorization test is performed by `AccessController.checkPermission()`. The effect is as if the `Subject.doAs()` method were never called, as is shown in Figure 9.8. Similar considerations apply to `Subject.doAsPrivileged()`.[3]

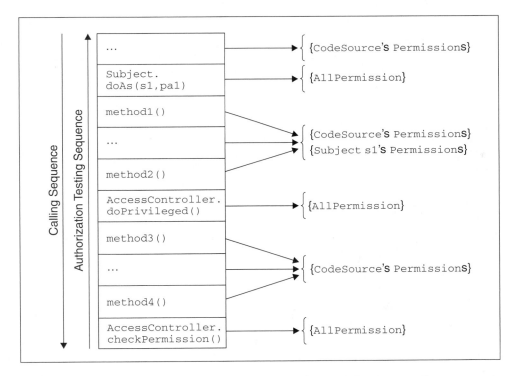

Figure 9.8. Effect of Calling `AccessController.doPrivileged()` after `Subject.doAs()`

---

3. This behavior may change in future Java releases, whereby the `Subject` will not be removed from the thread after a call to `AccessController.doPrivileged()`. Therefore, the `Subject` will be inspected during authorization tests.

9.4   JAAS and J2EE

As discussed so far in this chapter, JAAS addresses authentication and authorization functions in a Java environment. In previous chapters, we saw how J2EE security is defined and used. Within J2EE, the preferred approach for performing authentication, authorization, and delegation is declarative. In some cases, the declarative approach is insufficient. One example is a servlet performing a programmatic login. There are two approaches: using container-supplied APIs, and implementing the security policies within the application. When using the container-supplied APIs, the results—for example, authentication—will be consistent with the operations performed by the container. The disadvantage is that this approach is not standardized, and the code is likely to be nonportable.

When the security policy is implemented within the application, the preferred approach is to use the existing J2SE and JAAS security mechanisms. This guarantees portablity of the code, but the results—for example, authentication—may not be consistent with the container. For example, there is no formal relationship between the `getCallerPrincipal()` method in interface `javax.ejb.EJBContext`, as defined in the EJB specification, and the `Principal` objects contained within a `Subject`, if it exists, during the execution of an EJB method.

The following subsections explain how JAAS fits into a J2EE environment. They also discuss some of the technical issues developers should be aware of when using JAAS from within their J2EE applications.

9.4.1   Web Application Servers Executing in Various JVMs

A developer can use the JAAS functionality from within a J2EE application. This is required to be supported by J2EE-compliant WASs (see Section 2.3.1 on page 33). What this implies is that developers can use JAAS from within their applications, including performing logins and authorization tests. There are container-specific configuration issues that deployers must consider. For example, updating the Java policy file may not affect the `Permissions` granted to a `Subject`. This occurs when the WAS has its own `Policy` implementation—for example, an existing authentication/authorization infrastructure—or a more sophisticated mechanism to specify policies that do not rely on the default policy file implementation. There are also product-specific ways to configure `LoginModules`.

The J2EE specification allows J2EE applications to use the JAAS API. However, the J2EE specification does not require J2EE containers to use JAAS for their authentication and authorization mechanisms. This implies that using JAAS within a J2EE application need not have any effect on the security context of an executing J2EE application. For example, if a servlet invokes an enterprise bean within a `Subject.doAs()` method block, the identity under which the enterprise bean is invoked need not be the identity represented by the `Subject` instance. Therefore, the effective identity within a J2EE environment need not be the identity represented within the `Subject`. Container-supplied APIs may offer solutions to the problem of programmatic delegation but at the cost of nonportability.

9.4.2 JAAS `Subject` in a J2EE Environment

In Section 9.3.2.1 on page 317, we explained how an application can access authenticated-user information by calling the `Subject.getSubject()` method. This method returns a `Subject` instance containing the credentials and `Principal`s of the entity currently executing on the thread. J2EE WASs are themselves Java applications. Also, beginning with V1.3, J2EE has supported JAAS. Application developers may therefore assume that a WAS uses JAAS to perform authentication.[4] Based on these assumptions, a servlet or an enterprise bean may incorrectly attempt to access the authenticated `Subject` information by calling `Subject.get-Subject()`. Such a call may result in a `null` being returned, because the WAS is not required to implement its authentication using JAAS and may not have dispatched the servlet or enterprise bean from within a `Subject.doAs()` call.

`Subject.doAs()` provides the capability to execute downstream method calls under the identity of the specified `Subject`. However, this is true only if the calls are localized within a single JVM. In case of a servlet invoking an enterprise bean, the call is likely to traverse process and JVM boundaries. Therefore, the identity under which a target enterprise bean is invoked may not be the same as the identity that was logged in as a result of the call to `LoginContext.login()`.

9.4.3 Bridging the Gap

When originally defined, the J2EE authorization model was different from the Java 2 security permission model (see Section 8.6 on page 267). To bridge the gap between the J2EE and J2SE security models, Java Specification Request (JSR)[5] 115, "Java Authorization Contract for Containers," has defined J2EE roles as sets of Java 2 `Permission`s and their use in authorization for resource access. The specification has also defined how the Java 2 permission model and JAAS can be used to address authorization requirements from within a J2EE environment.

JSR 115 does not resolve all the outstanding issues between J2EE and J2SE security. In particular, the process of authentication within a J2EE container is still

---

4. Section 15.2.2 on page 531 discusses how J2EE containers can be designed to use JAAS to perform authentication.
5. JSR details can be found at `http://www.jcp.org`.

not required to be based on JAAS. However, JSR 196, "Java Authentication Service Provider Interface for Containers," is expected to focus on how JAAS is used to address J2EE authentication requirements. JSR 196 will also help address some of the issues discussed in this chapter, including the relationship between the `Principal` object resulting from `getCallerPrincipal()` and the list of `Principals` within the `Subject` instance that resulted from the user authentication.

9.4.4 Enterprise Security Policy Management

Once security policies are defined, the next challenge is creating an authorization policy store that scales well. Large enterprises often have many deployed applications spread across a set of heterogeneous operating platforms and J2EE-container vendors. Without the appropriate administration tools, it is practically impossible to provide a single and consistent view of the security policy in such complex distributed heterogeneous environments. One approach, as explored by JSR 115 and the security-services vendors, is to define security-services contracts for J2EE containers. These contracts, in the form of APIs, allow the J2EE containers to plug in security services from multiple vendors. The vendors providing the security services also provide the security-service management in distributed computing environments. In this way, it is possible to consistently manage the security policy of distributed heterogeneous environments across the enterprise. One example of such security-service management is provided by Tivoli Access Manager, formerly called Tivoli Policy Director.

9.5 Additional Support for Pluggable Authentication

In addition to JAAS, the Generic Security Services API[6] and Simple Authentication and Security Layer (SASL) define frameworks that provide additional support for pluggable authentication. Specifically, these authentication frameworks were designed for network communication protocols. Details of using these security services can be found in the documentation for the Java 2 SDK V1.4. Support for Kerberos and its integration with JAAS are also described in the Java 2 SDK V1.4 documentation.

---

6. See Request for Comments (RFC) 2853 at `http://www.ietf.org/rfc/rfc2853.txt`.

ENTERPRISE JAVA
AND CRYPTOGRAPHY

The Theory of Cryptography

ONE of the essential ingredients of e-business and enterprise computing is cryptography. Cryptography plays a critical role in J2SE and J2EE security, as Part IV of this book demonstrates.

This chapter explains the theory of cryptography that will be used in Chapters 11, 12, and 13. First, this chapter describes secret-key cryptographic systems, as they are at the heart of most cryptographic services, including bulk-data encryption, owing to their inherent performance advantage. Next is an overview of public-key encryption, which is essential for conducting e-business, particularly across public networks, because of the relative ease of distributing cryptographic keys. In Chapter 11, secret- and public-key cryptography services are described in the context of the standard Java APIs: the Java Cryptography Architecture and the Java Cryptography Extension.

For readers who may feel intimidated by the mathematical jargon associated with cryptography, we have tried to explain the mathematics associated with cryptography in a clear and simple way. Our intent is to demystify the concepts and terms surrounding cryptography.

10.1 The Purpose of Cryptography

The purpose of cryptography is to protect data transmitted in the likely presence of an adversary. As shown in Figure 10.1, a *cryptographic transformation of data* is a procedure by which plaintext data is disguised, or *encrypted*, resulting in an altered text, called *ciphertext*, that does not reveal the original input. The ciphertext can be reverse-transformed by a designated recipient so that the original plaintext can be recovered.

Cryptography plays an essential role in

- **Authentication.** This process to prove the identity of an entity can be based on *something you know*, such as a password; *something you have*,

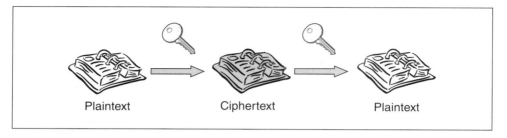

Figure 10.1. The Process of Encryption and Decryption

such as an encryption key or card; *something you are*, such as biometric measurements, including retinal scans or voice recognition; or any combination of these.

- **Data confidentiality.**   With this property, information is not made available or disclosed to unauthorized individuals, entities, or processes. When two or more parties are involved in a communication, the purpose of confidentiality is to guarantee that only those parties can understand the data exchanged. Confidentiality is enforced by encryption.

- **Data integrity.**   This property refers to data that has not been changed, destroyed, or lost in an unauthorized or accidental manner. The need for data integrity is especially evident if data is transmitted across a nonsecure network, such as the Internet, where a man-in-the-middle attack can easily be mounted. Integrity is enforced by mathematical functions applied to the message being transmitted.

- **Nonrepudiation.**   *Repudiation* is the denial by one of the entities involved in a communication of having participated in all or part of the communication. *Nonrepudiation* is protection against repudiation and can be of two types.

  - *Nonrepudiation with proof of origin* provides the recipient of data with evidence that proves the origin of the data and thus protects the recipient against an attempt by the originator to falsely deny sending the data. Its purpose is to prove that a particular transaction took place, by establishing accountability of information about a particular event or action to its originating entity.

  - *Nonrepudiation with proof of receipt* provides the originator of data with evidence proving that data was received as addressed and thus protects the originator against an attempt by the recipient to falsely deny receiving the data.

In most cases, the term *nonrepudiation* is used as a synonym of *non-repudiation with proof of origin*. Like integrity, nonrepudiation is based on mathematical functions applied to the data being generated during the transaction.

Keeping secrets is a long-standing tradition in politics, the military, and commerce. The invention of public-key cryptography in the 1970s has enabled electronic commerce to blossom in systems based on public networks, such as the Internet.

There are two primary approaches to cryptography (see Figure 10.2). In secret-key cryptography, the key used to decrypt the ciphertext is the same as the key that was used to encrypt the original plaintext. In public-key cryptography, the key used to decrypt the ciphertext is different from but related to the key that was used to encrypt the original plaintext.

Each approach has its strengths and weaknesses. Many of the cryptographic services enterprise applications need use both approaches. However, most application developers will not be aware of the underlying machinery that is deployed. For example, most users of SSL-enabled Web browsers are not aware that both public- and secret-key cryptography are essential parts of the SSL protocol.

Naively, we can think about cryptography primarily as a means for keeping and exchanging secrets. This is the confidentiality property that cryptography affords us. However, other essential cryptographic services are provided. When exchanging a message, whether encrypted or not, we often want to verify its integrity. Someone, particularly in public networks, may have modified the message. Data-integrity verification includes authenticating the origin of the message. Was the message from the source that we think sent the message? Once we accept that the message is from an authenticated entity and was not modified after being created, we also want to consider whether the sender can repudiate—deny sending—the message by claiming that someone stole the cryptographic key used to

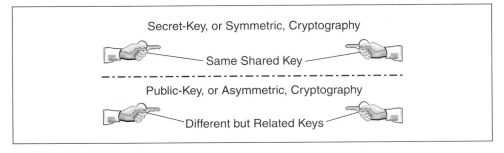

Figure 10.2. Secret-Key and Public-Key Encryption

authenticate the message. Therefore, nonrepudiation is an essential feature of cryptographic systems e-businesses use.

10.2 Secret-Key Cryptography

In *secret-key cryptography*, a sequence of bits, called the *secret key*, is used as an input to a mathematical function to encrypt a plaintext message; the same key is also used to decrypt the resulting ciphertext message and obtain the original plaintext (see Figure 10.3). As the same key is used to both encrypt and decrypt data, a secret key is also called a *symmetric key*.

10.2.1 Algorithms and Techniques

In this section, we examine the most common cryptographic algorithms that are based on the use of a secret key.

10.2.1.1 Substitutions and Transpositions

Some very early cryptographic algorithms manipulated the original plaintext, character by character, using the techniques of substitution and transposition.

- A *substitution*, or *permutation*, replaces a character of the input stream by a character from the alphabet set of the target ciphertext.

- A *transposition* replaces a character from the original plaintext by another character of that same plaintext. This results in shuffling yet still preserving the characters of the original plaintext.

An example of a substitution is the famous Caesar Cipher, which is said to have been used by Julius Caesar to communicate with his army. The Caesar

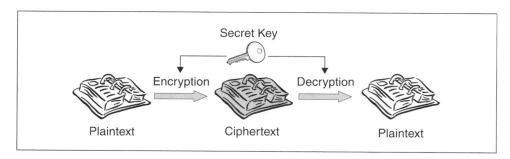

Figure 10.3. Secret-Key Encryption and Decryption

Cipher replaces each character of the input text by the third character to its right in the alphabet set. In Figure 10.4, the value 3 is added to the position of the input character; then modulo 26 is taken to yield the replacement character. If we assign numerical equivalents of 0–25 to the 26-letter alphabet A–Z, the transformation sends each plain character with position P onto the character with position $f(P) := P + 3 \pmod{26}$.

A *transposition cipher* consists of breaking the original plaintext into separate blocks first. A deterministic procedure is then applied to shuffle characters across different blocks. For example, a transposition can split the secret message "PHONE HOME" into the two separate blocks "PHONE" and " HOME". Then, characters are cyclically shuffled across the two blocks to result in the ciphertext of "POMHE HOEN". Another example of a simple transposition cipher consists of writing the plaintext along a two-dimensional matrix of fixed rows and columns and then simply transposing the matrix, as shown in Figure 10.5.

Original	A B C D E F G H I J K L M N O P Q R S T U V W X Y Z
Substitution	D E F G H I J K L M N O P Q R S T U V W X Y Z A B C

Figure 10.4. The Caesar Cipher

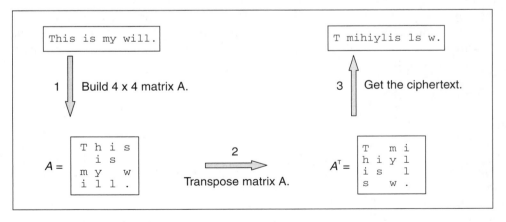

Figure 10.5. Transposition Matrix

Generally, transposition ciphers are easy to break. However, composing them by setting the result of one transposition as the input of another one greatly enhances the ciphering against attacks.

With the age of computers, early modern cryptography carried on these same concepts, using the various elementary transformations that we have listed. The primary difference is that these transformations now apply at the bit level of the binary representation of data instead of characters only.

10.2.1.2   The XOR Operation

A common transformation is the exclusive OR (XOR) operation, denoted by the symbols XOR, or $\oplus$. XOR is a bitwise function that maps an element of $\{0, 1\} \times \{0, 1\}$ onto the set $\{0, 1\}$, as shown in Figure 10.6. If we interpret the second operand as a key value, the XOR operation can be thought of as a bit-level substitution based on the bit values of the key. With such an assumption, XOR sends a 0 or 1 to itself when the corresponding key bit is 0 and inverts a 0 into a 1 and a 1 into a 0 when the corresponding key bit is 1.

The last property implies that when using a fixed-key value, the XOR operation can be applied to encipher a plaintext, which can then be recovered by simply applying the XOR operation to the ciphertext with the same key value. This property has led to the proliferation of many variants of weak encryption methods that rely solely on the simple XOR operation and thus are easily breakable.

Figure 10.7 shows how to XOR blocks of some plaintext P with a fixed-length key K, leading to ciphertext P'. The figure also shows that if P' is then XORed with K, the original plaintext P is produced.

Knowing a block of plaintext and its XOR transformation directly leads to K, by way of XORing the plaintext with the corresponding ciphertext, as shown in Figure 10.8. Similarly, by knowing two ciphertext blocks P' and Q' alone, one can XOR them together to yield the XOR of the corresponding plaintext blocks P and Q, as in Figure 10.9.

XOR:$\{0,1\} \times \{0,1\} \rightarrow \{0,1\}$

XOR	0	1
0	0	1
1	1	0

Figure 10.6.   The XOR Operation Table

```
          P = 1 0 1 0 1 1 0 0 0 1 0 1 1 1 1 0 0 1 0 1 0 0 0 1

                K = 1 1 0 0 0 1 0 1
```

P	1 0 1 0 1 1 0 0	0 1 0 1 1 1 1 0	0 1 0 1 0 0 0 1
XOR K	1 1 0 0 0 1 0 1	1 1 0 0 0 1 0 1	1 1 0 0 0 1 0 1
= P'	0 1 1 0 1 0 0 1	1 0 0 1 1 0 1 1	1 0 0 1 0 1 0 0

```
       P' = 0 1 1 0 1 0 0 1 1 0 0 1 1 0 1 1 1 0 0 1 0 1 0 0
```

P'	0 1 1 0 1 0 0 1	1 0 0 1 1 0 1 1	1 0 0 1 0 1 0 0
XOR K	1 1 0 0 0 1 0 1	1 1 0 0 0 1 0 1	1 1 0 0 0 1 0 1
= P	1 0 1 0 1 1 0 0	0 1 0 1 1 1 1 0	0 1 0 1 0 0 0 1

Figure 10.7.   XORing Plaintext Blocks with a Fixed-Length Key

P block	1 0 1 0 1 1 0 0
XOR P' block	0 1 1 0 1 0 0 1
K	1 1 0 0 0 1 0 1

Figure 10.8.   How to Get the Fixed-Length Key by XORing a Plaintext Block with Its Corresponding Ciphertext Block

P block	1 0 1 0 1 1 0 0		Q block	0 1 0 1 1 1 1 0
P' block	0 1 1 0 1 0 0 1		Q' block	1 0 0 1 1 0 1 1

P block XOR Q block	1 1 1 1 0 0 1 0
P' block XOR Q' block	1 1 1 1 0 0 1 0

Figure 10.9.   Ciphertext-Block XOR and Plaintext-Block XOR Equality

Therefore, examining the bit patterns of $P \oplus Q$ can easily result in recovering one of the plaintexts by knowing some information about the other. The plaintext can then be xored with its ciphertext to yield the keystream, where the *keystream* is the key used to encipher the plaintexts.

Despite the simplicity of the xor operation and the weakness of encryption algorithms that use it with fixed keys, there is a way to make the sole use of such basic operation result in a perfect encryption scheme. A *one-time pad* is a key of randomly generated digits that is used only once. Use of such a key yields a perfect cipher. Such a cipher is provably secure against attacks in which a code breaker has knowledge of a set of ciphertexts.

The security of the one-time pad stems from the fact that the uncertainty in attempting to guess the keystream is equal to that of directly guessing the plaintext. Note, however, that the length of the keystream for the one-time pad is equal to that of the plaintext being encrypted. Such a property makes it difficult to maintain and distribute keys, which could be very long. This difficulty has led to the development of stream ciphers whereby the key is pseudorandomly generated from a fixed secret key.

10.2.1.3 Stream Ciphers

Stream ciphers are geared for use when memory buffering is limited or when characters are individually transformed as they become available for transmission. Because stream ciphers generally transform plaintext bits independently from one another, error propagation remains limited in the event of a transmission error. For example, the xor operation lends itself to be used as a stream cipher.

10.2.1.4 Block Ciphers

Block ciphers divide a plaintext into identically sized blocks. Generally, the blocks are of length greater than or equal to 64 bits. The same transformations are applied to each block to perform the encryption.

All the widely known secret-key block-cipher algorithms exhibit the cryptographic properties desired in a block cipher. Foremost of these is the fact that each bit of the ciphertext should depend on all key bits. Changing any key bit should result in a 50 percent chance of changing any resulting ciphertext bit. Furthermore, no statistical relationships should be inferrable between a plaintext and its corresponding ciphertext. In the reminder of this section, we present the most common secret-key block-cipher algorithms.

Feistel Ciphers.   A *Feistel cipher* uses a noninvertible function f, obtained as a sequence of substitutions and transpositions. A Feistel cipher consists of the following basic steps:

1. A plaintext message m is divided into two separate blocks of equal size: the *left block*, L, and the *right block*, R.

2. The original message, m, is transformed into an intermediate message, m', in which the left block, L', is the same as R, and the right block, R', is $L \oplus f(R)$, where the symbol $\oplus$, as usual, denotes the XOR operation.

These two steps are shown in Figure 10.10. Even though f is a noninvertible function, this design permits recovering m from m' by concatenating $R' \oplus f(L') = R' \oplus f(R) = L$ with $L' = R$.

Steps 1 and 2 must be iteratively repeated a number of times for a Feistel cipher to be secure. The number of iterations depends on the strength of the function f. It is possible to prove that, even with the strongest-possible function f, the iterations must be at least three in order for the Feistel cipher to be reliable.

DES. One of the most widely recognized secret-key block ciphers is the Data Encryption Standard (DES) algorithm. DES was developed by IBM cryptographers in the early 1970s and was adopted as a U.S. government standard in 1976. DES is intended for the protection of sensitive but unclassified electronic information. Because it uses the same key for both encryption and decryption, the algorithm is referred to as a *symmetric cipher*.

DES is a block cipher in which a 64-bit input plaintext block is transformed into a corresponding 64-bit ciphertext output. DES uses a 56-bit key expressed as a 64-bit quantity in which the least relevant bit in each of the 8 bytes is used for parity checking. DES is a Feistel algorithm that iterates over the data 16 times, using a combination of permutation and substitution transformations along with standard arithmetic and logical operations, such as XOR, based on the key value.

For many years, the DES algorithm withstood attacks. Recently, as the result of increased speed of computing systems, DES has succumbed to brute-force attack on several occasions, demonstrating its vulnerability to exhaustive searching of the key space.

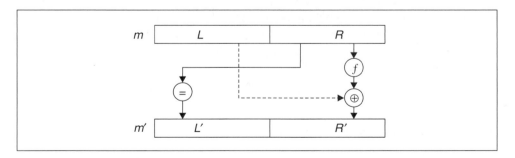

Figure 10.10. Basic Steps of a Feistel Cipher Algorithm

Triple-DES.   *Triple-DES* is the DES algorithm applied three times, using either two or three keys.

- With two keys, Triple-DES proceeds by using the first key to encrypt a block of data. The second key is then used to decrypt the result of the previous encryption. Finally, the first key is once more used to encrypt the result from the second step. Formally, let us indicate the encrypting and decrypting functions based on a given key k with E_k and D_k, respectively. If k_1 and k_2 are the two Triple-DES keys and if m is the message to be encrypted, the encrypted message m' is obtained as

$$E_{k_1}(D_{k_2}(E_{k_1}(m)))$$

To decrypt m' and obtain the original plaintext m, it is necessary to compute

$$D_{k_1}(E_{k_2}(D_{k_1}(m')))$$

- The three-key Triple-DES, stronger than the two-key Triple-DES, uses a separate key for each of the three steps described. With the notation that we have introduced, if k_1, k_2, and k_3 are three distinct keys, a plaintext message m is encrypted into its corresponding ciphertext message m' by

$$E_{k_3}(D_{k_2}(E_{k_1}(m)))$$

To decrypt m' and obtain the original plaintext m, it is then necessary to compute

$$D_{k_1}(E_{k_2}(D_{k_3}(m')))$$

In Triple-DES, the second key is used for decryption rather than for encryption to allow Triple-DES to be compatible with DES. A system using Triple-DES can still initiate a communication with a system using DES by using only one key k. Formally, by choosing $k_1 = k_2 = k_3 = k$, the ciphertext m' corresponding to a plaintext message m is obtained from

$$E_k(D_k(E_k(m))) = E_k(m)$$

By contrast, m is obtained from m' by computing

$$D_k(E_k(D_k(m'))) = D_k(m')$$

This shows that Triple-DES with only one key reduces itself to DES.

IDEA. Although less visible than DES, the International Data Encryption Algorithm (IDEA) has been classified by some contemporary cryptographers as the most secure and reliable block algorithm. Like DES, IDEA encrypts plaintext data organized in 64-bit input blocks and for each, outputs a corresponding 64-bit ciphertext block. IDEA uses the same algorithm for encryption and decryption, with a change in the key schedule during encryption. Unlike DES, IDEA uses a 128-bit secret key and dominantly uses operations from three algebraic groups; XOR, addition modulo 2^{16}, and multiplication modulo $2^{16} + 1$. These operations are combined to make eight computationally identical rounds, followed by an output transformation resulting in the final ciphertext.

Rijndael. Recently chosen as the Advanced Encryption Standard (AES), a replacement of DES by the U.S. government, *Rijndael* is an iterated block cipher with a variable block length and a variable key length, both of which can independently be 128, 192, or 256 bits. The strong points of Rijndael are its simple and elegant design and its being efficient and fast on modern processors. Rijndael uses only simple whole-byte operations on single- and 4-byte words and requires a relatively small amount of memory for its implementation. It is suitable for implementations on a wide range of processors, including 8-bit hardware, and power- and space-restricted hardware, such as smart cards. It lends itself well to parallel processing and pipelined multiarithmetic logic unit processors.

A major feature of the Rijndael algorithm is that it presents a departure from the traditional Feistel ciphers. In such ciphers, some of the bits in the intermediate states of a cipher are transposed unchanged. The Rijndael algorithm does not adopt the Feistel structure. Instead, each round of transformations is composed of three distinct invertible subtransformations that treat each bit of the intermediate state of the cipher in a uniform and similar way.

10.2.1.5 Modes of Operation
Modes of operation are cryptographic techniques using block ciphers to encrypt messages that are longer than the size of the block. The most common modes of operation are electronic codebook (ECB) and cipher block chaining (CBC).

ECB. With the ECB mode of operation, a message is divided into blocks of equal size. Each block is then encrypted using a secret key. Figure 10.11 shows how ECB works, assuming the following.

1. The original message m is divided into n blocks $m_1, m_2, ..., m_n$.
2. For all $i = 1, 2, ..., n$, the plaintext block m_i is encrypted into a ciphertext block c_i with a secret key k. The encryption function associated with k is indicated with E_k. In ECB mode, the block-cipher algorithm typically used for encryption is DES.

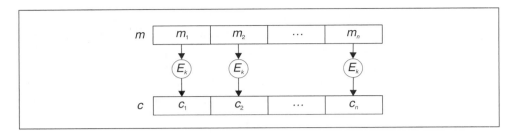

Figure 10.11. ECB Mode

3. The ciphertext blocks $c_1, c_2, \ldots, c_n$ are concatenated to form the cipher-text c corresponding to the message m.

ECB presents some limitations because each ciphertext block depends on one plaintext block only, not on the entire message.

CBC. Given a secret key k, the CBC mode of operation works as follows (see Figure 10.12).

1. The original message m is divided into n blocks $m_1, m_2, \ldots, m_n$.

2. A randomly chosen block of data is selected as the *initial vector v*. This initial vector must be known to the receiver as well. Therefore, a possibility is for both the sender and the receiver to be able to generate v independently as a function of the key k.

3. The first ciphertext block, c_1, is obtained by XORing v with m_1 and encrypting the result of the XOR operation with the secret key k. In other words,

$$c_1 = E_k(v \oplus m_1)$$

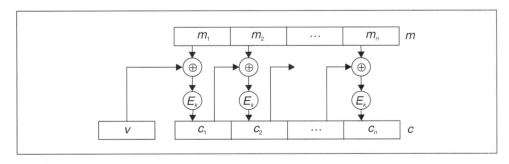

Figure 10.12. CBC Mode

where E_k is the encrypting function associated with the key k.

4. For all $i = 2, \ldots, n$, the ciphertext block c_i is obtained by XORing the plaintext block m_i with the ciphertext block c_{i-1} and encrypting the result of the XOR operation with the secret key k. In other words,

$$c_i = E_k(c_{i-1} \oplus m_i)$$

5. The ciphertext blocks $c_1, c_2, \ldots, c_n$ are concatenated to form the ciphertext c of the message m.

One of the key characteristics of CBC is that it uses a chaining mechanism that causes the decryption of a block of ciphertext to depend on all the preceding ciphertext blocks.

10.2.2   Secret-Key Security Attributes

This section examines the security implications of using secret-key cryptography.

10.2.2.1   Key Space

The strength of modern secret-key encryption methods no longer rests in the secrecy of the algorithm being used but rather in the secrecy of the encryption key. Breaking such cryptographic systems, therefore, can be achieved using a *brute-force attack*, the process of exhaustive searches over the *key space*. The latter is the set of all possible key values that a particular enciphering method can take.

For example, a generalization of the Caesar Cipher is an arbitrary permutation over the English alphabet. This results in 26! (factorial) possible keys corresponding to each of the permutations. Further constraining the permutation method to one that simply maps each letter in the alphabet to one at a fixed number of positions to its right (with a wraparound) and by enciphering each letter at a time (block length = 1), the key space narrows down to the much smaller set of the first 26 integers, $\{1, 2, \ldots, 26\}$. It should be noted, however, that the level of a secret-key encryption algorithm's security is not necessarily proportional to the size of the key space. For example, even though 26! is a very large number, it is possible to break the generalization of the Caesar Cipher by means of statistical analysis.

Most common secret-key cryptographic systems use unique, randomly generated, fixed-size keys. These systems can certainly be exposed to the exhaustive search of the key space. A necessary, although not sufficient, condition for any such cryptographic systems to be secure is that the key space be large enough to preclude exhaustive search attacks using computing power available today and for the foreseeable future. As ironic as it may sound, efficiency of enciphering methods will aid in the exhaustive brute-force search attacks.

10.2.2.2 Confidentiality

Using a secret-key algorithm to encipher the plaintext form of some data content allows only entities with the correct secret key to decrypt and hence retrieve the original form of the disguised data. Reliability of the confidentiality service in this case depends on the strength of the encryption algorithm and, perhaps more important, the length of the key used. The long lifetime of a secret key also might help diminish assurance in such a confidentiality service. Increasing the frequency with which a key is used increases the likelihood that an exhaustive key-search attack will succeed. Most modern systems make use of secret keys that remain valid for only the lifetime of a particular communication session.

10.2.2.3 Nonrepudiation

Secret-key cryptography alone is not sufficient to prevent the denial of an action that has taken place, such as the initiation of an electronic transaction. Although one can apply data privacy in such a scenario, the fundamental flaw of a nonrepudiation scheme based on secret-key cryptography alone is inherent in the fact that the secret key is dispensed to more than one party.

10.2.2.4 Data Integrity and Data-Origin Authentication

At a much lesser cost than encrypting the entirety of a plaintext, data integrity and data-origin authentication can be afforded by a secret cryptographic scheme using a message authentication code (MAC) function. The basic idea is to attach to each message m that is sent across a network the result $h(m)$ of a mathematical function h applied to the message m itself. If an error has occurred during the message transmission, such that the received message a is different from the message m that was originally sent, the message receiver will be able to detect the anomaly by independently computing $h(a)$ and comparing it to $h(m)$ (see Figure 10.13).

The main component of a MAC function is a hash digest function (see Figure 10.14). Hash digest functions are considered one of the fundamental primitives in modern cryptography. By definition, a *hash digest function* is a deterministic function that maps a message of arbitrary length to a string of fixed length n. Typically, n is 128 or 160 bits. The result is commonly known as a *message digest*. As the original data is often longer than its hash value, this result is sometimes also referred to as the original message's *fingerprint*.

Of course, a hash digest function is inherently *noninjective*. This simply means that multiple messages will be mapping to the same digest. In fact, the universe of the messages that can be digested is potentially unlimited, whereas the universe of all the message digests is limited by the set of the 2^n strings with n bits. However, the fundamental premise is that, depending on the strength of the hashing algorithm, the hash value becomes a more compact representation of the original data. This means that, although virtually possible, it should be computa-

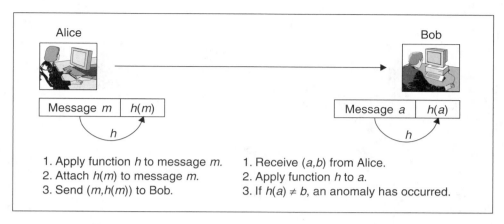

Alice

Bob

| Message *m* | *h(m)* |

h

| Message *a* | *h(a)* |

h

1. Apply function *h* to message *m*.
2. Attach *h(m)* to message *m*.
3. Send (*m,h(m)*) to Bob.

1. Receive (*a,b*) from Alice.
2. Apply function *h* to *a*.
3. If *h(a) ≠ b*, an anomaly has occurred.

Figure 10.13. Data-Integrity Verification: Basic Scenario

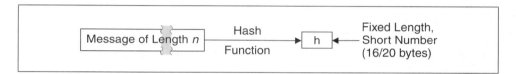

| Message of Length *n* | Hash Function → | *h* | ← Fixed Length, Short Number (16/20 bytes) |

Figure 10.14. Producing a Message Digest with a Hash Function

tionally infeasible to produce two messages having the same message digest or to produce any message having a given, prespecified target message digest.

Message Digest V5 (MD5) and Secure Hash Algorithm V1 (SHA-1) are the most widely used cryptographic hash functions. MD5 yields a 128-bit (16-byte) hash value, whereas SHA-1 results in a 160-bit (20-byte) digest. SHA-1 appears to be a cryptographically stronger function. On the other hand, MD5 edges SHA-1 in computational performance and thus has become the de facto standard.

Hash functions alone cannot guarantee data integrity, because they fail in guaranteeing *data-origin authentication*, defined as the ability to authenticate the originator of a message (see Figure 10.15). The problem with digest functions is that they are publicly available. If a message *m* is intercepted by an adversary after being transmitted by Alice, the adversary can change *m* into a different message, *m′*, compute *h(m′)*, and send Bob the pair (*m′, h(m′)*). By simply applying the function *h* to the received message *m′*, Bob has no means of detecting that an adversary has replaced *m* with *m′*.

Data-origin authentication is inherently supported by secret-key cryptography, provided that the key is shared by two entities only. When three or more parties share the same key, however, origin authenticity can no longer be provided by

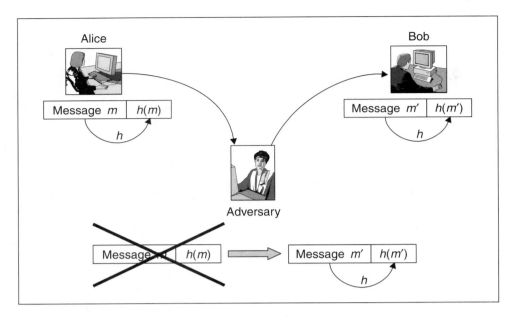

Figure 10.15. Data-Integrity Verification in the Presence of an Adversary

secret-key cryptography alone. Various secret-key-based authentication protocols have been developed to address this limitation. Public-key cryptography, described in Section 10.3 on page 359, provides a simpler and more elegant solution to this problem.

In contrast to using a pure and simple hash function to digest a message, a MAC function combines a hash digest fuction with secret-key encryption and yields a value that can be verified only by an entity having knowledge of the secret key. This way, a MAC function takes care of the problem described in Figure 10.15 and enables both data integrity and data-origin authentication.

Another simple solution to achieve data integrity and data-origin authentication is to apply a regular hash function h, such as SHA-1 or MD5, but rather than hashing the message m alone, the message is first concatenated with the key k, and then the result of the concatenation is hashed. In other words, the sender attaches to the message m the tag $h(k, m)$. This solution, however, exposes some theoretical weaknesses. A more reliable solution consists of attaching the tag $h(k, h(k, m))$.

A MAC can even be computed by using solely a secret-key block-cipher algorithm. For example, the last ciphertext block, encrypted in CBC mode, yields the final MAC value. This is a good choice for a MAC because one of the key characteristics of CBC is that it uses a chaining mechanism that causes the decryption of a block of ciphertext to depend on all the preceding ciphertext blocks. Therefore, the MAC so defined is a *compact* representation of the *entire* message that can be computed *only* by an entity having knowledge of the secret key. Known instances of this procedure use DES and Triple-DES, resulting in DES-MAC and Triple-DES-MAC, respectively. A MAC mechanism that uses a cryptographic hash function is also referred to as HMAC. HMAC is specified in RFC 2104.[1]

10.3 Public-Key Cryptography

Public-key cryptography emerged in the mid-1970s with the work published by Whitfield Diffie and Martin Hellman.[2] The concept is simple and elegant yet has had a huge impact on the science of cryptography and its application. *Public-key cryptography* is based on the notion that encryption keys are related pairs, private and public. The *private key* remains concealed by the key owner; the *public key* is freely disseminated to various partners. Data encrypted using the public key can be decrypted only by using the associated private key and vice versa. Because the key used to encrypt plaintext is different from the key used to decrypt the corresponding ciphertext, public-key cryptography is also known as *asymmetric cryptography.*

The premise behind public-key cryptography is that it should be computationally infeasible to obtain the private key by simply knowing the public key. Toward achieving this premise, modern public-key cryptography derives from sophisticated mathematical foundations based on the one-way functions existing in the abstractions of number theory.

A *one-way function* is an invertible function that is easy to compute but computationally difficult to invert. A *one-way trapdoor function* is a one-way function that can be easily inverted only if one knows a secret piece of information, known as the *trapdoor.* Encryption is the easy one-way trapdoor function; its inverse, decryption, is the difficult direction. Only with knowledge of the trapdoor—the private key—is decryption as easy as encryption. Two of these currently known one-way functions, factoring large numbers and computing discrete logarithms, form the basis of modern public-key cryptography. Factoring large numbers is a one-way trapdoor function, whereas computing discrete logarithms is a one-way function with no trapdoors.

---

1. See http://www.ietf.org/rfc/rfc2104.txt.
2. W. Diffie and M. E. Hellman. "New Directions in Cryptography," *IEEE Transactions on Information Theory* 22, 6, (1976): 644–654.

10.3.1 Algorithms and Techniques

This section examines the most common cryptographic algorithms that are based on the use of a public- and private-key pair.

10.3.1.1 RSA

The most famous of the well-known trapdoor one-way functions is based on the ease of multiplying two large prime numbers; the reverse process, factoring a very large number, is far more complex. This consideration is at the basis of Rivest-Shamir-Adleman (RSA), certainly the most widely used public-key encryption algorithm.

Basic RSA Concepts. A *prime number*, by definition, is an integer that has no positive divisors other than 1 and itself. A nonprime integer is called *composite*. Two integers $a \geq 1$ and $b \geq 2$ are said to be *relatively prime* if their greatest common divisor GCD(a, b) is 1. The number of elements in the set

$$\{a \in \mathbf{Z} : 1 \leq a < b, \text{GCD}(a, b) = 1\}$$

where $\mathbf{Z}$ is the set of all integers, is often denoted by $\phi(b)$. The function ϕ is called the *Euler phi-function*.

Every integer $b \geq 2$ can be *factored* as a product of powers of primes in a unique way. For example, $60 = 2^2 \times 3 \times 5$. Factoring *large numbers*—numbers that expressed in binary format take 1,024 bits or more—is known to be computationally infeasible with current computing technology. Consequently, the one-way trapdoor problem is to make a very large number a public knowledge and secretly maintain its prime factors. With this in mind, we can now summarize the widely adopted RSA public-key algorithm.

How the RSA Algorithm Works. In simple terms, the *RSA algorithm* centers on three integer numbers: the *public exponent*, e; the *private exponent*, d; and the *modulus*, n. The modulus is obtained as the product of two distinct, randomly picked, very large primes, p and q. A well-known result from number theory implies that $\phi(n) = (p - 1)(q - 1)$. The two numbers e and d are characterized by the fact that they are greater than 1 and smaller than $\phi(n)$. In addition, e must be relatively prime with $\phi(n)$, and it must also be $de = 1$ (mod $\phi(n)$), which means that d and e are the multiplicative inverse of the other modulo $\phi(n)$. The pair (e, n) is the RSA public key, whereas the pair (d, n) is the RSA private key.

A block of plaintext P whose numerical equivalent is less than the modulus is converted into a ciphertext block by the formula P^e (mod n). Conversely, a ciphertext block C is converted back to its corresponding plaintext representation by the formula C^d (mod n). These two formulas are the inverse of the other. Therefore, whatever is encrypted with the public key can be decrypted only with the corresponding private key; conversely, whatever is encrypted with the private key can be decrypted only with the corresponding public key.

To better understand how RSA works, let us consider an example involving small numbers. We randomly pick two prime numbers, $p = 7$ and $q = 11$. This implies that $n = p \times q = 77$ and $\phi(n) = (p - 1)(q - 1) = 60$. A valid choice for the public exponent is $e = 13$. By solving the equation $13d = 1 \pmod{60}$, we get $d = 37$. Therefore, the RSA public key in this case is the pair $(13, 77)$, and the corresponding RSA private key is the pair $(37, 77)$. Let us now consider the plaintext message $P = 9$. By encrypting it with the RSA public key, we obtain the ciphertext message $C = 9^{13} \pmod{77} = 58$. To decrypt this message, we have to apply the RSA private key and compute $58^{37} \pmod{77} = 9$, which yields the original plaintext P.

To encrypt or decrypt a message, the RSA algorithm uniquely represents a block of data in either a plaintext or ciphertext form as a very large number, which is then raised to a large power. Note here that the length of the block is appropriately sized so that the number representing the block is less than the modulus. Computing such exponentiations would be very time consuming were it not for an eloquent property that the operation of exponentiation in modular arithmetic exhibits. This property is known as the *modular exponentiation by the repeated squaring method.*

Note that the one-way trapdoor function discussed in this section requires deciding on whether a randomly picked very large integer is prime. Primality testing, however, is a much easier task than factorization. Several methods have been devised to determine the primality of an odd number p, the most trivial of which is to run through the odd numbers starting with 3 and determine whether any of such numbers divides p. The process should terminate when the square root of p, $\sqrt{p}$, is reached, because if p is not a prime, the smallest of its nontrivial factors must be less than or equal to $\sqrt{p}$. Owing to the time complexity that it requires, in practice this procedure is stopped much earlier before reaching $\sqrt{p}$ and is used as a first step in a series of more complicated, but faster, primality test methods.

Security Considerations.   Breaking the RSA algorithm is conjectured to be equivalent to factoring the product of two large prime numbers. The reason is that one has to extract the modulus n from the public-key value and proceed to factor it as the product of the two primes p and q. Knowing p and q, it would be easy to compute $\phi(n) = (p - 1)(q - 1)$, and the private key (d, n) could then be obtained by solving the equation $de = 1 \pmod{\phi(n)}$ for the unknown d. With the complexity of the fastest known factoring algorithm being in the order of $|n|$, where $|n|$ is the total number of the binary bits in the modulus n, this roughly means that, for example, every additional 10 bits make the modulus ten times more difficult to factor. Given the state of factoring numbers, it is believed that keys with 2,048 bits are secure into the future. The fastest known factoring algorithm to date is the *number field sieve*.

10.3.1.2 *Diffie-Hellman*

The Diffie-Hellman (DH) key-agreement algorithm is an elegant procedure for use by two entities establishing a secret cryptographic key over a public network without the risk of exposing or physically exchanging it. Indeed, DH presents a critical solution to the secret-key distribution problem. The security of the algorithm relates to the one-way function found in the discrete logarithm problem.

Basic DH Concepts.   Let q be a prime number. An integer α is called a *primitive root*, or *base generator* of q, if the numbers $\alpha \pmod q$, $\alpha^2 \pmod q$, ... , α^{q-1} (mod q) are distinct and consist of the integers from 1 to $q - 1$ in some permutations. For any integer y and a primitive root α of the prime number q, one can find a unique integer exponent x such that $y = \alpha^x \pmod q$. The exponent x is referred to as the *discrete logarithm* of y for the base α modulo q. This is a one-way function. In fact, computing y from x using this function is easy; for q about 1,000 bits long, this would take only a few thousand multiplications. However, the inverse function, $x = \log_\alpha y \pmod q$, which yields x from y, is computationally infeasible, as far as anyone knows; Diffie proved that with q still about 1,000 bits long and the best known algorithm, the discrete logarithm would take approximately 10^{30} operations.

How the DH Algorithm Works.   The mathematics encompassed in the DH key-agreement algorithm is fairly simple. Let q and α be as explained previously. These two numbers are publicly available. Suppose that Alice and Bob want to agree on a secret key. Alice generates as her private key a secret random number x_A such that $1 \le x_A < q$ and publishes the corresponding public key

$$y_A := \alpha^{x_A} \pmod q$$

Similarly, Bob generates as his private key a secret random number x_B such that $1 \le x_B < q$ and publishes the corresponding public key

$$y_B := \alpha^{x_B} \pmod q$$

The secret key for Alice and Bob is

$$K_{AB} := \alpha^{x_A x_B} \pmod q$$

Alice can obtain this key by getting y_B from a public directory and then computing

$$y_B{}^{x_A} (\text{mod } q) = \alpha^{x_B x_A} (\text{mod } q) = \alpha^{x_A x_B} (\text{mod } q) = K_{AB}$$

Bob computes the same secret key in a similar way.

One problem in the algorithm that we have just described consists of finding a primitive root α of a given prime number q. The definition of primitive root does not help from a computational point of view, because it requires computing $q - 1$ powers in the worst case for every attempt to find a primitive root. However, a known algebraic theorem proves that an integer α is a primitive root of 9 if $\alpha^i \neq 1$ for any integer $i \in \{1, ..., q - 1\}$ such that i is a divisor of $q - 1$. Therefore, the problem is reduced to factoring $q - 1$ and testing that $\alpha^i \neq 1$, where this time i varies only in the set of the divisors of $q - 1$. Unfortunately, as we discussed in Section 10.3.1.1 on page 360, factoring a large number is computationally infeasible too. In fact, this is exactly the one-way trapdoor function on which the security of the RSA algorithm relies. However, a solution to this problem for the DH algorithm consists of generating $q - 1$ before generating q itself. In other words, it is possible to generate $q - 1$ as the product of known primes—in which case, the factorization of $q - 1$ is known in advance—and subsequently test q for primality. As discussed in Section 10.3.1.1 on page 360, primality testing is a much easier task than factorization. An advantage of this algorithm is that its security does not depend on the secrecy of q and α. Once a pair of integers (q, α) has been found that satisfies the requirements described previously, the same pair can be published—in cryptography books, for example—and reused by algorithm implementors.

Security Considerations. With the algorithm described, Alice and Bob do not have to physically exchange keys over unsecure networks, because they can compute the same secret key independently of each other. An attacker would have to compute K_{AB} from the only public information available, y_A and y_B. No way to do this is known other than computing the discrete logarithm of y_A and y_B to find x_A and x_B, an operation that, as we said, is conjectured to be computationally infeasible even with the fastest known algorithm.

In order for Bob and Alice to be able to compute the same secret key independently of each other, they have to know each other's public keys. A general security problem that arises at this point is how to ascertain that the public key of an entity belongs to that entity. The DH algorithm does not offer a direct solution to this problem. However, we will see how to solve this problem in Section 10.3.4 on page 372.

10.3.1.3 Elliptic Curve

Recently, elliptic curves over finite fields have been proposed as another source of one-way trapdoor functions for use with existing public-key cryptographic systems.

Basic Elliptic-Curve Concepts. An *elliptic curve* in the plane x, y is the union of the singleton $\{O\}$ with the set of the points (x, y) of the plane satisfying an equation of the form

$$y^2 + axy + by = x^3 + cx^2 + dx + e$$

where a, b, c, d, and e are real numbers, and x and y take on values in the real numbers. The element O is called *point at infinity*. For our purpose, it is sufficient to consider equations of the form

$$y^2 = x^3 + ax + b$$

Figure 10.16 shows the elliptic curve with equation $y^2 = x^3 - x$.

A form of *addition* can be defined over the set of points of an elliptic curve by imposing that if any three points on an elliptic curve lie on a straight line, their sum is O. The operation of addition for an elliptic curve, indicated with the symbol +, is constructed on the following rules.

1. The point at infinity, O, is the *additive identity*. This means that $O = -O$, and for any point P on the elliptic curve, $P + O = O + P = P$.

2. A vertical line meets the elliptic curve at two points with the same coordinates, say $P_1 = (x, y)$ and $P_2 = (x, -y)$. The vertical line also meets the curve at its infinity point, O. This implies that $P_1 + P_2 + O = O$, and $P_1 = -P_2$. Therefore, the negative of a point is a point with the same x coordinate but negative y coordinate. This construction is illustrated in Figure 10.17.

3. If Q and R are two points with different x coordinates, draw a straight line between them and find the third point of intersection P_1. It is easily seen that P_1 exists and is unique, unless the line is tangent to the curve at either Q or R, in which case we take $P_1 = Q$ or $P_1 = R$, respectively. Because P_1, Q, and R lie on the same straight line, it must be $Q + R + P_1 = O$, which implies $Q + R = -P_1$. This construction is illustrated in Figure 10.17.

4. To double a point Q, draw the tangent line in Q and find the other point of intersection S. Then $Q + Q = 2Q = -S$. This construction is illustrated in Figure 10.17.

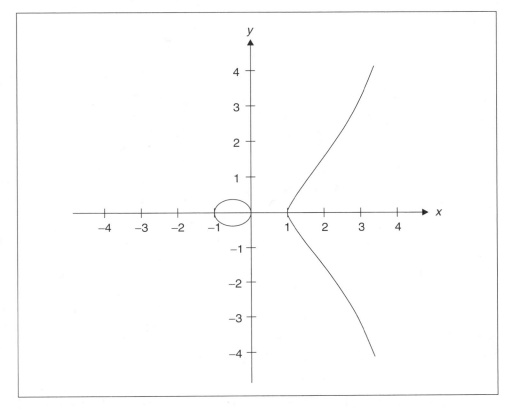

Figure 10.16. An Elliptic Curve

Figure 10.17 shows how to perform the addition operation on the elliptic curve $y^2 = x^3 - x$. It can be shown that if $4a^3 + 27b^2 \neq 0$, the operation of addition constructed on rules 1–4 has the following properties.

- **It is well defined.**   Given any two points P and Q on an elliptic curve, their sum $P + Q$ is still a point on the same elliptic curve.

- **It is associative.**   Given any three points P, Q, and R on an elliptic curve, $(P + Q) + R = P + (Q + R)$.

- **It is commutative.**   Given any two points P and Q on an elliptic curve, $P + Q = Q + P$.

- **It possesses a unity element.**   Rule 1 establishes that the unity element for the operation of addtion is the point at infinity, $\boldsymbol{O}$.

- **Every point on the elliptic curve has an inverse.**   Given any point P on an elliptic curve, rules 1 and 2 show how to construct its inverse, $-P$.

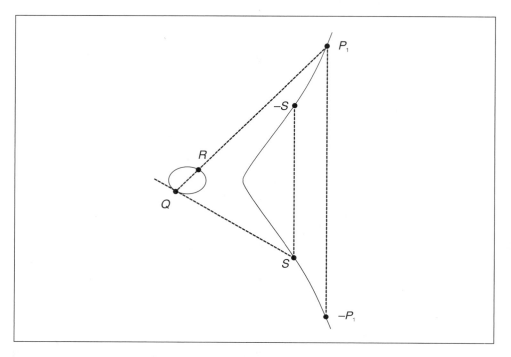

Figure 10.17. The Addition Operation on an Elliptic Curve

These properties can be summarized by saying that the set of the points of an elliptic curve, coupled with the operation of addition that we have just defined, is an *abelian group*. *Multiplication* of a point P on an elliptic curve by a positive integer k is defined as the sum of k copies of P. Thus $2P = P + P$, $3P = P + P + P$, and so on.

An elliptic curve can be defined on a finite field as well. Let $p > 3$ be a prime number. The *elliptic curve* $y^2 = x^3 + ax + b$ over $\mathbf{Z}_p$ is the set of solutions $(x, y) \in \mathbf{Z}_p \times \mathbf{Z}_p$ to the congruence $y^2 = x^3 + ax + b$ (mod p), where $a, b \in \mathbf{Z}_p$ are constants such that $4a^3 + 27b^2 \neq 0$ (mod p), together with a special point $\mathbf{0}$, called the *point at infinity*. *Addition* of two points on an elliptic curve and *multiplication* of a point for an integer are defined in a way that is similar to elliptic curves over real numbers.

Note that the equation of an elliptic curve over the finite field $\mathbf{Z}_p$ is defined as for real numbers. The only difference is that an elliptic curve $\mathbf{Z}_p$ is not continuous. Rather, the points that belong in the curve are only the pairs of non-negative integers in the quadrant from $(0, 0)$ to (p, p) that satisfy the equation modulo p.

Given an integer $k < p$ and the equation $Q = kP$, where P and Q are two points on an elliptic curve E over the finite field $\mathbf{Z}_p$, the one-way function here consists of the easy operation of computing Q given k and P. The inverse problem of finding k given P and Q is similar to the discrete logarithm problem and is, in practice, intractable.

The Elliptic-Curve Algorithm.   One straightforward application of the one-way function to DH is for two entities Alice and Bob to publicly agree on a point P on an elliptic curve E over a finite field $\mathbf{Z}_p$, where p is a very large prime number ($p \approx 2^{180}$). The criterion in selecting P is that the smallest integer value of n for which $np = \mathbf{O}$ be a very large prime number. The point P is known as the *generator point*. The elliptic curve and the generator point are parameters of the cryptosystem known to all the participants.

To generate the key, the initiating entity, Alice, picks a random large integer $a < n$, computes aP over E, and sends it to the entity Bob. The integer a is Alice's private key, whereas the point aP is her public key. Bob performs a similar computation with a random large number b and sends entity Alice the result of bP. The integer b is Bob's private key, whereas the point bP is his public key. Both entities then compute the secret key $K = abP$, which is still a point over E.

Security Considerations.   Given an elliptic curve E on a finite field $\mathbf{Z}_p$, where p is a very large prime number, the security of elliptic-curve cryptography depends on how difficult it is to determine the integer k given a point P on the curve and its multiple kP. The fastest known technique for taking the elliptic-curve logarithm is known as the *Pollard rho method*. With this algorithm, a considerably smaller key size can be used for elliptic-curve cryptography compared to RSA. Furthermore, it has been shown that for equal key size, the computational effort required for elliptic-curve cryptography and RSA is comparable. Therefore, there is a computational advantage to using elliptic-curve cryptography with a shorter key length than a comparably secure RSA.

10.3.2 Public-Key Security Attributes

This section examines the security implications of using public-key cryptography. Generally speaking, the strength of each algorithm is directly related to the type of the one-way function being used and the length of the cryptographic keys. Inverting the one-way functions we have discussed, namely, factoring a very large number and computing the discrete logarithm, is known to be practically infeasible within the computing means and the theoretic knowledge available today.

10.3.2.1 Confidentiality
The premise of the privacy service here is achieved by encrypting data, using the recipient's public key, and the fact that decryption can be done only by using the recipient's private key. For example, if Alice needs to send a confidential message

to Bob, she can encrypt it with Bob's public key, knowing that only Bob will be able to decrypt the ciphertext with his private key (see Figure 10.18).

Thus, only the recipient with knowledge of the private key is able to decrypt the enciphered data. It is worth noting that a privacy service strongly depends on the assurance that a public key is valid and legitimately belongs to the recipient.

One confidentiality problem that needs to be addressed by public-key encryption is the fact that in some cases, the plaintext corresponding to a given ciphertext can be easily understood. As an example, we consider the scenario in which Alice is a stock client and Bob a stockbroker, as shown in Figure 10.19.

Typically, Alice's messages are all likely to be of the type "Buy" or "Sell." Knowing this, an attacker could build a table mapping ciphertexts to plaintexts.

Figure 10.18. Public-Key Scenario

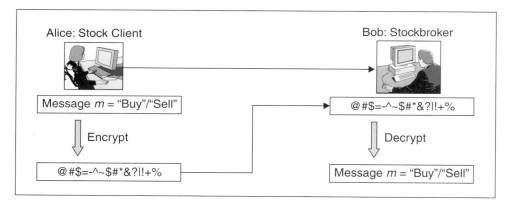

Figure 10.19. Scenario Requiring Message Randomization

This would break the confidentiality of the transmission. Even worse, the attacker could impersonate Alice and replace the ciphertext corresponding to "Buy" with the ciphertext corresponding to "Sell" and vice versa (see Figure 10.20).

This problem can be solved by *randomizing* the message. Before encrypting the plaintext message "Buy" or "Sell," the message-randomizing algorithm on Alice's side inserts a meaningless sequence of bits, which is randomly generated. As the ciphertext depends on the entire plaintext message, the ciphertexts produced by Alice are no longer recognizable. In addition, message randomization reduces the risks of message-prediction-and-replay-attacks (see footnote 6 on page 150).

10.3.2.2 *Data Integrity, Data-Origin Authentication, and Nonrepudiation*
As we said in Section 10.3.2.1 on page 367, privacy is provided by encrypting data, using a publicly available key, typically the recipient's public key. However, an eavesdropper may intercept the data, substitute new data, and encrypt it using the same public key. Simply applying a public-key algorithm to achieve privacy does not guarantee data integrity; nor does it guarantee data-origin authentication. In practice, digital signatures are the preferred method of achieving data integrity and data-origin authenticity. Another service that is inherently offered through digital signatures is nonrepudiation.

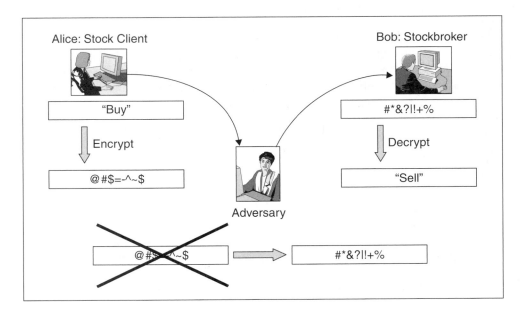

Figure 10.20. Message Randomization

10.3.3   Digital Signatures

The use of public-key cryptography combined with one-way hash functions enables the digital signing of documents. This process inherently enables data integrity and data-origin authentication and has the potential to withstand repudiation. In fact, using the private key of a public- and private-key pair to encrypt a data stream automatically binds the subject—a person or an entity—with the encrypted data.

The cost of encrypting an entire document in order to simply establish this binding can be prohibitive. Fortunately, digital signing of a document is a computationally affordable alternative, as it does not require encrypting the entire document.

If confidentiality is a requirement, the message originator, Alice, encrypts the message only once, with the public key of the receiver, Bob, thereby guaranteeing confidentiality, because the ciphertext can be decrypted only with the Bob's private key. However, data integrity, data-origin authentication, and nonrepudiation are not guaranteed, because anybody could have used Bob's public key to encrypt a different message, pretending that it was sent by Alice. To resolve this ambiguity, Alice attaches a digital signature to the encrypted message. The digital signature is obtained by applying a mathematical function to the plaintext message. This mathematical function depends on Alice's private key.

An eavesdropper who attempted to replace the transmitted data with new data could still encrypt the new data with Bob's public key but would not be able to use Alice's private key to generate Alice's digital signature. Once he receives the encrypted message and the digital signature, Bob decrypts the ciphertext with his own private key. Finally, he uses Alice's public key to verify Alice's digital signature. If the digital signature verifies, Bob knows that the original message has been sent by Alice and has not been compromised during transmission. Because Alice's private key has been used to compute the digital signature, this entire process guarantees data integrity, data-origin authentication, and nonrepudiation (see Figure 10.21).

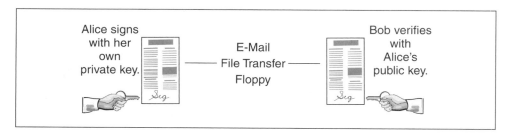

Figure 10.21. Digital-Signature Scenario

With the fundamental premise that the private key remains in the confines of its owner, verifying a digital signature using the associated public key certainly leaves no possibility for the originator to deny involvement. Denial, however, can always take place on the basis that a private key has been compromised. A strong nonrepudiation service never exposes the private keys it manages, even to the owner. Tamper-proof hardware modules for private keys become necessary for a legally binding nonrepudiation service.

If a confidentiality service is not needed, Alice can transmit the signed document to Bob in its cleartext form. The signature is provided to Bob for data-integrity verification, data-origin authentication, and nonrepudiation purposes.

The most well-known digital signature algorithms are RSA and Digital Signature Algorithm (DSA). These algorithms are discussed in the next two subsections.

10.3.3.1   RSA Signature

The RSA digital-signature algorithm proceeds along two main steps, as shown in Figure 10.22.

1. Using one of the common hashing algorithms, such as MD5 or SHA-1, a document is first digested into a much smaller representation: its hash value.

2. The hash value of the document, rather than the entire document itself, is then encrypted with the private key of the originator.

If confidentiality is needed, the document itself must be encrypted, as explained in Section 10.3.2.2 on page 369.

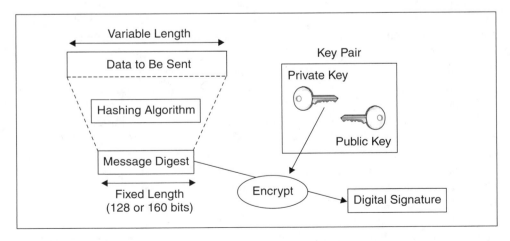

Figure 10.22. The Process of Computing a Message's RSA Digital Signature

10.3.3.2   DSA Signature

Other types of digital signatures rely on algorithms designed solely for signing but not encrypting. In other words, the digital signature is still obtained by encrypting the hash value of a document with the originator's private key, but the public and private key pair here can be used only for digital signing, not for encrypting arbitrary-size messages.

An example of this class of algorithms is the standard DSA, which computes a signature over an arbitrary-size input, using SHA-1 as a message digest, five public parameters, and a private key. DSA signatures have better performance characteristics than RSA does.

10.3.4   Digital Certificates

As we mention in Section 10.3.5 on page 375, authenticating the identity of a sending entity and protecting data to allow only authenticated and authorized receivers to view that data is an extremely important security requirement, especially for the exchange of security-sensitive data or when the nature of the transaction requires data-origin authentication and nonrepudiation. Encrypting a message with the receiver's public key guarantees confidentiality, whereas digitally signing a message by encrypting its hash value with the originator's public key guarantees data-origin authentication and nonrepudiation.

These scenarios are very attractive, but for them to work, it is necessary to have a means to bind a public- and private-key pair to its owner. To understand why, let us consider the following scenario. Alice wants to send Bob a confidential message in a secure manner over a public network. To do so, she needs to encrypt the message with Bob's public key. For sure, only Bob will be able to read the message once it is transmitted, because the message's ciphertext can be decrypted only with Bob's private key. However, how can Alice be sure that Bob is really Bob? Owning a public- and private-key pair does not give any assurance about the real identity of a person. Similarly, Bob may receive a signed message from Alice, and he can verify the digital signature's authenticity by decrypting it with Alice's public key, but how can he be sure that the entity that signed the message declaring to be Alice is really Alice?

A solution to this problem is to use digital certificates, which can be used to exchange public keys and to verify an entity's identity. An entity's *digital certificate* is a binary file that contains the entity's public key and Distinguished Name (DN), which uniquely identifies that entity, along with other pieces of information, such as the start and expiration dates of the certificate and the certificate's serial number (see Figure 10.23).

The international standard for public-key certificates is called X.509 (see Appendix B on page 553). This standard has evolved over time, and the latest version is V3. The most significant enhancement in X.509 V3 is the ability to add other,

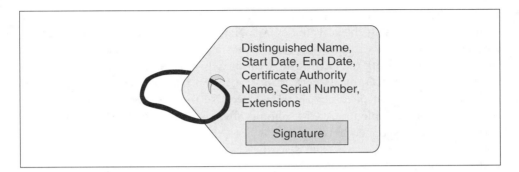

Figure 10.23. Information Contained in a Digital Certificate

arbitrary data in addition to the basic name, address, and organization identity fields of the DN. This is useful when constructing certificates for specific purposes. For example, a certificate could include a bank account number or credit card information.

Digital certificates are released by trusted third-party registry organizations called Certificate Authorities. These CAs are public organizations that are trusted by both the sender and the receiver participating in a secure communication. An entity, Alice, can receive her own certificate by generating a public- and private-key pair and by transmitting the public key along with a certificate request and proof of ownership of the public key to a CA. For serious applications, Alice can obtain a certificate only by applying in person and showing evidence of her identity. If Alice's request for a certificate is accepted, the CA wraps Alice's public key in a certificate and signs it with its own private key.

Alice can now convey her public key information to other entities by transmitting her certificate. A receiving entity, Bob, can verify the certificate's authenticity by verifying the CA's digital signature. This can be done without even contacting the CA, because CAs' public keys are available in all the most common client and server applications, such as Web browsers, Web servers, and other programs that require security. If the signature is verified, Bob is assured that the certificate really belongs to Alice. From this moment on, when he receives a message digitally signed by Alice, he knows that it is really Alice who signed it and transmitted it—data-origin authentication—and Alice will not be able to deny that the message originated from her—nonrepudiation. Similarly, by accessing Bob's certificate from a CA and by encrypting a message with Bob's public key, Alice is assured that only Bob, and no other person, will be able to decrypt the message—confidentiality.

As Figure 10.23 shows, certificates contain start and end dates. The validity of a certificate should not be too long, to minimize the risks associating with having inadvertently exposed the associated private key and to make sure that the current key strength still makes it computationally infeasible to compute the private key from the public key. If the private key associated with the public key in a certificate gets inadvertently exposed, a certificate's owner should make an immediate request for suspending the certificate's validity. In this case, the CA will add an entry for that certificate in its certificate revocation list. A CRL also enumerates those certificates that have been revoked because their owners failed to comply with specific requirements. A CRL should always include data explaining why a certificate was suspended or revoked.

In the scenario that we have described in this section, there is only one CA that the sender and the receiver participating in a secure communication use to verify each other's public key's authenticity. In real-life situations, there are chains of CAs, whereby each successive CA verifies and vouches for the public key of the next identity in the chain. In this case, a public-key certificate embodies a chain of trust. Consider the situation shown in Figure 10.24.

A system has received a request containing a chain of certificates, each of which is signed by the next higher CA in the chain. The system has also a collection of *root certificates* from trusted CAs. The system can then match the top of the chain in the request with one of these root certificates, say, Ham's. If the chain of signatures is intact, the receiver can infer that Nimrod is trustworthy and has

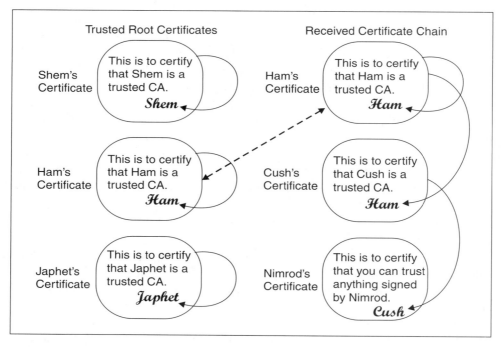

Figure 10.24. Certificate Hierarchy

inherited the trustworthiness from Ham. Note that one of the implications of a certificate chain is that the certificate at the top of the chain is *self-signed*.

10.3.5 Key Distribution

In public-key cryptography, an entity's private key never has to be exposed, whereas the corresponding public key is made publicly available. This makes it possible to obtain confidentiality, nonrepudiation, data-origin authentication, and data integrity without having to distribute the secret key. The main problem of public-key cryptography is that it is computationally expensive. Conversely, secret-key cryptography, described in Section 10.2 on page 346, offers better performance and scales well for Kerberos and distributed computing environment (DCE) security, even though its limitation lies in the fact that it becomes necessary to share the secret key across unsecure networks.

Combining public-key and secret-key cryptography yields the performance advantages of secret-key cryptography and the security enhancements of public-key cryptography, as shown in Figure 10.25. One algorithm that combines public-key and secret-key cryptography is DH (see Section 10.3.1.2 on page 362), which allows two parties to independently compute the same secret key. To do this, each

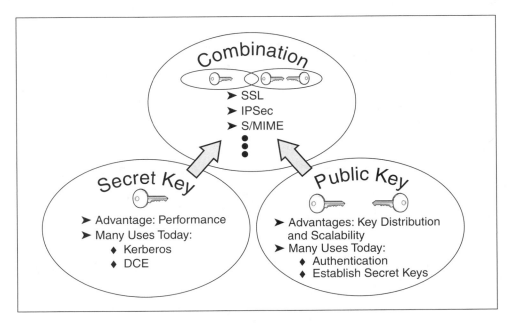

Figure 10.25. Combining Public-Key and Secret-Key Cryptography

entity uses its own private key and the other entity's public key. With Diffie-Helmann, the shared secret key is mathematically computed by the two parties, and there is no need to physically exchange it over the network.

Another way to use public-key cryptography for secure secret-key establishment over a public network is, essentially, to consider the secret key as the data that needs to be distributed with a privacy requirement. Thus, the secret key is encrypted using the public key of the target entity. The receiving entity uses its private key to decrypt the enciphered secret key and hence has established a common secret key with the sending entity. This is, for example, the approach used by the SSL and TLS protocols (see Section 13.1 on page 449). Other protocols that combine secret- and public-key cryptography are IPSec and S/MIME (see Section 12.2 on page 439).

Note that authenticating the identity of the sending entity is a strong security requirement. A breach in such a key-establishment mechanism risks exposing the entire cryptographic channel that follows key establishment.

The Java 2 Platform and Cryptography

FROM JDK V1.1 onward, Java provides general-purpose APIs and service provider interfaces (SPIs) for cryptographic functions, collectively known as Java Cryptography Architecture and Java Cryptography Extension. The JCA and JCE are based on a provider architecture that allows for multiple and interoperable cryptographic implementations.

Chapter 10 on page 343 described the sorts of problems for which cryptography can provide solutions and introduced the general concepts of secret- and public-key cryptography. In this chapter, we look in more detail at JCA and JCE and show how J2EE and J2SE applications can take advantage of the Java cryptography API.

11.1 The JCA and JCE Frameworks

The J2EE and J2SE APIs and runtime environments are shipped with security-related classes. The set of core classes in the Java 2 platform can be divided into two subsets:

1. Security-related core classes, which can be further subdivided as those related to access control and cryptography, respectively

2. Other core classes, which can be further subdivided as those providing message digest, digital signature, and certificate management; and those providing encryption, key exchange, and message authentication code (see Section 10.2.2.4 on page 356).

The first set of cryptography-related core classes is part of the JCA; the second set, part of the JCE. Together, the JCA and the JCE provide a platform-independent cryptography API.

Originally, the JCE was released separately as a standard extension to the Java 2 SDK, in accordance with the U.S. export control regulations. Starting with the Java 2 SDK V1.4, the JCE is shipped as part of the core classes in the package `javax.crypto` and its subpackages `javax.crypto.interfaces` and `java.crypto.spec`. However, at that time, only a weak-encryption version of the JCE could be exported outside the United States, whereas a strong-encryption version can now be exported too, as long as proper protection mechanisms are in place.[1]

11.1.1 Terms and Definitions

A few terms need to be explained in order to become familiar with the JCA and JCE. These terms are engine, algorithm, and provider.

- **Engine.** This term is used to depict an abstract representation of a cryptographic service that does not have a concrete implementation. A cryptographic service is always associated with a particular algorithm and can have one of the following functions:

  - To provide cryptographic operations, such as those for digital signatures or message digests

  - To generate or supply the cryptographic material—keys or parameters—required for cryptographic operations

  - To generate and manage data objects, such as certificates or databases of keys and certificates, called *keystores*, that encapsulate cryptographic keys in a secure fashion

    Message digests (see Section 10.2.2.4 on page 356) and digital signatures (see Section 10.3.3 on page 370) are examples of engines. In the JCA and JCE, engines are represented by classes called *engine classes*. Users of the JCA and JCE API request and use instances of the engine classes to carry out corresponding operations.

- **Algorithm.** An *algorithm* can be looked on as an implementation of an engine. For instance, the MD5 algorithm is one of the implementations accessible through the `java.security.MessageDigest` engine class, which provides access to the functionality of a message digest regardless

---

1. *Cipher strength* is controlled by the size of the key used in the encryption algorithm. Symmetric encryption is defined to be *weak* if the key length is 40 bits or less. A key of this size can be cracked in a matter of hours with quite modest computing facilities. Each extra bit doubles the key space, so a key size of 64 bits is 16 million times tougher than 40 bits. A similar rule applies to public-key encryption, where a 512-bit modulus is inadequate, but a 1,024-bit modulus is expected to remain effective for the next 10 years, at least for commercial use.

of the underlying algorithm. The internal implementation of the MD5 algorithm can vary depending on the source that provides the MD5 algorithm class.

- **Provider.** The term cryptographic service provider (CSP), or simply *provider*, refers to a package or a set of packages that supply a concrete implementation of a subset of the cryptographic services supported by the Java security API. These packages must implement one or more cryptographic services, such as digital signature, message digest, and key conversion. Although every provider can choose how to implement a particular cryptographic service, the API exposed must be the same. Each set of algorithm classes from a particular source is managed by an instance of the `java.security.Provider` class. Installed providers are listed in the `java.security` properties file present in the `lib/security` subdirectory of the Java home directory.

From this brief discussion, one can see that to form a complete provider package, cryptographic solutions require a whole collection of tools and functions, which include not only the encryption algorithms themselves but also functions for message digests, certificate management, and key generation.

11.1.2 The Principles of JCA and JCE

The JCA and the JCE are frameworks for accessing and developing cryptographic functionality for the Java platform. This functionality encompasses the parts of the Java 2 security API related to cryptography. The JCA and the JCE were designed around four principles: implementation independence, implementation interoperability, algorithm independence, and algorithm extensibility.

11.1.2.1 Implementation Independence
Implementation independence allows a Java program to use cryptographic functions without having to deal with their implementation. This is achieved by using a provider-based architecture. The JCA and the JCE allow any number of vendors to register their own implementations of the algorithms. For example, if a particular application uses the MD5 implementation supplied by provider *A* and if it is later decided that the implementation supplied by provider *B* would be more appropriate, the application code does not need to be changed. Providers can be configured declaratively. Therefore, the choice of one provider over another does not influence the code of an application (see Figure 11.1).

The provider infrastructure permits implementations of various algorithms to be found at runtime, without any changes to the code. Thanks to the principle of

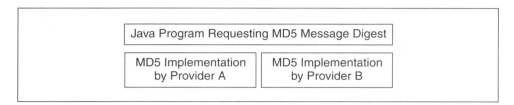

Figure 11.1. Implementation Independence

implementation independence, providers may be updated transparently to the application: for example, when faster or more secure versions are available.

11.1.2.2 *Implementation Interoperability*

Implementation interoperability means that various implementations can work with one another, use one another's keys, or verify one another's signatures. For example, if user Alice signs a document using a program that relies on the DSA implementation supplied by provider *A*, user Bob can verify the authenticity of that signature with his own program, even if it relies on the DSA implementation supplied by provider *B* (see Figure 11.2). Similarly, for the same algorithm, a key generated by one provider would be usable by another.

11.1.2.3 *Algorithm Independence*

Algorithm independence is achieved by defining types of cryptographic services and introducing classes that provide the functionality of these cryptographic services. These classes are called *engine classes*. An engine class defines API methods that allow applications to access the specific type of cryptographic service it provides. The implementations supplied by providers implement the corresponding SPI classes. Examples of engine classes are the `MessageDigest`, `Signature`, and `KeyFactory` classes in package `java.security`; the corresponding SPI classes are `MessageDigestSpi`, `SignatureSpi`, and `KeyFactorySpi`, still in package `java.security`. Representing all functions of a given type by a generic engine class masks the idiosyncrasies of the algorithm behind a standardized Java class behavior. Thanks to the principle of algorithm independence, implementations of

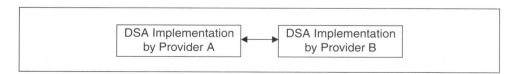

Figure 11.2. Implementation Interoperability

various algorithms providing the same cryptographic functions must expose the same API.

For example, an implementation of the MD5 algorithm and an implementation of SHA-1 need to expose the same API because, even though MD5 and SHA-1 are different algorithms, they both represent the same cryptographic service (see Figure 11.3). Application code invokes the `MessageDigest` API class, specifying the desired algorithm. The `MessageDigest` API class transparently invokes the `MessageDigestSpi` class supplying the implementation for the specified algorithm.

As Figure 11.3 shows, application code needs to interact only with API engine classes. Providers transparently supply the various cryptographic service implementations through the SPI provider classes.

If an application needs to generate MD5 message digests, the `getInstance()` factory method in the `MessageDigest` API can be invoked, specifying, for example, that the MD5 algorithm should be used. If the application developer later decides that SHA-1 should be used in place of MD5, the call to `getInstance()` should be changed to reflect the requirement for SHA-1, but all the other `MessageDigest` method calls can stay the same.

11.1.2.4 Algorithm Extensibility

Algorithm extensibility (Figure 11.4) means that new algorithms that fit in one of the supported engine classes can easily be added. For example, if a new message-digest algorithm is invented and an implemenentation of that algorithm becomes

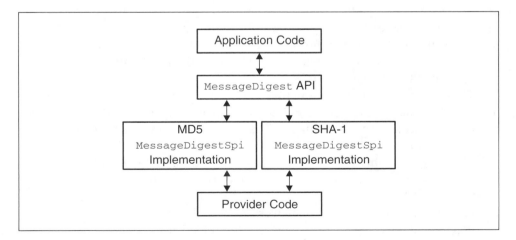

Figure 11.3. Algorithm Independence

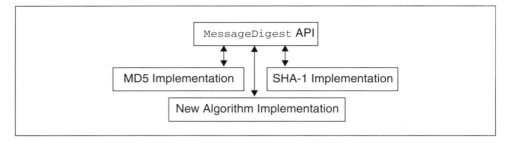

Figure 11.4. Algorithm Extensibility

available, that implementation can be plugged into the JCA and JCE frameworks as long as it is compliant with the `MessageDigest` API.

11.1.3   JCA and JCE Providers

The concept of provider is essential in the JCA and the JCE. In this section, we look at the design behind the concept of provider and study how to manage providers in the Java language.

11.1.3.1   Design

A framework that supports multiple underlying implementation modules needs to be coupled with the supported modules in some fashion. The coupling can be very rigid or very flexible and capable of selecting more than one module for use. At one extreme is a monolithic framework that is so tightly bound to a single module as to preclude the use of other modules or even different implementations of the same module. At the other end of the spectrum is a highly extensible and configurable framework offering seamless and near-effortless pluggability of different modules and their implementations.

The JCA and the JCE are examples of the latter type of framework. They use a CSP infrastructure to support various implementations of cryptographic algorithms and other security mechanisms. The CSP architecture was introduced in the Java 2 SDK V1.2.

Modules in a framework provide services that are used by the framework and ultimately by applications that use the framework. Therefore, the framework has to interface with its pluggable modules. The framework/module interface forms the basic coupling between the framework itself and a module.

For pluggability, extensibility, and module independence, the JCA and JCE provider architectures use SPIs. An SPI is a set of Java-language interfaces and abstract classes used to provide the implementation of one or more cryptographic services. JCA and JCE providers are pluggable modules, and each of them provides concrete implementations of some SPI methods.

The design of the SPI depends on the kind of framework being developed. The design dictates whether a module implements all or a subset of the SPI. The design also determines the granularity of pluggable modules. Object-oriented and Java-language class and interface design principles play a major role in the design of the SPI.

The set of SPIs used by the JCA and JCE is very granular. The `java.security` package and its subpackages contain many SPI interfaces that pluggable JCA security providers can implement. Similarly, the `javax.crypto` package and its subpackages contain many SPI interfaces that pluggable JCE security providers can implement.

11.1.3.2   Implementation

The JCA `Provider` class in the `java.security` package defines the concept of a provider. This abstract class must be subclassed by specific providers. The constructor of a `Provider` class sets the values of various properties that are required for the Java security API to look up the algorithms or other facilities implemented by the provider. Each `Provider` class instance has a case-sensitive name, a version number, and a string description of the provider and its services. These three pieces of information can be obtained by calling the methods `getName()`, `getVersion()`, and `getInfo()`, respectively. Additionally, the `Provider` class has methods for accessing information about the implementations of the algorithms, such as key generation, conversion and management facilities, signature generation, and message digest creation.

A provider is said to be a *main provider* if it implements all the SPI methods. Every provider must exhibit a *master class*, which is a subclass of `java.security.Provider`. The only requirement of a master class is that it must have a default constructor so that it can be loaded by the JCA and JCE infrastructure when the JVM starts up. The essential function of a master class is to define property/value pairs, in which each property is an SPI label and the corresponding value is the name of a class that implements that SPI.

For each cryptographic service, a particular implementation is requested and instantiated by calling a `getInstance()` factory static method on the corresponding engine class, specifying the name of the desired algorithm and, optionally, the name of the `Provider` whose implementation is desired. If none is specified, `getInstance()` relies on the `java.security.Security` class to search the registered providers for an implementation of the requested cryptographic service associated with the named algorithm. In any JVM, providers are installed in a given preference order specified in the `java.security` file. Listing 11.1 shows the fragment of a `java.security` file enumerating all the providers installed in a Java 2 Runtime Environment (J2RE) V1.4.

Listing 11.1. Fragment of a `java.security` File Listing the Providers Installed on a J2RE

```
security.provider.1=com.ibm.jsse.IBMJSSEProvider
security.provider.2=com.ibm.crypto.provider.IBMJCE
security.provider.3=com.ibm.security.jgss.IBMJGSSProvider
security.provider.4=com.ibm.security.cert.IBMCertPath
```

This `java.security` file fragment enables the following four IBM providers:

1. `IBMJSSEProvider`, supplying the Java implementation of the Secure Sockets Layer and Transport Layer Security protocols for use by applications importing the Java Secure Socket Extension API (see Chapter 13 on page 449)

2. `IBMJCE`, supplying the implementation for the cryptographic services supported by the JCA and JCE

3. `IBMJGSSProvider`, supplying the implementation for Generic Security Services (see Section 9.5 on page 340)

4. `IBMCertPath`, supplying the implementation for `CertPath` (see Section 1.1.4 on page 8)

The order in which the providers are enumerated in the `java.security` file is also the one in which the `Security` class searches them when no specific provider is requested. If the implementation is found in the first provider, that implementation is used. If it is not found, an implementation is searched for in the second provider, and so on. If an implementation is not found in any provider, a `java.security.NoSuchAlgorithmException` is raised. Calls to `getInstance()` methods that include a `Provider` argument enable developers to specify from which provider they want an algorithm. A program can also obtain an array of all the installed `Provider`s using the `java.security.Security.getProviders()` static method; the program can then choose a `Provider` from the returned array. Alternatively, it is possible to invoke the `Security.getProvider()` static method, which returns the `Provider` with the name specified in the argument or `null` if the specified `Provider` is not found.

Listing 11.2 enumerates all the providers installed on your Java 2 SDK system and shows for each of them the name, version number, and general information on the cryptographic services supported and the algorithms implemented.

Listing 11.2. `GetProviderInfo.java`

```java
import java.security.Provider;
import java.security.Security;

class GetProviderInfo
{
    public static void main(String[] args)
    {
        System.out.println
            ("Providers installed on your system:");
        System.out.println("-------------------------------");
        Provider[] providerList = Security.getProviders();

        for (int i = 0; i < providerList.length; i++)
        {
            System.out.println("[" + (i + 1) +
                "] - Provider name: " +
                providerList[i].getName());
            System.out.println("Provider version number: " +
                providerList[i].getVersion());
            System.out.println("Provider information:\n" +
                providerList[i].getInfo());
            System.out.println("-------------------------");
        }
    }
}
```

As you can see, the GetProviderInfo Java program uses the `getProviders()` method in the `Security` class and builds an array of `Provider` objects with all the providers installed on the system. Then, on each `Provider` object, the program invokes the methods `getName()`, `getVersion()`, and `getInfo()` to get the provider's name, version number, and general information, respectively. Listing 11.3 shows how you can discover some more information by adding the following lines of code to the `for` loop of `GetProviderInfo.java`.

Listing 11.3. Additional Code to Be Added to `GetProviderInfo.java`

```java
Enumeration properties = providerList[i].propertyNames();

while (properties.hasMoreElements())
{
    String key, value;
    key = (String) properties.nextElement();
    value = providerList[i].getProperty(key);
    System.out.println("Key: " + key + " - Value: " + value);
}
```

These additional lines of code make use of the fact that the `Provider` class extends `java.util.Properties` and so inherits the `propertyNames()` method, which returns a `java.util.Enumeration` object. The `while` loop goes through all the properties of the `Provider` objects installed on the system and prints a list of the keys and values, from which you can understand the cryptographic services supported by the providers installed on your system and the algorithms implemented. For this code to work, `GetProviderInfo.java` must also import `java.util.Enumeration`.

Let us now consider a scenario in which an application needs an implementation of the MD5 message-digest algorithm. The application will typically obtain an instance of the `MessageDigest` engine class and pass the `java.lang.String` `"MD5"` as the argument to the `getInstance()` factory method:

```
MessageDigest md = MessageDigest.getInstance("MD5");
```

Internally, the `getInstance()` method asks the `Security` class to supply the required object. As no specific `Provider` has been passed as an additional argument to the `getInstance()` method, the `Security` class in turn asks all the providers in the sequence they are listed in the `java.security` file, until a provider implementing the requested algorithm is found. A provider manages the individual algorithm classes. When the first provider in the list receives the request from the `Security` class, two things can happen.

1. If it has an implementation of the MD5 message-digest algorithm, the provider will reply to the `Security` class with the requested algorithm class name.

2. If the provider does not have an implementation for the MD5 message digest algorithm, the `Security` class will ask the second provider in the list, and so on, until a provider with the requested implementation is found, if any. If the `Security` class cannot find any implementation of the MD5 message-digest algorithm, a `NoSuchAlgorithmException` is raised.

If an MD5 implementation has been found by one of the providers in the list, the `Security` class passes the MD5 implementation to the `getInstance()` method of the `MessageDigest` class, which returns a `MessageDigest` object, `md`. The `MessageDigest` object is now ready to be used. For example, if an array of bytes, say, `inputData`, has to be hashed into a digest using the MD5 algorithm, the `update()` method for the `MessageDigest` object will be used:

```
md.update(inputData);
```

To compute the digest value, the `digest()` method for the `MessageDigest` object will be used:

```
byte[] digest = md.digest();
```

This way, we have demonstrated how the provider architecture allows for implementation and algorithm independence in the case of the message digest cryptographic service. The same procedure is adopted with any other cryptographic service, such as digital signature and key-pair generation. Figure 11.5 shows how vendor and algorithm independence are achieved when a particular Java application requests the implementation of a key-pair generation algorithm.

11.1.3.3   Configuration and Management

Providers can be installed by first copying the provider package into the file system and then configuring the provider.

Copy the Provider Package.   Simply place the JAR file(s) containing the provider library classes anywhere on the application class path or even on the boot class path. However, the best solution is to supply the provider library as an installed or bundled extension, by placing the JAR file(s) in the extension class path.

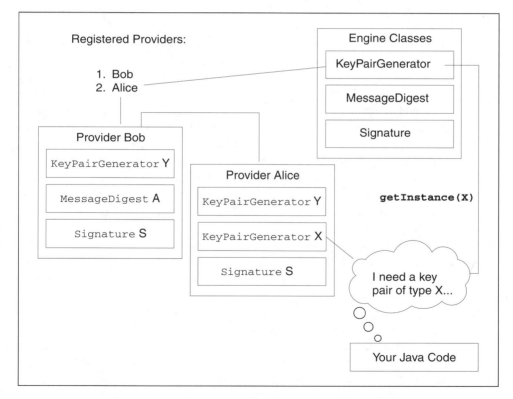

Figure 11.5.   Implementation and Algorithm Independence

Configure the Provider.   For this, you simply need to add the provider to your list of approved providers. This can be done in two ways.

1. **Static configuration.**   A provider configuration can be done statically by adding the provider to the security provider list in the `java.security` file. The order number with which the provider is added to the list is very important; if an implementation is supplied in multiple providers, the implementation of the provider with the higher preference—corresponding to the lower order number—is chosen by the JVM. In the same way, a provider is removed by simply deleting the entry corresponding to it in the `java.security` file.

   The configuration information in the `java.security` file is static insofar as it is effective in a Java runtime. Like most text-file-based configuration information, it is read once when the runtime starts. Any subsequent modification to the file is ignored until after the Java runtime has been restarted.

2. **Dynamic configuration.**   Fortunately, the JCA and JCE provider infrastructures enable dynamic configuration of master provider modules. In fact, providers may also be registered dynamically, after the Java runtime has started up. To do so, it is necessary to call either the `addProvider()` or the `insertProviderAt()` static method in the `Security` class. The `addProvider()` method adds a new provider at the end of the list of the installed providers. On the other hand, the `insertProviderAt()` method adds a new provider at a specified position in the array of providers. If the given provider is installed in the requested position, the provider that used to be at that position, and all the providers with a position greater than that, are shifted up one position, toward the end of the list of the installed providers. Both methods return the preference position in which the provider was added, or `-1` if the provider was not added because it was already installed.

   If the preference position of a provider has to be changed, the provider must be first removed and then inserted back at the new preference position. A provider can be removed by calling the `removeProvider()` method of the `Security` class.

   Note that the dynamic provider registration is not persistent and can be done only by trusted programs or, in other words, programs that have been granted the necessary `Permissions` (see Section 8.2 on page 258). To add a provider whose name is indicated with *name* or to insert it in a specified position in the list, the `Permission` required is a `java.security.SecurityPermission` `"insertProvider.name"`. To remove it, the `Permission` required is a `java.security.SecurityPermission` `"removeProvider.name"`.

11.1.4 Engine and SPI Classes

The provider architecture of JCA and JCE has been designed to allow implementation and algorithm independence. This way, implementations of various cryptographic services can be found at runtime, without any changes to the code. For this reason, abstract representations of cryptographic services are offered through generic engine classes. The engine classes are the interfaces between the user code and the implementations of the underlying algorithms offered by the installed providers, as shown in Figure 11.6.

The following engine classes are defined on the Java 2 platform as part of the JCA framework:

- **java.security.MessageDigest.** Used to calculate the message digest (hash) of specified data.

- **java.security.Signature.** Used to digitally sign data and verify digital signatures.

- **java.security.KeyPairGenerator.** Used to generate a pair of public and private keys suitable for a specified algorithm.

- **java.security.KeyFactory.** Used to convert *keys*—opaque cryptographic keys of type `java.security.Key`—into *key specifications*—transparent representations of the underlying key material—and vice versa.

  An *opaque key representation* is one in which you have no direct access to the key material that constitues a key. Therefore, an opaque key

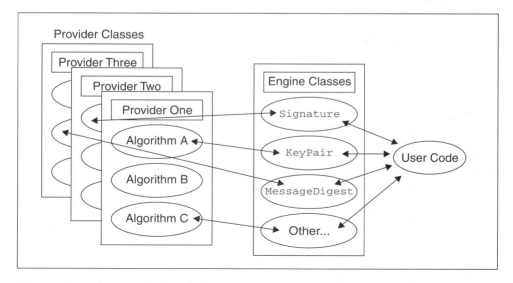

Figure 11.6. User Code, Engine Classes, and Providers

representation gives you limited access to the key itself. An encoded form of the key is available, but the parameters used to generate the key are not. A *transparent key representation* is one in which you can access each parameter value in the set individually, through one of the `get` methods defined in the corresponding specification class. For example, both classes `RSAPublicKeySpec` and `RSAPrivateKeySpec` in package `java.security.spec` define a method `getModulus()` to access the modulus n used in the RSA algorithm. In addition, `RSAPublicKeySpec` defines method `getPublicExponent()` to allow access to the public exponent e, and `RSAPrivateKeySpec` defines method `getPrivateExponent()` to allow access to the private exponent d.

A `KeyFactory` object can also be used to translate a `Key` object, whose provider may be unknown or potentially untrusted, into a corresponding `Key` object of this `KeyFactory`.

- **`java.security.KeyStore`.** Used to create and manage keystores.

- **`java.security.AlgorithmParameters`.** Used to manage the parameters for a particular algorithm, including parameter encoding and decoding.

- **`java.security.AlgorithmParameterGenerator`.** Used to generate a set of parameters suitable for a specified algorithm.

- **`java.security.SecureRandom`.** Used to generate random or pseudo-random numbers.

- **`java.security.certificate.CertificateFactory`.** Used to create public-key certificates and certificate revocation lists.

- **`java.security.cert.CertPathBuilder`.** Used to build certificate chains.

- **`java.security.cert.CertPathValidator`.** Used to validate certificate chains.

- **`java.security.cert.CertStore`.** Used to retrieve certificates and CRLs from a repository.

In both the JCA and the JCE, an instance of an engine class encapsulates the implementation of a cryptographic service by one of the providers installed on the Java platform. The engine classes defined on the Java 2 platform as part of the JCE are as follows:

- **`javax.crypto.Cipher`.** Provides the functionality of a cryptographic cipher for encryption and decryption.

- **`javax.crypto.ExemptionMechanism`.** Provides the functionality of an exemption mechanism. Programs that use an *exemption mechanism* may be granted stronger encryption capabilities than those that do not.

- **`javax.crypto.KeyAgreement`.** Provides the functionality of a key-agreement or key-exchange protocol.

- **`javax.crypto.KeyGenerator`.** Provides the functionality of a symmetric key generator.

- **`javax.crypto.Mac`.** Provides the functionality of a MAC algorithm.

- **`javax.crypto.SecretKeyFactory`.** Represents a factory for secret keys.

Each engine class can be instantiated by using the `getInstance()` static factory method. If you pass this method a single argument, it must be the name of the algorithm to be used. In this case, the `getInstance()` method will ask the `Security` class to find the first provider in the preference list offering an implementation of that algorithm. Otherwise, you can force this decision and specify two arguments; in this case, along with the algorithm, you will explicitly pass in the `Provider` name or the `Provider` instance.

An engine class provides the methods to enable applications to access the specific cryptographic service it provides, independent of the particular type of cryptographic algorithm. The `MessageDigest` engine class, for example, provides access to the functionality for all message-digest algorithms, such as MD5, SHA-1, and so on. The application interfaces supplied by an engine class are implemented in terms of the corresponding SPI. That is, each engine class has a corresponding abstract SPI class, which defines the methods that cryptographic service providers must implement. The name of each SPI class is the same as that of the corresponding engine class, followed by `Spi`. For example, the SPI class corresponding to the `Signature` engine class is `SignatureSpi`. Each SPI class in the Java core API is abstract. It is the responsibility of a provider to subclass it and supply a concrete implementation for it.

To supply the implementation of a particular type of service, for a specific algorithm, a provider must subclass the corresponding SPI class and supply implementations for all the abstract methods. By convention, the abstract methods in the SPI class all begin with `engine` and are declared `protected`. For example, the `SignatureSpi` class defines abstract methods, such as `engineInitVerify()` and `engineInitSign()`. An instance of an engine class—the *API object* obtained by calling the `getInstance()` factory method on the engine class itself—encapsulates as a private field an instance of the corresponding SPI class, the *SPI object*. The implementations of the API object's methods invoke the corresponding methods in the encapsulated SPI object. For example, when called by an application, the `digest()` method of a `MessageDigest` API object calls the `engineDigest()` method on the `MessageDigestSpi` object encapsulated in it. Similarly, when the `updateDigest()` method of a `MessageDigest` API object is called, the method calls the `engineUpdateDigest()` method on the `MessageDigestSpi` object encapsulated in it. This scenario is shown in Figure 11.7.

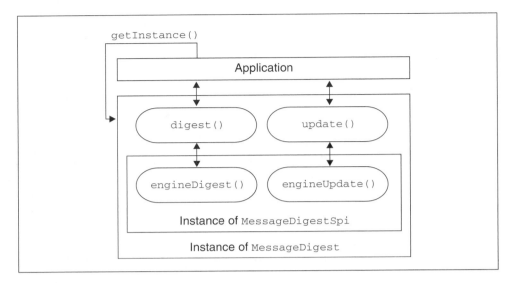

Figure 11.7. `MessageDigest` Engine and SPI Classes

11.2 The JCA API

This section explains how to use the most important JCA API classes from within Java programs in a J2EE environment.

11.2.1 The `java.security.SecureRandom` Class

This class provides a cryptographically strong pseudorandom number generator (PRNG). The package `java.security` also offers the class `SecureRandomSpi`, which defines the SPI for `SecureRandom`. This SPI can be used for more advanced `SecureRandom` implementations, such as true random number generator (TRNG). Let us consider the following instruction:

```
SecureRandom r = new SecureRandom();
```

This instruction obtains a `SecureRandom` object containing the implementation from the highest-priority installed security provider that has a `SecureRandom` implementation. Another way to instantiate a `SecureRandom` object is via the static method `getInstance()`, supplying the algorithm and optionally the provider implementing that algorithm:

```
SecureRandom random =
    SecureRandom.getInstance("IBMSecureRandom", "IBMJCE");
```

The `SecureRandom` implementation attempts to completely randomize the internal state of the generator itself unless the caller follows the call to the `get-Instance()` method with a call to the `setSeed()` method. When calling `set-Seed()`, the given seed supplements, rather than replaces, the existing seed. Thus, repeated calls are guaranteed never to reduce randomness.

The sample code in Listing 11.8 on page 402 shows how to use the `SecureRandom` class to initialize a `KeyPairGenerator` object. The examples in Listing 11.4 on page 395 and Listing 11.5 on page 395 demonstrate how to make calls to `setSeed()`.

11.2.2   The `java.security.Key` Interface

The package `java.security` offers several interfaces and classes to provide key generation and management. The `Key` interface is the top-level interface for all opaque keys. In fact, this interface defines the functionality shared by all opaque key objects. Because the key representation offered by the `Key` interface is opaque, this interface defines only three methods—`getAlgorithm()`, `getEncoded()`, and `getFormat()`—which correspond to the three characteristics of any opaque key:

1. **An algorithm.**   The key algorithm is usually an encryption or asymmetric operation algorithm, such as DSA or RSA. The name of the algorithm of a `Key` is obtained calling the `getAlgorithm()` method.

2. **An encoded form.**   This is an external encoded form for the `Key`. An external encoded format is used when a standard representation of the key is needed outside the JVM, as when transmitting the key to another party. The key is encoded according to a standard format, such as X.509 or PKCS#8 and is returned using the `getEncoded()` method as an array of bytes.

3. **A Format.**   The name of the format of the encoded key is returned by the `getFormat()` method as a `String` object.

11.2.3   The `PublicKey` and `PrivateKey` Interfaces in Package `java.security`

The `PrivateKey` and `PublicKey` interfaces in package `java.security` extend the `Key` interface and contain no methods or constants but merely serve to group—and provide type safety for—all public- and private-key interfaces. The specialized public- and private-key interfaces, such as the `DSAPublicKey` and `DSAPrivateKey` interfaces in the `java.security.interfaces` package, extend `PublicKey` and `PrivateKey`, respectively. All the sample code presented in Section 11.2.9 on page 400 shows how to use the `PublicKey` and `PrivateKey` interfaces.

11.2.4   The `java.security.KeyFactory` Class

The `java.security` package also contains classes to manage keys and key pairs; the `KeyFactory` class, for example, is used to convert keys into key specifications (and vice versa), and the `KeyFactorySpi` class is used to define the SPI for the `KeyFactory` class. A representation of key material is *opaque* if it does not expose any direct access to the key material fields.

A `KeyFactory` is bidirectional. This means that it allows you to build an opaque key object from given key material (specification) or to retrieve the underlying key material of a key object in a suitable format. A `KeyFactory` object can be created using the static `KeyFactory.getInstance()` method. From a key specification, you can generate the keys by using the `generatePublic()` and `generatePrivate()` methods. To get the key specification from a `KeyFactory`, you can use the `getKeySpec()` method. Sample code using the `KeyFactory` class is available in Listing 11.9 on page 406.

11.2.5   The `java.security.KeyPair` Class

The `KeyPair` class is used to hold a public key and a private key. The class provides `getPrivate()` and `getPublic()` methods to get the private and the public keys, respectively. This class does not enforce any security and, when initialized, should be treated like a `PrivateKey`. Sample code using the `KeyPair` class is shown in Listing 11.8 on page 402.

11.2.6   The `java.security.KeyPairGenerator` Class

The `KeyPairGenerator` class is used to generate key pairs, whereas the `KeyPairGeneratorSpi` class is used to define the SPI for the `KeyPairGenerator` class. A `KeyPairGenerator` object can be created using the `getInstance()` static factory method for the `KeyPairGenerator` class. A `KeyPairGenerator` object must be initialized before it can generate keys. To do this, four methods are provided, all of them called `initialize()` but each having a different signature. The four `initialize()` methods allow you to

- Generate a key pair in an algorithm-independent manner or in an algorithm-specific manner

- Provide a specific source of randomness or use the `java.security.SecureRandom` implementation of the highest-priority installed provider as the source of randomness

When you initialize a key pair in an algorithm-independent manner, you specify the key size. If you initialize in an algorithm-specific way, you supply the `AlgorithmParameterSpec` to the generator.

In the algorithm-independent case (Listing 11.4), it is up to the provider to determine the algorithm-specific parameters to be associated with each of the keys. The provider may use precomputed parameter values or may generate new values.

Listing 11.4. Algorithm-Independent Key-Pair Initialization

```
KeyPairGenerator kGen = KeyPairGenerator.getInstance("DSA");
SecureRandom rd =
    SecureRandom.getInstance("IBMSecureRandom", "IBMJCE");
rd.setSeed(userSeed);
kGen.initialize(1024, rd);
```

In the algorithm-specific case, the user supplies the parameters to initialize a key pair (Listing 11.5).

Listing 11.5. Algorithm-Specific Key-Pair Initialization

```
KeyPairGenerator kGen = KeyPairGenerator.getInstance("DSA");
DSAParameterSpec dsaSpec = new DSAParameterSpec(p, q, g);
SecureRandom rd =
    SecureRandom.getInstance("IBMSecureRandom", "IBMJCE");
rd.setSeed(userSeed);
kGen.initialize(dsaSpec, rd);
```

Note that `java.security.KeyPairGenerator`, `java.security.Secure-Random`, and `java.security.spec.DSAParameterSpec` must be explicitly imported in order for the preceding code fragments to work properly. Listing 11.8 on page 402 presents a complete example of `KeyPairGenerator` use.

11.2.7 The `java.security.KeyStore` Class

A *keystore* is a database of private keys and their associated certificates or certificate chains, which authenticate the corresponding public keys. The JCA provides the `KeyStore` API to manage keystores and to represent in-memory collections of keys and certificates, whereas the `KeyStoreSpi` class defines the SPI for the `KeyStore` class. You can generate a `KeyStore` object by using the static `get-Instance()` factory method. When generating a `KeyStore` object, you must specify the `KeyStore` type as a parameter to the `getInstance()` method. The type indicates the format in which certificates and keys are stored in the keystore.

The default keystore implementation, provided in the reference implementation of Java 2 SDK, is a flat file, using a proprietary keystore type or format, named Java keystore (JKS). This format protects the integrity of the entire keystore with a keystore password. A hash value of the entire keystore is used to protect the keystore from alteration. The keystore itself is not encrypted; the hash value is used only to detect whether the keystore has been altered by unauthorized entities. However, each private key in the keystore is encrypted with a separate password, which may be identical to the keystore password. With the JCE keystore (JCEKS) implemented by IBM and shipped as part of the IBM JCE, the keystore itself is encrypted. Other common implementations use the PKCS#12 standard (see Section 12.1.7 on page 437).

To load a `KeyStore` object from a `java.io.InputStream`, the `load()` method is provided. The `store()` method can be used to store the keystore to a `java.io.OutputStream`. Additionally, the `KeyStore` class exposes methods to get and set keys and certificates from a given keystore. For instance, `aliases()` lists all the alias names in the keystore, `deleteEntry()` deletes the entry identified by a specific alias from the keystore, and `getKey()` gets the key associated with a given alias from the keystore.

Although the Java 2 SDK offers the `keytool` utility to manage keystores, sometimes it is necessary to manage a keystore programmatically. For example, a J2EE application may need to access a keystore to obtain the public key of an entity to verify a digital signature. Listing 11.6 shows how to load a `KeyStore` object, get a digital certificate with alias `marco` from it, and store that certificate into another `KeyStore` object. The code comments explain the operations in detail.

Listing 11.6. How to Use the `KeyStore` Class

```java
import java.security.KeyStore;

import java.security.cert.X509Certificate;

import java.io.FileInputStream;
import java.io.FileOutputStream;


// Other code goes here...

// Create the KeyStore object
KeyStore ks1 = KeyStore.getInstance("JKS", "IBMJCE");
String keypass = "marcop";
char[] pwd = keypass.toCharArray();

// Load the keystore from the file system
FileInputStream fis1 = new FileInputStream("keystore1");
ks1.load(fis1, pwd);

// Get the certificate from the keystore with alias marco
X509Certificate cert =
    (X509Certificate) ks1.getCertificate("marco");
```

```
// Store the same certificate in the other keystore.

// Create the KeyStore object.
KeyStore ks2 = KeyStore.getInstance("JKS", "IBMJCE");
FileInputStream fis2 = new FileInputStream("keystore2");

// Load the keystore.
ks2.load(fis2, pwd);

// Insert the certificate in the keystore.
ks2.setCertificateEntry("marco", cert);

// Store the keystore.
FileOutputStream fos2 = new FileOutputStream("keystore2");
ks2.store(fos2, pwd);

// Other code goes here...
```

The purpose of this code fragment is to show how to use the Java security API to manage keystores. For simplicity, we have assumed the following.

- The keystore from which the certificate is loaded is called keystore1, and the one to which the certificate is stored is called keystore2. Both of these files are assumed to be located in the directory from which the program is launched. The file names are hard-coded.

- Both keystores are of type JKS.

- All passwords are set to marcop, and this value is hard-coded. Because the source code of servlets and enterprise beans is not accessible from the client, there are no risks of decompilation attacks.

- In keystore1, the key pair and the certificate wrapping the public key are associated with an alias called marco.

The code fragment in Listing 11.6 loads keystore1, gets the certificate associated with the alias marco, inserts this certificate into keystore2, and stores the destination keystore into the file system. Listing 11.10 on page 408 provides another example showing how to use the KeyStore class.

11.2.8 The `java.security.MessageDigest` Class

An example of an engine class is the java.security.MessageDigest class, which provides access to message-digest algorithms. The MessageDigest class provides the functionality of cryptographically secure message digests, such as SHA-1 or MD5, whereas the MessageDigestSpi class defines the SPI for the MessageDigest class. The package java.security also offers the DigestInputStream and DigestOutputStream classes for reading and writing digest information.

As we explained in Section 10.2.2.4 on page 356, a cryptographically secure message digest takes arbitrary-sized input—a byte array—and generates a fixed-sized output—the *message digest*, or *hash*. A digest has the following properties.

- It should be computationally infeasible to find two messages that hash to the same value.

- The digest must not reveal anything about the input that was used to generate it.

With the `MessageDigest` class, as with all the other engine classes, you can obtain an object by using the `getInstance()` static factory method. You must supply either the algorithm or the algorithm and the provider. The following line of code constructs a `MessageDigest` object initialized to use the SHA-1 algorithm:

```
MessageDigest md = MessageDigest.getInstance("SHA1");
```

A caller may optionally specify the name of a provider, which will guarantee that the implementation of the algorithm requested is from the named provider, as in the following line of code:

```
MessageDigest md = MessageDigest.getInstance("SHA1", "IBMJCE");
```

The JCA is case insensitive with regard to algorithm names. Therefore, passing the parameter `"SHA1"` or `"Sha1"` would have still returned a `MessageDigest` object initialized to use the SHA-1 algorithm.

The `MessageDigest` class provides an `update()` method that is used to update `MessageDigest` objects with the data to be digested. Finally, the data is digested using the `digest()` method. Figure 11.8 summarizes the sequence of actions that

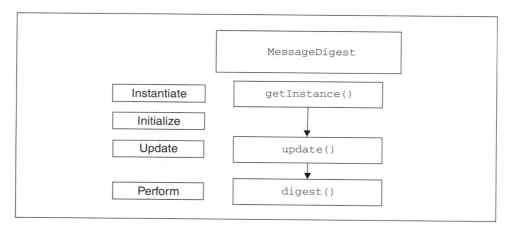

Figure 11.8. Actions Taken on a `MessageDigest` Object and Corresponding Methods

need to be taken on a `MessageDigest` object to compute the digest of a message, as well as the corresponding methods that need to be invoked in order for those actions to take place.

Note that a `MessageDigest` object starts out initialized. In other words, a call to `getInstance()` returns an initialized `MessageDigest` object. As Figure 11.8 shows, no additional initialization is needed, and the object is ready to use.

The code fragment in Listing 11.7, which could be embedded in any J2EE application, shows how to use the `MessageDigest` class in practice.

Listing 11.7. How to Use the `MessageDigest` Class

```java
import java.security.MessageDigest;

import java.io.File;
import java.io.FileInputStream;
import java.io.FileOutputStream;
import java.io.BufferedInputStream;
import java.io.BufferedOutputStream;


// Other code goes here...

// Obtain a MessageDigest object initialized to use.
MessageDigest md = MessageDigest.getInstance("SHA1");

// Get the file to be digested.
File inputFile = new File("C:\\CONFIG.SYS");
FileInputStream cfis = new FileInputStream(inputFile);
BufferedInputStream cbis = new BufferedInputStream(cfis);
byte[] cbuff = new byte[1024];

while (cbis.available() != 0)
{
    int len = cbis.read(cbuff);

    // Update the digest with the data to be digested
    md.update(cbuff, 0, len);
}

cbis.close();
cfis.close();

// Finally, calculate the digest.
byte[] digest = md.digest();

// Write the digest information to a file.
File outputFile = new File("C:\\digest.txt");
FileOutputStream cfos = new FileOutputStream(outputFile);
BufferedOutputStream cbos = new BufferedOutputStream(cfos);
cbos.write(digest);
cbos.close();
cfos.close();

// Other code goes here...
```

The code in Listing 11.7 calculates the digest of the contents of the file `C:\CON-FIG.SYS` and stores it in the file `C:\digest.txt`.

11.2.9 The `java.security.Signature` Class

The `java.security.Signature` class is an engine class that is designed to provide the functionality of a cryptographic digital-signature algorithm, such as RSA or DSA. As we explained in Section 10.3.3 on page 370, a cryptographically secure signature algorithm takes arbitrary-sized input and a private key and generates a relatively short, often fixed-sized, string of bytes, called the *signature*, with the following properties.

- Given the public key corresponding to the private key used to generate the signature, it should be possible to verify the authenticity and integrity of the input.

- The signature and the public key do not reveal anything about the private key that was used to generate the signature.

A `Signature` object can be used to sign data, as well as to validate a signature of signed data.

`Signature` objects are stateful. This means that a `Signature` object is always in a particular state; only a single type of operation may be performed until the state is changed. States are represented as final static fields of type `int`. The three states `Signature` objects may have are UNINITIALIZED, SIGN, and VERIFY. When the `Signature` object is created, it is in the UNINITIALIZED state. As we will see shortly, the `Signature` class defines two initialization methods, `initSign()` and `initVerify()`, which change the state to SIGN and VERIFY, respectively.

To obtain a `Signature` object for signing or verifying a signature, the first step is to create a `Signature` instance. As with all engine classes, the way to get a `Signature` object for a particular type of signature algorithm is to call the `get-Instance()` static factory method on the `Signature` class, as in the following code line:

```
Signature signature = Signature.getInstance("SHA1withDSA");
```

A caller may optionally specify the name of a provider, which will guarantee that the implementation of the algorithm requested is from the named provider, as in the following line of code:

```
Signature signature = Signature.getInstance("SHA1withDSA", "IBMJCE");
```

Unlike a `MessageDigest` object, when a `Signature` object is created, it is in the UNINITIALIZED state and must be initialized before it can be used. The initialization method depends on whether the object is first going to be used for signing or for verification.

- If the `Signature` object is going to be used for signing, it must first be initialized with the private key of the entity whose signature is going to be generated. This initialization is done by calling the method `initSign()`, which takes a `java.security.PrivateKey` object as a parameter. When it is called, this method puts the `Signature` object in the `SIGN` state.

- If instead the `Signature` object is going to be used for verification, it must first be initialized with the public key of the entity whose signature is going to be verified. This initialization is done by calling the method `initVerify()`, which takes a `java.security.PublicKey` object as a parameter. When it is called, this method puts the `Signature` object in the `VERIFY` state.

Once a `Signature` object has been initialized, you can either sign data or verify the signature of previously signed data.

- If it has been initialized for signing, which implies that it is in the `SIGN` state, the `Signature` object can be supplied the data to be signed. This is done by making one or more calls to the `update()` method. Calls to this method should be made until all the data to be signed has been supplied to the `Signature` object. At this point, to generate the signature, it is enough to call the `sign()` method, which takes no parameters and returns an array of bytes representing the digital signature of all the data updated.

- Once data has been signed, the `Signature` class can be used again, this time to verify the signed data. To start the process, it is necessary to use a `Signature` object implementing the same algorithm implemented by the `Signature` object that was used to sign the data. This new `Signature` object must have been initialized for signature verification, which implies that it is in the `VERIFY` state. The data to be verified, as opposed to the signature itself, is supplied to this `Signature` object by making one or more calls to one of the `update()` methods. Calls to this method should be made repeatedly until all the data has been supplied to the `Signature` object. At this point, the signature can then be verified by calling the `verify()` method, which takes as its only parameter an array of bytes representing the digital signature associated with the data updated. This method returns a `boolean` value: `true` if the signature was verified and `false` if not.

Figure 11.9 summarizes the various phases involved in the use of the `Signature` class, showing what actions need to be taken to sign data or verify a signature, along with the corresponding methods.

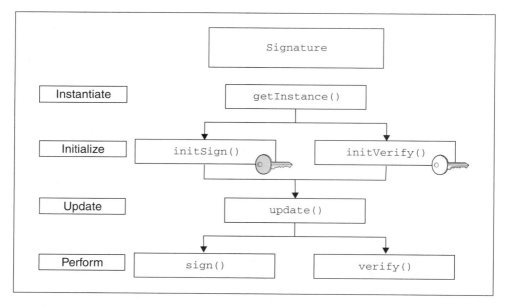

Figure 11.9. Actions Taken on a `Signature` Object and Corresponding Methods

The code fragment shown in Listing 11.8 demonstrates how to create a key pair, use the private key in the pair to sign a document, and store the signature and the public key in two separate files.

Listing 11.8. How to Use the `Signature` Class for Signature Generation

```
import java.security.KeyPair;
import java.security.KeyPairGenerator;
import java.security.SecureRandom;
import java.security.PublicKey;
import java.security.PrivateKey;
import java.security.Signature;

import java.io.FileInputStream;
import java.io.BufferedInputStream;
import java.io.FileOutputStream


// Other code goes here...

// Create the key pair.
KeyPairGenerator kpg = KeyPairGenerator.getInstance
    ("DSA", "IBMJCE");
SecureRandom r = new SecureRandom();
kpg.initialize(1024, r);
KeyPair kp = kpg.generateKeyPair();
```

```
// Get the generated keys.
PrivateKey priv = kp.getPrivate();
PublicKey publ = kp.getPublic();

// Intialize the Signature object with the private key.
Signature dsasig = Signature.getInstance
   ("SHA1withDSA", "IBMJCE");
dsasig.initSign(priv);

// Get the file to be signed.
FileInputStream fis = new FileInputStream(inputFile);
BufferedInputStream bis = new BufferedInputStream(fis);
byte[] buff = new byte[1024];
int len;

// Update the Signature object with the data to be signed.
while (bis.available() != 0)
{
    len=bis.read(buff);
    dsasig.update(buff, 0, len);
}

// Close the BufferedInputStream and the FileInputStream.
bis.close();
fis.close();

// Get the signature as a byte array.
byte[] realSignature = dsasig.sign();

// Write the signature to a file.
FileOutputStream fos = new FileOutputStream(signatureFile);
fos.write(realSignature);
fos.close();

// Write the public key to a file.
byte[] pkey = publ.getEncoded();
FileOutputStream keyfos = new FileOutputStream(publicKeyFile);
keyfos.write(pkey);
keyfos.close();

// Other code goes here...
```

This code fragment could be embedded in any J2EE application that needs to sign a file. The comments embedded in the code explain what the code does. A detailed explanation follows.

In this program, a `KeyPairGenerator` generates keys for the DSA signature algorithm. The `KeyPairGenerator` class is used to generate a public- and private-key pair. In general, `KeyPairGenerator`s are constructed using one of the two `getInstance()` factory methods provided in the `KeyPairGenerator` class. A `KeyPairGenerator` for a particular algorithm creates a public- and private-key pair that can be used with this algorithm and also associates algorithm-specific parameters with each of the generated keys. In the code of Listing 11.8, we generate a `KeyPairGenerator` object by implementing the DSA algorithm provided by the IBM provider:

```
KeyPairGenerator kpg =
    KeyPairGenerator.getInstance("DSA", "IBMJCE");
```

Then, we initialize the `KeyPairGenerator` with a random number. The source of randomness is an instance of the `SecureRandom` class. This class provides a cryptographically strong random-number generator. To get an instance of this class, you can use the `getInstance()` method, specifying the secure random generation algorithm and the provider that supplies it:

```
SecureRandom r =
    SecureRandom.getInstance("IBMSecureRandom", "IBMJCE");
```

Another option, which is the option selected for this example, is to call the `SecureRandom` constructor directly:

```
SecureRandom r = new SecureRandom();
```

This instruction obtains a `SecureRandom` object containing the implementation from the highest-priority installed provider that has a `SecureRandom` implementation.

We can now create the key pair by using the `generateKeyPair()` method on the `KeyPairGeneration` object. The key size is set to 1,024 bits:

```
kpg.initialize(1024, r);
KeyPair kp = kpg.generateKeyPair();
```

The private and the public keys can be retrieved by using the `getPrivateKey()` and the `getPublicKey()` methods of the `KeyPair` class, respectively:

```
PrivateKey priv = kp.getPrivate();
PublicKey publ = kp.getPublic();
```

The `Signature` object is generated by using the `getInstance()` factory method of the `Signature` class. We need to provide the signing algorithm and the provider name. Then, we associate the private key to be used for signing by using the `initSign()` method:

```
Signature dsasig = Signature.getInstance("SHA1withDSA", "IBMJCE");
dsasig.initSign(priv);
```

Next, we get the file to be signed. The signature can be generated by using the sign() method after all the data has been updated. As we have explained, once generated, a Signature object has three phases. For signing data:

1. It must be initialized with a private key, using the initSign() method.

2. It must be updated with the data to be signed, using the update() method:

```
dsasig.update(buff, 0, len);
```

3. The final phase is to sign the data, using the sign() method:

```
byte[] realsignature = dsasig.sign();
```

Signature verification consists of similar phases.

1. The initialization is done with the public key rather than the private key and is performed by calling initVerify() rather than initSign().

2. The update is done with the data to be verified rather than the data to be signed.

3. The sign() method is replaced by the verify() method.

The final step is to save the signature generated and the public key to two files. We need to get the public key in its encoded format before writing it to the file. This can be done using the getEncoded() method provided in the Key interface:

```
byte[] pkey = publ.getEncoded();
```

Note that the names of the three files used in the code fragment of Listing 11.8 on page 402 should be defined somewhere else in the program:

1. The variable inputFile indicates the input file to be signed.

2. The variable signatureFile indicates the file where the signature will be written.

3. The variable publicKeyFile indicates the file where the public key will be written.

It is not necessary that the signatureFile and the publicKeyFile files exist. The code creates them automatically.

Once generated, the three files can be sent to the receiver, who will verify the signature through a J2EE application containing the code fragment shown in Listing 11.9.

Listing 11.9. How to Use the `Signature` Class for Signature Verification

```
import java.security.Signature;
import java.security.KeyFactory;
import java.security.PublicKey;

import java.security.spec.X509EncodedKeySpec;

import java,io.FileInputStream;
import java.io.BufferedInputStream;


// Other code goes here...

// inputFile is the file whose contents have been signed.
FileInputStream fis = new FileInputStream(inputFile);

// signatureFile is the file containing the signature.
FileInputStream sfis = new FileInputStream(signatureFile);

// publicKeyFile is the file containing the signer's public
// key.
FileInputStream pfis = new FileInputStream(publicKeyFile);

// Get the public key of the sender.
byte[] encKey = new byte[pfis.available()];
pfis.read(encKey);
pfis.close();
X509EncodedKeySpec pubKeySpec =
    new X509EncodedKeySpec(encKey);
KeyFactory keyFac = KeyFactory.getInstance("DSA", "IBMJCE");
PublicKey pubKey = keyFac.generatePublic(pubKeySpec);

// Get the signature from signatureFile.
byte[] sigToVerify = new byte[sfis.available()];
sfis.read(sigToVerify);
sfis.close();

// Initialize the Signature object for signature verification.
Signature sig =
    Signature.getInstance("SHA1withDSA", "IBMJCE");
sig.initVerify(pubKey);

// Update the Signature object with the data to be verified.
BufferedInputStream buf = new BufferedInputStream(fis);
byte[] buff = new byte[1024];
int len;

while(buf.available() != 0)
{
    len = buf.read(buff);
    sig.update(buff, 0, len);
}

buf.close();
fis.close();
```

```
// Verify the signature.
boolean verifies = sig.verify(sigToVerify);

if (verifies)
    System.out.println("Signature verification succeeded.");
else
    System.out.println("Signature verification failed.");

// Other code goes here...
```

This code fragment could be embedded in any J2EE application that needs to verify the digital signature of a file.

The comments embedded in the code explain what the code does. A detailed explanation follows.

First, we must import the encoded public-key bytes from the file containing the public key and convert them to a PublicKey. Hence, we read the key bytes, instantiate the DSA public key by using the KeyFactory class, and generate the key from it:

```
byte[] encKey = new byte[pfis.available()];
pfis.read(encKey);
pfis.close();
X509EncodedKeySpec pubKeySpec = new X509EncodedKeySpec(encKey);
KeyFactory keyFac = KeyFactory.getInstance("DSA", "IBMJCE");
PublicKey pubkey = keyFac.generatePublic(pubKeySpec);
```

The X509EncodedKeySpec class represents the Distinguished Encoding Rules (DER) encoding of a public or private key, according to the format specified in the X.509 standard. The public key can be created from it using the KeyFactory class. This class is used to convert keys—opaque cryptographic keys of type Key—into key specifications—transparent representations of the underlying key material—and vice versa. We specify the DSA key algorithm and the IBM provider and use the generatePublic() method to generate the PublicKey.

The rest of the code fragment is similar to what needs to be done to sign the contents of a file (see Listing 11.8 on page 402). The only difference is that this time, the Signature is initialized with this PublicKey in place of the PrivateKey, and the sign() method is replaced by the verify() method.

The three files inputFile, signatureFile, and publicKeyFile, used in the code fragment of Listing 11.9 on page 406, should be defined somewhere else in the program. This time, all three files must exist in advance and should be the same files used by the code fragment of Listing 11.8. This way, we are simulating a scenario in which a sender generates a signature and then sends the original file to a receiver, along with the signature and the public key.

The expected output should be as follows.

- If none of the three files has been altered after the signature was applied, the program should display the following:

```
Signature verification succeeded.
```

- If you change the contents of any of the three files, the program displays the following message:

```
Signature verification failed.
```

In particular, if you modify the signature file so that it no longer respects the signature format, the code fragment of Listing 11.9 will throw a `java.security.SignatureException`.

This scenario demonstrates how you can successfully use the Java 2 APIs in a J2EE environment to send documents with proof of data integrity and authenticity.

If you wish to load the keys from a keystore rather than generating them, you can use the code fragment in Listing 11.10 in place of the one shown in Listing 11.8.

Listing 11.10. Using `Signature` and `KeyStore` for Signature Generation

```
import java.security.KeyStore;
import java.security.Signature;
import java.security.PrivateKey;

import java.security.cert.X509Certificate;

import java.io.FileInputStream
import java.io.BufferedInputStream;
import java.io.FileOutputStream;


// Other code goes here...

// Access the default keystore in the user home directory.
String s1 = System.getProperty("user.home");
String s2 = System.getProperty("file.separator");
FileInputStream fisk = new FileInputStream(s1 + s2 +
    ".keystore");
KeyStore ks = KeyStore.getInstance("JKS", "IBMJCE");

// Access the private key and the certificate of the signer.
String keypass = "marcop";
char[] pwd = new char[keypass.length()];
keypass.getChars(0, keypass.length(), pwd, 0);
ks.load(fisk, pwd);
String alias = "marco";
```

```
PrivateKey priv = (PrivateKey) ks.getKey(alias, pwd);
X509Certificate cert = (X509Certificate)
    ks.getCertificate(alias);

// Intialize the Signature object.
Signature sig =
    Signature.getInstance("SHA1withDSA", "IBMJCE");
sig.initSign(priv);

// Get the file to be signed.
FileInputStream fis = new FileInputStream(inputFile);
BufferedInputStream bis=new BufferedInputStream(fis);
byte[] buff = new byte[1024];
int len;

// Update the Signature object with the data to be signed.
while (bis.available() != 0)
{
    len = bis.read(buff);
    sig.update(buff, 0, len);
}

// Close the BufferedInputStream and the FileInputStream.
bis.close();
fis.close();

// Produce the actual signature.
byte[] realSignature = sig.sign();

// Write the signature to a file.
FileOutputStream fos = new FileOutputStream(signatureFile);
fos.write(realSignature);
fos.close();

// Write the certificate to a file.
byte[] encCert = cert.getEncoded();
FileOutputStream certfos = new FileOutputStream(certFile);
certfos.write(encCert);
certfos.close();

// Other code goes here...
```

This code fragment could be embedded in any J2EE application that needs to sign the contents of a file with a private key obtained from a keystore. The comments embedded in the code explain what the code does.

You can see that this code fragment is very similar to the one shown in Listing 11.8 on page 402. The only difference here is that, in place of generating keys, we load an existing keystore and use keys already created and present in it. The program is configured to retrieve the keystore from the user home directory. System variables are used to grant code portability across the platforms.

You can generate a keystore by using the `-genkey` option of the `keytool` command line utility. When you run this sample code, ensure that you have generated a keystore called `.keystore` on your user home directory. This file name and location are the default for the keystore creation performed by the `-genkey` command of the `keytool` utility.

This code fragment also shows how to get the certificate associated with a specified alias and save it into a file so that it can be sent to the receiver for verification. The alias here is set to `marco`.

We generate the `KeyStore` object by using the `getInstance()` factory method for the `KeyStore` class. The implementation we use is JKS, and the provider is the IBM provider:

```
String s1 = System.getProperty("user.home");
String s2 = System.getProperty("file.separator");
FileInputStream fisk = new FileInputStream(s1 + s2 + ".keystore");
KeyStore ks = KeyStore.getInstance("JKS", "IBMJCE");
```

Next, we load the keystore, using the `load()` method, and supply the keystore password, which is hard-coded as `marcop`:

```
ks.load(fisk, pwd);
```

Finally, we get the `PrivateKey`, with the `getKey()` method, and the `Certificate`, with the `getCertificate()` method, associated with the intended alias:

```
PrivateKey priv = (PrivateKey) ks.getKey(alias, pwd);
X509Certificate certs = (X509Certificate) ks.getCertificate(alias);
```

Note that three pieces of information should be provided by the program embedding this code fragment:

1. The input file to be signed, indicated by the `inputFile` variable
2. The file where the signature will be written, indicated by the `signatureFile` variable
3. The file where the certificate will be written, indicated by the `certFile` variable

Note that it is not necessary that the signature file or the file to which the certificate is exported exist. The program creates them automatically.

At this point, the three files can be sent to the receiver, who will use the code fragment in Listing 11.11 to verify the signature.

Listing 11.11. `Signature` and `X509Certificate` Used for Signature Verification

```
import java.security.Signature;
import java.security.PublicKey

import java.security.cert.CertificateFactory;
import java.security.cert.X509Certificate;

import java.io.FileInputStream;
import java.io.BufferedInputStream;


// Other code goes here...

// inputFile is the file whose contents have been signed.
FileInputStream fis = new FileInputStream(inputFile);

// signatureFile is the file containing the signature.
FileInputStream sfis = new FileInputStream(signatureFile);

// certFile is the file containing the signer's certificate.
FileInputStream cfis = new FileInputStream(certFile);

// Get the certificate from the certificate file.
CertificateFactory cf =
    CertificateFactory.getInstance("X.509");
X509Certificate cert =
    (X509Certificate) cf.generateCertificate(cfis);
cfis.close();

// Get the public key from the certificate.
PublicKey pubkey = cert.getPublicKey();

// Get the signature from the signature file.
byte[] sigToVerify = new byte[sfis.available()];
sfis.read(sigToVerify);
sfis.close();

// Generate a Signature object by calling the getInstance()
// factory method.
Signature sig =
    Signature.getInstance("SHA1withDSA", "IBMJCE");

// Initialize the Signature object for Signature verification.
dsasig.initVerify(pubkey);

// Update the Signature object with the data to be verified.
BufferedInputStream buf = new BufferedInputStream(fis);
byte[] buff = new byte[1024];
int len;

while (buf.available() != 0)
{
    len = buf.read(buff);
    dsasig.update(buff, 0, len);
}
```

(continues)

Listing 11.11.   `Signature` and `X509Certificate` Used for Signature
                     Verification (*continued*)

```
buf.close();
fis.close();

// Verify the signature.
boolean verifies = dsasig.verify(sigToVerify);

if (verifies)
    System.out.println("Signature verification succeeded.");
else
    System.out.println("Signature verification failed.");

// Other code goes here...
```

This code fragment is similar to the one shown in Listing 11.9 on page 406.
However, instead of retrieving the signer's public key from a file for signature verification, this code shows how to retrieve the signer's public key from the signer's X.509 certificate, using the `getPublicKey()` method in class `X509Certificate`. The public key is then used to initialize the `Signature` object for signature verification.

The three files `inputFile`, `signatureFile`, and `certFile`, used in the code fragment of Listing 11.11, should be defined somewhere else in the program. Note that this time, all three files must exist in advance and should be the same files used by the code fragment of Listing 11.10 on page 408. This way, we are simulating a scenario in which a sender generates a signature and then sends the original file to a receiver, along with the signature and the certificate.

The expected output should be as follows.

- If none of the three files has been altered after the signature was applied, the program should display the following:

  ```
  Signature verification succeeded.
  ```

- If you change the contents of any of the three files, the program displays the following message:

  ```
  Signature verification failed.
  ```

  In particular, if you modify the signature file so that it no longer respects the signature format, the code fragment of Listing 11.9 on page 406 will throw a `java.security.SignatureException`.

This example demonstrates how you can successfully integrate the Java 2 APIs with local security structures, such as keystores and certificates, to send documents with proof of data integrity and authenticity.

11.2.10   The `AlgorithmParameters` and `AlgorithmParameterGenerator` Classes in Package `java.security`

The `AlgorithmParameters` class is an engine class that provides an opaque representation of cryptographic parameters. An *opaque representation of cryptographic parameters* is one in which you have no direct access to the parameter fields; you can get only the name of the algorithm associated with the parameter set and some kind of encoding for the parameter set itself. By contrast, with a *transparent representation of cryptographic parameters*, you can access each value individually, through one of the `get` methods defined in the corresponding specification class. However, you can call the `AlgorithmParameters.getParameterSpec()` method to convert an `AlgorithmParameters` object to a transparent specification.

The package `java.security` also provides the `AlgorithmParameterGenerator` and `AlgorithmParameterGeneratorSpi` classes.

- The `AlgorithmParameterGenerator` class is used to generate a set of parameters to be used with a certain algorithm. Parameter generators are constructed using the `getInstance()` factory methods.

- The `AlgorithmParameterGeneratorSpi` class defines the SPI for the `AlgorithmParameterGenerator` class.

11.2.11   The `java.security.SignedObject` Class

`SignedObject` is a class for creating runtime `Object`s whose integrity cannot be compromised without being detected. Specifically, a `SignedObject` contains another serializable `Object` and its signature. A `SignedObject` is a *deep copy*, in serialized form, of an original `Object`. Once the copy is made, further manipulation of the original `Object` has no side effect on the copy and vice versa.

To create a `SignedObject`, it is first necessary to generate a `java.security.Signature` object by calling the `getInstance()` method in the `Signature` class. A `SignedObject` can then be constructed by calling the constructor for the `SignedObject` class, passing it the `Object` to be signed, a `PrivateKey` for signing, and the `Signature` object previously constructed. The constructor of the `SignedObject` class automatically initializes the `Signature` object for signing. Therefore, there is no need to call the `initSign()` method on the `Signature` object.

Having received a `SignedObject`, the integrity of the `Object` that it wraps can be verified by calling the `verify()` method on the `SignedObject` itself. This method requires a `PublicKey` and a `Signature` object for `Signature` verification. For this verification process to succeed, the `PublicKey` passed to the `verify()` method must be the one that corresponds to the `PrivateKey` that was used to construct the `SignedObject`. The `verify()` method of the `SignedObject` class automatically initializes the `Signature` object for signature verification. Therefore, there is no need to call the `initVerify()` method on the `Signature` object.

For flexibility reasons, the constructor and `verify()` method of the `Signed-Object` class allow for customized `Signature` engines, which can implement signature algorithms that are not installed formally as part of a CSP. However, it is crucial that the programmer writing the verifier code be aware of what `Signature` engine is being used, as its own implementation of the `verify()` method is invoked to verify a signature. In fact, a malicious `Signature` may choose to always return `true` on verification in an attempt to bypass a security check.

Potential applications of `SignedObject` include the following.

- It can be used internally to any Java runtime as an *unforgeable authorization token*—one that can be passed around without fear that the token can be maliciously modified without being detected.

- It can be used to sign and serialize data for storage outside the Java runtime: for example, storing critical access-control data on disk.

- Nested `SignedObjects` can be used to construct a logical sequence of signatures, resembling a chain of authorization and delegation.

11.2.12   The `java.security.spec` Package

This package contains classes and interfaces for key specifications and algorithm parameter specifications. For example, `DSAPrivateKeySpec`, which is a specification class for keys using the DSA algorithm, defines `getX()`, `getP()`, `getQ()`, and `getG()` methods to access the private key x; and the DSA algorithm parameters, used to calculate the key: the prime p, the subprime q, and the base g. This is contrasted with an opaque representation of key material, as defined by the `Key` interface discussed in Section 11.2.2 on page 393, in which you have no direct access to the key-material fields.

This package contains key specifications for DSA public and private keys, RSA public and private keys, PKCS#8 private keys in DER-encoded format, and X.509 public and private keys in DER-encoded format (see Listing 11.9 on page 406). The package also provides an algorithm parameter specification class, `DSAParameterSpec`, which specifies the set of parameters used with the DSA algorithm. An example of `DSAParameterSpec` use is provided in Listing 11.5 on page 395.

The interfaces provided are `AlgorithmParameterSpec` and `KeySpec`.

- The `AlgorithmParameterSpec` interface is a specification of cryptographic parameters. It groups all parameter specifications. All parameter specifications, such as the `DSAParameterSpec` class provided in the same package, must implement it. This interface does not contain any methods or constants. Its only purpose is to group, and provide type safety for, all parameter specifications.

- The `KeySpec` interface is a specification of the key material that constitutes a cryptographic key. All key specifications must implement this interface, which does not contain any methods or constants. In fact, the only purpose of the `KeySpec` interface is to group, and provide type safety for, all key specifications.

11.2.13   The `java.security.cert` Package

This package provides classes to manage and handle digital certificates and CRLs, and provides separate classes for managing X.509 certificates and X.509 CRLs (see Section 10.3.4 on page 372).

- The abstract `Certificate` class can be used to manage various types of identity certificates, whereas the abstract `X509Certificate` class, which extends `Certificate` and implements the `X509Extension` interface, is specifically for X.509 certificates. Sample code using the `X509-Certificate` class is given in Listing 11.6 on page 396, Listing 11.10 on page 408, and Listing 11.11 on page 411.

- The `CRL` class is an abstraction of a CRL (see Section 10.3.4 on page 372). CRLs have different formats but important common uses. For example, all CRLs share the functionality of listing revoked certificates and can be queried on whether they list a given certificate. Specialized CRL types can be defined by subclassing this abstract class. An example is the `X509CRL` class, which extends `CRL` and implements the `X509Extension` interface. An `X509CRLEntry` class is provided for a revoked certificate entry in an X.509 CRL.

- The `java.security.cert` package also provides a `CertificateFactory` class to generate certificates and `CRL` objects from their encodings, and a `CertificateFactorySpi` class to define the SPI for the `Certificate-Factory` class. `CertificateFactory` objects can be instantiated using the `getInstance()` method. Then, the `generateCertificate()` and the `generateCRL()` methods can be used to create a `Certificate` and a `CRL` object, respectively. An example of `CertificateFactory` use is offered by the code fragment in Listing 11.11 on page 411.

11.2.14 The `java.security.interfaces` Package

This package contains only interfaces, which are used for generating DSA and RSA keys.

- The `DSAKey`, `DSAPrivateKey`, and `DSAPublicKey` interfaces provide the standard interfaces to DSA keys. The package also provides a `DSAKeyPairGenerator` interface for generating DSA key pairs and a `DSAParams` interface for generating a DSA-specific set of key parameters, which define a DSA key family.

- The `RSAPublicKey` and `RSAPrivateKey` interfaces are for RSA keys. The package also contains a class named `RSAPrivateCrtKey`, which is the interface to an RSA private key, as defined in the PKCS#1 standard (see Section 12.1.1 on page 435), using the Chinese Remainder Theorem (CRT) information values.

11.3 The JCE API

The JCE framework and implementations for encryption, key generation, key agreement, and MAC algorithms supplement the message digest and digital-signature interfaces and implementations provided in the JCA. Support for encryption includes symmetric, asymmetric, block, and stream ciphers. The software also supports secure streams and sealed—encrypted—objects. JCE was previously shipped as a standard extension to the Java 2 SDK V1.2 and 1.3 but has now been integrated into the Java 2 SDK V1.4.

JCE is based on the same design principles found elsewhere in the JCA: implementation independence and interoperability, and algorithm independence and extensibility (see Section 11.1.2 on page 379). Additionally, the JCE uses the same provider architecture (see Section 11.1.3 on page 382). Providers signed by a trusted entity can be plugged into the JCE framework, and new algorithms can be added seamlessly.

The JCE includes two software components:

1. A framework that defines and supports cryptographic services that providers can supply implementations for. This framework includes everything in the `javax.crypto` package and its subpackages `javax.crypto.spec` and `javax.crypto.interfaces`.

2. A provider supplying the implementation for a number of cryptographic services.

The JCE API covers

- **Encryption and decryption.**   The JCE provides support for both symmetric and asymmetric encryption and for password-based encryption (PBE).[2] Encryption and decryption are performed using a cipher. A *cipher* is an object capable of carrying out encryption and decryption according to an *encryption scheme*, or algorithm.

- **Key agreement.**   A *key agreement* is a protocol by which two or more parties can establish the same cryptographic keys without having to exchange any secret information. An example of a key-agreement protocol is offered by the Diffie-Hellman (DH) algorithm (see Section 10.3.1.2 on page 362).

- **MAC.**   As we discussed in Section 10.2.2.4 on page 356, a MAC provides a way to check the integrity of information transmitted over or stored in an unreliable medium, based on a secret key. Typically, MACs are used between two parties that share a secret key in order to validate information transmitted between them.

The JCE provider consists of the main package `javax.crypto` and its two subpackages `javax.crypto.spec` and `javax.crypto.interfaces`.

- The `javax.crypto` package forms the main body of the JCE class structure. The package consists primarily of classes that represent the concepts of cipher, key agreement, and MAC, and their corresponding SPI classes.

- The `javax.crypto.spec` package consists of various key-specification and algorithm parameter specification classes.

- The `javax.crypto.interfaces` package contains the `DHKey` interface and its subinterfaces, `DHPrivateKey` and `DHPublicKey`. These are the interfaces for the keys based on the DH algorithm (see Section 10.3.1.2 on page 362). This package contains also the interface `PBEKey`, for password-based keys.

11.3.1   The `javax.crypto.Cipher` Class

The `javax.crypto.Cipher` engine class forms the core of the JCE framework. This class provides the functionality of a cryptographic cipher used for encryption and decryption. Like other engine classes, the `Cipher` class is instantiated using its `getInstance()` static factory method. This method takes as argument a `String`

---

2. PBE derives an encryption key from a password. In order to make the task of getting from password to key very time consuming for an attacker, most PBE implementations will mix in a random number, known as a *salt,* to create the key.

object that represents a transformation. A *transformation* is a string that describes the operation or set of operations to be performed on the given input to produce some output. A transformation always includes the name of a cryptographic algorithm, which may be followed by a mode and padding scheme. Therefore, a transformation is of the form `algorithm/mode/padding` or just `algorithm`. For example, the following is a valid way to create a `Cipher` object:

```
Cipher c = Cipher.getInstance("DES/CBC/PKCS5Padding");
```

This `Cipher` object will be used for encryption or decryption using the DES algorithm with CBC mode of operation. Algorithms usually operate on blocks having a predefined size. Plaintext packets whose length is not a multiple of that size must be *padded* according to a specified *padding scheme* prior to encryption. The `Cipher` c above uses a padding scheme known as PKCS5Padding (see Section 12.1.2 on page 435).

If mode and padding are not specified, provider-specific default values are used. Optionally, `getInstance()` can accept, as a second argument, the name of the provider after the transformation parameter.

A `Cipher` object obtained from `getInstance()` must be initialized for *encryption, decryption, wrap*, or *unwrap mode*. These modes are defined as final `int` constants in the `Cipher` class. These four modes can be referenced by their symbolic names: ENCRYPT_MODE, DECRYPT_MODE, WRAP_MODE, and UNWRAP_MODE, respectively. The `Cipher` will perform a different function, based on its initialized mode.

- If the `Cipher` has been initialized in encryption mode, it will perform encryption of data.

- If the `Cipher` has been initialized in decryption mode, it will perform decryption of data.

- If the `Cipher` has been initialized in wrap mode, it will be used to wrap a `java.security.Key` object into bytes so that the key can be securely transported.

- If the `Cipher` has been initialized in unwrap mode, it will be used to unwrap a previously wrapped key into a `java.security.Key` object.

A `Cipher` object is initialized by calling the `init()` method. When this happens, the object loses all previously acquired states. In other words, initializing a `Cipher` is equivalent to creating a new instance of that `Cipher` and initializing it.

Data can be encrypted or decrypted in one step (*single-part* operation) or in multiple steps (*multiple-part* operation). This depends on whether you call the `do-Final()` or the `update()` method, respectively. A multiple-part operation is useful if the exact length of the data is not known in advance or if the data is too long to be stored in memory all at once.

11.3.2 The `CipherInputStream` and `CipherOutputStream` Classes in the `javax.crypto` Package

The JCE introduces the concept of secure streams, which combine a `java.io.InputStream` or a `java.io.OutputStream` with a `Cipher` object. Secure streams are provided by the `CipherInputStream` and `CipherOutputStream` classes.

- **CipherInputStream.** The `javax.crypto.CipherInputStream` class is a `java.io.FilterInputStream` that encrypts or decrypts the data passing through it. The class is composed of an `InputStream`, or one of its subclasses, and a `Cipher`. `CipherInputStream` represents a secure `InputStream` into which a `Cipher` object has been interposed. The `read()` methods of `CipherInputStream` return data that is read from the underlying `InputStream` but has additionally been processed by the embedded `Cipher` object, as shown in Figure 11.10.

  Note that the `Cipher` object must be fully initialized before being used by a `CipherInputStream`. For example, if the embedded `Cipher` has been initialized for decryption, the `CipherInputStream` will attempt to decrypt the data it reads from the underlying `InputStream` before returning it to the application.

- **CipherOutputStream.** The `javax.crypto.CipherOutputStream` class is a `java.io.FilterOutputStream` that encrypts or decrypts the data passing through it. The class is composed of an `OutputStream`, or one of its subclasses, and a `Cipher`. `CipherOutputStream` represents a secure `OutputStream` into which a `Cipher` object has been interposed. The `write()` methods of `CipherOutputStream` first process the data with the

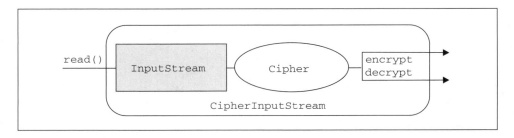

Figure 11.10. Representation of a `CipherInputStream`

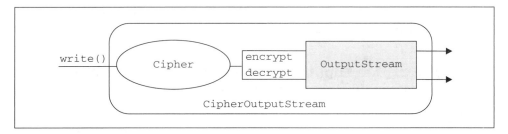

Figure 11.11. Representation of a `CipherOutputStream`

embedded `Cipher` object before writing it out to the underlying `Output-Stream`, as shown in Figure 11.11.

The `Cipher` object must be fully initialized before being used by a `CipherOutputStream`. For example, if the embedded `Cipher` has been initialized for encryption, the `CipherOutputStream` will encrypt its data before writing it out to the underlying `OutputStream`.

The code fragment in Listing 11.12 shows how to

1. Read data from an input file, `inputFile`
2. Encrypt it, using a `Cipher` object, `cipher1`, initialized for the DES algorithm in encrypt mode
3. Decrypt it, using another `Cipher` object, `cipher2`, initialized for the DES algorithm in decrypt mode
4. Print the result of the decryption, which is the same as the original plaintext, to an output file, `outputFile`

The code makes use of the `CipherInputStream` class to encrypt and decrypt data passing through a `FileInputStream`.

Listing 11.12. How to Use the `CipherInputStream` API

```
import java.io.FileInputStream;
import java.io.FileOutputStream;

import java.security.Key;

import javax.crypto.Cipher;
import javax.crypto.KeyGenerator;
import javax.crypto.CipherInputStream;
```

```
// Other code goes here...

// Generate Cipher objects for encryption and decryption.
Cipher cipher1 = Cipher.getInstance("DES");
Cipher cipher2 = Cipher.getInstance("DES");

// Generate a KeyGenerator object.
KeyGenerator kg = KeyGenerator.getInstance("DES");

// Generate a DES key.
Key desKey = kg.generateKey();

// Initialize the Cipher objects.
cipher1.init(Cipher.ENCRYPT_MODE, desKey);
cipher2.init(Cipher.DECRYPT_MODE, desKey);

// Create the encrypting CipherInputStream.
FileInputStream fis = new FileInputStream(inputFile);
CipherInputStream cis1 = new CipherInputStream(fis, cipher1);

// Create the decrypting CipherInputStream.
CipherInputStream cis2 = new CipherInputStream
    (cis1, cipher2);

// Write the decrypted data to output file.
FileOutputStream fos = new FileOutputStream(outputFile);
byte[] b2 = new byte[1024];
int i2 = cis2.read(b2);

while (i2 != -1)
{
    fos.write(b2, 0, i2);
    i2 = cis2.read(b2);
}

// Close the streams.
fos.close();
cis1.close();
cis2.close();

// Other code goes here...
```

11.3.3 The `javax.crypto.SecretKey` Interface

The JCE offers a set of classes and interfaces to manage secret keys. At the root of the hierarchy is the `javax.crypto.SecretKey` interface, which contains no methods or constants. Its only purpose is to group and provide type safety for secret, or symmetric, keys. Provider implementations of this interface must overwrite the `equals()` and `hashCode()` methods inherited from `java.lang.Object`, so that secret keys are compared on the basis of their underlying key material, not on reference. Because it extends the `Key` interface (see Section 11.2.2 on page 393), this interface is an opaque representation of a symmetric key.

11.3.4 The `javax.crypto.spec.SecretKeySpec` Class

The `javax.crypto.spec.SecretKeySpec` class specifies a secret key in a provider-independent fashion. The class can be used to construct a `SecretKey` from a byte array, without the need to go through a provider-based `SecretKey-Factory`. This class is useful only for raw secret keys that have been pregenerated, can be represented as a byte array, and have no key parameters associated with them: for example, DES or Triple-DES keys. This class is a transparent representation of a symmetric key.

11.3.5 The `javax.crypto.KeyGenerator` Class

As we saw in Section 11.2.6 on page 394, the `KeyPairGenerator` class is used to generate a pair of public and private keys. The JCE provides for a `KeyGenerator` engine class, which is used to generate secret keys for symmetric algorithms. `Key-Generator` objects are created using the `getInstance()` factory method of the `KeyGenerator` class. Note that a factory method is by definition static.

The `getInstance()` method takes as its argument the name of a symmetric algorithm for which a secret key is to be generated. Optionally, a package provider name may be specified. If only an algorithm name is specified, the system will determine whether an implementation of the requested key-generator algorithm is available in the environment; if there is more than one, the preferred one will be selected. If both an algorithm name and a package provider are specified, the system will determine whether an implementation of the requested key-generator algorithm is in the package requested and throw a `NoSuchAlgorithmException` if there is not. A `KeyGenerator` for a particular symmetric-key algorithm creates a symmetric key that can be used with that algorithm and associates algorithm-specific parameters, if any, with the generated key.

11.3.6 The `javax.crypto.SecretKeyFactory` Class

The `javax.crypto.SecretKeyFactory` class represents a factory for secret keys. A `KeyFactory` (see Section 11.2.4 on page 394) is bidirectional, which means that it allows building an opaque `Key` object from a given key specification—key material—or retrieving the underlying key material of a `Key` object in a suitable format. In general, a `KeyFactory` is used to convert keys—opaque cryptographic keys of type `Key`—into key specifications—transparent representations of the underlying key material—and vice versa. In particular, `SecretKeyFactory` operates only on secret, or symmetric, keys, whereas a `KeyFactory` object processes both the public- and the private-key components of a key pair.

Objects of type `java.security.Key`—an interface of which `PublicKey`, `PrivateKey` (see Section 11.2.3 on page 393) and `SecretKey` (see Section 11.3.3 on page 421) are subinterfaces—are opaque key objects; you cannot tell how they are implemented. The underlying implementation is provider dependent and may be software or hardware based. `KeyFactory` allows providers to supply their own implementations of cryptographic keys. For example, suppose that you have a key specification for a DH public key, consisting of the public value y, the prime modulus q, and the base generator α (see Section 10.3.1.2 on page 362). If you feed the same specification to DH `KeyFactory` objects from various providers, the resulting `PublicKey` objects will most likely have different underlying implementations.

A provider should document the key specifications supported by its `Secret-KeyFactory`.

- The `SecretKeyFactory` for DES keys supplied by the IBM provider supports the `javax.crypto.spec.DESKeySpec` class as a transparent representation of DES keys.

- The `SecretKeyFactory` for Triple-DES keys supports `javax.crypto.spec.DESedeKeySpec` as a transparent representation of Triple-DES keys.

- The `SecretKeyFactory` for PBE keys supports `javax.crypto.spec.PBEKeySpec` as a transparent representation of the underlying password.

11.3.7 The `javax.crypto.SealedObject` Class

This class enables a programmer to create a `Serializable Object` and protect its confidentiality with a cryptographic algorithm. This provides a way of storing `Serializable Object`s safely.

Given any `Object` whose class implements the `java.io.Serializable` interface, one can create a `SealedObject` that encapsulates the original `Object`, in serialized format—a *deep copy* of the `Object`—and seals, or encrypts, its serialized contents, using a cryptographic algorithm, such as DES, to protect the `Object`'s confidentiality. The encrypted content can later be decrypted and deserialized, yielding the original `Object`.

This class provides a variety of options for decrypting a `SealedObject` and recovering it in its original form. The original `Object` can be recovered by either passing the same `Cipher` object appropriately initialized with the same key and algorithm parameters as used for encryption or by passing only the decryption key; in this case, the appropriate `Cipher` object is automatically created with the decryption key and the same algorithm parameters that were stored in the sealed object.

The code fragment in Listing 11.13, which could be embedded in any J2EE application, illustrates the use of the `SealedObject` class.

Listing 11.13. How to Use the `SealedObject` Class

```
import java.security.Key;

import javax.crypto.Cipher;
import javax.crypto.KeyGenerator;
import javax.crypto.SealedObject;


// Other code goes here...

// Generate Cipher objects for encoding and decoding.
Cipher cipher1 = Cipher.getInstance("DES");
Cipher cipher2 = Cipher.getInstance("DES");

// Generate a KeyGenerator object.
KeyGenerator kg = KeyGenerator.getInstance("DES");

// generate a DES key.
Key desKey = kg.generateKey();

// Initialize the Ciphers for encryption and decryption.
cipher1.init(Cipher.ENCRYPT_MODE, mykey);
cipher2.init(Cipher.DECRYPT_MODE, mykey);

// Seal a String object.
SealedObject s = new SealedObject
    ("SSN 123-456-7890", cipher1);

// Recover the sealed String object
String s1 = (String) s.getObject(cipher2);
System.out.println ("The sealed object is: " + s1);

// Other code goes here...
```

11.3.8 The `javax.crypto.KeyAgreement` Class

Whenever two or more parties decide to initiate a secure conversation over a non-secure communication channel using secret-key encryption, they need to use the same secret key—which is called the *session key*—without transmitting it in the clear over the channel. To achieve this result, public-key encryption can be used to transmit the session key securely.

An alternative is to use a *key agreement*, a protocol that allows two or more parties to calculate the same secret value without exchanging it directly. Therefore, the parties share the same secret key and can encrypt the communication using symmetric encryption. The most famous of these protocols is the DH algorithm (see Section 10.3.1.2 on page 362).

The `javax.crypto.KeyAgreement` class provides the functionality of a key-agreement protocol. The keys involved in establishing a shared secret key are created by `KeyPairGenerator` or `KeyGenerator`, a `KeyFactory`, or as a result from an intermediate phase of the key-agreement protocol.

Each party involved in the key agreement has to create a `KeyAgreement` object. This can be done using the `getInstance()` factory method of the `Key-Agreement` engine class. This method accepts as its argument a `String` representing a key-agreement algorithm as parameter. Optionally, you can specify a provider as the second argument.

- If only an algorithm name is specified, the system will determine whether an implementation of the requested key-agreement algorithm is available in the environment; if there is more than one, the preferred one will be selected.

- If both an algorithm name and a package provider are specified, the system will determine whether an implementation of the requested key-agreement algorithm is in the package requested and throw a `NoSuchAlgorithm-Exception` if there is not.

If the DH algorithm is used, a DH private key is used to initialize the `Key-Agreement` object. Additional initialization information may contain a source of randomness and/or a set of algorithm parameters.

Every key-agreement protocol consists of a number of phases that need to be executed by each party involved in the key agreement. The `doPhase()` method is used to execute the next phase in the key agreement. This method takes two arguments: a `Key` and a `boolean`.

1. The `Key` argument contains the key to be processed by that phase. In most cases, this is the public key of one of the other parties involved in the key agreement or an intermediate key that was generated by a previous phase. The `doPhase()` method may return an intermediate key that you may have to send to the other parties of this key agreement, so they can process it in a subsequent phase.

2. The `boolean` parameter specifies whether the phase to be executed is the last one in the key agreement. A value of `false` indicates that this is not the last phase of the key agreement, and that more phases are to follow. A value of `true` indicates that this is the last phase of the key agreement and that the key agreement is completed.

After each party has executed all the required key-agreement phases, the key agreement can compute the shared secret by calling the `generateSecret()` method.

11.3.9   The `javax.crypto.Mac` Class

The `Mac` class provides the functionality of a MAC (see Section 10.2.2.4 on page 356). As with all other engine classes in the API, `Mac` objects are created using the `getInstance()` factory methods of the `Mac` class. A factory method is a static method that returns an instance of a class; in this case, an instance of `Mac` that provides the requested MAC algorithm. The `getInstance()` method takes as its argument the name of a MAC algorithm. Optionally, a package provider name may be specified.

- If only an algorithm name is specified, the system will determine whether an implementation of the requested MAC algorithm is available in the environment; if there is more than one, the preferred one will be selcted.

- If both an algorithm name and a package provider are specified, the system will determine whether an implementation of the requested MAC algorithm is in the package requested, and throw a `NoSuchAlgorithmException` if there is not.

11.4 JCE in Practice

Listing 11.12 on page 420 showed how to encrypt and then decrypt the contents of a file in the same code fragment. However, real-life situations are more complex. A realistic situation would be when two persons—say, Bob and Alice—are situated at two different locations and want to exchange data safely by encrypting it during transmission. In this case, there will be two different programs for encryption and decryption. It should be noted that sending a secret key along with the encrypted message would be like locking jewels in a box and then sending the key along with the locked box of jewels. A secure solution is for Bob and Alice to generate the same secret key independently. The general steps required in this process are as follows.

1. Bob and Alice establish a secret key between themselves, without transmitting it over the network.

2. Bob runs a program that encrypts data using the secret key and sends the encrypted data over the network to Alice.

3. Alice runs a program that uses the secret key to decrypt the data encrypted by Bob.

The following list describes in more detail the steps involved in this process.

1. Both Bob and Alice generate a key pair using the DH algorithm. The private key in this key pair is used to initiate a `KeyAgreement` object by either party.

2. The public key generated in the key pair is encoded and stored in a file by both parties. Both parties now send this file to each other.

3. Using the public key belonging to Alice and Bob's own private key, Bob's `KeyAgreement` object generates a secret key using the DES algorithm.

4. Similarly, using the public key belonging to Bob and Alice's own private key, Alice's `KeyAgreement` object generates the same secret key, also using the DES algorithm.

5. Using the secret key, Bob encrypts the confidential data he wants to send to Alice and stores the encrypted data in a file. The encryption is done using a `Cipher` object that is initialized in the encrypt mode. The file containing the encrypted data is then transmitted over the network to Alice.

6. Using the secret key, Alice decrypts the data that she has received from Bob and stores the decrypted data in a file. The decryption is done using a `Cipher` object at Alice's end, which is initialized in the decrypt mode.

11.4.1   Bob's Program

Listing 11.14 shows the code fragment embedded in Bob's J2EE application. This code is responsible for

1. Generating Bob's public and private key pair

2. Storing Bob's public key to a file, `bobPublicKeyFile`—simulating Bob's publishing his public key

3. Obtaining Alice's public key from a file, `alicePublicKeyFile`—simulating the receiving of Alice's public key from Alice or from a Certificate Authority (see Section 10.3.4 on page 372)

4. Calculating the shared secret key based on Bob's private key and Alice's public key

5. Encrypting with the secret key an input `String` object: `inputString`

6. Storing the encrypted string to a file, `cipherFile`—simulating the sending of the encrypted string to Alice

Listing 11.14.   Bob's Code Fragment for Encryption

```
import java.io.FileInputStream;
import java.io.FileOutputStream;

import java.security.AlgorithmParameterGenerator;
import java.security.AlgorithmParameters;
import java.security.KeyPairGenerator;
import java.security.KeyPair;
import java.security.KeyFactory;
import java.security.PublicKey;
```

(continues)

Listing 11.14.   Bob's Code Fragment for Encryption (*continued*)

```
import java.security.spec.X509EncodedKeySpec;

import javax.crypto.KeyAgreement
import javax.crypto.Cipher;
import javax.crypto.SecretKey;

import javax.crypto.spec.DHParameterSpec;


// Other code goes here...

// Generate the AlgorithmParameterGenerator object.
AlgorithmParameterGenerator gen =
    AlgorithmParameterGenerator.getInstance("DH");
gen.init(512);

// Generate the AlgorithmParameters.
AlgorithmParameters parameters = gen.generateParameters();
DHParameterSpec paramSpec = (DHParameterSpec)
    parameters.getParameterSpec(DHParameterSpec.class);

// Generate and initialize the KeyPair.
KeyPairGenerator kpg = KeyPairGenerator.getInstance("DH");
kpg.initialize(paramSpec);
KeyPair kp = kpg.generateKeyPair();

// Write the PublicKey to a file.
byte[] pubKeyEnc = kp.getPublic().getEncoded();
FileOutputStream fos = new
    FileOutputStream(bobPublicKeyFile);
fos.write(pubKeyEnc);
fos.close();

// Generate and initialize the KeyAgreement object.
KeyAgreement ka = KeyAgreement.getInstance("DH");
ka.init(kp.getPrivate());

// Wait for Alice's public key.
boolean read = false;

while(!read)
    try
    {
        FileInputStream fis = new
            FileInputStream("alicePublicKeyFile");
        fis.close();
        read = true;
    }
    catch (Exception e)
    {
        System.out.println(e);
    }
```

```
// Get Alice's PublicKey.
FileInputStream pfis = new
FileInputStream("alicePublicKeyFile");
byte[] encKey = new byte[pfis.available()];
pfis.read(encKey);
pfis.close();
X509EncodedKeySpec pubKeySpec = new
    X509EncodedKeySpec(encKey);
KeyFactory kf = KeyFactory.getInstance("DH");
PublicKey alicePubKey = kf.generatePublic(pubKeySpec);

// Generate the SecretKey.
ka.doPhase(alicePubKey, true);
SecretKey secretKey = ka.generateSecret("DES");

// Generate and initialize the Cipher object.
Cipher cipher = Cipher.getInstance("DES/ECB/PKCS5Padding");
cipher.init(Cipher.ENCRYPT_MODE, secretKey);

// Store the encrypted data in a file.
byte[] data = inputString.getBytes();
byte[] cipherData = cipher.doFinal(data);
FileOutputStream cfos = new FileOutputStream("cipherFile");
cfos.write(cipherData);
cfos.close();

// Other code goes here...
```

11.4.2 Alice's Program

Listing 11.15 shows the code fragment embedded in Alice's J2EE application. This code is responsible for

1. Obtaining Bob's public key from a file, `bobPublicKeyFile`—simulating the receiving of Bob's public key from Bob or from a CA

2. Generating Alice's public- and private-key pair

3. Storing Alice's public key to a file, `alicePublicKeyFile`—which simulates Alice's publishing her own public key

4. Calculating the shared secret key based on Alice's private key and Bob's public key

5. Getting the encrypted string generated by Bob from a file, `cipherFile`—simulating the receiving of the encrypted string from Bob

6. Decrypting the encrypted string and storing the decrypted contents to a file: `dataFile`

Listing 11.15. Alice's Code Fragment for Decryption

```
import java.io.FileInputStream;
import java.io.FileOutputStream;

import java.security.AlgorithmParameterGenerator;
import java.security.AlgorithmParameters;
import java.security.KeyPairGenerator;
import java.security.KeyPair;
import java.security.KeyFactory;
import java.security.PublicKey;

import java.security.spec.X509EncodedKeySpec;

import javax.crypto.KeyAgreement;
import javax.crypto.Cipher;
import javax.crypto.SecretKey;

import javax.crypto.spec.DHParameterSpec;

import import javax.crypto.interfaces.DHPublicKey;


// Other code goes here...

// Wait for Bob's public key. This is done by looping until
// Bob's public key is received.
boolean over = false;

while (!over)
    try
    {
        FileInputStream pfis1 =
            new FileInputStream("bobPublicKeyFile");
        pfis1.close();
        over = true;
    }
    catch (Exception e)
    {
        System.out.println(e);
    }

// Get Bob's PublicKey.
FileInputStream pfis = new FileInputStream("bobPublicKeyFile");
byte[] encKey = new byte[pfis.available()];
pfis.read(encKey);
pfis.close();
X509EncodedKeySpec pubKeySpec =
    new X509EncodedKeySpec(encKey);
KeyFactory kf = KeyFactory.getInstance("DH");
PublicKey bobPubKey = kf.generatePublic(pubKeySpec);

// Get the parameters of Bob's PublicKey.
DHParameterSpec paramSpec =
    ((DHPublicKey) bobPubKey).getParams();
```

```
// Generate Alice's KeyPair.
KeyPairGenerator kpg = KeyPairGenerator.getInstance("DH");
kpg.initialize(paramSpec);
KeyPair kp = kpg.generateKeyPair();

// Get Alice's PublicKey and store it to a file.
byte[] pubKeyEnc = kp.getPublic().getEncoded();
FileOutputStream fos =
    new FileOutputStream("alicePublicKeyFile");
fos.write(pubKeyEnc);
fos.close();

// Generate and initialize the KeyAgreement object.
KeyAgreement ka = KeyAgreement.getInstance("DH");
ka.init(kp.getPrivate());

// Generate the shared SecretKey
ka.doPhase(bobPubKey, true);
SecretKey secKey = ka.generateSecret("DES");

// Generate and initialize a Cipher object.
Cipher cipher = Cipher.getInstance("DES/ECB/PKCS5Padding");

cipher.init(Cipher.DECRYPT_MODE, secKey);

// Wait for the file produced by Bob containing the encrypted
// data.
boolean read = false;

while (!read)
try
{
    FileInputStream cfis = new FileInputStream("cipherFile");
    cfis.close();
    read = true;
}
catch(Exception e)
{
}

// Get the file produced by Bob containing the encrypted
// data.
FileInputStream cfis = new FileInputStream("cipherFile");
byte[] cipherData = new byte[cfis.available()];
cfis.read(cipherData);
cfis.close();

// Decrypt Bob's encrypted data and store the decrypted data
// to a file.
byte[] data = cipher.doFinal(cipherData);
FileOutputStream dfos = new FileOutputStream("dataFile");
dfos.write(data);
dfos.close();
```

11.5 Security Considerations

Within a J2EE environment, the security server is the primary user of the JCA to validate signatures on transactions and certificates. However, all primary and secondary objects within the J2EE environment can make use of the capabilities of the JCA and the JCE. For example, an enterprise bean could sign data using a `java.security.Signature` instance or encrypt data using a `javax.crypto.Cipher` instance. The JCA and JCE play a fundamental role to any Java application that implements secret- or public-key security.

PKCS and S/MIME in J2EE

Public-key cryptography is seeing wide application and acceptance in e-business applications. One thing is increasingly clear: If public-key cryptography is to be effective in e-business, standards must be interoperable. Even though vendors may agree on the basic public-key algorithms and protocols, compatibility between implementations is not guaranteed. Interoperability requires strict adherence to an agreed-on standard format for transferred data. The Public-Key Cryptography Standards provide such a basis for interoperability.

These PKCS standards include both algorithm-specific and algorithm-independent implementation standards. Two of the many algorithms supported are Rivest-Shamir-Adleman (see Section 10.3.1.1 on page 360) and Diffie-Hellman key exchange (see Section 10.3.1.2 on page 362). However, only RSA and DH are specifically detailed. The PKCS standards also define an algorithm-independent syntax for digital signatures, digital envelopes—for encryption—and extended certificates. This enables someone implementing any cryptographic algorithm whatsoever to conform to a standard syntax and thus achieve interoperability.

This chapter addresses the most widely used PKCS standards, which consist of a number of components: PKCS#1, PKCS#5, PKCS#7, PKCS#8, PKCS#9, PKCS#10, and PKCS#12. The PKCS standards are specifications produced by RSA Laboratories in cooperation with secure-system developers worldwide for the purpose of accelerating the deployment of public-key cryptography.

The Multipurpose Internet Mail Extensions provide an extensible standard to send messages and data across the Internet. MIME messages, however, lack most security guarantees, which would be essential to flow confidential data across the unsecured pathways of the Internet. The Secure/Multipurpose Internet Mail Extensions specifications remedy this by building on the PKCS#7 standard to provide signing and encryption to MIME-based messages. The S/MIME specification also provides support for certification request objects conforming to the PKCS#10 standard. In the Java world, S/MIME uses the Java implementations of PKCS#7 and PKCS#10.

The S/MIME specification was designed to be easily integrated into e-mail and messaging products, such as Lotus Notes. In this chapter, we examine how S/MIME builds security on top of the industry-standard MIME protocol, using equally important industry standards for cryptography: the PKCS. The industry has embraced PKCS and S/MIME as the standard techniques through which these types of security objects can be created, packaged, and delivered. Many Java implementations of these standards have emerged and are widely used in today's electronic transactions. The adoption of PKCS and S/MIME has come at a cost, though, as the interoperability of S/MIME was slow in coming, owing to incomplete specifications.

12.1 PKCS Overview

RSA and a consortium of companies developed the first portions of PKCS in 1991. The set of PKCS standards has expanded and matured to encompass everything from defining encryption techniques (PKCS#1 and PKCS#5) to the exchange of personal information (PKCS#12). The current set of standards from RSA also includes PKCS#7, which describes how signed and encrypted data should be presented; and PKCS#8, which defines the format for private keys, including encrypted private keys. PKCS#9 defines a set of attributes used by many of the PKCS standards.

PKCS is widely used in today's e-business transactions even if the application programmer is not aware of it. The primary PKCS standards that we have introduced here are useful in themselves but can be aggregated and expanded in a standard fashion to allow more complex application. For example, one way a user can request a certificate from a Certificate Authority is for that user to send his or her public key in a PKCS#10 object to the CA.[1] Once the request is approved, the CA issues a certificate that is wrapped in a PKCS#7-formatted object.

The Java Cryptography Architecture and the Java Cryptography Extension provide the basis for fundamental security operations, such as message digest, digital signature, encryption, and digital-certificate creation. These operations make heavy uses of PKCS. The PKCS standards give cryptographic service providers a formal framework to bring the right level of public-key technology and interoperability into JCA and JCE providers.

---

1. A certificate request could be made using the Certificate Management Protocol (CMP) as well. CMP is defined in Request for Comments (RFC) 2510 at `http://www.ietf.org/rfc/rfc2510.txt`.

The following sections give a brief overview of the purpose of each of the relevant PKCS standards. This discussion is followed by scenarios showing how the PKCS standards are often used in practice in e-business applications.

12.1.1 PKCS#1: RSA Cryptography Standard

Two popular types of public-key algorithms are Digital Signature Algorithm (DSA) (see Section 10.3.3.2 on page 372) and RSA (see Section 10.3.3.1 on page 371). DSA can be used to sign messages by encrypting the hash of the data, although it cannot be used to encrypt data in general. In contrast, RSA provides a more general-purpose encryption solution, including a standard for using RSA public and private keys for encryption. DSA is not widely used today.

The fundamental building block for all public-key cryptography is PKCS#1, which defines a method for encrypting data using the RSA public-key cryptosystem. PKCS#1 describes RSA key generation, key syntax, the encryption process, the decryption process, signature algorithms, and object identifiers that can be implemented by various JCA and JCE providers. PKCS#1 is also used in the construction of digital signatures and digital envelopes, as described in PKCS#7. PKCS#1 describes a syntax that is very important for interoperability: the public-key syntax, used in certificates, and the private-key syntax, used typically in PKCS#8 private-key information.

12.1.2 PKCS#5: Password-Based Cryptography Standard

PKCS#5 is similar to PKCS#1 in that it describes a standard for encryption. However, instead of defining standards for public-key encryption, PKCS#5 describes standards for password-based encryption. In particular, PKCS#5 specifies how to use passwords or text to generate symmetric keys. Although not directly related to public keys, the algorithms introduced in PKCS#5 are used by other PKCS standards that use or store public and private key pairs, such as encrypting a private-key object with a password.

PKCS#5 defines how a password and a random number, known as a *salt*, are to be mixed together to form a symmetric key. In PKCS#5, the password and the salt are digested to produce 16 or 20 bytes of data. PKCS#5 also defines the password format.

PBE involves generating a symmetric key from a password and using it for encryption. Usually, though, a password does not have enough effective random bits to qualify as a candidate for a key or even a random seed to generate a key. For example, each character of an 8-byte alphanumeric password that also allows case-sensitive letters has the equivalent of slightly less than 6 bits of randomness.

For 8-character passwords, this is far less than the required key size of a block cipher, such as DES.

Therefore, a good PBE implementation not only uses the password but also mixes in a salt to create the key. Normally, the mixing is a message digest. This makes the task of getting from password to key very time consuming for a hacker performing a dictionary attack.[2] Digesting a password with a salt helps thwart dictionary attacks. With a salt, the attacker has to create a dictionary of keys generated from each password, but each password then has to have a dictionary of each possible salt. Additionally, using an iterative function in the process of generating a symmetric key makes it more difficult for an attacker to find the key.

12.1.3   PKCS#7: Cryptographic Message Syntax Standard

A simple security operation, such as signing a message and verifying the signature, requires many attributes and objects. To name just a few, the signer and the verifier of the message must know the signature algorithm, signer's certificate, original message, and signature bytes. PKCS#7 specifies how to package this information in a standard format, allowing senders to encode the objects and receivers to decode the information in a predictable, interoperable way, using independent implementations.

This standard covers a variety of complex objects, including but not limited to `SignedData` and `EnvelopedData`, which are used for sending signed and encrypted data, respectively, to recipients in a trusted manner, as we will see in Section 12.3.1 on page 442. These objects can wrap each other, providing even more flexibility, extensibility, and functionality. For example, a message can be sealed, which involves creating a `SignedData` object with the data that in turn is encrypted within an `EnvelopedData` object. After decrypting and verifying the message, the recipient of a sealed message gets the security guarantees of both the signing and encryption processes, not just one or the other.

12.1.4   PKCS#8: Private-Key Information Syntax Standard

Public keys are meant to be shared freely. Certificates bare them for the world to view, as public keys are crucial to the verification process. Private keys, on the other hand, are meant to be hidden or stored securely. The owners of private keys should not store them unprotected for others to causally view or maliciously use.

---

2. In a *dictionary attack*, an attacker puts together a dictionary of keys generated from likely passwords and tries out each key on encrypted data. Using PBE without mixing in a salt would greatly reduce the amount of work to find the key and might make it feasible to recover encrypted material.

PKCS#8 provides standard definitions for encoding and decoding private keys either in raw form or, preferably, in an encrypted format.

12.1.5   PKCS#9: Selected Attribute Types

The various PKCS standards include many common attributes, such as `Content-Type` and `MessageDigest`. PKCS#9 defines these common attributes.

12.1.6   PKCS#10: Certification Request Syntax Standard

Public keys form the basis of digital certificates, which are created by CAs. However, a standard format is needed for a user to request a certificate. PKCS#10 provides a standard to request certificates from a CA. In particular, PKCS#10 describes the format of a certificate request. The process is typically started by running a key-pair generator from within an application, such as a Web browser or a Java program. A key-pair generator creates a public- and private-key pair (see, for example, Section 11.2.6 on page 394). The application squirrels away the private key and bundles the public key and accompanying attributes into a PKCS#10 object, which is then sent to the CA as the formal certification request.

Interestingly, the CA leverages the PKCS#7 standard to send back the generated certificate to the user's application within a `SignedData` object, as PKCS#10 does not specify a return format. The application takes the certificate and associated private key and stores both into a certificate database, or keystore (see Section 11.2.7 on page 395).

12.1.7   PKCS#12: Personal Information Exchange Syntax Standard

Today, in many cases, keys are stored in a vendor-specific way. Therefore, applications need to be able to share the same keys while avoiding the use of proprietary formats. The solution is PKCS#12. This standard describes a transfer syntax for personal-identity information, including private keys, certificates, miscellaneous secrets, and extensions. This standard also allows applications to import, export, and exercise a single set of personal information. The personal information specified by a PKCS#12 standard is protected by privacy and/or integrity modes.

A browser stores trusted-parties certificates into a certificate database. These certificates are typically self-signed certificates belonging to trusted CAs. Popular browsers, such as Netscape Communicator and Microsoft Internet Explorer, also store users' key pairs and certificates in this database. The keys and certificates that are stored in a browser are for secure-transaction assurance in the Internet.

For instance, to authenticate the possessor of a Web site, the user of a Web browser can establish a successful SSL connection with server authentication between the Web browser and the Web server hosting the Web site (see Section 13.1 on page 449). Authenticating the server requires obtaining the server's certificate and verifying that it has been signed by a trusted party (see Section 13.1.2 on page 452). As another example, a user can authenticate a seller on the Internet, based on the seller's certificate. If the seller's certificate has been signed by a trusted party, the seller can be considered authenticated.

Sensitive information, such as passwords and credit card numbers, is protected by cryptographic means. However, the keys and certificates that are stored in the browser are limited for use only within the browser. Other applications generally do not have access to the information stored in a browser's keystore. Besides that limitation, keys and certificates are usually obtained from the Internet through a third party, such as VeriSign. A user cannot easily generate a key pair and be certified by a CA off line. Even if a user has a key in the browser's database, that key cannot be used without using the browser. This limits the use of the keys.

However, browsers implement key-import and key-export functions, and PKCS#12 is one of the formats that common browsers support. Using the PKCS#12 format, a browser can export protected keys and certificates to files. Applications can therefore obtain the necessary information from such files. Usually, the information is protected in PKCS#12 format by a password using PBE. This is similar to the concept of a Java keystore: In the J2SE reference implementaiton, keystores are protected by a password that only intended users possess (see Section 11.2.7 on page 395).

As PKCS#12 is a complex specification, implementing it in each application is not feasible. For that reason, instead of having a vendor-specific Java keystore, a Java keystore that implements the PKCS#12 specification greatly improves the usability and interoperability of keys and certificates stored in a browser.

PKCS#12 provides for the bundling of various object information into one object. Although PKCS#12 objects can be used for a variety of applications, Web browsers use this standard to export a certificate and its associated private key in a confidential yet standard-based fashion. The user can import the created PKCS#12 file into a different certificate database, such as that belonging to a user directory or another Web browser's certificate database. As the file includes the sensitive private key, users can encrypt and thus protect the PKCS#12 file with a key or with a password, leveraging the PBE-based algorithms defined in the PKCS#5 standard.

12.2   S/MIME Overview

The S/MIME standard offers a consistent way to send and receive secure MIME data. S/MIME provides the following cryptographic security services for electronic messaging applications: authentication; message integrity and nonrepudiation of origin, using digital signatures; and privacy and data security, using encryption.

S/MIME can be used by traditional mail clients to add cryptographic services to mail that is sent and to interpret cryptographic services in mail that is received. However, S/MIME is not restricted to mail but can be used with any transport mechanism that transports MIME data, such as HTTP. As such, S/MIME takes advantage of the object-based features of MIME and allows secure messages to be exchanged in mixed-transport systems.

Many of the difficulties early implementers faced with the S/MIME standard were caused by incomplete specifications. The S/MIME specifications, through several long iterations, have not been verified to be implementable and interoperable by many vendors. RSA has also created S/MIME compliance tests, along with an `S/MIME` seal that states that an implementation has passed S/MIME compliance testing.

12.3   Signing and Verifying Transactions with PKCS and S/MIME

With its platform independence and ease of programming, the Java language has become the language of e-business. The basic security objects, which include keys, certificates, message digests, and digital signatures, along with the related algorithms, are included as part of the JCA, as described in Section 11.1 on page 377. Objects and algorithms that deal with general-purpose encryption are part of the JCE, as described in Section 11.3 on page 416.

Most Internet and intranet transactions are conducted using one or more of the PKCS standards described in Section 12.1 on page 434. A well-designed GUI will not expose the PKCS implementations to users needing to know that PKCS standards and objects are being used under the covers. Even though they may be hidden by a GUI, the PKCS standards play a key role in ensuring that transactions are secure. In particular, most e-business transactions make use of the objects defined by PKCS#1 and PKCS#7.

Let us say that Bob wants to use his e-mail application to send a signed message to Alice. All Bob needs to do is compose the message and check the **Sign** box before sending the e-mail, as shown in Figure 12.1. When Alice receives the message, her e-mail application displays the message and an icon indicating that

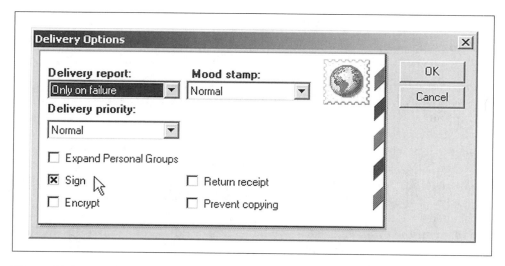

Figure 12.1. Signing an E-Mail Message through a GUI

the message was signed and verified. Alice can rest assured that Bob sent the message and that the contents were not tampered with in transit.

Sending signed data is a simple process for the user but is more complicated under the GUI. Developers of e-mail programs and any application that sends and receives signed data need to be involved in the intricacies of the signing and verification process.

Before delving into the details of the transaction, let us first examine the use of S/MIME. To send secure messages between parties, developers have created S/MIME implementations that extend the MIME standard. The S/MIME standard builds on the PKCS standards to allow applications to send secure data through such public mail protocols as SMTP. Today's applications implement the S/MIME V2 specifications. Work on the V3 specifications is under way.

S/MIME V2 builds on the PKCS#7 and PKCS#10 objects. The MIME file extensions convey the following types of supported objects:

- `7m`—`EnvelopedData` or `SignedData` with contents
- `p7s`—`SignedData` with signature(s) only
- `p7c`—`SignedData` with certificate(s) only
- `p10`—`CertificationRequest` object

Figure 12.2 shows how Bob can use an application, such as an e-mail program, to sign and send a message to Alice.

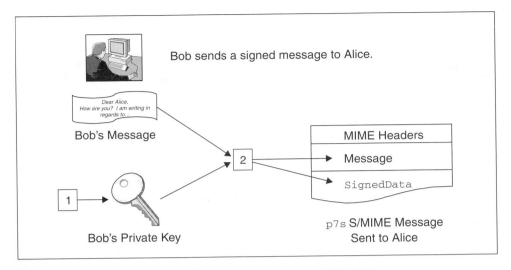

Figure 12.2. Sending a Signed Message with PKCS and S/MIME

Once Bob composes his message and clicks **Send**, the application extracts Bob's private key from the application's defined certificate database, as depicted in step 1 of Figure 12.2. The application then feeds the private key and message contents into a signing algorithm, such as MD5withRSA, and generates a signature. This signature, along with other information, is bundled into a signature-only `SignedData` object. Before sending the message, the application constructs a `p7s` S/MIME message with MIME header information, original message, and `Signed-Data` object, as depicted in step 2 of Figure 12.2. The MIME header includes such information as the content transfer encoding, which is base64 encoded for PKCS objects (see footnote 2 on page 77). Finally, the application sends the S/MIME message to Alice via SMTP.

Figure 12.3 shows how Alice's application receives and verifies Bob's message. Alice's application first verifies the MIME headers in the S/MIME message, as depicted in step 1 of Figure 12.3. If the headers indicate a `pkcs7-signature` type, the application extracts the signer's certificate corresponding to each `Sign-erInfo` object from the `SignedData` object and verifies it by tracing the certificate chain back to a known trusted root CA, as shown in step 2 of Figure 12.3. If the certificate is verified, the application extracts the signer's public key from the certificate and obtains the signature from each `SignerInfo` object in the `SignedData` object, as depicted in step 3 of Figure 12.3. The application verifies each signature with the message and corresponding public key, returning `true` or displaying a "Signed and Verified" GUI if the verification was successful.

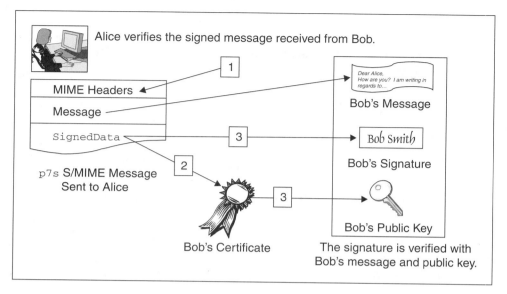

Figure 12.3. Verifying a Signed Message with PKCS and S/MIME

12.3.1 Considerations on the PKCS#7 Standard

As we have seen, the PKCS#7 standard includes a host of widely used objects. The most popular objects are `EnvelopedData` and `SignedData`.

An `EnvelopedData` object allows a sender to encrypt data with a secret key. Typically, the application that creates the `EnvelopedData` object automatically creates the secret key so that the caller does not need to generate it. The secret key is also encrypted for each recipient, using the recipient's public key. Once the `EnvelopedData` object arrives, each recipient can use his or her private key to decrypt the secret key, which in turn can be used to decrypt the data. Popular encryption algorithms include Rivest's Cipher V2 (RC2), DES, and Triple-DES.

A `SignedData` object allows a sender to package and sign data and a recipient to verify the signed data. This object contains a number of attributes and subobjects.

1. The top layer is composed of the digest algorithm, encapsulated contents, a set of certificates, and a set of CRLs. Applications can use CRLs to determine whether the certificates are still valid and have not been revoked by the issuing CAs.

2. A set of `SignerInfo` objects forms the second layer. Each `SignerInfo` object includes the issuer and serial number corresponding to a certificate

in the parent `SignedData` certificate set, the message-digest and digital-signature algorithms, signed and unsigned attributes, and the signature value itself. Popular message-digest and digital-signature algorithms include SHA1withSA and MD5withRSA.

Note that not all fields are required. For example, CRLs are rarely packaged with `SignedData` objects. Additionally, the `SignedData` object is structured to allow more than one user or entity to sign the data. Each signer is represented by a `SignerInfo` object. No matter how many users sign the data, the `SignedData` object does not replicate the data to be signed. The data is enclosed once at the top layer in the encapsulated contents.

The fact that not all fields are required means that applications can use the `SignedData` object in a variety of forms.

1. The first form a `SignedData` object can take packages the signed contents and at least one signature. When populated with contents and one or more `SignerInfo` objects, recipients of the `SignedData` object can verify that the contents were signed by the entities whose certificates correspond to the `SignerInfo` objects.

2. However, senders often construct the `SignedData` object without contents and wind up sending the contents along with the separate `SignedData` object to recipients. This second form is known as a *signature-only* `SignedData` object (`p7s` type). A signature-only `SignedData` object contains the signature value and information about the signer to allow recipients to take these values along with the detached message and verify the signature normally. Recipients cannot use the `SignedData` object itself to verify the signature on each `SignerInfo` object, as the verification algorithm requires the detached contents to be included as part of its parameters.

3. The third most popular form of the `SignedData` object is known as *certificate-only* (`p7s` type). Section 12.1.6 on page 437 discussed how users can send a PKCS#10 message to a CA to request a certificate. In response, the CA sends back a certificate-only `SignedData` object. This object contains only a certificate, not any signed contents or `SignerInfo` objects, as there were no contents to sign.

The PKCS#7 standard allows objects to be wrapped within other objects. For example, a user can seal a message first by signing the message—by creating a `SignedData` object—and then encrypting the `SignedData` object by creating an `EnvelopedData` object that takes the `SignedData` object as its contents to encrypt.

To unseal a message, a recipient first decrypts the sealed object to gain access to the `SignedData` and then verifies the signature for each of the `SignerInfo` objects contained in the `SignedData` object before extracting the enclosed message.

The PKCS#7 standard has continued to evolve. The most recent version of the standard is reflected in Request for Comments 2630.[3] This version upgrades the objects and attributes to support additional functionality.

12.3.2   Using PKCS and S/MIME

Section 11.2.9 on page 400 includes several examples showing how to use the JCA API and algorithms to create and verify digital signatures. What about a higher-level application using public and private keys? To accomplish this, we need to build on the technology and algorithms of public and private keys and use the PKCS and S/MIME standards. PKCS#7 defines how the various objects that compose signed data should be packaged for interoperability. Although we could accomplish signing data without the PKCS standards, we would not have a uniform way for all parties to group together the various objects and encode and decode them for interoperability. The `SignedData` object defines how the original message, the signing certificate, and the signature information should be packaged together. The S/MIME standards build on the PKCS standards, including PKCS#7, to define how `SignedData` should be sent using the already established MIME standards.

The Java pseudocode in Listing 12.1 and Listing 12.2 shows how much easier it is to sign and verify data using the PKCS#7 `SignedData` object than with the fundamental security objects available with the JCA.

Listing 12.1. Signing Data with PKCS and S/MIME in Java

```
// Encapsulate the data to sign.
Data data = new Data();
data.setBytes(message);
ContentInfo ci = new ContentInfo(data);

// Create the SignedData object and simultaneously generate
// the digital signature.
SignedData sd = new SignedData(ci, signingCert,
    signingPrivateKey, signingAlgorithm);
```

---

3. See `http://www.ietf.org/rfc/rfc2630.txt`.

Listing 12.2. Signature Verification with PKCS and S/MIME in Java

```
// Verify the signature by retrieving one of the signing
// certificates from the SignedData object. Note that the
// SignedData object could store more than one signature
// depending upon the number of different signers of the
// content. The issuerDNAndSN variable corresponds to
// the unique identifier of a certificate (its issuer's
// Distinguished Name (DN) and Serial Number (SN).
Certificate cert = sd.getCertificate(issuerDNAndSN);

// The PKCS method verify() on the SignedData object
// automatically extracts the public key from the certificate.
// The SignedData object already contains the original content
// and algorithms used to create the signature.
if (sd.verify(cert))
    return true;
```

12.4 Encrypting Transactions with PKCS and S/MIME

The signing process encrypts the hash of the data, not the data itself. Section 12.3 on page 439 did not cover encrypting general-purpose data, but the technologies are similar. Public and private keys are typically used in conjunction with secret keys to send encrypted messages, as secret-key algorithms encrypt and decrypt data much more quickly than public-key algorithms do. The PKCS standards also specify how to package encrypted data in a uniform fashion for interoperability.

For example, to send an encrypted message, the sender or the sender's application would generate a unique secret key for the transaction, encrypt the message with the secret key, and encrypt the secret key with the recipient's public key before sending the encrypted message and encrypted secret key to the recipient. The recipient decrypts the encrypted secret key with the recipient's private key and uses the decrypted secret key to decrypt the message. Someone other than the intended recipient who captures the encrypted message could not decrypt the message, as only the intended recipient holds the private key that can be used to unlock the encrypted secret key. Could the original message have been encrypted with the recipient's public key, forgoing the secret key altogether? Yes, but as mentioned earlier, secret keys are much faster at encrypting and decrypting bulk data.

With PKCS and S/MIME, senders can encrypt a message as a one-step operation. Alternatively, senders could combine the signing and encryption process to create a message that is first signed by the sender and then encrypted before being sent to the intended recipients.

12.5 Security Considerations

The growing opportunity in e-business brings with it a growth in threats over the Internet. The possibility that the message you receive may not be from the person advertised on the message is very real. Senders need to guarantee to recipients that their messages can be authenticated and integrity verified. The technologies of public keys along with signature algorithms provide this degree of trust as part of the Java platform through the JCA. Additional standards, such as PKCS and S/MIME, help developers work with these security objects and resources at a higher level to deliver successful and secure e-business solutions.

The PKCS standards play an important role in some of the basic security infrastructures used by most companies today, such as SSL and TLS protocols (see Section 13.1 on page 449). It is important to make sure that these protocols' implementations contain the most current versions of the PKCS standards. In June 1998, a flaw was found in a PKCS#1 implementation that was used in all the implementations of SSL. The flaw would have allowed sophisticated intruders to use the PKCS#1 implementation vulnerability to recover secret information from an SSL-encrypted session.

12.6 Future Directions

The PKCS and S/MIME standards continue to evolve as the technology and environment around them change. An example of this is the influence that mobile devices have on S/MIME and each of the PKCS standards. In fact, mobile devices have specific requirements for small footprints and low computationally intense functions. As these devices become more pervasive, their effects on existing technologies, such as PKCS and S/MIME, increase.

In addition, there are no standards addressing the handling of such objects as text or files where they are to be considered as real objects—in the computer programming sense of having inheritance, having life cycle, and being capable of audit. Current standards address themselves only to the application of a security layer, usually as a temporary envelope that is seamlessly discarded, rather than persisting once it has been checked.

We are some time away from seeing formal standards in this area, mainly because technical standards are still focused on how technical mechanisms are supposed to function. They leave it up to the implementer to find the best way, if there is one, of applying the standard to a business requirement. As technical-standard writers are not usually businesspeople, it may be some time before that world aligns itself with normal commercial or personal requirements. The technical community needs to spend more time implementing business-based solutions that can be made to operate quickly and without substantial costs and gain practical experience before setting new standards.

CHAPTER 13

The SSL and TLS Protocols in a J2EE Environment

In Chapter 11 on page 377, we discussed the capabilities for invoking cryptographic functions from within Java code. However, most programmers and application designers would prefer to work with ready-built cryptographic protocols rather than have to create them from the basic elements of encryption and digital signatures.

Secure Sockets Layer is the most widely used protocol for implementing cryptography in the Web. The advantage of a protocol such as SSL is that it removes the need for the application developer to deal with the nuts and bolts of cryptography. J2EE can make use of this function in two ways: by using the SSL support built into the J2EE products and/or by using an SSL library from within the J2EE programs. This chapter explains how SSL works and describes how a J2EE environment can use the advantages SSL offers.

13.1 The SSL and TLS Protocols

SSL is a standard protocol proposed and developed by Netscape[1] in 1994 for implementing cryptography and enabling secure transmission on the Web. The primary goal of the SSL protocol is to provide privacy and reliability between two communicating parties. SSL is now under the control of the international standards organization, the Internet Engineering Task Force (IETF), which has renamed SSL to Transport Layer Security (TLS). The TLS first specification,[2]

---

1. The Internet draft of the SSL V3.0 specification is available at `http://home.netscape.com/eng/ssl3/draft302.txt`.
2. See Request for Comments (RFC) 2246 at `http://www.ietf.org/rfc/rfc2246.txt`.

version 1.0, was released in January 1999.[3] TLS V1.0 is a modest upgrade to the SSL V3.0, which is the most recent version of SSL. For the purposes of this book, the differences between SSL V3.0 and TLS V1.0 are insignificant. Therefore, in the remainder of this chapter, we will refer to this protocol as SSL, which is the name this protocol has become known as.

SSL provides a secure alternative to the standard TCP/IP sockets protocol. In fact, SSL is not a drop-in replacement, because the application has to specify additional cryptographic information. Nonetheless, it is not a large step for an application that uses regular sockets to be converted to SSL. Although the most common implementation of SSL is for HTTP, several other application protocols have also been adapted.

SSL has two security aims: to authenticate the server and the client by using public-key signatures and digital certificates[4] and to provide an encrypted connection for the client and the server to exchange messages securely.

The SSL connection is private and reliable. Encryption is used after an initial handshake to define a secret key. Message-integrity checks are maintained.

In SSL, symmetric cryptography is used for data encryption, whereas asymmetric, or public-key, cryptography is used to authenticate the identities of the communicating parties and to encrypt the shared encryption key when an SSL session is established. This way, the shared encryption key can be exchanged in a secure manner, and client and server can be sure that only they know the shared secret key. Also, you have the advantage that client and server can encrypt and decrypt the communication flow with a single encryption key, which is much faster than using asymmetric encryption.

In this way, SSL is able to provide

- **Privacy.**   The connection is made private by encrypting the data to be exchanged between the client and the server. In other words, only they can decrypt it and make sense of the data. This allows for secure transfer of private information, such as credit card numbers, passwords, secret contracts, and so on.

- **Data Integrity.**   The SSL connection is reliable. The message transport includes a message-integrity check based on a secure hash function. So there is virtually no possibility of data corruption without detection.

- **Authenticity.**   An SSL session typically involves server authentication, which means that the client can authenticate the server. Optionally, an

---

3. The draft specification of TLS V1.1 was released in March 2003.

4. This is optional. SSL client authentication needs to take place only if a server explicitly requires it. As we discuss in step 3 on page 453, even server authentication may be not required in some cases.

authenticated server can authenticate the client too. Mutual authentication implies that the information is guaranteed to be exchanged only between the intended parties. The authentication mechanism is based on the exchange of digital certificates.

- **Nonrepudiation.**   Digital signatures and certificates together imply nonrepudiation. This establishes accountability of information about a particular event or action to its originating entity, and the communications between the parties can be proved later.

For more information about these points, refer to Section 10.1 on page 343.

SSL comprises two protocols: the record protocol and the handshake protocol.

13.1.1   The Record Protocol

The *record protocol* defines the way that messages passed between the client and the server are encapsulated. At any time, the record protocol has a set of parameters associated with it, known as a *cipher suite*, which defines the cryptographic methods being used.

The SSL standard defines a number of cipher suites. The names describe their content. For example, the cipher suite named SSL_RSA_EXPORT_WITH_RC4_40_MD5 uses

- Rivest-Shamir-Adleman (RSA) public-key encryption for key exchange with an export-strength modulus (see Section 10.3.1.1 on page 360)
- Rivest's Cipher V4 (RC4) for bulk data encryption, using a 40-bit export-strength key
- Message Digest V5 (MD5) hashing to ensure data integrity (see Section 10.2.2.4 on page 356)

Note that a cipher suite determines the type of key-exchange algorithm used, the encryption algorithm used, the digest algorithm used, and the cipher strength.

The SSL protocol can use various digital-signature algorithms for authentication of communication parties. SSL provides various key-exchange mechanisms that allow for the sharing of secret keys used to encrypt the data to be communicated. Furthermore, SSL can make use of a variety of algorithms for encryption and hashing. These various cryptographic options defined by SSL are described by SSL cipher suites. For example, cipher suite SSL_RSA_WITH_RC4_128_MD5 implies an RSA key-exchange mechanism with unlimited strength, an RC4 128-bit encryption algorithm, and an MD5 hash function. On the other hand, cipher suite SSL_RSA_EXPORT_WITH_RC4_40_MD5 implies an RSA 512-bit key exchange mechanism, an RC4 40-bit encryption algorithm, and an MD5 hash function.

13.1.2   The Handshake Protocol

When the SSL record protocol session is first established, it has a default cipher suite of `SSL_NULL_WITH_NULL_NULL`, or no encryption at all. This is where the SSL *handshake protocol* comes in. It defines a series of messages in which the client and the server negotiate the type of connection they can support, perform authentication, and generate a bulk-encryption key. At the end of the handshake, they exchange `ChangeCipherSpec` messages, which switch the current cipher suite of the record protocol to the one they negotiated. This process is shown in Figure 13.1.

In Figure 13.1, only the server is authenticated, so the client does not need to provide a certificate. If client authentication is required, the handshake is a little longer. In that case, the client also sends its certificate or a `no_certificate` message to the server.

Let us now see more details on how an SSL session is activated. The major elements in an SSL connection are

- The cipher suites that are enabled
- The compression methods that can be used; the *compression algorithms* are used to compress the SSL data and should be lossless
- Digital certificates and private keys, used for authentication and verification
- Trusted signers, that is, the repository of trusted signer certificates, used to verify the other entities' certificates
- Trusted sites, or the repository of trusted site certificates

To speed up connection establishment, the SSL protocol allows reuse of cryptographic parameters of previously established communication sessions between a client and a server. For this reason, SSL also maintains a *session cache*.

The steps involved in an SSL transaction before the communication of data begins are as follows.

1. The client sends the server a `Client Hello` message. This message contains a request for a connection, along with the client capabilities, such as the version of SSL, the cipher suites, and the data-compression methods it supports.

2. The server responds with a `Server Hello` message. This message includes the cipher suite and the compression method it has chosen for the connection, and the session ID for the connection. Normally, the server chooses the strongest common cipher suite. If unable to find a cipher suite that both the client and the server support, the server sends a handshake-failure message and closes the connection.

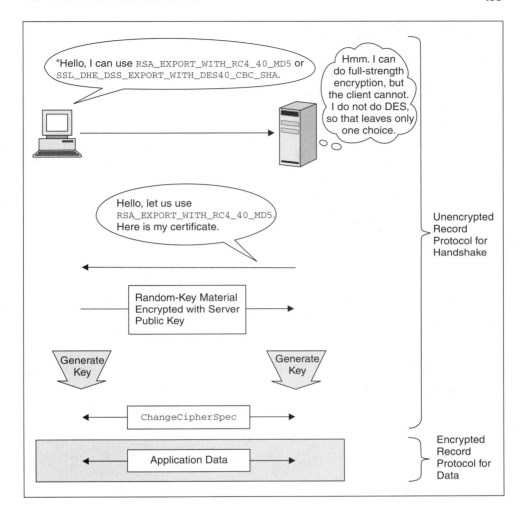

Figure 13.1. The SSL Handshake

3. The server sends its certificate if it is to be authenticated, and the client verifies it. Optionally, the client sends its certificate too, and the server verifies it.

   When a secure connection requiring SSL server authentication is being established, the server sends a certificate chain[5] to the client to

------

5. The CA that signed a certificate might not be a known or trusted entity. Hence, for verification purposes, the certificates of the CA, and of the CA that certified this CA, would be required. This is known as a *certificate chain* (see Section 10.3.4 on page 372).

prove its identity. The SSL client will pursue the connection establishment to the server only if it can authenticate the server, or, in other words, verify the signature on the server's certificate. In order to verify that signature, the SSL client needs to trust the server site itself or at least one of the signers in the certificate chain provided by the server.[6] After verifying the server certificate, the client uses the public key of the server in the next steps of the SSL handshake protocol.

SSL client authentication follows the same procedure: If an SSL server requires client authentication, the client sends to the server a certificate chain to prove its identity, and the server has to verify it.

We discussed SSL cipher suites earlier in this section. Almost all the SSL cipher suites, with the exception of some anonymous ones, require server authentication and allow client authentication.

4. The client sends a `ClientKeyExchange` message. This random-key material is encrypted with the server's public key. This material is used to create the symmetric key to be used for this session, and the fact that it is encrypted with the server's public key is to allow a secure transmission across the network. The server must verify that the same key is not already in use with any other client. If this is the case, the server asks the client for another random key.

5. When client and server agree on a common symmetric key for encrypting the communication, the client sends a `ChangeCipherSpec` message indicating the confirmation that it is ready to communicate. This message is followed by a `Finished` message.

6. In response, the server sends its own `ChangeCipherSpec` message indicating the confirmation that it is ready to communicate. This message is followed by a `Finished` message.

Now the client and the server can start communicating in secure mode.

13.2 HTTPS

HTTP can be carried over SSL. The resulting protocol is known as HTTPS. To access SSL Web sites from a browser, a user needs to specify `https` in place of

---

6. In the certificate chain provided by the server, only one of all the certificates needs to be trusted in order for the server itself to be authenticated. However, some SSL implementations, including some JSSE providers, also require that all those certificates be successfully *validated*. On those implementations, the authentication process will fail, for example, if any of the certificates in the certificate chain provided by the server has expired.

`http` in the URL location, so that the browser is forced to use HTTPS. This represents one of the most common APIs to SSL on the client side. It layers HTTP over SSL. The default TCP port at which a Web server listens for HTTP connections is 80; for HTTPS, it is 443. The URL class in the `java.net` core package supports HTTPS URLs without any modification.

13.3   Using the SSL Support Built into J2EE Products

The SSL protocol has a very important role in J2EE security. The SSL support built into a J2EE product helps reduce the burden on programmers, because SSL can be declaratively activated when the communication between the client and the server needs to be protected. In this section, we see when SSL protection should be turned on to guarantee privacy, data integrity, authenticity, and nonrepudiation.

13.3.1   SSL to Protect User ID and Password during Authentication

In a J2EE environment, user authentication is a fundamental security issue. One of the most common forms of user authentication requires a user to authenticate by submitting to the server a valid user ID and password pair. J2EE products support two methods of authentication based on user ID and password: HTTP authentication and form-based authentication.

With HTTP authentication, the user ID and password are transmitted as part of an HTTP header. There are two HTTP basic authentication modes: *basic*, if user ID and password are transmitted as cleartext, and *digest*, if a hash value of the password, rather than the password itself, is transmitted to the server.

With form-based authentication, the server retrieves the user ID and password information from the client through an HTML form. The user ID and password are transmitted as cleartext.

Therefore, with HTTP basic authentication and form-based authentication, it is highly recommended that, to protect the confidentiality of the credentials, the authentication transaction take place over an HTTPS connection. Note that with these forms of authentication, SSL is not used to authenticate the client but only to protect the communication between the client and the server. For this reason, it is not necessary for the server to require client authentication. Typically, in these scenarios, user ID and password information is transmitted over an SSL session with server-side authentication only. Protecting the authentication transaction with SSL can be done declaratively, using the support for SSL built into the J2EE product.

J2EE also supports Java clients that allow the user ID and password to flow across an IIOP message. Using the CSIv2 protocol (see Section 3.3 on page 61), the user ID and password pair is in a GSSUP token within the CSIv2 ESTABLISH_CONTEXT message. In order for this communication to be protected, transport-level SSL is recommended.

13.3.2 SSL in Certificate-Based Authentication

As we discussed in Section 13.1.2 on page 452, when a Web server is configured to require client authentication over SSL, the client and the server mutually authenticate by using each other's digital certificates. The certificates are exchanged during the SSL handshake.

In a public-key cryptosystem, the private key of a client is known only to its owner. The private key stays with the client and is never sent over the network, and it is its owner's responsibility to ensure that no one can have access to it. Therefore, the possession of a private key is a valid form of client authentication. A successful negotiation of an SSL connection between the client and the server implies that the client's certificate is signed by a CA trusted by the server and that the client who presented the certificate possesses the private key corresponding to the public key wrapped in the client certificate. As a client's certificate is associated with a specific principal on the client side, the client's certificate in a successful SSL handshake is considered a valid form of client authentication.

The client-certificate contents can be used to derive the identity of the requester. The SSL server uses the client's digital certificate to represent a unique user, a group of users, or an organization. This way, client digital certificates can be used to infer the identity of the clients and to prove authenticity when performing authorization checks.

In a J2EE environment, it is possible to set the authentication method for a Web application to be certificate based by declaratively configuring the deployment descriptor in the Web application's Web module. This can be done by setting the auth-method element in the login-config descriptor to the value CLIENT-CERT, as shown in Listing 4.7 on page 121.

After a successful certificate-based authentication, the client's identity information is available to programs running on the J2EE product. Those programs can use that information to customize the level of security in relation to the client's identity. For example, based on the identity of the client, a servlet may enforce a specific level of access control or may interact with an enterprise bean to retrieve information on that specific client from a database. In Section 4.8.3 on page 140, we showed that the Java Servlet API allows servlets to retrieve several pieces of information about the client's identity, such as

- The client's digital certificates and digital certificates of all the CAs in the certificate chain

- The size of the key used to establish the SSL connection
- The cipher suite used to establish the SSL connection

An example of a servlet retrieving client-identity information after a successful certificate-based authentication is shown in Listing 4.19 on page 141.

13.3.3   Reverse Proxy Server and WAS Mutual Authentication

Several enterprise topologies are designed in such a way that an SSL connection is established between a client and a secure reverse proxy server located in a demilitarized zone (see Section 2.2 on page 29 and Section 6.2.4 on page 195). In such environments, it is the reverse proxy server that participates in the SSL handshake. The J2EE Web application server designated to handle the requests from the client does not participate in the handshake.

Therefore, the reverse proxy server is responsible for authenticating the client by deriving the client's identity from the client's digital certificate. Subsequently, the reverse proxy server transmits the client's identity information to the WAS designated to handle the requests from the client. Therefore, two security issues need to be addressed.

1. The client's identity information should be encrypted while in transit between the reverse proxy server and the WAS.

2. A trust relationship between the reverse proxy server and all the WASs in the clustered environment must be properly designed.

Both of these requirements are met in a declarative way by establishing a mutual-authentication SSL connection between the reverse proxy server and each WAS in the clustered environment.

SSL support is also useful when two WASs need to exchange confidential information. For example, there may be clustered WASs sharing the same Web contents and load balanced by a dispatcher machine. In this case, client session information needs to be shared across the WAS nodes to prevent loss of authentication information. To obtain data confidentiality and integrity on untrusted networks, SSL can be turned on. This scenario is depicted in Figure 13.2.

13.3.4   SSL in Cookie-Based Single Sign-On

As we observed in Section 4.5.2 on page 123, when the authentication method is form based, SSO can be achieved by setting an HTTP cookie with authentication information on the client system (see Section 4.10.2.1 on page 148). For data confidentiality and integrity reasons, SSL should be used when this type of SSO is

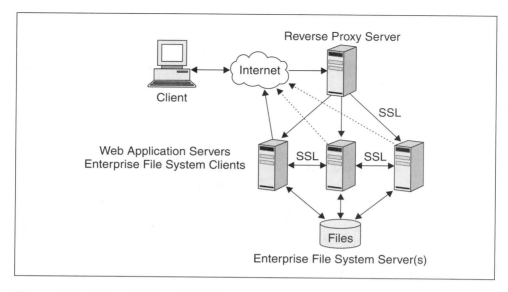

Figure 13.2. Using SSL in a J2EE Clustered Topology

required. An SSL connection prevents unauthorized parties from acquiring the token from the network flow and guarantees data integrity.

The safest approach is to ensure that an SSL connection is established every time a cookie is created and stored on the client. This assurance can be obtained declaratively by properly configuring the server. Similarly, an SSL connection should be active every time the authentication information stored in the cookie is transferred from the client to the server. This second requirement can be met by making the cookie *secure*, which means that its Secure attribute is set. The client interprets this as an indication that the cookie should be sent back to the server only by using a secure protocol, such as HTTPS or SSL.

13.3.5 Single Sign-On with Certificate-Based Authentication

If authentication is certificate based, a single SSL connection is maintained across multiple HTTPS requests. Therefore, the client's identity information is available on every request, and there is no need to prompt the user to resubmit it every time. SSO in these scenarios is implicitly guaranteed by the fact that all the HTTP requests are carried over the same SSL session.

The only problem with this approach is when an enterprise includes multiple organizations, each having its own HTTP server belonging to a different Domain Name Service system. In this case, an SSL session between a client and a server cannot be transferred from that server to another. The second server should engage in a new SSL handshake with the client, at which point the user at the client system will be required to resubmit authentication information as part of the client's certificate. Therefore, the SSO intrinsically supported by certificate-based authentication cannot be used in these environments.

13.3.6   SSL to Protect the Communication Channel

So far, we have seen how SSL can be declaratively used in a J2EE environment to protect authentication information. However, SSL was designed and implemented primarily to protect any type of security-sensitive information flowing between a client and a server, not only authentication data. For example, credit card or social security numbers entered on an HTML form should not be transferred as cleartext from a client to a server. Data confidentiality, integrity, authenticity, and non-repudiation are essential requirements with these types of transactions. There are two possible ways to meet these requirements: to secure the communication channel in a declarative way and to protect the data using cryptography in a programmatic way.

The second approach requires special client-side capabilities that may not be available in a Web browser environment. The first approach—to secure the communication channel in a declarative way—is obtained by using SSL. In a J2EE environment, a Deployer can specify that the URL request for a particular Web application must be accessed only over a secure channel by properly configuring the Web application's deployment descriptor in the Web application's Web module. This can be done by setting the `transport-guarantee` element in the `user-data-constraint` descriptor to `INTEGRAL` or `CONFIDENTIAL`, as shown in Listing 4.12 on page 133. In this case, the Web container will redirect the request to be resubmitted over HTTPS, enforcing integrity and confidentiality on the transport layer of the communication between the client and the server. As we observed in Section 3.10.1.2 on page 92, the values `INTEGRAL` and `CONFIDENTIAL` are treated as equivalent; they both indicate the requirement for an SSL connection.

13.4   Using SSL from within J2EE Programs

Using the SSL support built into a J2EE product is a very simple and effective approach but in some cases may have some limits because the communication between the client and the server can use only the capabilities offered by the J2EE container. A direct SSL socket connection between client and server allows more sophisticated and responsive applications. For example, a Java servlet can communicate through an SSL connection and interoperate with other services and processes that are not necessarily written in the Java language. This can be done by using a Java package that provides SSL function.

13.4.1 JSSE

The Java Secure Socket Extension is a set of Java packages and APIs that enable the use of SSL from within Java programs.[7] JSSE provides a framework and an implementation for the SSL and TLS protocols and includes functionality for data encryption, server authentication, message integrity, and optional client authentication. Using JSSE, developers can enforce secure passage of data between a client and a server running any application protocol over TCP/IP, such as HTTP, TELNET, or FTP.

From a programmatic point of view, the main advantage of using JSSE is that a programmer does not have to bother with the details of the record and handshake protocols and with the encryption and decryption of the information exchanged. The underlying JSSE implementation will take care of those details at runtime. This way, the risk of creating subtle but dangerous security vulnerabilities is minimized. Moreover, JSSE simplifies application development by providing developers with a building block that can be integrated directly into existing applications. As SSL and TLS are standard protocols, Java programs using JSSE can communicate via SSL with other processes and services that may not have been written in the Java language.

The JSSE design resembles that of the Java Cryptography Architecture and Java Cryptography Extension (see Section 11.1 on page 377). Like the JCA and the JCE, JSSE provides both an API framework and an implementation of that API and is designed so that any vendor's implementation can be installed and used without having to recompile the application. JSSE uses the same provider architecture defined in the JCA and the JCE (see Section 11.1.3 on page 382). This enables applications to be vendor neutral, implementation independent, and, whenever possible, algorithm independent.

The JSSE API consists of the package `javax.net` and its subpackage `javax.net.ssl`. This API supplements the core network and cryptographic services defined in the `java.net` and `java.security` packages by providing extended networking socket classes, trust managers (see Section 13.4.2), key managers, SSL contexts, and a socket-factory framework for encapsulating socket-creation behavior. This API supports SSL V2.0 and V3.0, TLS V1.0, and HTTPS. These security

---

7. JSSE was originally shipped as a standard extension to the J2SE V1.2 and V1.3 platforms. JSSE has been integrated into the J2SE platform starting with J2SE V1.4. JSSE is not an integral part of J2EE, but J2EE applications can use it as explained in Section 4.10.1 on page 145.

protocols encapsulate a normal bidirectional stream socket, and the JSSE API adds transparent support for authentication, encryption, and data-integrity protection.

In Section 4.10.1 on page 145, we studied how servlets can become HTTPS clients by invoking an HTTPS URL programmatically. In Section 13.5 on page 462, we show how a servlet can use the JSSE API.

13.4.2   Trust Managers

A *trust manager* is a software component responsible for deciding whether the credentials presented by a peer during an authentication process should be considered trusted. In JSSE, trust managers are represented as implementations of the `javax.net.ssl.TrustManager` interface. `TrustManager` instances are created by either using a `javax.net.ssl.TrustManagerFactory` object or instantiating a class implementing the `TrustManager` interface.

13.4.3   Truststores

A *truststore* is a regular keystore that is used when authenticating a peer to decide whether the peer should be trusted. In JSSE, truststores are represented as `java.security.KeyStore` objects (see Section 11.2.7 on page 395). As the entries in a truststore are used to make trust decisions during an authentication process, an entry should be added to a truststore only by a system administrator and only if the entity represented by that entity is considered trusted.

The J2SE reference implementation comes with a default truststore file called `cacerts`, located in the `lib/security` subdirectory of the Java home directory. This file contains the digital certificates of common CAs, such as VeriSign and Thawte. The default password to access and modify this truststore is `changeit`. Users of a Java system can specify a different truststore by setting the system property `javax.net.ssl.trustStore` to the truststore file of their preference. This can be done programmatically, through a call to `java.lang.System.set-Property()`, or statically, using the `-Djavax.net.ssl.trustStore` option of the `java` command.

Often, it is useful to keep regular keystore files separated from truststore files. A regular keystore file contains private information, such as an entity's own certificates and corresponding private keys, whereas a truststore contains public information, such as that entity's trusted certificate entries, including CA certificates. Using two different files instead of a single keystore file provides for a cleaner separation between an entity's own certificate and key entries and other entities' certificates. This physical separation, which reflects the logical distinction of private- and public-key material, gives system administrators more flexibility in managing the security of the system. For example, a truststore file could be made write protected so that only system administrators are allowed to add entries to it. Conversely, a user's keystore can be write accessible to its owner.

13.5 Examples

The SSL support built into a J2EE container may sometimes be insufficient to address the security requirements of a Web application. J2EE programs with the possibility to engage in SSL sessions autonomously are more flexible and may allow addressing those security requirements that are not met by the hosting J2EE product. For example, a servlet may need to contact a remote program to retrieve a secret number and then transfer that number to a client, as shown in Figure 13.3.

Although the HTTP communication between the servlet and the client can be protected via HTTPS declaratively, this solution may not be an option in the communication between the servlet and the remote secret-number generator. To protect this communication, the servlet and the secret-number generator need to establish an SSL connection independently of the servlet container. The sample code in this section demonstrates this scenario, showing how to use the JSSE API from within a servlet.

The code in this section also shows how to convert an unsecure socket connection to a secure socket connection that uses the SSL protocol. In fact, in many cases, programs need to be modified because they were originally written without thinking of any security implications or because security requirements arose afterward. In the scenario we describe, a possibility could be to retrieve the secret number from the remote server through a regular socket connection—one that does not use any form of encryption. In such a case, however, eavesdroppers could get at the random number easily and even change it and communicate a different value to the servlet. It is therefore necessary to activate a form of protection, such as SSL, to guarantee data integrity and authenticity.

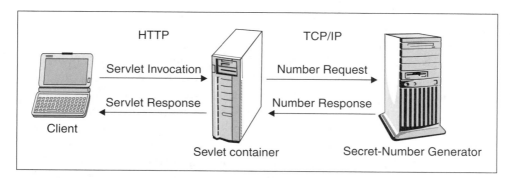

Figure 13.3. Scenario Favorable for Using SSL from a Servlet

13.5.1 Basic Scenario without SSL

The sample code in Listing 13.1 shows how to implement a servlet, Secret-NumberServlet, that communicates with an external server using an unsecure socket. The SecretNumberServlet program is activated when its `init()` method is executed by the servlet container. The servlet container communicates to the servlet the host name of the external server responsible for generating the secret number and the port number on which the external server is listening. When a client contacts the servlet, the servlet's `service()` method is invoked. At that point, the servlet opens an unsecure socket connection with the external server, retrieves the secret number, and communicates it back to the client through the servlet container.

As we have already observed, the communication between the client and the servlet can be protected using HTTPS. However, the communication between the servlet and the external server must be protected programmatically. The example in this section does not do that. The servlet and the external server communicate using a regular TCP/IP socket connection. Therefore, use of this servlet is indicated in those network topologies in which the servlet container and external server are located in a protected network—one in which wire tapping is unfeasible. Section 13.5.2 on page 468 shows how the code presented in this section can be made secure using SSL.

Listing 13.1. `SecretNumberServlet.java`

```
import java.io.InputStream;
import java.io.IOException;
import java.io.DataInputStream;

import java.net.Socket;
import java.net.UnknownHostException;

import javax.servlet.ServletConfig;
import javax.servlet.ServletException;
import javax.servlet.ServletOutputStream;

import javax.servlet.http.HttpServlet;
import javax.servlet.http.HttpServletRequest;
import javax.servlet.http.HttpServletResponse;


/**
 * This servlet connects to an external server, retrieves
 * from it a secret number, and communicates it to the
 * client. The communication between the servlet and the
 * external server is not protected. Therefore, usage of
 * this servlet is indicated when the servlet container and
 * external server are located in the same intranet.
 */
```

(continues)

Listing 13.1. `SecretNumberServlet.java` (*continued*)

```java
public class SecretNumberServlet extends HttpServlet
{
    private String server;
    private int port;

    /**
     * Initializes the servlet by setting the initialization
     * parameters: the external server host name and port
     * number.
     *
     * @param config a ServletConfig object used by the
     *        servlet container to pass information to the
     *        servlet during initialization.
     * @throws ServletException if the servlet intialization
     *         cannot be executed.
     */
    public void init(ServletConfig config)
        throws ServletException
    {
        super.init(config);

        try
        {
            port = (new Integer(getInitParameter("port"))).
                intValue();
        }
        catch (NumberFormatException nfe)
        {
            log("<port> must be a parsable integer");
            throw new ServletException(nfe.getMessage());
        }

        String server = getInitParameter("server");
    }

    /**
     * Opens a socket connection with the external server,
     * retrieves the secret number generated from the
     * external server, and communicates it to the client.
     * This method is executed each time a client invokes
     * the servlet.
     *
     * @param request an HttpServletRequest object
     *        containing information about the client's
     *        request.
     * @param response an HttpServletResponse object in
     *        which the servlet stores information to be
     *        sent to the client.
     * @throws ServletException if an exception occurs that
     *         interferes with the servlet's normal
     *         operation.
     * @throws IOException if an I/O exception occurs.
     */
```

```
public void service(HttpServletRequest request,
    HttpServletResponse response)
    throws ServletException, IOException
{
    log("Requesting connection from " + server +
        " on port " + port + "...");
    Socket s = null;

    try
    {
        // Open socket connection with the external
        // server.
        s = new Socket(server, port);
    }
    catch (UnknownHostException uhe)
    {
        log("Server " + server + " is unknown");
        throw new ServletException(uhe.getMessage());
    }

    log("Connected to server " + server);

    // Get the secret number from the external server.
    InputStream in = s.getInputStream();
    DataInputStream dis = new DataInputStream(in);
    int secretNumber = dis.readInt();

    // Send the response to the client in HTML format.
    ServletOutputStream out =
        response.getOutputStream();
    response.setContentType("text/html");
    out.println("<HTML><HEAD><TITLE>" +
        "Secret Number Page</TITLE></HEAD></HTML>");
    out.println("<BODY><H1>Secret Number: " +
        secretNumber + "</H1></BODY>");
    out.println("</HTML>");
    dis.close();
    in.close();
    s.close();
}
}
```

The servlet SecretNumberServlet in Listing 13.1 can be deployed in any J2EE-compliant Web container. During deployment, the initialization parameters `server` and `port` must be set to the fully qualified host name of the server machine and the number of the port on which the server is listening, respectively.

Listing 13.2 shows the code of the server program responsible for generating random numbers and communicating them to its clients.

Listing 13.2. `Server.java`

```java
import java.io.OutputStream;
import java.io.IOException;
import java.io.DataOutputStream;

import java.util.Random;

import java.net.Socket;
import java.net.ServerSocket;


/**
 * Server class for random number generation. This server
 * runs as a process that external client applications can
 * contact by opening an appropriate socket. Every time a
 * client contacts the server application, a new Thread is
 * generated. The server application produces a new random
 * number, communicates it to the client, and closes the
 * connection with the client.
 */
public class Server extends Thread
{
    private Socket client;
    private static Random randomGenerator = new Random();

    /**
     * Public constructor. Initializes the server by setting
     * the Socket to communicate with the client.
     *
     * @param client a Socket object representing the
     *        client application this server is
     *        communicating with.
     */
    public Server(Socket client)
    {
        this.client = client;
    }

    /**
     * Generates a random number and communicates it to the
     * the client.
     */
    public void run()
    {
        int secretNumber = randomGenerator.nextInt();
        System.out.println("Secret Number: " + secretNumber);

        try
        {
            OutputStream out = client.getOutputStream();
            DataOutputStream dos = new DataOutputStream(out);
            dos.writeInt(secretNumber);
            dos.flush();
            dos.close();
            out.close();
            client.close();
        }
```

```java
        catch(IOException e)
        {
            System.out.println(e);
        }
    }

    /**
     * Launches the server application. This method expects
     * the port number to be passed on the command line.
     *
     * @param args a String[] array whose first element
     *         must represent the port number this server
     *         will be listening on. The port number is
     *         expected to be an integer between 1025 and
     *         65536. Values not in this range will cause the
     *         application to quit.
     */
    public static void main(String args[])
    {
        if (args.length == 0)
        {
            System.out.println("Usage: java Server <port>");
            System.exit(0);
        }

        int port = 0;

        try
        {
            port = (new Integer(args[0])).intValue();
        }
        catch (NumberFormatException nfe)
        {
            System.out.println("Usage: java Server <port>");
            System.out.println
                ("<port> must be a parsable integer");
            System.exit(0);
        }

        if (port <= 1024 || port > 65536)
        {
            System.out.println("Usage: java Server <port>");
            System.out.println
                ("<port> must be an integer in the range " +
                "1025-65536");
            System.exit(0);
        }

        System.out.println("Server starting...");
        ServerSocket ss = null;
        // Try to start the server. At this point, problems
        // may arise if another process is already listening
        // on the selected port.
        try
        {
            ss = new ServerSocket(port);
        }
```

(continues)

Listing 13.2. `Server.java`   *(continued)*

```
        catch (IOException ioe)
        {
            System.out.println
                ("There is already a server running on port " +
                port + "\n" + ioe);
            System.exit(0);
        }

        System.out.println
            ("Server started on port " + port);
        System.out.println("Waiting for clients...");

        // Start an endless loop in which the server is
        // constantly waiting for clients to connect.
        while (true)
        {
            Socket client = null;

            try
            {
                client = ss.accept();
            }
            catch (IOException ioe)
            {
                System.out.println("Unable to accept " +
                    "connection from client\n" + ioe);
                System.exit(0);
            }

            System.out.println
                ("Request from client received...");
            Server server = new Server(client);
            server.start();
        }
    }
}
```

The server code in Listing 13.2 can be launched from the command line by entering the command

`java Server port`

where *port* is a valid TCP port number not already in use in the range, 1025–65536.

13.5.2   Scenarios with SSL

This section shows how the code shown in Section 13.5.1 on page 463 can be modified so that the communication between the servlet and the external server is protected by the SSL protocol. Both the servlet and the server application that we are going to present here use the SSL support provided through the JSSE API.

The code presented in this section has the same structure as the code in Section 13.5.1. However, to use secure sockets, both the servlet and the external server need to use an SSL socket factory. The servlet uses the `javax.net.ssl.SSLSocketFactory` class to generate a `javax.net.ssl.SSLSocket` object and communicate with the external server. The external server uses the `javax.net.ssl.SSLServerSocketFactory` class to generate a `javax.net.ssl.SSLServerSocket` and communicate with the servlet. Because SSL is used to protect the communication between the servlet and the external servlet, the secret number generated by the external servlet is encrypted before being sent to the servlet and is transmitted in a confidential manner.

The external server that generates the secret number is a regular Java application that can run on any J2SE platform. As we noticed in footnote 7 on page 460, starting with J2SE V1.4, JSSE is an integral part of the J2SE platform. Therefore, no modification is necessary to a J2SE V1.4 platform to enable the external server to run on it. However, JSSE is not an integral part of a J2EE platform. Therefore, to enable the servlets presented in this section to make use of JSSE, the Web container hosting the servlets must have the JSSE API installed and available in the Java runtime class path with the necessary authorizations granted. Typically, the JSSE is added as an extension. Additionally, a JSSE provider must be installed and configured for use by the J2EE programs that need to establish SSL connections (see Listing 11.1 on page 384 and Section 11.1.3.3 on page 387).

13.5.2.1 *Scenario with No Authentication*

In this section, we assume for simplicity that the external server does not require any authentication. (In Section 13.5.2.2 on page 476 and Section 13.5.2.3 on page 484, we show how to enforce SSL authentication.) Additionally, as in this example, we do not provide certificates for the external server that generates secret numbers, we enable the anonymous cipher suite `SSL_DH_anon_EXPORT_WITH_DES40_CBC_SHA` in both the client and the server. Anonymous cipher suites are supported by most JSSE providers even though not all the JSSE providers enable them.[8] As we said in step 3 on page 453, neither the client nor the server is authenticated in anonymous cipher suites.

---

8. Sun Microsystems' JSSE provider supports anonymous cipher suites, which by default are enabled. However, anonymous cipher suites do not enforce authentication. Therefore, they are not considered secure. For this reason, IBM's JSSE provider supports anonymous cipher suites but by default does not enable them. Someone who wants to use anonymous cipher suites with the IBM JSSE provider will have to write a trust manager (see Section 13.4.2 on page 461).

Enabling an additional cipher suite is accomplished through the following steps.

1. All the enabled cipher suites, in the form of an array of `String` objects, are obtained from the `SSLSocket` representing the communication. The `SSLSocket` class offers the `getEnabledCipherSuites()` method for this purpose.

2. The additional cipher suite is added to the array.

3. The array of cipher suite `Strings` augmented with the additional cipher suite is passed as a parameter to the `SSLSocket`'s `setEnabledCipher-Suites()` method.

When the cipher suite that the client and the server negotiate during the SSL handshake is not an anonymous cipher suite, the server can disable SSL client authentication by passing the `boolean false` to the `setNeedClientAuth()` method on the `SSLServerSocket` object responsible for the communication with the client.

The servlet code is shown in Listing 13.3.

Listing 13.3. `SSLSecretNumberServlet.java`

```java
import java.io.InputStream;
import java.io.IOException;
import java.io.DataInputStream;

import javax.net.ssl.SSLSocket;
import javax.net.ssl.SSLSocketFactory;

import javax.servlet.ServletConfig;
import javax.servlet.ServletException;
import javax.servlet.ServletOutputStream;

import javax.servlet.http.HttpServlet;
import javax.servlet.http.HttpServletRequest;
import javax.servlet.http.HttpServletResponse;


/**
 * This servlet connects to an external server, retrieves
 * from it a secret number, and communicates it to the
 * client. The communication between the servlet and the
 * external server is SSL-protected. Therefore, usage of
 * this servlet is indicated when the information exchanged
 * between the servlet container and external server demands
 * confidentiality.
 */
public class SSLSecretNumberServlet extends HttpServlet
{
    private String server;
    private int port;
```

```
/**
 * Initializes the servlet by setting the initialization
 * parameters, the external server host name and port
 * number.
 *
 * @param config a ServletConfig object used by the
 *        servlet container to pass information to the
 *        servlet during initialization.
 * @throws ServletException if the servlet initialization
 *         cannot be executed.
 */
public void init(ServletConfig config)
    throws ServletException
{
    super.init(config);

    try
    {
        port = (new Integer(getInitParameter("port"))).
            intValue();
    }
    catch (NumberFormatException nfe)
    {
        log("<port> must be a parsable integer");
        throw new ServletException(nfe.getMessage());
    }

    String server = getInitParameter("server");
}

/**
 * Opens a secure socket connection with the external
 * server, retrieves the secret number generated from
 * the external server, and communicates it to the
 * client. This method is executed each time a client
 * invokes the servlet.
 *
 * @param request an HttpServletRequest object
 *        containing information about the client's
 *        request.
 * @param response an HttpServletResponse object in
 *        which the servlet stores information to be
 *        sent to the client.
 * @throws ServletException if an exception occurs that
 *         interferes with the servlet's normal
 *         operation.
 * @throws IOException if an I/O exception occurs,
 *         preventing this method from executing.
 */
public void service(HttpServletRequest request,
    HttpServletResponse response)
    throws ServletException, IOException
{
    log("Requesting connection from " + server +
        " on port " + port + "...");
    SSLSocket s = null;
```

(*continues*)

Listing 13.3. `SSLSecretNumberServlet.java`   (*continued*)

```
        SSLSocketFactory sslFact = (SSLSocketFactory)
            SSLSocketFactory.getDefault();

        try
        {
            // Open socket connection with the external server.
            s = (SSLSocket) sslFact.createSocket(server, port);
        }
        catch (IOException ioe)
        {
            log("Server " + server + " is unknown");
            throw new ServletException(ioe.getMessage());
        }

        // Enable anonymous cipher suite
        String[] cipherSuites = s.getEnabledCipherSuites();
        String[] encs = new String[cipherSuites.length + 1];

        for (int i = 0; i < cipherSuites.length; i++)
            encs[i] = cipherSuites[i];
        encs[cipherSuites.length] =
            "SSL_DH_anon_EXPORT_WITH_DES40_CBC_SHA";
        s.setEnabledCipherSuites(encs);
        log("Connected to server " + server);

        // Get the secret number from the external server.
        InputStream in = s.getInputStream();
        DataInputStream dis = new DataInputStream(in);
        int secretNumber = dis.readInt();

        // Send the response to the client in HTML format.
        ServletOutputStream out = response.getOutputStream();
        response.setContentType("text/html");
        out.println("<HTML><HEAD><TITLE>" +
            "Secret Number Page</TITLE></HEAD></HTML>");
        out.println("<BODY><H1>Secret Number: " +
            secretNumber + "</H1></BODY>");
        out.println("</HTML>");
        dis.close();
        in.close();
        s.close();
    }
}
```

The servlet SSLSecretNumberServlet in Listing 13.3 can be deployed in any J2EE-compliant, JSSE-enabled Web container. During deployment, the initialization parameters `server` and `port` must be set to the fully qualified host name of the server machine and the number of the port on which the server is listening, respectively.

Listing 13.4 shows the code of the server program responsible for generating random numbers and communicating them to its clients through SSL socket connections.

Listing 13.4. `SSLServer.java`

```java
import java.io.OutputStream;
import java.io.IOException;
import java.io.DataOutputStream;

import java.util.Random;

import javax.net.ssl.SSLSocket;
import javax.net.ssl.SSLServerSocket;
import javax.net.ssl.SSLServerSocketFactory;


/**
 * Server class for random number generation. This server
 * runs as a process that external client applications can
 * contact by opening an appropriate socket. Every time a
 * client contacts the server application, a new Thread is
 * generated. The server application produces a new random
 * number, communicates it to the client, and closes the
 * connection with the client. The communication between
 * the server and client is protected by SSL. An anonymous
 * cipher suite is enabled.
 */
public class SSLServer extends Thread
{
    private SSLSocket client;
    private static Random randomGenerator = new Random();

    /**
     * Public constructor. Initializes the server by setting
     * the Socket to communicate with the client.
     *
     * @param client an SSLSocket object representing the
     *        client application this server is
     *        communicating with.
     */
    public SSLServer(SSLSocket c)
    {
        this.client = c;
    }

    /**
     * Generates a random number and communicates it to the
     * the client. The communication is protected by SSL.
     */
    public void run()
    {
        int secretNumber = randomGenerator.nextInt();
        System.out.println("Secret Number: " + secretNumber);

        try
        {
            OutputStream out = client.getOutputStream();
            DataOutputStream dos = new DataOutputStream(out);
            dos.writeInt(secretNumber);
            dos.flush();
```

(continues)

Listing 13.4. `SSLServer.java`   (*continued*)

```java
                dos.close();
                out.close();
                client.close();
            }
            catch(IOException e)
            {
                System.out.println(e);
            }
        }
    }

    /**
     * Launches the server application. This method expects
     * the port number to be passed on the command line.
     *
     * @param args a String[] array whose first element
     *          must represent the port number this server
     *          will be listening on. The port number is
     *          expected to be an integer between 1025 and
     *          65536. Values not in this range will cause the
     *          application to quit.
     */
    public static void main(String args[])
    {
        if (args.length == 0)
        {
            System.out.println("Usage: java Server <port>");
            System.exit(0);
        }

        int port = 0;

        try
        {
            port = (new Integer(args[0])).intValue();
        }
        catch (NumberFormatException nfe)
        {
            System.out.println("Usage: java Server <port>");
            System.out.println
                ("<port> must be a parsable integer");
            System.exit(0);
        }

        if (port <= 1024 || port > 65536)
        {
            System.out.println("Usage: java Server <port>");
            System.out.println
                ("<port> must be an integer in the range " +
                "1025-65536");
            System.exit(0);
        }
        System.out.println("Server starting...");
        SSLServerSocketFactory sslSrvFact =
            (SSLServerSocketFactory)
            SSLServerSocketFactory.getDefault();
        SSLServerSocket ss = null;
```

```
        // Try to start the server. At this point, problems
        // may arise if another process is already listening
        // on the selected port.
        try
        {
            ss = (SSLServerSocket)
                sslSrvFact.createServerSocket(port);
        }
        catch (IOException ioe)
        {
            System.out.println
                ("There is already a server running on port " +
                port + "\n" + ioe);
            System.exit(0);
        }

        System.out.println
            ("Server started on port " + port);
        System.out.println("Waiting for clients...");

        // Enable anonymous cipher suite
        String[] cipherSuites =
            ss.getEnabledCipherSuites();

        String[] encs = new String[cipherSuites.length + 1];
        for (int i = 0; i < cipherSuites.length; i++)
            encs[i] = cipherSuites[i];

        encs[cipherSuites.length] =
            "SSL_DH_anon_EXPORT_WITH_DES40_CBC_SHA";
        ss.setEnabledCipherSuites(encs);

        // Start an endless loop in which the server is
        // constantly waiting for clients to connect.
        while (true)
        {
            SSLSocket client = null;

            try
            {
                client = (SSLSocket) ss.accept();
            }
            catch (IOException ioe)
            {
                System.out.println("Unable to accept " +
                    "connection from client\n" + ioe);
                System.exit(0);
            }

            System.out.println
                ("Request from client received...");
            SSLServer server = new SSLServer(client);
            server.start();
        }
    }
}
```

The server code in Listing 13.4 can be launched from the command line by entering the command

```
java SSLServer port
```

where *port* is a valid TCP port number not already in use in the range 1025–65536.

13.5.2.2   *Scenario with SSL Server Authentication*

Using anonymous cipher suites as we did in Section 13.5.2.1 on page 469 is not recommended, because neither the server nor the client is authenticated. The only advantage in using anonymous cipher suites is that the communication between the client and the server is encrypted.

In this section, we show how the servlet and the external server presented in Listings 13.3 and 13.4, respectively, can be modified so that the external server is authenticated. For SSL server authentication to work, the external server must present the servlet with a valid certificate from its own keystore. In order for the servlet to trust the server, at least one of the certificates in the certificate chain of the server certificate must be in the servlet's truststore.

From an implementation perspective, these two requirements imply the following two points, respectively.

1. The servlet must create a `javax.net.ssl.SSLContext` and initialize it with a `TrustManagerFactory` object. The `TrustManagerFactory` must have been previously initialized with a `KeyStore` object and the password to access the keystore file. The `KeyStore` object represents the truststore against which the servlet will attempt to authenticate the external server. At this point, the `SSLContext` can be used to generate an `SSLSocketFactory`, which is responsible for creating `SSLSockets`, as in Listing 13.3.

2. Similarly, the server must create an `SSLContext` and initialize it with a `javax.net.ssl.KeyManagerFactory` object. The `KeyManagerFactory` object itself must have been previously initialized with a `KeyStore` object and the password to access the keystore file. The `KeyStore` object represents the keystore from which the server will extract the certificate that will be presented to the servlet for server authentication. At this point, the `SSLContext` can be used to generate an `SSLServerSocketFactory`, which is responsible for creating `SSLServerSockets`, as in Listing 13.4.

Section 8.1.2.2 on page 256 explains how to use the `keytool` command line utility to export certificates from a keystore, importing trusted certificates into a truststore, and obtain a certificate issued by a CA.

The servlet code is shown in Listing 13.5.

Listing 13.5. `SSLSecretNumberServletWithServerAuth.java`

```
import java.io.InputStream;
import java.io.IOException;
import java.io.DataInputStream;
import java.io.FileInputStream;

import java.security.KeyStore;

import javax.net.ssl.SSLContext;
import javax.net.ssl.TrustManagerFactory;
import javax.net.ssl.SSLSocket;
import javax.net.ssl.SSLSession;
import javax.net.ssl.SSLSocketFactory;

import javax.servlet.ServletConfig;
import javax.servlet.ServletException;
import javax.servlet.ServletOutputStream;

import javax.servlet.http.HttpServlet;
import javax.servlet.http.HttpServletRequest;
import javax.servlet.http.HttpServletResponse;


/**
 * This servlet connects to an external server, retrieves
 * from it a secret number, and communicates it to the
 * client. The communication between the servlet and the
 * external server is SSL-protected and supports SSL server
 * authentication. Therefore, usage of this servlet is
 * indicated when the information exchanged between the
 * servlet container and external server demands
 * confidentiality and server authentication.
 */
public class SSLSecretNumberServletWithServerAuth
    extends HttpServlet
{
    private String server;
    private int port;

    /**
     * Initializes the servlet by setting the initialization
     * parameters and the external server host name and port
     * number.
     *
     * @param config a ServletConfig object used by the servlet
     *        container to pass information to the servlet
     *        during the initialization process.
     * @throws ServletException if the servlet initialization
     *        cannot be executed.
     */
    public void init(ServletConfig config)
        throws ServletException
    {
        super.init(config);
        try
        {
```

(continues)

Listing 13.5. `SSLSecretNumberServletWithServerAuth.java`   (*continued*)

```
            port = (new Integer(getInitParameter("port"))).
                intValue();
        }
        catch (NumberFormatException nfe)
        {
            log("<port> must be a parsable integer");
            throw new ServletException(nfe.getMessage());
        }

        String server = getInitParameter("server");
    }

    /**
     * Opens a secure socket connection with the external
     * server, retrieves the secret number generated from the
     * external server, and communicates it to the client. This
     * method is executed each time a client invokes the
     * servlet.
     *
     * @param request an HttpServletRequest object containing
     *          information about the client's request.
     * @param response an HttpServletResponse object in which
     *          the servlet stores information to be sent to
     *          the client.
     * @throws ServletException if an exception occurs that
     *          interferes with the servlet's normal operation.
     * @throws IOException if an I/O exception occurs.
     */
    public void service(HttpServletRequest request,
        HttpServletResponse response)
        throws ServletException, IOException
    {
        log("Requesting connection from " + server +
            " on port " + port + "...");

        // The keystore password is hardcoded
        char[] passwd = "xyz123".toCharArray();

        SSLSocket s = null;

        try
        {
            // Create an SSLContext instance implementing the
            // TLS protocol.
            SSLContext ctx = SSLContext.getInstance("TLS");

            // Create a TrustManagerFactory implementing the
            // X.509 key management algorithm.
            TrustManagerFactory tmf =
                TrustManagerFactory.getInstance("IbmX509");

            // Create a KeyStore instance implementing the
            // Java KeyStore (JKS) algorithm.
            KeyStore ks = KeyStore.getInstance("JKS");
```

```
            // Load the KeyStore file trustStoreFile,
            // representing the truststore that the servlet
            // will use to authenticate the server
            ks.load(new FileInputStream("trustStoreFile"),
                passwd);

            // Initialize the TrustManagerFactory object with
            // the KeyStore.
            tmf.init(ks);

            // Initialize the SSLContext with the
            // KeyManagerFactory.
            ctx.init(null, tmf.getTrustManagers(), null);

            // Create an SSLSocketFactory instance from the
            // SSLContext and generate an SSLSocket from it
            SSLSocketFactory sslFact = ctx.getSocketFactory();
            s = (SSLSocket)
                sslFact.createSocket(server, port);
        }
        catch (Exception e)
        {
            // Catch any Exception and turn it into a
            // ServletException
            throw new ServletException(e.getMessage());
        }

        SSLSession session = s.getSession();
        log("Connected to server " + server + "\nCipher suite:"
            + session.getCipherSuite());

        // Get the secret number from the external server.
        InputStream in = s.getInputStream();
        DataInputStream dis = new DataInputStream(in);
        int secretNumber = dis.readInt();

        // Send the response to the client in HTML format.
        ServletOutputStream out = response.getOutputStream();
        response.setContentType("text/html");
        out.println("<HTML><HEAD><TITLE>" +
            "Secret Number Page</TITLE></HEAD></HTML>");
        out.println("<BODY><H1>Secret Number: " +
            secretNumber + "</H1></BODY>");
        out.println("</HTML>");
        dis.close();
        in.close();
        s.close();
    }
}
```

The servlet SSLSecretNumberServletWithServerAuth in Listing 13.5 can be deployed in any J2EE-compliant, JSSE-enabled Web container. During deployment, the initialization parameters server and port must be set to the fully qualified host name of the server machine and the number of the port on which the server is listening, respectively.

This servlet requires the presence of a truststore file in the same directory as the servlet class. The truststore file name is hard-coded as `trustStoreFile` and the password to access it as `xyz123`. The J2SE and J2EE reference implementations provide the `keytool` command line utility to manage keystores (see Section 8.1.2.2 on page 256). In particular, the `-genkey` option of this command can be used to create a new keystore.

Listing 13.6 shows the code of the server program responsible for generating random numbers and communicating them to its clients through SSL socket connections in which server authentication is enabled.

Listing 13.6. `SSLServerWithServerAuth.java`

```
import java.io.OutputStream;
import java.io.IOException;
import java.io.DataOutputStream;
import java.io.FileInputStream;

import java.util.Random;

import javax.net.ssl.SSLSocket;
import javax.net.ssl.SSLSession;
import javax.net.ssl.SSLServerSocket;
import javax.net.ssl.SSLServerSocketFactory;
import javax.net.ssl.SSLContext;
import javax.net.ssl.KeyManagerFactory;

import java.security.KeyStore;


/**
 * Server class for random number generation. This server
 * runs as a process that external client applications can
 * contact by opening an appropriate socket. Every time a
 * client contacts the server application, a new Thread is
 * generated. The server application produces a new random
 * number, communicates it to the client, and closes the
 * connection with the client. The communication between
 * the server and client is protected by SSL. Server
 * authentication is enabled.
 */
public class SSLServerWithServerAuth extends Thread
{
    private SSLSocket client;
    private static Random randomGenerator = new Random();

    /**
     * Public constructor. Initializes the server by setting
     * the Socket to communicate with the client.
     *
     * @param client an SSLSocket object representing the
     *            client application this server is
     *            communicating with.
     */
```

```
    public SSLServerWithServerAuth(SSLSocket c)
    {
        this.client = c;
    }

    /**
     * Generates a random number and communicates it to the
     * the client. The communication is protected by SSL.
     */
    public void run()
    {
        int secretNumber = randomGenerator.nextInt();
        System.out.println("Secret Number: " + secretNumber);

        try
        {
            OutputStream out = client.getOutputStream();
            DataOutputStream dos = new DataOutputStream(out);
            dos.writeInt(secretNumber);
            dos.flush();
            dos.close();
            out.close();
            client.close();
        }
        catch (IOException e)
        {
            System.out.println(e);
        }
    }

    /**
     * Launches the server application. This method expects
     * the port number to be passed on the command line.
     *
     * @param args a String[] array whose first element
     *        must represent the port number this server
     *        will be listening on. The port number is
     *        expected to be an integer between 1025 and
     *        65536. Values not in this range will cause the
     *        application to quit.
     */
    public static void main(String args[])
    {
        if (args.length == 0)
        {
            System.out.println("Usage: java Server <port>");
            System.exit(0);
        }

        int port = 0;

        try
        {
            port = (new Integer(args[0])).intValue();
        }
        catch (NumberFormatException nfe)
        {
```

(continues)

Listing 13.6. `SSLServerWithServerAuth.java`   (*continued*)

```
        System.out.println("Usage: java Server <port>");
        System.out.println
            ("<port> must be a parsable integer");
        System.exit(0);
    }

    if (port <= 1024 || port > 65536)
    {
        System.out.println("Usage: java Server <port>");
        System.out.println
            ("<port> must be an integer in the range " +
            "1025-65536");
        System.exit(0);
    }

    // The keystore password is hardcoded
    char[] passwd = "abc123".toCharArray();

    SSLContext ctx = null;

    try
    {
        // Create an SSLContext instance implementing
        // the TLS protocol.
        ctx = SSLContext.getInstance("TLS");

        // Create a KeyManagerFactory implementing the
        // X.509 key management algorithm.
        KeyManagerFactory kmf =
            KeyManagerFactory.getInstance("IbmX509");

        // Open up the KeyStore in order to present the
        // server's certificates to the client.
        KeyStore ks = KeyStore.getInstance("JKS");

        // Load the KeyStore file keyStoreFile
        ks.load (new FileInputStream("keyStoreFile"),
            passwd);

        // Initialize the KeyManagerFactory object with
        // the KeyStore.
        kmf.init(ks, passwd);

        // Initialize the SSLContext with the
        // KeyManagerFactory.
        ctx.init(kmf.getKeyManagers(), null, null);
    }
    catch (Exception e)
    {
        System.out.println
            ("Unable to initialize SSLContext " +
            e.getMessage());
        System.exit(0);
    }
```

```
        System.out.println("Server starting...");

        // Create an SSLServerSocketFactory instance from
        // the SSLContext and generate an SSLServerSocket
        // from it.
        SSLServerSocketFactory sslSrvFact =
            ctx.getServerSocketFactory();
        SSLServerSocket ss = null;

        // Try to start the server. At this point, problems
        // may arise if another process is already listening
        // on the selected port.
        try
        {
            ss = (SSLServerSocket)
                sslSrvFact.createServerSocket(port);
        }
        catch (IOException ioe)
        {
            System.out.println
                ("There is already a server running on " +
                " port " + port + "\n" + ioe);
            System.exit(0);
        }

        System.out.println("Server started on port " +
            port);
        System.out.println("Waiting for clients...");

        // Start an endless loop in which the server is
        // constantly waiting for clients to connect.
        while (true)
        {
            SSLSocket client = null;

            try
            {
                client = (SSLSocket) ss.accept();
                SSLSession session = client.getSession();
                System.out.println ("Connected. Cipher suite: "
                    + session.getCipherSuite());
            }
            catch (IOException ioe)
            {
                System.out.println("Unable to accept " +
                    "connection from client\n" + ioe);
                System.exit(0);
            }
            System.out.println
                ("Request from client received...");
            SSLServerWithServerAuth server =
                new SSLServerWithServerAuth(client);
            server.start();
        }
    }
}
```

The server code in Listing 13.6 requires the presence of a keystore file in the same directory as the server class. The keystore file name is hard-coded as `key-StoreFile` and the password to access it as `abc123`.

This server can be launched from the command line by entering the command.

```
java SSLServerWithServerAuth port
```

where *port* is a valid TCP port number not already in use in the range 1025–65536.

13.5.2.3 Scenario with Both SSL Server and Client Authentication

This section presents the scenario in which both SSL server and client authentications are required. Note the following.

1. As in Section 13.5.2.2 on page 476, in order for SSL server authentication to succeed, the external server must present the servlet with a valid certificate from its own keystore, and at least one of the certificates in the certificate chain of the server certificate must be present in the servlet's truststore.

2. In addition, because this time SSL client authentication is required, the servlet also must present the server a valid certificate from its own keystore; for the server to trust the servlet, at least one of the certificates in the certificate chain of the client must be present in the server's truststore.

From an implementation perspective, these two requirements imply the following two points, respectively.

1. The servlet must create an `SSLContext` and initialize it with a `Key-ManagerFactory` object and a `TrustManagerFactory` object.

    *   The `KeyManagerFactory` must have been previously initialized with a `KeyStore` object and the password to access the keystore file. The `Key-Store` object represents the keystore from which the servlet will extract the certificate to present to the server to perform client authentication.

    *   The `TrustManagerFactory` must have been previously initialized with a `KeyStore` object and the password to access the keystore file. The `KeyStore` object represents the truststore against which the servlet will attempt to authenticate the external server to perform server authentication.

    At this point, the `SSLContext` can be used to generate an `SSLSocket-Factory`, which is responsible for creating `SSLSockets` as in the examples of Listings 13.3 and 13.5.

2. Similarly, the server must create an `SSLContext` and initialize it with a `KeyManagerFactory` object and a `TrustManagerFactory` object.

   - The `KeyManagerFactory` must have been previously initialized with a `KeyStore` object and the password to access the keystore file. The `KeyStore` object represents the keystore from which the server will extract the certificate to present to the servlet to perform server authentication.

   - The `TrustManagerFactory` must have been previously initialized with a `KeyStore` object and the password to access the keystore file. The `KeyStore` object represents the truststore against which the server will attempt to authenticate the servlet to perform client authentication.

   At this point, the `SSLContext` can be used to generate an `SSLServerSocketFactory`, which is responsible for creating `SSLServerSocket`s as in the examples of Listing 13.4 and 13.6.

The complete servlet code is shown in Listing 13.7.

Listing 13.7. `SSLSecretNumberServletWithServerAndClientAuth.java`

```java
import java.io.InputStream;
import java.io.IOException;
import java.io.DataInputStream;
import java.io.FileInputStream;

import java.security.KeyStore;

import javax.net.ssl.SSLContext;
import javax.net.ssl.TrustManagerFactory;
import javax.net.ssl.KeyManagerFactory;
import javax.net.ssl.SSLSocket;
import javax.net.ssl.SSLSession;
import javax.net.ssl.SSLSocketFactory;

import javax.servlet.ServletConfig;
import javax.servlet.ServletException;
import javax.servlet.ServletOutputStream;

import javax.servlet.http.HttpServlet;
import javax.servlet.http.HttpServletRequest;
import javax.servlet.http.HttpServletResponse;


/**
 * This servlet connects to an external server, retrieves
 * from it a secret number, and communicates it to the
 * client. The communication between the servlet and the
 * external server is SSL-protected. Both SSL client and
 * server authentications are enabled. Therefore, usage of
 * this servlet is indicated when the information exchanged
 * between the servlet container and external server demands
 * authentication and confidentiality.
 */
```

(continues)

Listing 13.7. `SSLSecretNumberServletWithServerAndClientAuth.`
`java` (*continued*)

```java
public class SSLSecretNumberServletWithServerAndClientAuth
    extends HttpServlet
{
    private String server;
    private int port;

    /**
     * Initializes the servlet by setting the initialization
     * parameters, the external server host name and port
     * number.
     *
     * @param config a ServletConfig object used by the servlet
     *         container to pass information to the servlet
     *         during initialization.
     * @throws ServletException if the servlet initialization
     *         cannot be executed.
     */
    public void init(ServletConfig config)
        throws ServletException
    {
        super.init(config);

        try
        {
            port = (new Integer(getInitParameter("port"))).
                intValue();
        }
        catch (NumberFormatException nfe)
        {
            log("port must be a parsable integer");
            throw new ServletException(nfe.getMessage());
        }

        String server = getInitParameter("server");
    }

    /**
     * Opens a secure socket connection with the external
     * server, retrieves the secret number generated from
     * the external server, and communicates it to the
     * client. This method is executed each time a client
     * invokes the servlet.
     *
     * @param request an HttpServletRequest object
     *         containing information about the client's
     *         request.
     * @param response an HttpServletResponse object in
     *         which the servlet stores information to be
     *         sent to the client.
     * @throws ServletException if an exception occurs that
     *         interferes with the servlet's normal
     *         operation.
     * @throws IOException if an I/O exception occurs.
     */
```

```
public void service(HttpServletRequest request,
    HttpServletResponse response)
    throws ServletException, IOException
{
    log("Requesting connection from " + server +
        " on port " + port + "...");

    // The truststore and keystore passwords are
    // both hardcoded
    char[] passwd = "xyz123".toCharArray();
    char[] passwd2 = "client123".toCharArray();

    SSLSocket s = null;

    try
    {
        // Create an SSLContext instance implementing
        // the TLS protocol.
        SSLContext ctx = SSLContext.getInstance("TLS");
        // Create a TrustManagerFactory implementing the
        // X.509 key management algorithm.
        TrustManagerFactory tmf =
            TrustManagerFactory.getInstance("IbmX509");

        // Create a KeyStore instance implementing the
        // Java KeyStore (JKS) algorithm.
        KeyStore ks = KeyStore.getInstance("JKS");

        // Load the KeyStore file keyStoreFile.
        ks.load(new
            FileInputStream("trustStoreFile"), passwd);

        // Initialize the TrustManagerFactory object with
        // the KeyStore.
        tmf.init(ks);

        // Since the server requires client authentication
        // the client must present its own certificate to
        // the server.

        // Create a KeyManagerFactory implementing the
        // X.509 key management algorithm.
        KeyManagerFactory kmf =
            KeyManagerFactory.getInstance("IbmX509");

        // Create a KeyStore instance implementing the
        // Java KeyStore (JKS) algorithm.
        KeyStore ks2 = KeyStore.getInstance("JKS");

        //  Load the KeyStore file keyClientStore
        ks2.load(new FileInputStream("keyClientStore"),
            passwd2);

        // Initialize the KeyManagerFactory object with
        // the KeyStore.
        kmf.init(ks2, passwd2);
```

(continues)

Listing 13.7. `SSLSecretNumberServletWithServerAndClientAuth.`
`java` (*continued*)

```
            // Initialize the SSLContext with the
            // KeyManagerFactory and TrustManagerFactory.
            ctx.init(kmf.getKeyManagers(),
                tmf.getTrustManagers(), null);

            // Create an SSLSocketFactory instance from the
            // SSLContext and generate an SSLSocket from it.
            SSLSocketFactory sslFact = ctx.getSocketFactory();
            s = (SSLSocket) sslFact.createSocket
                (server, port);
        }
        catch (Exception e)
        {
            // Catch any Exception and turn it into a
            // ServletException
            throw new ServletException(e.getMessage());
        }

        SSLSession session = s.getSession();
        log("Connected to server " + server + "\nCipher suite:"
            + session.getCipherSuite());

        // Get the secret number from the external server.
        InputStream in = s.getInputStream();
        DataInputStream dis = new DataInputStream(in);
        int secretNumber = dis.readInt();

        // Send the response to the client in HTML format.
        ServletOutputStream out = response.getOutputStream();
        response.setContentType("text/html");
        out.println("<HTML><HEAD><TITLE>" +
            "Secret Number Page</TITLE></HEAD></HTML>");
        out.println("<BODY><H1>Secret Number: " +
            secretNumber + "</H1></BODY>");
        out.println("</HTML>");
        dis.close();
        in.close();
        s.close();
    }
}
```

This servlet requires the presence of a keystore file and a truststore file in the same directory as the servlet class. The keystore file name is hard-coded as `key-ClientStore` and the password to access it as `client123`. The truststore file name is hard-coded as `trustStoreFile` and the password to access it as `xyz123`.

The server code is shown in Listing 13.8.

Listing 13.8. `SSLServerWithServerAndClientAuth.java`

```java
import java.io.OutputStream;
import java.io.IOException;
import java.io.DataOutputStream;
import java.io.FileInputStream;

import java.util.Random;

import javax.net.ssl.SSLSocket;
import javax.net.ssl.SSLSession;
import javax.net.ssl.SSLServerSocket;
import javax.net.ssl.SSLServerSocketFactory;
import javax.net.ssl.SSLContext;
import javax.net.ssl.KeyManagerFactory;
import javax.net.ssl.TrustManagerFactory;

import java.security.KeyStore;


/**
 * Server class for random number generation. This server
 * runs as a process that external client applications can
 * contact by opening an appropriate socket. Every time a
 * client contacts the server application, a new Thread is
 * generated. The server application produces a new random
 * number, communicates it to the client, and closes the
 * connection with the client. The communication between
 * the server and client is protected by SSL. This server
 * supports server authentication and requires client
 * authentication.
 */
public class SSLServerWithServerAndClientAuth extends Thread
{
    private SSLSocket client;
    private static Random randomGenerator = new Random();

    /**
     * Public constructor. Initializes the server by setting
     * the Socket to communicate with the client.
     *
     * @param client an SSLSocket object representing the
     *         client application this server is
     *         communicating with.
     */
    public SSLServerWithServerAndClientAuth(SSLSocket c)
    {
        this.client = c;
    }

    /**
     * Generates a random number and communicates it to the
     * the client. The communication is protected by SSL.
     */
    public void run()
    {
```

(continues)

Listing 13.8. `SSLServerWithServerAndClientAuth.java` (*continued*)

```java
        int secretNumber = randomGenerator.nextInt();
        System.out.println("Secret Number:" + secretNumber);

        try
        {
            OutputStream out = client.getOutputStream();
            DataOutputStream dos = new DataOutputStream(out);
            dos.writeInt(secretNumber);
            dos.flush();
            dos.close();
            out.close();
            client.close();
        }
        catch (IOException e)
        {
            System.out.println(e);
        }
    }
    /**
     * Launches the server application. This method expects
     * the port number to be passed on the command line.
     *
     * @param args a String[] array whose first element
     *        must represent the port number this server
     *        will be listening on. The port number is
     *        expected to be an integer between 1025 and
     *        65536. Values not in this range will cause the
     *        application to quit.
     */
    public static void main(String args[])
    {
        if (args.length == 0)
        {
            System.out.println("Usage: java Server <port>");
            System.exit(0);
        }

        int port = 0;

        try
        {
            port = (new Integer(args[0])).intValue();
        }
        catch (NumberFormatException nfe)
        {
            System.out.println("Usage: java Server <port>");
            System.out.println
                ("<port> must be a parsable integer");
            System.exit(0);
        }

        if (port <= 1024 || port > 65536)
        {
```

```
        System.out.println("Usage: java Server <port>");
        System.out.println
            ("<port> must be an integer in the range " +
            "1025-65536");
        System.exit(0);
    }

    // The keystore and truststore passwords are
    // both hardcoded
    char[] passwd = "abc123".toCharArray();
    char[] passwd2 = "trust123".toCharArray();

    SSLContext ctx = null;

    try
    {
        // Create an SSLContext instance implementing
        // the TLS protocol.
        ctx = SSLContext.getInstance("TLS");

        // Create a KeyManagerFactory implementing the
        // X.509 key management algorithm.
        KeyManagerFactory kmf =
            KeyManagerFactory.getInstance("IbmX509");

        // Open up the KeyStore in order to present the
        // Server's certificates to the client
        KeyStore ks = KeyStore.getInstance("JKS");

        // Load the KeyStore file keyStoreFile
        ks.load (new FileInputStream("keyStoreFile"),
            passwd);

        // Initialize the KeyManagerFactory object with
        // the KeyStore.
        kmf.init(ks, passwd);

        // Create a TrustManagerFactory implementing the
        // X.509 key management algorithm.
        TrustManagerFactory tmf =
            TrustManagerFactory.getInstance("IbmX509");

        // Since client authentication will be requested,
        // the server must be able to trust the client.
        KeyStore ts = KeyStore.getInstance("JKS");
        ts.load (new FileInputStream("trustServerStore"),
            passwd2);

        // Initialize the TrustManagerFactory object with
        // the TrustStore
        tmf.init(ts);
        // Initialize the SSLContext with the
        // KeyManagerFactory and TrustManagerFactory
        ctx.init(kmf.getKeyManagers(),
            tmf.getTrustManagers(), null);
```

(continues)

Listing 13.8. `SSLServerWithServerAndClientAuth.java`   (*continued*)

```
        }
        catch (Exception e)
        {
            System.out.println
                ("Unable to initialize SSLContext " +
                e.getMessage());
            System.exit(0);
        }

        System.out.println("Server starting...");

        // Create an SSLServerSocketFactory instance from the
        // SSLContext and generate an SSLServerSocket from it.

        SSLServerSocketFactory sslSrvFact =
            ctx.getServerSocketFactory();
        SSLServerSocket ss = null;

        // Try to start the server. At this point, problems
        // may arise if another process is already listening
        // on the selected port.
        try
        {
            ss = (SSLServerSocket)
                sslSrvFact.createServerSocket(port);

            // Require client authentication
            ss.setNeedClientAuth(true);
        }
        catch (IOException ioe)
        {
            System.out.println
                ("There is already a server running on port "
                + port + "\n" + ioe);
            System.exit(0);
        }

        System.out.println("Server started on port " + port);
        System.out.println("Waiting for clients...");

        // Start an endless loop in which the server is
        // constantly waiting for clients to connect.
        while (true)
        {
            SSLSocket client = null;

            try
            {
                client = (SSLSocket)ss.accept();
                SSLSession session = client.getSession();
                System.out.println("Connected.  Cipher Suite: " +
                    session.getCipherSuite());
            }
            catch (IOException ioe)
            {
```

```
                    System.out.println("Unable to accept " +
                        "connection from client\n" + ioe);
                    System.exit(0);
                }

                System.out.println
                    ("Request from client received...");
                SSLServerWithServerAndClientAuth server =
                    new SSLServerWithServerAndClientAuth(client);
                server.start();
            }
        }
    }
```

This server requires the presence of a keystore file and a truststore file in the same directory as the server class. The keystore file name is hard-coded as `key-StoreFile` and the password to access it as `abc123`. The truststore file name is hard-coded as `trustServerStore` and the password to access it as `trust123`.

The server code in Listing 13.8 can be launched from the command line by entering the command

`java SSLServerWithServerAndClientAuth` *port*

where *port* is a valid TCP port number not already in use in the range 1025–65536.

13.6 Summary

The history of the World Wide Web is based on pragmatism. For example, no one would argue that sending uncompressed American Standard Code for Information Interchange (ASCII) text data on sessions that are set up and torn down for every single transaction is efficient in any way. However, this is what HTTP does, and it is very successful. The reason for its success is that it is simple enough to allow many different systems to interoperate without problems of differing syntax. The cost of simplicity is in network overhead and a limited transaction model.

Using cryptography in the Java language offers a similar dilemma. It is possible to write a secure application using a toolkit of basic functions. Such an application can be very sophisticated, but it will also be complex. Alternatively, using SSL URL connections (as described in Section 4.10.1 on page 145) offers a way to simplify the application but at the cost of application function. SSL Java packages provide a middle way, retaining simplicity but allowing more flexible application design.

ADVANCED TOPICS

CHAPTER 14

Enterprise Security
for Web Services

THE eXtensible Markup Language (XML), because of its simplicity and flexibility, is expected to facilitate Internet business-to-business (B2B) messaging. One big concern that enterprises have in doing Internet B2B messaging is security. The Internet is a public network, without protection against such attacks as eavesdropping and forgery. If messages are stolen, replayed, or modified during transmission, B2B messaging becomes useless. Fortunately, the recent advancement of Web Services security has remedied most of the security problems in communication.

Various XML security technologies are enhancing security by introducing new features, such as digital signatures, elementwise encryption, and access control, that are beyond the capability of a transport-level security protocol, such as the SSL.

In this chapter, we delve into the dynamics of e-business and how companies will have to make their products and services available over the Internet to remain competitive. In particular, we focus on Web Services technology. A *Web service*[1] is an interface that describes a collection of network-accessible operations based on open Internet standards. Web Services technology has the potential to enable application integration at a higher level in the protocol stack. The key to reaching this level is the definition of a de facto program-to-program communication model, built on Web Services standards, such as XML, Simple Object Access Protocol (SOAP), Web Services Description Language (WSDL), and the Universal

---

1. A note on terminology: We capitalize the word *Services* when we refer to the Web Services technology. We do not capitalize the word *service* when we refer to a specific Web service.

Description, Discovery and Integration (UDDI)[2] standard, a cross-industry initiative designed to accelerate and broaden B2B integration and commerce on the Internet. The UDDI model uses standard protocols, such as HTTP and Java RMI-IIOP. To fully support e-business, extensions are needed for security, reliable messaging, quality of service (QOS), and management for each layer of the Web Services stack.

14.1 XML

One of the appeals of XML is its structured semantics and schema-driven nature, which allows creating an abstraction from computer-based security terms to more human-readable policy terms. This feature is especially useful when XML is used to make access-control decisions. More important, perhaps, is the belief that in the near future, XML will enable software computer agents to parse information and make risk-based judgments about interactions without human intervention.

When security is defined in platform-specific security terms, policies that do not reflect the cross-platform trust needs of the business have a higher risk of being established. Using XML, it is possible to enable organizations to define policies and express them as XML documents. Sections of these XML documents can be encrypted, and all or parts of the documents themselves can be digitally signed by one or more entities and then interpreted by the recipients using local security mechanisms. Various implementations can map from the XML description to a local platform-specific policy-enforcement mechanism without requiring changes to the infrastructure.

Issues such as single sign-on have been plaguing the computer security industry for years (see Section 4.5.2 on page 123). The problem arises from each system's building its own mechanism for identifying users or principals. Humans are often the weakest link in any security model, and the burden of maintaining multiple identities has caused users to find creative ways of subverting the security mechanisms set up to protect them. A digitally signed XML token that asserts the identity of a user and type of authentication that the user has performed and that has been verified by a trusted authority allows building platform-independent models whereby a user authenticates once, and the proof of that authentication can then be asserted to others who share the same administrative domain. If these assertions are part of a larger trust model, decisions about the named user can be

---

2. The UDDI standard is an industry initiative that is working to enable businesses to quickly, easily, and dynamically find and transact with one another. UDDI enables a business to describe its business and its services, discover other businesses that offer desired services, and integrate with these other businesses. For more details, see http://www.uddi.org/.

made without revealing keys or requiring the same security implementation on every platform.

Another area in which XML offers consistent value is Trading Partner Agreement (TPA). The electronic data interchange (EDI)[3] community has struggled with how to express the agreements between trading partners and has been held back by the complexity of configurations. The work in the Security Assertion Markup Language (SAML) within the Organization for the Advancement of Structured Information Standards (OASIS)[4] has set the standard for exchanging authentication and authorization information between domains. Also driven by OASIS is the eXtensible Access Control Markup Language (XACML), a security standard that allows developers to write and enforce information-access rules.

14.2 SOAP

SOAP[5] is a simple, lightweight, and extendable XML-based mechanism for exchanging structured data between network applications on top of widely used Internet standards, such as XML, and transport-independent protocols. SOAP consists of two parts:

1. An *envelope* that defines a framework for describing what is in a message and who should deal with it

2. A *set of encoding rules* defining a serialization mechanism that can be used to exchange instances of application-defined data types

SOAP can be used in combination with, or *reenveloped* by, a variety of network protocols, such as HTTP, RMI-IIOP, SMTP, and FTP. However, the only bindings we refer to in this chapter are SOAP in combination with HTTP and HTTP Extension Framework.[6] SOAP is designed to support a modular architec-

---

3. EDI is a set of protocols for conducting highly structured interorganization exchanges, such as for making purchases or initiating loan requests.

4. See http://www.oasis-open.org.

5. D. Box, D. Ehnebuske, G. Kakivaya, A. Layman, N. Mendelsohn, H. Frystyk Nielsen, S. Thatte, and D. Winer. "Simple Object Access Protocol (SOAP) 1.1." World Wide Web Consortium Submission, May 2000. http://www.w3.org/TR/SOAP/.

6. The HTTP Extension Framework describes a generic extension mechanism for the HTTP protocol, addressing the tension between private agreement and public specification and accommodating dynamic extension of HTTP clients and servers by software components. The kinds of extensions capable of being introduced include extending a single HTTP message, defining new encodings, initiating HTTP-derived protocols for new applications, and switching to protocols that, once initiated, run independently of the original protocol stack. For more details, see http://www.w3.org/Protocols/HTTP/ietf-http-ext/.

ture rather than to be a complete silo like other protocols, such as DCE and CORBA.

A SOAP envelope is used to wrap a SOAP message. A SOAP envelope is defined in an `Envelope` XML element and enables one to add a large variety of metainformation to the message, such as transaction IDs, message-routing information, and message security. The modular architecture of SOAP allows routing and security technologies to be defined in separate documents: the Web Services Addressing specification (WS-Addressing) and the Web Services Security specification (WS-Security), respectively. A SOAP envelope consists of two parts: an optional SOAP header, defined in the `Header` subelement, and a mandatory SOAP body, defined in the `Body` subelement.

1. The *SOAP header* provides a generic mechanism for adding features to a SOAP message. All immediate child elements of the SOAP `Header` element are called *header entries*.

2. The *SOAP body* provides a simple mechanism for exchanging information intended for the ultimate recipient of the message. Typical uses of the body element include marshaling RPC calls and error reporting.

Thus, SOAP can be considered to introduce another layer between the transport layer—for example, HTTP—and the application layer—for example, business data—and the SOAP header makes a convenient place for conveying message metainformation and the application payload.

14.3   WSDL

WSDL[7] is essentially an XML interface definition language (IDL) that provides a way to describe the function and the interface of a service. An IDL is an XML format for describing network services as a set of end points operating on messages containing either document-oriented or procedure-oriented information. The operations and the messages are described abstractly and then bound to a concrete network protocol and message format to define an end point. Related concrete end points are combined into abstract end points, or services. WSDL is extensible to allow the description of end points and their messages regardless of what message formats or network protocols are used to communicate. However, the only described bindings are for SOAP V1.1 and the HTTP GET and POST methods.

The WSDL service information can be extracted from a UDDI business service entry or may be obtained from other service repository sources. Regardless of the source, both the runtime and development tools can use WSDL to determine

---

7. See http://www.w3.org/TR/wsdl.

runtime bindings to a service. This information can be used to build the logic to access the service either directly from the client or through generated code stubs.

WSDL has the potential to be extended[8] to consider the definition of the context needed by a business's execution environment. This includes the business's security. Without these extensions, people will make assumptions about security in the runtime environment of a Web service. However, if these security assertions are defined in terms of XML, it will be possible to have a common interpretation of the security attributes in different implementations and begin to allow the full description of the Web service to be discovered, as described in the Web Services Policy Framework specification (WS-Policy).

14.4 Security for Web Services: Motivations

The Web Services model proposes to use the widely available public Internet for conducting business transactions. The notion of conducting business on a public network is a double-edged sword. On the one hand, doing so makes it easy to do business with anyone on the network, with the speed and efficiency we have seen in Internet e-mail. On the other hand, just as we must lock our cars when parking in most major cities, we need to protect ourselves from opportunistic crime, which comes with the power of open access to everybody.

Security is not an absolute. It is not technically possible to guarantee 100 percent security in any situation. Improving security in an e-business solution is based on many identifiable techniques, each designed as a countermeasure against various kinds of risks: digital certificates to guarantee authenticity and integrity, encryption methods to ensure confidentiality, tickets for authorizing access, and many more. But even using all available techniques, one can never guarantee that a particular application is absolutely 100 percent secure.

Security requirements vary by application. For example, you might notice a camera that records the license plate of your rental car at the parking lot exit. Such a system provides an automatic audit trail of cars leaving the lot. This is a unique requirement for the physical security of a rental car agency but may not apply to your business.

Security technologies do not come for free. Adding credentials to a message makes the message longer, thereby adding overhead in transmission, routing, and processing a received message. You may need a newer version of your middleware to support a particular security technology, and upgrading requires work and sometimes a fee to the software vendor. Pragmatically, though, the main cost is in processing time. The pricing for secure messaging—cryptography—is expensive, and the price for interoperable messaging—CanonicalizatioN (C14N), which

---

8. See `http://xml.coverpages.org/wsfl.html`.

consists of bringing an XML document to its canonical form[9]—is even more expensive.

This leads us to a difficult question: "How much should we do to make an application sufficiently secure to be comfortable using the public Internet for message exchange?" As you would expect, the answer is not simple, because different problems require different solutions. Essentially, you should do enough to make the application reasonably secure, and not more. For example, suppose that you can buy a digital certificate to guarantee the integrity and authenticity of a purchase. A certificate that costs $50 is probably a good investment for a transaction involving $5,000,000 but is likely to be overkill for a transaction of $5. Security involves risk assessment and making trade-offs based on cost and value of the security measures available.

14.5 Security Technologies

When existing applications evolve into Web services, some of the security constraints and trust models of those applications will need to be carried forward and expressed within current implementations of Web services. To accomplish this result, it is necessary to integrate the work begun in the various Web Services security toolkits, which offer a range of security technologies from basic authentication to XML Signature support. As these security technologies themselves become services, and as workflow becomes the primary application paradigm for dynamic application integration, security services will evolve into core elements of a secure application workflow.

A variety of security technologies are being adopted as standards. Following is a brief overview of these standards and how they can be used.

- XML Signature is a standard for securely binding a claim to a set of bits. The XML Signature specification[10] allows for XML documents to be signed in a standard way, with a variety of digital-signature algorithms. Digital signatures can be used for validation of messages and for non-repudiation.

- SAML, a blending of the formerly competing Authentication Markup Language (AuthML) and Security Services Markup Language (S2ML), is an industry standard that, together with other standards, forms the basis for secure e-commerce transactions through XML. SAML is being developed to provide a common language for the sharing of security services between

---

9. Canonical XML is described at http://www.w3.org/TR/xml-c14n.
10. See RFC 3275 at http://www.ietf.org/rfc/rfc3275.txt.

companies engaged in B2B and business-to-consumer (B2C) transactions. SAML allows companies to exchange authentication, authorization, and profile information with their customers, partners, or suppliers, regardless of the security systems or e-commerce platforms they have in place.

- The goal of XML Encryption[11] is to enable encrypting XML fragments. XML Encryption allows for encrypting the parts of an XML document while leaving other parts unencrypted, encrypting a whole XML document, and *superencrypting* XML data—encrypting an XML document when some of its elements have already been encrypted.

- WS-Security is a standard set of SOAP extensions that can be used when building secure Web services to implement integrity and confidentiality. This set of extensions, which is depicted in Table 14.1 on page 509, is also referred to as the Web Services Security Language.

As part of the Java Community Process (JCP), four Java Specification Requests (JSRs)[12] are in progress:

1. JSR 105, "XML Digital Signature APIs"
2. JSR 106, "XML Digital Encryption APIs"
3. JSR 155, "Web Services Security Assertions"
4. JSR 183, "Web Services Message Security APIs"

These four JSRs leverage the standards body work and define the Java API standards for each respective technology. This standardizes the interfaces in each vendor's Web Services toolkit.

14.5.1   XML and Cryptography

XML has become the standard for data exchange. SOAP has become the de facto standard as a means of sending XML messages.

An area of rapid growth is security. The Web Services security challenge is to understand and assess the risk involved in securing a Web-based service today, building on existing security technologies, and at the same time tracking emerging standards and understanding how they will be used to offset the risk in new Web services. Any security model must illustrate how data can flow through an application and network topology to meet the requirements defined by the business without exposing the data to undue risk. A Web service security model must support protocol-independent declarative security policies that Web service providers

---

11. See http://www.w3.org/TR/xmlenc-core/.
12. JSR details can be found at http://www.jcp.org.

can enforce, as well as descriptive security policies attached to the service definitions that clients can use in order to securely access the Web service.

Several standards bodies are actively involved in examining the issues and in developing standards. The main relevant developments here are

- XML Encryption, XML Signature, and XML Key Management Specification (XKMS), all driven by the World Wide Web Consortium (W3C)

- WS-Security, XACML, and SAML, driven by OASIS

We will concentrate on XML Signature and XML Encryption.

Several standard digital signature formats are available today (see Section 10.3.3 on page 370). The most widely used one is Public-Key Cryptography Standards (PKCS) #7 (PKCS#7) (see Section 12.1.3 on page 436), which is used in such standards as S/MIME (see Section 12.2 on page 439) and RosettaNet.[13]

The PKCS#7 syntax is based on Abstract Syntax Notation 1 (ASN.1), which takes a binary bit string as the data to be signed. The type of the data being signed is irrelevant as far as the signature's validity is concerned. As any signature algorithm is expensive to apply directly to a large amount of data, a hash value is first calculated for the entire data, and then the hash value is signed (see Section 10.3.3.1 on page 371 and Section 10.3.3.2 on page 372). Typically, even a single bit change in the bit string results in a completely different hash value, as we observed in Section 10.2.2.4 on page 356. Therefore, any modification of the data invalidates the signature.

For signing XML documents, a joint working group between the IETF[14] and the W3C has defined the XML Digital Signature standard. XML Digital Signature is an XML grammar for signing data regardless of whether the data object is included within an XML document. Likewise, the XML Encryption specification defines a means of representing encrypted data as XML content. XML Encryption supports elementwise encryption. This way, it is possible to encrypt an entire XML document or only parts of it.

As with general encryption scenarios, an XML document as a whole can be digitally signed without problem. However, difficulty arises when parts of a document need to be signed, perhaps by different people, and when this needs to be done in conjunction with selective encryption. To digitally sign an XML document, you first must calculate the hash value of the document. It is possible to take an XML document as a character string, and thus a bit string, and compute its hash

---

13. Named after the ancient Rosetta stone, which helped decipher hieroglyphics, RosettaNet is a consortium whose goal is to design and implement industrywide, open e-business process standards on the Internet. The consortium includes IBM, Microsoft, Intel, and Oracle. For more information, see `http://www.rosettanet.org`.

14. See `http://www.ietf.org`.

value. The problem with this approach is that logically, the same XML document can be represented in many different ways because of XML's flexibility regarding character encoding, white-space handling, and so on.

To address the problem of surface string deviation, the joint working group of XML Digital Signature defined XML C14N, which introduces a set of rules about how an XML document can be represented as a character string in a standard way, so that equivalent XML documents have exactly the same C14N representation, and nonequivalent XML documents have different C14N representations.

There are additional problems as well. One of the strengths of XML languages is that searching is clear and unambiguous: The document type declaration (DTD),[15] or *schema*, provides information as to the relevant syntax. If a document subsection, including tags, is encrypted as a whole, the ability to search for data relevant to those tags is lost. Further, if the tags are themselves encrypted, they may, being known, be useful as material for mounting plaintext attacks against the cryptography used.

In Listing 14.1, an XML Digital Signature example, the `SignedInfo` element points to the data that is signed, and the `SignatureValue` element contains the actual signature. Note that the canonicalization method is also specified. This way, the receiver knows exactly what algorithm was used to generate the signature. The same algorithm must be used to validate the signature.

Listing 14.1. Example of XML Digital Signature

```
<Signature xmlns="http://www.w3.org/2000/09/xmldsig#">
<SignedInfo>
<CanonicalizationMethod Algorithm=
    "http://www.w3.org/2001/10/xml-exc-c14n#"/>
<SignatureMethod Algorithm=
    "http://www.w3.org/2000/09/xmldsig#rsa-sha1"/>
<Reference URI=
    "#wssecurity_body_id_2601212934311668096_1040651106378">
<Transforms>
    <Transform Algorithm=
        "http://www.w3.org/2001/10/xml-exc-c14n#"/>
</Transforms>
<DigestMethod Algorithm=
    "http://www.w3.org/2000/09/xmldsig#sha1"/>
<DigestValue>AWQKpmksMpzzT4PxcizO980gVHw=</DigestValue>
</Reference>
</SignedInfo>
<SignatureValue>
    bNhT+DsNN9PR [binary data has been truncated]
</SignatureValue>
</Signature>
```

---

15. The XML document type declaration contains or points to markup declarations that provide a grammar for a class of documents. This grammar is known as a DTD.

14.5.2 WS-Security

WS-Security provides a set of mechanisms to help developers of Web services secure SOAP message exchanges. Specifically, WS-Security describes enhancements to the existing SOAP messaging to provide *quality of protection* through the application of message integrity, message confidentiality, and single-message authentication to SOAP messages. These basic mechanisms can be combined to accommodate building a wide variety of security models using cryptographic technologies.

A *claim* is a declaration made by an entity—for example, about an entity's name, identity, key, group, privilege, capability, and so on. A *security token* is a collection of claims. Examples of security tokens include an X.509 certificate, a Kerberos ticket, and a user ID. WS-Security provides a general-purpose mechanism for associating security tokens with messages. However, WS-security does not require a specific type of security token. WS-Security is designed to be extensible—for example, by supporting multiple security-token formats—to accommodate a variety of authentication and authorization mechanisms.

Let us consider the following security scenario. A requester provides proof of identity and a signed claim of having a particular business certification. A Web service, on receiving such a message, could then determine what kind of trust to place in the claim, based on the signature.

Additionally, WS-Security describes how to encode binary security tokens and attach them to SOAP messages. In particular, the WS-Security specification esplains how to encode X.509 digital certificates (see Section 10.3.4 on page 372), Kerberos tickets, and opaque encrypted keys (see Section 11.1.4 on page 389) as samples of various binary token types. Kerberos tickets and X.509 certificates are used by developers to add authentication mechanisms to many Web applications. With WS-Security, the domain of these mechanisms can be extended by carrying authentication information in Web Services requests. WS-Security also includes extensibility mechanisms that can be used to further describe the security tokens included with a message. In this sense, WS-Security is a building block that can be used in conjunction with other Web Services protocols to address a wide variety of application security requirements.

Message integrity is provided by leveraging XML Signature and security tokens to ensure that messages have originated from the appropriate sender and were not modified in transit. WS-Security also extends XML Signature by introducing a mechanism to reference attached tokens to bind signatures to claims. Similarly, message confidentiality leverages XML Encryption and security tokens to keep portions of SOAP messages confidential.

The SOAP messaging model is based on an extensible framework. SOAP-based specifications are designed to be composed with one another to provide a rich messaging environment. As such, WS-Security by itself does not provide a complete security solution but can be used in conjunction with other Web service and application-specific mechanisms to accommodate a wide variety of existing and future security models and encryption technologies.

14.6 Web Services Security Model Principles

Web services can be accessed by sending SOAP messages to service end points identified by URIs, requesting specific actions, and receiving SOAP-message responses, including fault indications. Within this context, the broad goal of securing Web services breaks into the subsidiary goals of providing facilities for securing the integrity and confidentiality of the messages and for ensuring that the service acts only on requests in messages that express the claims required by policies.

Today, the SSL and TLS protocols are used to provide transport-level security for Web Services applications. These protocols offer several security features, including authentication, data integrity, and data confidentiality and enable point-to-point secure sessions. As a network-layer standard for transport security, IPSec may become important for Web Services. Like SSL and TLS, IPSec also provides secure sessions with application-level authentication, data integrity, and data confidentiality.

Today's Web Services application topologies include a broad combination of mobile devices, gateways, proxies, load balancers, DMZs, outsourced data centers, and globally distributed, dynamically configured systems (see Section 2.1 on page 23 and Section 6.2 on page 192). All these systems rely on the ability of message-processing intermediaries to forward messages. Specifically, the SOAP messaging model operates on logical end points that abstract the physical network and application infrastructure and therefore frequently incorporates a multihop topology with intermediate actors or roles.

When data is received and forwarded by an intermediary beyond the transport layer, both the integrity of data and any security information that flows with it may be lost. This forces any upstream message processors to rely on the security evaluations made by previous intermediaries and to completely trust their handling of the content of messages. The key point here is that sensitive information is transferred into the clear and is vulnerable to attack—combined with the fact that these intermediary systems are often edge processors, which makes them more susceptible to attack. Therefore, a comprehensive Web Services security architecture needs a mechanism that provides end-to-end security as opposed to point-to-point security. A comparison of these two approaches is shown in Figure 14.1. Successful Web Services security solutions will be able to leverage

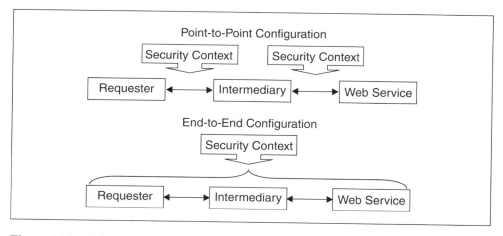

Figure 14.1.   Point-to-Point and End-to-End Configurations

network-, transport-, and application-layer security mechanisms to provide a comprehensive suite of security capabilities.

The Web Services security model described herein enables us to achieve these goals by a process in which

- A Web service can require that an incoming message prove a set of claims. If a message arrives without having the required claims, the service may ignore or reject the message.

- A requester can send messages with proof of the required claims by associating security tokens with the messages. Thus, messages both demand a specific action and prove that their sender or sender's delegate has the claim to demand the action.

- When a requester does not have the required claims, the requester or someone on the requester's behalf can try to obtain the necessary claims by contacting other Web services. These *security-token services* may in turn require their own set of claims. Security-token services broker trust between trust domains by issuing security tokens.

This model is illustrated in Figure 14.2, showing that any requester may also be a service and that the security-token service may also fully be a Web service, including expressing policy and requiring security tokens.

This general *messaging security model*—claims, policies, and security tokens—subsumes and supports several more specific models, such as identity-based security, access-control lists, and capabilities-based security. The model allows use of existing technologies, such as X.509 public-key certificates, Kerberos

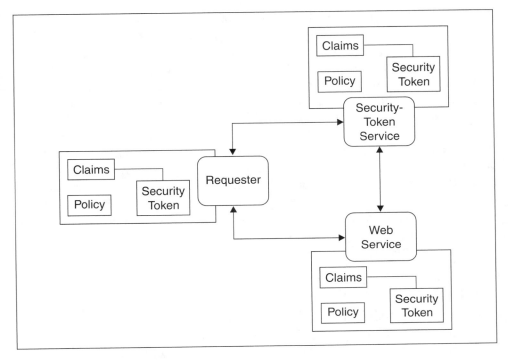

Figure 14.2. Web Services Security Model

shared-secret tickets, and even password digests, and provides an integrating abstraction allowing systems to build a bridge between security technologies. The general model is sufficient to construct higher-level key exchange, authentication, authorization, auditing, and trust mechanisms.

One of the security principles expressed in Figure 14.1 and introduced in WS-Security is the ability to provide an end-to-end propagation of a security context. This constitutes the goals and cornerstone for the Web Services security model shown in Figure 14.2. The set of the Web Services security specifications is shown in Table 14.1.

Table 14.1. Web Services Security Specifications

Layers	Specifications		
Federation	WS-SecureConversation	WS-Federation	WS-Authorization
Policy	WS-Policy	WS-Trust	WS-Privacy
Security		WS-Security	
Foundation		SOAP	

WS-Security provides the basis for the other security specifications, including a comprehensive Web Services messaging security model as described in Table 14.1. Layered on this is a *policy layer*, which includes WS-Policy, the Web Services Trust Language specification (WS-Trust), and Web Services Privacy Language specification (WS-Privacy). Together, these initial specifications provide the foundation on which to establish comprehensive, secure, and interoperable Web services across trust domains.

Building on these initial specifications, the *federation layer* includes specifications for *federated security*, which includes a Web Services Secure Conversation Language specification (WS-SecureConversation), a Web Services Federation Language specification (WS-Federation), and a Web Services Authorization Language specification (WS-Authorization). The combination of these security specifications enables many scenarios (such as the one described in Section 14.8 on page 518) that would be difficult to implement with today's basic security mechanisms.

14.6.1 Web Services Message Security

A *signed security token* is asserted and cryptographically signed by a specific authority. For example, an X.509 certificate, which asserts a binding between one's identity and public key, is an example of a signed security token. Similarly, a Kerberos ticket represents a signed security token. Conversely, a user ID is an unsigned security token.

A SOAP header provides a mechanism for associating the signature with the claims in a security token. There are several things to note.

- Such a binding is limited to those elements covered by the signature.

- This mechanism does not specify a particular method for authentication; it simply indicates that security tokens may be bound to messages.

- The message recipient may or may not trust the security tokens or may trust them only partially.

- These security-model mechanisms are not a complete solution by themselves; additional specifications are required for a complete security solution.

As we have observed, security-token claims can be either endorsed by an authority or left unendorsed. A set of endorsed claims is usually represented as a signed security token that is digitally signed or cryptographically protected by the authority. A security token can be *pushed*, or carried in a message, or the security token can be a reference that the receiver can use to *pull* the claim from the referenced authority.

Another aspect of a security model is the articulation of a trust relationship. Security tokens are useful within a trust domain. A trust domain can be articulated through a manual process, an agreement, or the implementation of a set of rules enforcing the trust policy. An unendorsed claim can thus be trusted given any established trusted channel between the sender and the receiver. For example, the unendorsed claim that the sender is Bob is sufficient for a certain receiver to believe that the sender is in fact Bob, if the sender and the receiver use a connection with a sufficient protection and there is a trusted channel between them (see page 522).

One special type of unendorsed claim is a *proof-of-possession*, data that is used in a proof process to demonstrate the sender's knowledge of information that should be known only to the claiming sender of a security token. Such a claim produces evidence that the sender has a particular piece of knowledge that is known to, or verifiable by, only appropriate actors. For example, a user ID and password pair is a security token with this type of claim. When a proof-of-possession is involved, the receiver decides whether the evidence produced is sufficient proof. This type of evidence is sometimes combined with other security tokens to prove the claims of the sender. Note that a digital signature applied to a message for the purposes of message integrity can also be interpreted as evidence of possession of part of the key pair, although in the WS-Security specification, a digital signature is not considered as a type of security token.

Protecting the message content from unauthorized access (*confidentiality*) and/or modification (*integrity*) are primary security concerns. The WS-Security specification provides a means to protect a message by encrypting and/or digitally signing the contents of the body or the header of the message.

- Message confidentiality leverages XML Encryption in conjunction with security tokens to keep portions of a SOAP message confidential. The encryption mechanisms are designed to support additional encryption processes and operations by multiple actors.

- Message integrity is provided by leveraging XML Signature in conjunction with security tokens to ensure that messages are transmitted without modifications. The integrity mechanisms are designed to support multiple signatures, potentially by multiple actors, and to be extensible to support additional signature formats.

14.6.2 WS-Policy

WS-Policy provides a general-purpose framework and corresponding syntax to describe and communicate the policies of a Web service. WS-Policy defines a base set of constructs that can be used and extended by other Web Services specifications to describe a broad range of service requirements, preferences, and capabilities.

The Web Services policy specification, detailed in Figure 14.3, includes

- The WS-Policy document, which defines the general grammar for expressing Web services policies

- The Web Services Policy Attachment specification (WS-PolicyAttachment) document, which defines how to attach these policies to Web services

- Two policy-assertion documents: the Web Services General Policy Assertions Language specification (WS-PolicyAssertions) and the Web Services Security Policy Language specification (WS-SecurityPolicy)

WS-Policy is designed to allow extensibility. *Policy* is a broad term that encompasses a range of disciplines, such as security, reliability, and privacy. Similarly, the ability to express policies is not limited to the expression of general policies or security policies. The set of WS-Policy specifications shown in Figure 14.3 adds another mechanism to the WS-Security portfolio, but policy expression is not limited to security policies. The intent is for the basic policy framework to accommodate the expression of domain-specific policy languages in a way that leverages domain knowledge within a consistent Web Services framework.

WS-PolicyAttachment offers several ways to advertise policy assertions for Web services. It builds on the existing WSDL and UDDI specifications but also supports extensibility. It allows for combining domain-specific policies with common policies for Web services. A typical example is a requesting Web service that may look for a service provider that offers processing in a particular human language, such as Italian. The requesting Web service thus applies a policy assertion—the need for Italian-language support. The provider could also make this assertion by advertising that it can offer its service in Italian. The WS-Policy-Assertions language offers this type of common policy expression by defining a generic set of policy assertions for Web services.

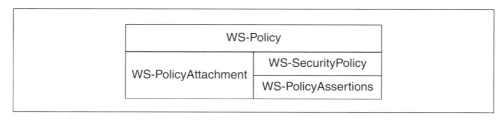

Figure 14.3. Set of WS-Policy Specifications

Security is a domain. To illustrate security policies, the WS-SecurityPolicy specification expresses assertions needed to support security tokens, integrity, and confidentiality as defined in WS-Security.

As we discuss in Section 14.6.3, in the Web Services paradigm, the trust between a service requester and a service provider is established through the exchange of information between the two parties in an expected and understood manner. The description of this expected behavior within the security space can be called a *trust policy*. The WS-Policy framework supports trust partners' expressing and exchanging their statements of trust. Often, this expression of a broad level of trust between entities is built on the exchange of security tokens to provide the elements for a secure conversation.

14.6.3   WS-Trust

The WS-Trust specification starts the work of defining trust relationships by defining a set of interfaces for requesting security tokens. It is designed to support the creation of multiple security-token formats, as described in WS-Security, to accommodate a variety of security practices, including authentication, authorization, and secure conversations.

In general, a Web service has a policy applied to it, receives a message from a requester that possibly includes security tokens, and may have some protection applied to it using Web Services security mechanisms. For example, a Web service security configuration requires that the Web service requester provide an authorization token in order to access certain service enhancements. The authorization token might be generated by a security-token service, which takes in a proof of identity and a request for a signed claim that the named identity has a particular business certification. This authorization token can then be supplied in a request to the Web service, which has expressed trust in such a signed claim.

The trust engine of a Web service performs the following key steps:

1. Verifies that the claims in the token are sufficient to comply with the policy and that the message conforms to the policy.

2. Verifies that the claims are proved by the signatures, that is, performed with keys associated with the necessary attributes. In brokered trust models, the signature may verify the identity not of the claimant but of the intermediary, who may simply assert the identity of the claimant. The claims are either proved or not, based on policy.

3. Verifies that the issuers of the security tokens, including all related and ancestral security tokens, are trusted to issue the claims they have made. The trust engine may need to send tokens to a security-token service in order to exchange them for other security tokens it can use directly in its

evaluation. This step may include token-signature hierarchy validation, performed by validating a CA chain (see Section 10.3.4 on page 372).

If these conditions are met and the requester is authorized to perform the operation, the Web service can process the Web service request within the specified trust model.

Asserting trust can be done in many ways, and assessing the presence of a trust relationship can be done by either of two methods. WS-Trust describes these two methods, which depend on whether the assessment is based on information from within a message flow (*in-band*) or external to a message flow (*out-of-band*).

1. **In-band.**   As part of a message flow, a request may be made of a security-token service to exchange a security token, or some proof, of one form for another. The exchange request can be made either by a requester or by another party on the requester's behalf. The security-token service trusts the provided security token—because, for example, it trusts the issuing authority of the provided security token, and if the request can prove possession of that security token, the exchange is processed by the security-token service. This is an example of an *in-band direct-trust relationship*.

    In the case of a *delegated request*—one in which another party, the *delegate*, provides the request to a service on behalf of the requester—the delegate may need to make a request to a security-token service to exchange the original token provided by the client for one that is acceptable to the target service. The exchanging security-token service may in turn submit a request to another security-token service to generate the new token. The generating security-token service may not need to directly trust the authority that issued the original token. In that case, the exchanging security-token service would trust the original token authority, and the generating security-token service would trust the exchanging security-token service.

2. **Out-of-Band.**   An administrator or other trusted authority may designate that all tokens of a certain type are trusted. The security-token service maintains this trust axiom and can communicate it to trust engines to make their own trust decisions or can revoke it later. Alternatively, the security-token service may provide this function as a service to trusting services.

14.6.4 WS-SecureConversation

WS-SecureConversation takes the designation of trust based on security tokens to the next level by demonstrating how tokens can be used within the context of these policy-defined trusted relationships to allow requesters and providers to securely exchange information over the duration of a conversation. Whereas WS-Trust defines the behavior of overall trust relationships, WS-SecureConversation focuses on defining a security context—security token—for secure communications.

14.6.5   WS-Privacy

The purpose of WS-Privacy is to descibe the syntax and semantics for binding privacy policies to Web services and instances of data in messages. The main emphasis of WS-Privacy lies in enabling policies to be processed by Web service providers and requesters, in contrast to interfacing to human users on a precise meaning and on usability in chains of Web services within or across enterprises. WS-Privacy builds on WS-Policy and related standards. WS-Privacy does not define a new privacy-policy language but offers the means to bind such existing languages to a Web service.

14.6.6   WS-Federation

Federation is the overall term used to refer to the set of distinct, heterogeneous enterprises that wish to provide a user with a single-sign-on, ease-of-use experience. Enterprises can be corporate entities, Internet service providers, or associations of individuals. A federated environment differs from a traditional single-sign-on environment in that no preestablished rules limit how enterprises transfer information about a user. Policy rules may have been preestablished for an enterprise's participation in the federation. Within a federated environment, enterprises provide services that deal with authenticating users, accepting *authentication assertions*—also referred to as *authentication tokens*—supplied by other enterprises, and providing some form of translation of the identity of the vouched-for user into one that is understood within the local enterprise. Therefore, the goal of WS-Federation is to define mechanisms that are used to enable identity, attribute, authentication, and authorization federation across trust domains.

14.6.7   WS-Authorization

The purpose of WS-Authorization is to describe how access policies for a Web service are specified and managed. In particular, the goal is to describe how claims may be specified within security tokens and how these claims will be interpreted at the end point.

The goal of WS-Authorization is to be flexible and extensible with respect to both authorization format and authorization language. This enables the widest range of scenarios and ensures the long-term viability of the security framework.

14.6.8 Example

Let us use a travel agency scenario to illustrate some of these concepts. Fabrikam456 Travel Agency Company offers its travel services through several business portals to provide air, hotel, and car rental services to its customers. Fabrikam456 needs to establish trust relationships with its partners through these portals.

Fabrikam456 would like to offer an integrated set of services to its customers whereby a requester could submit a single request for hotel, airline, and vehicle. Fabrikam456 would like also the flexibility to extend the services for its partners on the basis of a variety of criteria: gold service, preferred customers, and so on. The policy for one of its partners, RentalCars456, might include a security policy requirement for a RentalCars456 security token to establish the user's identity, as well as a business application requirement stating the cancellation policy for reservations. The policy for another partner, UnitedCars456, might include a requirement for UnitedCars456 preferred-customer numbers.

Because Fabrikam456 supports various business relationships, it needs to be able to determine which travel services to invoke for which customer. How can the WS-Security standards help in automating the trust relationships for Fabrikam456 to quickly and securely offer integrated travel services as part of the customer's trusted portal environment?

Fabrikam456 could assume the registration tasks for all its partners and issue customers a Fabrikam456 user name and identifier. In this case, Fabrikam456 provides a veneer for its partners. Before a request is processed, Fabrikam456 checks the policy for a partner—for example, RentalCars456—notifies the user of the cancellation policy, and asks whether the request should be processed. Once approved, the request could be augmented by Fabrikam456 with additional security tokens, based on the user's identity, the privacy policy, and other business policies. For example, suppose that the user is an employee of a certain company, qualifies for gold service, and has a credit limit of $10,000. Fabrikam456 needs to have established trust relationships with the relevant companies and determine which additional tokens need to be supplied with each reservation request.

Alternatively, Fabrikam456 could act as a clearinghouse, redirect all requests from each user to any partner, and let the partner challenge the user for authentication and notify the customer of the policy. Although Fabrikam456 as a clearinghouse might earn advertising revenue, it needs to provide value as a travel service. In this second scenario, Fabrikam456 could offer a security-token service for its new business partners. For example, RentalCars456 may prefer to outsource the management of user information. In this case, RentalCars456 sees the advantage of not doing its own credit processing and may choose to take advantage of Fabrikam456's additional service by taking each authenticated request and calling the security-token service to retrieve credit approval from Fabrikam456.

Credit services might require additional security measures. WS-Security-Policy assertions give Fabrikam456 and RentalCars456 the ability to express additional security policies that the messages between Fabrikam456 and Rental-Cars456, which both adhere to the WS-Security specification, must provide. For example, RentalCars456 may require that all credit assertions be digitally signed and contain an expiration time.

14.7 Application Patterns

This section examines two patterns of evolving Web services from existing Web applications.

1. One pattern is the *browser-to-server pattern*, which wraps an existing application as a service using a SOAP message as the service invocation. The Web server provides a runtime execution container that defines its own security model with policy information derived from a deployment descriptor configured by the Deployer of the Web application (see Section 3.7.3 on page 70). This pattern typically includes a mechanism for associating the identity of the invoking entity—the Web browser client—with the executing application instance and allows the application to continue to function as it did before.

   In the J2EE instance, this would manifest itself as the creation of a CSIv2 identity assertion (see Section 3.12 on page 97). A CSIv2 identity assertion uses an *implicit trust model* in the sense that the client and the server rely on the middleware configuration to ensure that the identity is established within a security context provided by the J2EE environment itself. An advantage of this model is that the runtime maintains the ID-mapping and name-assertion lifetime constraints, whereas mechanisms for maintaining a valid token can be provided by the middleware. A disadvantage is that the model for delegating an identity requires that the delegated application-level identity be the same as the invocation identity of the intermediary and hence the security context. This creates a coupling between the middleware and the application-level delegation logic—the run-as deployment descriptor element in J2EE—and another coupling between the middleware and the requirement for the security context to support cascaded delegation, auditing, and nonrepudiation.

2. The second pattern involves rewriting the application with a modular design to create smaller tasks that can be combined in different ways to perform more complicated transactions. Each component is able to externalize its output into a *message* that the following component can take as

input. This pattern uses SOAP messages to trigger each event. The messaging agents and message queues can be built into the runtime server below the application level. Sometimes, the messaging agents become the security-aware part of the runtime and control the flow of information along its path, based on security attributes in the header of the message.

Sometimes, the security attributes get added into the message structure itself, as is the case with digital signatures. The trust model for this type of messaging relies on the specification of an explicit trust model. In this model, the trust will be *explicit*, or *direct*, in the sense that the client and the server rely on coupling the identity information along with the message explicitly and thus do not rely on the underlying security context. This requires that the service handler be able to establish the identity of the caller, based on the WS-Security `UsernameToken` element, which is specified in the SOAP header, and based on the trust on the entity that created the assertion tokens. Thus, in a direct, or explicit, trust model, an authentication/authorization authority has to be known and digitally sign the assertions at the time of the authentication/authorization event. A certificate associated with the signature can be used to identify the trusted authority and validate the signature. A trusted timestamp is included to indicate the assertion validity period. An advantage of this type of trust model is that the message can pass through multiple intermediaries. Authorization and delegation decisions can be made in a standard way by the intermediaries without modifying the name assertion of the originator of the message request.

If implemented in an *enveloped* way, it is also possible to build audit trails capable of asserting evidence of nonrepudiation, as each intermediary could wrap a message with its own name assertion. A disadvantage of this model is that the end point has to do some additional processing to make sure that the originator name assertion is valid both from a trust standpoint and a time standpoint.

Both patterns implement security in the runtime, and both rely on a mapping of an external form of an identity into a runtime interpretation of that identity and into a set of rules about the identity and its capabilities. The differences relate to who does the mapping and whether the information is in an externalized form that can be middleware independent and persistent.

14.8 Use Scenario

Let us take a very simple scenario whereby a travel agency system contacts an airlines reservation system in order to complete a travel transaction request. The two applications—the Travel Agency Web service and the Airlines Web service, respectively—use XML to exchange travel itinerary information and payment details, using a well-understood industry-standard specification. The industry specification states that when making reservations, the applications always mark them with the `makeReservation` tag.

The Fabrikam456 Travel Agency Company's application is designed to accept a reservation request with a `makeReservation` tag from a customer. Based on the airline details requested, the application will contact the airline's reservation service. The Airlines456 Company's application is designed to perform a transaction under which a reservation for the passenger is made and charged to the credit card system. Note that the airline can even contact the credit card company's charging service in order to perform that operation.

A user surfs for the best-possible travel deal and decides to purchase the ticket from the Fabrikam456 Travel Agency Company. The user submits a request to access the agency's reservation Web service by specifying the itinerary and credit card details in a SOAP message marked with a `makeReservation` tag. The agency application requests a reservation to be made to the airline reservation system by sending in a booking request from the agency, providing both the agency's details and the passenger's details. When the airline system receives the booking request, the application looks in the database for the availability of seats for that particular itinerary. Using XML, the airline application will return a response after making the reservation in its back-end system. The response marks the details with record-locator number and fare basic code details, using the `recordLocator` tag, as shown next:

```
<recordLocator>ABCXYZ123</recordLocator>
```

When the travel agency receives the message from the airline, the application scans it for the `recordLocator` tag. On finding it, the application passes the data into its system to issue a ticket to the end user.

The Web service that provides the reservation service in a service network can be combined with other Web services, such as a weather Web service to obtain the weather forecast for the travel destination, and a credit Web service to charge the end user for the travel expense. This way, Fabrikam456 Travel Agency Company can automatically issue tickets and schedule ticket delivery with shipping companies through the Fabrikam456 Web service.

This example describes a simple Web service in which two or more functions cooperate through the Web, and the nature of their cooperation adapts to parameters provided by a particular request. As you can see, Web Services technology provides a framework for *loosely coupled*, or *dynamic*, application integration.

14.9 Web Services Provider Security

In the previous section, we showed how loosely coupled applications can be integrated to provide a Web Services-based e-business solution. Users can invoke Web services using one of the supported protocols. For example, users can submit their SOAP requests over HTTP, and the requests are processed by the Web service engine. When Web services are used to provide business-related data, the data needs to be secured like any other data.

The Web application server that hosts the Web service engines can support various protocols. Sometimes, owing to the bundling of security with protocols, we need to begin to categorize the tasks to be performed as either transport-layer or message-layer security tasks and assign them to the appropriate handlers.

- A *transport-protocol-specific handler* can process protocol-specific information. In the case of HTTP, the handler might perform HTTP authentication and establish the context prior to the SOAP engine's getting a chance to process the message.

- A *transport-protocol-agnostic handler* can perform authorization based on authentication information, regardless of the transport. In the case of message-level security, the SOAP engine would handle the security tokens in the SOAP message, establish a security context, validate the signatures, and decrypt the message, as appropriate.

Once the user is authenticated, the Web service security provider should determine whether the invoking user has the authority to invoke the service. This authorization decision is based on the authorization policy associated with the Web service. In a J2EE environment, where the service is likely implemented as an enterprise bean, the authorization policy for the enterprise bean would be based on J2EE roles.

14.9.1 User Authentication

In order to secure access to a Web service, the user requesting the service needs to be identified through an underlying authentication mechanism, as shown in Figure 14.4.

An identity needs to be associated with a request in order to enforce authorization policies. A Web service security configuration should declare authentication policies that specify how to retrieve and verify the user credentials, or *authentication data*.

- In the J2EE security model, the login configuration policy specifies how a user's authentication data is retrieved (see Section 3.9.1 on page 76 and

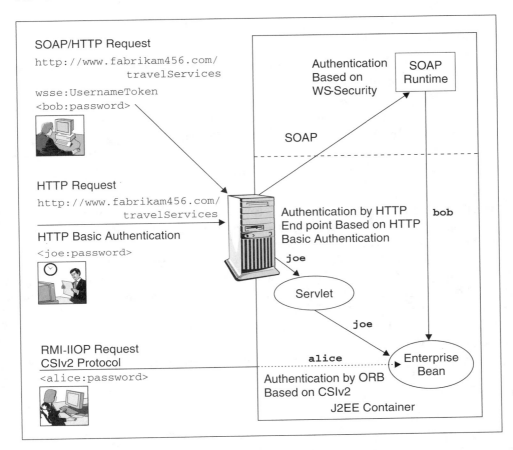

Figure 14.4. Web Services Authentication

Section 4.5.1 on page 113), whereas policies specific to the operational environment will dictate how the user gets authenticated—for example, using the Kerberos authentication mechanism.

- In the WS-Security model, the login configuration should address not only authentication of *immediate clients*—clients submitting the request directly to the service—but also the mode in which an end client's identity may be part of the request. (Requests can traverse through many intermediaries.) This information is necessary for both the client—to submit the credential information in a format understood by the server—and the server—to retrieve the credential information from the transport layer or message itself.

The WSDL definition of the service may include security constraints on how the credential information is expected to be provided or retrieved. These constraints will be expressed by the runtime, using WS-Policy and the related specifications.

- An HTTP-bound service can expect data to be supplied through HTTP basic authentication.

- In the case of a Web service that can be accessed through an intermediary, the configuration should indicate that the credential information is expected as part of the message itself. For instance, the configuration can say that the authentication information is expected in the WS-Security message header, which is represented by the `wsse:Security` XML element in the SOAP header.

Based on these two possibilities, we can categorize that authentication data as supplied using transport-level security or message-level security, as when it is part of the WS-Security header.

Depending on the topology, a user may get authenticated by the Web service engine or up front before the Web service engine is handed the request. For example, when a user submits a request to the servlet that dispatches the Web service request, the user might be challenged by a front-end secure reverse proxy server, using the HTTP 401 challenge mechanism to prompt the user to submit a user ID and password pair.

In order to handle the authentication data that gets passed around through various means, a Web service engine can support both transport-level and message-level security.

- In a J2EE environment in which HTTP is the transport protocol used, the HTTP-specific handler, a servlet, can invoke the `getUserPrincipal()` method in the `javax.servlet.http.HttpServletRequest` interface to retrieve the identity of the user. If the user is not already authenticated as far as the underlying system is concerned, the container should authenticate the user, based on the credentials sent over the transport: for example, the user ID and password in the HTTP header.

- If the authentication credentials are sent over in the message itself, the SOAP engine will retrieve that authentication data and validate the assertion. In such cases, it may be possible to specify the authentication method as part of the Web service deployment descriptor. In other words, a Web service can be protected through mechanisms that are similar to expressing the `login-config` element in the `web.xml` deployment descriptor for a Web resource (see Section 3.9.1 on page 76 and Section 4.5.1 on page 113). Even though this option is not a J2EE standard yet, mechanisms specific to the Web service provider will be available to provide it. For example, IBM WebSphere[16] provides a mechanism whereby authentication, signature, and encryption requirements for protecting a Web service can be specified as part of a deployment descriptor that gets packaged with the Web service.

14.9.2 Authorization Enforcement

The authorization policies of a Web service can be enforced according to the authorization policies of the application environment. For example, when a Web service is implemented as an enterprise bean, the EJB authorization rules of the J2EE environment will apply.

In order for the Web service provider to enforce security constraints on Web services, the security policies need to be declaratively conveyed to the runtime authorization policy end point to ensure portability of the service from one WAS to another. Using this approach, the Web service provider infrastructure can take care of defining the security policies, and the Web service developers need not know how to programmatically enforce all possible authorization policies. This helps a service to be deployed in various servers, and the appropriate mechanism will be expected to enforce the policies.

As shown in Figure 14.5, user Bob, who is a registered Customer, is granted the permission to make travel reservations using TravelService. This security policy should be declared in the deployment descriptor of the service implementation—in this case, TravelServiceBean, which is the enterprise bean providing the implementation behind the TravelService Web service. This is demonstrated by the deployment descriptor fragment in Listing 14.2.

Listing 14.2. Web Service Deployment Descriptor Fragment

```
<method-permission>
    <role-name>Customer</role-name>
    <method>
        <ejb-name>TravelServiceBean</ejb-name>
        <method-name>makeReservation</method-name>
    </method>
</method-permission>
```

In order for an authorization check to succeed, the user invoking the service should have at least one of the roles required to access the Web service. The mechanisms by which users and user groups are granted application roles are specific to the operational environment.

---

16. See http://www.ibm.com/websphere.

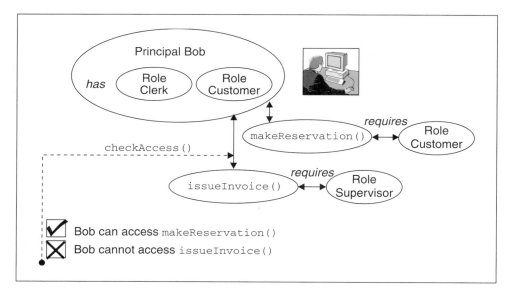

Figure 14.5. Authorization Scenario

As the scenario of Figure 14.5 and the deployment descriptor fragment of Listing 14.2 show, the `makeReservation()` method on the TravelServiceBean implementation behind the TravelService Web service requires the role Customer. For example, if user Bob makes a request, his identity gets asserted in the WS-Security header. The security authorization handler will make the authorization decision, based on the asserted identity of the caller invoking the service. The ability to specify the authorization policy declaratively helps decouple the application security policy from organizational security policies while still effectively enforcing overall application security requirements.

Given that the authorization may be based on the service implementation, better protection is achieved by implementing the service as an enterprise bean and using the EJB role-based authorization facilities. If the service implementation is a Java bean,[17] the EJB role-based authorization does not apply. If SOAP is used in combination with HTTP (see Section 14.2 on page 499), one can protect the URL that leads to the SOAP engine processing the request. For example, in the TravelService scenario described earlier, if the service implementation is a Java bean and SOAP is used in combination with HTTP, one can protect the URL `http://www.fabrikam456.com/travelServices`. Note that this does not allow for operation-level, or method-level, protection. Also, if many services can be

---

17. See `http://java.sun.com/products/javabeans/`.

accessed through the same URI (`/travelServices`), they all will have the same protection characteristics.

In conclusion, security should be considered not only after implementing a Web service but also before making the decision on how the Web service should be implemented. As technology evolves, it is possible that more fine-grained authorization can be applied, based on the SOAP message contents. At that point, the authorization mechanisms built around the Web service implementation can be combined with those based on the SOAP message contents.

14.10 Security Considerations

A Web Services security model should address security issues starting from an end client to a target service, including the intermediary services that route the service requests. This chapter has proposed a mechanism for the client to provide authentication data, based on the service definition, and at the same time, for the service provider to retrieve that data. A proposed authorization approach, based on a declarative authorization policy model, can be used by the service provider to enforce authorization constraints. Understanding the necessity and complexity in established trust in the Web Services model, this chapter has also proposed how XML Signature and XML Encryption can be used to achieve a level of trust. Additionally, this chapter has illustrated that, as part of its evolution, the Web Services paradigm for application development can be seen as an opportunity to introduce a method of coupling security technologies—authentication, authorization, digital signatures, and so on—with business trust issues, such as PKI policy, role-based access control, and firewalls. This leads to the creation of core Web security services configured through policies expressed in XML. As the base Web Services technology evolves, more complex scenarios will need to be thought about and handled in the future.

14.11 Futures

As work to secure Web services continues, we can also consider this an opportunity to evaluate Web Services offerings through the lens of risk assessment. No Web service is impenetrable to attack. Every offering of a Web service implies the notion of risk; whether on the Internet or on an intranet, there is always a risk when a Web service interface is externally exposed. The following questions arise.

- What is the scope of the exposure?
- How can the exposure be offset against the potential value of the service?
- Who is responsible for the enforcement of any countermeasures used to prevent the service interface from being exploited?

To be able to supply a complete Web Services environment in which risk assessment and policy enforcement are an integral component will depend on several initiatives continuing to evolve as de facto standards.

- Workflow needs to develop an integrated security model into its processing model.

- Some analysis will need to be done to see whether XML schemas can be used to formalize security models through the definition of security types.

- WSDL V1.2 needs to be extended to contain security attributes and, potentially, policy information as outlined in WS-Policy. Specifically, the area of specifying PKI policies will be important for interoperability in the more dynamic Web services that involve late binding.

- The emerging W3C and OASIS activities to define the processing rules and key-management services for XML applications must be well integrated with the other Web Services specifications.

CHAPTER **15**

Security Considerations for Container Providers

ANY sound specification should be backed by a solid implementation that adheres to the specification; is secure, reliable, and administrable; and performs well. A J2EE container implementation should provide these qualities while adhering to the J2EE specification. This chapter discusses security considerations that a container provider should take into account while designing and implementing a J2EE container. This chapter also provides an approach to implementing a container runtime by making use of available technologies, including Java security technologies. For example, authentication, authorization, and delegation facilities within a J2EE container can be implemented based on existing Java security technologies.

This chapter starts by discussing the environment in which J2EE containers are deployed and then discusses how JAAS `LoginModules` can provide a modular and pluggable mechanism to achieve authentication. Authorization implementation comprises administration facilities and a runtime implementation. This chapter discusses an interpretation of security roles as a set of permissions and explains how to achieve better administration, as well as the abstraction of various organizational roles that are involved in application development, deployment, and administration.

15.1 Understanding the Environment

In order to architect a J2EE-compliant hosting environment—in other words, a Web application server—it is important to understand the environment in which it will be deployed. Such an environment may have to support a set of authentication mechanisms that generate credentials to represent an identity, user registries that contain the user account information, authorization policies that need to be managed, authorization providers that should be accommodated to make access decisions, and secure communication between processes. Understanding a secure end-to-end request flow helps in making sense of these requirements.

Figure 15.1 depicts the end-to-end flow of a J2EE request and shows the security aspects of such a flow (see also Section 3.12 on page 97). A request from an HTTP client typically gets routed through an HTTP listener and dispatcher, such as a Web server, to an appropriate Web container that handles the incoming request. A secure request will typically be submitted over an HTTP connection over the SSL protocol—an HTTPS request. In these cases, the Web server will act as the SSL termination point. The Web server can either be a stand-alone unit or a component in the Web container listening to HTTP requests. In the case of a stand-alone Web server, a request to a J2EE resource, such as a servlet, will be routed to an appropriate Web container.

Based on servlet matching rules, the Web container will process the request and associate a Web application with the request. The user will be authenticated based on the URL pattern and the protection policy of the URI defined in that Web application. After successful authentication, access to the resource will be allowed

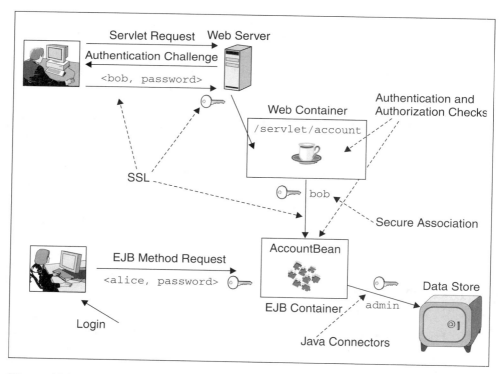

Figure 15.1. End-to-End Security Request Flow

if the user submitting the request is granted one of the required roles associated with the URI. The Web container is then responsible for setting the security context for proceeding with the execution of the servlet. The Web container is also responsible for satisfying the requirements of programmatic APIs, such as the `getUserPrincipal()` and the `isUserInRole()` servlet methods in the `javax.servlet.http.HttpServletRequest` interface.

When the servlet invokes an enterprise bean, the request is forwarded to the EJB container, possibly in a different Web application server. In this case, the Web container and the EJB container should initiate a secure session to establish a trust relationship between them. As part of the secure association, the communication link between the containers should be over a secure channel: for example, an SSL session. If this request is over IIOP, the CSIv2 protocol can be used to establish the secure association between the containers. Once such a session is established, the identity of the requester—or the resultant identity based on the delegation policy—is forwarded to the EJB container.

When a request for an EJB invocation arrives at an EJB container, the container is responsible for validating the user identity propagated by the Web container. Once the credential is validated and a security context is established, authorization to the EJB request will be enforced by the container, based on the authorization policies associated with the enterprise bean. As in the case of a Web application, the security context will be maintained so that the container can satisfy the requirements of programmatic APIs, such as the `getCallerPrincipal()` and the `isCallerInRole()` methods in the `javax.ejb.EJBContext` interface.

Sometimes, business logic implemented as an enterprise bean needs to access non-J2EE applications or data stores. In such a case, the Connection Manager implementation of the container must adhere to the Java connector framework and facilitate the mapping of the requesting identity to an identity, or credential, that can be used by the target resource adapter.

The end-to-end security scenario discussed in this section provides some context to help J2EE Container Providers to implement the runtime. The following sections illustrate an approach to building a WAS, using Java-based security technologies where appropriate.

15.2 Authentication

The purpose of authentication is to verify the identity of a requesting entity. Typically, this entity is an end user requesting access to a resource, such as a URL or an enterprise bean. Authentication in enterprise environments may also include authenticating other entities, such as servers. For example, in order to trust a Web container, an EJB may end up authenticating an identity associated with the Web container.

The process of authentication involves verifying the authentication data provided by an identity. Authentication data may be a user ID and password pair or a security credential, such as an X.509 certificate, a Kerberos ticket, or other forms of acceptable credentials. Based on the security level of an environment, identity may also be asserted.[1] In such cases, the validity of the assertion will be based on the trust relationship between the asserting authority and the validating end point.

15.2.1 Authentication Mechanisms

A J2EE container's authentication framework typically consists of an authentication mechanism and a user registry (see Figure 15.2). The authentication mechanism is responsible for processing authentication data. The result of this process is a set of authenticated credentials. Depending on the type of authentication mechanism and the authentication data, the authentication mechanism may in turn consult a user registry to verify the authentication data. For example, if the authentication data is a user ID and password pair and if the user registry is an LDAP directory, the authentication mechanism will verify the password by performing an LDAP bind against the directory. A successful authentication will result in a set of authenticated credentials. If Kerberos is an authentication mechanism, the resultant credential will be a Keberos ticket.

Considering the flow of request given in Figure 15.1 on page 528, the user ID and password will be validated by the Web container. On successful authentication, the credential—for example, a Kerberos ticket—will be propagated for the

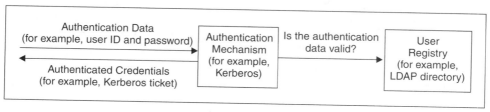

Figure 15.2. The Process of Authentication

---

1. *Identity assertion* is the foundation of a general-purpose impersonation mechanism that makes it possible for an intermediary to act on behalf of an identity other than itself. An intermediary's authority to act on behalf of another identity may be based on trust by the target in the intermediary, or on trust by the target in a privilege authority that endorses the intermediary to act as proxy for the asserted identity. Identity assertion may be used by an intermediary to assume the identity of its callers in its calls.

downstream requests. When the request is handled by the EJB container, it will perform authentication by validating the Kerberos ticket.

15.2.2 Using JAAS `LoginModules`

In a Java environment, the implementation of an authentication mechanism can be realized through one or more login modules, implemented in JAAS as objects of type `javax.security.auth.spi.LoginModule` (see Chapter 9 on page 289). WASs can use the JAAS framework to authenticate a set of credentials through a login module. The result of a login is a JAAS subject, implemented as an object of type `javax.security.auth.Subject`. The authenticated credential can be part of the `Subject` that is returned from the `LoginModule`. Using JAAS `LoginModules` allows for an extensible framework so that any `LoginModule` can be plugged into the container environment and possibly even be stacked with other `LoginModules`.

In the context of CSIv2, enough information needs to be propagated from one container to another so that an identity can be established within the second container. In this case, a credential from a JAAS `Subject` can be extracted and serialized as a security token for use by the CSIv2 protocol. On the receiving end, a `Subject` can be reconstructed by validating the incoming token, using the configured `LoginModule`. This approach allows `LoginModules` to be used for authentication and validation, thus facilitating authentication and delegation in a secure end-to-end request flow.

15.2.3 User Information

A J2EE container is responsible for answering the queries through the J2EE APIs, such as the EJB methods `isCallerInRole()` and `getCallerPrincipal()`, and the servlet methods `isUserInRole()` and `getUserPrincipal()`. In the case of `getCallerPrincipal()` and `getUserPrincipal()`, the object to be returned is a `java.security.Principal`. Applications using this mechanism to obtain the user name call the `getName()` method on the returned `Principal` object. The container should return a user name that is useful for the application. For example, when using an LDAP directory for authentication, `getName()` should return the Distinguished Name of the user. As enterprise environments may consist of multiple user registries, it may also be useful to provide a user name qualified by the name of the security domain.

15.2.4 Single Sign-On

Propagating identity to downstream servers allows user identity to be available to applications accessed within a call chain. In the case of HTTP, many Web applications can be hosted in different Web containers. In such scenarios, the Web containers are required to provide a mechanism to maintain user identity across HTTP requests. If the same credential is made available across requests to Web containers, a user will not be prompted more than once for authentication data. This addresses the need for single sign-on for HTTP requests.

User idenity across HTTP request can be maintained in at least two ways.

1. One way is to pass the credential as an HTTP cookie or part of the URL through a URL-rewriting mechanism. With this approach, the credential is sent back to the user, and the browser will send it back to the servers to which it sends requests. Servers can extract this information from the HTTP request, establish the requesting identity by validating the incoming credential, and authorize requests accordingly. If HTTP cookies are used, their configuration should consider the possibility of replay attacks, man-in-the-middle attacks, and so on. Using the `Secure` field of the cookie will ensure that such sensitive cookies are never transmitted in the clear but only over an HTTPS connection.

2. An alternative approach in the case of J2EE is to store the credential in a `javax.servlet.http.HTTPSession` object. This approach has the advantage of letting the credential maintenance rely on the session maintenance and the infrastructure behind it. The disadvantage is that if a session is hijacked, the credentials inside it will be too.

Maintaining *application-state information* (session) independent of *authentication-state information* (credential) makes it possible to achieve SSO across J2EE and non-J2EE applications as well. It is also desirable to span multiple application sessions across a single authentication state and vice versa. This enables the HTTP session timeout to be independent of the authentication credential timeout. Therefore, it is advantageous to have the ability to maintain HTTP session state information and authentication state information independently of each other.

15.3 Authorization

Authorization in a J2EE environment is based on the concept of roles. A user who has been granted at least one of the required roles is allowed to access a resource, such as a method in an enterprise bean. In the J2EE deployment descriptor, role names are associated with a set of method permissions and security constraints. The containers are responsible for mapping users and groups to these roles so that an authorization decision can be made when a resource is accessed. There are at least two ways to implement a role-based authorization engine: the role-permission model and the role-privilege model.

The role-permission interpretation of the J2EE security model considers a *role* to be a set of permissions and uses the role name defined in the `method-permission` and `security-constraint` descriptors as the label to a set of permissions. A permission defines a resource—the enterprise bean to which a `method-permission` descriptor applies or a URI described in a `security-constraint` descriptor—and a set of actions—remote EJB methods or HTTP methods. For example, a Teller role may be associated with a set of permissions to invoke the `getBalance()` method on an `AccountBean` enterprise bean and to perform a GET invocation over HTTP to a `/finance/account` URI. If multiple `method-permission` descriptors refer to the same role, they are consolidated so that a single set of permissions is associated with the role name, likely within the scope of that application.

Administrators define authorization policies for the roles in their application. This is done by associating subjects to a role, an operation that grants each subject the permissions associated with that role. This effectively grants the subject access to the enterprise bean methods and to the URIs permitted by that role.

The *method-permission table* represents the association of a role to a set of permissions (see Table 3.1 on page 84). Based on the J2EE security model, a method can be accessed by a user who has at least one of the roles associated with the method. The roles associated with a method form the set of *required roles* to perform an action. The roles associated with a subject form the set of *granted roles* to that subject. A subject will be allowed to perform an action if the subject's granted roles contain *at least* one of the required roles to perform that action.

An *authorization table*, or *protection matrix*, represents the association of a role to subjects (see Table 3.2 on page 84). In such a table, the role is defined as the *security object*, and users and groups are defined as *security subjects*.

According to the J2EE security model, it is responsibility of the Application Assembler to associate actions on protected resources to sets of required roles. The Deployer refines and configures the policies specified by the Application Assembler when the application is installed into a WAS. Association of roles to subjects can be performed when the application gets installed in a WAS or at a later time, as part of security administration.

An alternative approach to implement role-based authorization is to treat a role as a privilege attribute, typically a user group. For example, if a role name is Manager, a user group named Manager should be defined in the user registry. This model has advantages and disadvantages.

- This approach has the advantage of maintaining only one table—the method-permission table—because the subject who is assigned a role is implicitly a user group that has the identical name. In the example given in

Table 3.1 on page 84, user groups with the names Teller and Supervisor will be defined in the user registry.

- This approach has the disadvantage that for every role defined in an application, a user group needs to be defined in the system. If two applications use the same role name, care should be taken to ensure that the users who are members of a user group identical to the defined role names are allowed to access both applications.

  Additionally, in order to manage users and groups in a user registry and associate them at will with user groups named identical to roles, the user registry would need to support nested groups. For example, if the Supervisor role should be assigned to the HRManagers user group, the HRManagers user group should be a subgroup of the Supervisor user group. This may be difficult to achieve in practice because not every user registry supports nested groups. Thus, unlike the role-permission model, the role-privilege model imposes a structure on the underlying user registry.

Regardless of which model is used to achieve role-based authorization, the container runtime will need to make runtime authorization decisions each time an attempt is made to access a resource. For example, when the `getBalance()` method in the AccountBean enterprise bean is invoked, the container must make an authorization decision to verify whether the invocation is allowed. As the J2SE permission security model (see Chapter 8 on page 253) augmented by JAAS (see Chapter 9 on page 289) is rich enough to check permissions based on a subject, it is logical to use the J2SE permission model to perform access checks. Therefore, containers can invoke the `java.lang.SecurityManager`'s `checkPermission()` method. This also implies that J2EE resources and methods will need to be modeled by different permission types. In Java 2, permissions are implemented as `java.security.Permission` objects (see Section 8.2 on page 258).

The process of authorization starts from the time of application installation. When an application is installed, the deployment descriptor information that is stored with the application is read by the container deployment tools. The subject-to-role mapping is effectively managed using the tools provided by the container and/or security provider. Such tools must allow changing the permission-to-role mapping. Effectively, a set of policy management tools will help manage the security policies associated with authorization to access the various J2EE components. When a resource is accessed, the container will consult the authorization runtime provided by the security provider to verify whether the user accessing a resource can be allowed to perform the operation. The security provider may be the same vendor as the container provider or a different one. These steps are illustrated in Figure 15.3.

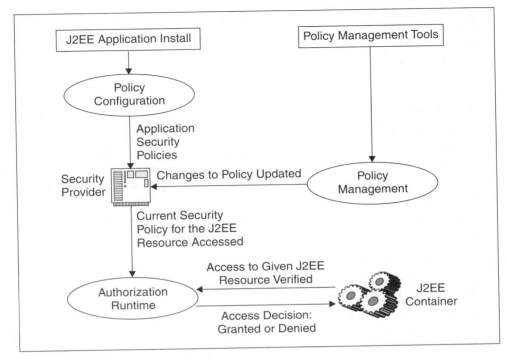

Figure 15.3.   Authorization in a J2EE Container

   The advantage of using the J2SE/JAAS Permission model is that a single security provider can perform both J2SE permission checks—for example, for accesses to the file system—and J2EE permission checks—for example, to execute EJB methods. Part of the design of authorization engines is to create `java.security.Policy` objects. Similar to how `LoginModules` can be used as an approach to allow multiple authentication mechanisms to be used by a container, one of many `Policy` implementations can be used by the container when making an access check on a resource.

15.4   Secure Communication

Secure communication channels are an important part of a secure environment. As SSL is a widely accepted secure transport protocol, communication between containers can be encrypted using SSL. This will ensure that the data transmitted over the wire will be kept confidential so that no unauthorized user can gain access to the information while data is in transit. It will also ensure the integrity of any data sent between containers; in other words, it will ensure that data is not modified by unauthorized users during transit. SSL can also be used for secure communication from the containers to external servers, such as LDAP directories, to ensure an end-to-end secure communication.

15.4.1 Using JSSE

JSSE is a Java implementation of the SSL protocol (see Section 13.4.1 on page 460). Java-based WASs can use JSSE to achieve secure communication between the servers. Keys can be kept secure by selecting an appropriate keystore type. For instance, if a hardware keystore provides a way to store keys securely, JSSE can be configured to use that keystore. Similarly, through a custom keystore, it is possible to centrally manage keys in distributed computing environments.

15.4.2 Client Certificates

According to the servlet specification, Web containers must allow users to authenticate themselves using client certificates. In such cases, in addition to a Web server authenticating to a Web client—typically, a Web browser—when an SSL connection is established between them, the client will be required to authenticate to the server, using a client certificate. Because a Web server can be independent of a Web container, the HTTP end point—that is, the Web server—needs to be configured to require client certificate. However, because an SSL connection can perform either server authentication or mutual authentication, a separate SSL port needs to be assigned to accept client certificates.

Figure 15.4 illustrates the process of client-certificate authentication using SSL. As the figure shows, the steps for SSL client authentication are as follows.

1. The authentication process starts when a user makes a request to a Web server, using HTTPS.

2. On receiving the request, the Web server responds by presenting its server certificate to the client.

3. The Web client verifies the server certificate.

4. The Web server then requests a client certificate.

5. The client browser presents the client certificate to the server on behalf of the user.

6. The server attemtps to verify the user's identity, based on the contents of the client certificate.

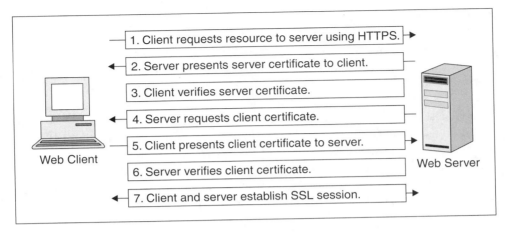

Figure 15.4. Client-Certificate Authentication Using SSL

7. If the server verifies the user's identity successfully, the client will be able to access the protected resources on the server over an encrypted SSL connection.

A Web container depends on the HTTP end point—typically, the Web server—to authenticate the client. This implies that the Web container may not engage in the SSL handshake, which is performed exclusively by the HTTP listener—the Web server, in this case. Therefore, when a resource is accessed in the Web container, the SSL connection is already established. Given this configuration, the Web container will have to trust the Web server to have performed a valid SSL handshake and deliver the accurate information related to the SSL session, such as the contents of the X.509 client certificate, to the Web container. Given that a servlet can access information pertaining to the client certificate using the APIs and attributes defined in the Java Servlet specification, the information that is related to the SSL session is used by the Web container to answer such queries from a servlet.

15.5 Secure Association

Securing the communication between containers is one part of a secure exchange of information. In addition to establishing an SSL session, it is important for the servers that host containers to verify the identity of the servers with which they are communicating. In the request flow depicted in Figure 15.1 on page 528, the Web container should validate the EJB container before propagating the request to invoke an enterprise bean. It is equally important for the EJB container to validate the trust it has on the invoking container. What is needed to provide such a trusted link is the facility to establish a secure association between the layers and to ensure secure interoperablity.

If WASs communicate over IIOP, the WASs themselves can use CSIv2 to establish a secure association. If HTTP is used, the client and the server can engage in mutual-authentication SSL via HTTPS. Alternatively, the client can send its identity to the server as part of the HTTP header over a server-side SSL connection (see Section 3.11 on page 95). In general, appropriate security mechanisms should be used to ensure a secure and trusted communication link between the conversing servers, depending on the protocol of communication.

15.6 Access to System Resources

Depending on the trust level on the deployed applications, one would have to protect malicious applications from accessing system resources, such as files and sockets, as well as resources within the container, such as internal data structures used by the container. The Java 2 security model can be used to achieve this level of security (see Chapter 8 on page 253). By granting appropriate Java permissions to trusted applications, as well as by checking for relevant permissions when a protected resource is being accessed, the container can protect sensitive resources. For example, if the container is configured to provide access to the class-loading mechanism or other internal classes only to trusted applications, the container can define and check for the relevant permissions before allowing access.

In addition to checking for permissions before accessing sensitive resources, the container should provide the right context when such checks are performed. For example, to maintain location transparency, so that local or remote enterprise beans behave the same way when permissions are checked, the container needs to limit the `java.security.ProtectionDomain`s on the call stack when authorization tests are performed (see Section 8.5 on page 265). As an example, let us consider two applications: ApplicationA and ApplicationB. Furthermore, let us assume that ApplicationA calls ApplicationB and that ApplicationB accesses a resource R1 requiring permission P1. When a call to the `SecurityManager`'s `checkPermission()` method is made to check whether P1 is granted, the `java.security.AccessController` class will check all the `ProtectionDomain`s on the call stack. In the case of local calls, ApplicationA (the caller) will be on the stack when such a check is performed. Therefore, both ApplicationA and ApplicationB will be on the call stack. However, if ApplicationA invokes ApplicationB remotely, ApplicationA will not be in the call stack and hence will not affect the authorization evaluation.

In order to maintain location transparency, the container needs to perform an `AccessController.doPrivileged()` call at the boundary where ApplicationA calls into ApplicationB, as shown in Figure 15.5. Invoking `doPrivileged()` sets up the environment such that ApplicationA's `ProtectionDomain` will not be on the stack, regardless of whether ApplicationA calls ApplicationB locally or remotely.

Containers are also expected to insert necessary `AccessController.do-Privileged()` calls so that applications are not required to be granted a Permission for a task that the container is expected to perform. For instance, if the container has configuration information in a directory `/config`, the container should retrieve configuration information from the files in that directory without requiring that the permissions be granted to applications. In order to achieve this, containers should access such container-specific resources within an `Access-Controller.doPrivileged()` call, as shown in Figure 15.6.

This ensures that only the container is required to be granted necessary Permissions to access the resources required to perform its tasks. Applications will not be required to be granted those Permissions.

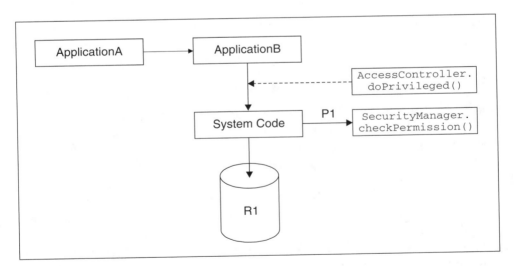

Figure 15.5. Accessing System Resources

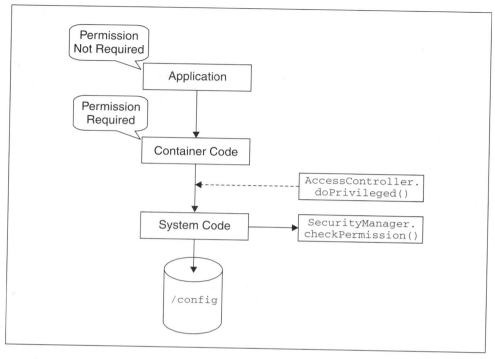

Figure 15.6.   Preventing Permission-Requirement Propagation

15.7 Mapping Identities at Connector Boundaries

The Java Connector Architecture allows for applications to access resources—typically, non-J2EE applications—in an architected fashion. For every resource that is accessed, a resource adapter is expected to be registered with the J2EE container. Applications obtain connections to these resources by using the appropriate resource adapter.

Back-end systems are likely to have their own security mechanisms to secure access to those resources. In many cases, these adapters expect some form of credential to be made available when creating a connection. Typically, the credential is in the form of a user ID and password pair. Therefore, a user ID and password pair are made available to the resource adapter when a connection is created. The JCA framework provides two ways to make the credential available to the resource adapters.

1. In an application-managed authentication, the application will explicitly pass a user ID and password when it requests connections.

2. In a container-managed authentication, the container will make a user ID and password pair available to the resource adapter.

In the context of this discussion, the container-managed authentication is of particular interest.

A J2EE application is allowed to create connections to any non-J2EE application using JCA. For example, an application can connect to a database by using a JDBC resource adapter. In such cases, the user ID and password pair that are made available to the connection are based on many factors, including the resource adapter type—in this example, JDBC—and target instance—for example, DB2 database AccountDB hosted on machine with hostname `accounts.accountinc.com`.

Consider a user, Bob, accessing a J2EE application that in turn accesses a database. One end of the spectrum is where all the users in the J2EE container environment are mapped to a single identity when accessing the resource adapter—for example, the identity `db2admin`. This is the case of a *many-to-one mapping* per resource adapter. On the other end of the spectrum is where the user's identity is effectively propagated to the third tier. This gives rise to a *one-to-one mapping* of identities at the JCA boundary. For example, the identity `bob` on J2EE container hosted in `ibm.com` is mapped to the identity `bobsmith` in the database domain. Of course, there can be other possible mappings in this spectrum. For example, all managers have a `manager_user` identity when accessing the database, whereas others have a `restricted_user` identity.

In order for the J2EE container to accommodate the wide spectrum of the mapping that is required and to allow for a flexible and extensible architecture, the container must allow for an identity/credential mapping facility at the JCA boundary. An example of this is illustrated in Figure 15.7.

As shown in Figure 15.7, the currently executing identity, which may in turn be based on the delegation policies associated with a J2EE component, will be considered along with the target resource adapter characteristics. The mapping layer is expected to use this information to make a decision as to which identity is to be used when accessing back-end applications. The back-end applications in Figure 15.7 are a database, an IBM Customer Information Control System, and an enterprise resource planning application. In some cases, the client's credential may be propagated to the back-end application without any change. For example, if the back-end application accepts a Kerberos credential, a Kerberos ticket associated with the user accessing the J2EE application may be propagated to the resource adapter, thus giving rise to a one-to-one mapping effectively.

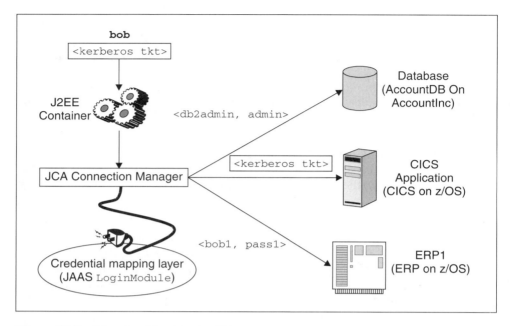

Figure 15.7. Mapping Identities in JCA

In order to accommodate such varied scenarios flexibly, the implementation of the mapping layer can be effectively achieved as a JAAS `LoginModule`. A container can use a `LoginModule` so that it can map the identity, represented as a JAAS `Subject` under which the business logic is performed, to a different identity, resulting in a JAAS `Subject`, based on the target system being connected to.

CHAPTER 16

Epilogue

In this book, we have described the security of the Java 2 Enterprise Edition platform. After introducing the general concepts of Java and network security, we have outlined the security of the core J2EE technologies: Java Servlet, JavaServer Pages, and Enterprise JavaBeans. Then, we covered the architecture of Java 2 Standard Edition security and the Java 2 permission model, showing how it is augmented by Java Authentication and Authorization Service. Given that cryptography has become an essential part in any security system, we have detailed the general concepts of secret-key and public-key cryptography and have shown how these technologies can be used in the Java Cryptography Architecture, Java Cryptography Extension, Java Secure Socket Extension, Public-Key Cryptography Standards, and Secure/Multipurpose Internet Mail Extensions. Finally, we have discussed the security implications of the emerging Web Services technology in a J2EE environment and have concluded by showing what security considerations a J2EE container provider should take into account when designing and developing a J2EE product.

This short chapter represents the epilogue of this long adventure through enterprise Java security. We believe that J2EE is a powerful platform to create secure computer systems. Because of its unique design, J2EE offers many safety and security advantages over alternative approaches. In this book, we have illustrated this fact and, we hope, given you some insight into how to create secure enterprise Java applications, how to use J2EE to protect assets, and how to do so securely.

P A R T   V I

APPENDIXES

APPENDIX **A**

Security of Distributed Object Architectures

COMMON Gateway Interface (CGI) programs use a transaction model: The client issues a transaction request and then waits until the server returns the results. Distributed object architectures offer a more elegant approach; the *object space* that an applet or an application is working with is extended to include objects on different systems. Client-side Java and server-side Java can be combined to create a fully distributed architecture, in which functions can be split between the client and the server to optimize processing and network loads.

Distributed object architectures have a number of advantages, including security advantages, over more conventional transactional systems. For example, you can design systems in which mission-critical objects may be kept safe behind a firewall, with access allowed only via method calls from clients. This is far safer than shipping data out of the organization to multiple clients who may simultaneously make changes.

To aid in the creation of distributed architectures, Java provides a toolkit called Remote Method Invocation (RMI). This toolkit extends the Java object model to the network by allowing objects in one JVM to invoke methods seamlessly on objects in another, remote, JVM. The remote JVM can, in turn, invoke other remote objects.

A.1 RMI

RMI support in Java 2 is provided by the `java.rmi` package and its four sub-packages: `java.rmi.activation`, `java.rmi.dgc`, `java.rmi.registry`, and `java.rmi.server`. With RMI, an object, *B*, residing on the server may be manipulated by another object, *A*, on a remote client. Object *B* doesn't really exist on the client; rather, an alternative object is used as a kind of *stunt double*. This *stub*, or *proxy object*, provides the same interface as the real object *B* but under the covers uses the RMI services to pass method requests over the network to the real object *B*. Object *A* therefore doesn't need to know whether object *B* is local or remote (see Figure A.1).

If another object, *C*, needs to be passed between the client and the server—for instance, as a parameter for a method—RMI uses a technique called *object serialization* to flatten the object, turning it into a stream of bytes. These bytes are sent to the RMI system on the remote machine, which rebuilds the object *C* and passes it into the method call. Return values from methods are handled in the same way.

A simple naming service, the RMI registry, is provided to connect clients and servers, using a URL-style of names, such as `//host:port/name`. A client asks for the remote objects, and the remote server returns the stub object to the client. Developers use the `rmic` compiler to generate the matching stub and skeleton classes for a remote object.

This means that it becomes possible to write distributed applications, with little need to be aware of exactly where the software will be executed. A `Remote-Exception` may be thrown on error conditions; otherwise, the program need not be aware that portions are executing remotely.

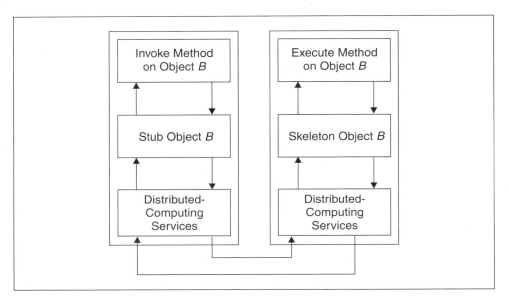

Figure A.1.   Invoking a Method with RMI

A.2 Stubs and Skeletons

In RMI, an object residing on a server machine may be manipulated by another object residing on a remote client machine. The terms *client* and *server* here apply only for this single call, because in a later transaction, the machine that acted as the server can also act as a client and request an RMI from another machine, which would be the server for this new interaction. When it wants to invoke a remote method, a client object calls a Java method that is encapsulated in a surrogate object called the *stub*. The stub resides on the same machine as the client. The stub then uses the Java object serialization mechanism to send data in a format suitable for transporting the parameters and the method call to a process on the server. The stub builds an information block that consists of

- An identifier of the remote object to be used
- An operation number, describing the method to be called
- The marshalled[1] parameters

This information block is sent to the server. A *skeleton* object residing at the server end receives this information block and takes the appropriate actions:

- Unmarshals the parameters sent by the stub
- Calls the appropriate method on the object residing on the server
- Captures any `Exceptions` generated owing to the call on the server or any return value to be sent back to the stub on the client
- Sends a block in a marshalled form back to the client

Now, the stub receives the response from the skeleton and unmarshals the return value or the `Exceptions`. The stub is also responsible for passing the return value or the `Exception` to the process that called the stub initially.

Starting with Java 2 SDK, Standard Edition, V1.2, an additional stub protocol has been introduced that eliminates the need for skeletons in environments that involve the Java 2 SDK platform only. Instead, generic code is used to carry out the duties performed by skeletons in the JDK V1.1.

A.3 RMI Registry

How does the stub get a handle to the server skeleton object on the server machine? This happens through the *RMI registry*, a simple server-side name server

---

1. *Marshalling* is the mechanism of encoding the parameters into a format appropriate to transport objects across the network.

that allows remote clients to get a reference to a remote object. The RMI registry is typically used only to locate the first remote object to which an RMI client needs to talk. In turn, that first object would provide application-specific support for finding other objects. Once a remote object is registered on the server, callers can look up the object by name, obtain a remote object reference, and then remotely invoke methods on the object. At the server end, the RMI server source code must bind the server object with a reference to the object and a name, which is a unique string on the RMI registry.

Note that for security reasons, an application can bind or unbind only to a registry running on the same host. This prevents a client from removing or over-writing any of the entries in a server's remote registry. A lookup, however, can be done from any host.

A.4   The Security of RMI

RMI appears to be a straightforward way of creating a distributed application. But there are a number of security issues.[2]

- RMI has a simple approach to creating the connection between the client and the server. Objects are serialized and transmitted over the network. They are not encrypted, so anyone on the network could read all the data being transferred.

- There is no authentication; a client simply requests an object, or stub, and the server supplies it. Subsequent communication is assumed to be from the same client.

- There is no access control to the objects.

- There are no security checks on the registry itself; it assumes that any caller is allowed to make requests.

- Objects are not persistent; the references are valid only during the lifetime of the process that created the remote object.

- Stubs are assumed to be matched to skeletons; however, programs could be constructed to simulate the RMI network calls, while allowing any data to be placed in the requests.

- Network and server errors will generate `Exceptions`, so applications must be prepared to handle them.

---

2. At the time of writing this book, the Java RMI Security Extension is a proposed standard extension to add security to Java RMI. Most of the problems listed here, such as lack of authentication, will be solved by the Java RMI Security Extension.

- There is no version control between stubs and skeletons; thus, it is possible for a client to use a down-level stub to access a more recent skeleton, breaking release-to-release binary compatibility.

- A `SecurityManager` must be set before a remote class can be loaded. For Java applets, the `SecurityManager` is defined by the Web browser or the Applet Viewer. For Java applications, the `SecurityManager` can be defined on the command line invocation with the `-Djava.security.manager` option, or it can be defined programmatically within the application itself. The standard Java API provides a `java.rmi.RMISecurityManager` class, which merely extends `java.lang.SecurityManager` but does not make any extra checks. If you require a security policy that is either more or less restrictive, you will need to create your own `SecurityManager`.

If the client and the server are connected through one or more firewalls, additional issues need to be considered (see Section 2.4 on page 36).

As we discussed in Chapter 5 on page 157, an enterprise bean is typically accessed using RMI-IIOP, which uses the RMI APIs as just described, but also provides security through the CSIv2 protocol. For the rest, we recommend that you use RMI only in pure intranet configurations or for applications in which it cannot usefully be attacked. An intercompany chat system may be a reasonable use of RMI. Closely coupled internal systems might use RMI, if the appropriate access controls are put in place by network and firewall design. But the lack of authentication and access control in the raw RMI must limit its wider use in secure applications.

If you need to create a secure distributed application, you should investigate alternatives to RMI. The CORBA implementations available today provide heavier-weight remote execution methods, and other suppliers can provide alternatives to RMI.

X.509 Digital Certificates

X.509, one of the most common formats for signed certificates, is used largely by Sun Microsystems, Microsoft, VeriSign, IBM, and many other companies for signing e-mail messages, authenticating program code, and certifying many other types of data. In its simplest form, an X.509 certificate contains the following data:

- The certificate format version—X.509 V1, V2, or V3.

- The certificate serial number.

- The identifier of the signature algorithm—the algorithm the CA used to sign the certificate. The identifier consists of the algorithm ID and the parameters passed to the algorithm.

- The X.500 name of the signer of the certificate. This entity is normally a CA. Using this certificate implies trusting the entity that signed this certificate. In some cases, such as root or top-level CA certificates, the issuer signs its own certificate.

- The period of validity: begin date and end date. Each certificate is valid for only a limited amount of time, described by a start date and time and an end date and time. This period can be as short as a few seconds or almost as long as a century.

- The name of the certified entity: The X.500 Distinguished Name of the entity whose public key the certificate identifies. This field conforms to the X.500 standard, so it is intended to be unique across the Internet (see Section 4.5.1.3 on page 120).

- The public key of the certified identity: The public key of the entity being named, together with an algorithm identifier that specifies which public-key cryptosystem this key belongs to and any associated key parameters.

- The signature: the hash code of all the preceding fields, encoded with the signer's private key. Thus, the signer guarantees that a given entity has a particular public key.

All the data in a certificate is encoded using two related standards: Abstract Syntax Notation 1 and Distinguished Encoding Rules.

B.1   X.509 Certificate Versions

Several modifications have been made to the features and information content of X.509 certificate versions.

1. X.509 V1 has been available since 1988, is widely deployed, and is the most generic.

2. X.509 V2 introduced the concept of subject and issuer unique identifiers to handle the possibility of reuse of subject and/or issuer names over time.

3. X.509 V3, available since 1996, supports the notion of extensions, whereby anyone can define an extension and include it in the certificate. Some common extensions in use today are

   - KeyUsage, which limits the use of the keys to particular purposes, such as signing only. The associated private key should be used only for signing certificates, not for SSL.

   - AlternativeNames, which allows other identities to also be associated with this public key: for example, DNS names, e-mail addresses, or IP addresses.

Technical Acronyms Used in This Book

A

ACID	atomicity, consistency, isolation, durability
ACM	Association for Computing Machinery
AES	Advanced Encryption Standard
API	application programming interface
APPC	Advanced Peer-to-Peer Communication
AS/400	Application System/400
ASCII	American Standard Code for Information Interchange
ASN	Abstract Syntax Notation
ASN.1	ASN 1
ATM	automatic teller machine
AWT	Abstract Windowing Toolkit
AuthML	Authentication Markup Language

B

B2B	business-to-business
B2C	business-to-consumer
BMP	bean-managed persistence

C

C14N	CanonicalizatioN
CA	Certificate Authority
CATT	Center for Advanced Technology in Telecommunications

CBC	cipher block chaining
CBR	call-by-reference
CBV	call-by-value
CD-ROM	Compact disk–read-only memory
CGI	Common Gateway Interface
CICS	Customer Information Control System
CMP	Certificate Management Protocol
CMP	container-managed persistence
CN	Common Name
COBOL	Common Business Oriented Language
COM	Component Object Model
CORBA	Common Object Request Broker Architecture
CPU	central processing unit
CRL	certificate revocation list
CRT	Chinese Remainder Theorem
CSI	Common Secure Interoperability
CSIv2	CSI Version 2
CSP	cryptographic service provider
CSR	Certificate Signing Request

D

DCE	distributed-computing environment
DCOM	Distributed Component Object Model
DER	Distinguished Encoding Rules
DES	Data Encryption Standard
DH	Diffie-Hellman
DMZ	demilitarized zone
DN	Distinguished Name
DNS	Domain Name Service
DSA	Digital Signature Algorithm
DTD	document type declaration

E

EAR	Enterprise Archive
ECB	electronic codebook
ECI	External Call Interface
EDI	electronic data interchange
EIS	enterprise information system
EJB	Enterprise JavaBeans
EPI	External Presentation Interface
ERP	enterprise resource planning

F

FDDI	Fiber Distributed Data Interface
FTP	File Transfer Protocol

G

GIF	Graphics Interchange Format
GSS	Generic Security Services (GSS)
GSS-API	GSS Application Programming Interface
GSSUP	GSS Username Password
GUI	graphical user interface

H

HTML	Hypertext Markup Language
HTTP	Hypertext Transfer Protocol
HTTPS	HTTP over Secure Socket Layer

I

I/O	input/output
IBM	International Business Machines
ICAPI	Internet Connection Application Programming Interface
IDEA	International Data Encryption Algorithm
IDL	interface definition language
IEEE	Institute of Electrical and Electronics Engineers
IETF	Internet Engineering Task Force
IIOP	Internet Inter-Object Request Broker Protocol
IP	Internet Protocol
IPSec	IP Security
ISP	Internet service provider
IT	information technology

J

J2EE	Java 2 Enterprise Edition
J2RE	Java 2 Runtime Environment
J2SDK	Java 2 Software Development Kit
JAAS	Java Authentication and Authorization Service
JAR	Java Archive
JCA	Java Connector Architecture
JCA	Java Cryptography Architecture
JCE	Java Cryptography Extension

JCEKS	JCE keystore
JCP	Java Community Process
JDBC	Java Database Connectivity
JDK	Java Development Kit
JGSS	Java Generic Security Services
JGSS-API	JGSS Application Programming Interface
JIT	just-in-time
JKS	Java keystore
JMS	Java Message Service
JNDI	Java Naming and Directory Interface
JRE	Java Runtime Environment
JSP	JavaServer Pages
JSR	Java Specification Request
JSSE	Java Secure Socket Extension
JVM	Java virtual machine

K

KB	kilobyte

L

LAN	local area network
LDAP	Lightweight Directory Access Protocol

M

MAC	media access control
MAC	message authentication code
MD5	Message Digest V5
MD5withRSA	Message Digest V5 with Rivest-Shamir-Adleman
MIME	Multipurpose Internet Mail Extensions
MIT	Massachusetts Institute of Technology
MQ	message queuing
MVC	Model-View-Controller
MVS	multiple virtual storage

N

NCSA	National Center for Supercomputing Applications
NCSA	National Computer Security Association
NSAPI	Netscape Connection Application Programming Interface

NetBIOS	Network Basic Input Output System
NetREXX	Net Restructured Extended Executor

O

OASIS	Organization for the Advancement of Structured Information Standards
OGSA	Open Grid Services Architecture
OMG	Object Management Group
OO	object-oriented
OOPSLA	Object-Oriented Programming, Systems, Languages, and Applications
ORB	Object Request Broker
OS	operating system
OS/2	Operating System 2
OS/390	Operating System 390
OSI	Open Systems Interconnection
OU	organizational unit

P

PAM	Pluggable Authentication Module
PBE	password-based encryption
PC	personal computer
PDA	personal digital assistant
PKCS	Public-Key Cryptography Standards
PKI	Public Key Infrastructure
PRNG	Pseudorandom Number Generator

Q

QoS	quality of service

R

RACF	Resource Access Control Facility
RC2	Rivest's Cipher V2
RC4	Rivest's Cipher V4
RDBMS	relational database management system
RFC	Request for Comments
RMI	Remote Method Invocation
RMI-IIOP	RMI over Internet Inter-Object Request Broker
ROM	read-only memory
RSA	Rivest-Shamir-Adleman

S

S/MIME	Secure/Multipurpose Internet Mail Extensions
S2ML	Security Services Markup Language
SASL	Simple Authentication and Security Layer
SDK	Software Development Kit
SHA-1	Secure Hash Algorithm V1
SHA1withDSA	SHA-1 with Digital Signature Algorithm
SMTP	Simple Mail Transfer Protocol
SNA	Systems Network Architecture
SOAP	Simple Object Access Protocol
SOCKS	SOCKet Secure
SPI	service provider interface
SQLJ	Structured Query Language for Java
SSL	Secure Sockets Layer
SSO	single sign-on

T

TCP	Transmission Control Protocol
TCP/IP	TCP/Internet Protocol
TLS	Transport Layer Security
TPA	Trading Partner Agreement
TRNG	true random number generator

U

UDDI	Universal Description, Discovery and Integration
UDP	User Datagram Protocol
URI	universal resource identifier
URL	uniform resource locator

V

VDU	visual display unit
VM	Virtual Machine
VPN	virtual private network

W

W3C	World Wide Web Consortium
WAR	Web Archive
WAS	Web application server

WS-Addressing	Web Services Addressing specification
WS-Policy	Web Services Policy Framework specification
WS-PolicyAssertions	Web Services General Policy Assertions Language specification
WS-PolicyAttachment	Web Services Policy Attachment specification
WS-SecureConversation	Web Services Secure Conversation Language specification
WS-Security	Web Services Security specification
WS-SecurityPolicy	Web Services Security Policy Language specification
WS-Trust	Web Services Trust Language specification
WSDL	Web Services Description Language
WWW	World Wide Web

X

XACML	eXtensible Access Control Markup Language
XKMS	XML Key Management Specification
XML	eXtensible Markup Language
XOR	eXclusive OR

Sources Used in This Book

THIS book draws and expands on material from the following sources:

- M. Hondo, N. Nagaratnam, and A. Nadalin. "Securing Web Services," *IBM Systems Journal* 41, 2, 2002.
- L. Koved, A. Nadalin, D. Deal, and T. Lawson. "The evolution of Java security," *IBM Systems Journal* 37, 3, 1998.
- L. Koved, A. Nadalin, N. Nagaratnam, M. Pistoia, and T. Shrader. "The Security Challenges for Enterprise Java in an e-Business Environment," *IBM Systems Journal* 40, 1, 2001.
- A. Nadalin and N. Nagaratnam. "J2EE Security: A WebSphere 4.0 Perspective," *IBM DeveloperToolbox Technical Magazine*. October 2001. http://www.ibm.com/developerworks.
- A. Nadalin, T. Shrader, and B. Rich. "Java Cryptography Part 1: Encryption and Decryption," *IBM DeveloperToolbox Technical Magazine*. December 1999. http://www.ibm.com/developerworks.
- A. Nadalin, T. Shrader, and B. Rich. "Java Cryptography Part II: Key Generation and Management," *IBM DeveloperToolbox Technical Magazine*. March 2000. http://www.ibm.com/developerworks.
- A. Nadalin, T. Shrader, and B. Rich. "Java Cryptography Part III: Implementing Your Own Provider," *IBM DeveloperToolbox Technical Magazine*. June 2000. http://www.ibm.com/developerworks.
- A. Nadalin, T. Shrader, and B. Rich. "Java Cryptography Part IV: JCE Export Considerations," *IBM DeveloperToolbox Technical Magazine*. September 2000. http://www.ibm.com/developerworks.
- M. Pistoia, D. F. Reller, D. Gupta, M. Nagnur, and A. K. Ramani. *Java 2 Network Security*. (Upper Saddle River, NJ: Prentice-Hall, 1999).
- T. Shrader, A. Nadalin, and B. Rich. "When Cryptographic Messages Go Bad," *IBM DeveloperToolbox Technical Magazine*. June 2000. http://www.ibm.com/developerworks.

Index

0-201-44099-7

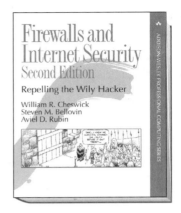

0-201-63466-X

0-201-76175-0

0-321-13620-9

0-201-76176-9

0-321-10895-7